# The Assassination
of Europe, 1918–1942

## Also by Howard M. Sachar

*The Course of Modern Jewish History*

*Aliyah: The Peoples of Israel*

*From the Ends of the Earth: The Peoples of Israel*

*The Emergence of the Middle East: 1914–1924*

*Europe Leaves the Middle East, 1936–1954*

*A History of Israel: From the Rise of Zionism to Our Time*

*The Man on the Camel: A Novel*

*Egypt and Israel*

*Diaspora: An Inquiry into the Contemporary Jewish World*

*A History of Israel, Volume II: From the Aftermath of the Yom Kippur War*

*The Rise of Israel: A Documentary Record from the Nineteenth Century to 1948: A Facsimile Series Reproducing over 1,900 documents in 39 volumes, Volume 1*

*A History of the Jews in America*

*Farewell Espana: The World of the Sephardim Remembered*

*Israel and Europe: An Appraisal in History*

*Dreamland: Europeans and Jews in the Aftermath of the Great War*

*A History of the Jews in the Modern World*

# The Assassination of Europe, 1918–1942

## A Political History

Howard M. Sachar

UNIVERSITY OF TORONTO PRESS

Copyright © University of Toronto Press 2015
Higher Education Division

www.utppublishing.com

All rights reserved. The use of any part of this publication reproduced, transmitted in any form or by any means, electronic, mechanical, photocopying, recording, or otherwise, or stored in a retrieval system, without prior written consent of the publisher—or in the case of photocopying, a licence from Access Copyright (Canadian Copyright Licensing Agency), One Yonge Street, Suite 1900, Toronto, Ontario M5E 1E5—is an infringement of the copyright law.

Library and Archives Canada Cataloguing in Publication

Sachar, Howard Morley, 1928–, author
   The assassination of Europe, 1918–1942 : a political history / Howard M. Sachar.

Includes bibliographical references and index.
Issued in print and electronic formats.
ISBN 978-1-4426-0919-8 (bound).—ISBN 978-1-4426-0918-1 (pbk.).—
ISBN 978-1-4426-0920-4 (pdf).—ISBN 978-1-4426-0921-1 (epub)

   1. Europe—Politics and government—1918–1945.  2. Political violence—Europe—History—20th century.  3. Europe—History—1918–1945.  I. Title.

D720.S23 2014               940.5               C2014-903885-2
                                                                                      C2014-903886-0

We welcome comments and suggestions regarding any aspect of our publications—please feel free to contact us at news@utphighereducation.com or visit our Internet site at www.utppublishing.com.

*North America*
5201 Dufferin Street
North York, Ontario, Canada, M3H 5T8

2250 Military Road
Tonawanda, New York, USA, 14150

ORDERS PHONE: 1–800–565–9523
ORDERS FAX: 1–800–221–9985
ORDERS E-MAIL: utpbooks@utpress.utoronto.ca

*UK, Ireland, and continental Europe*
NBN International
Estover Road, Plymouth, PL6 7PY, UK
ORDERS PHONE: 44 (0) 1752 202301
ORDERS FAX: 44 (0) 1752 202333
ORDERS E-MAIL: enquiries@nbninternational.com

Every effort has been made to contact copyright holders; in the event of an error or omission, please notify the publisher.

This book is printed on paper containing 100% post-consumer material.

The University of Toronto Press acknowledges the financial support for its publishing activities of the Government of Canada through the Canada Book Fund.

Printed in the United States of America.

*For my newest grandchildren, Mia, Isabelle, and Sophia*

*and*

*For Jane Garrett, my editorial muse of nearly 40 years.*

CONTENTS

*List of Illustrations* ix

*Preface* xi

*Stylistic Note* xiii

CHAPTER ONE: Social Democracy's White Terror  1

CHAPTER TWO: The Death of Giacomo Matteotti  31

CHAPTER THREE: A Posthumous Imperial Vengeance  67

CHAPTER FOUR: Who Killed Sergei Kirov?  106

CHAPTER FIVE: "Richard III" in Germany  142

CHAPTER SIX: A Return Visit from Austria's Tatterdemalion Son  182

CHAPTER SEVEN: All Roads Lead to Rome  224

CHAPTER EIGHT: Gallic *Fraternité* under the Third Republic  262

CHAPTER NINE: The Hunt for Leon Trotsky  297

CHAPTER TEN: Gallic *Fraternité* under Vichy's Armistice  331

CHAPTER ELEVEN: The Humanist of Yesterday  379

*Bibliography*  405

*Index*  435

ILLUSTRATIONS

**Maps**

1 Germany's Losses by the Treaty of Versailles  36
2 Italian Postwar Gains  77
3 New Nations of Reconstructed Central Europe  239
4 Occupied and Vichy France  336

**Photographs**

Rosa Luxemburg, 1907  18
Kurt Eisner 1919  24
Giacomo Matteotti c. 1924  55
Matthias Erzberger with Members of the German Armistice Commission at Spa, c. 1918–19  88
Walther Rathenau at the Genoa Conference, 1922  104
Walther Rathenau's State Funeral, Berlin, June 27, 1922  105
Sergei Kirov with Joseph Stalin and His Daughter Svetlana  135
Ernst Röhm, c. 1934  178
Engelbert Dollfuss at a Heimwehr Rally in Innsbruck Two Weeks Before His Assassination in 1934  213
King Aleksandar I with French Foreign Minister Louis Barthou  255
Carlo and Nello Rosselli, 1934  292
Leon Trotsky Dying in Hospital after the Attack by Ramón Mercader, August 20, 1940  327
Georges Mandel Speaking at an Inauguration Ceremony, November 16, 1938  370
Stefan and Lotte Zweig, Shown in their Home after their Deaths on February 22, 1942  401

PREFACE

In the aftermath of the "Great European War," political observers and cultural mandarins alike gallantly persisted in defining the tradition of "humanism" as Europe's signature accomplishment. These commentators acknowledged that the Continent's economic and demographic resources had been grievously depleted by the epic carnage of 1914–18. Nevertheless, from their austere perspective, Europe's path to revival could still have been accomplished essentially by a reenergized commitment to democracy and collective security. The same aspiration had been given eloquent resonance by an "outsider," President Woodrow Wilson of the United States. But Europeans regarded Wilson's preachments as gratuitous. For them, it was still unthinkable that the Old World itself, the former "Concert of Europe," with its conflated and idealized record of political and economic leadership, could fail to achieve rehabilitation by dint of its own cumulative experience, resilience, and sheer historical *gravitas*.

Yet fail the Old World did, for the image of a European family once living in "concert" was a myth. The glowering hatreds that engendered the late war—Germans against Slavs, Roman Catholics against Eastern Orthodox, gentiles against Jews, poor against rich, conquerors against conquered—were neither trivial nor susceptible to assuagement either before or after the armistices of 1918. Rather, the demons survived and grew. If they were incapable of wreaking their havoc in the immediate aftermath of the postwar "peace" conferences, there were other, equally functional paths to "rectification" and revenge.

It was the ensuing chain reaction of political homicides that inflicted the coup de grâce on postwar Europe's "proud tower" of political and moral leadership. The post-armistice era was no ordinary one of nationalist or ethnic rivalries. Under the façade of constitutions and peace treaties, sovereign governments and underground cabals in their desperation and hatred evidently countenanced nothing less than the physical eradication of their political, national, or "racial" enemies. Their targets included kings and commoners, civilians and soldiers, military recruits and senior commanders, political legmen and party chairmen, businessmen and academicians, journalists and belletrists—and ultimately a train of victims' families: husbands, wives, and children.

Indeed, it was this sinister new dimension that was even less imaginable in a postwar Europe ostensibly committed to the security and dignity of its member nations, of the latter's borders, governments, and populations. But the fulfillment of that worshipful vow apparently required a far wider scope of political and economic "integration" than the peacemakers of 1919–21 were prepared to acknowledge. It was ultimately the twentieth century's defining tragedy that a reconfiguration of such magnitude would have to await the end of another, even more apocalyptic war.

In the course of preparing this volume, I have profited from the generous advice of several esteemed academic colleagues. Among these are Professor R. Emmet Kennedy, for chapters on France; Professor Steven Beller, for the chapter on Austria; Professor Milan Vega, for the chapter on Yugoslavia; Professor Muriel Atkin and the late Professor Vladimir Petrov, for chapters on Russia.

Additionally, my warm thanks go out to Ms. Natalie Fingerhut, senior acquisitions editor of the University of Toronto Press; to Ms. Judith Earnshaw and Ms. Karen Taylor, freelance editors; and to Ms. Beate Schwirtlich, the press's production editor; to Ms. Huyen K. To and Mr. Glenn Canner, interlibrary loan directors of George Washington University's Gellman Library; to Mr. William Sartain, director emeritus of the Stack and Reader Division of that incomparable cathedral of bibliographical resources, the United States Library of Congress, for rewarding many times over my own (and doubtless innumerable others of my authorial colleagues') migration to the nation's capital; and finally, to my wife, Eliana Steimatzky Sachar, for patiently and devotedly "engineering" this volume to its editorial destination.

H.M.S.<br>Kensington, Maryland

## STYLISTIC NOTE

For the convenience of English-language readers, the indiscriminate capitalization of German nouns has been discarded. The exceptions are proper nouns and such historical movements, titles, or institutions as *Weltpolitik*, Sturm Abteilung, Reichswehr, *Anschluss*, or *Gleichschaltung*. Political identifications (whether "socialist," "communist," or "fascist") are capitalized only for actual party membership.

In chapters dealing with Russia or Yugoslavia, the spelling of South Slavic surnames generally is left intact, although with some of the diacritical marks eliminated. The major exception is Lev Trotski, whose prominence even in the years of his exile has transformed virtually all his subsequent Western biographical references into "Leon Trotsky."

Foreign words or expressions that appear often in English are italicized, if at all, only in their first appearance.

CHAPTER ONE

# Social Democracy's White Terror

*"Rosa Luxemburg and Karl Liebknecht have carried out their ultimate revolution."*

## THE EDUCATION OF ROSA LUXEMBURG

On May 31, 1919, the partly decomposed body of a woman was spotted in one of the locks of Berlin's Landwehr Canal. The corpse was retrieved and taken to the city morgue, where it was swiftly announced to be that of Rosa Luxemburg. Two weeks later, on the designated occasion of Luxemburg's interment, mourners in seemingly endless thousands filed by to pay their respects to a woman who had emerged as a legend of socialist idealism.

In her native Poland, the image of the woman rebel was an indelible feature of Luxemburg's formative years. She was eight years old in 1879 when Vera Zasulich walked into the office of General Fyodor Trepov, military governor of St. Petersburg, and shot him at point-blank range. She was ten years old when Sophia Perovskaya, herself the daughter of a Russian general, was executed for participating in the assassination of Tsar Alexander II. When Luxemburg was graduated from gymnasium, the twenty-one-year-old Maria Bohusz, a leader of "Proletariat," the first Polish workers' party, died in Siberian exile. Siberian exile was the fate also of Aleksandra Jentya, daughter of a Jewish physician and cofounder of Proletariat. Indeed, it was in the battle for social emancipation even more than for political equality or national independence that Polish, Russian, and Jewish revolutionaries achieved their greatest visibility. By the late nineteenth century, the very term, socialism, betokened a new era of elementary human justice for all the downtrodden of the earth, worker and peasant, man and woman, Jew and gentile. Rosa Luxemburg early on was caught up in that ferment.

The youngest of five children of a middle-class Jewish timber merchant, Rosalia Luksemburg (her registered name) was born in 1871 in a small Hasidic townlet in the Lublin province of tsarist Poland. Her family, atypically, was Polish speaking and secular. Traveling often to Germany on business, her father insisted on sending his three sons to Berlin for a Western gymnasium education, and in 1873 he moved his entire family to Warsaw for that city's cultural ambience. Even in Warsaw, however, Rosa Luxemburg's life was painfully constricted. When she was five, a hip ailment was inaccurately diagnosed as tubercular (the malformation later was proved to be genetic), and she was confined to bed in a cast for nearly a year. The treatment left her with one leg shorter than the other, and with a permanent dwarf-like gait. It also left her exposed to continual taunting by schoolmates. Characteristically, she became an overachiever. Upon finishing at the top of her class, she won acceptance under the minuscule Jewish quota to a prestigious state gymnasium. Here again she overcame the derision of Polish fellow students to graduate with highest honors.

By then, Luxemburg had become thoroughly immersed in a revolutionary socialist movement that was enveloping much of Eastern Europe's younger generation. Under continual police surveillance, she also risked the imprisonment or Siberian exile that were meted out to innumerable other revolutionaries of her generation. Terrified for her safety, her parents then arranged for her to be smuggled across the Austrian frontier. It was a useful move. Upon reaching Vienna, Luxemburg managed to support herself as a governess for the children of an affluent Jewish family, and within eighteen months she had saved enough to travel on to Switzerland. Here it was, at the age of nineteen, that she enrolled in the social science faculty at the University of Zurich. The new world that opened out to her then was one not only of intellectual discovery but of social equality among students of all backgrounds. At the turn of the century, Zurich was a hotbed of émigré socialists, including such future

East European luminaries as Georgi Plekhanov, Julius Martov (originally Iulii Tsederbaum), and Vladimir Lenin.

Rosa Luxemburg's most intimate "soul mate" among these kindred spirits was Leo Jogiches, the son of a prosperous and cultured Vilna Jewish family. Shortly after finishing gymnasium, Jogiches had founded the Vilna branch of the revolutionary-terrorist Narodnaya Volya (People's Will) party. He paid with jail time. Upon release from his second confinement, in 1889, the young man departed for Switzerland. There he joined the flood of other expatriates registering at the University of Zurich. In Jogiches's case, however, matriculation was the barest formality. Almost from the moment of his arrival, he hurled himself with characteristic zeal into socialist activism. Luxemburg soon joined his personal coterie, and with him in 1892 founded a new subsection, the SDKP, the "Social Democratic Party of the Kingdom of Poland and Lithuania." It was a far-leftist faction that rejected the official Polish Socialist Party for its "diversionary" insistence on linking socialism with Poland's struggle for political independence.

Other members of Jogiches's entourage tended to be fellow students, at least half of them Jews who also had struggled in Poland under the double incubus of tsarist political oppression and Polish antisemitism. For Rosa Luxemburg, moreover, ideology was fortified by tough-minded historicism. In the dissertation she would present in 1898 for her doctorate, and that almost simultaneously would achieve publication both in Switzerland and Germany, she provided compelling evidence that the economic growth of tsarist Poland always had been indissolubly linked to the vast Russian market. All the more reason, she argued, for Russia's Polish provinces not to be pried loose "artificially" from their surrounding Russian hinterland.[1] To the end of her life, Luxemburg's socialism was defined by its single-minded internationalism.

The young woman's ideological bond with Jogiches meanwhile took on a new dimension. In 1892, the two began living together. Despite her unprepossessing physical appearance, Luxemburg evidently overwhelmed Jogiches by sheer intellectual brilliance and moral strength. For her, in turn, Jogiches's ideological passion, his ascetic face, burning eyes, and temperamental aloofness made him a kind of Dostoyevskian hero, a man able to engulf her mind and heart. Her letters to him when they were apart were suggestive. Enclosing a draft of an article she had written, she would implore: "Help, for heaven's

---

[1] Rosa Luxemburg, *Die industrielle Entwicklung Polens* (doctoral dissertation, University of Zurich, 1898), *passim*.

sake, help. . . . I know you'll pick up the main thread immediately and add the finishing touches. . . . Just give me a few new ideas." More passionately: "I feel the way you do. I dream about being near you, my only love. I struggle with myself, struggle hard, and still I need you. . . . My golden one."[2]

In organizational resourcefulness, however, Luxemburg far transcended the mood-ridden, pathologically secretive Jogiches, who never managed to earn a single degree or even to develop his own SDKP party faction. It was she, not he, who became a dynamic and respected voice within the world of émigré socialism. Its members flocked to listen as she addressed their conferences in Switzerland and Germany. Indeed, for her audience, Luxemburg was a revelation: as a student, a Pole, a Jew, a woman. Emile Vandervelde, Belgium's Socialist Party chairman, left a description of her in 1894, as she addressed a Socialist congress in Zurich:

> She rose from among the delegates at the back and stood on a chair to make herself heard. Small and looking very frail in a summer dress, which managed effectively to conceal her physical defects, she advocated her cause with such magnetism and such appealing words that she won the majority of the Congress at once and they raised their hands in favor of the acceptance of her mandate.[3]

In Berlin, the party's venerable founding leaders, Karl Liebknecht and August Bebel, brought Luxemburg into their inner circle. In turn, upon receiving her doctorate in 1898, she made the decision to move to Germany on a permanent basis. The heartland of European socialism and the home of the Continent's first, best-funded, and largest Social Democratic Party, Germany offered a matchless arena for her talents. Luxemburg's impending separation from Jogiches, still in Switzerland and engaged in his party commitments, plainly was not an easy step for her. It was their mutual agreement, however, that he would join her "presently" in Germany.

There were bureaucratic obstacles that first had to be overcome. As a citizen of the tsarist empire, Luxemburg was vulnerable at any time to extradition from Germany as a political radical. Her best hope of security was to acquire

---

[2] Elżbieta Ettinger, *Comrade and Lover: Rosa Luxemburg's Letters to Leo Jogiches* (Cambridge, MA: MIT Press, 1979), xix.

[3] Paul Frölich, *Rosa Luxemburg: Her Life and Work*, trans. Edward FitzGerald (London: Victor Gollancz, 1940), 52–53.

German citizenship. But when her efforts to surmount Germany's rigorous naturalization barriers foundered, she turned to a more direct route. She would marry a German, thus instantly acquiring her husband's nationality. The designated partner was one Gustav Lübeck, the son of German socialist friends living in Zurich. Jogiches countenanced the move. The marriage then took place in April 1898 in the Basel City Hall and for all practical purposes ended immediately afterward.[4] The "newlyweds" separated on the steps of the building, never to see each other again. The following month, "Dr. Rosalia Lübeck" departed Switzerland for Germany, to enter a world with dramatically extended political vistas.

## "RED ROSA" IN GERMANY

Upon arriving in her new Berlin domicile, Luxemburg initially was dispatched on her Social Democratic career with a modest assignment as party organizer among the Polish-speaking workers of Posen. Characteristically, she hurled herself into the task with energy and passion, and within months became the party's recognized authority on East European affairs. But Luxemburg's activities soon extended beyond the Social Democrats' "Polish" section. Admired for her doctoral credentials, brilliant mind, and linguistic fluency in German, Polish, and Russian, she became a contributor to party newspapers and a much sought-after lecturer before party audiences. Altogether, the young woman's intellectual acumen was dazzling (in 1899, it was she who formulated the term "imperialism" before John Hobson officially invented the word to describe the global shift in world politics).

Luxemburg's influence also soon made itself felt in the party leadership's stance on "revisionism." In the 1880s and 1890s, Eduard Bernstein, a former German bank clerk and a registered Social Democrat, had been living and working in England. From his personal experience in this "workshop of the world," he had been drawn to the conclusion that capitalism apparently was not approaching imminent collapse, as Karl Marx had contended. In a series of articles, enlarged in 1899 into a book, *Die Voraussetzungen des Sozialismus und die Aufgaben der Sozialdemokratie* (translated in England as *Evolutionary Socialism*), Bernstein elaborated on his thesis that capitalism, in its uneven but steady enhancement of prosperity throughout all echelons of industrial societies, was gaining, not losing, strength. In Germany, too, Bernstein suggested, the working class could share in that prosperity if it abandoned

---

4 Karl Kautsky, *Briefe an Karl und Luise Kautsky* (Berlin: E. Laub, 1923), 380.

revolutionary aims and concentrated upon winning middle-class support for gradual reforms within the existing capitalist order. In effect, Bernstein was advocating a "revision" of classical Marxism through a voluntary, peaceful reconciliation between socialism and capitalism.⁵

For Luxemburg, however, "revisionism" was heresy. In 1898 and 1899, riposting to Bernstein in a vigorous series of articles, she skewered his arguments as "doctrinal complacency" and went further even than Karl Marx, arguing that capitalism would collapse not only as a consequence of inevitable social laws but also through the vigorous and indispensable leadership of an activist proletariat.⁶ For Wilhelm Liebknecht and August Bebel, the Social Democrats' senior eminences, Luxemburg's eloquence and faith in the masses stiffened their effort to kept the party officially committed to the goal of revolution.⁷ Indeed, by the early twentieth century, she herself was achieving recognition as one of those eminences, and becoming a perennial in her party's delegations to international Socialist congresses.

Thus, in 1904, Luxemburg joined Bebel and Liebknecht at the biennial Congress of the Second International meeting in Amsterdam. Returning from Amsterdam to Berlin, however, she was greeted by the Prussian police and ushered forthwith to prison.⁸ The year before, she had been convicted of lèse-majesté for "insulting the kaiser" in one of her political speeches. Although she had appealed the court judgment, her effort had been rejected. Now she would have to serve her six-week sentence. Luxemburg survived the ordeal uncomplainingly. Indeed, the imprisonment actually fortified her "revolutionary" bona fides. Upon being released, she was scarcely able to meet the enlarged demand for her speeches and articles.

Luxemburg's growing fame took its toll on her relationship with Jogiches, however. Although in 1900 he succumbed to her pleas and rejoined her in Berlin, he chafed at his subordinate role, functioning invariably in "Red Rosa's" shadow, lacking a profession or even a persona to compare with hers. After two years, Jogiches returned to Poland, eventually to participate in that country's 1905 October uprising against tsarist oppression. Despite her reservations on Polish "particularism," Luxemburg dutifully followed him. Both were promptly arrested and jailed for radical activity. Both their families managed to provide "bail"—bribe money—for their release, but Luxemburg

---

5 Carl E. Schorske, *German Social Democracy, 1905–1917: The Development of the Great Schism*, Harvard Historical Studies No. 65 (Cambridge, MA: Harvard University Press, 1955), 16–24.
6 Frölich, *Rosa Luxemburg*, 64–66.
7 Frölich, *Rosa Luxemburg*, 12, 16.
8 Karl Kautsky, *Briefe*, 55.

then acknowledged her inability to influence future events in the East. She returned to Germany, but this time alone. Jogiches, still in Poland, had been rearrested within a week of his original release. He would spend another two years in prison before managing to escape and return to Germany. By then, however, the sequence of separations had left Luxemburg emotionally drained. Upon Jogiches's eventual return to Berlin in late 1907, she would not take him back.

Whatever Luxemburg's inner turmoil, the years between 1907 and 1914 became her most intellectually productive. She published two volumes on political economy and churned out a seemingly endless torrent of articles for party journals. Yet her ideological influence had begun to wane in this period. She had remained an unremittingly orthodox Marxist; but even as Germany's Social Democratic leadership continued to pay lip service to the Marxist ideal of a class revolution, the party rank and file were accommodating to Germany's burgeoning prosperity. As Eduard Bernstein had predicted, German workers began to question the need any longer for more than progressive social-welfare legislation. By the early twentieth century, the purists who stood with Luxemburg in maintaining the revolutionary faith comprised a respected but visibly shrinking group. "We Marxists," she acknowledged in a letter to her friends Karl and Luise Kautsky, "are unfortunately becoming thin on the ground in Germany...."[9]

Indeed, in August, 1914, with the sequence of events following the assassination of Franz Ferdinand in Sarajevo, Germany's Social Democrats officially and decisively abandoned their historic commitment even to socialist internationalism. Their party caucus voted to support the government's war budget.[10] Only two members of the executive council remained devoted heart and soul to the revolutionary cause. One of these was Karl Liebknecht, son of the late party chairman, Wilhelm Liebknecht. The other was Luxemburg. Yet their doctrinal orthodoxy availed little against Germany's mounting patriotic frenzy.[11]

## THE IMPRISONED REBEL

For Luxemburg herself, moreover, political isolation was exacerbated by legal vulnerability. In September 1913, she had declaimed to a party audience: "If they think we are going to lift the weapons of murder against our French and

---

9 Kautsky, *Briefe*, 113.
10 Fred Ölsner, *Rosa Luxemburg: Eine kritische biographische Skizze*, 2nd ed. (Berlin: Dietz, 1951), 165 ff.
11 Ölsner, *Rosa Luxemburg*, 165 ff.

other brethren, then we shall shout: 'We will not do it.'"[12] Immediately she was arrested for incitement. On February 20, 1914, in spite of her defiant and lengthy defense before a Berlin court, she was sentenced to a year's imprisonment, to which could be added an indeterminate period of "protective custody." The appeal process stayed Luxemburg's incarceration for a year; but in February 1915, six months after the war began, her sentence was confirmed. She was dispatched to Berlin's Alexanderplatz prison to serve her time.[13]

Initially, Luxemburg's imprisonment was far from unbearable. She was allowed reading material and permitted to accept food parcels from friends and to correspond freely. She managed also to engage in political writing and, in April 1915, to produce the first comprehensive antiwar essay to be circulated in Germany. Bearing the signature "Junius" (after a legendary early Roman pacifist), the pamphlet was a furious denunciation of war and imperialism, of capitalist "exploitation" and the "swindle of national self-determination." In her wrath, Luxemburg did not spare the "craven" Social Democrat leadership itself, "shamed, dishonored, wading in blood and dripping with filth. . . . In the era of imperialism there can be no more [justified] national wars."[14] The pamphlet awaited publication for nearly six months, until Luxemburg's first, brief release from prison (p. 9). But even in its early, privately mimeographed version, "Junius" was a source of reinvigoration for the party's beleaguered Marxist purists.

Indeed, in August 1914, upon the Reichswehr's invasion of neutral Belgium, the schism among Germany's Social Democrats began to widen. When asked in late 1915 to approve an extension of war credits, a far larger minority, 44 of the party's 110 Reichstag deputies, voted against the request. Two years later, in April 1917, the Social Democratic veterans Karl Kautsky and Hugo Haase, joining with the famed "revisionist," Edouard Bernstein, led eighteen formerly "orthodox" deputies in seceding from the mother party and organizing their own antiwar faction, the "Independent Social Democratic Party." Yet even the "Independents" were not prepared to disgorge Germany's recent military gains in Eastern Europe. Only one group was. A year earlier, a tiny splinter faction within the Social Democrats assumed the title "Spartakusbund." Named for the leader of a Roman slave rebellion of antiquity and inspired by Luxemburg's "Junius" pamphlet as well as her ongoing

---

12 J.P. Nettl, *Rosa Luxemburg*, 2 vols. (London: Oxford University Press, 1966), 2: 481. For more on Liebknecht and Luxemburg challenging German war frenzy, see Schorske, *German Social Democracy*, 297–305.
13 Nettl, *Rosa Luxemburg*, 2: 488–92.
14 Rosa Luxemburg, *Die Krise der Sozialdemokratie*, 2nd ed. (Berlin: Verlag Rote Fahne, 1919), 12, 16.

succession of defiant prison letters, the "Spartacists" gathered in Luxemburg's vacant Berlin apartment to endorse her uncompromising commitment to peace and social revolution.

In April 1916, with time off for good behavior, Luxemburg secured an early release from prison. Then, unhesitatingly, she hurled herself again into the propaganda campaign to repudiate all territorial annexations and to bring the war to an end. Several weeks later, joining Karl Liebknecht in organizing a mass demonstration of ten thousand people in Berlin on behalf of "peace, bread, and freedom," she exhorted the Reichswehr to lay down its weapons. In response, the government promptly stripped Liebknecht of his Reichstag seat and sentenced him to four years in prison. Three months afterward, in July 1916, Luxemburg also was put under "protective custody," this time without trial. Carried off at first to Berlin's women's prison on the Branimstrasse, she was later transferred to Wronski prison, near Posen, far to the east. She would not know freedom again until the end of the war.

As in her original confinement, Luxemburg's circumstances at Wronski initially were not inhumane. She was allowed to correspond (subject to military censorship) and to receive food parcels. Her most devoted intermediary remained Leo Jogiches. Now working underground and incognito in Germany, Jogiches was in his element as a conspirator of revolution. If love between the two had long since expired, their mutual respect had not flagged, nor had their commitment to a shared political goal. In March 1918, when Jogiches himself was arrested and imprisoned, Luxemburg promptly entreated her correspondents to send him every parcel of food they had intended for her.

Meanwhile, five months earlier, in November 1917, Luxemburg's first reaction to news of Russia's Bolshevik Revolution was one of almost inexpressible joy. With her Spartacist comrades in arms, she exhorted the SPD majority to give unstinting support to the Bolshevik experiment. "On the whole," she wrote, "the events [in Russia] are glorious and will have immeasurable results."[15] Yet, as the weeks passed, Luxemburg's reservations about Vladimir Lenin's emergent dictatorship began to grow (p. 14). "Freedom only for the supporters of the [Bolshevik] government," she protested in one of her smuggled articles, "only for the members of one party—however numerous they may be—is no freedom at all."[16]

---

15  Nettl, *Rosa Luxemburg*, 2: 488–92.
16  Rosa Luxemburg, *Die russische Revolution* (Berlin: Verlag Gesellschaft und Erziehung, 1922), 3–4.

Since the summer of 1917, too, Luxemburg had been forced to confront other, more intimate difficulties. Until then, she had reacted to the boredom of prison life by endless reading and writing. Given the run of the prison, she had been allowed even to cultivate her own flower garden outside her cell. But in July 1917, Luxemburg was transferred from Wronski to the town prison of Breslau. There her incarceration became far more rigorous. At times she was reduced to sending her messages on the torn pages of French poetry books. Her secret "ink" was her own urine. Her health worsened. By the last year of her confinement, at the age of forty-seven, her hair had turned completely white.

## FAREWELL, THE HOHENZOLLERNS

It was the Treaty of Brest-Litovsk, signed on March 3, 1918, that confirmed Russia's departure from the war and the territorial amputation of fully a third of the former tsarist empire and almost half of its population (p. 75). Yet, almost simultaneously, as American troops arrived in increasing numbers to augment the French and British armies, Germany's Reichswehr experienced a palpable exhaustion of its manpower reserves. By then, too, the nation's population was subsisting on marginal food and fuel rations. Civilians had become pale and hollow-eyed, debilitated from lack of nourishment and the attendant diseases of malnutrition. Hence, in the aftermath of Brest-Litovsk, General Erich Ludendorff, assuming command of Germany's armies on the Western Front, persuaded Field Marshal Paul von Hindenburg and even Kaiser Wilhelm II that it was essential to launch a final "hammer blow" to break the back of the Western Allies.

In the late spring and summer of 1918, Ludendorff nearly pulled off his gamble. Five German army corps managed to drive back the French and British armies some forty miles. In mid-July, reprising its offensive of four years earlier, the Reichswehr then advanced to a bend in the Marne River only 45 miles from Paris. But this time Marshal Ferdinand Foch, the Allies' supreme commander, had carefully prepared his counterattack. On July 18, his sudden offensive, in which nine fresh American divisions also participated, took Ludendorff and his staff entirely by surprise. Soon afterward the "Second Battle of the Marne" developed into the Allies' climactic victory. From then on, their armies never lost the initiative. On August 8, "the black day of the Reichswehr," the entire Western Front was rolled back toward the German border; and on September 29, as the Allied forces approached the Rhine, Ludendorff's nerve broke. Only an immediate armistice could save Germany, he warned his shaken emperor.

In fact, the decision to seek an armistice was the consequence not only of military vulnerability but of social and political revolution. On October 3, 1918, the kaiser reluctantly agreed to appoint a new chancellor, Prince Maximilian of Baden, a liberal with a mandate to begin a more thorough political democratization of the Reich. It was presumed that the strategy would restore the nation's fighting morale (p. 68). But the transformation had been delayed too long. On November 3, the German naval squadrons at Kiel mutinied. Defying orders to put out to sea for one last, climactic battle, their crews instead hoisted red flags as they seized control of their ships. From Kiel, the mutiny spread to the other naval bases of northern Germany. By late autumn, military and civilian revolution erupted in Bavaria, which was directly exposed to Allied invasion from the south.

It was then, on November 9, that tens of thousands of Germans, civilians and soldiers alike, converged on the Hohenzollern royal palace at Potsdam, demanding an immediate end to the war on pain of mass violence. At this point, too, Friedrich Ebert, a former saddle maker who had risen through the years to chairmanship of the Social Democratic Party, "suggested" to Prince Maximilian that the government forthwith be turned over to the Social Democrats. The chancellor abruptly resigned his office in favor of Ebert himself. Ebert then proceeded directly to the formation of his cabinet. In the process, moreover, he resolved not only to end the war but to dispense with the imperial throne itself.

Indeed, the latter decision was influenced by both domestic politics and the diplomatic stance of the United States government, and specifically by that of its president, Woodrow Wilson. As early as October 4, 1918, when Germany's first oblique armistice feelers reached Washington, Wilson had let it be known that he would refuse to countenance any negotiations with a Germany led by a "war-mongering regime." The implication was plain that, first and foremost, the kaiser himself would have to go (p. 12). The ultimatum presented a quandary both for Chancellor Ebert and for the imperial general staff. With Germany in the throes of mass revolt, Wilhelm II seemingly had been the last remaining bulwark against the nation's "bolshevization." But during the night hours of November 8–9, from the imperial command headquarters at Spa, Belgium, Hindenburg left it to his recently appointed deputy, Quartermaster General Wilhelm Gröner, to confer by telephone with Chancellor Ebert in Berlin. If the kaiser consented to leave the throne, Gröner asked, would Ebert accept the armistice, protect Germany from Bolshevik anarchy, and let the army come home peacefully? Ebert agreed on the spot.

But the chancellor, negotiating with the far-leftist Independent Socialists, was forced to grapple with a challenge of his own, one that he presented to General Gröner. What would be the attitude of the military high command toward his, Ebert's, new Social Democrat government? Would the Reichswehr pledge its unconditional allegiance to that government? Hereupon, requesting a few minutes to confer with Hindenburg, Gröner shortly called back to confirm that indeed "orders have been given for the army to deal with your government in a cooperative and forbearing spirit."[17] These telephonic conversations apparently would spare the Socialist revolution from lapsing into bolshevism and the army command from imposing a possible dictatorship on Germany.[18]

Accordingly, on the same afternoon of November 9, Hindenburg himself led a cortege of senior officers into Spa's imperial salon, where the kaiser and his family had been residing since October 29. There, formally and tearfully, the army commander requested the kaiser's abdication. Wilhelm remained silent for a few moments. Then, asking his visitors to await him in the anteroom, he conversed separately with his wife. After ten minutes he returned to announce his concurrence, even ruefully disclosing that, for the last several days, the family's personal belongings already had been packed. The following morning, November 10, Hindenburg released the news of the kaiser's abdication to the nation. Simultaneously, by prearrangement, Friedrich Ebert in Berlin appeared on the balcony of the chancellery building on the Ballplatz to proclaim the "official" birth of a new German Republic. Two hours later, in the early afternoon, the dethroned kaiser, together with his family and personal retinue, boarded the royal train (still bearing its escutcheons of cream and gold) and embarked for the sheltered retreat of neutral Holland.

## A VALEDICTORY FOR "RED ROSA"

That same November 10, in response to the demands of the three newly appointed Independent Socialists in his six-man coalition cabinet, Chancellor Ebert acknowledged that German political power should now be invested in workers' and soldiers' "soviets" (councils); and, further, that the cabinet itself would be retitled a "soviet," and its members would jettison the traditional nomenclature of "ministers" and henceforth be titled "people's commissars." Yet, at the same time, the chancellor and even his "Independent" colleagues

---

17 J.W. Wheeler-Bennett, *Wooden Titan: Hindenburg in Twenty Years of German History* (New York: W. Morrow & Co., 1936), 209.
18 Harold J. Gordon, Jr., *The Reichswehr and the German Republic, 1919–1926.* (Princeton, NJ: Princeton University Press, 1956), 209.

would not be pushed to the brink of bolshevism. They intended to honor their pledge to the army high command. Hence, two and a half weeks later, on December 1, the Ebert government moved further along the path of moderation. When the Social Democrats convened an incongruously named "Congress of Workers' and Soldiers' Councils" in Berlin, they chose voluntarily to renounce the emergency powers thrust in their hands by the November 9 revolution. Instead, at Ebert's initiative, the party members approved elections the next month for a national assembly, which then would formulate a democratic constitution for the new republic.

It was this latter decision, in turn, that stunned the party's fringe of Spartacist radicals. On December 13, outraged at the "abject surrender" of revolutionary authority, a Spartacist contingent of sailors and civilians launched an attempted break-in of the chancellery building. The assault was stopped in its tracks. Delivering on its part of the November 9 bargain with Ebert, the army exploited its still impressive reserves of firepower by killing and wounding scores of the assailants and putting the rest to flight. Whereupon, denouncing the "brutality" of the repression, the Independent Socialists left the government coalition, and Ebert for his part lost no time in filling their positions with his moderately oriented Social Democrats. Indeed, by then, except for ending the war and ushering in a new, democratic republic, the revolutionary phase of German socialism apparently was liquidating itself.

Yet the development also became the nightmare that Rosa Luxemburg, Karl Liebknecht, and their loyalists had most feared. As Luxemburg's "Junius" pamphlet had made clear, their purpose in establishing the Spartakusbund was classically and unequivocally Marxist, to "fuse the proletariat of all countries into one living revolutionary force."[19] Until the approaching end of the war, with Luxemburg and Liebknecht still languishing in prison, the league had sustained its revolutionary fervor under the interim direction of Franz Mehring, Klara Zetkin, and Leo Jogiches (until Jogiches's own imprisonment). But the Spartacist leadership, and tens of thousands of common German working people, well understood that Luxemburg and Liebknecht remained the heart and soul of the revolution.

Accordingly, on November 9, 1918, when Friedrich Ebert's government declared a general amnesty for political prisoners, a crowd of revolutionaries thronged the gates of Breslau prison to usher Rosa Luxemburg out to freedom.

---

19  Rudolf Coper, *Failure of a Revolution: Germany in 1918–1919* (Cambridge: Cambridge University Press, 1955), 53.

Although frail and ill, her eyesight still uncertain in the autumn sunlight, the tiny woman did not so much as await her return to Berlin before addressing a rapt mass meeting in Breslau's central square. The revolution would have to be carried to its logical victory of a classless society, she declaimed to uproarious cheers; there could be no return to the exploitative and chauvinistic old order. Then Luxemburg was brought back to the capital, where she was awaited at the Zoogarten railway station by a crowd that included two other newly released prisoners. These were Liebknecht and Jogiches. Gaunt and sunken-cheeked, Jogiches clasped his former lover to him. Their embrace was tearful—and elegiac.

Luxemburg's followers had provided office facilities for her in a commandeered right-wing publishing plant. There, she and Liebknecht immediately set about producing a Spartacist newspaper, *Die Rote Fahne* (*The Red Flag*). Working at white heat, as if there had been no wartime interregnum of imprisonment and illness, Luxemburg churned out articles and editorials, entreating her readers to organize a Red Guard, to expropriate hereditary wealth and absentee property, and, above all, to convene an "authentically revolutionary" soviet to replace Friedrich Ebert's "fraudulent," so-called Soviet of People's Commissars. But however fiery on the printed page, Luxemburg's program in fact was less than draconian. Although advocating a spontaneous mass upheaval by the nation's workers and farmers—in effect, by a majority of the German population—it sternly repudiated the kind of Bolshevik dictatorship then operating in Russia.

Three months earlier, while still in prison, Luxemburg had warned a visiting colleague, Paul Levi, that "freedom of the press, the rights of association and assembly, all have been outlawed for opponents of the Soviet regime. . . . [Yet] without a free and untrammeled press, without the unlimited right of association and assembly, the rule of the broad mass of the people is entirely unthinkable."[20] Now, picking up the same theme in her *Rote Fahne* editorials, Luxemburg reminded her followers that Lenin's dictatorship was

> worse than the disease it was supposed to cure. . . . Socialism by its very nature cannot be dictated [or] introduced by command. . . . Without general elections, without unrestricted freedom of the press and assembly, without a free exchange of opinions, life dies out in every public institution and only bureaucracy remains active.[21]

---

20  Rosa Luxemburg, *The Russian Revolution*, ed. Bertram D. Wolfe (Ann Arbor, MI: University of Michigan Press, 1961), 66–67.
21  Luxemburg, *The Russian Revolution*, 62–63, 70–71.

"The Bolsheviks," Luxemburg stated to Lenin's personal emissary, Karl Radek, "are welcome to keep their tactics for themselves."[22]

Meanwhile, although working by day at her well-protected editorial office in Berlin, Luxemburg was obliged at night to transfer her personal quarters from hotel to hotel to evade possible rightist murder attempts. On street corners and billboards, in newspapers and leaflets, she was denounced as a Bolshevik, a Jew, a devil, bent on destroying German "respectable" society. On one occasion a Freikorps—rightist, paramilitary—attempt to kidnap Luxemburg was repelled only at the last moment by her watchful Spartacist bodyguards. Throughout December 1918, antigovernment violence both of the Right and Left flickered periodically in Berlin and other German cities. On December 6, when a crowd of Spartacist loyalists launched a protest demonstration against the Ebert cabinet as "militarists-in-disguise," they were met by Freikorps machine-gun fire that left 187 civilians dead. In their outrage at the mayhem, the Independent Socialists then defected en bloc from Ebert's government.

These were the circumstances that persuaded Karl Liebknecht and other Spartacist leaders that their only remaining alternative was to negotiate a closer relationship with Soviet Russia. As the first step in this direction, they argued, the Spartakusbund itself should be transformed into Germany's first openly identified Communist party. Luxemburg and Jogiches opposed the move. It would lead inevitably to a Bolshevik-style, elitist revolution, they warned; and, in any event, the masses in Germany needed more indoctrination before they were ripe for that kind of upheaval. But on December 31, 1918, under Liebknecht's leadership, a rump Spartacist conference voted decisively to transform its little fraction into the "Kommunistische Partei Deutschlands"—although the nomenclature "Spartakusbund" was maintained in parentheses. At this juncture, the pace of revolution was accelerated beyond Luxemburg's control.

On the night of January 6, 1919, a joint committee of Communists and Independent Socialists followed Liebknecht's initiative, summoning workers to a general strike in preparation for a takeover of the government.[23] Upon being informed that her old comrade had embarked on a revolution without careful preparation or precautions against bloodshed, Luxemburg cried

---

22  Elżbieta Ettinger, *Rosa Luxemburg: A Life* (Boston: Beacon Press, 1986), 236.
23  Ossip K. Flechtheim, *Die KPD in die Weimarer Republik* (Offenbach: Bollwerk-Verlag, 1948), 12–18; see also Eric Waldman, *The Spartacist Uprising of 1919 and the Crisis of the German Socialist Movement* (Milwaukee: Marquette University Press, 1958), 93–98.

in protest: "How could you? What about our ideology, our program, our strategy?"[24]

Once the uprising began, however, and demonstrated an unexpected base of popular support, she and her staff at the *Rote Fahne* decided over Jogiches's objection that their only alternative was to support it with all possible energy.[25] "Act quickly," she editorialized. "The revolution demands it."[26] The appeal was ill-judged. Two days later, on January 8, 1919, the government launched a full-scale counteroffensive. Chancellor Ebert's defense commissar, Gustav Noske, himself a veteran Social Democrat, had long been chafing to settle scores with the "bolshies" who were maligning the name of honest workers. For that purpose, Noske relied extensively on the Freikorps. Numbering about one hundred thousand members nationwide, and soon to more than double in size, these right-wing war veterans functioned under regular army command. In Berlin, about thirty thousand of them, heavily armed with automatic weapons and artillery pieces, turned on the revolutionaries with a vengeance. By the time the four-day battle had ended, on January 12, over a thousand rebels lay dead, with many times that wounded, and both Freikorps paramilitaries and some eight thousand veteran Reichswehr troops remained in firm command of the capital.[27]

Two days later, Luxemburg's final *Rote Fahne* edition rolled off the mimeographs, this time at a secret hideaway in Berlin's middle-class Wilmersdorf district. Her editorial was a defiant affirmation that "the revolution marches over graves still to be occupied, over—victories and defeats—toward its great task."[28] By then, Luxemburg and Liebknecht had been making their separate ways from one retreat to another. On January 15, both took shelter in the apartment of old friends, the Marcussohn family. It was precarious sanctuary. Defense Commissar Noske had put a price of 100,000 marks on the two fugitive leaders. That very evening, a resident of the building informed police that strangers had been seen in the Marcussohn apartment, and at about 9:00 p.m. a Horse Guard military unit broke in and seized Luxemburg and Liebknecht.

---

24 Otto Friedrich, *Before the Deluge: A Portrait of Berlin in the 1920s* (New York: Avon, 1972). For the uprising of 1919 see pages 40–45; for the quotation, see page 63.
25 Nettl, *Rosa Luxemburg*, 2: 734.
26 Paul Frölich, *Rosa Luxemburg: Gedanke und Tat* (Frankfurt am Main: Europäische Vergasanstalt, 1967), 25, 28.
27 Gustav Noske, *Von Kiel bis Kapp* (Berlin: Verlag für Politik und Wirtschaf, 1920), *passim*.
28 Rosa Luxemburg, "Die Ordnung herrscht in Berlin," *Die Rote Fahne*, January 14, 1919; a different translation is available online at the *Marxist Internet Archive Library*, http://www.marxists.org/archive/luxemburg/1919/01/14.htm.

The Horse Guards had made their own headquarters in the Hotel Eden, near the municipal zoo, and there Luxemburg and Liebknecht were brought in for questioning. In the process, both prisoners were savagely beaten. When the "interrogation" ended, Captain Waldemar Pabst seemingly arranged for the two captives to be transferred to the Moabit district jail. Liebknecht and Luxemburg then were dragged separately out of a side exit. But as Liebknecht stumbled into an awaiting automobile, a pair of guards proceeded to club him senseless. Afterward, carried off in the darkness, he was shot dead and his body was dumped into an alley. At the Hotel Eden, a second automobile awaited Luxemburg. She had already lost consciousness before she was pulled into its back seat. When the car drove off, one of its occupants, Lieutenant Kurt Vogel, put a pistol to her head and shot her. The drive continued to the Liechtenstein Bridge, where she was thrown into the Landwehr Canal. Several hours later, a government news release stated that Liebknecht had been killed while "attempting to escape" and that Luxemburg's body had been seized by an "angry crowd" and disposed of at an "unknown place."[29]

Only Leo Jogiches entertained no illusions about Luxemburg's fate. That same evening of January 15, 1919, maintaining a hardened revolutionary's stoic demeanor, he dispatched a cryptic telegram to Lenin in Moscow: "Rosa Luxemburg and Karl Liebknecht have carried out their ultimate revolution."[30] The day before, Jogiches himself had been arrested, but had managed to escape without being identified. From his hideaway in a secret apartment, taking over sole leadership of the Spartacist resistance, he remained determined somehow to carry on its revolutionary mission. But there was little time to regroup. Elections for the new German republic's national assembly took place only a few days later, and the delegates subsequently proceeded from Berlin to Weimar to debate a new constitution under the "protection" of the Freikorps. At this point, Jogiches and his colleagues moved rapidly to launch a final strike, on March 3, 1919. There should be no violence, Jogiches warned, no provocation that Defense Commissar Noske could exploit to repeat the massacres of January.

But again the leadership lost control. Earlier, the Communists had cached away substantial quantities of weapons. Retrieving them now, they proceeded to launch attacks on Berlin's police stations. As in January, however,

---

29  E. J. Gumbel, *Vier Jahre politischer Mord* (Berlin: Verlag der neuen Gesellschaft, 1922), 81.
30  Howard M. Sachar, *Dreamland: Europeans and Jews in the Aftermath of the Great War* (New York: Alfred A. Knopf, 2002), 230. For a different translation of this telegram, see Richard M. Watt, *The Kings Depart: The German Revolution and the Treaty of Versailles, 1918–19* (Harmondsworth: Penguin, 1969), 303: "Rosa Luxemburg and Karl Liebknecht have carried out their ultimate revolutionary duty."

ROSA LUXEMBURG, 1907

Noske was ready and waiting. Indeed, by then the army had replenished the Freikorps's arsenal from its own remaining stocks of artillery, tanks, flame-throwers, and even airplanes. Two days of carnage then followed, claiming an additional six hundred civilian lives.[31] One of these was Jogiches's. He was seized on March 10 while paying a return visit to Luxemburg's apartment in search of her papers. Carried off to the Alexanderplatz police headquarters, he was beaten senseless and then shot.[32]

Nearly five months later, on May 31, 1919, when the winter ice had melted, a corpse was discovered and removed from the Landwehr Canal. It was

---

31  Friedrich, *Before the Deluge*, 101–2.
32  Nettl, *Rosa Luxemburg*, 2: 780.

subsequently announced to be Luxemburg's. Noske issued orders for the body to be buried secretly. But the press already had picked up the news. Paul Levi, who had assumed leadership of the Communist Party after Jogiche's murder, arranged for her body to be buried in the Friedrichsfelde cemetery, near those of Liebknecht, Jogiches, and twenty-nine of their fallen comrades. On the day of the interment, June 13, tens of thousands of mourners filed by to pay their respects to these victims of the winter violence. Seven years later, in June 1926, a memorial was unveiled to commemorate their last resting place.

It was only then, in the mid- and late-1920s, after a half-decade of comparative political quiescence, that all factions of Germany's ideological Left began giving retrospective attention to Luxemburg's career. Their initial evaluation was that she had lent her powerful intellect and acerbic pen to a heedless and senseless revolution. This interpretation, fostered during the Stalin era in denunciation of the so-called cosmopolitan internationalism of the Trotskyites, has largely been dispelled by modern scholarship. So, too, has the image of Luxemburg as a sulfurous political virago. The publication of several small volumes of her letters, entirely personal and of touchingly human and often poetic beauty, was enough to destroy the legend of a bloodthirsty "Red Rosa."[33] She was a sentimental woman, a passionate lover of Jogiches, a birdwatcher and flower cultivator, a woman to whom guards at her prison bade goodbye with tears in their eyes.

Indeed, from beginning to end, Luxemburg's alleged "political ruthlessness" was mobilized less on behalf of an abstract dialectic than for world peace and for the common people. Not for her the Leninist vision of war as the indispensable catalyst of revolution. The very notion of mass death and destruction, of a Bolshevik-style dictatorship, she regarded as intolerable. Today, Rosalia Luksemburg emerges as a courageous if single-minded personality, a woman who embraced the Marxist cause doubtless with historical naiveté but also with unique moral courage against a chauvinism that survived even within the socialist world. Jogiches was right. In a life of self-sacrifice, she had carried out her "ultimate revolution"—and paid her ultimate dues.

It was a supreme irony, therefore, that the obsequies bestowed at the memorial her friends and followers arranged at Luxemburg's designated grave might actually have been misplaced. On May 29, 2009, almost ninety years to the day when the retrieval of her body had been announced, Dr. Michael Tsokos, director of forensic medicine at Berlin's Charité hospital, informed

---

33   Lelio Basso, *Rosa Luxemburg: A Reappraisal* (New York: Praeger, 1975), 132 *ff*.

the press that he was virtually certain that an unidentified, headless cadaver, lately discovered in one of the hospital's basement vaults, was that of Rosa Luxemburg. While DNA evidence still was lacking, the bodily structure of a female with a twisted spine and one leg shorter than the other, together with the hastily noted date of recovery—May 31, 1919—all were commensurate with photographs and medical records of "Red Rosa."[34]

## THE AFTERSHOCKS OF REVOLUTION

### Bavaria

The "ultimate dues" also had been paid by others, even of the moderate Left. At 9:45 on February 21, 1919, Kurt Eisner, minister-president of Bavaria, postwar Germany's second largest province, departed his Munich office to attend the opening session two blocks away. Accompanying him during the short walk on the Promenadenplatz were two bodyguards and two political aides. None looked backward. Unnoticed, a young man then walked up softly behind the minister-president and fired a pistol bullet into his back, killing him instantly.

Eisner's death was preceded by that of Bavaria's monarchy. Formerly, even after entering Bismarck's newly established German Empire in 1871, Bavaria had been allowed to remain a semiautonomous kingdom and, to retain its own dynasty, the House of Wittelsbach. Yet its royalist government had not achieved the status of a constitutional monarchy, and its legislation remained obdurately conservative. Even in the months after the armistice and Bavaria's transformation into a *Land*—a province of republican Germany—this formidable citadel of Catholic conservatism remained a cultural extension of Habsburg Austria, and its citizenry only grudgingly tolerated progressive movements of any kind.[35] All the more ironic, therefore, that Bavaria emerged from the war as the first of Germany's Länder to inaugurate a Socialist government and, subsequently, to remain in the grip of political radicalism longer than any other German province.[36]

---

34 "Rosa Luxemburg Mystery: DNA of Great-Niece May Help Identify Headless Corpse," *Der Spiegel*, July 21, 2009, http://www.spiegel.de/international/germany/rosa-luxemburg-mystery-dna-of-great-niece-may-help-identify-headless-corpse-a-637385.html.
35 Alan Mitchell, *Revolution in Bavaria* (Princeton, NJ: Princeton University Press, 1965), 31.
36 Franz Schade, *Kurt Eisner und die bayerische Sozialdemokratie* (Hanover: Verlag fur Literature und Zeitgeschehen 1961), 13–14.

The process was guided by the far-leftist Independent Socialists (p. 8). Their chairman, Kurt Eisner, was as improbable a political phenomenon as the party itself. Eisner was neither a Bavarian nor a Catholic. Born in Berlin in 1867, he was the prototypical outsider, the son of Jewish lower-middle-class parents. Upon graduating from Berlin's Friedrich Wilhelm University, he found his métier in journalism; and, as a political columnist for the *Frankfurt Allgemeine Zeitung*, he staked out his ideological home in Social Democracy. From the outset of his journalistic career, Eisner's political essays spared no vested interest, neither the aristocracy, nor the great money lords, nor even the imperial kaiser. Indeed, in 1897, he was sentenced to a three-month jail term for lèse-majesté. Yet the brief incarceration became Eisner's stroke of good fortune. It won him the admiration of Wilhelm Liebknecht, the "grand old man" of Germany's Social Democratic Party. Upon Eisner's release, Liebknecht appointed him editorial director of the *Vorwärts*, Europe's most respected socialist newspaper, and within three years Eisner rose to the periodical's managing editorship.

His fall was almost as rapid. Despite his hostility toward Prussia's imperial court and Junker barons, Eisner was no less emphatic in his condemnation of "lawlessness," whether of the Right or the Left. In 1905, he refused editorial endorsement of a mass Social-Democratic "sympathy" demonstration on behalf of the Octobrist revolutionaries in tsarist Russia. Yet, in turn, Eisner's selective and incremental brand of revisionism offended old Liebknecht, who fired him.[37] Subsequently, out of work and out of favor with the party, and with a wife and five children to support, the thirty-eight-year-old journalist soon was obliged to earn his bread as a freelance writer outside Berlin. In 1910, leaving his family behind, he tried his luck in Munich. It was a useful move. His reputation as a fearless critic of "Prussian" militarism won him appointment as political editor of the *Münchener Post*, the organ of Bavarian socialism. Soon Eisner was back in his element. Although physically less than impressive—a short, small-boned, rather plump man of sallow complexion, with thinning hair, a full reddish beard already streaked with gray, and wearing thick, steel-rimmed glasses—he achieved grandiose moral dimensions with his fearless editorial attacks against Junker imperialism.[38]

When war began in 1914, Eisner avoided doctrinaire condemnation. "Now that tsarism has attacked Germany," he wrote, "we have no choice... [but] to annihilate

---

37  Friedrich Stampfer, *Erfahrungen und Erkenntnisse* (Cologne: Verlag für Politik und Wirtschaft, 1957), 109–12.
38  Kurt Eisner, "Religion des Sozialismus," in *Gesammelte Schriften*, vol. 2 (Berlin: Cassirer, 1919), 27–38.

the hereditary enemy of European civilisation."[39] Yet, within weeks, horrified by the Reichswehr's invasion of neutral Belgium, Eisner changed his tune and urged an end to the conflict. For his efforts, he was dismissed from his newspaper and reduced again to contributing intermittent guest articles. This time, however, upon breaking with Social Democracy's nationalist-collaborationist line, Eisner did so in full force, moving decisively to the political Left. In 1917, as a founding member of Germany's breakaway Independent Socialist Party, he became chairman of its Bavarian branch. The following year, leading a protest strike against the Empire's punitive—Brest-Litovsk—dismemberment of Russia, he was arrested again, convicted for incitement, and confined in the Stadelheim citadel for eight-and-a-half months.

For Eisner the episode became even more of a defining moment than his earlier, youthful imprisonment. As Bavarian socialism's first major political martyr, he soon acquired a near-legendary aura among his fellow "progressives." Indeed, it was a reputation he put to decisive use sooner than he expected. By the time he was set free in the last week of October 1918, Munich already was enveloped in chaos, with socialists of all colorations demanding an end to the war and the eradication of both monarchies, Bavaria's Wittelsbach and Imperial Germany's Hohenzollern. Eisner and his fellow "Independents" immediately assumed leadership in the campaign, organizing mass demonstrations on behalf of peace and republicanism. On November 7, at their direction, factories closed altogether throughout Bavaria's principal cities, and thousands of mutinous troops began mingling with striking workers, brandishing red flags, spontaneously forming joint "soviets." The next morning, in a procession of automobiles, King Ludwig III and the Bavarian royal family fled to neighboring Austria. With breathtaking audacity, Eisner then moved on his own to direct the course of the uprising, and without bothering to consult the leadership of Bavaria's mainstream Social-Democratic faction.

Escorted into the Bavarian Landtag on November 9 by a phalanx of Independent Socialist comrades, Eisner informed the assembled deputies, "in the name of the Soviet of Workers and Soldiers," that Bavaria was now an autonomous republic, shorn for good and always both of its Wittelsbach dynasty and its subservience to Berlin. All power henceforth was to be invested in a national—that is, a Bavarian—"soviet," over which he, Eisner, would preside as minister-president and foreign minister. Moreover, although promising free and democratic elections for a constitutional assembly, Eisner

---

39 Quoted in Roger Fletcher, *Revisionism and Empire: Socialist Imperialism in Germany, 1897–1914* (London: Allen & Unwin, 1984), 116, 179.

made clear that, in the "interim," his soviet would govern by "temporary decree."[40] No other political spokesman dared to challenge his audacious pronunciamento, especially when he followed it by inviting Erhard Auer, chairman of the mainstream Social Democrats, to join a socialist coalition government. Indeed, for the next few weeks of the early post-armistice, peace and order seemingly reigned in Bavaria.[41]

The appearance was altogether deceptive. No one in Eisner's "soviet" possessed meaningful executive experience. Its only "socialist" innovation was a blandly welfarist eight-hour day, accompanied by marginally improved factory working conditions and an increase in unemployment benefits. Otherwise, neither Eisner as minister-president, nor his colleagues—whether Social Democrat or Independent Socialist—evinced any particular willingness to tamper with Bavaria's great landed estates, its formidable industrial cartels, or its public utility monopolies. In Munich, as in Berlin, these issues were postponed for an indeterminate future. With little real comprehension of economics, Eisner simply acknowledged that "authentic" socialism would have to wait until most of Europe's other industrialized nations were comparably "socialized."

It was not only administrative or ideological confusion, however, that accounted for the minister-president's hesitancy. He well understood the vagaries of his political base. After all, no one had voted him into power. Indeed, his government was tolerated essentially on the premise that, if it cooperated faithfully in the forthcoming peace negotiations, it would be positioned to ensure lenient treatment from the Allies. But, to accomplish even this limited goal, Eisner and his colleagues assumed that they would have to distance themselves not only from the warmongering reputation of the former Reich but, if possible, from political links with "greater" Germany altogether—even with the presumably fraternal "soviet" of Chancellor Friedrich Ebert. Yet it was an ill-conceived assumption. When Eisner visited Berlin on November 23 and submitted to Ebert his proposal for an autonomous Bavarian foreign policy, the German chancellor all but exploded at this "act of treachery."[42] In turn, shaken and bitter, Eisner hurried back to Munich to announce that his government on its own was "severing diplomatic relations" with Berlin.[43] But this move, too, was as futile as it was impulsive. It evoked no special, forbearing

---

40 Hans Bayer, *Von der Novemberrevolution zur Räterepublik in München* (Berlin: Rütten & Loening, 1957), 2–12.
41 Schade, *Kurt Eisner*, 50–52.
42 Karl Schwend, *Bayern zwischen Monarchie und Diktatur: Beiträge zur bayerischen Frage in der Zeit von 1918 bis 1933* (Munich: R. Pflaum, 1954), 50–51.
43 Schwend, *Bayern*, 58.

# THE ASSASSINATION OF EUROPE

## KURT EISNER (LEFT), 1919

treatment from the Allies, who maintained their economic blockade as indiscriminately against Bavaria as against Germany at large.

Meanwhile, at the insistence of Bavaria's Social Democratic leadership, the date of January 12, 1919, had been set for Landtag elections. Indeed, campaigning already had started the previous December and would continue for the ensuing six weeks. But it was during that interval, too, that the Catholic Bavarians began to reappraise a government that was not only socialist, ineffectual, and predominantly Munich based but also substantially Jewish. Besides Eisner, they saw Gustav Landauer and Erich Mühsam sitting in Munich's six-man "central soviet," as well as other Jews who were prominent in the several variations of Bavarian socialism. The campaign literature and oratory of the non-Socialist parties, as well as editorials in the Bavarian press, left no doubt that the nation's reaction to the leftist experiment and its "alien" leadership was becoming increasingly uncongenial.[44]

Thus, when some 3 million Bavarians voted in the Landtag elections of January 12, the outcome proved a serious defeat for Eisner and his partners. The mainstream Social Democrats received the largest plurality of votes, followed closely by the various Catholic "confessional" parties. By contrast, Eisner and his fellow Independent Socialists won a pitiable three seats, only one more than the tiny Communist faction. For another month and a half, the minister-president trimmed and maneuvered, seeking frantically to reconstitute his precarious coalition, but to no avail. Eventually, at 9:45 a.m. on February 21, chastened and despondent, Eisner set out on the two-block walk from his foreign ministry office to the Landtag, where he intended to submit his government's resignation. With his short and tubby frame, his goatee and trademark oversized black hat, he was an easily recognizable figure. It was then that Eisner's youthful assailant crept up behind him and fired a series of pistol shots into his back, killing him instantly.

Eisner's bodyguard, in turn, shot and wounded the assassin. Afterward, the police rushed the young man to a hospital, where surgeons managed to save his life. It soon emerged that his name was Anton von Arco auf Valley. He was twenty-one years old, a former lieutenant of the Royal Guards, and a count—indeed, the son of Count Maximilian von Arco auf Valley, whose family could trace its patent of nobility back to the twelfth century. But Arco's mother was born Emily Freiin von Oppenheim, and thus he was also a half-Jew. Several days of police investigation produced one ostensible motive for his act of homicide. He had applied for membership in the Thule Gesellschaft,

---

44 Mitchell, *Revolution*, 123.

an ardently racist society named after a legendary Nordic *Ur* kingdom. Among its other members were the future Nazis Alfred Rosenberg and Rudolf Hess. Its emblem was the swastika. Hence, when Anton von Arco was discovered to be of part-Jewish origin, he was immediately rejected. As Rudolf von Sebottendorf, the society's president, explained later, Arco in his bitterness "evidently wanted to show that even a half-Jew could perform such a deed."[45]

In January 1920, when the young assassin finally was brought to trial, the court listened to extensive defense testimony that he had consummated "a noble deed." Whether the three judges agreed or not, on January 16 they sentenced Arco to death, then promptly commuted his sentence to life imprisonment. In fact, Arco's subsequent confinement in the Stadelheim fortress proved to be hardly more than an inconvenience. He was released in April 1924 for "good behavior," and received a hero's welcome home. Years later, in 1941, the Nazis proclaimed him an "honorary Aryan."

## A Posthumous Bavarian Nightmare

One hour after the original fatal shooting of February 21, 1919, Alois Lindner, a member of Bavaria's far-leftist Revolutionary Workers' Soviet, entered the central chamber of the Landtag building and approached one of its seated deputies, Erhard Auer, leader of the Bavarian Social Democratic Party. Removing a pistol from his pocket, Lindner shot Auer point-blank, severely wounding him, although not fatally. There was no apparent ideological connection between these double shootings; but, in the ensuing political uncertainty, Bavaria's original Central Soviet immediately issued a fiat of martial law. To alleviate public misgivings, it was decided that the newly elected Landtag would be recalled into session "as soon as conditions permit." But the assembly was not allowed to convene until late March 1919. Its first act then was to inaugurate a new cabinet, functioning under the chancellorship of a veteran, mainline Social Democrat, Johannes Hoffmann. At its opening session, the Hoffmann government resignedly agreed to accept Germany's newly formulated Weimar Constitution (p. 29). Bavaria, in consequence, terminated its brief career as an autonomous republic and became a *Land*, in the manner of Germany's other regional provinces.

Yet the Hoffmann administration, under whatever political nomenclature, soon proved as ineffectual as the recent Eisner soviet in coping with Bavaria's massive unemployment and raging inflation. Over the next weeks, the Independent Socialists and other far-leftists called for the establishment of an

---

45 Quoted in David Luhrssen, *Hammer of the Gods: The Thule Society and the Birth of Nazism* (Washington, DC: Potomac Books, 2012), 115.

"authentic" soviet and a new "people's army"—in effect, a new revolution. The time for this move was propitious, they believed. Although Germany's Spartacist uprising in Berlin had been crushed the previous January, the threat of worker insurrections still continued in the Ruhr Valley, while a Communist regime under Bela Kun lately had assumed control in neighboring Hungary, thus giving proof that revolution could succeed outside Soviet Russia. Hence, on April 4, 1919, a crowd of defiant radicals gathered in Munich's Löwenbräu beer hall to press for a "bona fide" socialist government; and, three days later, political power shifted almost by default to a far-leftist council of some one hundred members. It was this council, in turn, that lost no time in proclaiming its constituency the "Soviet Republic of Bavaria." Reasserting its independence of Berlin, and before the confused Munich police force could intervene, the self-appointed regime then promptly sent the Hoffmann government fleeing to the town of Bamberg, in northern Bavaria.

None of the guiding spirits of the new cabal, neither Gustav Landauer, Erich Mühsam, nor Ernst Toller, was so much as a native Bavarian. They were Jewish intellectuals from elsewhere in Germany. Moreover, their unquestioned Marxist idealism was almost entirely vitiated by lack of a coherent governing vision. Issuing a stream of edicts, these "coffee-house anarchists" (as Toller later ruefully dubbed his colleagues)[46] ordered the mobilization of an armed workers' militia, the regulation of all food supplies, the nationalization of Bavaria's newspapers, and even the confiscation of all homes possessing more than three rooms. As these measures were duly enacted, food and fuel were swiftly exhausted, and the regime's pronunciamentos soon were ignored by a confused and frightened citizenry. The "commissar for foreign affairs," Franz Lipp, fecklessly appealed to Berlin for help, complaining that the late Hoffmann government had exhibited the gall even to abscond with the key to the commissarial men's room.

Less than a week and a half later, an adventure that had begun as opéra bouffe ended in tragedy. On April 17, 1919, with the support of a makeshift "Red Militia," a small junta of Communist Party members, led by a triumvirate of hardened Russian-born Bolsheviks—Tovia Axelrod, Max Levien, and Eugene Leviné—confronted Landauer and his colleagues to announce that the latter's "pseudo-soviet" was finished and that a "pure" soviet now would establish a government. So began the third and final mutation of Bavarian socialism.[47] Indeed, it began with a wave of forceful intimidation. Munich's

---

46 Ernst Toller, *I Was a German: The Autobiography of a Revolutionary*, trans Edward Crankshaw (New York: W. Morrow, 1934), 149–50.

47 Rosa Leviné-Meyer, *Aus der Münchener Rätezeit* (Berlin: Vereinigung Internationaler Verlags-Anstalten, 1925), 12–16.

Stadelheim fortress soon was filled with hostages from middle-class and aristocratic families. Schools were closed, opposition newspapers were banned, and an official "Bavarian Red Army" was organized out of the twenty thousand militiamen who had remained in a state of semi-mobilization from the two predecessor administrations.

In Bamberg, on April 20, only three days into this latest—"pure"—soviet experiment, Johannes Hoffmann's "government in exile" turned to Berlin for help. Hoffmann himself traveled north to meet with the German defense minister, the formidable Gustav Noske. Noske, in turn, secured the republican cabinet's approval for dispatching a substantial German expeditionary force to confront the "bolshies"—provided Hoffmann abandoned all further "*quatsch*" ("nonsense") about Bavarian autonomy. Hoffmann agreed on the spot. Accordingly, in the last week of April 1919, thirty thousand veteran Reichswehr troops under the command of General Walther von Lüttwitz began its drive to the south. Crossing the Bavarian frontier on April 30, the seasoned and disciplined military force embarked on a meticulously coordinated offensive against Munich, blasting the capital's defenders with heavy artillery and aerial bombardment. The rebels held out for three days; but on May 2 resistance crumbled and the expeditionary force successfully occupied the city.

At this point, on its own initiative but supplemented by some twelve thousand Freikorps paramilitaries, the army launched upon an indiscriminate "White Terror," combing Munich for "Reds," whether hard-core Communists or Socialist moderates. Within a six-day period, at least a thousand people were slaughtered. Finally, on May 23, the Hoffmann émigré government was permitted to return from Bamberg, and both Reichswehr and Freikorps regiments then departed Munich. Yet, even afterward, the hunt continued for suspected radicals, whether of the latest "pure" soviet, of its predecessor "coffee-house" Bavarian Soviet Republic, or even of Eisner's anodyne social-welfare "soviet." Captives were indiscriminately killed or imprisoned, among them Gustav Landauer (beaten to death), Erich Mühsam (tortured and partially blinded in prison), and Ernst Toller (imprisoned, later exiled, and eventually reduced to penury and suicide). The terror did not gutter out until early summer of 1919.

*Germany*

By then, the ordeal of "normalization" had taken its toll on Germany at large. As far back as January 19, 1919, a few days after suppression of the original Communist (Spartacist) uprising in Berlin, 30 million Germans had gone to the polls for the country's first postwar national election. Their ballots produced a solid triumph for Friedrich Ebert and the Social Democratic moderates. With a dominating plurality of 163 deputies (out of 421), Ebert anticipated that the first Nationalversammlung (national assembly) also would function as a constitutional assembly and formulate a revised basic law for the emergent new government. To accomplish that purpose, the chancellor secured the deputies' permission to shift the assembly's venue away from Berlin—still flickering with intermittent Communist violence—to sedate, provincial Weimar, with its humanistic legacies of Goethe, Schiller, and Herder.

It was in Weimar, too, on February 10, four days after assembling in the town's dignified old National Theater, that the delegates formally honored Ebert with the title of "President of the new German Republic." In Ebert's place, his close associate, Philipp Scheidemann, was elected chancellor of the left-center coalition government (no longer bearing the provocative title "soviet"). It required an additional six weeks to formulate and approve the draft of the new republican constitution. But at last, in early April 1919, the delegates reconvened in Berlin as a normally functioning legislature, although the constitution permitted retention of the nostalgic title "Reichstag."

Ten weeks later yet, on June 28, 1919, in Versailles's Hall of Mirrors, a German delegation signed a peace treaty with the Allies. The document was not forbearing (p. 83). In its apparent implacability, the treaty evoked such rage and despair among large segments of the German people that, in March 1920, a group of disgruntled nationalists launched yet another uprising, this time against the new "Weimar"—republican—government. Fronted by Wolfgang Kapp, a mid-level functionary of the former imperial foreign ministry, and accompanied by the revered General Erich Ludendorff, the conspirators seized control of the chancellery building (p. 146). But on this occasion, and in stark contrast to their role in suppressing Germany's (and Bavaria's) far-leftist governments, both the Reichswehr and the Freikorps paramilitaries declined to intervene.[48] They did not have to. The insurrection guttered out after a few days when Germany's labor unions mounted a nationwide strike that effectively paralyzed Kapp's efforts to run the economy.

Both before and after this latest fiasco, the republican government's leadership—Ebert, Scheidemann, and the Social Democrats—remained ideologically committed to fundamental and long-delayed reforms. Among these were liberalization of the civil service and the army general staff and dismantlement of Germany's interlocked Junker estates and industrial cartels. Fearful, however, of opening the door once again to "bolshevism," the cabinet hesitated to embark on any of these steps. Indeed, the ministers' fear

---

48  Gordon, *The Reichswehr*, 98.

soon became a self-fulfilling scenario. In March 1921, over the objections of Paul Levi, who had briefly served as Communist Party leader after the death of Leo Jogiches and who had favored peaceful consolidation over further acts of revolutionary violence, the hard-core Communists once again arose as if from the dead to mount a final offensive.[49]

The uprising ostensibly was ignited by the government's "preemptive" raids on local Communist Party offices, especially in the industrial Ruhr Valley; but its authentic purpose may have been to demonstrate loyalty to Soviet Russia's "Third International," whose spokesmen were calling for Red uprisings elsewhere in Europe. The previous February, under pressure from German communism's ultra-left wing, a new party chairman, Heinrich Brandler, had been selected. Under Brandler's fiery leadership, the Communist executive immediately set about organizing a "Red Army" of some fifty thousand workers. Its goal was to mount a show of strength by assaulting military posts and police stations throughout the entire Ruhr industrial basin. But the move was as futile as it was impetuous. Once again, with the approval of the Social Democratic government, both the Freikorps and the Reichswehr struck back with cold ferocity. This time, over a thousand workers—men, women, children, even Red Cross nurses—were mowed down within the space of a week. For the next decade, until the advent of the Great European Depression, the Communist Party would not reemerge as a meaningful political alternative in Germany.

But neither would the Social Democrats. The year before, in the Reichstag elections of June 1920, their party lost over sixty seats. The smaller, ostensibly moderate parties, the German Democratic Party (DDP) and even the Catholic Center Party (Zentrum), also lost badly. In contrast, two far-rightist factions, the German People's Party (DVP) and the German National People's Party (DNVP), more than doubled their total strength. Although in 1928 the Weimar coalition regained a precarious majority in the Reichstag, its control was both fragile and brief. The economic depression of the following year spelled finis for the nation's precarious democracy. Socially polarized by then, Germany had created a political monster, a Reichstag that henceforth would live on through the 1920s and early 1930s without an authentically democratic base. In the end, the Weimar Republic could transcend neither the dead weight of its autocratic past nor the crippled legacy of its anarchic birth.

---

49 Paul Levi, *Unser Weg: Wider den Putschismus*, 2nd ed. (Berlin: Seehof, 1921), 7.

CHAPTER TWO

# The Death of Giacomo Matteotti

*"And now, get ready to deliver my funeral oration."*

## A MARCH ON ROME

On October 16, 1922, meeting privately in his Milan headquarters with a dozen of his senior advisors, Benito Mussolini, chairman of Italy's Fascist Party, gave firm and final approval for a plot to seize control of his nation's government. Eight days later, a quadrumvirate of Mussolini's principal "war lords"—Emilio De Bono, Cesare De Vecchi, Italo Balbo, Michele Bianchi—refined their party's strategy for the impending political coup. It would proceed in two stages. On October 27, three columns of some eighty thousand black-shirted Fascist paramilitaries would set about occupying the municipal buildings and transportation centers of Italy's principal cities. The second and largest of these columns would converge on Rome by train, bus, private automobile, or on foot. Once in the capital, they would demand the resignation of the government's rickety and ineffectual liberal cabinet and move, if necessary by force, to seize the reins of power.

Accordingly, on October 25–26, by telephone and telegraph, Mussolini made ready to launch the scheduled operation. By nightfall of the 27th, the Fascist mobilization was in full swing. The second of the three designated columns assembled in Rome's eastern suburbs in preparation for a descent on parliament and the royal palace. But instead of comprising its anticipated forty thousand participants, the column numbered barely fourteen thousand and was equipped with only a motley collection of light arms. It soon became clear to government scouts that the rag-tag assemblage was vulnerable to dispersal even by the few army units that were bivouacked at the capital's outskirts. Indeed, at the palace, military aides were unanimous in assuring Italy's diminutive king, Vittorio Emanuele III, that his army was prepared and capable of moving preemptively before the Fascists could so much as set foot in a single government building.

But it was on the same night of October 27, that Luigi Facta[1], Italy's prime minister, suffered a crisis of confidence. Unwilling to preside over a bloodletting, Facta tendered his resignation. At the same time, however, he urged Vittorio Emanuele to proclaim a "state of siege"—in effect, a warning—that he, the king, was prepared to authorize military resistance. Facta's proposal was endorsed by the army chief of staff, General Umberto Pugliese.[2] Although confused by Facta's mixed signals, Pugliese "guaranteed" Vittorio Emanuele that the army could easily disperse Mussolini's followers.

By then, however, the king himself was beginning to share his prime minister's ambivalence. He had heard rumors that his own cousin, the Duke of Aosta, whose personal craving for the throne was an open secret, had enlisted the support of key army leaders to join forces with the Fascists. At all costs, Vittorio Emanuele now wished to avoid a provocation that might unite the opposition. If there were still time to negotiate a compromise with the Fascist leadership, he preferred to seize the opportunity. Hence, the king instructed his aides to telegraph a proposal to Mussolini. Under its terms, Antonio Salandra, a former wartime prime minister of pronounced rightist sympathies, would form a coalition government in which the Fascist Party would be entitled to play a "prominent" role. The telegram was duly sent off.

But no sooner had the offer reached Mussolini than he contemptuously rejected it.[3] He had no objection to joining Salandra in a coalition government, he wired back; but he was adamant that the Fascist Party must play

---

1 Angelo Rossi, *The Rise of Italian Fascism, 1918–1922* (London: Methuen, 1938), 296.
2 Anthony Rhodes, *D'Annunzio: The Poet as Superman* (New York: McDowell, Obolensky, 1959), 33.
3 Benito Mussolini, *My Autobiography* (London: Hutchinson & Co., 1928), 181.

the leading role in such a coalition and that he, Mussolini, must be appointed prime minister. He insisted, moreover, upon being granted one year of "emergency" powers to govern without parliamentary interference. The audacity of the Fascist leader's demands was unprecedented. Italy's monarchy, after all, functioned under a constitution. Nevertheless, as Mussolini debated the formulation of his proposed government, his political intimates agreed that he should stand firm; for the king after all had exposed his own weakness by his unwillingness to summon the army. Accordingly, in the early hours of October 29, when a second royal appeal reached him, Mussolini once again rejected the notion of joining a Salandra administration.

For all his bravura, however, the Fascist leader still was unwilling to risk traveling to Rome. Instead, he lingered in his Milan office, his chauffeur prepared to speed him across the Swiss border should the king exhibit a last-minute access of courage and summon the army. But even as he was temporizing, the crisis suddenly resolved itself. Late that same morning, Salandra personally advised the king to let Mussolini form a government. It would not survive long in any case, he predicted; the Fascists were a rabble of inept *lazzaroni*, after all, and he, Salandra, would be waiting in the wings when the Fascists' putative "government" collapsed. The king grasped at the suggestion with relief. That same afternoon, his private secretary placed a long-distance call to the Fascist leader, confirming that "His Majesty" was prepared to receive Signor Mussolini the following afternoon. Jubilant, Mussolini immediately telephoned his wife to pack his bags. That same evening he entrained for Rome.

He arrived at noon of the following day and was greeted at the railroad station by a cortege of senior Fascist officials. Disdaining to change his party's trademark black shirt and boots, or even to stop off at his reserved hotel suite for a quick bath, Mussolini and his party escort sped off at once for the palace. There the king was waiting in the royal reception chamber. He greeted his visitors politely. After a preliminary exchange of courtesies, he invited Mussolini to form a coalition government. Accepting on the spot, the Fascist leader promised to return within a few hours to submit a list of his preferred fellow ministers.

At 7:00 p.m., bathed and shaven and wearing a borrowed frock coat, Mussolini was driven back to the palace to deliver his choice of political partners. In fact, the list had been selected at his party meeting a week and a half earlier. It projected Mussolini himself in the multifold roles of prime minister, foreign minister, and interior minister. As a gesture of placation, however, the document consigned other senior portfolios, including the war and interior ministries, to non-Fascists (p. 48) and expressed Mussolini's willingness to govern through parliament (which as yet included only a small minority of "registered" Fascist party members). Hereupon, relieved and presumably gratified at the gesture of "forbearance," Vittorio Emanuele needed less than two hours to confer with Salandra and with other veteran political leaders before granting his royal consent.

It was also in this unlikely sequence of events that Benito Mussolini vaulted to the pinnacle of Italian political life after having served no more than an eighteen-month apprenticeship in parliament.[4] Moreover, he accomplished the feat without provoking a civil war, and with a miscellany of followers that was still ill-armed, ill-fed, and ill-coordinated either in ideology or strategy.

## A RESTIVENESS OF THE UNWASHED

Political commentators were left to speculate how the gamble was pulled off. What had rendered a presumably constitutional government vulnerable to a miscellany of tatterdemalion paramilitaries? In historical perspective, the reasons may not have been arcane. Lack of political coherence was central among them. Even in an age of romantic nationalism, the Italian people's *Risorgimento*, its "surge" toward national unity, had been accomplished comparatively late in the nineteenth century and, at that, was left uncompleted. Since 1870, when Rome officially became the nation's capital, until the end of the World War, as many as 3 million ethnic Italians remained either under direct Austrian sovereignty or under the de facto governance of others of the Habsburg Empire's subject communities. It was in consequence of that amorphous double servitude that a substantial minority of the Italian population had experienced neither the political equality that the Austrian government had granted the Hungarians nor as much as the administrative quasi-autonomy that the empire had ceded to millions of Croats, Slovenes, Bohemians, Moravians, or others of its Slavic populations.

Moreover, even within the enlarged, post-1870 borders of the newly independent Italian nation, with its core population of some 30 million, a scant half-million of its citizens possessed voting rights. It was not until 1881 that the nation's parliament enacted its first electoral reform legislation, and well afterward that the number of eligible voters rose to barely 3 million. Indeed, final universal—male—suffrage was enacted only in 1912. During the intervening years, public office had remained the privilege of the "political class," the minority of

---

4 Giorgio Pini and Duilio Susmel, *Mussolini, l'uomo e l'opera*, 3 vols. (Florence: La Fenice, 1953–1955), 2: 255–56.

wealthy estate owners who had consolidated their political power during the *Risorgimento*. Decades after the original (and distinctly minimalist) franchise reform of 1881, these privileged *latifundisti* continued to function in a political climate of rampant bribery, ballot manipulation, and intimidation. The rest of the population, still overwhelmingly peasant based and semiliterate, remained politically inchoate.

As elsewhere in Western Europe, however, economic modernization eventually challenged the old social order. By the opening of the twentieth century, Italy's estate owners had begun to introduce capitalist methods and modern machinery to their holdings. The ensuing adoption of mechanized farming produced a swelling outflow of tenant farmers. Economically redundant, these displaced peasants in turn began to flood into Genoa, Turin, Milan, Rome, and other of Italy's larger cities, where they shortly coalesced into a substantial urban working class. It was in response to their growing restiveness that the first serious efforts were generated to reform the nation's political culture.

Among the minority of officeholders who gave attention to this volatile new proletariat was Giovanni Giolitti. As chairman of his nation's Liberal Party, Giolitti had served three terms as prime minister over the turn of the century and had emerged as Italy's dominant political figure of the prewar era. In 1912, it was he who first sought to accommodate the nation's still unfocused economic and political restiveness by sponsoring and driving through an electoral reform bill that tripled the number of Italy's voters to almost 9 million. In the process, Giolitti also began to address the need for land distribution and factory reforms. Yet even these tentative steps toward self-government and economic improvement were not sufficient to dissipate the nation's rising political impatience. It was rather the Italian Socialist Party, founded in 1892, that unexpectedly emerged in ensuing years into the dominant political force among urban and agricultural workers alike. Indeed, socialism's advances in the 1913 parliamentary elections, and its near-revolutionary militance in the nation at large, dramatically exposed the modesty of the Italian Liberal Party's (PLI) earlier electoral and social achievements.

Less than a year later, moreover, the outbreak of World War I introduced a new and even more complicating factor into Italian politics. When hostilities began, it was Italy, alone of the larger European nations, that underwent extended public debate over the issue of intervention or neutrality. Since 1882, when Germany's Chancellor Bismarck completed his ingenious diplomatic spider web, the Italian government was obligated by its membership in the "Triple Alliance" to come to the aid of its treaty partners, Germany and Austria, in the event of war. But, in the ensuing years, most of Italy's Socialist leadership,

## GERMANY'S LOSSES BY THE TREATY OF VERSAILLES

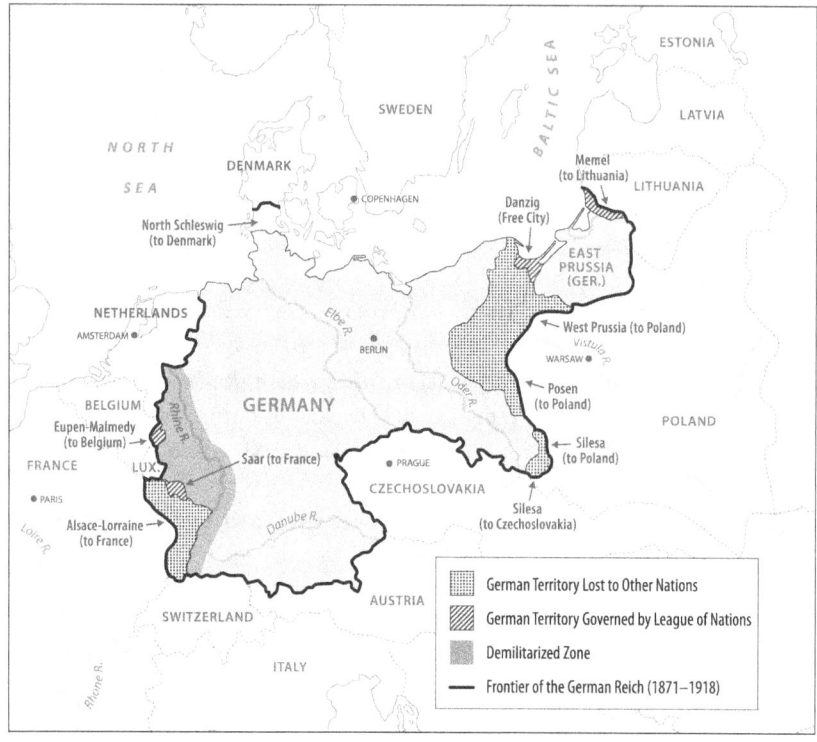

together with the Giolitti Liberals and the rightist Catholic parties, had come to oppose military intervention at the side of the autocratic Central Powers. Indeed, by the summer of 1914, when war erupted in Europe, even the conservative wing of the Liberal Party, led by Prime Minister Antonio Salandra and Foreign Minister Sidney Sonnino, were inclined to a cautious neutrality.

Salandra and Sonnino based their reservations on a legalistic loophole. It was ostensibly the failure of the Austrians to "consult" Italy before their decision to go to war. Yet this vapid rationalization failed to camouflage the Italian government's authentic change of position. This was the shift in the Italian people's own nationalist priorities. For most of the nineteenth century, their salient objective had been the unification of the Italian nation under a centralist Italian monarchy. By the turn of the century, however, that priority had extended from internal unification to the "reclamation" of the substantial Italian-speaking communities still living in neighboring lands, particularly in South Tyrol, the Habsburg-ruled mountain terrain to Italy's northwest, and in the "Trentino," the Habsburg-ruled coastal area of the northeastern bend of the Adriatic Sea, including the "queen city" of Trieste (see map, p. 36). Both regions encompassed some 2 million Italian speakers, and Rome's political leadership—indeed, the Italian nation at large—came alive at the belated prospect of reclaiming these "family lands."

Eventually, on April 26, 1915, after months of hard bargaining, the Salandra government and France and England (the two Western members of the Triple Entente) acknowledged this newly kindled Italian irredentism by signing a compact, the "Treaty of London." Ostensibly secret, the document's contents shortly leaked to the public. In return for the nation's entrance into war against the Austrian and German empires, the treaty stated, the Entente and, presumably, its Russian partner, would award Italy the latter's major territorial desiderata in the hitherto Austrian-ruled South Tyrol and Adriatic coastal basin. For Prime Minister Vittorio Orlando's Liberal government, it was an unrefusable offer. Indeed, with the exception of the Socialists, who opposed military intervention in the war as a matter of Marxist principle, the Italian population at large greeted the treaty's provisions enthusiastically. Four weeks later, on May 23, the Italian government repudiated its membership in the Triple Alliance with finality by entering the war at the side of France and Britain.

## YOUNG MUSSOLINI

In fact, the commitment to join the war proved almost suicidal, both in the short and long terms. From a population of 38 million, 6 million Italians were conscripted into the army. Four million of them saw combat against Austria, particularly in the South Tyrolean border regions of the Dolomite mountains. Before the war ended, an estimated 650,000 of these troops had been killed, over a million wounded, and 600,000 taken prisoner. In the battle of Caporetto alone, in October 1917, not fewer than 100,000 Italians died, 300,000 were wounded, and 300,000 more were captured by the Austrians, whose army proceeded afterward to penetrate deep into northern Italy. Although reversed in the closing weeks of the war, these defeats and casualties shocked Italian public opinion and impelled the government into a belated public-relations campaign, promising its troops postwar compensation in the form of "land and work."

But the promise was not fulfilled. Although some of the nation's ensuing domestic turmoil was evoked by the Entente Powers' refusal to accede to Italy's engorged nationalist expectations (p. 43),[5] far more of its chagrin

---

[5] H. James Burgwyn, *The Legend of the Mutilated Victory: Italy, the Great War, and the Paris Peace Conference* (Westport, CT: Greenwood Press, 1993), *passim*.

reflected the government's foundering effort to integrate over 4 million veterans into the postwar economy. Prime Minister Orlando's vow to provide employment was not achieved—neither by him nor by his immediate successors in office. There was no way that the flood of demobilized Italian soldiers could be integrated en masse into the nation's still underdeveloped economic infrastructure (p. 43). In turn, their mounting despair provided an opportune opening for a shrewd political demagogue. Neighbors and friends afterward maintained that Benito Mussolini was a natural for the role.

He was a product of the "Romagna," the former Vatican-ruled sector of pre-*Risorgimento* Italy. As late as 1883, the year of his birth in the townlet of Forlì, the region's economy was still peasant based, and its politics characteristically were a fusion of intense antimonarchism and anticlericalism.[6] Mussolini's father, a semiliterate blacksmith and part-time innkeeper who barely could feed his growing family, compensated for private failures with political bluster. He was an unregenerate partisan of the nation's anarchist-syndicalist faction, and his son, Benito, had been a silent participant in his father's stormy party meetings. It was Benito's mother, a former school teacher, who insisted that their son be educated away from home (and presumably away from her husband's radical politics). At first, she selected a tuition-free boarding school operated by the monkish Silesian order. It was an unfortunate choice, for young Mussolini proved to be a rebellious student and a frequent runaway. But later, as an adolescent, he performed reasonably well at a state secondary school closer to home. Upon receiving his diploma at age 18, he subsequently managed to secure appointment as an elementary-school substitute teacher in Gualtari, a "Red" commune in the Po Valley.

After a year of threadbare employment, however, Mussolini was obliged to join the tens of thousands of other impoverished young Italians who crossed the border to Switzerland in search of better opportunities (although, by no coincidence, he made the decision shortly before becoming eligible for—peacetime—military conscription). Indeed, he soon paid the price for his twilight émigré status. The only work he could find was as an intermittent hod carrier. More frequently, he was unemployed altogether and reduced to scavenging for food in garbage cans and sleeping under bridges or in public lavatories.[7] It was almost inevitable, too, in light of his family background, that Mussolini spent much of his Swiss vagabondage in the company of revolutionaries, many of whom were fellow émigrés from elsewhere in Europe. One of

---

6 Pini and Susmel, *Mussolini*, 1: 42.
7 Margherita Sarfatti, *Dux* (Milan: Mondadori, 1926), 53.

these was Angelica Balabanoff, a Ukrainian-born socialist theorist and party organizer, for whom he did odd jobs and whose colleague he later became in Italy (p. 41). Periodically, he was fined and expelled from one Swiss canton to another for haranguing his fellow expatriates with anticlerical tirades.[8]

In December 1904, however, the Italian government declared a general amnesty for draft evaders, on condition that they present themselves forthwith for military service. After his two sterile years as an émigré roustabout, Mussolini decided to accept the offer. Fortunately for him, his army billet near Verona was not onerous. It left him ample time for reading, both classic socialist tracts and works of general history. In January 1905, upon finishing his tour of military duty, Mussolini returned to Switzerland, this time as a teacher's assistant in a school for expatriate Italian children. Later yet, upon passing a French-language examination, he secured employment in an even more "respectable" cantonal school in Geneva. But if the teaching vocation was genteel, Mussolini characteristically insisted on jeopardizing it with his anticlerical rabble-rousing.[9] Again, he was periodically fined or threatened with arrest.

## THE EDITOR

Early in 1909, the 26-year-old Mussolini was hired as editor of a threadbare Socialist Party journal in the "Trentino," the mountainous, extensively Italian-populated region of Habsburg South Tyrol. In journalism, it appeared at first that he had found his true métier, for his prose was racy and arresting. As in Switzerland, however, it was his temperament hardly less than his political radicalism that threatened to do him in. His editorials brimmed with anticlerical vituperation, and in short order his gutter language—for example, his description of the Vatican as "a gang of robbers" and of a well-known priest as a "hydrophobic dog,"—tried the patience even of the lackadaisical Habsburg authorities.[10] In September 1909, Mussolini was deported back to integral Italy. But again the young firebrand was not discountenanced. This time he was returning with the panache of a martyred revolutionary. In his private life, too, he appeared to be making a statement. He persuaded the 18-year-old Rachele Guidi, daughter of an impoverished tenant farmer, to

---

8  Mussolini, *My Autobiography*, 24.
9  Adolf Dresler, *Mussolini als Journalist* (Leipzig: De Gruyter, 1938), 8–11; see also Ivone Kirkpatrick, *Mussolini: Study of a Demagogue* (London: Odhams Books, 1964), 51.
10  Kirkpatrick, *Mussolini*, 48.

move in with him (not bothering to legalize their union in a registry office, let alone in a church).

By 1911, finally, the modest reputation that Mussolini had achieved as a radical in the Trentino secured him the post of secretary of a local Socialist Party branch in Forlì, near his original birthplace. With the appointment came the editorship of the party's weekly newspaper. Although comprising only four pages, and lacking other employees, Mussolini relished the opportunity to be his own man. Henceforth, it was from his modest Forlì bailiwick that he managed to cut an increasingly influential figure in the papal Romagna, where diatribes against church and monarchy already were a routine staple of the regional culture. Indeed, in his editorial support of violence as a political weapon, Mussolini's vehemence was even more compelling than the "norm." In 1911, he editorially applauded the assassination of Pyotr Stolypin, Russia's reactionary prime minister. In the same year, and with comparable vehemence, he denounced the Giolitti cabinet for embarking on its military conquest of Libya. Equating the imperialist adventure, as symbolized by "the national flag," with "a rag to be planted on a dunghill," Mussolini appealed for a general strike against the government and for workers to erect street barricades and tear up railway tracks.[11] Although the exhortation managed only to provoke a few local demonstrations, this time it also sufficed to get the young editor convicted for "incitement" and sentenced to a year's imprisonment.

The episode actually proved the "making" of Mussolini. Upon his release (after five months), he found that the publicity of his trial and imprisonment had attracted more than local attention. Indeed, the party's central leadership acclaimed him as one of its heroes and in 1912 appointed him to the editorial board of *Avanti*, the leading organ of Italian socialism. A few months later, Mussolini's racy prose elevated him to the newspaper's senior editorship. *Avanti*'s headquarters were in Milan, one of Italy's few prosperous and dynamic cities. It was consequently in Milan, assured at last of a decent salary, that the young editor lost no time in settling his growing family in a comfortable middle-class apartment and embarking upon his new assignment in an equally comfortable suite of editorial offices.

Mussolini was as fortunate in his staff as in the amenities of home and profession. His former mentor, Angelica Balabanoff, who had preceded him from Switzerland to Milan, became his deputy editor (although remaining his senior

---

11 Mussolini, from an article in *La Lotta di Classe*, quoted in translation in Gaudens Megaro, *Mussolini in the Making* (Boston: Houghton Mifflin, 1938), 253.

in the Socialist Central Committee). Cesare Sarfatti, a prominent socialist (and husband of Margherita Sarfatti, who later would become the most influential of Mussolini's mistresses), described him at this stage as "a wonderful young man, spare of figure, hard, fiery, most original . . . a man with a great future before him."[12] The forecast seemingly was vindicated. Mussolini's editorship at the *Avanti* was hardly less than spectacular. Within two years, his lead articles, colorful in style and even more in invective, played a decisive role in quintupling the paper's circulation, from 20,000 to almost 100,000.

Altogether, the Socialists were gaining ground on the Italian political scene. In 1913 alone they mounted 900 strikes; and in the national elections of that year the party doubled its parliamentary representation, to 53 seats. In June 1914, worker restiveness in Italy peaked with a general strike that closed down virtually all of the nation's communications. In this instance, under police harassment, the demonstrations and stoppages collapsed after a week. Yet, even in failure, Mussolini drew an enduring lesson from the episode. It was respect for armed strength and contempt for the masses, not excluding the "working" masses. Moreover, he himself had emerged from the fiasco with his reputation enhanced as a political firebrand and electrifying orator. An admirer, Leda Rafanelli, described him as confiding in her:

> I desire to be somebody, do you understand me? . . . I want to rise to the top. . . . The background in which I was raised enslaved me. . . . I must rise, I must make a leap forward, to the top.[13]

In the end, it was this ambition, more than ideology, principle, or personal loyalty, that determined Mussolini's future career.

### THE CHAUVINIST

Two months after the June strike, war broke out in Europe. The Socialist Party officially voted in favor of neutrality. So did Mussolini, together with a majority of Italians. But in August 1914 the heroism of French troops in the Battle of the Marne significantly influenced Italy's emotional conversion to the side of France, Italy's "Latin Sister"; and the 1915 diplomatic negotiations

---

12 Margherita Sarfatti, *The Life of Benito Mussolini*, trans. Frederic Whyte (New York: Frederick A. Stokes, 1925), 176.

13 Leda Rafanelli, *Una donna e Mussolini* (Milan: Rizzoli, 1946), 67–69; see also Pini and Susmel, *Mussolini*, 1: 201–4.

that subsequently produced the Treaty of London, with its basket of territorial inducements, turned the tide of Italian public opinion even more decisively in favor of the Triple Entente (p. 37).

Mussolini, however, apparently did not await sentimental or territorial inducements before taking a personal stand.[14] As early as October 1914, without alerting members of the Socialist executive, all of whom were committed to peace as an axiom of party ideology, the young editor suddenly made a decisive leap toward pro-Entente interventionism. His editorial in *Avanti* that month denounced as "backward-looking" a policy of absolute neutrality. "Do we, as men and as Socialists," he declaimed, "want to be inert spectators of this huge drama? Or do we want to be . . . the protagonists?"[15] Mussolini's volte face, without forewarning or consultation, profoundly shocked his colleagues. Indeed, the next day he was summoned before the Socialist executive to defend himself. His tortured explanations were rejected. Then and there, all his former comrades, including Angelica Balabanoff, demanded and secured Mussolini's resignation as *Avanti's* editor; and, in December, charging him with accepting French bribes, Italy's Socialist Congress voted to expel him from the party.

Were the accusations of bribery valid? In February 1915, a party commission of inquiry cleared Mussolini of the charge. Yet the previous November, less than a month after resigning his editorship, he had reemerged as editor of a new, pro-war daily, *Il Popolo d'Italia*. It developed only later that a visiting French goodwill mission, learning of Mussolini's intended new publishing venture, had offered him a 100,000-lire "loan," and he had accepted it gratefully.[16] From then on, while still identifying himself as a "philosophical" socialist, Mussolini made a point of ingratiating himself with his French benefactors. Indeed, in the first issue of *Il Popolo d'Italia*, he advanced the notion of a revolutionary war, a struggle committed less to the overthrow of the bourgeoisie than to the creation of a new, more energetic and efficient society. It was with this rationale, by the early spring of 1915, that the one-time fiery antimonarchist and antimilitarist steered *Il Popolo d'Italia* on a sacred mission of intervention on the side of the Allies.

In September 1915, four months after Italy's entrance into the war, Mussolini himself was conscripted into the army. His ensuing military record was unexceptionable. As an infantryman, he spent the next 18 months facing

---

14  Pini and Susmel, *Mussolini*, 1: 236–37.
15  Sarfatti, *Dux*, 200.
16  Gaetano Salvemini, *Mussolini diplomatico* (Bari: Laterza, 1952), 200–1.

the Austrians in the trenches of the Dolomite Mountains. In February 1917, he was wounded by mortar shrapnel in a training accident (an event that he later termed "the most beautiful moment of my life").[17] Eventually, after a six-month period of recuperation, Mussolini received his honorable discharge; and in September of the same year he was back in Milan, seeking ways to revive his career as a journalist and editor. In the pages of *Il Popolo d'Italia*, he marked time by embellishing his image as the consummate patriot and haranguing his readers in behalf of "patriotism," "loyalty," "discipline."

By the time Allied victory was achieved, it became clear that the outcome fell significantly short of meeting Italian expectations. A major factor was the rebuff suffered by the nation's diplomats at the Paris Peace Conference, when the Allied representatives proved unwilling to deliver fully on the 1915 Treaty of London (p. 37). More anguishing still, however, was Italy's abrupt transition from a wartime to a peacetime economy. Even before the final armistice, the nation's war industries began reducing their production quotas. By spring of 1919, as discharged veterans returned home en masse, ostensibly in the prime of their lives, they were almost immediately transformed into a restless army of hundreds of thousands of unemployed men. It was not long before their frustration began generating violent protest strikes, notably in the industrialized northern regions of Piedmont and Lombardy. With Italy's early postwar governments at a loss to deal with the turmoil, the nation's parliament ricocheted from one political crisis to another.

## THE FASCIST

By the early postwar, Mussolini too had revised his political stance of the moment. In March 1919, he summoned to his press headquarters in Milan a diverse aggregation of some fifty men. Included among them were intellectuals, nationalists, ex-socialists, anarcho-syndicalists, republicans, old-school conservatives, discharged veterans from elite military units, as well as simply curious or confused young adventurers. Although Mussolini and his cohorts gave them a glamorous title, "Fasci di Combattimento" ("Combat Squads"), and proclaimed as their symbol the ancient Roman emblem of lictors bound to a mace, the group's initial agenda was as heterogeneous as its participants.

At first blush, that program appeared to be a mélange of bland social welfarism and neo-socialism. Favoring an eight-hour day, old age pensions,

---

17   Sarfatti, *Dux*, 185; see also Ivon de Begnac, *Palazzo Venezia: Storia di un Regime* (Rome: La Rocca, 1950), 128.

medical insurance, and nationalization of the arms industry, it also demanded special taxes on war profits, the apportionment of "excess" latifundia acreage to tenant farmers, and the confiscation of all church property. Yet the program stopped short of embracing "Marxist bolshevism," and countenanced in its stead a vibrant revisionist nationalism, with an emphasis upon direct, violent action. Indeed, its program soon emerged as a seductive alternative to Italy's existing political parties, with their farrago of opportunistic slogans and legions of professional office seekers.[18] Mussolini made this point as early as April 1919, when he dispatched his armed followers to pillage the Milan offices of his former party newspaper, *Avanti*.[19]

Throughout most of 1919, however, for all his bravado, the young agitator failed to win a substantial popular following. Within the nationalist camp, it was Gabriele D'Annunzio, poet and war hero, who dominated the political arena with his buccaneering foray into Fiume (pp. 230–31). In the November 1919 parliamentary elections, the Socialist Party and the new Italian Popular (Catholic) Party (PPI) registered the most impressive gains. By contrast, the Fascists garnered less than 10 per cent of the ballots. Mussolini himself, who represented his incipient party as a candidate from Milan, collected a pitiable 4,000 votes out of the 270,000 cast locally and thus failed to win a seat in the Chamber of Deputies. *Avanti*, by then restored to "safe" hands, reported derisively: "A corpse in a state of decomposition was fished out of the canal yesterday. It appears to be that of Mussolini."[20] The newspaper then organized a mock funeral procession for its former editor through Milan's streets.[21]

But the Socialists also were overplaying their hand. Late in 1919, speculating that the time was ripe for a dramatic anticapitalist gesture, they launched a series of clamorous strikes that adopted the anarcho-syndicalist tactic of "requisitioning" private property, laying claim to large factories and smaller workshops alike. At the same time, the party's subsidiary "peasants leagues," operating on the Ferrara-Bologna plain, embarked on a campaign of agrarian terrorism, commandeering landed estates, even entire villages. In the end, these escalating work stoppages and expropriations sharpened the Socialist leadership's long-standing internal conflict between moderate reformers and hard-edged militants. In their party congress of December 1919, it was the latter who voted to join the Moscow-sponsored Third International; and a year

---

18   Dino Grandi, *Le origini e la missione del fascismo* (Bologna: L. Cappelli, 1922), 52.
19   Massimo Rocca, *Come il fascismo divenne una dittatura* (Milan: Edizioni Librarie Italiane, 1952), 77.
20   Anthony Cardoza, *Benito Mussolini: The First Fascist* (New York: Pearson Longman, 2006), 40.
21   Cesare Rossi, *Mussolini com'era* (Rome: Ruffolo, 1947), 87, 88.

later they veered even further to the camp of radicalism, withdrawing from the Socialist ranks altogether to form the Italian Communist Party.

Predictably, these developments on the political Left generated acute concern among Italy's "respectable" middle-class and Catholic traditionalists. In January 1921, with the return of the indestructible Giovanni Giolitti to the prime ministry, the government coalition, nominally in Liberal hands, began taking a firmer stand against worker and peasant "hooliganism." The approach was presently emulated by factory and estate owners, who recruited and armed their own private strong-arm bands. Among the latter were Mussolini's black-shirted *squadristi*. Thirsting for revenge, these Fascist enforcers launched a series of punitive expeditions against their Socialist and Communist enemies, torching the latter's political, newspaper, and union offices and beating their personnel with truncheons or forcibly dosing them with castor oil. Several of the victims died of their mistreatment.

By spring 1921, Fascist Party membership had soared within the space of a year from less than 10,000 to 300,000, with some 2,000 party branches operating throughout Italy. By then, too, Benito Mussolini had emerged as the dominant figure in the network of these local and provincial *Fasci*. Perhaps more than any of his associates, he recognized that fascism had generated two parallel reservoirs of support: one consisting mainly of army veterans, students, and members of the urban middle class and the other drawing to its ranks *latifundisti*, together with a sizeable minority even of peasant farmers. In appraising the party's membership potential, Mussolini shrewdly adapted his program to these ostensibly disparate factions, putting his emphasis variously on discipline, law and order, and the "sacredness" of property rights, as well as on irredentist nationalism (p. 37).[22] The strategy paid off. In Italy's ensuing summer election of 1921, 35 Fascists—including, for the first time, Mussolini himself—were elected to parliament, more than twice the party's earlier total.

For Mussolini, however, the veneer of legislative authority was always a sham. Under the direction of Italo Balbo, a much-decorated war hero and by then Mussolini's principal lieutenant, Fascist "paramilitary operations"— in effect, rampant hooliganism—continued and intensified. By early 1922, Balbo's widening raids against Socialist and Communist Party offices and politicians were becoming a frontal threat both to other parties and to the authority of the state itself. Thus, in February, Balbo issued an

---

22 Benito Mussolini, *The Political and Social Doctrine of Fascism*, trans. Jane Soames (London: Hogarth, 1933), as quoted in Kirkpatrick, *Mussolini*, 81.

"ultimatum": if the national government did not immediately embark on a public-works project in Ferrara, a town suffering acutely from unemployment, he would launch a "demonstration." But when the cabinet nonetheless declined to act, Balbo proceeded to lead 60,000 black-shirted *Fascisti* in a march through the town center, closing down Ferrara's public utilities until a thoroughly intimidated Prime Minister Ivanoe Bonomi—a liberal socialist from the Italian Reform Socialist Party (PSRI) who lately had replaced Giolitti—came up with a series of regional-improvement projects. During the late winter of 1921, Fascist offensives also were directed against the recalcitrant municipalities of Parma and others of northern Italy's smaller cities, all but paralyzing their economies. When Prime Minister Bonomi threatened to call in the army, his warnings palpably rang hollow. By then, fascism was making serious inroads among the army's officer class (pp. 43–44).[23]

Mussolini himself, meanwhile, was traveling throughout Europe to meet the continent's statesmen—Aristide Briand, Gustav Stresemann, Walther Rathenau—as if he were a colleague representing a shadow government of his own. He was not far off the mark. By February 1922, it was an open secret that Italy's current Liberal-Socialist coalition was faltering, weakened by soaring unemployment and a precipitous fall of the lira. Hence, on February 25, King Vittorio Emanuele and his advisers gambled on replacing Ivanoe Bonomi, the government's indecisive prime minister of the moment, with Luigi Facta, a veteran Liberal workhorse. It was a mystifying choice. Facta at best was a hack provincial politician whose earlier tenure as finance minister was notably undistinguished.

Indeed, Facta's appointment proved the beginning of the end of Italy's fragile parliamentary democracy. Within 24 hours of the king's announcement, the Socialist-Labor Alliance registered its own protest by declaring a general strike in the nation's largest cities. Here Mussolini sensed his opening. Addressing a mass meeting of black-shirted *Fascisti* in Rome's Piazza Venezia, he issued an ultimatum to the new Facta coalition. It was to quash the work stoppage without delay or "face the consequences." But when the government still dithered, the Fascists themselves proceeded to take over and operate public services. The strike then collapsed ignominiously, and the Fascists became instant public heroes. Moreover, they exploited their popularity by launching political coups in Italy's principal northern cities. In Milan, they seized the town hall and expelled the Socialist administration. In Rome,

---

23   De Begnac, *Palazzo*, vii.

local Fascist chieftains invited a nationalist hero, Gabriele D'Annunzio, who had briefly led a celebrated postwar occupation of the Dalmatian coastal port of Fiume (pp. 230–31), to appear on the capital's city hall balcony and denounce the government before a packed crowd.

By October 1922, the number of registered Fascist Party members had grown to an impressive 700,000. At that point, Mussolini suddenly ordered his followers to cease their campaign of political intimidation and adopt an "interim" strategy of respectability.[24] On the 16th of the month, conferring with the party's executive committee in Milan, he entered into his first detailed discussions of a prospective march on Rome. A week and a half later, after further party meetings in Naples, the scenario was put into action, and it was three days afterward that Mussolini assumed the office of prime minister of Italy.

## THE STATESMAN

At age 39, he was the youngest prime minister in his nation's history. Outside of Lombardy and the former Papal States, he was also the least known to his countrymen, for he had been the leader of his Fascist movement for less than four years and a member of the Chamber of Deputies for only 18 months. Yet, by the time he engineered his coup, Mussolini had transcended at least the more obvious deprivations of his youth. Although lacking a university education, he had used his years in Switzerland and the Habsburg Trentino to acquire a conversational fluency in French and German. During his brief membership in the Chamber of Deputies, he had developed an uncanny instinct both for private deal making and public demagoguery. In the end, however, if this unknown roughneck had vaulted within a matter of months to the leadership of his party and government, the achievement reflected less Mussolini's political acuity than the Italian people's frustration with their dashed territorial hopes for the postwar and with the failure of the nation's politicians to cope with the country's economic chaos. Their quest palpably was for a strong man with a steady hand.

Even after the October "March on Rome," the Chamber of Deputies theoretically was capable of marshaling enough votes to unseat Mussolini. By then, however, the parties of the Right and Center were cautiously willing to share governing authority with the Fascist minority faction, even to grant the Fascist demand for "temporary" emergency powers (p. 33).[25] Indeed,

---

24  Simona Colarizi, *Dopoguerra e fascismo in Puglia, 1919–1926* (Bari: Laterza, 1971), 156.
25  Antonio Salandra, *Il diario di Salandra*, ed. Gian Battista Gifuni (Milan: Pan, 1969), 32.

Mussolini himself made their decision easier, for he appeared prepared to meet them halfway. He consigned the ministry of agriculture to the recently elected leader of the Liberal Party, Giuseppe De Capitani d'Arzago, and the colonial ministry and the under-secretariat of the treasury to veteran members of the Nationalist Party. In appointing Alberto De Stefani, formerly a stalwart of the Center Party, as minister of the treasury, he chose a man who earlier had proved to be Italy's ablest and most popular finance minister. The right wing of the Catholic party also joined the government.

Although Mussolini rejected Communist participation, and the Socialists declined to share in his coalition, the Italian Social Democrats willingly accepted several of the less important cabinet ministries. Indeed, Mussolini had only three Fascists, excluding himself, in his cabinet, and he personally took over only the prime ministry and the ministries of the interior and foreign affairs, although he distributed among his Fascist colleagues other key posts in the national administration: secretaryships, regional prefectures, and police commands. In this pragmatic fashion, the young prime minister for the ensuing two years presided over a series of widely based coalition administrations.[26]

Moreover, despite his conglomerate political base, Mussolini's initial administrative accomplishments were not trivial. He ensured "order" by selectively raising police salaries, and streamlined the bureaucracy by dismissing some 35,000 redundant civil servants. He placed much emphasis upon enhancing Italy's lackadaisical public-transportation system (thereby winning domestic and foreign praise as "the man who made the trains run on time"). By the end of the fiscal year 1923, Minister of Finance De Stefani could assure parliament that the value of the lira was approaching its first postwar stabilization. By then, too, the paying membership of the Fascist Party had climbed to an unprecedented 800,000, and much of the Italian population seemed to breathe more easily with the dynamic young leader at the helm of government.

That leader was also in some respects a "new" Mussolini. Although short, compact, and prematurely bald, with a prognathous jaw and protuberant eyes, Mussolini as prime minister exuded power and sheer animal vitality, an aura reinforced by his vigorous and authoritative public-speaking style. Even before taking office, he had also taken pains to overcome the rough edges of his harsh early years. He bathed daily now, refined his table manners, wore the subdued civilian garb that befitted a "statesman." In conversation with leaders of other parties, he was courteous, even charming. In public, addressing the Chamber of Deputies or audiences at ceremonial occasions, he projected the

---

26  De Begnac, *Palazzo*, 235.

image of an indomitable *"Duce"* (leader), a title that he himself increasingly encouraged. Withal, Mussolini's life style remained modest. As prime minister, he was entitled to a comfortable apartment and vacation villa, but he evinced no apparent taste for luxury. Six days a week, arriving at his office in the Palazzo Venezia shortly after 8:00 a.m., he worked usually without interruption until mid-evening. He did not smoke or drink.

To some extent, Mussolini's spartan regimen was also dictated by health problems. He had contracted syphilis as a youth (although he was later cured), and in 1925 he fell seriously ill with gastric ulcers, an affliction that plagued him intermittently for the rest of his life. Although he did not smoke or drink, his one flagrant indulgence in any case was not of personal luxury or of financial peculation but of insatiable sexual dissoluteness. In December 1922, to keep his trysts with Margherita Sarfatti, he rented a suite in Rome's Grand Hotel. Emilio De Bono, commander of the Fascist militia and a valued friend, on occasion tactfully pleaded with the prime minister to be more discreet in his private behavior. Yet, to the end of his life, promiscuity was an extravagance that Mussolini could not transcend.

Whatever his lapses, the young prime minister appeared to be providing his fellow Italians with an uncharacteristic interlude of political stability, thus vindicating the bargain he had reached in October with King Vittorio Emanuele and the nation's leading political parties. Since parliament had delegated "emergency" powers to the Fascist government in October 1922, it had not met for the ensuing ten and a half months, and the nation apparently had benefitted by the respite. Thus, in late August 1923, Mussolini decided to exploit that success. With only six weeks remaining on his political grace period, he introduced a startling new bill on legislative "reform." By its provisions, any party obtaining at least 25 per cent of the votes in a popular election would automatically be entitled to not less than two-thirds of the seats in the Chamber of Deputies.

Mussolini's rationale for this "enabling act" was the need to block a return to the former disruptiveness of minority parties, with their habit of toppling government coalitions virtually at will. Indeed, he regarded the initiative as indispensable to his program of "discipline" and "order." The Fascists currently held a modest 47 seats in the Chamber, even in the aftermath of their recent fusion with the Nationalists. But if the party could do marginally better in the ensuing election, reaching the proposed 25 per cent threshold, it would achieve the leverage the prime minister insisted he needed to control his parliamentary agenda. Indeed, to ensure that threshold, Mussolini raised the veiled threat of "recessing" parliament in the event he failed to win majority support for his bill.

The threat possibly was gratuitous. With their own extensive experience of legislative paralysis, the old political veterans—Giolitti, Orlando, and Salandra—acceded to the bill without protest.[27] Yet there were others, notably the deputies of the Socialist and Catholic parties, who needed "persuasion." Thus, as the parliamentary debates gained momentum in August 1923, uniformed Fascist enforcers manned the doorways and crowded the galleries, their hands resting ominously on their holsters.[28] Whatever the inducement, at summer's end the Chamber of Deputies passed the "enabling act" by an impressive majority. Afterward, following a circumspect interregnum of an additional four months, Mussolini prepared to exploit the new law. His supporters introduced a bill to dissolve parliament and hold new elections on April 6, 1924.

The Fascists almost certainly would have won the scheduled election in any case; but they ensured that industrialists were "encouraged" to contribute large sums to the Fascist Party, and that candidates of other, predominantly centrist and leftist factions were "persuaded" to drop out. One Socialist candidate suffered a mysterious, fatal poisoning. On election day, black-shirted goons closely monitored persons entering the polling stations, and many ballot boxes unaccountably disappeared.[29] When the votes were tabulated, they registered approximately 4.5 million for Mussolini's conglomerate list and a total of 3.5 million for the 19 other parties. In this fashion, the Fascist-Nationalist partnership automatically garnered 355 seats, against the other parties' accumulated total of 180. Although few Italians could then have predicted ensuing developments, the election of April 6, 1924, turned out to be the last one Mussolini would countenance in his remaining 19 years of power.

## THE DENUNCIATION

By the spring of 1924, Cesare Rossi, director of the government press bureau, had emerged as one of the prime minister's most intimate collaborators. Rising in the Fascist ranks as a journalist in his native Pescia, Rossi had won Mussolini's confidence for his resourcefulness in putting a benevolent face on the government's program of political intimidation. Subsequently, as director of the government press bureau, he functioned for all practical

---

27  Maurice Pernot, *L'expérience italienne* (Paris: B. Grasset, 1924), 232–34.
28  Emilio Lussu, *Enter Mussolini: Observations and Adventures of an Anti-Fascist*, trans. Marion Rawson (London: Methuen & Co., 1936), 172.
29  Carlo Silvestri, *Matteotti, Mussolini, e il dramma italiano* (1947; repr., Milan: Cavallotti, 1981), 72.

purposes as the prime minister's alter ego. It came as a profound shock, therefore, on June 16, 1924, when Rossi, of all Mussolini's inner circle, suddenly was arrested and jailed on government orders. The charge was not revealed. Indeed, six months later, on December 28, the shock was compounded when *Il Mundo*, Italy's most respected mass-circulation newspaper, published crucial extracts of a secret Rossi memorandum. Running to 14 pages, the document ascribed to the prime minister himself the most scandalous of the outrages leading up to the recent parliamentary election of April 6. "All that has occurred," it stated, "was done by Mussolini's orders or with his concurrence."[30]

The events cited by Rossi (and quoted in *Il Mundo*) included the wide-ranging series of physical attacks carried out on prominent anti-Fascist politicians and newspaper editors; the terrorization of the latter's staffs and families, and the pillage or destruction of their party headquarters and publishing offices. In his litany of allegations, Rossi singled out Emilio De Bono, commander of the Fascist militia, as the official most responsible for blocking inquiries into the cited offenses.[31] But until the press release of December 28, one crime apparently had escaped Mussolini's and De Bono's preemptive veil of *omertà*—of enforced silence—and, accordingly, formed Rossi's most sensational charge. It related to the abduction of one of the parliament's most prominent members, Giacomo Matteotti, secretary of Italy's far-leftist "Unitary" Socialist Party (PSU).

Matteotti was 39 years old in 1924. Photographs of him revealed a slim, handsome man, with luminous eyes and an ingratiating smile. The son of a progressive middle-class family and a graduate of the University of Bologna Law School, he had opted early on for a public career by establishing several labor confederations along the Po Valley. As a committed Socialist, he had also opposed Italy's entrance into the war. Refusing to serve in the army, he was duly punished by a two-year internment in a Sicilian work farm. In the national disillusionment of the postwar, however, Matteotti's brief prison record became emblematic of his ideological integrity. Indeed, he evoked more than ordinary deference upon his first election to the Chamber of Deputies in 1919, when his colleagues selected him as cochairman of the "United Socialists," the party's far-leftist component. A devoted husband and father of two small children, Matteotti was an equally loyal friend to

---

30 Angelica Balabanoff, *Il traditore* (Rome: G. Popolizio, 1942), 189.
31 Salvemini, *Mussolini diplomatico*, 232–33.

his Socialist comrades.[32] In 1921 and again in 1924, he was overwhelmingly reelected both to parliament and to his faction's leadership.

By 1924, too, Matteotti had embarked on an energetic campaign against fascism. In the effort, he managed to produce documented evidence of the movement's duplicities and brutalities. His concise booklet, *The Fascists Exposed: The First Year of Fascist Domination*, cited facts and figures of some 150 murders and other acts of recent Fascist thuggery. The essay was translated and printed simultaneously in England by the British Labour Party and in Belgium by that nation's Socialist Party. In scalded reaction, then, *Il Popolo d'Italia*, the Fascists' official house organ (pp. 42–43), published an editorial on May 4 warning that "Matteotti, that infamous swindler, that well-known coward and despicable liar, would do well to be careful . . . [for] one day his brains may be beaten out. . . ." Matteotti's response to the threat was characteristic. He delivered it in parliament on May 30, when the president of the Chamber of Deputies called for a motion confirming the results of the recent election, the first countenanced under Mussolini's new "enabling" legislation. Indeed, Mussolini himself was attending the parliamentary session as a gesture of the importance he gave the motion.

Taking the floor in the ensuing debate, Matteotti launched into a fierce denunciation of the raw violence that Fascist militiamen had mounted against opposition parties during the election campaign and demanded a scrupulous reexamination of the ballot results. As he spoke, the Fascist delegates repeatedly interrupted in shouted insults and desk-pounding. Undaunted, Matteotti continued his verbal attack for two hours and concluded by accusing Mussolini personally of orchestrating the Fascist campaign of "hooliganism." At that point, livid with rage, Mussolini jumped up from the prime ministerial dais and shouted: "You deserve a charge of lead in the back"—a riposte that evoked thunderous cheers from his Fascist supporters.[33] Matteotti's proposal then was voted down by a voice vote of 285 to 172. Preparing to depart the Chamber, Matteotti whispered to Giovanni Cosattini, a Socialist colleague seated next to him: "And now, get ready to deliver my funeral oration."[34]

Later that same afternoon, in the lobby of the Chamber, Cesare Rossi, Mussolini's press chief, was overheard venting his rage against Matteotti. "The government has made a serious mistake in not having [Matteotti] . . .

---

32  Lucio Battistrada, *Il delitto Matteotti* (Bologna: Cappelli, 1973), 21–23.
33  Silvestri, *Matteotti, Mussolini*, 117–18.
34  Salvemini, *Mussolini diplomatico*, 246.

shot at the outset," he muttered to a colleague. Then he added, "[B]ut what it failed to do before, it can still do now."[35] As it was, on June 3, five members of the Socialist opposition were assaulted and beaten, and, as late as June 9, Mussolini, in his office, was overheard muttering to one of his "enforcers," Amerigo Dumini, that the *Ceka*—the Fascist Party's political police—should "hurry up and do something to justify its existence."[36]

On May 31, the day following Matteotti's peroration in the Chamber of Deputies, Giovanni Marinelli, the party treasurer, arranged the release from a Neapolitan prison of one Otto Thierschwald. Thierschwald was a common gangster who had supplemented his "earnings" by performing occasional strong-arm work for the Fascist Party. Now, as he was leaving prison, the warden handed him an envelope. Together with a rail ticket and a small amount of cash, its contents included typed instructions. These were to depart immediately for Rome and to proceed from the capital's train station to the nearby Hotel Dragoni. There, he was to inquire at the concierge's desk for a "Signor Bianchi."

Thierschwald duly entrained for the capital. The "Signor Bianchi" who greeted him in the lobby of the Hotel Dragoni was Amerigo Dumini. A hulking young army veteran, Dumini, like Thierschwald, was a professional gangster. In the prewar, he had worked for two years in the United States as a drug dealer in St. Louis. Subsequently, after returning to Italy to perform his military service, he had found his métier as a Fascist strong-arm man; and since 1922 he also had been employed in the government press bureau as personal assistant to the press chief, Cesare Rossi. Besides Rossi, Dumini, and Thierschwald, the other key participants in the unfolding conspiracy were Giovanni Marinelli, the party treasurer who had arranged Thierschwald's release, and Albino Volpi, a veteran jailbird who had achieved an extensive record for burglary, theft, army desertion, and the homicidal bludgeoning in 1921 of a Socialist workman (for which he had been acquitted as a result of Mussolini's personal court testimony on his behalf). The group's joint target now was Matteotti.

## THE MURDER

The plot was carefully prepared. On June 4, Dumini, Volpi, and Thierschwald inconspicuously took up their positions around Matteotti's modest apartment building on Via Pisanelli, in Rome's Lungotevere district. Their assignment

---

35 Elizabeth Wiskemann, *The Rome-Berlin Axis* (London: Collins, 1966), 247.
36 Silvestri, *Matteotti, Mussolini*, 117–81.

was to survey and record Matteotti's schedule of arrivals and departures. Five days later, Dumini asked Filippo Filippelli, editor of a leading Fascist newspaper, *Il Corriere Italiano*, for permission to borrow the latter's Lancia automobile for several days. Apparently not privy to the conspiracy, Filippelli consented. The next afternoon, June 10, Dumini, Volpi, Thierschwald, and two other itinerant "enforcers," Giuseppe Viola and Augusto Malacria, drove to Via Pisanelli and parked near Matteotti's building.

Some 40 minutes later, at 4:30 p.m., leaving his apartment to walk to parliament, Matteotti passed the awaiting Lancia. According to an elderly garbage collector, who happened to be gazing out the window of his nearby apartment, three men suddenly leaped from the automobile, seized Matteotti, and grappled him into the back seat. Shouting for help, Matteotti at the last moment before the vehicle raced off managed to fling a card out of its rear window.[37] The card later was found to be a railroad pass bearing his name, one of the hundreds issued to parliamentary deputies. The horrified garbage collector, who had witnessed the entire incident and had managed to jot down the number of the Lancia's license plate, rushed to Matteotti's apartment to inform the latter's wife, Velia. Velia Matteotti instantly telephoned the police. Arriving within minutes, and retrieving Matteotti's railway pass, the police interviewed the garbage collector and recorded his notes of the automobile's license number. It was a simple matter afterward to trace the vehicle to the editor, Filippelli. In turn, upon police questioning the same evening, Filippelli confirmed that the vehicle was his, although he denied knowledge of the reported abduction. Then he telephoned Cesare Rossi, informing the press chief of the incident.

Notwithstanding Rossi's later testimony (p. 51), it was improbable that Mussolini had been notified in advance of the plot, although he probably would not have objected if Matteotti had been severely threatened or even beaten. But later that evening, when Filippelli and Emilio De Bono, commander of the Fascist militia, informed the prime minister that "things had gone wrong" and that Matteotti evidently had been abducted and the police already had been informed, Mussolini furiously cursed out De Bono: "*Porca madonna, bastava avessero pisciato sulla targa* [Damn it, all they had to do was piss over the license plate]".[38] At midnight, Giovanni Marinelli, the party treasurer, telephoned Mussolini to report that Matteotti had been not only abducted but probably slain.

---

37 Alessandro Schiavi, *La vita e l'opera di Giacomo Matteotti* (Rome: Opere Nuove, 1957), 157–58.
38 Cesare Rossi, *Il delitto Matteotti* (Milan: Ceschina, 1965), 55–56, 102.

## THE DEATH OF GIACOMO MATTEOTTI

GIACOMO MATTEOTTI (CENTER), C. 1924.

By early morning of June 11, even the Fascist press carried the police report of Matteotti's abduction and possible murder. Mussolini, in turn, ordered his aides to circulate rumors that Matteotti had escaped abroad. But it was too late to block afternoon newspapers from printing even more sensational news: that the police had just taken into custody four of Matteotti's suspected five assailants. Within the ensuing three days, the public also learned that others who had been arrested included Aldo Finzi, the undersecretary of the interior; Filippo Naldi, a prominent Fascist journalist who was close to the party hierarchs; and the editor Filippo Filippelli.

On June 12, interrogated by the police, Filippelli was able (and apparently eager) to divulge the crucial information of Matteotti's abduction. According to the police transcript of the interview, on the evening of June 10 Amerigo Dumini had come into Filippelli's office to return the editor's automobile. "Filippelli," Dumini whispered, "there has been a sad bungle.... Matteotti died today."[39] Dumini went on to explain that he and his four henchmen had intended simply to carry Matteotti off and give him a sound thrashing; but when Matteotti put up a struggle, he was beaten so fiercely that he expired. Racing out of town, the group then had spent the early evening hours searching for a remote place to drop the body before eventually selecting a copse of trees 14 miles south of Rome. As he related this chain of events, Dumini warned Filippelli that the latter's Lancia was covered with blood stains and had to be disposed of quickly. Appalled and shaken, Filippelli agreed, and stored the automobile temporarily in his garage.[40]

With this police transcript, Mauro Del' Giudice, chairman of the municipality's investigative panel, immediately ordered the arrest of potential suspects. These included Giovanni Marinelli, the party treasurer; Cesare Rossi, chief of the prime minister's press bureau; Aldo Finzi, undersecretary of the interior; Amerigo Dumini and the four other gangsters-abductors; and even the palpably innocent Filippo Filippelli. By the evening of June 13, all but one of the individuals privy to the crime were behind bars in the capital's Regina Coeli prison. The exception was Cesare Rossi, who had gone into hiding; but on June 16 he too surrendered to the police. Indeed, from the moment he was jailed, Rossi became a changed man. Far from remaining Mussolini's faithful acolyte, he cooperated fully in the interrogation. During the ensuing weeks, in his cell, he would augment his depositions with extensive supplementary information that he added to a private "memoir" (p. 51).

Meanwhile, several of the other prisoners also broke ranks, even in their preliminary grilling, and corroborated Rossi's initial testimony. They confirmed that, three days before the June 10 abduction, the plainclothes detectives, who had provided surveillance of Matteotti's apartment building, had

---

39 Quoted in Kirkpatrick, *Mussolini: Study of a Demagogue*, 213.
40 Gaetano Salvemini, *The Fascist Dictatorship in Italy* (New York: H. Fertig, 1967), 262.

suddenly been withdrawn. The order, they insisted, had come directly from the ministry of the interior, whose portfolio was held by Mussolini himself (although Aldo Finzi, the ministry's undersecretary, indignantly—and probably truthfully—denied any knowledge of the order).

## AN EQUIVOCATION OF PUBLIC REACTION

If Rossi and most of the other prisoners were falling over each other to implicate Mussolini, their testimony reflected not only their desperation to evade prosecution but their assumption that Mussolini himself would not survive politically long enough to make them scapegoats. At the time of the Matteotti abduction, during the second year of Fascist government, the prime minister was the chieftain only of his own Fascist Party. Undeniably, it was the party that dominated the government, and Mussolini also could rely for support on the timidity of a rather dull-witted king, on a timorous church hierarchy, as well as on the rapacity of an assortment of business leaders and ambitious senior military officers (pp. 43–44). Yet, as late as June 1924, the nation's public institutions—its free speech, free press, free party activity, free elections—had managed to survive. Italy's civil service, too, even its police force, still remained extensively staffed by non-Fascists.

With this fact in mind, a majority of the country's other political leaders similarly anticipated that Mussolini could not survive the Matteotti crisis. It is certain, too, that the prime minister himself recognized his acute political vulnerability. On the afternoon of June 13, he had received Matteotti's distraught wife in his parliamentary office and assured her that he would exert every effort to discover her husband's whereabouts and that those guilty of his "abduction"—he could not admit his awareness that Matteotti probably was dead—would receive maximum sentences. Following this conversation, at 6:00 p.m., Mussolini then entered the Chamber of Deputies to answer his accusers. In his ensuing 20-minute speech, he forcefully declaimed:

> Only . . . my deadliest enemies, who have spent long nights thinking up diabolical plans, could [be responsible] for this crime, which fills all of us with horror and revulsion. . . . [Justice] will be done. It must be done, for this crime is anti-Fascist and anti-national. . . . [I]t is a crime of degrading bestiality.[41]

Mussolini plainly was terrified.

---

41 Salvemini, *The Fascist Dictatorship*, 265.

So, initially, were the senior members of his party. Near midnight of the same June 13, the Fascist Grand Council held an emergency session in Rome. As much on the defensive as Mussolini, these traditionally swaggering political bosses issued a communiqué expressing their revulsion at the "alleged" crime and calling for the arrest and punishment of all those responsible for Matteotti's "presumed" abduction. The next morning, Luigi Federzoni, chairman of the Nationalist Party (a junior partner of the Fascists), visited privately with Mussolini to urge him to curtail the arrogant behavior of the provincial Fascist "Grand Councillors" and their private armies. Federzoni himself then volunteered to replace Mussolini as minister of the interior, with a mandate to usher in an ensuing "post-Fascist" period of normalization. The shaken prime minister agreed on the spot, and then and there dictated an announcement of the political change.

But the storm did not abate. Telegrams and letters of alarm arrived from all parts of the nation, including from such eminent public figures as the musical conductor Arturo Toscanini and the philosopher and Senate member Benedetto Croce (who initially had accepted Mussolini's accession with silent forbearance); from Léon Blum in France, from Ramsay MacDonald and Arthur Henderson in England, and from other prominent European socialists. Years later, Mussolini confided to his private physician that as few as 20 determined men could have overthrown his regime during the summer crisis of 1924.[42]

If the prime minister did not break then in the vortex of national and international recrimination, it was possibly due to the "neutrality" of several of Italy's most venerated institutions. One of these was the monarchy. In Spain on a state visit, King Vittorio Emanuele was alerted by the Italian ambassador to the uproar at home and to the escalating clamor for Mussolini's replacement. "These things ought not to be brought to me," the king protested. "I am not a judge."[43] Then he changed the subject, describing an enthusiastic letter he had just received from his daughter, who was on a hunting expedition in the Alps. As for the Vatican, its reaction was hesitant, but essentially noncommittal. As Cardinal Pietro Gasparri, the Vatican secretary of state, declared to the Belgian ambassador: "His Holiness [Pius XI] is very sorry about the

---

42 Charles F. Delzell, *Mussolini's Enemies: The Italian Anti-Fascist Resistance* (Princeton, NJ: Princeton University Press, 1961), 14.

43 Jay Robert Nash, ed., *The Great Pictorial History of World Crime* (Wilmette, IL: History Inc., 2004), 1: 124.

whole affair, but does not see how he can lend himself to a maneuver that would ally the Holy See with the Socialists."[44]

On June 24, in a Senate ceremony commemorating the (presumed) murder victim, Mussolini spoke eloquently again of his determination to seek punishment against any suspects in the crime, no matter how exalted their station. Deciding then to grant him the benefit of the doubt, the senators (this time including Benedetto Croce) responded with a vote of confidence. Four Liberals in the Senate actually consented to join a reconstructed government under Mussolini. But the Chamber of Deputies proved more intransigent. The week before, on June 18, a coalition of some 150 members of various parties, from the Catholic Italian People's Party on the Right to the Communist Party of Italy on the Left and even including a handful of repentant former Mussolini supporters, refused to participate in the hypocrisy of a Fascist-sponsored commemorative ceremony for Matteotti. Instead, Filippo Turati, the revered intellectual "voice" of the Socialist Party, led his fellow dissenters out of the Chamber, simultaneously invoking ancient Roman history and the memorable last stand of Gaius Gracchus and the Plebes on the Aventine Hill. As an act of protest, Turati and the current "Aventinians" proceeded then to form an alternate, rump caucus in the parliament building's reception foyer.

But later, when the Communist "Aventinians" moved to have the secessionists named a legal parliament, the more moderate Aventine leadership balked, and even the former Liberal ex-premiers, Giolitti, Salandra, and Orlando, who had remained in the Chamber but had become openly critical of Mussolini after Matteotti's murder, refused any longer to support Turati's defectors. Mussolini subsequently confessed that, lacking their refusal, he would have found his position untenable. As it was, the most authoritative remaining spokesman of the Aventinians was another Liberal, Giovanni Amendola, who had supplanted Turati as the faction's chairman. A 42-year-old Neapolitan deputy, a former professor of philosophy at the University of Bologna, and a decorated artillery officer in the late war, Amendola had been elected to the Chamber in 1919. His greatest political ambition, he had proclaimed, was to forge a powerful "Democratic Union" that would include revisionist Marxists, liberal Catholics, and other moderates. During the

---

44 Roy MacGregor-Hastie, *The Day of the Lion: The Life and Death of Fascist Italy: 1922–1945* (New York: Coward-McCann, 1963), 165; also David I. Kertzer, *The Pope and Mussolini: The Secret History of Pius XI and the Rise of Fascism in Europe* (New York: Random House, 2014), *passim*.

summer of 1924, following Matteotti's abduction, Amendola had carried on an incessant campaign against Mussolini and the Fascists in the columns of *Il Mundo*, repeatedly entreating King Vittorio Emanuele to call new general elections. But the king had remained adamant, insisting that his intercession simply would "open the way" for the Bolsheviks or, at the very least, for his unbeloved cousin, the Duke of Aosta, his rival for the throne.

In mid-August 1924, as the Aventinians continued to dither, confusedly seeking a way to unseat Mussolini, a political bombshell suddenly burst. A group of picnickers had stumbled across Matteotti's body in the woods south of Rome. A subsequent autopsy verified that Matteotti had indeed been murdered, by knife and truncheon. Hereupon, the police accelerated their interrogation of the gangster Amerigo Dumini and of his fellow prisoners. By the time the extensive grilling was completed, on November 24, the investigating magistrate had filled no less than 44 volumes of testimony and remanded the collection of accused prisoners for trial.

A month later still, on December 28, 1924, in the interval between investigation and trial, *Il Mundo* published Cesare Rossi's secret "memoir," which implicated Mussolini in personally laying the groundwork for Matteotti's abduction. Rossi's wife had smuggled the document out of Regine Coeli prison two days earlier, after visiting her husband, and turned it over to Giovanni Amendola, the Aventinian leader. Amendola and his fellow protestors were confident by then that the revelations would force Mussolini's departure from the prime ministry and possibly even assure his imprisonment.

## THE COUNTERATTACK

Instead, on January 3, 1925, the prime minister struck back. Two weeks earlier, he had been confronted in his office by 50 members of the Fascist Grand Council. In contrast to its last emergency meeting of June 13, 1924, the Council on this occasion challenged Mussolini to "be a man" and go on the offensive. The threat was all but explicit that, if he declined, the members themselves would unseat him as party chairman. But this time, Mussolini required no persuasion. He assured the assembled chieftains that he shared their impatience and that he would soon take action. That same day, he kept his promise. In an impassioned two-hour speech before the Chamber of Deputies, he assumed full responsibility for his past campaign of intimidation and violence, including the threats, beatings, and pillage of the opposition's offices and homes. These tactics would now be resumed, he shouted, for they represented the "only way" to bring order and prosperity back to Italy.

Within 48 hours, moreover, in fulfillment of Mussolini's threat, Fascist militiamen were given free rein to begin a campaign of intensified repression. In the larger cities, phalanxes of Blackshirts began wading into meetings of opposition parties, laying about them with truncheons. Simultaneously, the government imposed heavy censorship on opposition newspapers and then enforced the measure by confiscating their offices and printing plants. In February, the three remaining non-Fascists in Mussolini's cabinet were replaced by "reliable" members of his own party. Municipal governments and regional prefectures that formerly had been elective were summarily replaced by appointed officials, all Fascists. Finally, the police were given extended powers of arrest and detention, and a special branch of the police, the OVRA, began wiretapping suspected opposition politicians and other public figures, even searching their homes and intermittently rounding them up for "detailed interrogation."

By the spring of 1925, the Aventinian dissidents could sense the shifting political climate. Their popular support had begun to wane. On the Left, the Communists had been the first to defect, as the party ordered its deputies to return to the Chamber in the wake of the failed attempt to have the Aventinian secessionists proclaim themselves Italy's legal parliament. On the Right, the Vatican began openly condemning the Aventinians of playing into the hands of the secularist Left. Then, in July 1925, Giovanni Amendola, the Aventinian leader, although refraining from a direct accusation against Mussolini, loosed a final denunciation against Emilio De Bono, the Fascist militia commander who had managed thus far to avoid indictment and had returned to the Mussolini's good graces. A week later, 30 militiamen converged on Amendola at his Riviera vacation spa and beat him within an inch of his life. Shortly afterward, his family transported him France, settling him in Cannes, where he remained a semi-paralyzed invalid until he expired in April 1926, at the age of 44. His death, less than two years after Matteotti's, deprived the Aventinians of their most respected spokesman. The group's members soon dispersed. In November 1926, the Fascist-controlled Chamber of Deputies passed a law that effectively stripped all "deserters," that is, all former Aventinians, of their parliamentary seats.

Even then, the case against Matteotti's accused murderers could not easily be dropped. In earlier months, Mussolini had issued too many assurances to the contrary, and public opinion both in Italy and abroad was still a factor. Thus, in January 1926, after a last, brief postponement, the trial of suspects finally got underway. Its venue, however, no longer was Rome but the Adriatic coastal town of Chieti, one of the smallest provincial capitals in Italy. Far from the spotlight, Chieti was difficult to reach by railroad. It possessed only two small hotels, enabling the police more easily to scrutinize guest registers. Meanwhile, the original chairman of the three-judge panel, Mauro Del' Giudice, a veteran and much respected jurist, had been transferred from Rome to a minor prosecutorial office in Sicily. His replacement in Chieti was an obscure provincial magistrate who, not coincidentally, was the brother-in-law of Roberto Farinacci, secretary-general of the Fascist Party.

The previous July 31, 1925, only days after the preliminary judicial indictments, and before the scheduled opening of the formal trial, the government had issued a decree granting amnesty to all those who had been arraigned for "premeditated political murder" in the event that evidence could not be provided that the defendants had "specifically" intended to kill their victims. Under this interpretation, while Matteotti's seizure by Dumini and the latter's four accomplices manifestly was premeditated, the captive's actual death was proclaimed to have arisen from "unforeseen circumstances," and the defendants therefore could be charged only for the crime of abduction. Once the Chieti trial resumed, both the prosecution and the panel of three judges similarly agreed that Rossi and Marinelli, although responsible for plotting a crime of violence, had not themselves been proven to have committed the abduction, let alone a premeditated murder, and thereby also came within the "extended" scope of the amnesty. The two men were accordingly released *sine die*.

During the trial's second week, Matteotti's widow, Velia, seated in the courtroom as plaintiff in a simultaneous civil action against the defendants (a procedure allowed under Italian law), understood exactly the farce that was unfolding. In her despair, she finally petitioned the judges to allow her to withdraw from the proceedings. Her words gained her a shared immortality with her late husband's:

> My Lords: The murder of Giacomo Matteotti was a tragedy for me and my children, but still more for free and civilized Italy. I thought at first that justice would not be sought in vain. This trust was the only consolation left me in my deep sorrow. For this reason, I stood as plaintiff. . . . I did not seek revenge. I merely asked for justice. Men deny it to me, but history and God will grant [it]. . . . I beg Your Lordships to exempt me from the terrible ordeal of appearing any longer in this court.[45]

Velia Matteotti's petition was summarily granted.

---

45 Salvemini, *The Fascist Dictatorship*, 292–93.

As the trial proceeded, the defense lawyers seemed to have no difficulty in convincing the panel of judges that Dumini and his strong-arm accomplices in Filippelli's automobile, while still vulnerable to the charge of abduction, were unaware that Matteotti had been suffering from a disease (allegedly, borderline diabetes) "which contributed to his death." In light of this "information," four of the prisoners were released seven weeks later. Only Dumini himself, as the professional criminal who had recruited the kidnappers, was sentenced to an additional six months behind bars.[46] Upon his release in late 1926, however, he laid siege to Mussolini's office for a "promised" promotion. Hence, in an effort to sue the Fascist Central Committee, Dumini "confided" to several members of the Fascist Central Committee his knowledge of Mussolini's "personal" guilt for the murder. When the "confidants" then ratted on Dumini to the government, he was rearrested, retried for "perjury," and sentenced to an additional 15 years of imprisonment (although, during his ensuing confinement, the government paid "hush money" to his family).[47]

Meanwhile, Cesare Rossi, Mussolini's erstwhile aide and subsequent betrayer, did not escape punishment of another sort. In disgrace with the party for the testimony he had provided the political opposition, he emigrated to France in February 1926, where he subsequently freelanced as a political journalist and developed associations with other Italian political émigrés. But, in August 1928, Fascist agents lured Rossi into a visit to family members and friends in the Italian-speaking enclave of Campione on the Swiss side of Lake Lugano. There he was seized, drugged, and carried back to Italy in the trunk of an automobile. Once in Rome, he was charged with "conspiring to assassinate the prime minister" and condemned by a Fascist "special tribunal" to 30 years of imprisonment.

## FROM PRIME MINISTER TO DUCE

By early 1926, a three-year process was underway that would complete the transformation of Italy from an erstwhile neo-parliamentary state into an undisguised dictatorship. The Fascist Grand Council became an official state organ, presided over by Mussolini in his enlarged multifold role as party chairman, prime minister, and minister (by then) of no less than eight other government ministries. In 1929, under his detailed orchestration, the last vestiges of the old constitutional order disappeared with the abrogation of the

---

46 For a concise version of trial testimony, see Schiavi, *La vita*, 274–305.
47 Amerigo Dumini, *Diciassette colpi* (Milan: Longanesi, 1951), 79, 255.

Chamber of Deputies and its replacement with a nonelected "parliament" consisting of 400 Fascist deputies nominated by the Fascist Grand Council— the members of which themselves were nominated exclusively by Mussolini and his advisors.

By the late 1920s, local self-government was similarly abolished. Henceforth, government-appointed "prefects" would replace all formerly elected mayors.[48] Among other innovations, augmented police powers allowed for the "relocation" of dissidents, and the death penalty was reintroduced (although rarely invoked) for all "political" crimes—that is, all anti-government and antiparty transgressions. In 1926, a "Special Tribunal for the Defense of the Fascist State" was instituted. During the ensuing 17 years of Mussolini's incumbency, it was this body that handed down more than 13,000 convictions against "political criminals."

On the few occasions when Mussolini compromised with the existing hierarchy of Italy's political, economic, and religious institutions, he did so in ways that substantially consolidated his rule. Besides the monarchy itself, these included the senior army command, the oligarchs of industry and landed estates, the "white aristocracy" of the monarchical court, and the "black aristocracy" of the papal court. Mussolini shrewdly proceeded to combine their vested interests with his own. Thus, he enlarged the powers both of the government and of the capitalist classes by the "Vidoni Palace" agreement of 1925 and the corporations laws of 1926. The former excluded non-Fascist unions from representing workers either in industry or agriculture. The latter created 12 national "corporations" encompassing all major sectors of the economy. Although labor nominally was categorized as one of these sectors, it was consigned in effect to the mercy of the agricultural and industrial cartels. Free to determine employees' wages and working conditions, the cartels in turn bonded to the government in gratitude and loyalty.

Propitiation of the Vatican was a rather more complicated matter. Since 1870, when the late King Vittorio Emanuele II officially had proclaimed Rome as the capital of Italy, the popes in turn had proclaimed themselves "prisoners" in the Vatican. This self-defined martyrdom reflected not only papal aggrievement at having been shorn of political sovereignty over the "holy" city, let alone over the full amplitude of the "Romagna" (the former Papal States). It evinced, as well, the humiliation of being offered a compensatory Vatican ministate at the hands of a secular Italian monarchy. A sovereignty that was unilaterally guaranteed by the Italian government presumably also

---

48  Romualdo Rossi, *Mussolini nudo alla meta* (Rome: Edizioni de La rinascita d'Italia, 1944), 68.

could be rescinded by the same government. Indeed, during the late nineteenth and early twentieth centuries, all Italian governments had insisted on this interpretation as a guarantee of Vatican noninterference in Italy's secular affairs; even as, in "reprisal," one pope after another declined to recognize the House of Savoy as Italy's reigning dynasty.

Yet, from the beginning of his prime ministry, Mussolini, the former anticlerical firebrand, had demonstrated the same eagerness to assuage the papacy as in his dealings with the monarchy, the army, and the nation's capitalist establishment. In the effort, he reintroduced the catechism in state schools, exempted the clergy from taxation, outlawed the Freemasons, and prohibited the sale of birth-control equipment. Appeasement of the Vatican extended even into the Duce's private life. In 1925, he and his "wife" Rachele were officially "remarried" in a Catholic ceremony (p. 39) and had their children baptized in the church. With Mussolini's dictatorship in place and with the shrewd, militantly conservative Achille Ratti lately ensconced on the papal throne as Pius XI, the Fascist government and the Holy See began exploring a more flexible modus vivendi.

The bargaining was tortuous, but, in February 1929, an accommodation finally was reached. It consisted of two documents: the Lateran "Treaty" and the Lateran "Concordat." By the terms of the treaty, the Vatican would renounce all claim to the former Papal States and accept the House of Savoy as the reigning monarchy of Italy. The Italian government, in turn, would pay the Vatican 1,750,000 lire (part of which the papacy agreed to invest in Italian government bonds) and recognize the Vatican as an independent state possessing full territorial sovereignty within its own 109 acres, the attendant authority to establish its own diplomatic relations with other governments. The second document, the Lateran "Concordat," defined the rights of the two states in the realm of educational and spiritual matters. The Italian government recognized Catholicism as the official religion of the Kingdom of Italy, with religious education to be made mandatory in all Italian schools. Jurisdiction over marriage, apart from legal separation, was transferred to church courts. Proselytization by non-Catholic "sects" could be made a penal offense, as could dancing and other "uproarious" events during Lent. This agreement achieved, the pontiff could only express satisfaction, declaring to his counselors that Mussolini was a "man sent by Providence."[49]

---

49 Kertzer, *Pope and Mussolini: The Secret History*, 111; Anthony Rhodes, *The Vatican in the Age of Dictators* (London: Hodder and Stoughton, 1973), 46.

Yet the more benign—and popular—achievements of Mussolini's government were not trivial. They included a wide assortment of social-welfare programs. State insurance was provided against unemployment, illness, and old age. Housing and employment also were made available for low-income families. As the Duce widened his ambitious commitment to public works, projects also included giant swamp-drainage campaigns, the construction of hundreds of bridges and aqueducts, thousands of miles of new highways, and massive new government buildings and monuments—all intended not only to provide employment and infrastructure improvement but to remind the nation at large of the power of the Fascist regime.

In that reminder, too, the cult of the Duce was promoted assiduously. Newspapers, newsreels, radio broadcasts, school textbooks, and wall billboards praised Mussolini as the "divine Caesar," the modern man of the people, a genius, a loving father figure. Public discussion was encouraged that touted Mussolini's intellectual, musical, athletic, even sexual prowess. Architects of the Duce cult overlooked no detail in crafting his image. A 1934 editorial in *Il Popolo d'Italia* was characteristic:

> He sees, he foresees, he senses, measures, acts. . . . He tames fortune, masters destiny. . . . He has created a people. He has aroused a Nation. He has organized a State, has fused a block of will, of hearts, of souls, of powers. Everything takes breath and movement from Him, because it is He, the Hero.[50]

A "hero" who before long would not be content to limit his will to the frontiers of his native land.

---

50  Cardoza, *Benito*, 77.

CHAPTER THREE

# A Posthumous Imperial Vengeance

*"Today we still need you, but in a few months, when the overall situation will have changed, we will get rid of you."*

## AN EMISSARY TO THE ALLIES

On the morning of November 7, 1918, a procession of three automobiles left Germany's advanced military headquarters in Spa, Belgium, and under flags of truce set out for France's Compiègne Forest. Two of the automobiles carried members of the Reichswehr general staff. In the third car sat two civilians, attired in striped trousers and frock jackets. Senior among this pair was Matthias Erzberger, chairman of the "progressive" wing of Germany's Center (Catholic) Party and minister without portfolio in the imperial cabinet. The previous afternoon, at the behest of the imperial chancellor, Prince Maximilian of Baden (p. 11), he had been authorized to seek an armistice with the Allied Powers.

A stocky, middle-sized man of 43, adorned with a precisely manicured moustache and a beribboned pince-nez, Erzberger appeared notably solemn this day. Three weeks before, he had sat at the bedside of his son, Oskar, as the young officer cadet expired of influenza in a military hospital. Notwithstanding his loss, Erzberger had been selected by his cabinet colleagues as the person best qualified to negotiate with Germany's enemies. Through neutral emissaries, President Woodrow Wilson of the United States had made clear that neither he nor other Allied leaders would sign an armistice with the "Junker militarists" who had led the Central Powers into their "war of aggression" (p. 11). Both in Germany and among the Allied enemies, Erzberger had emerged as a vocal and influential advocate of peace, and thus he counted it as his duty now to accept his government's request.

In view of Germany's right-wing charge later that the Reichswehr had been intent on continuing the struggle but had been "stabbed in the back" by Communists and Jews, it was ironic that the self-same "Junker militarists" had themselves been the first to propose an armistice. Two months earlier, on August 11, 1918, the Allied armies had launched a pulverizing attack on the Western Front and had shattered 16 German divisions in the first 10 days of the offensive. In late September, Germany's co-belligerents, Austria, Bulgaria, and Turkey, their armies similarly in tatters, began initiating peace feelers of their own. By then even Quartermaster-General Erich Ludendorff, the Reichswehr's most uncompromising expansionist, was advocating an armistice at virtually any price; and on September 28 he had convinced Field Marshal Paul von Hindenburg, the Reichswehr commander in chief, that no feasible alternative remained.

In the spring and summer of 1918, moreover, German factory workers had begun laying down their tools, and housewives were marching through the streets, clanging the empty pots and pans that betokened their empty pantries (p. 10). Hence, on September 29, under pressure from both his personal counselors and the political opposition, Kaiser Wilhelm II at last announced his acceptance of an unambivalently parliamentary regime, with all government ministers, including for the first time the chancellor, the foreign minister, and the war minister, to be responsible exclusively to the Reichstag. Four days later, Prince Maximilian of Baden, unaffiliated politically but a man of respected liberal inclinations, was sworn in as chancellor of the newly democratized government. It was in the midst of this social and political turmoil that the kaiser sought breathing room for his dynasty, which had emerged in the eyes of Allied statesmen as the very embodiment of Prussian militarism.

But for the German people the gestures of democratization had come too late. On October 28, mutiny erupted at the Kiel naval base, then at other naval bases, and subsequently both military and civilian insurrections gained momentum in Germany's largest cities. It was under these conflicting pressures, on November 6, that Matthias Erzberger was asked to seek an armistice. The next day he prepared to set out from Spa, accompanied in the lead automobile by Count Alfred von Oberndorff, a senior foreign ministry official. As the two men were about to drive off, Field Marshal Hindenburg, tears in his eyes, suddenly grasped Erzberger's hand and whispered: "May God travel with you and help you in attaining the best that still can be attained for the Fatherland."[1] "From the Field Marshal's lips to God's ear," came Erzberger's muted response. The procession of automobiles then set out. The following afternoon, November 8, crossing French lines, it reached the town of Compiègne, where awaiting Algerian Zouaves directed its lead chauffeur to the advance headquarters of Marshal Ferdinand Foch, supreme commander of the Allied armies on the Western Front.

Somewhat incongruously, the headquarters were to be found in two rear carriages of the train used by Foch and his staff. The "generalissimo" himself stood outside, awaiting his visitors. He was flanked by General Maxime Weygand and two senior British naval officers, admirals Wemys and Hope, and their respective military aides. They greeted Erzberger and Oberndorff correctly, with salutes but no handshakes, and the mixed group entered the train's last carriage and took their seats. General Weygand then commenced reading out the armistice terms that Foch had formulated during the preceding week in a series of inter-Allied conferences with British, Italian, and American officials.

## AN APOSTLE OF AMBIVALENCE

Foch's intelligence staff had done extensive background research on Erzberger. If the German emissary had come as an apostle of peace and reconciliation, his authentic instincts could have been viewed at least as ambivalent. Three and a half years before, in February 1915, in his role as spokesman for the Reichstag's Centrist faction, Erzberger had declared in the party's monthly circular:

> The waging of war is a rough and brutal craft. . . . [T]he application of drastic measures is the quickest road to peace. Procrastination and hesitation, softness and consideration . . . [for the enemy] all constitute inexcusable weakness. Resolute, ruthless action is the earmark of strength and the certain road to

---

[1] Klaus Epstein, *Matthias Erzberger and the Dilemma of German Democracy* (Princeton, NJ: Princeton University Press, 1959), 274.

victory.... [England] ... has mobilized its allies and satellites ... from the white, yellow, brown, red . . . and even the *gefleckte* [mixed] races and sends them against Germany in the name of civilization. Every day that England continues to [interdict] our foodstuffs . . . by her naval blockade should be answered by our dirigibles bringing terror and death into the ranks of the English people.[2]

To that uncompromising end, in October 1916, Erzberger had secured a Reichstag motion declaring that "[i]f it is decided to initiate a ruthless submarine campaign, the [chancellor] can be certain of the support of the Reichstag." The resolution marked in effect the delegates' abdication of power to Chancellor Theobold von Bethmann-Hollweg and, specifically, to the military quasi-dictatorship of Hindenburg and Ludendorff.[3]

Yet Erzberger was a more complicated man than the Allies or even his own political colleagues would have suspected. Born in 1875 in a small village in Württemberg, the son of a Catholic tailor, he was the eldest of six children. None could afford a university education. Nevertheless, after attending a teacher's seminar, Erzberger qualified as an instructor in one of his province's Catholic primary schools. Soon, too, he became a leader in Württemberg's Catholic labor movement, which in 1896 sent him to study economics at the Catholic University in Freiburg, Switzerland. Seven years later, at the age of 28, devout in his religiosity and widely respected for his work ethic, Erzberger became the Center Party's regional nominee for the Reichstag. Upon winning election, he also became the Reichstag's youngest member.

In short order, Erzberger won recognition as a vigorous and respected spokesman of his party's "moderate," socially conscious wing. With his agile mind and phenomenal energy, the precocious deputy soon emerged as a favorite even of the ultraconservative Chancellor Bethmann-Hollweg. Indeed, in August 1914, after the outbreak of war, Bethmann-Hollweg appointed him the government's "director of information services," in effect, as propagandist in chief. Erzberger in turn managed his role so adeptly, with special emphasis on reaching Catholic audiences in neutral countries, and supported the government's annexationist policies with such apparent enthusiasm, that by 1915 his portfolio was elevated to cabinet status.

As early as the spring of that year, however, Germany's political parties began to diverge on the government's war aims.[4] The Conservatives and

---

2 Epstein, *Matthias Erzberger*, 410–11.
3 Epstein, *Matthias Erzberger*, 418.
4 Erich Otto Volkmann, ed., *Die Annexionsfragen des Welkrieges* (Berlin: Deutsches Verlagsgesellschaft für Politik und Geschichte, 1929), 48–69.

National Liberals favored harsh territorial annexations at the expense of the reeling Allies. In contrast, and true to their ideology, the Social Democrats favored a non-punitive peace. The Centrists and Progressive People's Party took an essentially opportunistic approach, favoring annexations as long as the military outlook remained favorable. Yet, by then, Erzberger himself had begun to reevaluate the government's hard line. Discreetly, he suggested that the foreign ministry might press its Austrian partner to adopt a more forthcoming approach towards its restless subject nationalities. Within the next two years, as the war devolved into a stalemate and casualties mounted by the hundreds of thousands, Erzberger became convinced that Britain too might opt out of the war if Germany were to forgo its annexationist policy in Belgium. Finally, in July 1917, he called on the government to renounce its territorial demands altogether.

Erzberger apparently was on safe political ground by then. Before delivering his speech in the Reichstag, he had persuaded his Centrist colleagues to join the Social Democrats and Progressives in support of his proposal. With this encouragement, on July 19, he submitted his "peace initiative" to a Reichstag vote. Almost miraculously, it won the endorsement of the new chancellor, Georg Michaelis, and then was passed by the Reichstag by a resounding majority of 212 to 126. But two days later, as Michaelis signed the non-annexation resolution, he added the caveat "as I interpret it." The army command had insisted upon the qualification—which thereby leached the Reichstag statement of any legislative significance. If Erzberger could take any solace from the government's dissembling, it was that Michaelis subsequently proved so compliant a rubber stamp of the military leadership that the kaiser himself replaced him as chancellor the following October with Count Georg von Hertling, the aged prime minister of Bavaria. With the kaiser's approbation, Hertling then appointed Richard von Kühlmann, a reputed moderate, as Germany's foreign minister. But the government's evident gravitation toward a forbearing peace had come too late for Erzberger, for it was followed within three weeks by the Bolshevik Revolution in Russia.

### RUSSIA LEAVES THE WAR

In November 1917, to consolidate that revolution, Vladimir Lenin, the leader of Russia's makeshift Soviet government (pp. 107–8), had sent out armistice feelers to the German High Command. In turn, General Max Hoffmann, Germany's Eastern Front commander, recommended to Hindenburg and Ludendorff that he be allowed to enter into a preliminary cease-fire with the Russians. The two senior Reichswehr commanders acquiesced. Parleys subsequently began on December 2, 1917, at General Hoffmann's advanced Ukrainian headquarters at Brest-Litovsk. The Russian delegation was led by a veteran Bolshevik, Adolf Joffe, with Lev Kamenev (p. 120) acting as his second in command. The initial meetings between the emissaries were equable. Hoffmann offered seemingly unexceptionable terms, suggesting that Germany would be receptive to a freeze on military action in the east, with both armies holding their current military positions until their governments could formulate a more "permanent" armistice—in effect, an operative peace treaty. When the Soviet delegates agreed, the date for "substantive" parleys then was set for December 22.

When those talks duly commenced 20 days later, Hoffmann was joined by Germany's Foreign Minister Kühlmann. Indeed, nearly 400 people eventually attended the conclave, representatives both of Russia and the full pleneum of the Central Powers—Austria, Turkey, and Bulgaria, as well as Germany. An atmosphere of collegiality seemingly prevailed. The various emissaries, military and civilian, were housed in the annexes of the Brest-Litovsk citadel, living in common dormitories and eating at a common mess table. The Germans placed automobiles at the disposal of the visiting delegates, including those from Russia. Hoffmann, Kühlmann, and their colleagues listened politely, too, as Adolf Joffe, the Russian delegation's senior spokesman, presented the diplomatic blueprint that Lenin and the Communist Central Committee had prepared during the three weeks of intervening cease-fire.

It was a formula based ostensibly on a "resolution" that Germany's Center and Social Democratic parties, and specifically Matthias Erzberger, had introduced in the Reichstag seven months before. It favored a cessation of hostilities without territorial annexations or financial indemnities. Although, at the time, the German military command and the kaiser himself had interposed qualifications that effectively torpedoed the proposal (p. 74), Joffe and the Russian delegates now professed to "accept" Erzberger's original resolution at its face value. They too endorsed the call for a peace without annexations or indemnities. Indeed, they added to it the general goal of freedom and independence for *all* nationalities—or at least the guarantee of "cultural national independence" if "administrative autonomy" was not possible.[5] By this embellishment, Joffe actually anticipated that the German and Austrian armies would relinquish their occupation of Poland, Ukraine, Lithuania, Latvia, and Courland, and return these formerly tsarist provinces to Russia.

---

5 Joffe's "Six Points" in translation, quoted in George Frost Kennan, *Soviet-American Relations, 1917–1920, Vol. 1 Russia Leaves the War* (Princeton, NJ: Princeton University Press, 1956), 220.

Afterward, the Soviet regime presumably would negotiate its own, federalized relationship with these provincial governments.

Acceptance of the Russian proposal actually was furthest from the minds of the German military command.[6] Nevertheless, General Hoffmann diplomatically finessed the issue three days later, on Christmas Day, by agreeing to accept the Communist formula "in principle." But on December 28, in consultation with Marshal Hindenburg and the kaiser, Ludendorff established the German government's authentic "negotiating" position. In a telegram to his country's delegation at Brest-Litovsk, Ludendorff directed that Hoffmann now "drive the spike" into the Soviet formula by insisting that the "border" nationalities should be given freedom to reach their own "direct understanding" with Germany and Austria.[7] Yet it soon became apparent that "direct understanding" was a euphemism for the amputation of these provinces from Russia and for their subsequent de facto vassalage under Germany and its partners. Moreover, as a token of "gratitude" for their "protection" from Russia, the border nationalities also would be expected to provide the Central Powers with vast amounts of grain and livestock, even as the Soviet government itself would be required to fork over to Germany and Austria the equivalent of one billion dollars in "reparations." Hereupon, shaken and outraged by the unanticipated magnitude of German demands, Joffe sought and obtained leave to return home for consultations with Lenin and the Communist Central Committee.

It was at this point, too, in the second week of January 1919, that Vladimir Lenin decided that a new and more authoritative Soviet negotiator was required. He replaced Joffe with Leon Trotsky, then serving as interim commissar for foreign affairs. As Lenin's most trusted surrogate, Trotsky presumably would find a way to wrest more forbearing terms from the Central Powers. But it did not happen. Upon traveling to Brest-Litovsk, Trotsky found himself confronting Foreign Minister Kühlmann; and Kühlmann, once thought a moderate, revealed himself to be hardly less obdurate than General Hoffmann, or even than the rapacious Ludendorff.[8] Indeed, he added Estonia to the list of border nationalities that were to be allowed to engage in "separate negotiations" with the Central Powers—in effect, to be severed from the Russian Empire.

---

6 Erich Ludendorff, *My War Memories, 1914–1918*, 2 vols. (London: Hutchinson & Co., 1919–1920), 2: 521.

7 Erich Ludendorff, *The General Staff and Its Problems: The History of the Relations between the High Command and the German Imperial Government as Revealed by Official Documents*, 2 vols. (London: Hutchinson & Co., 1920), 1: 524–28; see also, Wheeler-Bennett, *Brest-Litovsk*, 133–34.

8 Epstein, *Matthias Erzberger*, 237–38.

Trotsky reacted with bitterness and gall. Contemptuously skewering the formula of "separate negotiations" as the charade that it was, he warned that his government would sign neither a peace treaty nor even a provisional armistice on a basis that had no precedent in foreign affairs. Adhering to that position day after day, Trotsky cited each and every authority in international law, as well as a plenitude of examples from European history. By turns dynamic, scornful, almost diabolically brilliant, riding rings around Hoffmann and Kühlmann in the art of dialectic, Trotsky virtually brought the conference to a standstill. The American Red Cross representative in St. Petersburg, Colonel Raymond Robins, who was present as an observer at the Brest-Litovsk negotiations, wrote home: "If the German General Staff [think that they] bought Trotsky, they bought a lemon.... He's a four-kind son of a bitch, but the greatest Jew since Jesus Christ."[9] Eventually, on February 6, after three weeks of tense standoff, Kühlmann wired Berlin that he saw no alternative but to present Trotsky with a 24-hour ultimatum. It was to sign a peace treaty on Germany's terms or the Reichswehr would resume its offensive. In their headquarters at Spa, Ludendorff and Hindenburg heartily concurred.

Although the ultimatum was extended by four days, allowing Kühlmann to return to Berlin and leave the negotiating details to his subordinates, Trotsky riposted with an unanticipated ultimatum of his own. It was based on an ingenious alternate formula he had presented to Lenin and the Central Committee even before departing for Brest-Litovsk. This was to declare a state of "non-hostility" and the demobilization of the Russian Army. If the Reichswehr afterward should resume its offensive against "peaceful" Russia, Trotsky argued, Germany presumably would be exposed before Europe as an aggressor against a helpless Russian civilian population, against a people whose government already had committed itself to peace. Lenin had taken vigorous issue with Trotsky's formula, believing it to be unacceptably naive.[10] Under pressure from the Communist Central Committee, however, he had allowed Trotsky to take the gamble. Hence, on February 10, 1918, faced with the German delegation's unbudging stance, Trotsky revealed the card up his sleeve. He announced that his government had decided to "quit" the war. It would not resume hostilities against the Central Powers, he stated, but neither would it accept the proffered treaty.

---

9  Wheeler-Bennett, *Brest-Litovsk*, 152.
10  Leon Trotsky, *Lenin* (London: G.G. Harrap, 1925), 131–32; see also, Wheeler-Bennett, *Brest-Litovsk*, 195, and Orlando Figes, *A People's Tragedy: The Russian Revolution, 1891–1924* (London: Pimlico, 1996), 540–47.

Trotsky's announcement, of "no peace, no war," left the delegates of the Central Powers almost speechless. The formula was entirely alien to their experience, and their confusion was total. Had peace with Russia become an actual fact by virtue of Trotsky's astounding declaration? Or did the Powers remain in a state of war? Ironically, back in Berlin, Foreign Minister Kühlmann welcomed Trotsky's announcement. Believing that the end of hostilities was actually at hand, Kühlmann proposed to accept Trotsky's announcement of "withdrawal" from the war. In Vienna, moreover, its population on the verge of starvation, the Habsburg government ordered a celebratory ringing of church bells. But to Erzberger's subsequent dismay, Ludendorff and Hindenburg quickly overruled Kühlmann.[11] At their insistence, and the kaiser's, the order went out to the German delegation at Brest-Litovsk to "give the Russkies a taste of the whip."[12]

Accordingly, on February 18, the Reichswehr resumed its offensive. Within the week, facing no resistance, two of its army corps advanced another 150 miles eastward, virtually to the outskirts of St. Petersburg, thereby setting the Communist government scrambling to relocate itself to Moscow. By then, Trotsky and Lenin understood that the "no peace, no war" gamble had failed. The German terms would have to be accepted. On March 3, Trotsky assigned a deputy, Grigori Sokolnikov, to sign for him at Brest-Litovsk. The formality was completed in silence, with Sokolnikov's aide contemptuously blowing pipe smoke into General Hoffmann's face. The "negotiations" of two and a half months were over. Under the provisions of the "Treaty" of Brest-Litovsk—the euphemism of an "armistice" had been abandoned weeks before—Russia was obliged to forgo 32 per cent of its territories and 34 per cent of its former imperial population. Indeed, the document represented Europe's most punitive diplomatic surgery since the Treaty of Tilsit in 1807, when Napoleon had vivisected Prussia after the Battle of Jena.

For the Western Allies, on the other hand, the treaty would become pretext and precedent for the terms they themselves would impose on the Central Powers 15 months later.

## NEGOTIATING THE UNNEGOTIABLE

Indeed, within less than a half-year after the signing of the Brest-Litovsk Treaty, the pendulum of national opinion in Germany had begun to swing

---

11 See material on Richard von Kühlmann, in *Die Ursachen des Deutschen Zusammenbruches im Jahre 1918* (Berlin: Deutsches Verlagsgesellschaft für Politik und Geschichte, 1925), 1: 136–39.

12 Wheeler-Bennett, *Brest-Litovsk*, 199.

almost 180 degrees.[13] It was on October 3, 1918, as the climactic Allied offensive in the West gained momentum and as civil and military revolution erupted throughout Germany, that the kaiser appointed Prince Maximilian of Baden as chancellor of a new coalition government. A week later, "Prince Max" and his chastened cabinet authorized Matthias Erzberger to draft Germany's foreign-policy principles. Erzberger and his advisers completed the task within ten days. This time, the draft accepted virtually all of the Allies' territorial agenda. It acknowledged support for the restoration of Belgian sovereignty, with reparations to be paid to that little nation for the four years of German occupation and spoliation; the restoration of Lorraine (but not Alsace) to France; and a virtually total revision of the Brest-Litovsk Treaty (although on the basis of "genuine" self-determination for Ukraine and other non-Russian provinces), retaining for Germany only the Posen area of western Poland.[14]

The cabinet morosely voted its approval of Erzberger's draft and, on October 24, through Swedish intermediaries, the treaty prospectus was sent on to the Allied governments. By then, at Erzberger's request, no mention was made of the kaiser's recent abdication (p. 12);[15] but two days later, as a further token of its sincerity, the German government dismissed Ludendorff from his position in the Reichswehr High Command. Thereby vanished from the nation's inner councils a figure that the Allied governments widely regarded as the incarnation of ruthless and uncompromising German aggression. In response, Woodrow Wilson and the other Allied leaders sent word on November 5 that a sufficient basis had been laid for armistice negotiations.

On the next day, at Prince Max's recommendation, the cabinet asked Erzberger to continue his diplomatic mission by serving as chairman of Germany's armistice negotiating team. Although reluctant to take on a chore that undoubtedly would subject him to further nationalist denunciation, possibly even to political repudiation, Erzberger accepted the assignment.[16] After traveling to Spa later that afternoon and conferring with members of the Wehrmacht senior staff, he rested for the night. The following morning, November 7, together with Count Oberndorff and the modest retinue of

---

13  Volkmann, ed., *Die Annexionsfragen*, 128–58.
14  Epstein, *Matthias Erzberger*, 233–34; Wheeler-Bennett, *Brest-Litovsk*, 282, 298.
15  Erwin Gugelmeier, *Das schwarze Jahr, 1917–1918, Erlebtes aus dem letzten Kriegsjahr* (Freiberg: J. Bielefeld, 1926), 94.
16  Conrad Haussmann, *Schlaglichter: Reichstagsbriefe und Aufzeichnungen* (Frankfurt am Main: Frankfurter Societäts-Druckerei, 1924), 264.

ITALIAN POSTWAR GAINS

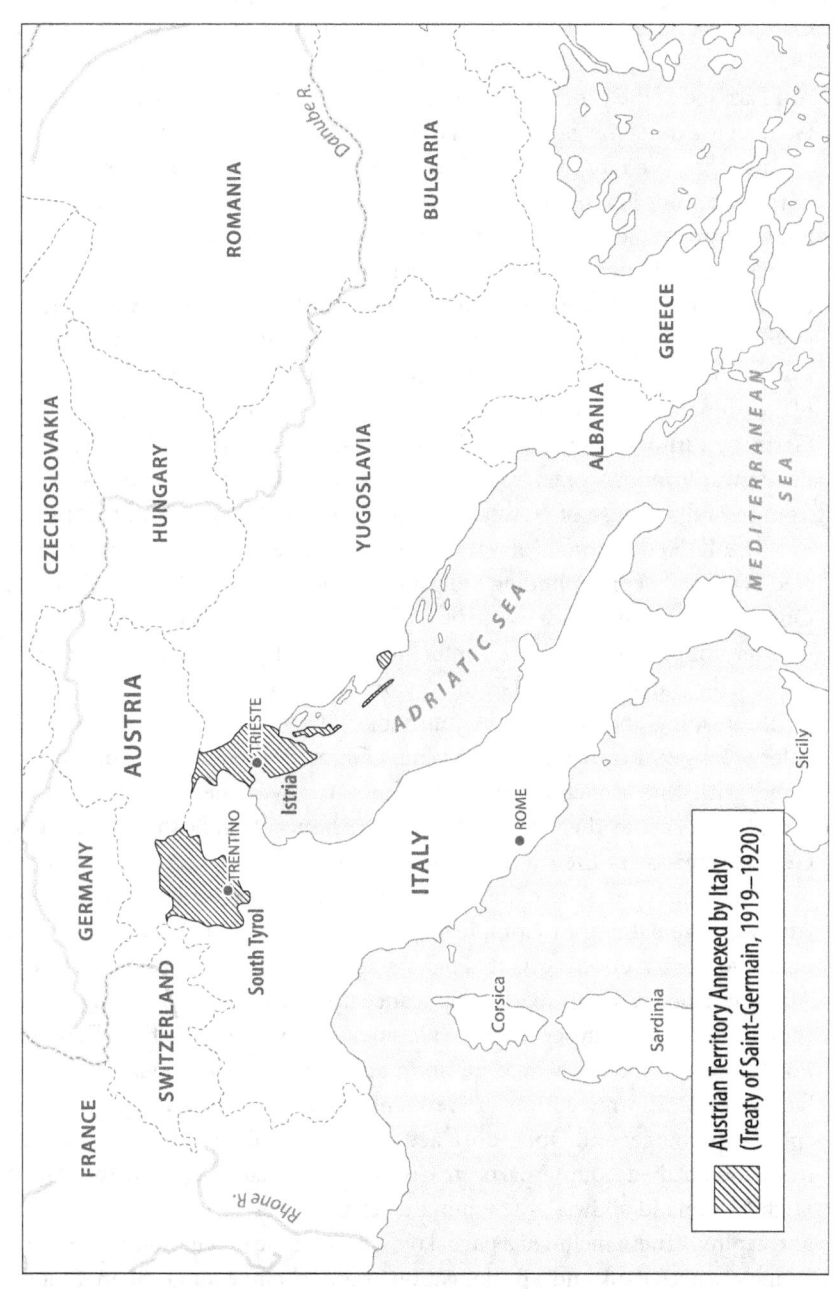

accompanying officers, he embarked on his crestfallen journey to Allied military headquarters. So it was, in the mid-morning of November 8, in the Compiègne Forest, that Marshal Foch ushered Erzberger and Oberndorff, as well as his own Allied entourage of officers, aides, and translators, into the rear carriage of the generalissimo's stationery military train. He then ordered General Maxime Weygand to read out the Allies' armistice terms.

These had been formulated in Paris between November 1 and November 4 during intensive inter-Allied consultations. The document's 34 provisions included complete German troop evacuation from Belgium and France (including *both* Alsace and Lorraine) and the immediate transfer to the Allies of hundreds of thousands of weapons, from small arms to airplanes and naval vessels, to be followed within the ensuing fortnight by 5,000 locomotives, 150,000 rail cars, and 10,000 trucks. German troop evacuation was required from the entire left bank of the Rhine, as well as from a 30- to 40-kilometer zone on the river's right bank. Germany's armies on the Eastern Front similarly were to be withdrawn behind the prewar frontiers—e.g., from the former tsarist Baltic provinces, as well as from the full expanse of German-occupied Poland, Ukraine, and Belorussia. Finally, all Allied prisoners of war should immediately be released and repatriated (without a corresponding obligation of reciprocity for German POWs). Once signed, the armistice was to be limited to 30 days, but with the possibility of extension, pending a peace conference and final peace treaty. Meanwhile, the Allied naval blockade of Germany would continue.

The reading and translations finished, Erzberger, Oberndorff, and their aides were given copies of the text in its German, French, and English versions, with the ultimatum that the German government would have to accept its terms in their entirety within 72 hours. Visibly shaken, the two German emissaries then were escorted to a telegraph office in the nearby town of Compiègne, where they were permitted to communicate with Berlin. Afterward, remaining in Compiègne, Erzberger and Oberndorff spent the next two days conferring with Foch's staff on possible concessions. If the Allies maintained their unrelenting stance, they protested, Germany would slide even further into economic ruin and, in that event, neither Germany nor the rest of Europe would be immune to possible bolshevization. They had a point. The revolution in Germany (p. 11) was escalating with such speed—Erzberger and Oberndorff actually learned of the kaiser's abdication from their Allied counterparts in Compiègne—that Foch and the Allied High Command allowed a few minimal changes before the armistice deadline expired. These included a partial reduction of the evacuation zone on the Rhine's eastern bank and a prolongation of the schedule for German military evacuation in Eastern Europe. Otherwise, the substance of the ultimatum remained unchanged.[17]

At 5:00 a.m. on November 11, after a three-hour deadline extension, the German emissaries signed the document, with Erzberger limiting himself to a brief, aggrieved condemnation of its "severity." The statement was ironic. The great majority of Germans actually had never experienced the authentic magnitude of their nation's defeat. Even now, in the wake of the armistice, the German people would not so much as set eyes on occupying Allied troops except within the "bridgeheads" of the Rhine and a thin sliver of the Rhineland east of the river. Allied contingents assuredly did not march in triumph into Berlin, as the Germans had marched into Paris in 1870. Rather, in November 1918, German soldiers were permitted to return home in good marching order, with crowds cheering them on their arrival. In Berlin, the new Social Democratic chancellor, Friedrich Ebert, greeted the arriving troops with the assurance "No enemy has conquered you!"[18]

Meanwhile, Erzberger, Oberndorff, and their attending aides similarly made their way back to Germany, maneuvering slowly through roads crowded with the retreating columns of troops. En route, stopping off at military headquarters in Spa on the afternoon of November 14 and reporting to Hindenburg and the senior military staff, Erzberger was at once surprised and gratified to receive the field marshal's effusive congratulations for his "successful"—but actually insignificant—modifications of the Allies' original armistice terms. In fact, Erzberger's task was not over. By the time he traveled from Spa back to Berlin on a train commandeered by soldiers waving red flags, the successor Ebert-Haase government had been in office for three and a half days. It was this Socialist coalition cabinet that decided to reappoint Erzberger, still a leader of the Centrist Party, as chairman of the German section of the international armistice commission, which the Allies had charged with the fulfillment of the Compiègne provisions. As Erzberger had feared, the extension of his role in this mournful task was to prove a fatal liability in his subsequent political career.

The armistice commission had established headquarters in the occupied Rhenish city of Trier, where its German staff alone comprised some 300 civilian and military officials. At Trier, Erzberger ate his bread with affliction. The

---

17  Epstein, *Matthias Erzberger*, 339.
18  Margaret MacMillan, *Paris 1919: Six Months that Changed the World* (New York: Random House, 2001), 137.

Allied occupation armies would maintain their economic blockade against Germany for more than eight months, until April 1919, with its grim human consequences of malnutrition and revolutionary unrest.[19] They kept the German POWs in internment for the same period. If some of these constraints were subsequently relaxed, the process was grudging and ceded essentially to extract further German territorial concessions. Meanwhile, neither Erzberger nor his staff members were granted the minimal diplomatic courtesies traditionally ceded to enemy emissaries. Between official meetings with their Allied counterparts, they were confined to their hotels and their own dining facilities, and were forbidden to receive mail.

To compound Erzberger's personal humiliation, news reached him that German public opinion was fastening on *him* as a traitor. Had *he* not placed himself at the head of the German armistice delegation, political leaders and newspaper editorials charged, thus exhibiting a lack of national dignity? Was *he* not bungling the current, ongoing negotiations, apparently failing to secure even the most trivial of concessions from the Allies? The accusations rankled. Nevertheless, as an experienced veteran of acrimonious Reichstag debate, Erzberger once again gave as good as he took. During the war, he noted acidly, his present critics were the fiercest advocates of annexing virtually all enemy territory, from the English Channel to the Caucasus. Did they still wish to press their country, with its shattered economy and broken military machine, into a renewal of hostilities? But Erzberger's critics were not to be silenced.

## THE PEACE TREATY

On January 18, 1919, with the armistice commission still in operation, a formal peace conference opened in Paris. This time, Germany's new Social-Democratic government excluded Erzberger from his country's delegation. Instead, the officials who were dispatched to the Allied Supreme Council were Germany's new foreign minister, Ulrich von Brockdorff-Rantzau, a professional diplomat who had replaced Georg von Hertling upon the establishment of the Weimar Republic, and Johann von Bernstorff, Germany's former ambassador to Washington. Yet even these two mid-level representatives were not accredited as "participants" in the Peace Conference, or allowed so much as to set foot in Paris for four months, until early May 1919. The Allied governments had made clear that Germany's emissaries had been invited

---

19 Suda Lorena Bane and Ralph Haswell Lutz, eds., *The Blockade of Germany after the Armistice, 1918–1919: Selected Documents* (Palo Alto, CA: Stanford University Press, 1942), v, 3–24, 430–95.

not to negotiate a treaty but only to read and accept its final text. Brockdorff-Rantzau, who on May 7 was allowed 90 minutes to peruse the completed document before meeting with the Allied leaders, could only express his shock and aggrievement—and his resentment of the absent Erzberger, who had "maneuvered" Germany into this corner.[20]

The treaty's provisions, most notably its Article 227 and 231, saddled Germany's government with a potentially back-breaking (if as yet unspecified) reparations debt and ceded all the former Reich's overseas colonies to its former enemies. In Europe itself, Alsace-Lorraine would revert back to France, Eupen-Malmédy to Belgium, and parts of East Prussia, Posen, and Upper Silesia to a resurrected and enlarged Poland. The Rhineland, although nominally remaining part of territorial Germany, would be placed under Allied military occupation for a period of not less than 15 years, while the Saar region, with its valuable mineral deposits and industrial plants, as well as the city of Danzig, with its extensive Polish population and its crucial maritime access to the Baltic Sea, would be "administered" by the League of Nations (from which Germany itself would be excluded). In addition, the German government would be required to deliver its "war criminals," including the ex-kaiser as well as many others of the nation's military and civilian leaders, to the Allies for trial. The treaty's rationale for these and other punitive measures was stated in its Article 231. It was Germany's moral responsibility for the war.

German indignation would focus ever after upon these two articles, 227 and 231, as *Schmachparagraphen* ("articles of shame"). Speaking for Germany's Social Democratic government, the newly appointed chancellor, Philipp Scheidemann (who had succeeded Friedrich Ebert upon the latter's elevation to the German presidency), called the Paris terms "unbearable, unrealizable, and unacceptable," and prophesied that "the hand should wither" that signed a treaty containing these provisions.[21] Nevertheless, although forgoing their demand for delivery of Germany's war criminals (including the abdicated kaiser), the Allies held fast to Article 227 and 231 as moral justification for the treaty's territorial and reparations demands.

It was ironic, however, that the list of these reparations, forming the lengthy continuation of Article 231, originally had served as a bone of contention among the Allied leaders themselves. In his "Fourteen Points," the bill of particulars Woodrow Wilson had submitted to the United States

---

20 Erich Brandenburg, *Deutschlands Kriegsziele* (Leipzig: Quelle & Meyer, 1920), 289.
21 Philipp Scheidemann, *Memoiren eines Sozialdemokraten*, 2 vols. (Dresden: C. Reissner, 1928), 1: 221.

Senate in January 1918 as his interpretation of Allied war objectives, the American president had firmly rejected the notion of demanding "indemnification" from the Central Powers. In diplomatic parlance, "indemnification" was synonymous with penalties. When the Prussian government imposed that kind of bill on France at the conclusion of the Franco-Prussian War, it had incurred widespread condemnation both in France and elsewhere in Western Europe. The president was not about to countenance it now. On the other hand, he found "reparations" legitimate, as these were payments that fell under the category of recompense for damages inflicted on civilians or civilian property.

On the Western Front, those damages had been imposed almost exclusively on France and Belgium, whose civilian properties had been pillaged by occupying German armies. Yet, under Wilson's definition, Great Britain would be excluded from reparations. Not a single German soldier had set foot on *British* territories, after all. Hereupon Britain's Prime Minister David Lloyd George finessed the distinction between "indemnification" and "reparations" by insisting that his government's pension payments to the families of fallen soldiers should also be categorized as "civilian" damages, thus making their recipients eligible for "reparations" to the tune of at least $110 billion (the French were asking for a minimum of $220 billion). For months, Wilson resisted Lloyd George's casuistry. In the end, however, exhausted by the protracted semantic wrangling and his own deteriorating health, the American president gave in. Against the advice of his legal adviser, John Foster Dulles, who condemned the British position as "illogical," Wilson exploded: "Logic! Logic! I don't give a damn for logic. I am going to include pensions."[22]

Yet the Germans themselves were hardly guiltless in these financial maneuvers. During the war, for political reasons, their government had kept the nation's tax rates low, relying instead on the sale of vast numbers of war bonds. The plan always had been for Germany to settle its public debt after victory, when it could transfer its costs to the defeated enemy. Indeed, on March 3, 1918, the government had done precisely that. The Treaty of Brest-Litovsk with Russia and the Treaty of Bucharest with Romania had consigned huge material resources to Germany, both in raw materials and

---

22   Hajo Holborn, "Diplomats and Diplomacy in the Early Weimar Republic," in *The Diplomats, 1919–1939*, ed. Gordon A. Craig and Felix Gilbert (Princeton: Princeton University Press, 1953), 123–71, see pages 141–44.

hard cash. Now, however, in the vanquished and prostrate Germany of 1919, the bill the government treasury owed its own citizens was coming due. Once again, the nation's right-wingers protested loudly against a rise of taxes or a government default on war bonds, even as its liberal and labor leaders pressed for increased benefits to veterans, widows, and orphans. In the end, the Weimar government meekly acquiesced to both demands, and Germany's fiscal deficit climbed still higher until, by summer of 1919, its bond-and-pension payments devoured not less than two-thirds of the national budget.

Both from his seat in the Reichstag and as a leader of the Center Party, Erzberger initially shared in the denunciation of the Versailles Treaty. But on June 16, 1919, the Allied leadership issued its last ultimatum: either the Germans would accept the treaty's provisions within seven days—by 7:00 p.m. of June 23—or their country would face military invasion. And still a majority of the German cabinet held out, including its Social-Democratic chancellor, Philipp Scheidemann. Hereupon, Erzberger, virtually alone among his ministerial colleagues, acknowledged that the government had run out of choices, that no alternative remained but to accept the Allies' terms.

At first, even Erzberger's own Center Party would not budge. On June 20, however, after Erzberger's two-hour conversation with President Friedrich Ebert, the latter finally consented to reshuffle the government coalition, replacing Chancellor Scheidemann with Gustav Bauer, a fellow Social Democrat who by then had persuaded his political colleagues to accept the treaty. Moreover, in his effort to win the Center Party over, Bauer bestowed upon Erzberger himself the portfolios of finance minister and vice-chancellor. At noon on June 23, with this new government configuration and with barely seven hours remaining on the Allied deadline, most of the cabinet disconsolately voted with the chancellor and Erzberger in favor of signing the treaty. Later that same afternoon, following the Reichstag's ratification of the cabinet's decision, the news was telegraphed to Brockdorff-Rantzau and Bernstorff in Paris. The two diplomats in turn relayed the information to the Allied representatives; and on June 28, in the Hall of Mirrors, the central gallery of the Palace of Versailles, they formally and ceremonially affixed their signatures to the peace treaty.

Five days earlier, after the Bauer government's original vote to accept the treaty, the dispirited German ministers prepared to leave the cabinet room. One of them, however, Friedrich Naumann, chairman of the German Democratic Party (DDP) that had resisted acceptance of the treaty almost to the end, approached Erzberger. "Today we still need you," Naumann whispered bitterly in Erzberger's ear, "but in a few months, when the overall situation will have changed, we will get rid of you."[23]

### ENEMIES IN WAITING

The rage of Erzberger's political enemies was soon to be inflamed even further. In June 1919, taking up his duties as vice-chancellor and finance minister, Erzberger embarked on a campaign to reverse the blunders of Germany's wartime leadership, and especially those of Karl Helfferich. It was Helfferich, as finance minister in the Bethmann-Hollweg government between 1915 and 1916, who had initiated the comfortable principle that Germany's enemies, not the German people, should pay the cost of the war after the Reich's anticipated victory.[24] But now, two and a half years later, upon becoming finance minister himself, Erzberger reminded the nation that the bill, present and future, had to be made good.

In preparing to achieve that goal, moreover, Erzberger did not hesitate to impose heavy, even confiscatory, taxes upon the wealthiest echelon of the nation's citizenry. The levies included progressive income taxes, war-profits taxes, and capital-gains taxes. Driving his initiatives through the Reichstag with relentless efficiency, Erzberger succeeded temporarily in stemming the flight of capital, even in restoring a measure of national financial stability. Yet, in the process, he incurred the animus of the landowning Junkers and the Ruhr's captains of industry. These economic oligarchs had been temporarily cowed by fear of bolshevism after Germany's military collapse; but in ensuing months, following suppression of the nation's leftist revolutions (pp. 12–18), they had regained much of their nerve.[25] By late 1919, they no longer bothered to mute their protests.

By then, too, galled by Erzberger's criticism and fiscal reforms, Karl Helfferich had become the Far Right's political spokesman in the Reichstag. He was a natural for the role. The son of an affluent Bavarian textile manufacturer, Helfferich had received a blue-chip university education in Munich, Berlin, and Strasbourg. Upon completing his doctorate in economics, he had been selected for specialized courses at the government's prestigious School for Colonial and Oriental Studies. In 1906, after a short teaching stint at

---

23 Epstein, *Matthias Erzberger*, 297–98.
24 Walther Lotz, *Die deutsche Staatsfinanzwirtschaft im Kriege* (Stuttgart: Deutsche Verlags-Anstalt, 1927), 117–22.
25 Epstein, *Matthias Erzberger*, 341 ff.

Munich's Maximilian II University, Helfferich was appointed a director of the German-dominated Anatolian Railway Company, Europe's largest transportation conglomerate. Two years later, he was similarly appointed to the board of the Deutsche Bank, again, Europe's largest.

By 1908, too, Helfferich had been elected to the Reichstag as a member of the Nationalist Party, where he soon overwhelmed his colleagues with his encyclopedic command of financial intricacies. Seven years later, in 1915, Chancellor Bethmann-Hollweg appointed Helfferich finance minister, and the following year added to the latter's portfolios the interior ministry and the vice-chancellorship. It was in these multifold responsibilities that Helfferich's intellectual gifts and prodigious work ethic established him as a favorite of both the chancellor and the kaiser. Yet his chilly arrogance made him personally unpopular even with his own Nationalist colleagues (many of whom dubbed him "the Jesuit in a frock coat"), and they declined to support his undisguised campaign for the chancellorship.

In the postwar summer of 1919, no longer a member of the government coalition but still a respected voice of the Reichstag's Nationalist faction, Helfferich launched into a series of press attacks against Erzberger. These were virtually unparalleled in their venom. Indeed, in his campaign, Helfferich mobilized all the charges levied piecemeal by Erzberger's enemies over the years, including defeatism, habitual mendacity, and "backstabbing" the Fatherland by his alleged eagerness to accept both the armistice and the even more detested Versailles Treaty. To these denunciations, Helfferich in December 1919 added the ad-hominem charge that Erzberger had enmeshed his political role as a government minister with his business responsibilities as a director of several banks, that he had profited financially from these entanglements, and that he also had been guilty of tax evasion. "One thing only can save the German people," Helfferich proclaimed in his newspaper offensive. "[A] single demand must be sounded with irresistible force everywhere in the country: 'Away with Erzberger!'"[26]

By then, his personal integrity impugned, Erzberger's lone evident recourse was to sue Helfferich for libel. This he did. The ensuing trial, held in Berlin, extended from January 29 to March 12, 1920, and was conducted against a background of sensational newspaper publicity and heated political passions that targeted the Versailles Treaty as much as Erzberger himself. Moreover, prosecutor and judge alike, both of them appointees of the former Wilhelminian Empire, hardly bothered to disguise their hostility to the

---

26 Epstein, *Matthias Erzberger*, 352.

new Weimar Republic or to Erzberger as its putative apologist.[27] On March 12, 1920, the court rendered its verdict. Although rejecting the accusation that Erzberger's wartime business relationships had been motivated by personal avarice, the judge ruled that Helfferich had substantiated the charges of Erzberger's "impropriety" in mingling politics with business. Except for the charge of tax evasion (a "technical" infraction for which Erzberger would have to pay a fine of 300 marks), Helfferich had achieved his purpose of tarnishing—in effect, crippling—Erzberger's reputation for financial probity.[28] Indeed, the outcome of the trial effectively ended Erzberger's cabinet career. Although retaining his seat in the Reichstag, he resigned immediately from the finance ministry and the vice-chancellorship to concentrate on the restoration of his good name.

It was ominous, too, that the court proceedings nearly had ended on their first day, January 29, when a young and evidently demented former naval cadet, Oltwig von Hirschfeld, fired a pistol at Erzberger as the latter was leaving the courtroom. The bullet wounds, in chest and shoulder, were severe but not fatal. Rushed to a nearby hospital, Erzberger underwent emergency surgery and survived. Within two weeks, he managed even to rejoin the trial, although in a wheelchair. But it was indicative of the nation's overwrought passions that, a month later (in February 1920), when Hirschfeld himself was brought to trial for attempted murder, his defense lawyers managed to convince the jury of their client's "patriotic idealism." Hence, although finding him guilty, the jurors recommended that he be granted leniency. The judge agreed, and sentenced Hirschfeld to a paltry 18 months imprisonment.

Even after the Helfferich trial, however, Erzberger still could rely on a staunch nucleus of political loyalists. Although he would not serve in the cabinet again, the liberal wing of the Center Party retained him as chairman of its Reichstag delegation. In that capacity, during the ensuing months, he became increasingly outspoken in his advocacy of workers' rights and in his criticism of the Junker landowners who had benefitted from the unearned increment of their estates. In foreign policy, too, Erzberger acknowledged Germany's moral obligation to pay reparations for its invasion of Belgium and its pillage of Belgium's and France's industrial and agricultural resources. While condemning many other features of the Versailles "*Diktat*," Erzberger

---

27 Fritz Zinnecke, "Zum Verständnis des Prozesses," in *Erzberger gegen Helfferich* (Berlin: Berliner Kommissionsbuchhandlung, 1920), 8–11.
28 *Erzberger gegen Helfferich*, 62–63, 66–67.

similarly took pains to warn his fellow Reichstag members that a stance of brazen defiance could prove economically and militarily suicidal.[29]

In the summer of 1921, exhausted by his official responsibilities and the emotional ordeal of defending his personal rectitude, Erzberger decided on a short vacation with his wife and two daughters. Their intended first destination was the Bavarian lakeside spa of Jordanbad. But upon learning of these plans and the family's decision to drive to Jordanbad in a roofless landau automobile, the police remonstrated with Erzberger. Indeed, ever since the Hirschfeld attack, they had cautioned him repeatedly that other assailants doubtless were on his trail. Would he now at long last accept an escort of plainclothes detectives? Once again, however, Erzberger declined the offer. He and his family then drove off imperturbably to Jordanbad. In fact, the trip passed without incident, and their ensuing 12 days at the resort were uneventful and restful.

On August 14, the Erzbergers left Jordanbad to spend the remainder of their August leisure at a Danubian rest home in Beuron, Austria. But on this occasion, three days into their stay, Erzberger was alerted by the management that it had received a telephone inquiry from an anonymous caller, seeking to learn of his whereabouts. At that point, Erzberger finally grasped that the police had not exaggerated. He was being tracked. Hence, within the hour, he and his wife and daughters checked out of the hotel and embarked on the drive back to Germany. Even then, however, the family was not prepared to forgo the last remaining days of its vacation. On August 19, the Erzbergers arrived in Bad Griesbach, a small German resort town at the foot of Kniebis Mountain. Here they registered at a modest chalet operated by Catholic nuns. They had vacationed at this sheltered inn before, and regarded it as entirely safe.

A week later, the family attended Mass at a local church. Afterward, Erzberger left his wife and daughters to join another guest for a mountain stroll. His companion was Karl Diez, a fellow Reichstag deputy and a member of Erzberger's Center Party. They discussed politics. But soon rain began to fall and the men turned back to town. Just out of sight, two strangers followed them. It developed later that these were former Reichswehr officers. They had been lingering in wait outside the church. When Erzberger and Diez embarked on their walk, the newcomers had remained behind for only a few moments before veering toward a shortcut through the wooded

---

29 Alfons Winz, *Erzberger zu den neuen Problemen der Gegenwart* (Singen: Singener Zeitung, 1921), 15–16.

MATTHIAS ERZBERGER (CENTER), WITH MEMBERS OF THE GERMAN ARMISTICE
COMMISSION AT SPA, C. 1918–19

mountain and then racing ahead of their prey. Some 30 minutes later, they emerged from the surrounding foliage to confront Erzberger. From a distance of less than three feet, both men then fired pistols directly into his chest. Erzberger tumbled down the path. The assailants followed, continuing to fire at their prostrate target at point-blank range before running off. Diez was left untouched. Erzberger died immediately.[30]

On August 31, his funeral took place in the neighboring town of Biberach, on the steps of the local Catholic church. Thirty thousand people attended. The eulogy was given by Germany's recently elected chancellor, Josef Wirth (p. 99), who described Erzberger, his Center Party comrade, as "a martyr for the cause of the German Republic and democracy."[31] Others took a different

---

30 For a detailed account of Erzberger's assassination, see Michail Krausnick and Günter Randecker, *Mord Erzberger!* [*Matthias Erzberger: Konkursverwalter des Kaiserreichs und Wegbereiter der Demokratie*] (Norderstedt: Books on Demand, 2005), *passim*.

31 Christoph E. Palmer and Thomas Schnabel, *Matthias Erzberger, 1875–1921: Patriot und Visionär* (Stuttgart: Hohenheim, 2007), 201.

view. Among them were the *Kreuzzeitung*, a prominent Junker-financed newspaper in East Prussia, which extolled the assassination, and the *Oletzkoer Zeitung*, journal of the rightist People's Party, which editorialized:

> Erzberger... has suffered the fate which the vast majority of patriotic Germans has long desired for him. Erzberger, the man who alone is responsible for the humiliating armistice; Erzberger, the man who is responsible for the Versailles "Treaty of Shame"... has at last secured the punishment suitable for a traitor.... We must sow hatred! We must learn to hate our enemies abroad, but we must also punish the domestic enemies of Germany with our hatred and our contempt.[32]

## A SCAPEGOAT MADE TO ORDER

Was Erzberger a sacrificial lamb in the cause of peace and democracy?

Five years earlier, in May 1916, it was the selfsame Erzberger, in his capacity as chairman of the moderate wing of the Center Party, who had stood up in the Reichstag to request the appointment of a new government committee. Its suggested task was to investigate the "over-proportion" of Jews employed in the offices and agencies of the war economy. By that request, the future martyr gave voice to a robust German antisemitism that had been suppurating during the years before and during the war.

In the Wilhelminian Empire, the "Jewish Question" had not suddenly vanished with the political equality that had been granted to this minority people in 1871. In ensuing years, and by the eve of the war, Jewish numbers in Germany had grown to approximately 510,000.[33] These included an influx of some 65,000 East European Jews, part of the much greater wave of 2 million Jews that was passing westward from Russia over the turn of the century in flight from tsarist oppression. Berlin's response to the surge of *Ostjuden* was not benign. Categorized by the Wilhelminian bureaucracy as less than economically useful, the bedraggled refugees frequently were shunted from one German *Land* to another.

Although the *ostjüdische* immigration was not the only or even the principal stimulus of German antisemitism in the last prewar decades, it offered still another weapon for racists such as Heinrich von Treitschke, Hermann

---

[32] Epstein, *Matthias Erzberger*, 388–89.
[33] Howard M. Sachar, *Dreamland: Europeans and Jews in the Aftermath of the Great War* (New York: Alfred A. Knopf, 2002), 206–7.

Ahlwardt, and Adolf Stöcker, who found political usefulness in execrating the "filth and degradation" carried into imperial Germany by these "Asians." The contumely was further inflamed by evidence that the newcomers, politically oppressed and economically redundant in the tsarist empire, frequently brought with them a vigorous radical ethos. In the first postwar years, they would suffer the consequences of their political extremism (p. 98). But so, too, would the "veterans" who comprised the majority of Germany's Jewish population.

These latter were characteristically and classically middle class. Most of them earned their livelihoods in business and (increasingly) in the professions. As compensation for their lingering social deprivations, moreover, German Jews frequently moved ahead in their vocations more urgently and rapidly than their gentile counterparts. As early as 1910, Berlin's 120,000 Jews, comprising a mere 5 per cent of the capital's population, paid 31 per cent of the city's municipal taxes. In Germany at large, nearly 25 per cent of the board members in ten major branches of the nation's industry and banking were Jews.[34] Yet this progress was still hobbled by an unspoken understanding that Jews would remain excluded from important areas of public life. Until the outbreak of war in 1914, it was rare for an unbaptized Jew to gain a diplomatic appointment, even a midlevel commission in the German army, or a university full professorship.

During the same prewar years, moreover, partisans of the older conservative-nationalist political factions began to grasp the usefulness of antisemitism as a device for luring white-collar and even many working-class voters away from the parties of liberalism and socialism. Accordingly, at their Tivoli Convention in 1892, Germany's Conservative Party leaders for the first time since the establishment of the empire adopted a specifically anti-Jewish plank, deprecating "Jewish influence" in national affairs. Over the turn of the century, too, the term *"Verjudung"* ("judaization") was applied increasingly to the growing role played by Jews in Germany's economic and cultural life.

Kaiser Wilhelm II personally would take no steps to deprive Jews of their recently acquired political rights. Indeed, from time to time he availed himself of the advice of such eminent Jewish businessmen as Albert Ballin, chairman of the Hamburg-American Packetboat Company; Max Warburg of the M. M. Warburg & Co. merchant bank; Carl Fürstenberg, of the Berliner Handels-Gesellschaft bank; and Walther Rathenau, chairman of the mighty AEG electricity conglomerate. Yet the kaiser hardly disguised his reservations on Jewish public visibility. "Jewish influence ... is increasing steadily," he observed in 1913. "Our efforts must indeed be directed towards ... restricting it as far as

---

34 Sachar, *Dreamland*, 206.

possible."[35] Chancellor Bethmann-Hollweg heartily agreed. Altogether, in the prewar years, the issue of disproportionate Jewish economic and cultural influence was emerging as a subject of open discussion—in the press, in the *Land* diets, even in the Reichstag.

If the National Liberal Party, traditionally the citadel of the nation's business elements, did not specifically embrace the upsurge of antisemitism, neither did its members trouble to condemn it. By the turn of the century, anchored to a vast and newly unified trading arena, the affluent German *Mittelstand* was beginning to restructure the party to conform with the military and economic triumphalism of the Hohenzollern Empire. In the process, whether instinctively or expediently, the National Liberals also began to embrace many of the traditional and rather more sinister values of the political Right. The phenomenon was a source of growing mystification and resentment for Germany's thoroughly acculturated Jewish majority. Most of the Jewish younger generation were products of "respectable" middle-class families, and by and large they themselves had started off as National Liberal loyalists. Lately, however, reacting to the "treason" of German political liberalism, Jews of all backgrounds tended increasingly to appraise the Social Democrats as an alternate political haven.

Together with their gentile colleagues, the overwhelming majority of Jewish Social Democrats were moderate "revisionists," abhorring the very notion of a Marxist revolution. They had virtually nothing in common with the East European Jewish radicals, such "buffalo Jew[s]" as Rosa Luxemburg or Leo Jogiches, who attached themselves to their party's original revolutionary faction.[36] Indeed, it was the mainstream of Jewish Social Democrats (whom antisemites nevertheless tarred with the label of radicalism) that produced the thoroughly respectable Reichstag delegates Hugo Haase and Ludwig Frank. Both men were native born, and both were idealists who commanded much respect among their fellow Social Democrats. Haase, a Baden lawyer who for years contributed his services pro bono to workers, was elected the party's deputy chairman in 1911 and its cochairman (with Friedrich Ebert) upon the death of August Bebel in 1913 (pp. 4, 6). But whether of the party's moderate or left wing, a growing Jewish minority within the Social Democrats was emerging not only as an influential political avant-garde but as a convenient bête noire for the parties of the hard-core German Right.

---

35 Peter Pulzer, *Jews and the German State: The Political History of a Minority, 1848–1933* (Detroit: Wayne State University Press, 2003), 120.

36 Peter Pulzer, *Jews and the German State*, 161.

## THE POLITICS OF PATRIOTISM

During the war period, the emergent image of the Jews as radical subversives might logically have been eclipsed by the more tangible evidence of their patriotism. Indeed, once hostilities began, German Jewry's various communal *Kulturverein* exhorted their members to "devote your resources to the Fatherland above and beyond the call of duty! . . . All of you—men and women—[must] place yourselves in [its service] . . . through personal help of every kind and through donations of money and property."[37] "I foresee a great victory for Germany and Germanism," exulted the novelist Jakob Wassermann in a diary entry of late August 1914. "Germany is becoming a world power."[38] For the prominent rabbi-philosopher Hermann Cohen, the Jews bore an obligation "piously to respect Germany, their spiritual home."[39]

Years later, Berlin's Jewish *Kulturverein* published statistics on the Jewish war record. These revealed that some 100,000 Jews had served in Germany's armed services, and that 12,000 had died in combat.[40] In numbers unimaginable before the war, Jews also were recruited for key public positions. The maritime capitalist Albert Ballin was charged with the establishment of a central acquisition agency, Reichseinkauf, for the purchase of crucial civilian materials. The economist Julius Hirsch directed the regulation of food prices. The industrialist Eduard Arnhold organized coal supplies through the Reichskohlenamt, even as another industrialist, Walther Rathenau, established and directed the war ministry's raw materials department. The renowned chemist (and later Nobel Prize laureate) Fritz Haber became the single most important organizer of the nation's scientists for the war effort.[41]

Notwithstanding this record, antisemitism flared up almost uncontrollably after August 1914. From the onset of hostilities, the Reichshammerbund (Imperial Hammer League), a chauvinist cabal led by Theodor Fritsch (later a prominent Nazi official) advocated a *Judenzählung*, a census to determine if Jews were making their "fair share" of sacrifices. Fritsch enjoyed support in high places. In December 1915, a conference of other influential reactionaries, including the future Nazis Count Ernst Reventlow and Adolf Bartels, approved

---

37  Peter Pulzer, *Jews and the German State*, 195.
38  Marta Karlweiss, ed., *Jakob Bassermann: Bild, Kampf und Werk* (Amsterdam: Querido Verlag, 1935), 241.
39  Howard M. Sachar, *A History of the Jews in the Modern World* (New York: Knopf, 2005), 316.
40  Tim Grady, *The German-Jewish Soldiers of the First World War in History and Memory* (Liverpool: Liverpool University Press, 2011), 59.
41  Fritz Richard Stern, *Einstein's German World* (Princeton, NJ: Princeton University Press, 1999), 119.

a research survey, "Die Juden im Reichswehr," for distribution among senior Reichswehr officers. For Reventlow, Fritsch, Bartels, and other far-rightists, the survey's ulterior purpose was to undermine the Bethmann-Hollweg government (itself firmly conservative) with evidence that it was permitting Jews to shirk military service, to serve in disproportionate numbers behind the lines, or to figure too prominently in the various civilian wartime supply corporations.

Although the government's reaction to Fritsch's census proposal was unenthusiastic, it would not specifically prohibit the Reichswehr from conducting its own survey. The *Judenzählung* consequently took place in May 1916. Its administrator was Lieutenant Colonel Max Bauer, a key member of General Ludendorff's staff. Bauer was cofounder of a xenophobic fringe group, the Alldeutscher Verband, and a politician manqué who had been instrumental in maneuvering Ludendorff's appointment as quartermaster-general. At his direction, Jewish soldiers were obliged now to fill out a questionnaire that pressed for details of where, how, and when they were performing their military service. A number of senior officers began indiscriminately transferring Jews under their command to front-line duty simply to avoid accusations of pro-Jewish favoritism.[42]

Before long, the Reichswehr inquiry produced an equivalent civilian proposal. It was a week after the *Judenzählung* had been activated that Matthias Erzberger, as chairman of the moderate wing of the Center Party, had stood in the Reichstag chamber to issue his own request for a government investigation of the "over-proportion" of Jews employed in the civilian offices and agencies of the war economy.[43] No Reichstag action was taken. Neither were the results of the military survey made public until 14 years after the war, when it was revealed that the number of Jewish casualties and medal recipients proportionally exceeded Jewish numbers in Germany at large. In 1916, however, the impact of these surveys and accusations on Jewish morale was devastating. "We have become marked men, second-class soldiers," agonized Ludwig Haas, a former Social Democratic Reichstag deputy, as he performed his military service as a lieutenant on the Eastern Front.[44] In shock, Dr. Hermann Cohen, a revered Judaic scholar, spoke of a "stab in the heart."[45] Ernst Simon, a future professor of philosophy who had volunteered

---

42 Egmont Zechlin, *Die deutsche Politik und die Juden im Ersten Weltkrieg* (Göttingen: Vandenhoeck & Ruprecht, 1969), 518–19.
43 Zechlin, *Die deutsche Politik*, 533.
44 Zechlin, *Die deutsche Politik*, 533.
45 Zechlin, *Die deutsche Politik*, 533–34.

for military service in the second week of the war, noted two years later that the *Judenzählung* evidently reflected "genuine popular attitudes."[46] Jewish soldiers, whatever their battlefield performance, could scarcely ignore the evidence of military distrust and extensive public racism.

### A MAN FOR ALL SEASONS

Neither could Jewish civilians. In the civilian sector, no individual had contributed more to the war effort than the industrialist Walther Rathenau. Neither did any other figure embody more of the contradictory legacies and vulnerabilities of Germany's most protean minority people. In August 1914, when hostilities began, Rathenau promptly endorsed the goal of an uncompromising and decisive victory. In December of that year, he urged Chancellor Bethmann-Hollweg to project Germany's war aim as the "complete political and economic reduction of France and England" and "[the imposition] of important [territorial] changes . . . and massive indemnities." Ironically, during the same war years in which he outlined a broadly compassionate economic agenda for cooperation between labor and management (p. 95), Rathenau went so far as to propose the forcible importation into Germany of thousands of Belgian laborers to work in German armaments factories.[47]

Both the Rathenau family and the German Empire owed each other much. Walther Rathenau's father, Emil, the owner of a small iron foundry in north Berlin, had become a successful manufacturer of steam engines. In 1881, attending the Paris Exhibition, the senior Rathenau witnessed Thomas Edison's new electric light bulb. On an impulse, and with borrowed funds, he purchased the German patent rights to the invention and, two years later, founded the company that became the Allgemeine Elektrizitäts Gesellschaft—AEG. Under Emil Rathenau's vigorous initiative, AEG flourished.[48] Walther Rathenau, born in 1867, was all but programmed by his father for the responsibilities of industrial leadership. After earning a doctorate in electrical engineering at the University of Berlin, the younger Rathenau was

---

46  Zechlin, *Die deutsche Politik*, 536.
47  David Felix, *Walther Rathenau and the Weimar Republic* (Baltimore, MD: Johns Hopkins Press, 1971), 51–52.
48  For the elder Rathenau's career, see Alois Riedler, *Emil Rathenau und das Werden der Grosswirtschaft* (Berlin: Springer, 1916), *passim*; see also Chapter 1 of Shulamit Volkov, *Walther Rathenau: The Life of Weimar's Fallen Statesman* (New Haven, CT: Yale University Press, 2012).

sent off for managerial apprenticeship in AEG branch factories at Neuhausen and Bitterfeld. Returning to Berlin ten years later, at the age of 32, he joined AEG's executive board.

Rathenau's relationship with his imperious father was not easy; but upon the death of an older brother in 1903 and Emil Rathenau's progressive physical incapacitation, Walther Rathenau became de facto chairman of the AEG board. Indeed, well before his father's death in 1915, the son had developed a legendary expertise in negotiating merger agreements. Under his direction, AEG by 1909 had become one of the world's largest industrial conglomerates, interlocked with 84 German firms and 24 foreign companies.[49] In the last decade before the war, the government and kaiser respectfully consulted Walther Rathenau on economic issues of key importance to the empire.[50]

Rathenau lived his role. In his palatial winter and summer homes, he entertained in appropriately regal style. A lifelong bachelor, cultured and charming, he made his way through society as purposefully as in business. In the process, his sense of his own worth was never modest. Edvard Munch's famous portrait of Rathenau reveals a tall man, his countenance fine-boned over an elegant goatee, standing haughtily in evening dress, cigar in hand. The Austrian novelist, Robert Musil, whose roman à clef, *The Man Without Qualities* [*Der Mann ohne Eigenschaften*] was based on Rathenau, described his hero as much more than a social dilettante. He conversed easily and incisively with others whose vocations were far from his own. Fluent in several languages, Rathenau much enjoyed corresponding with such renowned authors as André Gide, Hermann Hesse, Rainer Maria Rilke, Stefan Zweig, and Gerhart Hauptmann.

Altogether, Rathenau was not reticent in cultivating his own public image as a "lay" intellectual. Producing numerous journal articles on social and cultural themes of the day, he subsequently published these contributions in ten books, one of which, *In Days to Come* [*Von kommenden Dingen*], sold over 100,000 copies. Collectively, Rathenau's writings projected his vision of a "just" society in which "the equalization of property and income is a commandment of morality and economics," as he wrote in *In Days to Come*. He anticipated a Germany that would encourage workingmen to become better educated and raised in dignity, and an economy to be organized around

---

49 Peter Berglar, *Walther Rathenau: Seine Zeit, sein Werk, seine Persönlichkeit* (Bremen: Schünemann, 1970), 270–73.

50 Otto Friedrich, *Before the Deluge: A Portrait of Berlin in the 1920s* (New York: Harper & Row, 1972), 100.

nonprofit foundations. Rathenau offered no fiscal mechanism to achieve these less than modest goals. Indeed, his proposals comprised a rather vanilla exhortation to economic man: be good. But if skeptical critics dismissed Rathenau as a "prophet in a dinner jacket," few could doubt that he transcended most of his fellow tycoons in social compassion and public-spiritedness.[51]

At the same time, however, the qualities Rathenau brought to the war crisis were those of single-minded patriotism and cold-eyed economic efficiency. Focusing his attention on the empire's supply needs, he swiftly grasped that Britain's naval blockade required that Germany adopt emergency measures toward the accumulation of raw materials. When he pressed the issue with his government contacts, the war ministry authorized him to establish a raw-materials bureau. Initially, its office operated with a skeletal staff of a single lieutenant colonel and three junior civilian assistants. But in ensuing months its personnel swelled to over 200, as Rathenau commandeered widening quotas of vital supplies that extended from metals and chemicals to wool and rubber. Nothing of value to the war effort was left to the disposal of individual businessmen. In this fashion, Rathenau by some estimates kept the war economy functioning at least a year longer than the nation's resources would otherwise have permitted.[52]

Yet, in perspective, he nurtured few illusions about public reaction to his war service. Rathenau was a Jew, after all, although a thoroughly acculturated one, who set foot in synagogues only for the marriages or funerals of friends.[53] The author Stefan Zweig recalled of him: "Rarely have I sensed the tragedy of the Jew more strongly than in his personality which, with all its apparent superiority, was full of a deep unrest and uncertainty."[54] "Somewhere within him he felt fear lurking as his basic instinct," wrote his friend, Count Harry Kessler. "In those very years which were decisive for his future career, this lack of self-confidence was deepened by . . . the fact that he was a Jew and . . . [by] the harshness of the world."[55] On occasion, Rathenau himself would exaggerate his awareness of his minority status. Several years before the war, when Foreign Minister Bernhard von Bülow first met Rathenau at a social occasion (as Bülow wrote long afterward), "[Rathenau] approached

---

51  Felix, *Walther Rathenau*, 50.
52  For more on Rathenau's business, intellectual, and wartime accomplishments, see Paul Létourneau, *Walther Rathenau (1867–1922)* (Strasbourg: Presses Universitaires de Strasbourg, 1995), 137–41.
53  Létourneau, *Walther Rathenau*, 31–32.
54  Stefan Zweig, *The World of Yesterday* (New York: The Viking Press, 1943), 181.
55  Harry Kessler, *Walther Rathenau: His Life and Work* (New York: Harcourt, Brace and Company, 1930), 27.

[me] with a bow as impeccable as his attire.... 'Your Highness,' he murmured, in his becomingly modulated voice, 'before I am honored by the favor of your acquaintance, I must make ... a confession.' He paused briefly and then with charming deference, said: 'I am a Jew.'"[56]

Although Rathenau later spoke out forthrightly against opportunistic Jewish baptism,[57] he equally often apotheosized *"Deutschtum"* in ways that appeared to contrast invidiously with *"Judentum."*[58] Early in 1914, he was moved to write an epiphany of his love for Germany:

> Blond and steel-blue corn and air
> Blessed lakes the eyes of heaven
> Wooded vaults of dark fir
> Spindrift of pale dunes....
> Country, my Country, thou, my Love.[59]

Plainly, he was determined that his "love" not go unrequited.

## THE WAGES OF RESPECTABILITY

Yet it did. Even as the conservatives of the Wilhelminian Empire had found it useful to stigmatize liberalism as "Jewish," now, in the postwar years, far-rightists devised the strategy of characterizing the entire Weimar experiment as a "Jew Republic." In that effort, they orchestrated their antisemitic campaign with traditional German efficiency. Before the war, the empire's aggregation of reactionary parties, leagues, and cabals had never managed to produce a coordinated strategy. In February 1919, however, gathering in Hamburg as an antirevolutionary convention, a wide spectrum of these factions laid the groundwork for a "German People's League for Protection and Defiance" (Deutschvölkisch Schutz- und Trutzbund). In ensuing months, the league became the nucleus of the Community of German People's Unions (Gemeinschaft deutschvölkischer Bunde). By 1922 this "community"

---

56  Felix, *Walther Rathenau*, 51; see also Hans F. Löffler, *Walther Rathenau: Ein Europäer im Kaiserreich* (Berlin: Berlin Verlag A. Spitz, 1997), 16–57 *ff.*

57  Walther Rathenau, *Schriften und Reden*, ed. Hans Werner Richter (Frankfurt am Main: S. Fischer, 1964), 24–25.

58  Walther Rathenau, *Tagebuch 1907–1922*, ed. H. Pogge von Strandmann (Düsseldorf: Droste Verlag, 1967), 98–99.

59  James Joll, "Walther Rathenau: Prophet without a Cause," in *Intellectuals in Politics: Three Biographical Essays* (London: Weidenfeld and Nicolson, 1960), 59–129, see page 61.

had grown to 250,000 members in more than 200 branches that focused specifically on Jews: as putative subversives, malingerers, or profiteers during the war; as economic parasites or political radicals in the postwar; as "toadstool[s] on the Jewish oak"; and, above all, as the "secret political manipulators" behind the Weimar Republic itself.[60]

It was during the Weimar years, too, that "Aryan" racism acquired a new and highly politicized intensity. The pseudoscience extended well back into the nineteenth century, to the writings of Wilhelm Marr, who first coined the term "antisemitism" and applied it in 1879 in his apocalyptic and best-selling pamphlet, "The Victory of Judaism over Germanism [Der Sieg des Judenthums über das Germanenthum]." Afterward, the ex-Socialist Eugen Dühring gave the "racial struggle" against Jews a consistent ideological foundation. The renewal of German culture, Dühring argued, mandated a forthright repudiation of Jewish religious ideology and Jewish social mores, both characteristic of the "Semitic mind," and both thereby inimical to "Aryan civilization."

In the last prewar decades, it was the Aryan myth that became particularly attractive to the lower-middle class—the clerks, pensioners, and small shopkeepers who felt themselves threatened by the juggernaut of modern industrial capitalism, an "alien" force that presumably was subject to manipulation by an "alien" race. And in the havoc of the postwar, the concept of Aryanism appealed with special poignancy to the identical lower-middle class, the element most thoroughly deracinated by the inflation of the 1920s, and hence most prone to take compensatory solace in their own inflated racial pedigree.[61]

Germany's Jews, for their part, could have survived an antisemitism that remained essentially verbal and social. As late as 1923, the entire antisemitic vote, including ballots cast for the ultrarightist German National Party (by no means a one-issue faction) never exceeded 8 per cent. Physical attacks on "private" Jews still were comparatively rare. In 1923, however, as the French army occupied the Ruhr to compel German reparations payments, and as the value of Germany's currency imploded, rage suddenly boiled over. On November 5, a wave of impoverished citizens, blue collar and white collar alike, descended on Berlin's Scheunenviertel district, where numerous East European Jewish immigrant families lived and operated tiny shops and

---

60 Pulzer, *Jews and the German State*, 214.
61 Werner Eugen Mosse and Arnold Paucker, eds., *Deutsches Judentum in Krieg und Revolution, 1916–1923: Ein sammelband* (Tübingen: J.C.B. Mohr, 1971), 456–60.

market stalls. For the ensuing day and a half, the mob waded through the Scheunenviertel, attacking hundreds of Jewish proprietors and ransacking nearly a thousand Jewish enterprises before police managed to end the violence and looting.

Thuggery and pillage were not the only aberrations committed by the traditionally law-abiding German people. More ominous, in the revolutionary and counterrevolutionary hatreds of the postwar, was the growing frequency of political assassination. The Heidelberg historian E.J. Gumbel has calculated that, besides the murder of Matthias Erzberger, 375 political homicides were carried in Germany between 1918 and 1922, and overwhelmingly by the ideological Right. Many of those "executed" were Jews, and most of these were leftist Jews, among them Luxemburg, Jogiches, Landauer, Erich Mühsam, and Hugo Haase (the Independent Socialist who cochaired the original Ebert cabinet). In 1922 Maximilian Harden, editor of the moderate-progressive journal *Die Zukunft*, was beaten nearly to death by two strong-arm men. He survived, but was left permanently paralyzed. When the assailants were brought to trial, they argued that Harden had been disloyal to Germany as a writer of "unpatriotic" articles, and that, as a Jew who had changed his name from Witkowski, he had gotten no more than he deserved. The jury evidently agreed. It returned a verdict of "battery without intent to kill," and the court sentenced one defendant, the plotter, to a 57-month prison term and the other, the henchman, to a 33-month imprisonment.[62]

## A TARGET FOR ALL HATREDS

The assault on Harden may have appalled even "respectable" German ultraconservatives. Yet the profoundest shock was evoked by the fate of an eminence who embodied nearly every virtue of public-spirited German patriotism. As the war neared its end, Walther Rathenau had pleaded with the new chancellor, Prince Maximilian, to save the empire by rushing through a program of dramatic constitutional reforms. It did not happen in time, of course (pp. 10–11). Nevertheless, Rathenau accepted the birth of the new republic philosophically. Still in his early fifties, he was too restless and *engagé* to withdraw from national affairs. For the first (and last) time, he gave thought to campaigning for a seat in the new republican "Reichstag" as a candidate of the German Democratic

---

62 "Hard To Be an Apostate, Harden Tells Court," *The Advocate: American's Jewish Journal* 64 (December 30, 1922): 676.

Party—until the distrustful party leaders sabotaged the notion by assigning him a low, essentially unelectable slot on their list of nominees.[63]

Rathenau plainly remained an ambivalent figure in public consciousness. "Respectable" conservatives pigeonholed him as a rich Jewish intellectual manqué, while Social Democrats typed him merely as a successful industrialist of kindly instincts. Returning to his base at AEG, the chastened Rathenau for the while expressed his public concerns exclusively in writing. In December 1918, on the eve of the Paris Peace Conference, he published an "Open Letter to Colonel Edward House," President Woodrow Wilson's closest political adviser. "If vindictiveness [to Germany] prevails," Rathenau warned, "... a horde of [Bolshevik] desperadoes will be encamped before the doors of Western civilization."[64] In 1919, he found time to produce two small works, "Apologia" (an appendix to *Kritik der dreifachen Revolution*) and *Der Kaiser*, in which he deplored the polarization of German political life.

During the ensuing year, too, Josef Wirth gradually was drawn back into public service. Wirth, finance minister in the Social Democrat–dominated coalition government, consulted with Rathenau frequently. They soon became good friends. Then, in May 1921, Wirth himself became chancellor of a new Center Party–chaired coalition government. Immediately, he appointed Rathenau "minister of reconstruction"—in effect, minister for German reparations—and shortly afterward elevated him to foreign minister.[65]

In the latter capacity, less than a year later, Rathenau prepared to accompany Wirth to Genoa for a conference of European foreign ministers. The issue before the conference would be the critical one of jump-starting European economic reconstruction. For Germany, saddled with its punitive Versailles Treaty reparations debt, no issue could have been more urgent. As the ministers gathered in Genoa in the first week of April 1922, however, and Rathenau sought to find an opening to raise the reparations issue, he could make little headway. During the five days of proceedings, Britain's Prime Minister David Lloyd George, representing the most senior of Europe's financial powers and congenial in principle to the relaxation of war debts, found it "premature" to discuss Germany's reparations obligation.

---

63  Berglar, *Walther Rathenau*, 362–63.

64  Eric C. Kollman, "Walther Rathenau and German Foreign Policy: Thoughts and Actions," *The Journal of Modern History* 24, no. 2 (1952): 127–42, see page 136.

65  Kessler, *In the Twenties: The Diaries of Harry Kessler*, trans. Charles Kessler (London: Weidenfeld and Nicolson, 1971), 291, 323.

Then, shortly after midnight on April 16, Ago von Maltzan, director of the foreign ministry's Russian department, knocked on Rathenau's hotel room door. He brought astonishing news. Soviet Foreign Minister Georgi Chicherin had just telephoned to invite the German delegation to a private meeting with him in Rapallo, a nearby resort town. Still in pajamas, Rathenau and Maltzan then conferred immediately with Wirth in the latter's suite. After a lengthy discussion, agreement was reached that Rathenau should meet with Chicherin and "play the Russian card."[66]

The German and Soviet statesmen conferred that same afternoon. By 6:30 that evening, they had initialed the "Treaty of Rapallo." The document provided for a mutual repudiation of claims for war costs and damages, mutual trade on a most-favored-nation basis, and the immediate establishment of diplomatic relations. The accord thereby ended each nation's economic and international isolation[67] and allowed each a substantial new maneuverability vis-à-vis the Western Allies. Yet, notwithstanding all the Rapallo pact's advantages to Germany, its immediate consequence was to strip the Wirth government of the confidence it had sought among Western statesmen and to foreclose any alleviation of reparations. The consequences for Rathenau personally were graver yet. Long outraged by the very notion of *Erfüllungspolitik*, his rightist enemies now could denounce the foreign minister not only as a "Jew-pig", a defeatist, and a traitor but as a Bolshevik agent, who merited.

## "*KNALLT AB DEN WALTHER RATHENAU*" [KNOCK OFF WALTHER RATHENAU]

On the evening of June 23, 1922, Rathenau held a lengthy dinner meeting with one of his, and the late Erzberger's, harshest critics. It was the redoubtable Karl Helfferich, a minister of finance in the former imperial government and still chairman of the Reichstag's far-rightist Nationalist delegation. The discussion was exhaustive, as Rathenau sought to find a limited common diplomatic stance with Helfferich, and it continued inconclusively until the early hours of June 24. Exhausted, Rathenau slept later than usual the next morning, not leaving his home in Berlin's Grünewald suburb until 10:45. He was seated in

---

66 Wipert von Blücher, *Deutschlands Weg nach Rapallo* (Wiesbaden: Limes Verlag, 1951), 154–55.
67 Alfred Anderle, *Die deutsche Rapallo-Politik: Deutschsowjetische Beziehungen, 1922–1929* (Berlin: Rütten & Loening, 1962), 34; Carole Fink, *The Genoa Conference: European Diplomacy, 1921–1922* (Chapel Hill, NC: University of North Carolina Press, 1984), 72–75.

the back of an open limousine as his chauffeur pulled out of the driveway onto the main road. On a side street nearby, others were lying in wait.

The previous April, a 17-year-old gymnasium student, Hans Stubenrauch, had confided his intention of assassinating Rathenau to a classmate, Hans-Martin Günther, who promptly joined the plot. The son of a retired Reichswehr general, Stubenrauch was a member of the ultranationalist League of the Upright (Bund der Aufrechten). Upon news of Rathenau's return from the Genoa reparations conference on May 19, the two youths discussed their plan with a 25-year-old ex-naval officer, Erwin Kern, and the latter's friend, Hermann Fischer, also 25. Both Kern and Fischer reacted enthusiastically. Both were secret members of the Organization Consul, a right-wing terrorist society formed out of the Freikorps's notoriously racist Ehrhardt Brigade and a cabal fully sharing Stubenrauch's hatred of Rathenau. Through Hermann Fischer, Kern recruited yet another partner from the Organization Consul. This was Ernst-Werner Techow, 21, the son of a deceased Berlin magistrate. The young men then promptly set about formulating a plan for the murder.

On the evening of June 18, Stubenrauch, Kern, Günther, Fischer, and Techow, together with Techow's younger brother Gerd, age 16, and with still another chauvinistic romantic, Ernst von Salomon, age 21, who had been recruited at the last moment for his expert knowledge of escape routes—all met at the home of Techow's widowed mother to devise their ambush. The next day, eight others were consulted individually to add refinements to the plot. Finally, on the morning of June 24, six of the seven original conspirators parked their automobile on a side street leading to the Königsallee, the foreign minister's customary route from home to office. It was widely known that Rathenau was contemptuous of danger and had steadfastly refused all police protection. Indeed, Britain's ambassador to Berlin, Viscount Edgar D'Abernon, recalled that Rathenau had "time and again... told me that he was sure to be assassinated" but, "in the presence of known danger" had seemed almost eerily "fatalistic" about the prospect.[68]

Rathenau's presentiment was not mere posture. In late May, Chancellor Wirth received a visit from the papal nuncio, Monsignor Eugenio Pacelli (later to become Pope Pius XII). Without revealing names, Pacelli stated only that a priest had divulged to him a plot against the foreign minister. Wirth later gave Count Harry Kessler an account of the conversation:

---

68 Viscount Edgar Vincent D'Abernon, *Diary of an Ambassador: Rapallo to Dawes, 1922–1924* (Garden City, NY: Doubleday, 1929), 65–66.

[Pacelli] informed me simply and soberly in a few sentences that Rathenau's life was in danger. I could not question him; the interview had taken place in absolute privacy.... Then Rathenau himself was called in. I implored him... to abandon his resistance to increased police protection ... [but] he stubbornly refused.... With a calm such as I had never witnessed in him ... he stepped close to me, and placing both his hands on my shoulders, said "Dear friend, it is nothing. Who would do me any harm?"[69]

He received his answer at 10:50 a.m. on June 24.

As Rathenau's automobile reached the Königsallee, it slowed to cross a pair of streetcar tracks. At that moment, Techow, driving the assassination vehicle, pulled up beside the foreign minister's open limousine, aimed his pistol at close range, and fired off a quick succession of shots. Rathenau fell back. Fischer then stood up and hurled a grenade into the car. It exploded a few moments later, after the attackers' vehicle had sped off. Rathenau's chauffeur, miraculously unhurt, raced the limousine to a corner police station. A woman who had witnessed the attack, followed on foot. She was a nurse. Climbing into the vehicle's back seat, she attempted to staunch Rathenau's bleeding. Her efforts were unavailing. By the time an ambulance arrived, Rathenau had expired.

In the ensuing hours, Kern and Fischer, the two principal assassins, abandoned their car and fled Berlin for the Baltic port of Warnemünde, where they expected to book passage for Sweden. With no vessel available, however, they purchased bicycles and turned back southward. For almost a month, they hid in an abandoned castle in a dense, rarely traveled forest. But eventually, in late July, they were located and cornered in their shelter. As the police closed in, Kern was slain in an exchange of fire. Fischer shot himself. By then, the 13 surviving conspirators, active and marginal, had been rounded up and jailed.

Meanwhile, in the late morning and afternoon of June 25, when news of Rathenau's death first became generally known, workers in Berlin streamed out of the factories and began marching through the streets. Harry Kessler recalled: "Four deep, they marched in their hundreds and thousands, beneath their mourning banners, the red of socialism and the black-red-gold of the Republic, in one endless, disciplined procession ... wave after wave, from the early afternoon until late into the June sunset."[70] On June 27, the funeral

---

69  Kessler, *In the Twenties*, 363–64.
70  Kessler, *In the Twenties*, 388.

## WALTHER RATHENAU AT THE GENOA CONFERENCE, 1922

service was conducted in the Reichstag gallery. President Friedrich Ebert delivered the eulogy. Avoiding political accusations, he limited himself to a recitation of the accomplishments of the late industrialist and statesman.

In the autumn, the 13 jailed plotters underwent trial. All were found guilty of murder or of accessory to murder. Yet the judges, all appointees of the late Wilhelminian Empire, imposed sentences that were manifestly less than draconian. The severest, for 15 years, was meted out to the triggerman, Techow, who actually was set free after four years to resume his schooling; he eventually became a lawyer. Salomon's sentence, of eight years, was the lightest, although, perversely, he spent a year more of prison time than did Techow. Upon his release, he became a successful screenwriter, married a Jewish woman (who later was given "protected" status under the Nazis), and, following World War II, would publish the immensely popular autobiographical novel *Questionnaire* [*Fragebogen*], satirizing Allied efforts to denazify Germany.

In July 1933, 11 years after the deaths of Kern and Fischer, the recently inaugurated Nazi government mounted a solemn drum-and-trumpet parade to their graves. After dedicating the granite cenotaph that had been erected to their memory, the SS chieftain Heinrich Himmler delivered a memorial address. In its own way, with its sulfurous warning of vengeance, it validated the remarks delivered by Chancellor Josef Wirth, as he had addressed the

## A POSTHUMOUS IMPERIAL VENGEANCE

WALTHER RATHENAU'S STATE FUNERAL, BERLIN, JUNE 27, 1922

stunned members of the Reichstag on June 25, 1922, one day after Walther Rathenau's assassination and a few days before the late foreign minister's official funeral. As at the earlier obsequies to Matthias Erzberger, the chancellor's remarks did not take the form of a mere eulogy. Rather, they comprised a targeted and sulfurous denunciation both of the assassins and of their political agenda. "The real enemies of our country are those who instill this poison into our people." Wirth concluded bitterly, "We know where they are to be found. The enemy stands on the Right!—*Der Feind steht rechts!*"[71]

---

71 Josef Wirth, *Reden während der Kanzlerschaft*, introduction by Heinrich Hemmer (Berlin: Germania, 1925), 119.

CHAPTER FOUR

# Who Killed Sergei Kirov?

*"Old Russia was ceaselessly beaten for her backwardness.... She was beaten because to beat her was profitable."*

## THE FALL OF TSARDOM AND THE BOLSHEVIK REVOLUTION

In the course of World War I, the Russian army had mobilized 15.5 million troops and suffered an estimated 1.65 million killed and 3.85 million wounded. The deaths of civilians trapped in the war zones approached another 1.4 million. Losses of this magnitude might have been endured by a traditionally fatalistic Slavic population, but no longer when naked graft and venality compounded sloth and gross incompetence at the command level. More tragically yet, Tsar Nicholas II remained delusional in his estimation of his own strategic omniscience. In the autumn of 1915, he departed for the army's advance headquarters at Mogilev to assume personal direction of his nation's military effort. In effect, the government in St. Petersburg was left in the hands of Nicholas's wife, the Tsaritsa Alexandra, and of her closest "advisor," the louche Siberian faith healer, Grigori Rasputin. At Rasputin's suggestion, the empress in February 1916 dispatched a plea to her husband to appoint a new and presumably more competent prime minister, Boris Stürmer. The tsar acquiesced. In fact, Stürmer was a Baltic German of meager governmental experience and widely suspect political loyalties. This calamitous sequence of administrative decisions proved to be the turning point in the fate of the monarchy itself.

In January 1917, rumors began circulating that the tsar once again was preparing to prorogue the Duma, the contentious and ineffectual debating assembly that masqueraded as the nation's imperial parliament. The prospect of yet another dissolution, the third within 11 years, was intolerable even for conservative legislators. In February, a splinter group of rightist delegates joined the centrist Constitutional Democrats (Kadets) to demand the tsar's abdication. The issue was forced less than a month later when the palace garrison laid down its arms, refusing any longer to defend a manifestly bankrupt regime. It was at this point, on March 16, that the tsar gave up all further pretense to imperial authority and relinquished his throne. Within the week, the Duma simply declared itself the nation's "provisional government" and proceeded with the business of organizing a nation-wide election for a constitutional assembly.

But even as these plans were being laid, the provisional government faced a serious rival. This was the "Soviet [or council] of Workers' and Soldiers' Deputies," a group of Marxist militants that had spun off from its parent Social Democratic Party and had set about formulating its own, militantly collectivist, legislative agenda. The Soviet had assembled in St. Petersburg's Tauride Palace, across from the main hall where the "official" (if liberalized) Duma itself was holding its sessions. The uneasy relationship between Duma and Soviet produced a bicephalous arrangement that soon became dysfunctional, and all the more as the Duma's newly formed cabinet offered no practical blueprint for extricating Russia from a widely detested war.

Moreover, within the Soviet's ranks, the Bolshevik minority, committed to an immediate root-and-branch collectivization of the Russian economy (p. 110), was positioning itself as the Left's most radical faction. Its emergence was a consequence less of its economic program, however, and still less of its modest numbers, than of the audacity and ruthlessness of its guiding spirit, Vladimir Lenin. The son of middle-class parents, a lawyer, and a prominent spokesman for Russia's Social Democratic Party, Lenin had taken up temporary residence in England in 1903 to assume the chairmanship of the party's Bolshevik component, before returning to Russia shortly before the war to nurture the Bolsheviki on Russian soil.

Now, on January 18, 1918, aware that the ballot-counting in the recently completed Russian election for a constitutional assembly had produced no clear majority for any party, much less for the Soviet—and still less for the Soviet's Bolshevik faction—Lenin resolved to lead his core of dedicated followers in a preemptive move. Hence, as the assembly gathered at the Tauride Palace, Bolshevik soldiers and sailors packed the galleries, training their rifles and machine guns menacingly on the delegates and launching into a bedlam of imprecations and threats that effectively terminated further legislative proceedings. Within hours, a Bolshevik-dominated "Soviet of People's Commissars" replaced the Constituent Assembly. In this fashion, defying all national expectations and the modus operandi of almost all of Europe's earlier political upheavals, Lenin had well and truly maneuvered his minority of dedicated followers into a controlling political leadership of the largest nation in Europe.

## MILITARY HERO, SOVIET DUUMVIR

Between March 1917 and January 1918, proclaiming the "bourgeois" revolution over, the Bolshevik leader's first and most urgent objective was to withdraw Russia from the war. This he did, at Brest-Litovsk.[1] The territorial price was fearful (pp. 71–75), but Lenin was willing to pay it, anticipating that a general European peace subsequently would restore most of his country's lost provinces. His next challenge was to defend his new Bolshevik regime by moving preemptively against the regrouping armies of tsarist loyalists and other counterrevolutionaries.[2] This task, in turn, he entrusted to Leon Trotsky.

Trotsky appeared at first to be an unlikely choice. Born in 1879 as Lev Davidovich Bronshtein, in the Ukraine's Kherson province, he was the son of a Jewish farm couple and the grandson of one of the 40,000 Jews whom Tsar Alexander II, decades earlier, had lured to the empire's thinly populated southern provinces by offering them free land. The fifth of his family's surviving six children, young Bronshtein had experienced a difficult upbringing, quarreling often with his illiterate and brutal father. As a teenager, enrolled at an Odessa secondary school, he was swept up almost immediately in the revolutionary fervor of his late-nineteenth-century student generation. Afterward, upon leaving school, he preemptively severed all ties with his parents and changed his name to Lev Trotski—later becoming more widely known to the world at large as "Leon Trotsky."

---

1 Robert Wistrich, *Trotsky: Fate of a Revolutionary* (New York: Stein and Day, 1979), 78–79.
2 Edward H. Carr, *The Bolshevik Revolution* (Harmondsworth, UK: Penguin, 1966), 140–41.

For a few years, the youthful "Trotsky" became a *narodnik*, an agricultural populist, living and working among the peasants in a neighboring commune. Later, after a brief stint at the University of Odessa, he veered off into a more leftist political group, this one closer to the Socialist Revolutionary Party. By then, branded a radical by the tsarist government, Trotsky was confined to intermittent imprisonment.[3] It was in prison, too, in 1900, awaiting his impending deportation to Siberia, that he married a fellow prisoner, Alexandra Sokolovskaya, a young woman who had participated with him in antigovernment demonstrations. Shortly afterward, his new wife volunteered to accompany him on his exile. Their ensuing two daughters were born in Siberia.

It was also during this banishment that Trotsky, acquiring Marxist literature from comrades who shared his deportation and devouring the material by candlelight at night, found his ideological home at last in the Marxist Social Democratic Party.[4] From then on, his commitment to the revolutionary cause became his raison d'être. Indeed, it was in response to his impatience, in August 1902, two and a half years into his Siberian internment, that Alexandra persuaded her husband to escape on his own. She and their daughters would join him shortly, she promised. He did not object. Rather, supplied with funds from his wife's modest cache of rubles, Trotsky bribed a neighboring peasant to smuggle him out of the internees' compound in a hay cart.

His immediate destination lay just 13 miles away. It was a refueling stop on the Trans-Siberian Railroad. There, Trotsky waited less than two hours before the scheduled train arrived. As he boarded its last carriage undetected, and as the train subsequently proceeded westward on its four-day journey toward European Russia, sympathizers among its passengers supplied him with gifts of food and cash. Indeed, by October of the same year, Trotsky had managed not only to make his way across the Ural mountain chain but to smuggle himself across the tsarist empire's western border to Germany—and subsequently to arrange passage from Germany to England. It was in London, later the same month, that he turned up unannounced at the apartment of Vladimir Lenin, by then émigré chairman of Russian socialism's revolutionary faction and in self-exile since the tsarist government had banned the group's meetings.

Lenin received Trotsky warmly. The young man's reputation for socialist idealism had preceded him. Indeed, within the week, Lenin located a room for his

---

3 Howard M. Sachar, *A History of the Jews in the Modern World* (New York: Knopf, 2005), 327–29.
4 Isaac Deutscher, *The Prophet Armed: Trotsky 1879–1921* (London: Oxford University Press, 1954), 42–43.

young protégé, supplied him with rent and pocket money, and appointed him to the editorial board of *Iskra*, the émigré Social Democratic newspaper. From then on, under Lenin's patronage, Trotsky became an intimate of other prominent figures of the Russian Social Democratic Labor Party. At the party's 1903 Brussels Congress, one of the participants described the 24-year-old prodigy as "a lean, tallish man, with ... fierce eyes and a large, sensual, irregular mouth, perched on the [speaking] platform like a 'bird of prey'"; and he soon revealed himself to be a spellbinding intellectual and orator.[5]

It was at the same Brussels conclave, however, that a schism developed between Menshevik two-stage "gradualists," who advocated first a political revolution and only later a program of economic collectivization, and Bolshevik one-stage "extremists," who favored a sweeping one-stage political and economic revolution. As an orthodox Marxist, Trotsky still tended to identify with the Menshevik camp. Yet he was careful not to break off his respectful relationship with Lenin. The latter in turn remained continually impressed by Trotsky's ideological dedication and personal loyalty. Typical was the younger man's reaction to Russia's 1905 "October Revolution," the series of protest demonstrations that succeeded initially in extracting several marginal concessions from the tsarist government, including even a provisional legalization of the Social Democratic Party (p. 107). Although still listed as an escaped prisoner, Trotsky returned secretly to Russia. There he harangued his fellow socialists to reject Tsar Nicholas's "October Manifesto," with its fraudulent promise of constitutional reform, and instead to move without delay into an "authentic" political revolution. By then, with his hypnotic oratory and indifference to physical danger, Trotsky had achieved a reputation that elevated him above his party's factional divisions.[6]

Apparently it also elevated him above "bourgeois" domestic commitments. In the winter of 1905, when his wife and two young daughters managed to rejoin him in Moscow, Trotsky already had established a relationship with another woman, Natalia Sedova, with whom he would spend the next 35 years of his life. Although he and Alexandra remained in intermittent communication, he in St. Petersburg, she in Moscow, writing each other about their children, they never saw each other again.

During these prewar years, too, Trotsky's career began to achieve a drama that fiction rarely could match. In November 1906, living in Russia as an

---

5  Deutscher, *The Prophet Armed*, 70.
6  Wistrich, *Trotsky: Fate*, 64.

underground agitator, he was rearrested and sentenced again to Siberia, this time to life imprisonment. With other convicts, his horse-drawn police van carried him off once more to the rim of the polar circle. Shortly before reaching the penal colony of Obdorsk, however, and sensing that his choice this time was escape or almost certain death, Trotsky managed again to bribe a local peasant with money he had sewn into the soles of his shoes. The peasant secured a native guide, together with a sleigh and a team of reindeer. With this equipage, prisoner and guide traveled night and day for three weeks. Although changing teams of reindeer at villages en route, freezing and at times faint with hunger, they finally reached the Ural gap. Soon afterward, an "underground railroad" of Marxists smuggled Trotsky to safety, this time through Russia and across the Austrian border.

During the subsequent decade of frantic tsarist counterrevolution, Trotsky lived his exile in Vienna, where he earned a modest salary editing the émigré Social Democratic newspaper *Pravda*. Always the eloquent polemicist among his fellow émigrés, he also burnished his reputation this time as a lecturer before Social Democratic audiences in Central and Western Europe. His orations (in Russian, German, and French) were widely attended, and his editorials and essays were reprinted in the major European socialist journals. But with the onset of war in August 1914, Trotsky, Natalia Sedova, and—by then—their two young sons immediately exited the Austrian capital to avoid internment as enemy nationals. The family's subsequent destination was Zurich, the favored asylum of revolutionary exiles (pp. 2–3).

In fact, Trotsky's hiatus in neutral Switzerland was brief, lasting only three months. His first priority was income for his family, and eventually he managed to earn it from an unlikely source. With his prison record lying buried and unnoticed in the police files of the inept tsarist bureaucracy, Trotsky was taken on as the Paris war correspondent of the pro-war Ukrainian newspaper, *Kievskaya Mysl*. It was in Paris, too, under an assumed name, that he simultaneously published articles and editorials for socialist periodicals that baldly condemned the "capitalist" war.[7] In September 1915, he managed even to return briefly to Zurich to attend a conference of international socialist activists in the neighboring town of Zimmerwald, where the participants signed the celebrated "Zimmerwald Manifesto," predicting a well-deserved ruination for the "imperialist powers" on both sides in the war.[8] All the while,

---

7 See Louis Sinclair, *Trotsky: A Bibliography* (Aldershot, UK: Scolar Press, 1989).
8 Ian D. Thatcher, *Leon Trotsky and World War I: August 1914–February 1917* (Basingstoke, UK: Macmillan, 2000), 12–26.

Trotsky remained in the employ of the unsuspecting saber-rattling editors of *Kievskaya Mysl* and continued living in Paris with his family.

In November 1916, however, French censors at last spotted the disjunction between Trotsky's journalistic and political activities. He was promptly arrested for incitement and hustled with his wife and children across the frontier to neutral Spain, where the four were interned. But ten weeks later, under pressure from Spanish anarcho-syndicalists, the Madrid government relented and put Trotsky and his family on a ship bound for the United States.[9] By the time the four expatriates arrived in New York, in mid-January 1917, they apparently had reached a secure haven. Indeed, they were greeted enthusiastically by the city's colony of Russian socialist émigrés, who arranged lodgings for them in an East Side tenement and appointed Trotsky senior editor of their own local journal, *Novy Mir*. But even in the United States, Trotsky's sojourn lasted a mere two and a half months. When news arrived of Russia's March 1917 revolution, he was no less determined than Lenin to guide events in his native country. Again, his fellow expatriates came to the rescue, purchasing steamship tickets to Europe for him and his family. After an additional three weeks of Canadian interment as "political suspects" in Nova Scotia, the Trotskys eventually were allowed to depart. They arrived in Russia in early May.

Lenin had preceded Trotsky by a month. Within days of their reunion in "Petrograd" (the capital's fraternal wartime appellation), the two men reached agreement to put ideological disagreements aside in a common effort to overthrow Russia's provisional government and its current "Socialist Revolutionary" prime minister, the bland Aleksandr Kerensky. Hence, in July, when Lenin went into hiding in Finland after a premature coup attempt, Trotsky remained behind as caretaker of the Bolshevik cause. Although he himself suffered yet another brief imprisonment, this time at the hands of the Kerensky cabinet, he was released in September 1917. By then, the prime minister needed the soviets' help in quashing a threatened right-wing coup, led by Lavr Kornilov, a former tsarist general. Trotsky was able to deliver that support by winning over the loyalty of the capital's military garrison.[10] Thus, by October, when Lenin felt safe enough to return from his Finnish sanctuary, Trotsky had ensured that the ground was well laid for the ensuing Bolshevik seizure of power (pp. 106–8). By then, too, he shared with Lenin himself a virtual "duumvirate" of leadership in the revolutionary cause.

---

9 Thatcher, *Leon Trotsky*, 191–95.
10 W. Bruce Lincoln, *Passage through Armageddon: The Russians in War and Revolution* (New York: Simon and Schuster, 1986), 432.

## WAR HERO AND ALTER EGO

It was in April 1918, soon after the Brest-Litovsk Treaty had disengaged Russia from the European war, that the Central Committee of the "Communist" Party—a popular title lately adopted by the Soviet government to designate the triumph of "pure" socialism over Menshevik-Bolshevik factionalism—acted quickly to augment Trotsky's responsibilities. These included the commissariat of defense. No role could have been more vital, not even the party chairmanship. Contrary to Lenin's expectation, peace did not come to the new Soviet state, neither after the humiliation of Brest-Litovsk, nor after the general European armistices of October–November 1918, nor even after the Paris Peace Conference of 1919. Rather, during these years, the nation's territorial integrity was placed in even more jeopardy than it had been during the recent war; for, at the peace conference, most of the conquered, formerly tsarist imperial terrain had not been returned but was awarded instead to newly established "successor states." These included most of territorial Poland, as well as the former Baltic provinces of Latvia, Lithuania, and Estonia. In Finland, Ukraine, and Belarus, too, anticommunist governments proceeded to declare their full independence, as they did in formerly tsarist-ruled Uzbekistan and the Transcaucasus regions of Georgia, Armenia, and Azerbaijan.

In "integral" Russia itself, moreover, antirevolutionary troop units moved to wrest back political leadership on behalf of the tsarist dynasty. Thus, General M.V. Alekseev, a former imperial chief of military staff, began organizing a "White"—loyalist—army immediately after the Bolshevik Revolution. Soon, besides Lavr Kornilov in Russia, other former tsarist military commanders—Anton Denikin in southern Ukraine and Crimea, Nikolai Yudenich in the Baltic regions, Alexander Kolchak in Siberia—raised antirevolutionary armies of their own and established "White" enclaves throughout the vast, formerly tsarist Eurasian land mass. Indeed, for months at a time, the functional authority of Lenin's regime was reduced essentially to the areas immediately adjacent to Petrograd (St. Petersburg) and Moscow.

For the Bolshevik leadership, it was critical that a new, loyal, "Red" Army be created immediately. It was to meet this challenge that Trotsky, a transplanted Jewish civilian without previous training in conventional warfare, moved with a ruthless vigor more characteristic of an experienced military professional. Indeed, at the outset of his appointment as commissar of defense, rejecting all notions of communist egalitarianism, he insisted upon the establishment of a traditional military command structure and traditional military discipline. To achieve that goal, Trotsky even succeeded in recruiting some 50,000 former tsarist officers (although he assigned Communist Party political commissars to monitor their loyalty).[11] He was ruthless, too, in commandeering supplies and the nation's rail system for military needs.

Possibly the most effective of Trotsky's weapons, however, was his own well-tested personal charisma. He made a point of appearing at one military front after another, often standing on the roof of an armored car in the thick of battle, exhorting, challenging, rallying his troops.[12] Eventually, in the spring of 1921, after three years of civil and frontier warfare, resistance to the Communists began to diminish. The Red Army had regained control of some four-fifths of the prewar tsarist empire, with only the Baltic republics, Poland, and a slice of western Ukraine (preempted by newly independent Poland), lying permanently outside Soviet territory. The achievement was an extraordinary one. Indeed, in recognition of Trotsky's crucial role in defending the new Soviet state, the Communist Central Committee awarded him its first "Order of the Red Banner" and proclaimed him "Father of Victory."[13]

The cost of that victory had been appalling, however. Stripped of some of its most economically advanced border territories, Russia's industrial production by 1921 fell to barely one-sixth of its prewar level. Fuel remained in critically short supply. In the larger cities, electric power stations operated barely two days a week. Water mains functioned equally intermittently. To boil sewage for drinking and cooking water, people used the timber they hacked from their own trees, even from their own furniture. In its desperation to prevent starvation in the cities, the Soviet regime then resorted to "agricultural stations" where peasants were required to sell their produce and livestock at fixed prices. It was this latter measure, however, that was challenged virtually at its outset. Thousands of farm families limited their harvests to their immediate household needs and slaughtered their animals rather than surrender them to the stations.

The process of economic "collectivization" was equally slapdash and painful. Well before the government took title to private landholdings, the nation's peasants had set about a rule-of-thumb distribution among themselves. If the process reflected a certain elementary justice, it did little in the first revolutionary years to restore the productivity of Russia's economy. Neither did Lenin and Trotsky's landmark decision to "communize" industry and

---

11  Stephen Phillips, *Lenin and the Russian Revolution* (Oxford: Heinemann, 2000), 44.
12  Deutscher, *The Prophet Armed*, 442–45.
13  Victor Serge, *Mémoires d'un révolutionnaire, 1901–1941* (Paris: Éditions du Seuil, 1951), 101–2.

commerce. The two leaders initially had sought and obtained a Central Committee decree confiscating any enterprise with more than ten workers on its payroll. Banks similarly were taken over by the government, and their private accounts were sequestered. Little time passed, however, before these measures proved counterproductive. Indeed, they all but ensured the country's economic collapse. In the winter of 1921–22, one of the most traumatic famines in modern history descended on the Volga agricultural belt, taking between 2 and 3 million lives within the ensuing year and a half.[14] Instances of cannibalism were not unknown.

It was the impact of this enveloping mass starvation that finally induced Lenin, Trotsky, and the Communist Central Committee to retreat from their much-touted program of "war communism."[15] To encourage productivity both in farms and factories, the government embarked late in 1922 on a "New Economic Policy"—in effect, a retrogression from communism—that henceforth would tolerate modest individual agricultural holdings as well as a limited salary-and-income differential in the urban economy. Eventually, these emergency measures took effect. By 1923–24, in response to the "NEP's" emerging relaxations, the worst of the horror appeared to be easing. But at what cost! By then, as a consequence of mass starvation, the nation's social structure had been eviscerated beyond recognition.

## EMERGENCE OF AN ÉMINENCE GRISE

It was during these early years of military and economic trauma that a seemingly minor reorganization was instituted within the emerging Communist administration. In the winter of 1921–22, Lenin had established the office of party "secretariat" to provide a repository of personnel for the expanding government bureaucracy. In the spring, he appointed Joseph Stalin as the secretariat's first commissar. Ostensibly, Stalin's task was to serve as liaison with the multitiered Soviet governing apparatus, to assess its needs and provide it with reliable Communist staffers. But, in his hands, the office rapidly became a cache basin for his own political loyalists.

Stalin's aggressiveness in transforming himself into the Communist Party's bureaucrat in chief actually should have been predictable for those familiar with his background. Born in 1878 in the small Georgian village of Gori, he was christened Josip Djugashvili. His father was a shoemaker who

---

14 Timothy Snyder, "'Holocaust: The Ignored Reality': An Exchange," *New York Review of Books*, August 13, 2009.

15 Raphael R. Abramovich, *The Soviet Revolution* (London: George Allen & Unwin, 1962), 346–47.

in his drunken rages often beat his son unmercifully. His mother, hoping that the boy eventually would qualify for the priesthood (or at least escape her husband's brutal presence), enrolled him in a local church school. Afterward, when the boy reached adolescence, she managed to register him in the Tiflis Seminary. The institution had once been renowned as the region's "cradle of bishops."[16] By the early twentieth century, however, its decisive influence on the future Stalin was essentially its lessons of survival among bullying classmates and punitive priest-teachers. Indeed, it was not a coincidence that the school also was beginning to achieve notoriety as the cradle of atheists and revolutionaries. By Stalin's own later acknowledgment, in was in the seminary's dormitories and study halls that he and others of his classmates secretly became familiar with the writings of Karl Marx.

Thereafter, prowling Tiflis's railway depots and workshops, the teenage Stalin found an eager audience for his newly developed Marxist rhetoric. Yet it was not long, too, before his "extracurricular" activity was reported to the seminary administration. He was promptly expelled, together with some 20 other student radicals. Afterward, adopting the sobriquet of "Koba" (a fictitious Caucasian Robin Hood), Stalin soon emerged as the leader of his fellow expellees, devising protection rackets and controlling the streets in Tiflis's lower-middle-class residential districts.[17] Two years later, in 1901, he shifted his activities to Batum, a Georgian town on the Black Sea coast that a Rothschild-owned oil pipeline and refinery lately had transformed into a major international port. Finding work in the refinery, Stalin and his cronies allowed little time to pass before they set about dunning the company for pay raises. They were refused. Three months later, the refinery mysteriously caught fire. In the winter of 1902–3, however, when Stalin hinted of future "accidents," the Rothschild management had the precocious extortionist arrested, and a local court sentenced him to five years of Siberian exile.

But 19 months later still, at the onset of the October 1905 unrest, Stalin used false papers and his new false name to escape confinement and make his way back to Batum. There, he established his first meaningful contact with experienced Social Democratic emissaries and, in turn, promptly won their admiration as a gang leader who could raise money for the party. Indeed, when the 1905 "Octobrist" uprising failed and most of his companions were forced into hiding, Stalin remained in Batum to become the godfather of a small but useful extortion operation on the party's behalf. It was an enterprise that soon came to resemble a moderately successful Mafia

---

16  Simon S. Montefiore, *Young Stalin* (New York: Alfred A. Knopf, 2007), 32–33.
17  Montefiore, *Young Stalin*, 40–41.

family, engaging in currency counterfeiting, shakedowns, and protection rackets—even several bank robberies.[18]

In March 1908, the tsarist police tracked Stalin down and once again sentenced him to Siberian exile. But four months later, he escaped yet again, and for the ensuing half-decade his life devolved into one of plain and simple criminality. Although the young "mafioso's" feats were admired and exploited by the Social Democrats, the political ideology in his lawlessness was less than sophisticated.[19] It was not until his ninth arrest, in 1913, and his ensuing sentence to a four-year term of exile in Siberia that the comradeship Stalin developed among his Russian fellow prisoners finally transformed him from a provincial Georgian hooligan into a committed anti-tsarist revolutionary. Indeed, the period of the ensuing Russian Civil War climaxed the "making" of the authentic Stalin. In late 1917, shortly after the Kerensky government released him from prison, the successor Bolshevik regime appointed him director-general of food supplies for south Russia. During the ensuing months, reacting to the escalating conflict between "Reds" and "Whites," the young revolutionary transcended his essentially civilian role. In the process, too, he revealed the animating motif of his future career.

The clue was provided during the struggle for Tsaritsyn. As a key strategic city on the Lower Volga, Tsaritsyn (later to be retitled Stalingrad) was the gateway to the grain and oil of the north Caucasus. When the city seemed in danger of falling to White counterrevolutionaries, Lenin promoted Stalin from his status of food "director-general" for civilians to that of "commissar of supply," with sweeping military powers. Accordingly, in April 1918, in an armored train containing 400 Red Guards, Stalin arrived at Tsaritsyn to find the city rife with chaos and betrayal. At that point, suspecting counterrevolutionary activity among a group of some 200 ex-tsarist officers whom Trotsky had recruited (p. 114), Stalin immediately ordered the "traitors" herded onto a Volga barge and towed out to mid-river. At his orders, the barge's portals then were opened, and the vessel promptly sank with all its human cargo. "Death solves all problems," Stalin confided to his shocked comrades. "No man, no problem."[20]

Shortly afterward, Lenin had Stalin transferred to Moscow, assigning him to a series of increasingly pivotal administrative responsibilities: as commissar for nationalities, as commissar of the workers' and peasants' inspectorate,

---

18  Montefiore, *Young Stalin*, 135, 154.
19  Montefiore, *Young Stalin*, 91 ff.
20  Simon S. Montefiore, *Stalin: The Court of the Red Tsar* (New York: Knopf, 2004), 32–33.

then, successively, to the supreme revolutionary military council, to the Orgburo, to the Politburo (the latter functioning as the unofficial inner sanctum of the party leadership). Finally, in April 1922, Lenin appointed Stalin commissar of the Communist Secretariat, with the mandate of staffing the party's—in effect, the Communist state's—expanding bureaucracy. Indeed, in future years, Stalin used his latest position to recommend the appointment of some 10,000 party officials throughout the nation—and in the process converted the Secretariat into the de facto engine room of the Communist Party.[21]

Some of these appointees had been with Stalin since his early days in the Bolshevik underground. Grigori Ordzhonikidze ("Servo"), a veteran of the original "Georgian Mafia," would become Stalin's choice as commissar of heavy industry. Kliment Voroshilov, also one of Stalin's early cronies, eventually would replace Trotsky as commissar of defense (p. 113). Feliks Dzerzhinski, founder of the "Cheka"—the early Bolshevik political police—was a man whom Stalin had befriended in 1917. Another veteran comrade, Andrei Vyshinski, would become the chief prosecutor during the nation's subsequent "Great Terror" (pp. 124, 128–29). In this fashion, mistrustful of intellectuals, Stalin brought the clan-based and vendetta-ridden politics of the Caucasus into the Kremlin itself.[22] But even as he remembered his friends, it soon became evident that he would also not forget his critics or suspected rivals.

## A POLITICAL LESION OPENS

After the civil war, when Trotsky returned to Moscow on a permanent basis, no two men could have remained closer than he and Lenin. Their families occupied adjoining apartments in the Kremlin, sharing the same dining room and bathing facilities. Trotsky's children addressed the Lenins as "uncle" and "aunt." By then, the Russian public at large also had come to regard Lenin and Trotsky as a virtual "duumvirate." Trotsky's appearance and oratory at May Day military parades thrilled his listeners. Whether addressing audiences of simple "commoners" and civil servants or of scientists, physicians, librarians, or journalists, he remained unsurpassed as Russia's chief intellectual doyen. Thus, although still holding the position of defense commissar, Trotsky increasingly addressed the economic and social issues posed by the "NEP"

---

21 Robert Conquest, *The Great Terror: A Reassessment* (New York: Oxford University Press, 1990), 3, 5.
22 Montefiore, *Red Tsar*, 28, 35; For mistrust of intellectuals, see Wistrich, *Trotsky: Fate*, 125–26.

and other domestic programs, and functioned also as Lenin's alter ego in matters of Soviet foreign policy.

In the years 1921–22, occasional policy disagreements surfaced between the "duumvirate," on the one hand, and Stalin, on the other. Lenin and Trotsky favored a union of Soviet republics on a constitutionally equal basis. Stalin as party general secretary advocated a federation of Soviet republics in which Russia itself, as in tsarist times, would provide the central and authoritative governing direction. Although Stalin later withdrew his objections to the union model, his resentment of Trotsky's continuing seniority deepened, even as Trotsky's patronizing grandeur offended other veteran Bolsheviks, who tended to be more impressed with Stalin's hard-nosed "practicality." Then, on May 25, 1922, Lenin suffered a cerebral aneurysm. Until that moment, the Communist chairman had seemed to be impervious to ordinary physical dangers. Five years before, in August 1918, he had been wounded in an assassination attempt but had recovered within a month. This time, however, the stroke left him semi-paralyzed and bedridden.

Stalin accordingly lost no time in redoubling his effort to promote his own loyalists to influential party and government posts. But if Trotsky until then had failed to gauge Stalin's personal animus, it was ironic that Lenin himself may have been the more perceptive. Although confined to bed and wheelchair, and aware of Stalin's energy and administrative ability, he must also have sensed the extent of the Georgian's ruthless cunning. Indeed, in earlier months, Lenin had entreated Trotsky to accept the party vice-chairmanship; but the latter was unenthusiastic, preferring to exercise an ombudsman's free hand in wrestling with the nation's surfeit of challenges. In December 1922, however, Lenin, although not yet recovered from his stroke and speaking only with difficulty, implored Trotsky to reconsider the offer. This time Trotsky did not reject the proposal outright.

But it was in that same month that Stalin got wind of a message Lenin had sent Trotsky, congratulating the latter on winning Politburo support for a governmental monopoly on foreign trade. Stalin had opposed the measure. Furious, he instantly telephoned Nadya Krupskaya, Lenin's wife and personal secretary, berating her as a "syphilitic whore"—ostensibly for letting her husband concern himself with party affairs "in his state of health."[23] That very afternoon Lenin suffered a relapse. Although, four days later, he recovered enough strength to dictate another letter to the Central Committee, this one served, in effect, as his last political will and testament. Analyzing the

---

23  Montefiore, *Young Stalin*, 367.

merits and faults of each member of the party leadership, the document left an unambiguous description of Trotsky as his, Lenin's, "most able" colleague. Of Stalin, Lenin wrote only this: "Having become General Secretary, Stalin has concentrated immeasurable power in his hands, and I am not sure that he will always know how to use that power with sufficient caution." Afterward, on January 4, 1923, Lenin dictated a terse postscript, observing that "[Stalin's rudeness] has already become unbearable" and advising the Central Committee to remove him from office and to appoint "another man... more patient, more loyal, more politic... and attentive to comrades." The inference was plain that Trotsky was that man.[24]

Lenin's advice to the Central Committee was routed first to the Politburo. This was the party's inner sanctum, consisting of not more than a dozen senior officials. Grigori Zinoviev was widely considered its most influential member, after Lenin and Trotsky. Indeed, as chairman of the "Comintern," the nexus of communist parties outside the Soviet Union (pp. 30, 44, 124, 281, 301, 344), Zinoviev occupied official positions almost equivalent to Lenin's and Trotsky's in Russia itself, and was second only to Trotsky as a brilliant, multilingual orator. Another key Politburo figure, Lev Kamenev, a veteran Bolshevik, was chairman of the Moscow Soviet and served as the Politburo's chairman pro tem during Lenin's illness. Like Zinoviev, Kamenev harbored no personal animus against Trotsky, although he considered the latter imperious and arrogant. A comparable opinion was harbored by Nicholai Bukharin, editor of *Pravda*, the party journal.[25] Yet none of the three men was interested in more than preventing Trotsky from succeeding Lenin.

Trotsky himself gained his first inkling of these political reservations late in the winter of 1922 during a Politburo meeting in which Stalin assailed him for "defeatism" on the issue of a Russian-controlled "union" of soviet republics. Even at that late moment, however, cosseted in his sense of personal omniscience, Trotsky chose to ignore the danger signals. He made no effort to cultivate his own political faction. In any case, he anticipated Lenin's full recovery. But in late March of 1923, Lenin suffered a third stroke, leaving him entirely paralyzed and incapable even of speech. At this point, the "triumvirate"—Zinoviev, Kamenev, and Bukharin—packed the party Central Committee with protégés, thereby ensuring that Stalin was reappointed to his post as party first secretary.

---

24 Isaac Deutscher, *Prophet Unarmed: Trotsky, 1921–1929* (London: Oxford University Press, 1959). 70–71.
25 Stephen F. Cohen, *Bukharin and the Bolshevik Revolution: A Political Biography, 1888–1938* (New York: Knopf, 1973), 150–53.

## TROTSKY OUTFLANKED

In the summer of 1923, Moscow and Petrograd suddenly were shaken by industrial unrest. Workers' unions protested that their wages were penurious and that the NEP's "economic recovery" agenda (p. 115) was being carried out essentially at their expense. Whether or not these accusations were legitimate, the strikes imperiled the nation's still fragile economy. In an effort to defuse the threat, Stalin hastened to call an emergency meeting of the Politburo. With the support of his allies, he ordered Feliks Dzerzhinski, chairman of the Cheka, the party secret police, to infiltrate the nation's unions and arrest the "trouble-makers."[26] By then, however, belatedly apprized of the political conspiracy against him, Trotsky struck back. He accused Stalin of an effort to alienate the Communist leadership from the Soviet working population. At that point, the Politburo meetings swiftly degenerated into a farrago of accusations and counter-accusations.

News of the widening political schism leaked to the Central Committee. Genuinely alarmed, Zinoviev, Kamenev, and Bukharin at first promised to open the party to self-criticism and free discussion. But Trotsky was no longer deceived. During the autumn of 1923, in a series of articles released to the press, he openly attacked his critics and other members of the "Old Guard" for political opportunism and urged the party's younger members to assert themselves. Then, on December 8, fully nine months after being exposed to his rival's sub rosa campaign, Trotsky released an explosive message to the press. Accusing Stalin's cabal of fomenting "bureaucratic degeneration," he inveighed:

> Away with passive obedience, with mechanical leveling by the authorities, with suppression of personality, with servility, with careerism! . . . It [is] necessary to replace the mummified bureaucrats by fresh elements who are in close touch with the life of the party as a whole . . . [T]he new course must begin by making everyone feel that from now on nobody will dare terrorize the party.[27]

But Trotsky had waited too long. Stalin had completed his overhaul of the party machinery and had maneuvered his own loyalists into key positions in virtually every echelon of the Communist apparatus. These Stalin faithfuls

---

26 Roy Medvedev, *On Stalin and Stalinism* (London: Oxford University Press, 1979), 47–48.
27 Deutscher, *Prophet Unarmed*, 122–23.

in turn reacted to Trotsky's protest with a deafening barrage of counteraccusations: of "hatred" for the party organization, of "reckless" individualism, of "contumaciousness" toward the party veterans, of "disrespect" for the Bolshevik tradition, of notorious "underestimation" of the working class. Indeed, the counterattack all but openly implied that, at heart, Trotsky had remained a stranger in the party, an alien to Leninism, an agent of "petit-bourgeois" elements that had infected the party with their "deviationism."[28]

Emotionally exhausted by then, and possibly suffering from borderline pneumonia, Trotsky declined to reply. His physicians were insistent that he take a rest in a warmer climate, and eventually he heeded their advice. In January 1924, he and Natalia Sedova departed for the Black Sea resort of Sukhumi. But three days into their journey, a coded telegram awaited Trotsky at the Poltava rail stop. It was from Stalin, announcing that Lenin had died. Trotsky then wired back that he was returning immediately and asked that the funeral be delayed until his arrival. But a second telegram from Stalin asserted (mendaciously) that no time remained, that the funeral would have to take place the next day, and that Trotsky, meanwhile, would be well advised to continue on to Sukhumi and recover his health. Plainly, Stalin had his reasons for keeping Trotsky away from the elaborate, weeklong ceremonies. He intended that Trotsky's absence should be noted and criticized—as it was.[29] Not long afterward, Alexei Rykov, one of Lenin's former deputies, took Lenin's place as chairman of the Council of People's Commissars, the official "cabinet" of the Soviet government. Afterward, it was at Rykov's request, but palpably at Stalin's instigation, that all former Trotsky protégés in the secretariat were dismissed. No explanations were offered.

In the spring of 1924, Trotsky's health was sufficiently improved for him to return to Moscow. In May, he attended a special meeting of the Communist Central Committee. It was then that Nadya Krupskaya, Lenin's widow and an "honorary" member of the committee since her late husband's terminal illness, astonished the party veterans by taking the floor and reading aloud Lenin's political will and testament. The document included Lenin's castigation of Stalin and the suggestion that he be removed from his position as Communist first secretary. Stalin remained silent, visibly mortified that the document was being aired outside the intimate circle of the Politburo. But once again Zinoviev, Kamenev, and Bukharin hurried to his rescue. They implored their comrades to leave Stalin at his post, assuring them that he

---

28  Deutscher, *Prophet Unarmed*, 134.
29  Deutscher, *Prophet Unarmed*, 134.

had long since mended the behavior cited in Lenin's will. Thus, over Nadya Krupskaya's impassioned protest, the Central Committee voted by overwhelming majority to suppress Lenin's testament.

In late May, when the Thirteenth Congress of the Russian Communist Party formally assembled, it was the "triumvirs" again who led the packed crowd of over 1,000 party veterans in an orgy of anti-Trotsky denunciation. Indeed, at Stalin's initiative, they now loosed additional accusations. These included the charge that Trotsky lacked faith in the party's recent decisions to embark upon the "New Economic Policy," to forgo the "bankrupt" strategy of ongoing communist revolution in Western Europe, and to embrace Stalin's "patriotic" approach of "socialism in one country." Kamenev went so far as to demand that Trotsky, who was seated on the dais with other commissars, stand before the congress and "recant" his "anti-party behavior." At this point, Trotsky finally arose to address the congress members. He would accept any decision taken by the congress, he announced, but he would not "recant."[30] Then, pale and shaking, he walked out of the hall—and unwittingly into political quarantine.

## INTERNAL EXILE

For the time being, Trotsky was allowed to maintain his seat in the Politburo and to serve as chairman of several technical commissions. A moment of respite even occurred in December 1925. Lenin's widow had ensured that her late husband's political testament had been widely disseminated. It became evident afterward that many provincial branches of the party still remained loyal to Trotsky as a popular hero of the civil war and as Lenin's acclaimed alter ego. By June 1926, as these "oppositionists" were meeting, a significant minority of Central Committee members joined them. They defined themselves as champions of a Europe-wide socialist revolution (as opposed to the "chimera" of Stalin's version of "socialism in one country"), as defenders of the working class against the "*kulaks*" (capitalist farmers), the NEP "bourgeoisie," and the entrenched party bureaucracy. Taken aback by the protest, even Zinoviev and Kamenev were sobered. Timorously, they approached Trotsky to offer their discreet apologies for having impugned his efforts on behalf of the party.[31]

---

30 Leonard Schapiro, *The Communist Party of the Soviet Union* (New York: Random House, 1959), 307.
31 Wistrich, *Trotsky: Fate*, 133–34.

But the political countercampaign had come too late. By the summer of 1926, overbalanced with Stalinists, the Communist Central Committee retaliated by denouncing Zinoviev for his recent "heresy" and then deprived him of his Politburo seat. Although not yet expelled from the Politburo, Kamenev lost his voting rights. Ironically, Trotsky himself still kept his Politburo membership; but elsewhere, seeking to address crowds of "oppositionist" supporters, he was hooted and drowned out by Stalin's loyalists. Finally, in October, Kamenev and Zinoviev—sensing that they were being overwhelmed, that Trotsky's countercampaign was being stifled—approached Stalin with a proposal for a quid pro quo. They would relent in their opposition and accept "party discipline." In turn, the Politburo would readmit Zinoviev, restore Kamenev's voting rights, and cease its campaign of anti-Trotsky denunciation. After only momentary hesitation, Stalin agreed.

One week later he repudiated his agreement. In a stormy Politburo session, he accused the oppositionists of "undermining" socialism, of "sabotaging" the New Economic Policy, and of "bearing responsibility" for the party's failure to ignite communist revolutions in the West. The next day, at his request, the Central Committee formally deprived Trotsky of his seat in the Politburo and announced that Zinoviev would be stripped of his leadership of the Communist International. In January 1927, the Central Committee went further yet, confirming the expulsion from the Comintern of all "Trotskyites and Zinovievites" (soon to be a favored Stalinist epithet). Six months later, on August 1, Stalin dealt his trump card, insisting that the Central Committee strip party membership from Trotsky, Zinoviev, Kamenev, and all such "counterrevolutionaries" and "splitters." Although Trotsky subsequently was offered a hearing, his attempt to speak was drowned out by a storm of vituperation, with committee members flinging books and inkpots at him. Finally, on November 14, 1927, after a series of intermittent individual conferences, the Central Committee reassembled to endorse the expulsion from the party of Trotsky, Zinoviev, and Kamenev for their "counterrevolutionary insurrection."[32]

Trotsky had anticipated this bitter denouement. On November 12, senior officers of the GPU—the political police that had recently supplanted the revolutionary-era Cheka—informed him that he and Natalia Sedova would have to vacate their lodgings in the Kremlin. Complying without protest, the Trotskys then relocated to a tiny apartment on Granovski Street. It was the dwelling of a fellow "oppositionist," Adolf Joffe, Trotsky's friend and deputy at the Brest-Litovsk peace conference (and briefly married earlier to one of

---

32  Conquest, *The Great Terror: A Reassessment*, 11.

Trotsky's sisters). Two days later, following the Central Committee's decision to expel all "counterrevolutionaries" from the party, Joffe shot himself.[33] He had been penniless, depressed, and bed-ridden. When a large crowd of "oppositionists" accompanied his coffin to the cemetery, Stalin evidently reconsidered Trotsky's very presence in Moscow. On January 12, 1928, a GPU official arrived at the Granovski Street apartment to inform Trotsky that he and his family were being evicted from their temporary dwelling and, in fact, from European Russia altogether. They were to be deported to Alma Ata, the capital of Kazakhstan in Soviet Central Asia.[34]

Within the week, Trotsky, Natalia Sedova, and "Liova," their 22-year-old son (and Trotsky's namesake), were packed into a GPU van and sped off to Moscow's central railroad station. But to the consternation of their escort, several thousand of Trotsky's admirers braved Stalin's retaliation by waiting at the station entrance, even surging across the railroad tracks to block the train from moving. As the standoff continued, hour after hour, the GPU contingent finally was ordered to return the Trotskys to their lodgings for the night. But the next morning, transporting them back to the station, a reinforced GPU escort hustled the family members into their assigned rail carriage and locked them into their compartment. The locomotive whistle then sounded, the crowd began to disperse, and the train began its journey from the station marshaling yards for its Central Asian destination.

En route eastward, the accompanying GPU escort treated the Trotsky family members with deference. It was the weather that soon became their prime concern. Midway on their journey, at the village of Pishpek (renamed Frunze), a blizzard obliged the Trotskys and their guards to detrain. The remaining 160 miles to Alma Ata then had to be traversed by bus, truck, and horse sleigh, a trek across ice-covered hills and snow drifts that included night stops at selected frontier hostels. Only after four days of this ordeal did the group arrive at its destination.

## EXTERNAL EXILE

Hardly touched by civilization, the sleepy and slum-ridden community of Alma Ata was subject to earthquakes, floods, blizzards, and scorching summer heat waves; to dust clouds, plagues of insects, bouts of malaria—even

---

33  Deutscher, *The Prophet Unarmed*, 379.
34  Christopher Andrew and Oleg Gordievsky, *KGB: The Inside Story of Foreign Operations from Lenin to Gorbachev* (New York: HarperCollins, 1990), 115.

to cases of leprosy. On their escorted passage through the town center, the Trotskys encountered native Kazakhs sitting on the doorsteps of their bazaars, seeking to warm themselves in the intermittent sun, occasionally searching their bodies for lice. Fortunately, the GPU guard detail, seeking to mitigate the Trotskys' ordeal, continued to treat them with deference, providing them with a comfortable four-room apartment, later allowing them to rent a foothill dacha during the summer months. Trotsky's private library and archives were sent on to him from Moscow. He even received a modest official allowance, which he supplemented with publishers' advances for his impending German translation of the complete works of Marx and Engels.

From the beginning of his enforced departure, personal correspondence also figured significantly in Trotsky's writings. This included an extensive succession of letters to his former wife, Alexandra, to their two daughters, as well as to other family members. For months, he maintained an even wider correspondence with his admirers, entreating them at all costs to hold fast in their opposition to Stalin's emerging dictatorship. Although the GPU guard detail intercepted most of these letters, some of them were allowed to get through. Thus, in the autumn of 1928, relatives managed to send word of a family tragedy. Both Trotsky's daughters, Nina and Zina, had fallen ill—Nina, the younger, of tuberculosis, and Zina, the elder, of an undiagnosed neurological ailment. Subsequently, on November 19, 1928, news arrived that Nina had died the previous summer. At that moment, Trotsky's personal correspondence briefly lapsed.

On December 16, 1928, he was visited by a senior GPU official. The man had been dispatched from Moscow with an ultimatum: either Trotsky ceased his "counterrevolutionary" political propaganda or he would be transported to another residence. The threat of expulsion overseas was all but explicit. In this instance, however, Trotsky refused to back down. He acknowledged that family correspondence by then was pointless but insisted that communication with his followers would continue as a matter of ideological principle. When his reply was transmitted to Moscow, the reaction was predictable. On January 20, 1929, a full year since his deportation from Moscow, Trotsky was visited by the local GPU commander, who presented him with an expulsion order. It was irrevocable, the commander emphasized.[35] Indeed, "Comrade Trotsky" was to be deported from Alma Ata within 24 hours. When Trotsky asked for his intended destination, he was not answered. The deadline was extended for another day, allowing him to complete the packing of his archives; but, at dawn on January 22, Trotsky, Natalia, and their son Liova

---

35  Andrew and Gordievsky, *KGB*, 192–94.

were driven under military escort back on the same road they had used the previous year. The blizzard was even heavier this time, and several horses actually froze to death before the family reached the military base of Frunze.

At Frunze, the Trotskys were ushered to a rail siding, where a special train awaited them. Initially, they had been told only that they would be returned to Europe. Before the train embarked, however, the GPU officer revealed that their ultimate destination would be Istanbul, Turkey. At this point Trotsky's protest was vehement. He would go on a hunger strike, he insisted, even throw himself off the train, if he and his family were not allowed to return to Europe. Confused, the officer immediately telegraphed GPU headquarters in Moscow. Stalin himself was alerted. In a bizarre episode, the Trotskys waited at Frunze for 12 days—eating, washing, and sleeping in the rail depot as the Politburo again debated their fate. In the end, however, the expulsion order to Istanbul was upheld. The journey resumed.

The train raced southwestward, through the Ukraine to the Black Sea port of Odessa, the city of Trotsky's early youth. Once in Odessa, the family members were transported to the harbor, where a GPU detachment escorted them to their cabin on the awaiting Soviet coastal freighter *Ilyich*. The Trotskys were the *Ilyich*'s only passengers. Within the hour, hoisting anchor and slipping away from its dock, the vessel set forth in a wintery gale across the Black Sea. The family would not set foot in Russia again.

## THE REVOLUTION CONTINUES

Personal politics aside, Stalin's objective for the Soviet Union actually was not dissimilar to that of the late Lenin, or even of the exiled Trotsky. It was to regear his party and nation for an epic campaign of "building socialism." For almost a decade, Russia's class revolution had been stalled in midcourse. In the grim aftermath of revolution and civil war, the nation had undergone widespread privation. Confronting the Ukrainian famine that had taken the lives of between 2 and 3 million people (p. 115), Lenin and Trotsky had bowed to economic realities and suspended their original plans for the collectivization of Russian agriculture. Rather, in 1921, a "New Economic Policy" had been inaugurated (p. 115), allowing peasant farmers a cautious and qualified leeway to sell their own produce for private gain and permitting a modest differentiation of salaries between workers and managers. Stalin himself had been one of the firmest supporters of the NEP.

By the latter 1920s, however, if NEP quasi-capitalism had given the Soviet economy a breathing space, it had not yet achieved its goal of sustaining a tolerable standard of living for the nation's overwhelmingly agrarian population.

The so-called *kulaks*—farmers who had ended up owning supportable tracts of land—were distending the rural economy because of their ability to outproduce and underprice the harassed majority of mini-plot peasants. These latter, in any case, were breaking under the strain of the NEP's compulsory loans, taxes, and requisitions. Indeed, fully a decade after the overthrow of the tsarist empire, the Soviet Union appeared no closer than before the revolution to the party's widely proclaimed goal of an authentically socialist society. In Stalin's prognosis, a "coherent" program could be delayed no longer, an agenda that would sustain a viable agricultural population, feed the cities, raise industrial output, and, perhaps most importantly, build a widely based proletarian class that would function as guarantor of the Marxist revolution.

But the party secretary was influenced by still another factor that weighed on him as heavily as Marxist theory, economic pragmatism, or even political opportunism. This was national security. In a revealing speech to Soviet technocrats and leading business executives, given on February 4, 1931, Stalin expressly vowed that Russian backwardness would never again play into the hands of the nation's enemies:

> [O]ld Russia ... was ceaselessly beaten for her backwardness. She was beaten by the Mongol Khans, she was beaten by Turkish Beys, she was beaten by Swedish feudal lords, she was beaten by the Polish-Lithuanian *Pans* [gentry], she was beaten by Anglo-French capitalists, she was beaten ... by all—for her backwardness. For military backwardness, for cultural backwardness, for political backwardness, for industrial backwardness, for agricultural backwardness. She was beaten because to beat her was profitable and went unpunished.[36]

It was essentially these multiple political, economic, and security considerations that Stalin, in April 1929, had requested and received Central Committee endorsement for his program.

Both the effort and its consequences were epic—and traumatic. Over the ensuing decade, the Russian people were driven into the single most protracted economic transformation ever endured by a single nation in the history of modern Europe.[37] Throughout the countryside, between 4 and 5 million *kulaks*, the independent farmers whom the NEP originally had left in possession of their own plots, now were systematically driven from their farms, often literally at gunpoint, into *kolkhozes*—makeshift agricultural collectives. Here,

---

36 As quoted in Isaac Deutscher, *Stalin: A Political Biography* (New York: Oxford University Press, 1967), 328; but see also J. V. Stalin, *Works* (Moscow: Foreign Language Publishing House, 1954), 13: 40–41.
37 Conquest, *The Great Terror: A Reassessment*, 18.

they were set to work building their own dwellings and barns, then scratching a subsistence from the soil with party-owned tools and under the guidelines of party-decreed planting schedules. Again, as in 1919–22, the initial disruption of the scheme produced a major famine, particularly in the Ukraine, the nation's breadbasket, where the trauma took perhaps a million additional lives.

To compound Russia's agony, another 1.2 million of the surviving landowners, whom the government reviled as "capitalist parasites," were among the displaced peasant families that were transported to remote Central Asian and subarctic eastern regions in Kazakhstan and Siberia. There, under marginal, even subhuman conditions, they were set to work on public projects: digging canals, excavating mines, laying railroad tracks. Exposed to starvation and disease, often beaten and not infrequently imprisoned and shot (p. 134), these former "capitalist farmers" in their eastern exile suffered a mortality rate of an additional 600,000, bringing the death toll to at least 3 million, and by some estimates 4 million.[38] Nevertheless, by 1934, after a half-decade of relentless government-induced trauma, the collectivization of some two-thirds of the nation's arable land was an accomplished fact, and the *kulaks* as a class had indeed been virtually liquidated.

Almost simultaneously, in the same late 1920s and early 1930s, Stalin forged ahead in a parallel social transformation. Under a much-touted "Five-Year Plan," he also sought to revolutionize the Soviet industrial base, massively to enlarge its modest network of factories, electrification and transportation facilities, and steel mills and processing plants. In this goal, too, although with comparable brutality, Stalin achieved almost unqualified success. By 1934, despite innumerable bottlenecks and shortages in building material and worker housing, the infrastructure of the nation's heavy industry had increased by as much as 300 per cent. Indeed, five years later, with the completion of the second Five-Year Plan, the Soviet Union had replaced Great Britain in third place and trailed just behind Germany in the totality of its industrial production. In the process, during the same decade, the nation's urban population increased from 30 million to nearly 60 million.[39]

As Stalin had anticipated, too, the new industrial revolution had generated the widely based proletariat of factory workers that he and his fellow Marxists regarded as indispensable for a socialist economy.

---

38  Anne Applebaum, *GULAG: A History of the Soviet Concentration Camps* (London: Doubleday, 2003), 64, 521–22; Conquest, *The Great Terror: A Reassessment*, 19–20; For a more modest appraisal, see Timothy Snyder, *Bloodlands: Europe between Hitler and Stalin* (New York: Basic Books, 2010), 21–30, 53.

39  Isaac Deutscher, *The Prophet Outcast: Trotsky, 1929–1940* (New York: Oxford University Press 1963), 99n.

But at what human cost! Altogether, in the 1920s and early 1930s, the extended suffering of agricultural and industrial transplantation, of hunger and forced labor, as well as of imprisonments and executions (pp. 303–6), inflicted an estimated death toll on the Soviet population of between 12 million and 13 million persons.[40] It was a hemorrhage that represented as many as three times the combined fatalities suffered by the nation's population in World War I and the ensuing civil and border wars. In February 1936, the Supreme Soviet decreed a general census, which was carried out during the ensuing spring and summer months. When the results were tabulated, the population for the entire Soviet Union was calculated at 147 million. If the figure was accurate, it suggested that the nation's demographic resources had not increased in the ten years from 1926 to 1936 and that the birth rate during that period scarcely balanced the death rate inflicted by the postwar famines, the liquidation of "capitalist" farmers, the migration and congestion of the new industrial proletariat—all in addition to the massive Stalinist campaign of political imprisonments and executions (pp. 303–6).[41]

## A TACTICAL RETRENCHMENT

It was in the same decade, as he orchestrated his shock program of achievement and agony, that Stalin confronted a developing ideological opposition that was by no means trivial. This time, however, it was generated essentially by the political right wing within the Communist Central Committee. He acknowledged the challenge head-on as early as April 1929, when the economic turbulence of the first Five-Year Plan began to strike the cities. Addressing a Politburo meeting, the general secretary warned ominously: "Comrades . . . we must face reality. A factional cabal has been established within our party composed of [Nicholai] Bukharin, [Alexei] Rykov, [Mikhail] Tomsky, and [Martemyan] Ryutin . . . [that is] blocking our programs of industrialization and collectivization."[42] Thus, at Stalin's "request," the Politburo, and subsequently the Communist Central Committee, denounced these "right-wingers," removed them from their party positions, and consigned several of them to brief periods of house arrest.

Among the accused "cabal," Martemyan Ryutin, former secretary of the Moscow party branch and a self-styled political moderate, had emerged as an

---

40 Conquest, *The Great Terror: A Reassessment*, 24; compare Timothy Snyder's critiques in the *New York Review of Books*, August 13, 2009 and March 10, 2011.
41 F. Beck and W. Godin, *Russian Purge and the Extraction of Confession* (New York: Viking Press, 1951), 71.
42 Conquest, *The Great Terror: A Reassessment*, 24.

outspoken and incautious critic of Stalin's "ideological" cleansing. Indeed, he remained a critic even following his denunciation by the Communist Central Committee. In June 1932, a full three years after being relieved of his post in Moscow, Ryutin went much further than his party comrades in execrating the horror inflicted upon the *kulaks* and, indeed, upon the Soviet people at large. In that month, he courageously addressed a 15-page "Appeal to All Members of the All-Union Communist Party," followed by a 200-page bill of particulars (later to be known as the "Ryutin platform"). In these documents, the author called for an end to the program of enforced peasant collectivization, a relaxation of the exhausting pace of the industrial "Five-Year Plans," and a reinstatement of all previously expelled party members—even of Leon Trotsky!

The Ryutin platform by itself was enough to evoke Stalin's wrath. But its author sealed his fate when he audaciously called for the unseating of Stalin as the party's first secretary.[43] Although Ryutin circulated this appeal privately to a small number of trusted "Old Bolsheviks," including the "leftists" Kamenev and Zinoviev (p. 120), the GPU obtained copies of the document and delivered them to Stalin.[44] The chairman's reaction was all but reflexive. In October 1932, he ordered the arrest of Ryutin, as well as of some three dozen of the latter's fellow "conspirators." Nine days later, the Soviet leader called an emergency meeting of the Politburo to seek its approval for imposing the death sentence on Ryutin. This time, however, much to Stalin's astonishment and chagrin, a majority of Politburo members resisted his appeal. In no sense was their disapproval evoked by considerations of party ideology, let alone of human compassion. During the civil war, after all, most of these hardened Bolsheviks had shown little mercy in the wholesale elimination of "counter-revolutionaries," and they had supported Stalin's uncompromising economic transformations. They agreed, too, that all "defectors" should be expelled from the party, even condemned to varying terms of imprisonment.[45]

Nevertheless, a "centrist" bloc in this political inner sanctum was unwilling to violate Lenin's stricture against the corporal punishment of "loyal" Communists. Evidently, the group's argument was made with uncommon passion by Sergei Kirov, a man whose prominence as first secretary of the Leningrad branch of the Communist Party evoked special respect (pp. 133–34).[46] For the while, Stalin stayed his hand. Although 29 other of the

---

43 Conquest, *The Great Terror: A Reassessment*, 25–26.
44 Ante Ciliga, *The Russian Enigma* (London: Routledge, 1940), 279.
45 Abramovich, *The Soviet Revolution*, 353–54.
46 Conquest, *The Great Terror: A Reassessment*, 26; Cohen, *Bukharin*, 345.

"Old Bolsheviks" who were implicated with Ryutin, including Kamenev and Zinoviev, were stripped of their party positions and dispatched to exile beyond the Urals—and Ryutin himself was sentenced to a ten-year period of imprisonment—Stalin did not press the issue of execution. For the immediate future, the "Red Tsar" had other methods at his disposal for imposing his agenda on the party and the Soviet Union at large.[47]

One of these methods was civil purgation. In a particularly unlovely process, local party committees were encouraged to conduct "investigations" of their "errant" members, specifically, to cross-examine them in the presence of their colleagues. Far from being objective, the process allowed for old personal grievances to be avenged. In 1933 alone, as a result of these "collegial" inquisitions, some 800,000 party members were obliged to relinquish their party cards, with the grim economic consequence of forfeited employment and pensions. Additionally, tens of thousands of the most "suspect" defendants were consigned to the USSR's bleak Arctic regions for "special labor assignments" on canal and railroad construction.[48]

These years of stress and shock did not spare even Stalin's household. In November 1932, Nadezhda Alliluyeva, his second wife, interceded with him, protesting the brutality of the purges, arrests, and imprisonments that affected members even of her own extended family. Stalin silenced her so brutally that the young woman, suffering by then from chronic emotional stress, retrieved her husband's pistol from their bedroom dresser and fatally shot herself.[49]

## STALIN'S MYTHICAL ENEMY

By early 1934, it seemed that the worst of the nation's political and economic turmoil was beginning to abate. Addressing the Communist Central Committee in January of that year, Stalin adopted a forbearing tone. Emphasizing the need to "consolidate" earlier gains, he intimated that the Soviet economic transformation finally was about to enter a period of relaxation. This time he was not dissembling. The harshest phase of kulak transplantation had indeed wound down by then, and serious efforts apparently were underway to alleviate the desperate conditions of life and work in the network of jerry-built *kolkhozes*. In the cities, too, the initial "Five-Year Plan" for industrialization had been completed, and hints were circulated of an impending "Second Five-Year Plan" that would launch a long-delayed

---

47  Abramovich, *The Soviet Revolution*, 355.
48  Conquest, *The Great Terror: A Reassessment*, 26.
49  Montefiore, *Red Tsar*, 20.

improvement in workers' housing, public transportation, and consumer products. Finally, in a gesture of personal "magnanimity," Stalin allowed the reinstatement of several thousand of his critics, essentially in the lower echelons of the Communist bureaucracy. His former Politburo colleagues—Zinoviev, Kamenev, and Rykov—were not yet among those sharing in a full pardon; but they too were released from their imprisonment or Siberian confinement, even restored to their party membership.

Yet Stalin's "magnanimity" disguised an unexpected and sinister new feature. Those whom he had earlier marked as direct or oblique critics of his political leadership included not only the salient figures he had broken politically but other party stalwarts currently holding office and influence. In many instances, their very competence and popularity identified them as potential rivals for party leadership and thereby as future targets of Stalin's byzantinism. Was Sergei Kirov, the esteemed party first secretary for the Leningrad district, among these? Until today, the question remains an issue of scholarly disagreement.

By 1934, Kirov undoubtedly had accomplished much in his 48 years, and against many odds. Born Sergei Kostrikov in the provincial Caucasus town of Urzhum, he was the only son of a ne'er-do-well father who had abandoned his family when his child was eight months old. After his mother died six years later, the boy was given over to an orphanage. In 1901, however, a group of influential benefactors provided him with a scholarship to an industrial school in Kazan. Four years later, upon completing his course of studies, he was taken on as an "engineer's assistant" in Tomsk. It was also in Tomsk, however, that the young man became a Marxist and joined the underground Social Democratic Party. He paid the price. During the ensuing 1905 Octobrist uprising, he was arrested for "incitement" and sentenced to six months' imprisonment. Nevertheless, upon release, and after changing his name to "Kirov," the youthful revolutionary lost no time in resuming his career as a Bolshevik propagandist. Indeed, from then on, nothing deterred him in his radical commitments, not even a second, three-year term of tsarist imprisonment. In the wake of the Bolshevik Revolution, moreover, Kirov served with distinction as a Red infantry officer in the ensuing civil war. In 1921, he was appointed party secretary for Azerbaijan.

It was in the Caucasus, too, that Kirov came to know and respect Stalin, himself recently appointed as the party's first secretary. In 1926, Stalin rewarded the younger man's competence and loyalty by promoting him to the key party secretaryship for the District of Leningrad. Extending from the Estonian border to the Arctic Ocean, this "district" in the 1920s and early 1930s encompassed the largest industrial proletariat in the Soviet Union. Again, Kirov fully justified his appointment, presiding over the party's affairs with unsurpassed energy and efficiency. He also presided with a ruthlessness that rivaled Stalin's, for his bailiwick included the notorious Baltic-White Sea Canal construction project. Between 1929 and 1933, it was in this vast undertaking that approximately a quarter million laborers, predominantly deported *kulaks*, worked under appalling conditions, tens of thousands of them to die of their ordeal.[50]

By the early 1930s, Kirov was functioning not only as party secretary in Leningrad but as a newly elected member of the Communist Central Committee and, subsequently, of the Politburo. Dynamic, handsome, a compelling orator, he had already become a figure of national prominence. Indeed, in 1932, Kirov's views already commanded enough respect within the party to dissuade the Politburo from authorizing the punishment of Mikhail Ryutin (p. 131). Aside from this tactical disagreement, however, Stalin had no "objective" reason to distrust Kirov, for the younger man's personal devotion seemingly had remained intact, and he had not identified himself either with the party's "Right" or "Left." Yet, in Stalin's mind, was trust eclipsed by a mounting jealousy?

In future decades, this interpretation was advanced by several respected Western sovietologists. It was distinctly possible, however, that the latter's accounts were influenced by one of Stalin's most durable successors in office. This was Nikita Khrushchev, who was intent, years after Stalin's death, on besmirching the reputation of Stalin, a tyrant who had demeaned him, Khrushchev, reducing him to a buffoon in the inner sessions of the Central Committee. Other evaluations, however, published after Khrushchev's own eviction from office in 1964 and reflecting a more detailed access to the archival record of the late Stalin's rule, take issue with the image of Stalin as a man animated by jealousy of Kirov.[51]

Indeed, it was in the spring of 1934 that Stalin himself sought to persuade Kirov to become his personal deputy in Moscow. Kirov respectfully declined. Stalin persisted. That July, he hosted Kirov and his wife at his vacation dacha

---

50 See chapters 9 and 10 of Matthew E. Lenoe, *The Kirov Murder and Soviet History*, 2nd ed. (New Haven: Yale University Press, 2010).

51 For conspiratorial interpretations of Stalin's attitude toward Kirov, see Robert Conquest, *Stalin and the Kirov Murder* (New York: Oxford University Press, 1989). See also Roy Medvedev, *On Stalin and Stalinism*; Robert Tucker, *Stalin in Power* (New York: Norton, 1990); Amy W. Knight, *Who Killed Kirov?: The Kremlin's Greatest Mystery* (New York: Hill and Wang, 1999); and Orlando Figes, *A People's Tragedy: A History of the Russian Revolution* (New York: Viking, 1997).

For opposing views, exculpating Stalin from the alleged plot against Kirov, see J. Arch Getty and Oleg V. Naumov, *The Road to Terror: Stalin and the Self-Destruction of the Bolsheviks, 1932–1938* (New Haven: Yale University Press, 1999); Adam B. Ulam, *The Kirov Affair* (San Diego: Harcourt Brace Jovanovich, 1988); Alla A. Kirilina, *L'assassinat de Kirov: Destin d'un Stalinien, 1888–1934* (Paris: Édition Seuil, 1995); and Lenoe and Prozumenšikov, *The Kirov Murder and Soviet History*.

in the Black Sea resort of Sochi. As the two families sunbathed on the Sochi beachfront, Stalin again attempted to cajole the younger man into accepting his Moscow offer, even intimating that he envisaged Kirov as his eventual successor as party general secretary. After some hesitation, Kirov suggested a compromise. He offered to resettle in Moscow in late 1938 or early 1939, once the second industrial Five-Year Plan had been completed. This time Stalin promised to be patient.

## AN ASSASSINATION IN LENINGRAD

At 4:00 p.m. on December 1, 1934, an undersized and seemingly frail man in his early thirties entered Leningrad's Smolny Institute. A former school for daughters of the tsarist gentry, the "Smolny" after the Bolshevik Revolution had been converted into Communist Party headquarters for the Leningrad District. On this December afternoon, however, despite the Smolny's importance as a party nerve center, the guard posts flanking its collage of outer doors were unaccountably empty. Indeed, entering the ornate foyer, the visitor—later to be identified as one Leonid Nikolaev—continued to move freely past interior guard posts that were also unmanned. Reaching the central staircase, still unchallenged, he proceeded to the third floor. There, he loitered in a darkened hall corner, his hand resting on a Nagant army-issue automatic pistol in his coat pocket.

SERGEI KIROV (CENTER), WITH JOSEPH STALIN AND HIS DAUGHTER SVETLANA

Only minutes before, Sergei Kirov, after working at home to complete a report on a recent Central Party committee meeting in Moscow, had himself returned to the Smolny. Climbing the stairs to the third floor, Kirov entered the office of his aide, Mikhail Chudov. For some 20 minutes, the two men discussed the prospective report. Subsequently, Kirov left Chudov's office for his own adjoining executive suite. It was 4:30 p.m. As Kirov approached the door, Nikolaev, the little visitor, suddenly moved from his corner hiding place. Withdrawing his pistol, he proceeded then to fire two bullets directly into the party secretary's back. Kirov slumped to the floor. His assailant immediately attempted to fire a shot into his own head; but a carpenter working in the hall nearby threw himself at Nikolaev, and the gun went astray. Nikolaev then collapsed in a dead faint beside the prostrate Kirov. Within seconds, party officials were running out of their offices toward the two men. Several of them carried the stricken Kirov, who was breathing stertorously, to a sofa in his own office. Minutes later, he expired. Nikolaev, still unconscious, was kept pinioned to the hall floor.

In the next hours, questions arose. Once the assassin's identity was established from documents in his pocket, the critical issue was his motive. Only days later, after extensive police interrogation of Nikolaev's family and his former employers, did it become apparent that the man was at best a misfit, at worst a dupe. His height, five feet four, possibly reflected the effects of childhood malnutrition. It was learned that, as a teenager, Nikolaev had been accepted by the Red Army for combat in the civil war, but afterward, despite his party credentials, he had failed to make a success of his vocation as a staff electrician for Leningrad's emergent subway system. In March 1934, only months before the shooting, his superiors in Leningrad's Office of Transport had censured him for rejecting a temporary assignment outside the city and had deprived him of his party membership. Evidently, it was Nikolaev's unfocused resentment that had provoked his act of violence.

Even in the first minutes after the assassination, as party officials succeeded in reviving and questioning Nikolaev, the little assassin confessed that he had attempted to waylay the party secretary on three earlier occasions. The first of these was in the previous November, at Leningrad's central railroad station as Kirov awaited his wife's return from a family visit. Yet, on that occasion, Kirov's police escort apparently was too large for Nikolaev to risk an attack, and he departed the station. Two weeks afterward, however, Nikolaev had approached the Smolny itself in search of his prey. Once again he was blocked by guards and turned back, although without being searched.[52] But on December 1, 1934,

---

52  Walter G. Krivitsky, *I Was Stalin's Agent* (London: H. Hamilton, 1940), 183.

Nikolaev returned to the Smolny for his third and final attempt. This time he was not interrogated or even detained. Indeed, most of the guards had been transferred from their routine entry posts for assignment to the lecture hall on the building's top floor, where Kirov had been scheduled to deliver his report.

After the shooting, various rumors, exaggerations, and even bald fabrications were floated to account for the success of Nikolaev's act of homicide. Among these was speculation that the guards themselves were involved: either they neglected to search Nikolaev on the latter's previous Smolny visits; or they searched him, found his pistol, but returned it to him before sending him on his way; or they supplied him with a "courtesy" diagram of the Smolny's various offices, including Kirov's. Rumors circulated, too, that Mikhail Borisov, Kirov's faithful bodyguard, had mysteriously been absent from the Smolny when the murder took place (in fact, Borisov had been detained only momentarily at the building's entrance by a petitioner who was eager to acquire a lecture ticket). Whatever the variations of these accounts, the notion that a misfit like Nikolaev would be the chosen instrument of an elaborate murder plot was initially dismissed out of hand.

Within minutes of the assassination, meanwhile, news of Kirov's death was telephoned directly to the Kremlin. When Stalin was informed, his agitated first reaction was to order his private train, the "Red Arrow," to be made ready for his immediate departure to Leningrad. His second reaction was to order the preparation of an emergency decree that mandated the trial of accused terrorists within ten days of their arrest and subsequently their immediate execution "without appeal" in the event of a guilty verdict. As the party's general secretary, Stalin evidently considered it his prerogative to draft the decree (later to be known as the "December Law") without so much as a pro forma gesture of consultation with his colleagues in the Politburo. He simply telephoned its contents directly to Genrikh Yagoda, the recently appointed commissar of the NKVD, the department of state security.

Notwithstanding the "December Law's" apparently spontaneous origin, it was under the general imprimatur of this edict, and of its series of ensuing amendments and enlargements, that a horror would be unleashed on the Soviet population that would soon rival and ultimately surpass Russia's combined human sacrifices in the World War and in the nation's ensuing civil war (p. 127).[53]

That same evening of December 1, 1934, as Stalin entrained from Moscow, he was accompanied by a 13-man escort that included Yagoda, Nikolai Yezhov,

---

53   Montefiore, *Red Tsar*, 148.

Kliment Voroshilov, Vyacheslav Molotov, Andrei Zhdanov, and Andrei Vyshinski—all senior party eminences. The group reached Leningrad early the next morning, after a 16-hour trip. At the train station, it was awaited by a delegation led by Mikhail Chudov, who had functioned as Kirov's deputy, and Filip Medved, chairman of the Leningrad NKVD branch and the official personally responsible for the security of senior party officials. When Medved extended his hand in greeting, Stalin responded by punching the man's face.[54] Driven off then to the Smolny, the visitors ensconced themselves in the late Kirov's office. There, through the morning and most of the afternoon, Stalin himself took the lead in the interrogation.

Nikolaev was the first person to be brought in. Overwhelmed by the presence of the Soviet dictator, the confused little assassin could only reply that he was unable to account for his act of violence and that the police themselves should be questioned. After some 20 minutes of futile interrogation, Nikolaev was removed from the room.[55] Next to be grilled were the late Kirov's closest associates, Chudov and Medved. Why, they were asked, had Nikolaev not been imprisoned after his previous "visits" to the Smolny? Why had he not been searched for a weapon? No satisfactory answers were forthcoming. In the end, however, the central issue reduced itself to the lack of general security the day of the murder. Why had the Smolny's guard detail been missing? Why had Mikhail Borisov, Kirov's faithful bodyguard, not been at Kirov's side? Indeed, why was Borisov not presently available for questioning? Chudov and Medved then explained that he was undergoing cross-examination specifically on these issues at Leningrad's central police headquarters. Furious, Stalin ordered the police to bring Borisov before him without delay.

The visitors waited. Almost an hour passed before a police official finally entered the murdered Kirov's office. He brought astounding news. Only a few minutes before, he reported, the security van carrying Borisov back to the Smolny from central police headquarters had suffered a "traffic accident," and Borisov had been killed. At that point Stalin had heard enough. He ordered NKVD commissar Yagoda to remain in Leningrad with Medved and the latter's associates to "clear up matters." Stalin and the rest of his entourage also remained in Leningrad, but only overnight to attend Kirov's funeral. The ceremony took place the next morning in the neoclassical grandeur of the former capital's Tauride Palace. It was attended by party and municipal dignitaries, most of them still in shock and visibly moved by the death of their colleague.

---

54 Conquest, *The Great Terror: A Reassessment*, 40.
55 Roy Medvedev, *Let History Judge: The Origins and Consequences of Stalinism* (London: Spokesman Books, 1976), 159.

In the early afternoon of that same day, December 3, Stalin and his companions entrained for Moscow to arrange a more elaborate state funeral. Kirov's body traveled on the "Red Arrow" with them. In Moscow, it was embalmed for a scheduled public viewing two days later in the Kremlin's Hall of Columns. Subsequently, on the morning of the ceremony, when Stalin himself approached the open casket, he leaned forward to kiss Kirov's cheek.

## TRIAL AND PURGATION

Six days later, the Soviet press, which had been continuously and fulsomely publishing details of the assassination, cited the contents of Stalin's peremptory "December Law" (p. 137). In retrospect, the decree should have offered the clue to its ulterior purpose. Twenty-two years later, in February 1956 and four years after Stalin's own death, that purpose was ventilated before the Twentieth Congress of the Communist Party of the Soviet Union, when Nikita Khrushchev, by then the Communist Party general secretary, launched into his celebrated denunciation of Stalin's crimes (p. 134). In the case of the Kirov assassination, Khrushchev suggested, the December Law was designed to provide cover for Stalin's ensuing and massive purge of political enemies, rightist or leftist, past or present, actual or suspected. Although hardly a credible explanation of the Kirov assassination itself, Khrushchev's analysis withstands historical scrutiny for the murder's grim aftermath.

Indeed, it was under the harsh guidelines of the "December Law" that the NKVD moved without delay against the alleged "Leningrad terrorist center." On December 28–29, 1934, besides Nikolaev himself, 13 others—mainly the "delinquent guards" at the Smolny, as well as Borisov's police escort during the latter's fatal "automobile accident"—were tried by a secret "antiterrorist" court. The subsequent published account of the trial stated only that the defendants had confessed their crime, after which they had immediately been shot. Sixty-six other suspects were rounded up within the first two weeks of Kirov's assassination, including Nikolaev's pitiable and wholly innocent wife, his divorced former wife, his brother and sister-in-law, and other relatives and close friends. Most of these also were tried, summarily found guilty, and executed. Nikolaev's distraught second wife initially was confined to an institution for the mentally ill, but, months later, she too was shot. A sister, a cousin, another sister-in-law, and Nikolaev's 64-year-old mother, a semiliterate charwoman at the Leningrad tramway depot, were given harsh prison sentences for the crime of "passive collusion."

Yet, in the end, the principal victims of the expanding dragnet of 1934–35 were neither putative renegade collaborators, nor even the hapless Nikolaev and his extended family, but the far larger backlog of Stalin's once-and-future political enemies.[56] It was on these, plainly, that the Soviet dictator had set his sights as he laid the groundwork for a general purge. As early as December 3, 1934, an official letter from the Communist Central Committee, entitled "Lessons of the Events Connected with the Evil Murder of Comrade Kirov," was dispatched to the nation's regional party committees. The document identified Nikolaev as a secret "Zinovievite" and asserted that Zinoviev himself, together with Kamenev and the exiled Trotsky, were the éminences grises behind Kirov's murder.

The following day, December 4, the Kremlin issued a further announcement stating that 119 "White reactionaries" linked with the "Trotsky-Zinoviev-Kamenev clique" had also been arrested on charges of "preparing terrorist attacks against workers of the Soviet Union" and thus were to be remanded before the Soviet Supreme Court's military collegium. The choice of venue was significant. By Soviet law, the NKVD was a branch of the military, which allowed for swift and unappealable verdicts and sentences. Shortly afterward, and each ensuing day between December 5 and December 18, the Soviet press carried detailed accounts of the trial and the speedy execution of groups of "reactionaries" and "terrorists." Except for a half-dozen prominent journalists, most of the initially accused "terrorists" were second-level bureaucratic functionaries.[57]

On December 16, however, the former party stalwarts Zinoviev and Kamenev also were taken into custody. Indignantly protesting their innocence, they were dealt with cautiously at first and even were released on December 20 for lack of evidence. But on January 15, 1935, the associate public prosecutor, Genrikh Lyushkov, announced that the government had uncovered "conclusive proof" of the "counterrevolutionary activities" of Zinoviev, Kamenev, and 17 other "Trotskyites." All 19 of the accused subsequently were rounded up, marched into court and retried on the same charge. This time the defendants obsequiously confessed and publicly repented their guilt for "antiparty activities" (although not for Kirov's murder). Thereupon, Zinoviev was promptly sentenced to a ten-year stretch in prison, Kamenev to five years, and the other defendants to various lesser terms of imprisonment.

By late spring of 1935, Stalin had placed a score of his own acolytes in the crucial party committees of Ukraine and the Transcaucasian republics, as well as in his own central secretariat. With this defense in depth, he forged on in

---

56 Merle Fainsod, *How Russia is Ruled*, 2nd ed. (Cambridge, MA: Harvard University Press, 1963), 233 *ff*.

57 Robert Conquest, *Stalin and the Kirov Murder*, 77–94 *ff*.

his "coup d'état by inches."[58] By June, over 60,000 persons had been jailed, and, within the ensuing two months, most of these were dispatched to prison or to the iniquitous "Gulag Archipelago" of Trans-Ural work camps. Their places were taken immediately by some 40,000 other defendants, who underwent the identical process of summary trial and sentence. It was only during the late summer that arrests, imprisonments, or deportations to the Gulag momentarily eased, as Stalin consolidated his political power against suspected rivals.

Unannounced in this interregnum, however, a distortion of "judicial" procedures was being formulated to cope with "future eventualities." Independent of the formality of trial, prison sentences henceforth could be lengthened if evidence were discovered of alternative or "aggravated" crimes (it was under this modification that Kamenev subsequently had his original five-year sentence extended to ten years). Then, in April, 1935, a secret memorandum was circulated among party leaders, rendering "detainees" as young as 12 subject to the identical prison terms of adults. The innovation was ingenious. In short order, by threats against their children, it was used to blackmail confessions from Stalin's potential rivals. In June, moreover, an additional supplement to the criminal law declared family members responsible for crimes ostensibly committed by their relatives, even if they themselves were demonstrably innocent. Under this provision, Kamenev's wife was exiled to a village beyond the Urals; and the sentence was increasingly applied to thousands of other "tainted" relatives.

During the mid-1930s, finally, the KGB, the Committee for State Security, was established under the de facto chairmanship of Stalin himself, with the power to investigate all party members, to "liquidate enemies of the people," and to encourage citizens into denunciations of alleged "Trotskyites" and antiparty "splitters" (p. 124). Indeed, by the second half of the decade, suspicion was growing both in the Soviet Union and among "fellow travelers" abroad that the original Communist Party of the Bolshevik Revolution in effect had become a new Communist Party.[59] The "Old Bolshevik" fraternity of Marxist idealists evidently had been supplanted in governing authority and rebranded in preemptive guilt. In its stead, behind the Kremlin walls, lurked a presence who increasingly bore less resemblance to the venerated Lenin and more to the fearsome sixteenth-century Muscovite tsar, Ivan IV. It was this foreboding transformation that soon would become the Soviet people's direst nightmare.[60]

---

58 Conquest, *The Great Terror: A Reassessment*, 62–63.
59 Albert Glotzer, *Trotsky: Memoir and Critique* (Buffalo, NY: Prometheus Books), 178.
60 Lenoe and Prozumenšikov, *The Kirov Murder and Soviet History*, 670–92.

CHAPTER FIVE

# "Richard III" in Germany

*"Let the Führer do this thing himself."*

**YOUNG ADOLF**

In January 1923, after the Weimar Republic failed to meet the schedule of reparation payments mandated by the Treaty of Versailles, the government of France responded with a simple but draconian solution. It dispatched a legion of Belgian workers into the German Ruhr to operate that great industrial zone's mills and mines under French military direction and to carry off to France the required coal, steel, and timber shipments. The fragile German economy then imploded. In the most catastrophic European inflation of contemporary history, annuities and other pensions, insurance policies, accumulated savings in cash and securities—all were transformed into worthless paper. With their disappearance, Germany's lower-middle class, traditionally a bulwark of political conservatism, was left in ruin and desperation.

Not all German grievances could be attributed to French insecurity and revanchism. Some were self-inflicted. In the immediate postwar period, the Ebert and Scheidemann cabinets, themselves Social Democratic, had moved vigorously to quash a series of neo-Communist uprisings (pp. 29–30). Yet it was also the nation's succession of Social Democratic governments that failed to move with comparable decisiveness against the German Right— against Prussian Junkers, juridical and administrative officials of the former Wilhelminian Empire, bankers, industrialists, and senior Reichswehr commanders. Awed by these prestigious icons, the nation's leftist government never quite generated the resolve to curtail Germany's interlocking estates and industrial conglomerates or to dismiss the military and civilian officials who made no secret of their nostalgia for the abdicated kaiser.

Yet the ingredients of gestating National Socialism—Nazism—traced back not only to Social Democratic political timorousness but to the *Weltanschauung* of imperial Germany. Redolent with the teutophilia of mid-nineteenth-century romanticism, glittering in the benediction of Hegel, Nietzsche, Treitschke, and others of Germany's intellectual paladins, it was an ideology that fueled Bismarck's political wizardry in building Germany's imperial *Machstaat*. Moreover, during the fin-de-siècle years, the Pan-German League, in its commitment to an expansion of the Reich as far as the driving power of its industry and army would permit, also drew extensively for its rationale from the Aryan mythology of Eugen Dühring, Hermann Ahlwardt, Houston Stewart Chamberlain, and other racial supremacists. Whatever the varied interpretations of his biographers, there is historical consensus that Adolf Hitler's life was decisively shaped by his exposure to these influences.

It was a life, however, that also was shaped by more idiosyncratic factors. Born in 1888 in Braunau, Austria, the son of a Habsburg customs official who barely managed to provide for his family, Hitler experienced a youth riddled with frustrations. He was orphaned before he finished secondary school. Although he displayed a subsequent aptitude for art, and in 1907 traveled to Vienna in hope of studying at the capital's prestigious Academy of Fine Arts, he was denied admittance. Hence, for the ensuing six years, into his early twenties, young Hitler barely subsisted in Vienna on his late parents' modest pension, together with the proceeds from watercolors he occasionally managed to sell to art dealers.[1] In 1913, he tried his fortunes in Munich, where he continued to live penuriously until the following year. But, when the World War began, exultant at the prospect of combat and conquest, Hitler

---

1  Friedrich Reck-Malleczewen, *Diary of a Man in Despair* (New York: Macmillan, 1970), 29.

chose to enlist in the more formidable German Reichswehr, an alternative permitted by the Austrian and German governments. Indeed, during his ensuing four years on the Western Front, Corporal Hitler fought bravely. On the recommendation of his company commander, Lieutenant Hugo Gutmann (a Jew), he was awarded the Iron Cross.

In the last weeks of the war, Hitler fell victim to a gas attack and was confined briefly to a military hospital. Even then, remaining in uniform for several months after the armistice and his recuperation, he managed to earn pocket money working for the Reichswehr intelligence service. Despite its shrunken postwar resources, the army high command was intent on monitoring suspect leftist and other ostensibly treasonous elements, to which it attributed the nation's recent military defeat. Hitler's assignment was to prepare an evaluation of these elements. Here it was, in his lengthy memorandum of September 1919, that Hitler's attitude toward Jews first surfaced. The Jews, he insisted, were exploiters who specialized in undermining their host nations' moral health by infecting them with a kind of racial tuberculosis. In his prognosis, Germany's solution to this putative danger was to adopt an "antisemitism of reason," a series of juridical and administrative measures designed to eliminate Jews from all levels of the nation's economic and cultural life.

Beyond his professional frustrations and his exposure to the racism of prewar Vienna, were there clues in Hitler's personal life for this sudden eruption of antisemitism?[2] His mother's physician was a Jew and was esteemed by the family. In Vienna, Jews were virtually the only art dealers who purchased the young man's watercolors and treated him with consideration. It is the consensus of his biographers that Hitler's racism initially was less sociological than sexual in origin. "For hours," he wrote in *Mein Kampf*, the testament he produced during his later imprisonment (p. 151), "the black-haired Jew-boy, diabolical joy in his face, waits in ambush for the unsuspecting blonde girl whom he defiles with his blood...."[3] Elsewhere, Hitler wrote of the "nightmare vision of the seduction of hundreds of thousands of [Aryan] girls by repulsive, crook-legged Jew-bastards."[4] Later in *Mein Kampf*, he referred to Jews as "the seducers of our people" and described the phenomenon as *"Rassenschande,"* racial shame, which he equated with venereal disease.

---

2 Howard M. Sachar, *A History of the Jews in the Modern World* (New York: Knopf, 2005), 227–28.
3 Adolf Hitler, *Mein Kampf*, trans. Ralph Manheim (Boston: Houghton Mifflin, 1943), 325.
4 Quoted in William L. Shirer, *The Rise and Fall of the Third Reich* (New York: Simon & Schuster, 2011), 26.

Plainly, the fixation with *Rassenschande* occupied a central position in Hitler's mind. Relations in his own family were so convoluted as to border on incest.[5] It was uncertain whether his mother, Klara (Alois Hitler's third wife), was her husband's second cousin or niece; but the connection was intimate enough to require an episcopal dispensation for the couple to marry. In the 1920s, a love affair evidently developed between Hitler himself, who had settled in Munich by then, and his own niece, Geli Raubal, the daughter of his half-sister Angela. The liaison ended on September 19, 1931, when Geli was found dead in Hitler's apartment, shot with his army pistol. Was it murder or suicide? In his consuming despondency, Hitler afterward forbade any mention of the incident. Before and after this event, however, it was the fear of incest, of "blood poisoning," that seemed to have obsessed him.[6]

But "sociological" factors also played an important role in shaping Hitler's views on the Jewish minority (as he acknowledged in *Mein Kampf*). During his prewar years in Vienna, he had been repelled by the city's racial diversity, and specifically by its influx of East European Jews. It enraged him that the senseless constitutionalism of the Habsburg Empire permitted these "alien" types to be classed as citizens.[7] By then, he had become familiar with the anti-Jewish populism of Vienna's former mayor, Karl Lueger, and of the racist Pan-Germanism of the political theorist Georg von Schönerer. From these early encounters, by his own account, Hitler came to regard Jews as morally and physically repugnant and as a threat specifically to German women, whom they "defiled" with their blood. "Gradually I began to hate them," he acknowledged. "I was transformed from a weakly world citizen into a fanatical anti-Semite."[8]

It was after the war, subsisting as a Reichswehr informer in Munich, that Hitler came across an assortment of political eccentrics that piqued his interest. Consisting of several dozen beer drinkers, the clique first dubbed itself the German Labor Party. Its leaders, Anton Drexler, a lumberjack, and Gottfried Feder, a machinist, both early members of the racist Thule Society (p. 25), had come up with a populist, non-Marxist version of socialism that they apparently had borrowed from Karl Lueger's Christian Social Party. Hitler was particularly struck with their distinction between *"raffendes"* (predatory) capitalism, which was "Jewish," and *"schaffendes"* (creative, useful) capitalism,

---

5 Joachim C. Fest, *Hitler* (New York: Harcourt Brace Jovanovich, 1974), 27.

6 Hans Frank, *Im Angesicht des Galgens: Deutung Hitlers und seiner Zeit auf Grund eigener Erlebnisse und Erkenntnisse*, 2nd ed. (Neuhaus: Eigenverlag Brigitte Frank, 1955), 58.

7 Hitler, *Mein Kampf*, 55.

8 Hitler, *Mein Kampf*, 56.

which was "German and Christian."[9] Intrigued, he joined the group as the seventh member of its incipient executive committee.

Brimming with enthusiasm and indignation, surprising his colleagues and even himself with his newfound talent for oratory, Hitler managed in short order to co-opt the circle's leadership from Drexler and Feder.[10] It was he, personally, who also changed its title to the "National Socialist German Workers' Party" and broadened its program to include revision of the hated "*Diktat*" of Versailles. Within a month, adopting a legendary Indo-European ("Aryan") swastika as the party's insignia, he succeeded in propelling the "Nazi" membership to approximately 2,000.[11] In the spring of 1920, finally, Hitler left his army employment to work full time for the party, receiving his first marginal salary and paying his room rent from its dues.

## FROM FRINGE PARTY TO NATIONAL VISIBILITY

From the outset of his Nazi leadership, Hitler encouraged his colleagues to adopt the tactics of "visibility," by engaging in demonstrations, marches, street oratory, brawls, and even riots. These methods actually had not worked well for other extremist cabals. In March 1920, several hundred rightist militants, fronted by Dr. Wolfgang Kapp, a former mid-level civil servant in Germany's defunct imperial government, had seized control of the chancellery building in Berlin and proclaimed themselves Germany's new, "patriotic" government (p. 29). But without meaningful popular support, Kapp's effort soon was paralyzed by mass labor strikes. It collapsed within a week. In Bavaria, however, political circumstances were more hospitable to extremist movements. Exploiting this predominantly Catholic *Land*'s former history as an independent kingdom, as well as its citizens' disillusionment after their brief postwar exposure to a succession of leftist governments (pp. 22–28), a miscellany of rightist malcontents from all corners of the Weimar Republic began to gravitate to Bavaria's provincial militia and its private armies. There they flourished under the benevolent toleration of the *Land* administration. Indeed, by 1920–21, Bavaria's minister-president, Gustav von Kahr, had turned his province into a veritable Cave of Adullam for some 15 right-wing juntas and leagues that had set up shop there from elsewhere in Germany.[12]

---

9  Albrecht Tyrell, "Gottfried Feder and the NSDAP," in *The Shaping of the Nazi State*, ed. Peter D. Stachura (London: Taylor & Francis, 1978), 48–87, see pp. 54–55.
10  Hitler, *Mein Kampf*, 235, 390.
11  Fest, *Hitler*, 10–11.
12  Albrecht Tyrell, *Von "Trommler" zum "Führer"* (Munich: W. Fink, 1975), 191.

Salient among these was the Bavarian branch of the Freikorps, the citizens' voluntary corps that had been organized early in 1919 by a much-decorated Reichswehr veteran, Colonel Franz von Epp. Swelling within months to some 250,000 men, this intimidating militia played a central role in the Weimar Republic's success in crushing Bavaria's neo-Bolshevik regime (p. 28). Although the Freikorps eventually was dissolved under Allied pressure, a network of smaller but even more sinister paramilitary factions survived and thrived in the province. Overwhelmingly Reichswehr veterans from throughout Germany, many of their members yearned for the resuscitation of the defunct Wilhelminian Empire, and virtually all of them shared an intense anti-Marxism and antisemitism. The most prominent of these offshoots, "Organization Consul," led by Hermann Ehrhardt, an ex-Reichswehr captain and recent Freikorps militant, helped inspire the assassination both of Matthias Erzberger and of Foreign Minister Walther Rathenau. It was Ehrhardt, too, with another army veteran, Ernst Röhm, who was shortly to play a leading role in establishing the Nazis' own paramilitary organization, the Sturm Abteilung, a legion of brown-shirted "storm troopers."[13]

Adolf Hitler was among those who initially shared in the secret benediction of Gustav von Kahr. Although the latter's term of office as minister president had expired in 1921, in subsequent months, he continued to occupy the influential cabinet post of "security commissioner." It was in this latter capacity that he received Hitler personally on several occasions and adopted a forbearing attitude to Nazi defamations and demonstrations. Indeed, Kahr arranged for the appointment of Nazis to key roles in Bavaria's provincial administration, including that of Munich police chief. The previous year, in December 1920, the Nazis' emergence as primus inter pares among southern Germany's nationalist cabals was further strengthened by their purchase of the *Völkischer Beobachter*, a racist, nationalist semiweekly. Its editor, Dietrich Eckart, a poetaster-dramatist, virulent antisemite, and Hitler's mentor in personal manners and proper wardrobe, had borrowed the journal's 60,000-mark purchase price from his contacts among Germany's moneyed circles.[14] Within a year and a half, overflowing with sensationalist anti-Weimar "revelations" and antisemitic editorials, Eckart's tabloid-style

---

13  Wolfgang Sauer, "Die Mobilmachung des Gewalt," in *Die nationalsozialistische Machtergreifung: Studien zur Errichtung des totalitären Herrschaftssystems in Deutschland 1933/34*, ed. Karl Dietrich Bracher, Wolfgang Sauer, and Gerhard Schulz, 2nd ed. (Cologne: Westdeutscher Verlag, 1962), 831.

14  Tyrell, *Von "Trommler,"* 23, 194.

screed morphed into a daily newspaper that appeared in scores of Munich's street-corner kiosks.[15]

Yet the earliest stimulus for the Nazi Party could be traced neither to these organizational innovations nor even to Hitler's frenzied nationalist oratory and incendiary antisemitism. It was to all of these factors, operating in tandem with popular resentment of the Versailles *"Diktat"* that had amputated the Polish Corridor and imposed a grillwork of economic reparations on Germany, and to the French occupation of the Ruhr in 1923 and its accompanying lethal inflation. The nation's collective despair and hatred, in turn, were directed against the "predators of Versailles," against the "November criminals" who had "stabbed the nation in the back," and against those perennial bêtes noires, the Jews, who were "sucking the blood" of Germany's economy and "polluting" its Aryan bloodstream.[16] Finally, among all the nation's demagogues, it was Adolf Hitler, in his tortured genius, who articulated these multiple grievances more imaginatively, even hypnotically, than any of his contemporaries (p. 141).[17] By 1923, under his leadership, the Nazis had developed into a formidable avant-garde among Germany's radical nationalists. Its party treasury had grown to 173,000 gold marks.[18]

Not least of all, the Nazis had managed to enroll into their brown-shirted *Sturm Abteilung* some 35,000 men, almost half of them operating in Bavaria alone. These storm troopers in fact had become almost as numerous as the entire Bavarian police force, and even surpassed the modest Reichswehr units still billeted in southern Germany.[19] Moreover, the "SA" operated under a leader, Ernst Röhm, who functioned initially as Hitler's virtual alter ego. The son of a Munich family of veteran civil servants, Röhm had served as a Reichswehr noncommissioned officer during the war, where he proved himself a flamboyant daredevil in combat. Decorated for gallantry, he rose quickly to the rank of captain, and, toward the end of the war, he was promoted to the General Staff's military intelligence branch.[20] The stocky and florid Röhm hardly resembled the "Aryan" prototype of military hero. Although evincing few inhibitions about sparing the lives of his men, he demonstrated still less in inviting handsome young recruits to his

---

15 Dietrich Orlow, *History of the Nazi Party, 1919–1933* (Pittsburgh: University of Pittsburgh Press, 1969), 22.
16 Ian Kershaw, *Hitler* (New York: W.W. Norton, 1999–2001), 1: 154.
17 Kershaw, *Hitler*, 1: 149–53.
18 Fest, *Hitler*, 162; Orlow, *History of the Nazi Party*, 108 *ff*.
19 Sauer, "Die Mobilmachung," 831.
20 Ernst Röhm, *Die Geschichte eines Hochverräters* (Munich: F. Eher Nachf, 1934), 13–14.

bed. Yet Röhm had influential connections and knew how to exploit them. In the postwar years, as one of the first veterans to attend a meeting of the Nazi Party under Hitler's chairmanship, he was immediately impressed by the young Austrian agitator's racist-nationalist oratory. Joining the party himself, then, he subsequently made it his business to provide Hitler with contacts to politicians and military commanders, and to whatever armaments he could inveigle from his Reichswehr colleagues (in the process, acquiring a sobriquet within the Nazi Party as the "machine-gun king").[21]

During the autumn of 1923, moreover, Bavaria's Security Commissioner Kahr had intimated through Röhm that, if the Nazis wished to take the first step of mounting a *putsch*—an overthrow—of the Weimar government, he personally would cooperate on behalf of the Bavarian cabinet.[22] Hitler reacted enthusiastically to the hint. With Röhm, he suspected that General Otto von Lossow, who commanded the scattering of Reichswehr units in Bavaria, might be tempted to preempt leadership of an uprising if the Nazis did not move first. Accordingly, in the late afternoon of November 8, 1923, Hitler led his retinue of intimates, including Röhm and a dozen other storm troopers, into the Bürgerbräukeller, a Munich beer hall known to be favored by chauvinist rowdies. Jumping onto a table, melodramatically firing a pistol bullet into the ceiling, he announced to the startled customers that "the national revolution has begun."[23] Moments later, Hitler and his SA entourage exited the hall and proceeded directly to Gustav von Kahr's private residence.

This time, the security commissioner received Hitler and Röhm coldly. Offended at being confronted in his own home without prior appointment, he was not inclined at first to be chivvied into precipitous action. In mid-discussion, however, the three men were unexpectedly joined by the renowned General Erich Ludendorff, who assured Kahr that he too was prepared to march shoulder to shoulder with Hitler and Röhm.[24] Thus, after almost an hour of vigorous discussion, Kahr seemingly was won over and agreed not to obstruct the planned insurrection. The Nazi leaders then departed to make their preparations. But, shortly afterward, Kahr was summoned to an emergency meeting with Bavaria's current minister president, Eugen von Knilling (who had succeeded Kahr in that office), and a nucleus

---

21 Peter Longerich, *Die braunen Bataillone: Geschichte der SA* (Munich: Beck, 1989), 15–22.
22 Harold J. Gordon, *Hitler and the Beer Hall Putsch* (Princeton, NJ: Princeton University Press, 1972), 242–56.
23 Georg Franz-Willig, *Putsch und Verbotszeit der Hitlerbewegung, November 1923–Februar 1925* (Oldendorf: K.W. Schütz, 1977), 78, 79.
24 Fest, *Hitler*, 184–85.

of other cabinet colleagues. When Kahr apprized them of the impending Nazi putsch, he encountered strenuous objections. In a second meeting later the same night with General Lossow and a gathering of senior officers of the Reichswehr's Bavarian detachments, Kahr was taken aback by their contempt for Hitler and their outright refusal to serve under him. Losing his nerve, the security commissioner then retracted his earlier support for the uprising and proclaimed the Nazi Party "officially" dissolved.

Unaware, however, of this disavowal, Hitler, Röhm, and Ludendorff continued over the ensuing two days to mobilize their followers in anticipation of the "great march on Berlin." Joined by Anton Drexler and some 300 other Brownshirts, the procession then launched itself through Munich's central boulevards with the initial objective of "reclaiming" Bavaria's state offices. En route, the marchers suddenly were confronted by a phalanx of rifle-bearing police. Ludendorff continued imperturbably ahead. In turn, the confused police broke ranks to let the venerated general proceed with his companions. Minutes later, arriving at the city's Isar River bridge, Hitler, Ludendorff, and Röhm once again made a bombastic show of rallying their growing throng of storm troopers and accompanying followers. But this time they were met by a police fusillade, and in the exchange of volleys 14 of the marchers and four policemen were killed.[25]

It was only then that the rest of the Brownshirts, jettisoning their weapons, disbanded and scattered. Ludendorff surrendered immediately to the police, although later he was released upon giving "his word as an officer" to make himself available to the authorities. Röhm and Drexler also were arrested. Hitler, fleeing around a street corner, tripped and fell, dislocating his shoulder. At almost the same moment, however, he was bundled into an automobile driven by a fellow party member, who sped him to the suburban home of a friend and Nazi supporter, Ernst ("Putzi") Hanfstängl. But the refuge was brief. Two days later, Hitler was tracked down and arrested. In short order, he was carted off to Munich's Landsberg prison, where Röhm, Drexler, and seven others of the Nazi inner circle had preceded him in confinement.[26]

## CONVALESCENCE AND TRANSFORMATION

In prison, 10 of the 11 leading putsch conspirators waited nearly four months, until February 24, 1924, before their treason trial began at the Munich central courts building. The prosecution treaded with circumspection,

---

25  Franz-Willig, *Putsch und Verbotszeit*, 116.
26  Kershaw, *Hitler*, 1: 204–11.

especially with Ludendorff. The famed general had been driven in a private limousine to the courtroom, and there he was summarily exonerated by the reverential three-judge panel. Röhm was pronounced guilty, discharged from the Reichswehr, but also let off from additional imprisonment beyond the four months he already had served. Although most of the other defendants were summarily convicted, they, too, with the exceptions of Anton Drexler and Rudolf Hess (pp. 26, 146), were released on probation.

It was Hitler himself who disdained to plead his innocence. Taking the witness stand in his business suit, wearing his Iron Cross, he defiantly acknowledged his leadership role in the insurrection, and then declaimed on his favored theme: "There can be no question of treason in an action that aims to undo the November 1918 betrayal of this country."[27]

For four hours, rarely interrupted by prosecution or judges, Hitler in effect put the Weimar Republic on trial, prophesying its ultimate demise and a Nazi victory both in politics and history. The performance left even the chief prosecutor impressed. In his summation afterward, the latter benevolently observed that

> [Herr Hitler] is a highly gifted man, who has risen from humble beginnings to achieve a respected position in public life, the result of much hard work and dedication. He has devoted himself to the ideas he cherishes, to the point of self-sacrifice. As a soldier he did his duty to the utmost. He cannot be accused of having used [his] position ... in any self-serving way.[28]

In his refusal to plead his innocence, however, there was seemingly no juridical loophole for Hitler to avoid prison time. The panel of judges resignedly sentenced him to a five-year stint—but then left him eligible for parole after six months. As he exited the courthouse under guard, an awaiting crowd greeted him with cheers and flowers.

In Landsberg prison, Hitler then spent the next six months as he had spent the first four. Regarded as something of a hero equally by fellow inmates and guards, he was treated less as a convict than as a guest. After being assigned a spacious "VIP" cell, he was permitted to receive visitors (Ludendorff among them) for up to six hours a day.[29] In Landsberg, too, he found time to dictate his autobiographical and political testament, *Mein Kampf*, to Rudolf Hess,

---

27 Ernst Deuerlein, *Der Hitler-Putsch* (Stuttgart: Deutsche Verlags-Anstalt, 1962), 216.
28 Fest, *Hitler*, 192.
29 Ernst Hanfstängl, *15 Jahr mit Hitler: Zwischen Weissem und Braunem Haus* (Munich: Zürich Piper, 1980), 342.

a fellow Nazi prisoner and Hitler's rapt soul mate. It was in the pages of *Mein Kampf*, brimming with ferocious revanchism and even more sulfurous antisemitism, that Hitler offered a telling insight into his future political strategy. Far better to march "with the bayonets," he acknowledged, "than against them."[30] From then on, he asserted, he would abandon the strategy of armed revolution. The road to governing authority would run through the German electorate.

Hitler was paroled in December 1924. This time, however, as he departed Landsberg, only a dozen friends and followers were on hand to greet him and escort him to his spartan Munich apartment. For all his grandiose perorations in court and prison, the young Austrian's political future seemed foreclosed. Germany by then was returning to a shaky economic recovery, Allied reparations were being scaled down, factional extremism apparently was being consigned to the political wings. In Bavaria alone, during the previous six months, racist-nationalist splinter groups had lost nearly 70 per cent of their following, and the Nazi Party itself had virtually disintegrated, its members scattered, its offices and newspaper either banned or in financial arrears. Even the rowdy Sturm Abteilung units managed to stay afloat essentially in the guise of "sports" and "glee" clubs. Although the former Nazi stalwarts—Ernst Röhm, Alfred Rosenberg, Paul Joseph Goebbels, Julius Streicher, and Gregor and Otto Strasser (pp. 154–55)—succeeded in organizing a "National Socialist Freedom Party" as a front organization for a variety of nationalist-rightist factions, they displayed no apparent interest in restoring their former leader to the prominence he had won during the trial.

Hitler bided his time. He anticipated that these factions soon would be squabbling among themselves. On February 27, after letting two months go by, he scheduled his first post-imprisonment appearance at a Munich beer hall. Yet, with the notable exceptions of Hess and a former air force ace, Hermann Göring, most of his early followers shunned the meeting. Even Ernst Röhm, the Sturm Abteilung commander, who alone of the Nazi inner circle had been on an intimate, first-name basis with Hitler, remained hesitant to return to the party. Cashiered from the Reichswehr for his role in the Munich fiasco and lacking funds, he was obliged to rethink his old army connections. In fact, Hitler too was cautious about resuming their earlier friendship. He suspected that Röhm had always harbored the ambition to remake his SA paramilitaries into an "auxiliary army," a fighting force that would operate independently of the Nazi Party. Hitler had dismissed the notion as sheer fantasy. Better than a brawler

---

30  Hitler, *Mein Kampf*, 212.

like Röhm, he had learned from his abortive putsch attempt that a majority of Reichswehr officers sustained an abiding respect for their military oaths. They would not roll over for the SA. Indeed, a time might come when Hitler himself would need the Reichswehr's cooperation and military expertise.[31]

Provisionally, however, in April 1925, Hitler and Röhm agreed to a "reconciliation" meeting. Hitler had not forgotten all that he owed to Röhm in fund-raising, access to Reichswehr weaponry, and new members. Röhm, on the other hand, while still proclaiming his friendship for Hitler, revealed himself in the conference as stubborn and still unwilling to fit into the more "respectable" political structure Hitler had in mind. When he insisted on commanding a Sturm Abteilung that would be divorced from all Nazi political activity, it was Hitler who bridled. The two men soon reached an impasse.[32] Röhm then cut the conversation short. The following day, in a note to Hitler, he formally resigned both his Nazi Party membership and his leadership of the Sturm Abteilung. Two months later, he accepted an invitation to act as military advisor to the Bolivian army.[33] Hitler, in turn, let a year pass before he ventured to appoint a new SA leader. His choice this time was Captain Franz Pfeffer von Salomon, a presumed nonentity, who seemed willing to accept Hitler's redefinition of the force's role as essentially one of party propaganda, youth indoctrination, mass parades, and street brawling.

There were other issues that Hitler had to address. Even before the putsch debacle of November 8–9, 1923, Nazism had failed to take root in northern Germany, which had always distrusted the movement as a revival of Bavarian separatism. Originally, Gregor Strasser had functioned as Hitler's emissary in the north. A decorated Reichswehr veteran, Strasser had joined the Nazis in 1920. He too had participated in the 1923 insurrection and had served a few weeks of internment in Landsberg. He was shortly released, however, after being elected to the Bavarian Landtag. Afterward, Strasser's personal faction, the "National Socialist Freedom Party," with its populist and racist agenda, became something of a force in Germany. In the 1924 Reichstag elections, the party won close to 2 million votes and obtained 32 seats. Thus, when Hitler was released from prison, Strasser at first was unenthusiastic about accepting him again as senior spokesman of the Far Right. It was only in the autumn of 1925, when Hitler offered to appoint him party gauleiter for northern Germany, that Strasser was persuaded to rejoin

---

31 Sauer, "Die Mobilmachung," 836–37.
32 Hanfstängl, 15 Jahr, 342.
33 Röhm, Die Geschichte, 357–64.

the Nazis. Subsequently, from his Berlin headquarters, he worked in tandem with his brother, Otto, and with Alfred Rosenberg and Josef Goebbels, who coedited the *Völkischer Beobachter*, the party newspaper.

The Strassers and Rosenberg, however, had belonged to the left wing of the National Socialist German Workers' Party, and they continued to espouse its original populist, anticapitalist orientation. But, for Hitler, the stance had become increasingly counterproductive. During the months of his Landsberg detention, he had made up his mind to woo the capitalist Right, whose funds he regarded as indispensable.[34] Hence, by flattery and successive promotions, Hitler eventually convinced Goebbels to relinquish his neo-socialism in favor of single-minded nationalism, undiluted by any variety of Marxist ideology.[35] The Strasser brothers, too, apparently fell into line.[36] In late 1925, at a Nazi conference at Bamberg that was packed with Hitler appointees, the assembled delegates agreed to concentrate all their energies on propaganda and an increased party membership. Most important, they agreed to accept Hitler as their one and only *Führer*. Hence, from the Bamberg conference on, the rank and file assumed that there would be no further internecine battles over ideological principles.

Yet for all his dependence on the Strassers' organizational talents, Hitler continued to regard the brothers warily. His suspicions were well founded. In the late 1920s, with increasing disregard of their Bamberg pledge, both Gregor and Otto had resumed preaching their version of crude anticapitalism, with its envisaged nationalization of heavy industry. A new confrontation apparently was inevitable, for, by then, Hitler had won the tentative political support of such heavyweight industrialists as Alfred Hugenberg, Fritz Thyssen, Wilhelm Frick, Emil Kirdorf, Alfried Krupp von Bohlen, and even Hjalmar Schacht, president of the Reichsbank. The financial resources available to these men far surpassed the entirety of the dues paid by Nazi Party members.[37]

Thus, by 1930, as the Strassers resumed and increased their tycoon baiting, Hitler's patience ran out. On May 31 of that year, flanked by his dependable lieutenant and former prison mate Rudolf Hess, he summoned Gregor

---

34 Orlow, *History of the Nazi Party*, 173.
35 Joseph Goebbels, *Das Tagebuch von Joseph Goebbels, 1925/26*, Schriftenreihe der Vierteljahrshefte für Zeitgeschichte No. 1, ed. Helmut Heiber (Stuttgart: Deutsche Verlags-Anstalt, 1960), 92.
36 Otto Strasser, *Hitler und Ich* (Konstanz: J. Asmus, 1948), 113.
37 George W.F. Hallgarten, *Hitler, Reichswehr, und Industrie* (Frankfurt am Main: Europäische Verlagsanstalt, 1955), 130; see also Henry A. Turner, *German Big Business and the Rise of Hitler* (New York: Oxford University Press, 1985), 217–19.

Strasser to his private Berlin office in the Hotel Sanssouci. Strasser brought with him his uninvited brother, Otto. The four men argued heatedly. Hitler, berating the Strassers for placing their ideological program above his, "the Führer's," warned that he was not going to allow the whole party organization "to be destroyed by a few megalomaniac scriveners." The argument continued intermittently for seven hours, with both sides holding their ground.[38]

Hitler returned then to Munich. For several weeks he and the Strassers kept their peace. But in mid-June, Otto Strasser circulated a pamphlet among the party membership accusing Hitler of betraying the socialist ideal that was "at the heart of our common cause." This time Hitler moved decisively. He ordered Goebbels to expel Otto Strasser and the latter's followers from the party, "an organization which was not created for the doctrinaire games of political boy scouts, but . . . for a future Germany in which the concepts of class [differences] will have been eradicated."[39] On June 30, Goebbels dutifully assembled a meeting of Nazi leaders in Berlin. Alerted in advance, Strasser and his cohorts also turned up. But when they ventured to protest Hitler's "despotism," a group of Sturm Abteilung leaders forcibly ejected them from the hall. Several months later, Otto Strasser embarked on an attempt to form a "truly national" socialist movement, a separatist "Union of Revolutionary National Socialists." The experiment failed. In the Reichstag elections of September 1930, the "Union" did not win a single seat. Shortly afterward, Strasser left Germany for self-imposed exile in Czechoslovakia. At first, Gregor Strasser circumspectly disassociated himself from his brother's views, as did other prominent members of the party's left wing. But two years later, in December 1932, isolated and shunned by his suspicious colleagues, Gregor Strasser also tendered his resignation.[40]

## A PACT WITH THE DEVIL

As late as 1928, in any event, issues of Nazi ideology seemed increasingly irrelevant. The party by then was struggling to survive as a factor even in Germany's right-wing politics. Although it managed that year to achieve a membership of some 150,000 (drawing mainly from lower white-collar elements, artisans, and a minority of farm groups), its popularity apparently had reached its plateau. The raging German inflation of 1923–24 had been checked, the 1924 American-sponsored "Dawes Plan" had modified German

---

38 Reinhard Kühnl, *Die nationalsozialistische Linke, 1925–1930* (Meisenheim: A. Hain, 1966), 374.
39 Kühnl, *Die nationalsozialistische*, 374.
40 Martyn Housden, *Hitler: Profile of a Dictator* (New York: Routledge, 2001), 23.

reparations obligations, and the 1925 Stresemann-Briand nonaggression pact at Locarno (p. 346) evidently had opened a new era of Franco-German reconciliation. With a modest economic recovery under way and with industrial production by 1928 actually surpassing its prewar level, people were at work again, sitting in beer gardens on weekends, indulging themselves in family vacations. In the May 1928 Reichstag elections, the Nazis won a pitiable 2.6 per cent of the vote and seated only 12 deputies. Hitler himself, still lacking German citizenship, was not among them.

The turning point of the Nazi revival, as for that of the Communists, awaited the onset of the Great Depression, an economic catastrophe that affected Germany almost immediately. Between 1929 and 1932, unemployment in this nation of 53 million rose from some 2 million to over 9 million. It was not long before the country's political profile reflected its economic distention. For the first time, the Nazis began competing not only among industrial tycoons and lower-middle-class elements but among a significant minority of unemployed factory workers. Nazi storm troopers and Communist "enforcers" alike quickened the pace of their street brawls.[41] Between 1930 and 1932, Germany's courts were heavily backlogged with cases of civil disorder and incitement.[42] By then, too, the omens of Nazi resurgence were unmistakable. In the Reichstag election campaign of 1930, as Hitler and Goebbels jointly orchestrated the party's torchlight parades and pageantry, replete with military bands and uniformed, truncheon-bearing legions of storm troopers, their effort to mobilize the nation's wounded chauvinism did not go unrewarded. The Nazis won 107 seats in the Reichstag and transformed themselves almost overnight into Germany's third-largest party.

During 1932 alone, three additional public elections followed, two of them for president, one for a new Reichstag. Back in 1925, Field Marshal Paul von Hindenburg, as a candidate of the *Reichsbloc* coalition of nationalist parties, had been elected the nation's president upon the death of Friedrich Ebert (p. 11). But now, in March 1932, in Hindenburg's re-election campaign, Hitler himself had the temerity to challenge the revered field marshal for the presidential office. As anticipated, Hindenburg achieved his required plurality. Yet Hitler polled an astonishing 10.3 million votes and thereby forced a second, run-off election the following month. Here he accumulated over 13 million votes. Although Hindenburg managed this time to secure victory by an impressive 20 percentage-point margin, he accomplished the feat only with the last-minute support of the Democrats

---

41 Fest, *Hitler*, 272.
42 Frank, *Im Angesicht des Galgens*, 58.

and Centrists, who viewed the old Reichswehr commander as the lesser of political evils.

But finally, in the Reichstag election of July 1932, the Nazis garnered 12.7 million votes and 230 seats, the largest plurality won by any single party in the brief history of the Weimar Republic. During the campaigning, Hindenburg had been obliged to use his presidential, emergency-decree powers in an effort to ban the SA from its truculent intimidation or even from wearing its brown-shirted uniforms. By then, however, it was clear to the venerable president and his austere circle of Reichswehr intimates that "constitutional" measures alone could not indefinitely keep the Nazis from assuming executive power. Hitler's rabble-rousing coterie had to be kept from office at any cost and by any means.

Here it was that the intercession of General Kurt von Schleicher proved crucial. Serving as Hindenburg's minister of "defense information"—in effect, as the president's liaison with the Reichswehr—Schleicher came up with the brainstorm of appointing Franz von Papen as "interim" chancellor. As a minor Catholic aristocrat who functioned as leader of the Catholic Center Party's right wing, Papen as titular head of a "cabinet of barons" would serve in effect as a presidential puppet, and thus as a stopgap against a Nazi incumbency. Hindenburg accepted the idea. Would Hitler? After intensive consultations with Göring, Hess, and others of the Nazi inner circle, Hitler gave his unenthusiastic approval, and Papen consequently was able to assume the chancellorship on June 2, 1932.

In fact, the Nazi leader's approval was linked to a hard bargain, one that ultimately would outflank even the devious General Schleicher. It was for the government to lift the ban against Sturm Abteilung public activity. Upon discussing the proposal with Schleicher and Papen, Hindenburg reluctantly acquiesced. The concession almost immediately turned out to be political suicide for the nation's "respectable" rightists. From the moment the ban was lifted, on June 16, 1932, civil chaos resumed, then escalated into wild public clashes between SA Brownshirts and blue-collar Communist loyalists. By mid-July, nearly a hundred persons had been killed and more than a thousand seriously injured in street brawls and armed ambushes. The rule of law, and hence the credibility of the Weimar Republic itself, plainly was crumbling.

If evidence of the republic's fragility still was needed, it was produced by another legislative standoff, and hence by another Reichstag election, on July 31, 1932. Again, the exhausted democratic parties still could rely on considerable public support and their hairline majority; but the Nazis retained their previous intimidating control of 230 seats. Indeed, the Nazis and Communists had a cumulative majority of 53 per cent of the Reichstag membership. If the seats of the Nazis and the German National People's Party and the Center Party were counted together (a much more likely voting pattern) that figure rose to 56 per cent. Although Papen managed to retain his shaky chancellorship, Hitler by then was convinced that his Nazis held the balance of political power. Accordingly, on August 5, he met with General Schleicher, the president's liaison, and demanded that Hindenburg forthwith appoint him, Hitler, to the chancellorship and transfer to him the presidential power to rule by emergency decree. Upon hearing of the demand, Hindenburg was appalled. "That man for chancellor?" he spluttered. "Why, I'll appoint him a village postmaster, and then he can lick my ass on postage stamps for the rest of his days."[43] Even after nearly a week of pressure, the most the old president was persuaded to offer the Nazis was a vice-chancellorship in the current Papen government. Hitler instantly and contemptuously rejected the proposal.[44]

Nevertheless, Papen's own tenure as chancellor was functioning on borrowed time. His aristocratic pretensions and ineffectuality in decision making were beginning to exasperate his rightist coalition partners, and in September 1932 he was denied a Reichstag vote of confidence. A new election then had to be scheduled for early November—the fourth within the space of one year! As the fatigued German voting public geared up for still another contest, Hitler once again gave free rein to a renewed storm-trooper onslaught. This time, however, when the ballots were counted on the evening of November 6, it developed that the Nazis had suffered a percentage drop from 37.4 to 33.1. The law-abiding German voting public evidently had been repelled by SA brutality. Hitler had overplayed his hand. Moreover, in the resultant electoral deadlock, President Hindenburg seized the opportunity to appoint his personal éminence grise, the wily Schleicher, as "transitional" chancellor, with a mandate to solve the government crisis at least for the nearer future.

In tandem with Papen and his heterogeneity of rightist supporters, Schleicher then spent the ensuing three weeks patching together a coalition. Ironically, his scheme this time was to let Hitler occupy the post of chancellor but to surround him with a cabinet of conservatives from the Center Party and the German National People's Party (DNVP), including Papen himself, who would be relegated to the vice-chancellorship. Besides Hitler, only two

---

43  Ernst von Weizsäcker, *Erinnerungen* (Munich: Paul List, 1950), 103.
44  Weizsäcker, *Erinnerungen*, 105.

Nazis would be awarded ministerial portfolios: Wilhelm Frick, as minister of the interior, and Hermann Göring, as deputy minister president and Prussian minister of the interior. In this fashion, Schleicher and Papen expected to neutralize Hitler's influence, to engineer his eventual resignation, and thereby to eradicate for good and always the threat of a Nazi accession.

When the formula was brought to Hindenburg, the old president mulled it over. At last, with infinite reluctance, he gave his approval. Schleicher then approached Hitler with his scheme. This time the Nazi leader cautiously explored the idea with his party colleagues. Their initial reaction was negative. On January 26, 1933, however, after almost a month of protracted and frequently heated discussions, Hitler and his "shadow cabinet" decided after all, and with infinite lack of enthusiasm, to accept the offer as a "foot in the door." The decision was relayed to Schleicher and Hindenburg. Four days later, on January 30, the president officially appointed Hitler chancellor of a Nazi-Nationalist coalition government. That same evening, as thousands of torch-bearing SA Brownshirts marched exultantly along the Wilhelmstrasse, Adolf Hitler as Germany's new chancellor bowed for hours from a makeshift ceremonial balcony in the foreign ministry building. The "respectable" conservative politicians who had engineered his appointment remained largely unfazed. They were confident that they had brought a puppet to office.

At least one governmental eminence disagreed. On January 29, the eve of Hitler's investiture in office, the 85-year-old President Hindenburg roused himself from his senescence to observe bitterly to his outgoing "transitional" chancellor: "Schleicher, I solemnly prophecy that this accursed man [Hitler] will cast our nation into the abyss and bring [it] to inconceivable misery. Future generations will damn you in your grave for what you have done."[45]

### "A SIGN FROM HEAVEN"

Actually, Hitler himself was not yet confirmed in more than a precarious interim chancellorship. His ultimate benediction would have to await still another Reichstag election, this one scheduled for March 6, 1933. It was his conjecture that, if successful in his remaining five-week electoral campaign, he could manage to win a decisive, "functional" majority for his party. In embarking on the effort, moreover, the Nazi leader relied on the active support of Hermann Göring. In his own new role as Prussian minister of the interior,

---

45 Quoted in Kershaw, *Hitler*, 1: 427.

Göring imaginatively augmented his *Land* police force with SA "auxiliaries" and subsequently orchestrated the latter's reign of intensified terror against Communist and Social Democratic Party offices and public meetings. At the same time, Göring's thinly veiled threats against German business leaders elicited their "insurance" donations for Hitler's political campaign.

Then, on February 27, 1933, less than a week before the elections, there came a "sign from heaven" (as Göring himself described it). A wing of the Reichstag building mysteriously went up in flames. Despite the best efforts of Berlin's fire department, by nightfall much of the old building was reduced to a smoldering husk. It appeared later that the fire had been deliberately set. The arsonist was identified as one Marinus van der Lubbe, a mentally disturbed Dutch teenager. He had acted for no discernable political reason, although possibly with secret Nazi encouragement.[46]

Hitler, in any case, was determined to make political capital of the event. In a radio broadcast that same afternoon, the new chancellor announced to a confused and frightened nation that the police were in possession of "evidence" that the Communists had set the Reichstag ablaze as an opening move to "overthrow the government." Subsequently, at Hitler's urgent request, President Hindenburg agreed to issue yet another series of emergency decrees restricting freedom of speech, press, and assembly for six months if the crisis still continued. Entirely unofficially, however, SA Brownshirts were allowed to intensify their rampage of mayhem and terrorization. Again at Göring's initiative, some 25,000 Communists and Social Democratic Party members in Prussia alone were jailed in makeshift "holding pens."

Remarkably, in the ensuing March 6 Reichstag elections, the Communists still managed to win 81 seats and the Social Democrats fully 120 seats. This time, however, under Hitler's and Göring's "interpretation" of the emergency decrees, the Communists were denied access to their seats.[47] As a result, the Nazis and their coalition "partners" between them obtained a "working" legislative majority of 288 deputies. Indeed, for Hitler, the "partnership" was a mere technicality. Disdaining interparty consultations, he ordered swastika-adorned flags to be raised on government buildings, and then launched into a purge of his remaining political opponents. Everywhere the SA functioned as his vanguard, marching raucously through Berlin's central boulevards, besieging ministerial offices, coercing the resignation of mayors, police

---

46 Kershaw, *Hitler*, 1: 457–58.
47 Hans Mommsen, "The Reichstag Fire and Its Political Consequences," in *Republic to Reich: The Making of the Nazi Revolution*, ed. Hajo Holborn (New York: Pantheon Books, 1972), 129–222, see 129 *ff*.

commissioners, even entire provincial administrations, and replacing them with Nazi Party members.

Meanwhile, Joseph Goebbels, soon to be appointed Hitler's minister of "public enlightenment," brilliantly organized the pageantry for the installation of the Nazi-dominated government. The ceremonies began on the morning of March 23, 1933, with solemn state ceremonies at the Potsdam Garrison Church. President Hindenburg and Crown Prince August Wilhelm, a son of the exiled kaiser, gave their blessings to the Nazi-dominated regime, which was sworn into office with such unexpected pomp and majesty that millions of Germans were infused with the vision of a promising new era. The extravaganza continued into the afternoon when the Reichstag deputies, surrounded by 2,000 SA Brownshirts, assembled in their temporary quarters, the Kroll Opera House.

It was then that Hitler, exploiting the precedent adopted by Benito Mussolini in Italy (p. 49), submitted his own and even more drastic version of "enabling legislation." This was the "Law to Remove the Distress of the People and the State," more commonly known as the Enabling Act of 1933. The draft law would transfer to the chancellor all legislative authority for domestic and foreign affairs, ostensibly for a period of four years. With the endorsement of the Center and the German National People's parties (and presumably over the silent chagrin of President Hindenburg), the legislation then was rushed through the Reichstag's mandatory three readings in the space of 45 minutes, passing by a vote of 441 to 94. That same evening of March 23, 1933, the Reichsrat, the legislature's upper house, endorsed the law almost unanimously. Four months later, on July 14, the chancellory fastened a choke hold on Germany's government by issuing a broad catalog of "executive" decrees. Chief among these was an edict proclaiming the Nazi Party the nation's one and single "legal" party.

## *GLEICHSCHALTUNG*: NAZI "COORDINATION" OF GERMAN SOCIETY, 1933–34

### The Catholic Church

As chancellor, Hitler did not envisage simply a Nazi "state." He was determined to produce a Nazi "state of mind." To that end, Goebbels, as minister of "public enlightenment," organized a series of mass rallies that served as frenzied exercises in Hitler worship. Businessmen and workers, intellectuals and professionals, all vied with each other in apotheosizing the Nazi leader. Addressing a huge convention of Hitler Jugend (Hitler Youth) groups in

Munich, Rudolf Hess did not exaggerate the public mood, whether of apotheosis or intimidation, when he roared: "Adolf Hitler is Germany and Germany is Adolf Hitler. He who pledges himself to Adolf Hitler pledges himself to Germany."[48]

In this mood, too, Hitler proceeded to launch his vast program of *"Gleichschaltung"*—of subsuming all Germany's diverse and pluralistic institutions, whether cultural, religious, military, or paramilitary, into the cult and machinery of the *"Führerprinzip,"* the "leader principle." An early example of the process was the accommodation formulated between the Nazi regime and the Catholic Church. As recently as two years before Hitler's accession to power, a number of Germany's Catholic prelates had expressed apprehension at Nazi paganism and racism. To "pacify" their concerns at the source, Hitler sent Hermann Göring to Rome in May 1931 for an audience with Pope Pius XI. The pontiff received Göring cordially, praising the Nazis for taking a vigorous stand against bolshevism. Göring, in turn, reemphasized Hitler's "great regard" for the Catholic religion (which in fact he had denigrated in *Mein Kampf*).

Two years later, in the wake of his March 1933 electoral victory, Hitler dispatched Vice-Chancellor Papen to Rome to propose the formulation of a "concordat" between the Nazi Party and the Vatican, and thereby to elicit the support of Germany's (Catholic) Center Party in the forthcoming vote on the Enabling Act. The papal audience possibly was superfluous. Pius XI had given ear to Cardinal Eugenio Pacelli, his former nuncio in Germany and an unabashed admirer of German culture, when the latter observed that the Nazis might serve as a reliable bulwark against communism. Altogether, Pius XI saw little to fear from a political platform that had declared that the "National Socialist Party will not interfere in questions that lie outside of its political work." Notwithstanding the Führer's developing program of racism within Germany, his assertion had seemed reasonable to the pope and to many German Catholics, who envisaged Hitler as a leader in the same mold of the much-admired Mussolini.[49]

Conversely, there was much for the papacy to lose in opposing a concordat. If his negotiations with the Vatican failed, Hitler had intimated that he might approve the closure of Catholic schools and Catholic youth and social-action movements. Pius XI was listening. He instructed his current papal nuncio in Germany, Cardinal Cesare Orsenigo, to cooperate with the Nazis in crafting

---

48 Albrecht Tyrell, *Führer befiehl.... Selbstzeugnisse aus der "Kampfzeit" der NSDAP* (Düsseldorf: Droste, 1969), 173.

49 Klaus Scholder, *Die Kirchen und das Dritte Reich* (Frankfurt am Main: Propyläen, 1977), 279–80.

a political marriage of convenience. The ensuing "concordat," formulated between Orsenigo and Vice-Chancellor Papen over the spring and summer of 1933, was signed on July 20. By its terms, the German government guaranteed the church its right to operate Catholic schools in Germany, to exempt Catholic theological students from Germany's Labor Service Law, and to ensure "uninhibited freedom of action for all Catholic religious, cultural, and educational organizations"—with the proviso that these not function as political associations or federations.[50]

Yet, within two years of signing the concordat, the Nazi government repudiated the document both in spirit and substance.[51] Catholic schools were limited so rigorously in their doctrinal curriculum that they became virtually indistinguishable from state schools. The Catholic Youth Organization, dedicated to recreational and cultural activities, was swiftly "integrated" into the Hitler Jugend; Catholic pastoral journals and sermons were tightly scrutinized for evidence of political criticism, and priests were arrested if they failed to toe the Nazi line. In 1938, shortly before his death, a broken-hearted Pius XI would denounce the Nazi betrayal in a famous encyclical, *Mit brennender Sorge* [With Burning Anxiety]. By then, however, the denunciation would evoke no practical resonance.

## *The Jews*

Neither would the Nazi campaign against a much smaller and infinitely more vulnerable community. In 1933, numbering between 510,000 and 520,000, the Jews of Germany represented less than 1 per cent of the nation's population.[52] Yet their modest demography was belied by their visibility. In the postwar as in the prewar, over 70 per cent of German Jews lived in cities of 100,000 or more. Their vocational profile was overwhelmingly middle class. So was their economic vulnerability. During the inflation of the early 1920s, Jews suffered in identical proportions as non-Jews. In 1923, Berlin's Jewish *Kultusverein* had to maintain 19 soup kitchens and 5 homeless shelters; and, a decade later, the Depression left 60,000 German Jews unemployed and at least twice that many underemployed. As elsewhere in Western Europe,

---

50 Gerhard Weinberg, *Hitler's Foreign Policy: The Road to World War II, 1933–1939* (New York: Enigma, 2005), 68–71.

51 Anthony Rhodes, *The Vatican in the Age of Dictatorship, 1922–1945* (London: Hodder and Stoughton, 1973), 184–86.

52 "Jews in Prewar Germany," *United State Holocaust Memorial Museum*, http://www.ushmm.org/outreach/en/article.php?ModuleId=10007687.

however, non-Jews knew only what they saw; and, in good times and bad, they saw Jewish names on shops and professional offices. In the Depression, economic frustration alone would have exacerbated German antisemitism. Widely infused with "Aryan" racial propaganda, however, the animus soon achieved an unprecedented political dynamism even before the Nazi accession to power (pp. 97–98).

Indeed, Hitler's political success could not be attributed simply to the ruthlessness and ingenuity with which he manipulated his nation's incipient racism, for Jew-hatred was only one of several ingredients in the Nazi propaganda arsenal. Rather, it was Hitler's genius to link with antisemitism the full arsenal of the party's other weapons: chauvinism, Aryanism, populism, anti-bolshevism, white-collar paranoia. If antisemitism itself was incapable of decisively influencing the voting public, it was susceptible to combination with virtually all other putative enemies targeted on the Nazi agenda: the *Jewish* Bolshevik, the *Jewish* capitalist, the *Jewish* department-store owner, the *Jewish* "November criminal," and, perhaps most lethally, the *Jewish* blood polluter of an Aryan nation. As the historian Karl Schleunes has illustrated, antisemitism permitted Hitler to obfuscate the fact that Nazism attempted to be all things to all people.[53] These were the circumstances, both of racism and of political sleight of hand, that Hitler exploited in his campaign for the chancellorship—and beyond.

German Jewry lived the early months of the Nazi regime in a rictus of uncertainty. Would the ax fall on them? Perhaps not immediately. The new chancellor's initial priorities were to consolidate his political base, and he spoke only vaguely of depriving Jews of their "privileges" through "administrative, legal means." But Hitler also knew that eventually he had to propitiate those SA contingents that had played a key role in his ascent to power. In the wake of the Nazi victory, these uniformed rowdies brimmed over with explosive anti-Jewish zeal. Mere administrative measures scarcely were enough to assuage an element schooled in physical intimidation. Instead, during the first two weeks of March 1933, the SA on its own had embarked on a spontaneous anti-Jewish rampage. Local squads of Brownshirts, eager for blood and pillage, were abducting individual Jews and demanding ransom from the victims' families, dragging Jewish lawyers and doctors into the streets and disrobing them in public, or invading Jewish-owned department stores and creating havoc by intimidating their personnel and customers.

---

53 See Karl A. Schleunes, *The Twisted Road to Auschwitz: Nazi Policy to German Jews, 1933–1939* (Urbana, IL: University of Illinois Press, 1970), *passim*.

In his newly assumed "respectability" and "legality," Hitler did not approve these tactics. By their diversionary pandemonium, they threatened to sabotage the "legitimacy" of his regime. As a newly installed chancellor, however, he could not quite afford a showdown with an organization that had figured with such prominence in his rise to power. Instead, he sought to buy time by steering the SA leadership into less destructive channels. On March 26, at the suggestion of Julius Streicher, editor of the virulently antisemitic SA weekly *Der Stürmer* [The Stormer], Hitler acquiesced in a nationwide boycott of Jewish businesses and professional offices. Accordingly, an official "Boycott Day" was launched on April 1, 1934. Its sponsors' original intention, in fact, was to prolong the ban indefinitely (albeit peacefully) until Jews had been eliminated from the German economy altogether. But when rumors of the plan leaked on March 28, prices on the Berlin stock exchange dropped, and Foreign Minister Konstantin von Neurath urged Hitler to modify his approach. Hitler agreed and limited the boycott to a single day.

It was a day that began with the Sturm Abteilung taking up positions in front of every Jewish department store or medium-sized Jewish retail establishment and professional office in Berlin. Their intent was simply to "dissuade" citizens from entering. But all pretense of discipline soon was abandoned. Windows were broken, graffiti were painted on store windows, and acts of physical abuse became rampant. When the German public reacted coldly to this hooliganism, the boycott was canceled before the day was out (although not early enough to preclude shocked coverage in foreign newspapers).[54] From then on, anti-Jewish measures would follow bureaucratic, "legal" procedures. Although less raucous or brutal, the strategy soon outpaced mindless violence in accelerating the machinery of Jewish deracination.

## *The Reichswehr*

Hitler's racism focused not only on the Jews. It was also a central ingredient of his foreign policy and, specifically, in "rectifying" the territorial amputations of the Paris Peace Conference by "redeeming" German-speaking minorities in Eastern Europe's successor states. To achieve this objective, and in acute realization of his mistake in launching his 1923 putsch against the guns of the Reichswehr and police, Hitler a decade later resolved at all costs to ingratiate himself with Germany's military leadership. Thus, on February 2, 1933,

---

54 See, for example, Deborah E. Lipstadt, *Beyond Belief: The American Press and the Coming of the Holocaust, 1933–1945* (New York: Free Press, 1986) and Andrew Sharf, *The British Press and Jews under Nazi Rule* (London: Oxford University Press, 1964).

less than a week after assuming the chancellorship, he delivered a two-hour address to Germany's senior generals and admirals as they gathered at the home of General Kurt von Hammerstein, the Reichswehr chief of staff.

In his remarks, Hitler reassured the assembled officers that the armed services under no circumstances would be called upon again to take part in political-civil conflicts, as they had in the first year after the war. Thereafter, he promised, they could devote themselves exclusively to their central and "sacred" task of rearming the "new Germany." To this assurance, the generals and admirals gave respectful attention and prolonged applause. Thus, on April 4, as a further token of his commitment to the Reichswehr's seniority of status over the Sturm Abteilung and other paramilitary organizations, Hitler established the Reich Defense Council to spur his new and secret rearmament program. Three and a half months later, on July 20, he promulgated a new army law, abolishing the jurisdiction of the civil courts over military personnel and restoring to the officer corps its ancient semiautonomous prerogatives.

The measure of Hitler's dependence on the Reichswehr became dramatically evident on May 17, 1933, in his response to a League of Nations Disarmament Conference then taking place in Geneva. "Germany is entirely ready to renounce all offensive weapons," he had proclaimed, "if the [other] armed nations . . . will also destroy their offensive weapons." But if other nations did not match German disarmament, he added, he would withdraw Germany's delegation from the conference. It was a bold move. Under terms of the Treaty of Versailles, Germany was limited to an army of 100,000 men. By imposing his condition of parity, Hitler in effect was leaving the door open for his country's rearmament. Subsequently, he took pains further to reassure himself of Reichswehr support. Addressing a Nazi Party gathering on September 23, he reminded his listeners that

> one should particularly note the part played by our Reichswehr, for we all know well that, in the days of our [Nazi] revolution, if the army had not stood by our side, then we should not be standing here today. We can assure [our officers and men] that we shall never forget this, that we see in them the bearers of the tradition of our glorious old Reichswehr, and that with all our heart and all our powers we shall support the spirit of the [current] Reichswehr.[55]

In the ensuing weeks of deliberations at Geneva, when the Allied diplomats insisted on an interval of at least eight years to bring their own

---

55 William L. Shirer, *The Rise and Fall of the Third Reich* (New York: Simon and Schuster, 1960), 207.

armaments down to the level mandated for Germany, Hitler decided to make good on his earlier warning. On October 14, 1933, he simultaneously withdrew his delegation both from the Disarmament Conference and from the League of Nations altogether (p. 345). A day later, he ordered Germany's minister of defense, General Werner von Blomberg, to prepare for armed resistance should the League resort to military sanctions. It was a meaningless posture. The very notion of League military action was ludicrous. By invoking this mythical threat, however, the Nazi chancellor was deliberately tightening the bonds between the Reichswehr leadership and himself.

## The Sturm Abteilung

Nevertheless, even as the Nazi führer wooed Germany's military high command, another challenge refused to abate. It was the role of the Sturm Abteilung. During the late 1920s, Hitler had experienced a growing tension with Franz Pfeffer von Salomon, the man whom he had appointed in 1926 as Ernst Röhm's successor as SA commander. Little time had passed before Pfeffer, like Röhm before him, became restless under Hitler's uncompromising definition of the SA as a mere "auxiliary" paramilitary corps. For Pfeffer, too, the SA was the "crown jewel" of the Nazi movement, while the party's civilian apparatus was merely its "talking branch."[56] Indeed, in his exasperation at the limited funds Hitler made available to the SA, Pfeffer, on his own, set out to establish financial self-sufficiency for his 70,000 Brownshirts. On their behalf, he organized an independent SA insurance program, a series of independent SA housing projects, and a chain of SA clothing and food marts. The SA even marketed its own packets of razor blades and cigarettes, each bearing the SA logo. It was hardly the direction Hitler had anticipated for a "loyal party instrument."

Finally, in June 1930, tensions between the Nazi civilian bureaucracy and the Sturm Abteilung reached the flash point. In Berlin, the local SA leader, Walther Stennes, revolted against the party leaders by surrounding their Berlin headquarters on the Hedemannstrasse and locking several of their personnel in their offices. Among those incarcerated was Josef Goebbels, then functioning as party gauleiter for Berlin. When Goebbels subsequently telephoned Hitler with an hysterical plea for help, the Führer rushed up from Munich to assert his personal leadership over the SA (although promising

---

56 Turner, *German Big Business*, 117.

its rank and file more generous salary allotments). But when Stennes balked again, in January 1931, Hitler forthwith expelled him—and Franz Pfeffer, the SA chieftain—from the Nazi Party altogether.[57]

It was at this point, too, that the Führer decided to invite Ernst Röhm back from Bolivia to assume control of the SA's day-to-day operations as chief of staff. Sobered by his five years in the wilderness and grateful for Hitler's revived trust, Röhm unhesitatingly accepted the invitation. Returning to Germany, he promptly and vigorously imposed his brand of discipline upon the storm troopers.[58] When Hitler required every SA member to take an oath of loyalty to him personally, Röhm was the first to leap to his feet and repeat the pledge. In January 1933, following Hitler's appointment as chancellor, Röhm reiterated his loyalty to Hitler as Germany's "one and only Führer."[59]

Privately, however, Röhm and his lieutenants were galled by Hitler's transparent homage to the Reichswehr general staff, whom Röhm likened to "a bunch of Prussian old clods."[60] He was still unshakable in his conviction that the SA alone was capable of evading the military constraints of the Treaty of Versailles by functioning as the nucleus of a future revolutionary army, a "people's army," capable of performing for the Nazi state the role that France's conscript armies had performed for Napoleon. Yet, when Röhm circumspectly mentioned this issue, reminding Hitler that the Versailles Treaty had limited the Reichswehr to a pitiable 100,000-man "constabulary," while the SA in 1933 was projecting its own membership ultimately to reach 2 million, he could not seem to budge his old comrade. For the while, Röhm continued to profess his personal loyalty. Hitler, in turn, cultivated the SA leader's trust at every occasion. On January 1, 1934, after appointing Röhm to the Nazi cabinet as minister without portfolio, Hitler appended a personal note, using the familiar "du" salutation, and attributing the party's success to "such men as you . . . my friends and fellow combatants."[61]

But the fraternalism Hitler displayed to Röhm and the SA paled beside the deference he insisted on giving the Reichswehr senior command. Röhm could scarcely contain his frustration.[62] Again, as in the early 1920s, he launched his storm troopers on an increasingly clamorous series of parades and

---

57  Sauer, *Die Mobilmachung*, 844.
58  Heinz Höhne, *Mordsache Röhm* (Hamburg: Rowohlt, 1982), 61.
59  Sauer, *Die Mobilmachung*, 844.
60  Sauer, *Die Mobilmachung*, 846.
61  Adolf Hitler, *The Speeches of Adolf Hitler, April 1922–August 1939*, ed. Norman Hepburn Baynes (New York: Oxford University Press, 1942), 1: 289.
62  Höhne, *Mordsache Röhm*, 42.

demonstrations in Germany's larger cities, impervious to the exasperation his jack-booted lumpenproletariat evoked among the traditionally law-abiding German people. With comparable aggressiveness, Röhm sought out funds and supplies from his own contacts among Germany's industrial barons. In the process, he established his own task force, the SA Feldpolizei, to compete with Hitler's elitist SS (Schutzstaffel). He also created an autonomous SA judiciary with the power to impose its own sentences on SA miscreants. Denouncing the government for its hesitation in launching an "authentic," "people's" revolution, Röhm increasingly resorted to ad-hominem criticisms of Goebbels, Göring, Himmler, and Hess. By late 1933, even Hitler was not spared the SA chieftain's frustration. Röhm confided to his intimates:

> Adolf is rotten. He's betraying all of us. He only goes around with reactionaries. His old comrades aren't good enough for him, so he brings in these East Prussian generals.... They'll never have a new idea.... [Adolf] wants to inherit a ready-made army all set to go. He wants to have it all cobbled together by "experts." When I hear that word I blow my top.... [H]e's turning the [revolution] over to the Prussian generals ... to a bunch of old fogies who certainly aren't going to win the new war.[63]

In February 1934, Röhm climaxed a lengthy memorandum to the cabinet with the demand that the SA now serve as the foundation of a new "People's Army" and that the armed services, the Shutzstaffel (SS) and other security services be placed en bloc under a single ministry of defense over which, by implication, he, Röhm, should preside. At that point, reacting in outrage to the proposal, General Walther von Brauchitsch, the Reichswehr's recently appointed deputy chief of staff, sent a private note to Hindenburg to remind the old president that "[r]earmament [is] too serious and difficult a business to allow the participation of speculators, drunkards and homosexuals."[64] Indeed, during the winter and ensuing spring, the cabinet witnessed increasingly stormy confrontations between Röhm and Defense Minister Werner von Blomberg.[65] The SA leadership was posing a threat not only to the Reichswehr, Blomberg warned. In the scope and truculence of their demands, they also threatened Germany's efforts of clandestine rearmament.

---

63 Hermann Rauschning, *The Voice of Destruction* (New York: G.B. Putnam, 1940), 143.
64 Shirer, *The Rise and Fall*, 214.
65 Friedrich Hossbach, *Zwischen Wehrmacht und Hitler, 1934–1938* (Göttingen: Vandenhoeck & Ruprecht, 1965), 76.

Well seized of the Reichswehr's unease, Hitler was unwilling any longer to risk jeopardizing its loyalty. President Hindenburg, at age 86 and in failing health, already had crossed the threshold of senility. In the imminent likelihood of his death, the General Staff might be tempted to join other conservative elements in an effort to restore the monarchy. Hence, on April 4, receiving word that Hindenburg was indeed fading in and out of consciousness, Hitler recognized that a preemptive initiative no longer could be delayed.

## THE "DEUTSCHLAND PACT"

Five days later, on April 9, 1934, Hitler set out from Kiel to Königsberg on the battle cruiser *Deutschland*. He was accompanied by Defense Minister Blomberg, General Werner von Fritsch, and Admiral Erich Räder, the latter two supreme commanders, respectively, of the army and navy. Although the announced purpose of his voyage was to attend spring military maneuvers in East Prussia, Hitler's authentic mission was political. On board, he informed the senior officers of Hindenburg's worsening senility and bluntly proposed that he himself, with the public support of the Reichswehr, be recognized as Hindenburg's successor. In return, Hitler offered to block Röhm's ambitions by recognizing the Reichswehr as Germany's sole legitimate armed force and to launch forthwith on a dramatic expansion of the army and navy. Räder agreed to the proposal immediately. Although Fritsch asked to consult first with his senior officers, the consultation was held five weeks later at the spa of Bad Nauheim, and the assembled generals unanimously recommended endorsement. It was a decisive victory for Hitler, and all the more when the price to be paid was comparatively modest. It would be the sacrifice of the Sturm Abteilung.[66]

Even prior to the *"Deutschland* Pact," Hitler had taken preliminary steps to outflank Röhm. The previous January, he had ordered Rudolf Diels, chief of the secret state police (the incipient Gestapo), to gather incriminating information on Röhm and on the SA's terrorist activities. "This is the most important assignment you will ever receive," Hitler solemnly informed Diels.[67] In late February, at a joint meeting with Röhm, Defense Minister Blomberg, and Heinrich Himmler, commander of the SS, Hitler had repeated in general terms

---

66 Herbert Rosinski, *The German Army* (Washington, DC: The Infantry Journal, 1944), 222–23; see also J.W. Wheeler-Bennett, *The Nemesis of Power: The German Army in Politics, 1918–1945* (New York: St. Martin's Press, 1953), 313–14.
67 Fest, *Hitler*, 454.

# "RICHARD III" IN GERMANY

his formula for the division of authority between them, with the Brownshirts to be restricted to "political education" within Germany. Röhm had listened quietly. Shaking hands afterward with Hitler and the military leaders, he imperturbably partook of a "reconciliation breakfast" with them.

But to his intimates later that same day, Röhm all but exploded in exasperation against Hitler, "an idiot corporal"[68] who apparently did not comprehend that he, Röhm, "had the power of thirty divisions" behind him and that he was accumulating large amounts of weaponry on the international arms market in preparation for any action the Reichswehr might initiate. "After all," he scoffed, "the so-called Reichswehr is nothing but a pile of shit."[69] By then, Diels, Hitler's confidant, had already infiltrated a "mole" into Röhm's personal entourage. This was SA Obergruppenführer Viktor Lutze, who immediately transmitted to Diels a verbatim account of Röhm's tirade. Upon being informed, Hitler at first reacted calmly. "We must let matters ripen," he said.[70]

Throughout the spring of 1934, Röhm and his SA cronies intensified their preparations for a "second revolution." Even General Kurt von Schleicher, the former "interim" chancellor, who was apparently unable to endure his subsequent political obscurity, ventured to establish contact with Röhm and the intransigent Gregor Strasser. Schleicher reputedly was interested in negotiating a deal that would elevate him to the vice-chancellory in place of his old rival Franz von Papen. Röhm, in turn, would become minister of defense, and the SA would be amalgamated with the army. Yet this plot, too, was relayed to Hitler, who agreed then with Göring and Himmler that time no longer would permit matters to "ripen." Rather, on June 4, Hitler and Röhm held a climactic meeting. It lasted five hours and represented the Nazi leader's final attempt to reach an understanding with his "oldest" friend in the party. On this occasion, Röhm seemed to be conciliatory. Although he was soon to go off on a month's vacation at Bad Wiessee, a spa near Munich, he assured Hitler that, upon his return, he would "do everything possible to put things right."[71]

In Hitler's calculation, however, preemptive measures against the SA leadership could no longer be delayed, even with the *Deutschland* Pact" in hand and with Röhm's ostensible assurance of cooperation. It was all but certain that the SA leader would oppose Hitler's accession to the presidency upon Hindenburg's death. Beyond Röhm and the SA, moreover, the rejectionists

---

68 David C. Large, *Between Two Fires: Europe's Path in the 1930s* (New York: Norton, 1990), 119.
69 Höhne, *Mordsache Röhm*, 219.
70 Shirer, *The Rise and Fall*, 216–17.
71 Hanfstängl, *15 Jahr*, 340.

probably would include Vice-Chancellor Papen and the latter's Catholic Centrist loyalists, as well as the nation's Junker barons and, conceivably, even prominent members of the newer industrial and financial "aristocracy." Most of these men were known to favor a restoration of the Hohenzollern monarchy once Hindenburg expired. Indeed, on June 7, 1934, Papen visited Hindenburg at the latter's Neudeck estate to win the old president's endorsement for just such a restoration. Hindenburg seemed receptive. He would revise his last will and testament forthwith, he promised, to include Papen's recommendation. Then, bidding the vice-chancellor goodbye, Hindenburg seized the latter's hand: "Things are going badly, Papen," he whispered. "See what you can do to put them right."[72] Papen tried, a week and a half later, on June 17, 1934, in a speech he delivered at the University of Marburg.

Addressing a joint colloquium of the university's faculty and student body, Papen ventured an open challenge to Hitler in a speech he had formulated with the help of Edgar Jung, a professor of law and a widely respected Catholic intellectual. The vice-chancellor's voice trembled with emotion as he acknowledged that, while he himself had cooperated in "temporarily" bringing the Nazis to office, his purpose had been to clear the way for a "new spiritual and political elite" not, perish forbid, to introduce an "unbridled dictatorship . . . and a revolution against order, law, and religion." Then Papen rhetorically appealed to Hitler to distance himself from those who would produce circumstances of "perpetual chaos."[73]

Although the nation's press had effectively been censored by then, a few newspapers remained (most of them politically centrist) that risked publishing extracts of the vice-chancellor's address. Hitler now grasped the importance of moving swiftly and decisively against his enemies. Röhm and the SA were plainly foremost among these. On June 21, 1934, escorted by Minister of Defense Blomberg, Hitler paid court to Hindenburg at Neudeck to assess for himself the president's health. It was visibly failing. Propped up on cushions behind his desk, the old man was barely lucid. In the anteroom after the brief interview, Blomberg reminded Hitler of the military establishment's earlier commitment to deal firmly with the SA.[74] The reminder was superfluous. Even then, at Hitler's instructions, Göring, Himmler, and the latter's deputy, Reinhard Heydrich, were in the process of drawing up lists of "undesirables."[75]

---

72  Franz von Papen, *Der Wahrheit eine Gasse* (Munich: Paul List, 1952), 122.
73  Papen, *Der Wahrheit*, 310.
74  Hanfstängl, *15 Jahr*, 305.
75  Höhne, *Mordsache Röhm*, 239.

On June 27, further to convince the Reichswehr leadership of the need for solidarity with the government, Göring personally supplied Blomberg with Viktor Lutze's evidence of the SA conspiracy to mount a putsch (p. 171). Visibly alarmed, the defense minister then requested another conference with Hitler. The two met on the late morning of the same June 27. Blomberg, in his own name and that of General Fritsch, confirmed that the Reichswehr would stand behind Hitler "whatever the chancellor decided."[76] In reply, Hitler then assured Blomberg that he was arranging an early showdown with Röhm and Röhm's "gang." Although he did not clarify the nature of the "showdown," Blomberg by then trusted Hitler enough to publish a signed article of his own in the Nazi Party's *Völkischer Beobachter*. It appeared on June 29, affirming that "the Reichswehr... stands behind Adolf Hitler... who remains one of ours."[77]

## THE "NIGHT OF THE LONG KNIVES"

By the time Blomberg's article was published, the "showdown" already was in operation. Two days earlier, after his meeting with the defense minister, Hitler, Göring, Himmler, Heydrich, and members of the black-coated SS completed the details of their preemptive strike. Hitler then departed for Essen, ostensibly to attend the wedding of a regional SS gauleiter but actually (as he himself later confirmed) to "present an outward impression of absolute calm and to give no warning to the traitors."[78] That same evening, he telephoned Röhm at the latter's resort hotel in Bad Wiessee, directing him to summon all SA section leaders from throughout Germany for a "candid discussion" on June 30 with him, Hitler. Röhm unhesitatingly and enthusiastically agreed.

On the night of June 28, Hitler continued on from Essen to his hotel in the resort town of Bad Godesberg. The next morning, at his orders, Göring ordered Himmler to place all Gestapo units on full alert. Both men eagerly awaited evidence of storm-trooper defiance, a challenge that could be used for instant government retaliation. The morning hours passed without incident. In Bad Wiessee, Röhm evidently remained passive and unsuspecting.[79] But in Munich, late on the afternoon of the 29th, several hundred Brownshirts were summoned by anonymous handwritten notes (that possibly had been circulated by Gestapo chief Himmler) to exit their barracks

---

76 Max Gallo, *Night of the Long Knives* (New York: Harper & Row, 1972), 171–72.
77 Gallo, *Night*, 251–52.
78 Gallo, *Night*, 251–52.
79 Heinrich Bennecke, *Die Reichswehr und der "Röhm-Putsch,"* (Vienna: Günter Olzog, 1964), 85.

and appear on the city's main streets. The SA contingents duly followed these "suggestions" and proceeded to mill about confusedly. Upon confirming this development, Göring telephoned Hitler that an SA "mutiny" was indeed in progress.

Evidently, Hitler took the report with full seriousness. After consulting with Goebbels, who had accompanied him to Bad Godesberg, he ordered his personal airplane to be made ready at the nearby Bonn airport. Around midnight of July 29–30, accompanied by Goebbels and Goebbels's assistant Otto Dietrich, Hitler climbed into his Junkers transport plane and within minutes was en route to Munich. Approximately three and a half hours later, still before dawn on June 30, the craft touched down at Munich's suburban airport. It was awaited by a limousine and surrounded by a local escort of police motorcyclists. Before taking his car seat, Hitler instructed Goebbels to order the arrest of any SA leaders who had not yet departed for the scheduled Bad Wiessee conference. Then his procession set out for its initial destination, the "Brown House," the Nazi Party's national headquarters in Munich.

Once arrived, exhausted and anxious and acknowledging to the assembled party leaders that "[t]his is the darkest day of my life,"[80] the Führer then proceeded to berate them for letting the SA "run rampant" in Munich, "of all places, the capital of our movement." His ensuing orders were terse and unequivocal. All local SA commanders should be rounded up and jailed. If any of them resisted, he warned, they should be shot. Then, a few minutes later, as dawn broke, Hitler and Goebbels set out for Bad Wiessee in a three-automobile caravan flanked by the motorcycles of a police escort. At that early hour, the drive from Munich to the neighboring vacation community took barely 50 minutes. The sun was just coming up at 6:25 when the motorcade pulled to a stop at the Pension Hanselbauer, Röhm's chalet-style hotel.

As Hitler's chauffeur, Erich Kempka, later described the scene, the SS and police detectives burst into the lobby, shouting and gesticulating with their pistols. Kicking in the doors to hotel rooms, they routed the sleeping storm troopers from their beds. One Brownshirt, Edmund Heines, Röhm's personal aide, was found naked with a young recruit—"a disgusting scene," Josef Goebbels said later, "which made me feel like vomiting."[81] With the butts of their pistols, the intruders beat Heines to the floor, leaving his head a bloody pulp. Meanwhile, accompanied by two Munich detectives, Hitler himself entered Röhm's suite. He found the SA chief in bed alone (although later Goebbels would spread the false rumor that Röhm too had been asleep

---

80  Klaus Jürgen Müller, *Das Heer und Hitler* (Stuttgart: Deutsche Verlags-Anstalt, 1969), 125.
81  Albert Speer, *Inside the Third Reich* (New York: Macmillan, 1970), 51.

with a male lover). To his dumbfounded "old comrade," Hitler now shouted: "Röhm, you are under arrest!"[82] The detectives then hustled Röhm, still in his pajamas, out of his suite and into the hotel cellar. A few minutes later a procession of police vans transported the captives off to Munich, where they were thrown into prison.

Thus far, 64 SA personnel had been seized in the raid on Pension Hanselbauer; but within the ensuing hour and a half many more senior Brownshirts fell victim to the Nazi dragnet. By then, Hitler and Goebbels themselves were on their way back to Munich. En route, however, their caravan of police and SS vehicles encountered the rest of some 200 additional SA officers who were en route to Bad Wiessee for the anticipated meeting with Hitler and Röhm. These newcomers were now stopped at gunpoint, ordered into police vans, and transported to detention in the cellar of Munich's Lichterfelde Cadet Academy. Their incarceration was brief. Before the day was out, all were lined up in the academy courtyard and shot. Approximately a dozen of the original Pension Hanselbauer captives shared their fate.

That same afternoon, once back at Munich's "Brown House," Hitler directed Goebbels to telephone Göring in Berlin, signaling that a "wider" purge should promptly be carried out. The prospective victims included the scores of SA group leaders elsewhere in Germany who had not traveled to Bad Wiessee but who were known to be among Röhm's devoted lieutenants. By late afternoon, following Göring's directives, orders were dispatched to all SA regional and district leaders to report immediately to their command posts. The unsuspecting storm troopers duly complied. Awaiting them were armed contingents of Gestapo personnel who promptly bundled the group leaders into trucks, carried them to nearby parks and forests, and executed them.[83]

If Hitler seemed hesitant at first to do away with Röhm himself, he evinced no hesitation whatever in approving the elimination of others who were on Göring's and Himmler's lists of "undesirables." Notable among these was Gregor Strasser. In protesting the Nazi Party's abandonment of the "socialist" component of its program, Strasser and his brother Otto had endangered Hitler's courtship of Germany's industrial, banking, and landowning elites. Otto had since left the country. Gregor Strasser remained behind, in political pariahdom but seemingly not in personal danger. On the evening of June 30, however, under Göring's orders, a team of Gestapo detectives called on Strasser at his Berlin apartment and "invited" him to accompany them

---

82 Speer, *Inside the Third Reich*, 51–52.
83 Richard Bessel, *Political Violence and the Rise of Nazism: The Storm Troopers in Eastern Germany, 1925–1934* (New Haven, CT: Yale University Press, 1984), 228–39.

for a personal meeting with Hitler, who had just flown back from Munich. Assuming that the conference was to be one of reconciliation, Strasser willingly, even gratefully, joined the detectives in their automobile. His destination was not the chancellery, however, but the central Gestapo prison on Prinz Albechtstrasse. The moment Strasser was locked in a cell, one of the detectives aimed his pistol through the door's peephole and emptied its magazine into the prisoner. Strasser's death later was listed as "suicide."

General Kurt von Schleicher, the Machiavelli who had engineered the political accommodation between Papen, Hitler, and Hindenburg, was spending the morning of June 30 at his Berlin home in the company of his young wife. Friends had warned him to steer clear of public activity after Hitler's spectacular Reichstag triumph of March 6, 1933, and Schleicher's ensuing fall from power. Even so, the general could not resist meeting occasionally with his anti-Nazi contacts. Now, at about noon, five Gestapo men walked into his study and calmly shot him to death. As Schleicher's wife ran screaming into the room, they executed her as well. The subsequent Gestapo report to Himmler blandly explained that Schleicher had been killed while "resisting arrest" and that his wife unfortunately had fallen in the crossfire. A few months later, a maid who had witnessed the killings also was found dead, allegedly the victim of a "suicide."[84]

Meanwhile, Vice-Chancellor Papen, Schleicher's original coconspirator in bringing Hitler to office, was also "neutralized," although more circumspectly. On the same morning of June 30, he received a telephone call in his Berlin office from Hermann Göring's secretary, asking him to pay an urgent visit on Göring at the latter's personal apartment. Hitler recently had added to the list of Göring's titles that of "Reichsmarschall" of the air force. Hence, as Papen's limousine approached Göring's residence behind the air ministry's offices, he noticed that the entire complex was sealed off by SS guards.[85] Göring received Papen cordially but then informed him that the Führer had just flown to Munich to suppress an SA "putsch" and had entrusted him, Göring, with full powers to deal with the "rebels" in Berlin.[86] Indignant, Papen at first protested that it was he, as vice-chancellor, who was empowered to proclaim a state of emergency. Göring replied blandly, if evasively, that he himself had matters "well in hand" and that Papen would be well advised to return forthwith to his private residence and stay there until informed that it was safe to venture out. At that point Papen realized that he was being placed under house arrest.

---

84  Höhne, *Mordsache Röhm*, 288.
85  Speer, *Inside the Third Reich*, 51.
86  Papen, *Der Wahrheit*, 353–54.

Papen left Göring's apartment. Rather than travel immediately to his private residence, however, he rushed back to the vice-chancellory to secure his private papers. He was too late. The SS had already occupied his office, where they had shot Papen's press secretary for "offering resistance." A contingent of Göring's air-ministry guards subsequently arrived and "escorted" Papen to his home, which in the meanwhile had been occupied by the Prussian police. Here he was locked away, his telephone line cut, his mail intercepted.[87] It was only later that Papen realized that his enforced isolation probably was the Reichsmarschall's way of protecting him from the SS. Göring had no use for Papen, but he doubtless appreciated that the vice-chancellor was too well-connected for simple liquidation. Yet Göring entertained no second thoughts about disposing of Papen's intellectual guru, Edgar Jung, the law professor who had helped write the vice-chancellor's speech at the University of Marburg (p. 172). On July 1, the SS abducted Jung from his home in Berlin. Three days later, his bullet-riddled body was found behind a copse of trees in the capital's Oranienburg suburb.

Simple personal vengeance also played a role in Hitler's "Night of the Long Knives" (a term coined only later, evidently by Heinrich Himmler). On June 30 and July 1, 1934, as SS and Gestapo personnel were reviewing the lists supplied by Göring and Himmler and then imprisoning or shooting their victims, a separate Gestapo team descended on the Munich home of Gustav von Kahr. The former Bavarian minister-president had held the security portfolio in 1923 when he first supported, and then helped foil, Hitler's attempted putsch (pp. 143–50). Since 1926, Kahr had returned to private life and relative obscurity. But now, on June 30, 1934, the SS pulled the frail, 73-year-old man from his home, bundled him into an automobile, and carried him off toward the Munich suburb of Dachau. A few days later his body was found in a swamp. He had been axed to death.

It is of interest that Hitler displayed a certain lingering hesitation in dealing with the figure whose "treachery" was the ostensible cause of the wholesale purge. Ernst Röhm was among his oldest comrades, after all, the man whose organizational talents and Reichswehr contacts had provided indispensable support for the Nazi rise to power. Should he now be shot down like a dog? But in the end, it took Hitler less than 24 hours to succumb to Göring's persuasion. On the late afternoon of July 1, back in Berlin, he placed a telephone call to Munich. Answering the call was Theodor Eicke, commander of Munich's neighboring SS concentration camp in Dachau, where Röhm had been transferred during the night. Upon listening to Hitler's orders, Eicke led

---

87 Papen, *Der Wahrheit*, 354–55; Large, *Between Two Fires*, 126–27.

ERNST RÖHM, C. 1934

a three-man SS team into Röhm's cell. Pale and noticeably trembling, Röhm waited in silence as the group's commander, SS Hauptsturmführer Michael Lippert, laid a pistol on the cell table, remarking that "the Führer allows you ten minutes to draw the honorable conclusion." When Röhm said nothing, the men withdrew. Ten minutes went by, but no shot was heard. Eicke and Lippert then reentered the cell, their own guns drawn. Röhm was standing in the middle of the room, his shirt lying at his feet. Bare-chested, he proclaimed melodramatically, "Let the Führer do this thing himself." Immediately Lippert fired. As Röhm sank to the floor, he still was able to gasp—not "du, Adolf," but "Mein Führer, Mein Führer"—before Eicke finished him off.[88]

---

88  Höhne, *Mordsache Röhm*, 293–96; Erik Larson, *In the Garden of Beasts* (New York: Crown, 2011), 311, 313, 320.

The blood bath, which guttered out upon Röhm's execution, had claimed many scores of lives, of storm troopers and civilians alike. Among the latter were a former chancellor and 13 members of the Reichstag. Indeed, Göring and Himmler had extended the executions far beyond the ambit of "Röhm putschists." Hitler later referred to 77 "criminals" shot and killed. In contrast, *The White Book of the Purge*, published by German refugee émigrés in Paris, stated that 401 people had been killed, although it identified only 116 of them.[89] Whatever the true figure, it is certain that some of the victims were liquidated simply for having opposed Hitler in the past, others because they knew too much, and at least one because of mistaken identity.

At Goebbels's initiative, meanwhile, the press and radio offered their "official" versions of the rampant "homosexuality," "corruption," and "incipient mutiny" that the government ostensibly had eliminated.[90] Hitler himself, shaken by his own role in the Saint Bartholomew's–style massacre, chose to remain silent. But on July 13, again at Göring's behest, he agreed finally to deliver a speech of self-justification before the Reichstag. In an address lasting almost two hours, Hitler did not stint in his account of the "filthy depravities" that had characterized the personal behavior of Röhm and the latter's SA "intimates." Only upon reciting this litany of "depravities" did Hitler expand upon the threat the SA had presented to the nation, and particularly to the "heroic" Reichswehr, the "keeper of German honor . . . [t]he sole bearer of arms in the state."[91]

But Hitler's adulation of the armed forces was a gilding of the lily. As early as July 1, Defense Minister Blomberg, in a statement circulated to the Reichswehr, praised the "soldierly determination and noteworthy bravery" of the Führer in striking and crushing "the nation's traitors and turncoats."[92] President Hindenburg also had not awaited Hitler's Reichstag speech. The same July 1, in Hindenburg's name, the executive secretary of the presidential office had sent Hitler a telegram of congratulations "for your determined action and gallant personal intervention, which has nipped treason in the bud and rescued the German people from great danger."[93] It is noteworthy that these messages were dispatched even after the cold-blooded murder of General Schleicher, himself an ex-chancellor and one of the military's most prominent officers. Meanwhile, leaders of both the Catholic and Protestant

---

89 Franz Josef Heyen, *Nationalsozialismus im Alltag* (Boppard: Boldt, 1967), 197–98.
90 Speer, *Inside the Third Reich*, 52.
91 Gallo, *Night*, 294–95.
92 Max Domarus, *Der Reichstag und die Macht* (Würzburg: Selbstverlag, 1968), 405.
93 Domarus, *Der Reichstag*, 405.

churches, for the most part, remained silent or (in a few instances) congratulatory,[94] and Carl Schmitt, director of Germany's renowned Institute of International Law, actively praised Hitler's Reichstag speech in an article titled "The Führer Protects the Law."[95]

Meanwhile, throughout the same month of July 1934, the 87-year-old Hindenburg periodically would lapse into unconsciousness. On July 31, anticipating the president's imminent demise, Hitler presented his cabinet with a draft law of succession. To take effect upon Hindenburg's death, the document stipulated that the office of president should henceforth be united with that of chancellor. Later the same day, Hitler went to Neudeck to visit Hindenburg. Conversation was impossible. The president lay in a coma. Indeed, he died in the morning hours of August 2. Almost simultaneously, the chancellor's office issued a press release. According to a law enacted by the cabinet less than two days before, it stated, the offices of chancellor and president had been combined. Provisionally, Hitler had taken over the powers both of head of state and of commander in chief of the armed forces. But to give this preemptive transgression the veneer of "constitutional" authority, the announcement added that a plebiscite would take place on August 19, allowing the German people to vote on the governmental change.

On August 15, four days in advance of the scheduled plebiscite, Hindenburg's last political will and testament turned up, delivered to Hitler by none other than Franz von Papen. Its contents seemingly were "validated" three days later by the late president's son, Colonel Oskar von Hindenburg, in a radio address delivered to the nation on the eve of the plebiscite. In his broadcast, the younger Hindenburg declared, "My father himself had seen in Adolf Hitler his own direct successor as head of the German State, and I am acting according to my father's intentions when I call on all German men and women to vote for the transformation of my father's [presidential] office to the office of Führer and Reich Chancellor."[96]

The son's account was mendacious. The old field marshal actually had agreed to Papen's earlier recommendation that the monarchy be restored after his, the president's, own death, and he promised to include a clause to that effect in his political will and testament. But 12 years later, at the 1945–46 Nuremberg war crimes trials, Papen testified that Hindenburg afterward had preferred instead to make his recommendation of a monarchical restoration in the form

---

94 Otto Gritschneider, *Der Führer hat Sie zum Tode verurteilt. . . . Hitlers "Röhm-Putsch": Morde vor Gericht* (Munich: C.H. Beck, 1993), 72–73.
95 C. Schmitt, "Der Führer schützt das Recht," *Deutschen Juristenzeitung* 39, no. 15 (1934): 945–50.
96 Kershaw, *Hitler*, 1: 519.

of a separate letter to Hitler. After Hindenburg's funeral, Hitler had studied both documents, the official testament (without the monarchical recommendation) and the private letter (with the monarchical recommendation). He chose not to reveal the private letter. Instead, he instructed Oskar von Hindenburg to read only the public testament in the radio broadcast of August 18—and then to add his personal, and certainly false, allusion to his father's private wishes. Weeks later, Hitler had Oskar promoted from colonel to major general.

In the plebiscite of August 19, 1934, some 95 per cent of those who had registered went to the polls and, of these, 84.6 per cent voted approval of Hitler's usurpation of power. Afterward, Hitler himself went on the air to announce, worshipfully, that he could not accept the title of "President," inasmuch as the "greatness of the late Reichsmarschall" did not permit him to claim that honor for himself. Rather, he wished "in official as in unofficial communication" to continue to be addressed only as "Führer and Chancellor." Whatever his title, it had not awaited August 19 for the Reichswehr to offer Hitler its unconditional loyalty. On the day of Hindenburg's death, Defense Minister Blomberg ordered all Reichswehr officers and enlisted men to take an oath of allegiance to Adolf Hitler as their new commander in chief (the previous oath had been to "nation and fatherland"). There is scant evidence that they did so with reluctance. The *Deutschland* Pact" had promised them everything. From then on, gratefully and eagerly, they would set about fulfilling their anticipated role in the creation of Hitler's Third Reich.

CHAPTER SIX

# A Return Visit from Austria's Tatterdemalion Son

*"I have always wanted peace. . . .
Ask Mussolini to look after my wife and children."*

### A CONVOCATION OF STRANGERS

Vienna on the early morning of July 25, 1934, was half empty under a rising summer sun. Its renowned opera and most of its theaters were closed for the season. The Austrian government was operating at a pace somnolent even for its famously inefficient bureaucracy. The nation's president, Wilhelm Miklas, already had departed for vacation, leaving with his wife and seven children for their Carinthian holiday spa at Velden. Engelbert Dollfuss, Austria's chancellor, was still in the capital to attend a routine cabinet meeting scheduled for the late morning; but the session was due to be finished by noon, and he planned to be off for Italy by 2:00 p.m. He and his family had been invited to stay as house guests at Benito Mussolini's seaside retreat in Riccione. Indeed, the chancellor's wife and their two small children had preceded him to Riccione a week earlier; and, in anticipation of joining them, Dollfuss was taking swimming lessons from police physical-education instructors.

Most Austrians were gratified that Mussolini and Dollfuss had grown close. In their alarm at Adolf Hitler's expansionist ambitions, they tended to view with increasing skepticism the "moral" support tendered their little nation by Europe's other two champions of rightist authoritarianism, Pope Pius XI and Hungary's Regent Miklós Horthy. Mussolini, on the other hand, disposing of one of Europe's larger armies, appeared an eminently reliable patron. The previous summer, he had agreed to provide Austria with a generous financial subsidy, together with substantial quantities of small arms.[1] In any case, during these last days of July, as Hitler concentrated on the insubordination of Ernst Röhm and Germany's SA leadership, it appeared to most Austrians that the Nazi Führer had enough on his plate at home to inhibit him from foreign adventurism. Vienna's population had begun to relax then, and its coffee houses had begun filling up again.

Among these was the Café Weghuber, a favored gathering place for commercial and government personnel who worked in the capital's centrally located Lerchenfelderstrasse. At 8:15 on the morning of July 25, one of the arriving patrons was Johann Dobler, a slim, balding man of early middle age, dressed in the uniform of a senior police official. Dobler, in fact, was the police commissioner of Vienna's 16th district, and he had not entered the Weghuber for his traditional morning coffee but to use the café's telephone. In the booth, Dobler placed a call to the executive headquarters of the "Fatherland Front," a neo-fascist political party that only weeks before had been awarded ministerial status in Chancellor Dollfuss's cabinet (p. 194). When a secretary answered, Dobler asked to speak to the party's assistant director-general, a "Herr Stepan." "Herr Stepan is not yet in the office," was the reply. Dobler then left word for Stepan to postpone any of his impending appointments and rush to the Café Weghuber the moment he arrived. Returning to his table, the inspector then ordered his coffee.

One hour passed, then two. Periodically, Dobler arose to redial Stepan's office, but the answer was always the same: Herr Stepan had not yet arrived. In growing agitation, the police commissioner was weighing alternatives when a newcomer took a seat at a nearby table. The man's face seemed familiar. Within moments, Dobler recognized him as Karl Mahrer, an officer in the Heimwehr, a right-wing militia that served as the Fatherland Front's "defense arm" (p. 198). Hereupon Dobler resolved on a gamble. Approaching Mahrer,

---

1 Richard Lamb, *Mussolini as Diplomat* (New York: Fromm International, 1999), 101–2.

he introduced himself both as a police official and as a secret member of the Austrian Nazi Party. While Mahrer listened in growing astonishment, Dobler proceeded to confess that he, Dobler, was privy to a Nazi plot to launch a putsch—a takeover of the Austrian government—and to install a Nazi regime in its place. The plot, Dobler continued, was to be carried out that very morning, at 11:00 a.m., during a scheduled cabinet meeting at the chancellory.

At first disbelieving, Mahler asked why Dobler had approached him, a stranger, instead of immediately contacting his own subordinates in the police force. Dobler replied that the police themselves were riddled with closet Nazis. In fact, only recently they had murdered another potential informer in their ranks; and, for that reason, he, Dobler, had been attempting the entire morning—so far unsuccessfully—to telephone a "reliable" contact within the Heimwehr militia. But Mahler still was unconvinced. Why, he asked, should any credence be given to the "revelation" of a Nazi? "It's true that I was and still am a Nazi," Dobler acknowledged, "but now I have grave reservations about a plot that threatens to take the lives of government leaders. To my knowledge, such a contingency was never envisaged. It must be aborted."[2] The conversation went on for another few minutes. At last, Mahler reluctantly agreed to telephone his own Heimwehr superiors.

## AN IMPERIAL REMNANT

Inspector Dobler's revelations offered a mordant insight to the turmoil of his nation's postwar politics. Since the late nineteenth century, Austria's "core" German-speaking citizens had been acutely aware of their minority status within the Habsburg Empire and of their vulnerability to the nationalist aspirations of the realm's non-Austrian subjects. Yet it was the climactic military defeats of 1918 that transformed vulnerability into inevitability. Weeks even before the armistice of November 3, 1918, representatives of the empire's subject communities had been declaring their peoples' independence, one by one: the Ruthenians on October 10, the Galician Poles on October 15, the Bohemians and Slovaks on October 28, and the South Slavs on October 29. Within the period of a single month, Emperor Karl was obliged to accept these collective defections as faits accomplis and to renounce his throne both in the Austrian and Hungarian halves of his realm.[3] Although the monarch refrained

---

2  For details about the assassination, see Walter P. Maas, *Assassination in Vienna* (New York: Scribner, 1972).

3  Margaret MacMillan, *Paris 1919, Six Months That Changed the World* (New York: Random House, 2001), 242.

from issuing an official proclamation of abdication, hoping to keep the royal succession alive for his heirs, nothing had come of the forlorn maneuver.

Nor had anything resulted from an even more questionable political tactic. On October 30, 1918, in one of its final legislative acts, Austria's bloc of deputies in the imperial Habsburg Reichstag voted to reconstitute "German Austria" as a provisional "democratic republic" within the Greater Reich of neighboring Germany. In no way was the vote intended as a political challenge to the Allies. Rather, it was a pragmatic effort to sustain the viability of the vestigial Austrian homeland by merging it in the far larger German economy. The need for that relief could not have been more acute. Well after the November 3 armistice, even after the Allies consented to lift their blockade in March 1919 (half a year before a similar relaxation was applied to Germany), Austria's economy had virtually collapsed. Inflation was rampant and would soar in the ensuing 18 months by some 2,000 per cent.[4] Shops and homes were boarded up. Palaces were ransacked. Former government officials were reduced to shining shoes on the nation's street corners. Young women of good families were walking the streets, offering themselves to strangers for the price of a meal.[5] But regardless of the Austrian government's modest objective of a unified economy, the Allied Powers shot down the Reichstag's act of "joinder." They would not tolerate a reconfiguration of the late German-Austrian "Dual Alliance" in any alternate shape or form.[6]

At Paris, the statesmen of the Entente Powers turned their attention to Austria only after signing the Treaty of Versailles with Germany in June 1919. But two and a half months later, on September 10, the Austrians finally were handed their own bill of payment at Saint-Germain, another Parisian suburb. The document was not forbearing. It contained a parallel version of the war-guilt clause extracted from Germany. Although the attendant claim of financial reparations was less than one-third the size of Germany's, the territorial losses for Austria were much more severe. The major amputations, to be sure, had been achieved earlier by the spontaneous defection of the former Habsburg nationalities, including Hungary, Austria's imperial "partner." Indeed, these losses subsequently foreshadowed the Treaty of Trianon, which excised from "independent" Hungary the latter's plethora of Slavic subject peoples.

---

4 Bruce F. Pauley, *Hitler and the Forgotten Nazis* (Chapel Hill, NC: University of North Carolina Press), 6.

5 David Mitrany, *The Effect of the War on Southeastern Europe* (New Haven, CT: Yale University Press, 1936), 174.

6 Alfred D. Low, *The Anschluss Movement, 1918–1919, and the Paris Peace Conference* (Philadelphia, PA: American Philosophical Society, 1974), 314.

But even these losses were further compounded by the Peace Conference's transfer to Italy of the Alpine region of Habsburg South Tyrol, with the latter's sizeable majority of German-speaking inhabitants. Excised, too, was a substantial part of the Adriatic littoral, handed over by the Allies to the future Yugoslavia. By this succession of punishments, the Habsburg Empire was transformed from a mighty imperial conglomeration of 51 million inhabitants into a hunchbacked, residually Austrian, republic of a mere 7 million. Indeed, the city of Vienna alone encompassed fully a third of the nation's remaining population, and the capital's surrounding terrain was reduced to six diminutive provinces, most of them possessing arable soil, attractive scenery, and a modest scattering of small factories and workshops, but little else.

The economic consequences of these defections and treaty amputations were devastating. Before the war, the Hapsburg Empire had boasted highly developed resources—Bohemia's iron mines, textile plants, and stone quarries; Hungary's coal and wheat; the maritime and wharfage facilities of the Italian and South Slavic Adriatic provinces—together with an impressive network of railroads and a huge imperial bureaucracy. After the treaties of Saint-Germain and Trianon, however, most of this vast reticulation was gone. More painful yet, Austria was surrounded by its former subject nations, a majority still hostile and all intent on maintaining stiff tariff barriers and import quotas against the attenuated little republic's modest exports. So it was that postwar Austria was left threadbare and hungry, "too small to live, too large to die," as political commentators described its condition. Little wonder, even after the Peace Conference's veto, that the *Anschluss* movement, envisaging the union of Austria and Germany, remained alive and vibrant among a significant minority of Austrians.[7]

## AN IMPLOSION OF COALITION POLITICS

The nation's political structure was ill equipped to cope with these economic and political challenges. Within less than a week of Austria's surrender, Karl Renner, vice-chairman of the Reichstag's Social Democratic faction, won the support of his fellow deputies in establishing a provisional government for the newly declared "Austrian Democratic Republic." Afterward, the fledgling cabinet's first order of business was to schedule national elections for a constitutional convention that would transform itself into an operative parliament. The elections duly took place in February 1919. Nominally, the Social

---

7 Norbert Schausberger, *Der Griff nach Österreich: Der "Anschluss"* (Vienna: Jugend und Volk, 1978), 102–3.

Democrats emerged as the largest winners. Failing to gain an absolute majority, however, the party was obliged to enter into a coalition with the right-wing Christian Social Party (CS) and with other, smaller rightist factions. It was a political marriage of convenience that soon would prove unworkable, most notably in coping with the nation's grim economic and social issues.[8]

The Social Democratic Party had been established in the late 1880s and was largely the handiwork of middle-class Jewish intellectuals, among them the party's founder, Viktor Adler (who died only a day after the provisional republic was established), and Otto Bauer, a highly esteemed lawyer-economist who had been repatriated from a Russian prisoner-of-war camp in time to steer the Social Democrats toward an armistice and to acceptance of de facto independence for the empire's subject nationalities. Indeed, following the establishment of the remnant Austrian Republic, Bauer and his colleagues represented the Social Democrats' most influential leadership; and, upon Viktor Adler's premature death, Bauer became the party's chairman. Although another politician, Karl Renner, the product of an old Catholic family, served as the new republic's first chancellor, Bauer was the power broker who rapidly transcended his portfolio as foreign minister to orchestrate a major part of the new government's domestic agenda.[9] It was essentially at his initiative that the brief postwar period of Social-Democratic seniority produced the most sweeping working-class legislation in the nation's history, including an eight-hour workday, paid employee holidays, the prohibition of child labor and night work for women, and a vast increase in unemployment and health insurance.

Within 18 months of its adoption, however, the ambitious social-welfare program overreached itself. Financed by punitive taxes on business, the legislation did nothing to mitigate the truncated nation's devastating postwar inflation. Politically, it inflicted only humiliation on the "respectable," tradition-bound leadership and membership of the Christian Social Party, who found themselves in the unfamiliar role of a minority within the government coalition. Nevertheless, the moment of this rightist faction's apparent reincarnation came as early as the parliamentary elections of December 1920, when it managed to win a slim but functional majority. The accomplishment in no small measure reflected the Christian Socials' astute choice of their party chairman. This was Ignaz Seipel, a monsignor of the Catholic Church, a canny "priest-politician" who subsequently would dominate the Austrian

---

8 Sachar, *Dreamland*, 174.
9 Ernst Glaser, *Im Umfeld des Austromarxismus: Ein Beitrag zur Geistesgeschichte des österreichischen Sozialismus* (Vienna: Europaverlag, 1981), 371–91.

political landscape throughout most of the 1920s, serving as the nation's chancellor from 1922 to 1924 and again from 1926 to 1929.

Seipel's early background gave only a tentative clue to his impressive political future. Following his original ordination in 1899, he had earned a doctorate in moral theology at the University of Vienna, and, in 1908, he returned to the same university to teach courses in that subject and subsequently to chair his department. By 1918, too, Seipel's intellectual and administrative gifts evoked the interest not only of Austria's church hierarchy (which promoted him to monsignor) but of Emperor Karl, who recruited him to assist in the government's diplomatic explorations with the Allies, especially with Catholic France and Italy. For his efforts, the monsignor was appointed minister of social welfare in Austria's last imperial cabinet.

According to one appraisal, Seipel, "with his thin bloodless lips, hawk nose, and piercing eyes ... looked the part of a modern-day inquisitor."[10] But the impression was deceptive. The young prelate-academician actually had begun his political career as a moderate, and it was soon after the first postwar election of 1919, with its narrow Social Democratic majority, that he had participated congenially in the negotiations that produced the nation's early coalition government. Within 18 months, too, Seipel vaulted to prominence in the successor Christian Social Party administration, serving as foreign minister in the Johann Schober cabinet and then, in 1922, as his party's chairman and his nation's chancellor.[11] But even as head of his own government, Seipel made a point of muting his party's record of clerical royalism to concentrate on Austria's economic challenges. His emphasis, first and foremost, was to bring inflation under control, to legislate a more balanced program of rewards for small businessmen, and then to negotiate a government loan through the League of Nations. By 1929, when he retired from his second term as chancellor, Seipel largely had met these goals.

He had met them, however, only through the painful surgery of terminating numerous public-welfare projects and laying off thousands of redundant, formerly imperial, civil servants. If these measures produced a certain fragile economic stability, it soon became clear that Austria's salaried lower-middle class would be the first to pay. Indeed, during the mid-1920s, Christian Social politicians began concentrating upon the diversion of these white-collar frustrations. Their technique was a familiar one. They embraced their party's

---

10  David Clay Large, *Between Two Fires: Portraits of Europe in the 1930s* (New York: Norton, 1990), 63.
11  Klemens Von Klemperer, *Ignaz Seipel: Christian Statesman in a Time of Crisis* (Princeton, NJ: Princeton University Press, 1972), 75–79.

historic antisemitism with a ferocity that bore scant resemblance to the opportunistic populism of the party's nineteenth-century founder, Karl Lueger, the fin-de-siècle mayor of Vienna—and even less to Ignaz Seipel's aristocratic contempt for demagoguery.

Numbering some 200,000 (12 per cent) of greater Vienna's population of 1,865,000, Jews formed the capital's largest ethnic minority. Although essentially a middle-class element,[12] at least a third of Vienna's Jewish population were *Ostjuden*, recent immigrants from the late empire's Galician and Bukovinian provinces; and these newcomers tended to be quite poor, typically earning their livelihoods as proprietors of modest shops or market stalls.[13] Nevertheless, to most Austrians it appeared that retail stores and professional offices with Jewish names were proliferating in every business district of the capital. Before 1914, in the comparatively prosperous Austria of Emperor Franz Josef, a vocationally capitalist Jewish presence could be accepted or ignored. But not in the misery of early postwar Vienna, where a storm of *Judenhetze* rapidly assumed dimensions unprecedented in recent Austrian history.

Thus, in 1919, verbal abuse was superseded by a series of thuggish rampages through the commercial neighborhoods of Leopoldstadt, Vienna's quasi-ghetto quarter. Although the physical assaults ended when Jewish war veterans hastily organized a defense force, rallies and demonstrations against Jews, frequently initiated by Christian Social agitators, became distinctly more common.[14] Indeed, for two and a half ensuing years, the wave of antisemitic abuse endured, not subsiding until spring of 1923 when Chancellor Seipel warned his fellow party members that failure to conform to a more subdued and "respectable" behavior risked the punishment of Austrian credit on international financial exchanges.

Yet, if physical intimidation ebbed, Seipel's appeal for moderation of speech or thought rang hollow against both "alien" and "ideological" enemies. Austria's political landscape had taken definitive shape by the early 1920s, and its lineaments were ugly. Beyond the afflictions of xenophobia and the republic's complex, proportion-based electoral system, an even graver danger was the emergence of a series of paramilitary "defense" forces that sought to

---

12  Sachar, *Dreamland*, 179.

13  Hellmut Andics, *Der ewige Jude: Ursachen und Geschichte des Antisemitismus* (Vienna: Molden, 1968), 292; Leopold Goldhammner, *Die Juden Wiens: Eine statistische Studie* (Vienna: R. Löwit Verlag, 1927), 9.

14  Ivar Oxaal, Michael Pollak, and Gerhard Botz, eds., *Jews, Antisemitism, and Culture in Vienna* (London: Routledge & Kegan Paul, 1987), 156.

fill the vacuum of an organized army; for the Treaty of Saint-Germain had limited Austria's "official" armed forces to a negligible 30,000. One such private militia, springing up during the early postwar years, consisted of veterans' groups that were intent on protecting their family property against marauders, many of them South Slav irredentists but the majority of whom were themselves Austrian military veterans. By late 1918, these self-defense vigilantes had coalesced into the Heimwehr, or "home defense force." Although nominally apolitical, the Heimwehr almost from its outset functioned as the "enforcement branch" of the Christian Social Party.

Responding in turn to the threat of this armed right wing, the Social Democrats moved swiftly to organize a parallel defense constabulary of their own. This was the Schutzbund, or "Protective League," consisting almost exclusively of urban blue-collar workers. Thus it was, during the 1920s, that two quasi-armies came into existence, both functioning and clashing outside official government control, with the Heimwehr winning its recruits essentially in the agricultural hinterland and among the urban lower-middle class and the Schutzbund maintaining its base among the working classes of "Red" Vienna and of other, smaller Austrian cities. In July 1927, these rivalries produced a series of clashes. Beginning with scattered riots in the eastern province of Burgenland, they extended to Vienna itself and claimed 94 lives. Subsequently, the polarization and intermittent bloodshed between Heimwehr and Schutzbund—the "Blacks" and the "Reds"—would continue into the early 1930s.[15]

## THE "DUODECIMO" CHANCELLOR

During the initial violence of July 1927, it was Chancellor Seipel himself who had authorized the forceful suppression of the "Reds." In the process, he had become identified almost overnight as the "prelate without mercy." It was a curious sobriquet for a man who formerly had been admired for his political moderation and restraint. Yet the bloody summer collisions had dispelled the chancellor's lingering illusion that forbearance, or even parliamentary government itself, could survive in a nation as ideologically fractured as Austria. Altogether, the internecine clashes left Seipel emotionally drained and physically exhausted. In June 1929, he gave over the chancellorship to his fellow party member Ernst von Streeruwitz, saving only the foreign ministry for himself. Four months after that, the priest-politician left the government altogether, retiring to a monastery.

---

15  Klemperer, *Ignaz Seipel*, 266.

Seipel's timing was apt. He was spared the need to confront a new disaster that rivaled even the grim impoverishment of the early postwar years. This was Europe's Great Depression. In Austria, the calamity reached its full impact in May 1931 with the collapse of the Creditanstalt, Austria's (and Europe's) second largest banking conglomerate. The resulting economic free fall left the Social Democrats in disarray. Confronted by mass unemployment and the accompanying erosion of national and local tax bases, the party's postwar welfare programs no longer could meet the working population's most existential needs, even in "Red" Vienna. Yet the political right wing appeared equally at a loss. Between 1931 and 1932, as one Christian Social Party chancellor followed another in a vain effort to resolve the unemployment crisis, each ultimately was reduced to entreating the Social Democrats and other, smaller parties to participate in "emergency" political coalitions. The effort fell flat. Otto Bauer, still leader of the Social Democratic opposition, and still outraged by the "massacre" of July 1927, refused to share in administering the affairs of a "doomed" capitalism.[16]

Under these circumstances, in the wake of the nation's parliamentary elections of spring 1932, the government that emerged no longer remained the joint Christian Social–Social Democrat coalition of the immediate postwar but a confederacy this time exclusively of the Right. Indeed, to patch together their fragile majority, the Christian Social Party accepted into the government the Landbund, a peasant faction, and the Heimatbloc, an amalgam of ultra-reactionaries that functioned as the "political wing" of the uniformed Heimwehr militia. Even within this rickety junta, however, the Christian Social Party initially could muster only a one-man parliamentary majority to confirm its chairman, Engelbert Dollfuss, as Austria's new chancellor.

Dollfuss at first seemed an unlikely choice for political high office. At the age of 39, the youngest head of government in Europe, he was suspected of lacking the gravitas of an experienced statesman. Moreover, standing only four feet eleven inches, he inevitably became the butt of wags, who vied with each other in ridiculing him as "Millimetternich" or the "duodecimo chancellor." His family background, too, was hardly a consolation to a voting public still mourning its nation's lost heritage as the "aristocrat of European dynasties." Dollfuss was the illegitimate son of a peasant woman, Josefa Dollfuss, and an agricultural laborer whom her family had rejected for his even less impressive origins. When the child was one year old, a neighboring farmer, Leopold Schmutz, married Josefa and gave his family name to their ensuing children, although Engelbert Dollfuss himself inherited and

---

16   Sachar, *Dreamland*, p. 189.

kept his mother's maiden name as well as her dwarf-like stature. Like her, too, the boy became fervently religious. As a gymnasium student, he gave serious thought to a career in the priesthood. The temptation was eventually subsumed in young Dollfuss's extracurricular school activities, where he revealed a concomitant ardor for politics. Yet one passion energized the other. By the time he reached his second year at the University of Vienna theology faculty, Dollfuss had been elected president of the Catholic Student Club, and he was reelected even after transferring to the university's law faculty. In the end, however, it was the war that evoked the intense patriotism that became as much a defining marque of Dollfuss's public career as his piety or political acumen. He volunteered for the army. As a university student, he would routinely have been eligible for officer's training, but he was turned down for reasons of insufficient height. He reapplied. On his third effort, he was accepted, and was dispatched to the Italian front as a lieutenant of a machine-gun platoon. In the Tyroleon mountains, subsequently, Dollfuss displayed the courage under fire that won him two decorations.

Later, with the ensuing collapse of the empire and the end of the war, the young dynamo returned to chaotic, impoverished Austria, where he resumed his law studies at the University of Vienna and eventually was graduated as "Dr. Engelbert Dollfuss." Still in his twenties, and still a political overachiever, Dollfuss then gravitated instinctively to membership and energetic legwork in the Christian Social Party. In 1923, he was offered and accepted a government post as secretary of the Farmers' Union. The choice was astute. Drawing on his family's agrarian background, Dollfuss introduced Austrian farmers to the avant-garde soil technology that he had studied on visits to Germany, together with that nation's equally innovative agricultural marketing cooperatives and social insurance programs. For his efforts, Dollfuss achieved rapid political promotion. By 1931, he was appointed minister of agriculture, and, in the spring of 1932, the Christian Socials chose him as their party chairman. In that leadership role, the little dynamo organized the campaign that achieved his party's narrow electoral victory of May 12. He needed only eight more days to engineer the coalition of right-wing parties that brought him to the chancellorship.

A rather more daunting challenge for the new chancellor was the rescue of an Austrian economy that was floundering in the midst of a Europe-wide depression. Yet, within two months, addressing his nation's financial crisis with characteristic vigor and imagination, Dollfuss emulated Ignaz Seipel's earlier achievement by negotiating a 20-year loan agreement with the League of Nations. Collateralized by the Austrian railroad system, the agreement this time made available to the government 300 million gold schillings, an infusion that pulled the Creditanstalt out of its insolvency and made the bank's capital available again for business loans. Dollfuss subsequently protected these achievements by winning parliamentary approval for a series of rigorous financial reforms, including a deflationary monetary policy that evoked enthusiastic support from the nation's politically conservative majority.

No less crucially, the "duodecimo chancellor" in his legislative agenda managed at the same time to secure the warm approbation of the Vatican, and thereby of Austria's devoutly Catholic agricultural and small-town populations. These latter were specifically the elements that harbored the bitterest memories of Social Democratic rule in the war's immediate aftermath, an incumbency that had disestablished the church, laicized Austria's school system, and lifted the interdiction on divorces and interfaith marriages. It was hardly a secret, too, that Pope Pius XI enthusiastically supported Dollfuss's commitment to firm executive authority. Ruling the Holy See with a strong hand, the pontiff himself often had claimed for his inspiration Saint Augustine, whose tract, *Civitas Dei*, projected a vision of a state governed within the constraints of Christian discipline.

Indeed, it was in pursuit of that shared objective, on May 1, 1934, that Dollfuss signed an historic concordat with the Vatican. As in Mussolini's Lateran agreements (p. 65), the pact fully satisfied Pope Pius XI's requirements for marriage, education, and "public demeanor" and increased the government's financial aid to Austria's priesthood, its Catholic schools, and such lay associations as Catholic Action (the so-called Piusverein). In turn, addressing a visiting delegation of Catholic pilgrims, the pope gratefully noted that "[t]he Austrian people ... finally has the government it deserves."[17] The Social Democrats would view the concordat differently. For them, it represented the "Vaticanization of Austria."

## THE FASCIZATION OF AUSTRIA

Dollfuss's confrontation with political democracy in Austria was only marginally less aggressive than his policy of "Vaticanization." The process evolved in stages, beginning on October 1, 1932, with the chancellor's activation of the nation's "Enabling Law." Since 1867, it was this legislation that had allowed the imperial chancellor to govern independently for renewable six-month increments when the Reichstag was not in session. The measure was incorporated

---

17 James William Miller, *Engelbert Dollfuss als Agrarfachmann* (Vienna: Böhlau, 1989), 7.

afterward into the republican constitution of 1920. Twelve years later, confronting Austria's economic emergency, Dollfuss himself first invoked this enabling legislation in an executive decree requiring the Creditanstalt's stockholders to accept financial responsibility for repaying the bank's losses. He intervened again on March 4, 1933, when members of the Social Democratic faction in the upper house of parliament, incensed by the government's efforts to punish Austria's striking railroad workers, resigned their committee offices en bloc, thereby invoking an obscure legislative provision mandating new elections. Enraged by this "legalistic effrontery," Dollfuss reacted by announcing that parliament in effect had "dissolved itself," and therefore he was free to re-invoke the enabling legislation and to operate independently of the legislature for the sake of "preserving law and order."

In fact, the little chancellor's uncompromising authoritarianism signified the beginning of the end of Austria's republican experiment; for he subsequently announced that his emergency decrees would remain in effect until the political opposition agreed to a fundamental "revision" of the nation's constitution. When the Social Democrats and other political moderate-centrists bridled, Dollfuss in March and April of 1933 launched into his own de facto "revision." He suspended all party conventions, even of his own Christian Social Party. Following this decree by outlawing—and thus forcing underground—the Social Democrats' paramilitary Schutzbund, Dollfuss simultaneously confiscated one-third of the treasury of the Municipality of Vienna, the traditional stronghold of Austrian Social Democracy. In ensuing weeks, the chancellor and his cabinet went further yet in their authoritarian agenda: introducing a ban on labor unions; censoring the press; and abrogating habeas corpus, trial by jury, and the constitutional court. Finally, in September 1933, Dollfuss announced that henceforth his Christian-Social-dominated coalition, which included Pan-Germans and "Heimwehrer" (the paramilitary irregulars of the Christian Social Party), would govern not as separate constituencies but as an interlinked "Fatherland Front."

Yet, in taking these draconian measures and thereby effectively throttling the Austrian Republic's fragile democracy, Dollfuss was cultivating not only the approbation of the church hierarchy,[18] or even of his nation's agricultural and urban lower-middle classes. He was reacting also to the gravitational influence of Fascist Italy. Indeed, the Duce's corporative regime in many respects was the model Dollfuss hoped to install in Austria, even as he regarded Italian military support as essential for protecting his little

---

18 Miller, *Engelbert Dollfuss*, 22.

nation against Nazi Germany (pp. 219–20). Mussolini, for his part, cultivating his relationship with the Austrian chancellor, was exploiting his own priorities. Whatever the Duce's professed "ideological kinship" with Dollfuss, by the 1930s those priorities were essentially territorial and devoted to reclaiming the Adriatic regions originally promised to Italy in the 1915 Treaty of London (p. 37). Throughout the 1920s, Mussolini had refrained from pressing his expansionist itinerary. In those years, his government was preoccupied with domestic concerns, especially the consolidation of Fascist political control (pp. 47–50). Moreover, postwar Italy relied heavily on the international economy to stabilize its currency. The time had not yet come for adventurism or forfeiture of the admiration of conservative circles in France and Britain (who thus far tended to regard Mussolini as a "good European").

By the early 1930s, however, the Duce felt secure enough in his popular and governmental base to embark on a more revisionist and muscular foreign policy. In that effort, he discerned his first natural ally in Hungary, whose territory had been almost as mercilessly dissected by the Allied diplomats as Austria's and whose embittered and revanchist government was fast approaching the political authoritarianism of Italy's. Another potential ally for Italy was the Croatian enclave within the Yugoslav successor state, a community that nurtured an undisguised hatred of the realm's Serbian majority and monarchy (pp. 244–45). But between revisionist Italy, on the one side, and revisionist Hungary and Croatia, on the other, lay Austria. To complete his "nexus of resentment," Mussolini deemed it crucial to maneuver Austria into the Italian diplomatic orbit; and in that scheme he would have to pick and choose his political soul mates among his attenuated little neighbor's own population.

He found them in the ranks of Austria's ruling Christian Socials. Indeed, the Austrian government itself had taken the initiative in diplomatic overtures to Italy. In August 1922, during Ignaz Seipel's first term as Austria's chancellor, the "priest-politician" had traveled to Rome to consult with Italy's—pre-Mussolini—Facta government (p. 32) and to propose a currency-customs union between the two countries. Although the Allies vetoed the proposal, the idea was never abandoned, neither by political right-wingers in Austria nor by Italy's ensuing Fascist regime. Hence, in 1930, Austria's Streeruwitz cabinet succeeded in concluding a somewhat vapid "Treaty of Mutual Friendship and Cooperation" with the Mussolini cabinet; and when Dollfuss became chancellor two years later, he made three respectful pilgrimages to the Duce in Rome, similarly in quest of mutual areas of collaboration.

Mussolini did not hesitate in identifying those areas. Both on Dollfuss's visits and on other occasions, he entreated the Austrian chancellor to establish an unambiguously fascist government. Thus, in January 1934, the Duce sent his deputy foreign minister, Fulvio Suvich, to Vienna to beseech Dollfuss not to procrastinate in inflicting the coup de grâce on the Social Democrats and their political bailiwick in "Red Vienna." A week later, through the Italian ambassador in Austria, Mussolini intensified his pressure, warning Dollfuss not to miss "the current propitious moment" to "make good on the [authoritarian] promises he had given to Italy."[19] Dollfuss was listening. But as he embarked on his own domestic program of fascization, he was not eager to precipitate a full-blown civil war with the Social Democrats, or still less with their paramilitary militia, the Schutzbund (p. 190), which had gone underground but was still far from moribund.

Mussolini, however, was able to avail himself of other confederates to accomplish his expansionist agenda. Besides Austria's church hierarchy and the Christian Social Party, these included Austria's rightist Heimwehr. The constituency of this "home defense force" was both political and military. In its political incarnation, the Heimwehr was known as the Heimatbloc (p. 191) and comprised eight members of Dollfuss's newly proclaimed Fatherland Front. The Heimatbloc's military leadership, in turn, was divided between Major Emil Fey and Prince Ernst von Starhemberg. Fey, a decorated veteran of the Austrian army (although by descent a German of Brandenburger origin), was a hard-core militarist who doubled as cabinet minister of "state security" and—in Vienna—as commander simultaneously of the federal police, of locally based army units, as well as of the Heimwehr paramilitaries. Fey's political ally, the dashingly handsome Prince Ernst von Starhemberg, actually had founded the Heimwehr militia in the early postwar years and remained its national commander well into the 1930s. Accordingly, in his simultaneous role as deputy chairman of the Fatherland Front, Starhemberg, like Fey, was awarded a ministerial (if non-portfolio) seat in Dollfuss's cabinet.

Although unofficially recognized as "Mussolini's men in the cabinet," Fey and Starhemberg henceforth found no temperamental difficulty in working with Dollfuss to reach a common understanding with the Duce. For his part, Mussolini reciprocated that loyalty by providing the Heimwehr with sizeable quantities of Italian weapons and money. In 1932 alone, the deliveries included 50,000 rifles and 2,000 machine guns (most of these actually Austrian weapons captured in the World War). As Mussolini stated in a conversation with Starhemberg in June of the same year, "Our highest ideal in Fascist Italy is [one of] *'italianità,'* that is, the inculcation of Italian

---

19  Jens Petersen, "Das faschistische Italien und der 12. Februar 1934," in *Februar 1934: Ursachen, Fakten, Folgen* (Vienna: Verlag der Wiener Volksbuchhandlung, 1984), 518.

consciousness. You must create something of the sort in Austria. . . . Austria must play a new historic role in Europe."[20] The "new historic role" the Duce had in mind palpably was to bring Austria within the Italian orbit through a common fascist ideology. But neither Fey nor Starhemberg seemed to be discountenanced by this vision, as long as their joint ambition was to make a clean sweep of Austria's domestic political opposition.[21] Indeed, it was the initiative of the two Heimwehr leaders, as much as Dollfuss's or even Mussolini's, that precipitated a decisive confrontation with their common enemy, the Social Democratic Schutzbund.

## THE "*ITALIANITÀ*" OF AUSTRIA

In the predawn hours of February 12, 1934, a group of 20 policemen burst into the Hotel Schiff in Linz, the middle-sized provincial capital of Upper Austria. The hotel itself functioned as the unofficial headquarters of the recently banned Schutzbund. At the time of the police incursion, some 50 members of this clandestine leftist militia were sitting at a group of tables in one of the hotel's conference rooms, playing cards. But when the police commander announced that the Schutzbundler were under arrest, the latter immediately rushed for their own guns. In the ensuing hail of bullets, many on both sides were struck down. The police then issued a call for reinforcements, and, within the hour, a squad of Heimwehr irregulars arrived, augmented by a platoon of federal army troops bearing automatic weapons. The exchange of fire was heavy, but, in the early afternoon, the 38 surviving Schutzbundler surrendered. The violence was repeated in nearby Steyr, where the 600 employees of the town's Steyr-Werke, Austria's largest weapons factory, offered tough resistance to a combined Heimwehr-police-army assault. But here, too, after a day and a half of fighting, the workers capitulated.

News of the events in Upper Austria reached Vienna late that same February 12. The reaction of the Social Democratic leadership was all but reflexive. About mid-morning of the following day, the party executive ordered Vienna's streetcar drivers to halt service. It was the recognized signal for a general work stoppage in other major sectors of the capital's economy. Indeed, by mid-afternoon, Vienna's heating and electricity services were totally paralyzed. At the same time Julius Deutsch, the former Social

---

20 Fürst von Ernst Rüdiger Starhemberg, *Between Hitler and Mussolini: Memoirs of Ernst Rüdiger Prince Starhemberg* (New York: Harper, 1942), 105.
21 Rudolf Walter Litschel, *1934—Das Jahr der Irrungen* (Linz: Oberösterreichischer Landesverl, 1974), 42–45.

Democratic minister of defense and still de facto commander of his party's underground Schutzbund, ordered all his Viennese militia members to retrieve their stored weapons and congregate at selected points in the city. In reaction, Dollfuss seized upon the developing "insurrection" as a choice opportunity to outlaw his political enemies. Citing the Social Democrats' alleged "treason," the chancellor immediately proclaimed their party illegal and ordered its dissolution. He coupled his decree with orders for Vienna's Social Democratic mayor, Karl Seitz, to be removed from office and jailed.

It was at this juncture that events in Vienna passed from Dollfuss's control. The reincarnated leftist Schutzbund geared up for mass resistance. In the ensuing confrontation, between February 13 and February 15, Vienna became the scene of Austria's grimmest and most costly civil violence since the revolution of 1848. The fighting was concentrated at first in Floridasdorf, a northern, working-class suburb of the capital. Occupying the large municipal buildings near the Floridasdorf Bridge, and manning heavy machine guns, the Schutzbundler easily repulsed an initial police attack—and even launched a counterattack of their own that was halted only when Major Emil Fey, in his capacity as minister of "state security," ordered local army garrisons to use artillery. From then on, however, cannonades drove the workers out of their ramparts and forced them to retreat across the Danube, leaving behind hundreds of dead and wounded.

Subsequently, the most decisive single battle in the civil war shifted from the Floridasdorf Bridge to Vienna's Heiligenstadt quarter and, specifically, to the Karl-Marx-Hof. This mammoth workers project, encompassing 14 apartment buildings and occupying almost four square kilometers, was one of the most famous achievements of the postwar Social-Democratic government. Indeed, the Karl-Marx-Hof had become the very icon of "Red Vienna" and of the Social Democrats' dedication to the capital's proletarian majority. The battle opened on the evening of February 13 when the army began firing its mountain artillery at the center of the apartment complex. The next day, additional and heavier artillery pieces were trundled into position. Together with a battalion of infantry, and accompanied by a Heimwehr machine-gun company, the army pounded the workers' enclave without pause. The uneven struggle continued for 72 hours. Finally, in the late morning of February 15, the defenders raised white flags. By then Schutzbund resistance also had ended in Upper Austria.[22]

Throughout the country, during the three days of battle, approximately 600 workers had been killed and some 2,000 had been wounded; and 115

---

22 Paul R. Sweet, "Democracy and Counterrevolution in Austria," *Journal of Modern History* 22 (1950): 52–58.

Heimwehrer, police, and soldiers also had fallen. The Social Democratic leaders Julius Deutsch and Otto Bauer managed at the last moment to escape arrest by fleeing over the border to Czechoslovakia; but several thousand other leftist "rebels" fell into government hands. Dollfuss dealt with them mercilessly. Formerly known as a dictatorial but hardly a bloodthirsty man, the little chancellor now had become an unforgiving one. During the ensuing week, at his initiative, 21 "rebels" were tried, sentenced to death, and hanged. Although martial law was lifted on February 23, "treason" trials continued until mid-July. In all, over a thousand Social Democrats were sentenced to prison terms ranging from a few months to life. Meanwhile, the February 13 edict disbanding the Social Democratic Party was extended, removing from office all legislators, governors, and municipal functionaries whose positions had been based on Social Democratic electoral victories. Their places were taken by "dependable" members of the Fatherland Front.[23]

Finally, on May 1, 1934, Dollfuss climaxed his political and military purge by steering through a new constitution for the nation. The document not only reflected the influence of the Vatican and Mussolini but also, perhaps, expressed Austria's subliminal nostalgia for the lost Habsburg Empire. Its preface stated, "In the name of God Almighty, from Whom all right proceeds, the Austrian people receives this constitution for its Christian, German, Federal State." The term "Federal State [Bundesstaat Österreich]" was substituted for the previous "Republik Österreich," and its emblem again bore the late Habsburg double eagle. Much pageantry accompanied these changes, with parades flying the flags of Austria's seven future "estates." As analogues of Italy's "corporations," the estates manifestly were intended to operate as a virtual substitute for parliament. As for the "official" parliament, it was transformed into a one-chamber federal diet, with its attenuated membership of 59 persons limited to noblemen, priests, landowners, and senior public officials—and in any case fulfilled a mere advisory function.

Mussolini was gratified. Subsequently, he dispatched a personal letter to Dollfuss, pledging always to remain the chancellor's "faithful friend."

## OVERTURE TO A TERROR CAMPAIGN

By mid-spring of 1934, the Mussolini-Dollfuss relationship transcended even issues of political ideology. It also functioned undisguisedly as a strategic alliance, assuring the Duce of Austrian neutrality as he sought to advance Italy's

---

23 Large, *Between Two Fires*, 89–90.

cherished entryway into Yugoslavian Dalmatia (pp. 229–31). In turn, Dollfuss had to take into account Hitler's growing obsession not only with redressing the territorial amputations of the Paris Peace Conference but with the expansion of the Nazi "Third Reich." Almost certainly, Austria would be among the first victims of the Führer's prospective *Weltpolitik*.[24]

Indeed, it was in recognition of his strategic dependence on Mussolini that Dollfuss, together with Gyula Gömbös, the Hungarian prime minister (who shared the Duce's revisionist ambitions and similarly feared Hitler's), traveled to Italy in March 1934. With much fanfare, the two leaders joined Mussolini in signing the "Rome Protocols," pledging their three governments to "consult together" in the event of "changed political conditions." In the immediate aftermath of the ceremony, joint defense issues were addressed by the generals Jansa and Roatta, the respective Austrian and Italian military chiefs of staff. Italian military installations were strengthened on the Italo-Austrian frontier at the Brenner Pass, simultaneously with increased deliveries of Italian weaponry to the Austrian Heimwehr.[25]

For Austrian citizens, these mutual commitments and military assignments conceivably would have been strengthened even further if the Dollfuss government had succeeded in fostering a general sense of Austrian patriotism. But in the postwar, the sentiment had not managed to bestir the nation's core German-speaking population. It had taken the form, rather, of sentimental loyalty to the late Habsburg Empire. During the 1920s and 1930s, although the internecine hatred between Austria's Social Democrats and Christian Socials did nothing to foster a passion for national unity, neither, on the other hand, did it animate a political gravitation toward Nazi Germany. The temptations of *Anschluss* had been limited essentially to the immediate postwar years and were stirred by the perceived economic advantages of Austria's joinder with Germany's liberal Weimar Republic.

Indeed, when the topic of union with Germany resurfaced in Austria in 1929, at the onset of the Great Depression, most of its Austrian political supporters continued to identify with the nation's "German People's Party." Although this party shared briefly in Dollfuss's Fatherland Front, few even of these "Pan-Germans" could manage to generate enthusiasm for Nazism's truculent hooliganism. The Heimwehr, too, resisted the temptation to go the German route. As late as 1934, Prince Starhemberg, the militia's commander,

---

24 Alan Cassels, *Mussolini's Early Diplomacy* (Princeton, NJ: Princeton University Press, 1970), 146–74.
25 Lajos Kerekes, *Abenddämmerung einer Demokratie: Mussolini, Gömbös und die Heimwehr* (Vienna: Europa Verlag, 1966), 116–19.

stated, "For us there will be no Anschluss because we know that Anschluss means nothing other than the degrading of Austria to the status of a colony of Prussian Berlin."[26]

At first, Dollfuss too had entertained ambivalent feelings about the German connection. Although in his wartime military service he was single minded in his Austrian patriotism, during the economic and political malaise of the early 1920s he was amenable briefly to a limited confederative association with the Weimar Republic. He was married to a German woman and maintained congenial relations with his German in-laws and German friends. Hence, in February 1933, soon after Hitler took office as Germany's chancellor, Dollfuss approached the Nazi leader indirectly with the proposal that the German government assume a share of Austria's $200 million loan-repayment obligation to the League of Nations (p. 188). In return, he offered to strengthen his government's diplomatic relationship with Berlin and, by implication, loosen its exclusive diplomatic reliance on Rome.

But Hitler scornfully rejected these overtures. The relationship he had in mind with Austria was one he would accomplish on his own terms. Years before, in 1920 and 1921, returning briefly from Germany to address local gatherings of Austria's minuscule "German National Socialist Workers' Party," the young Adolf Hitler was obsessed with a private image of hapless little Austria functioning as a modest, even attenuated, regional enclave in his anticipated "Greater German Reich." The vision almost certainly evinced the resentment he nurtured against the "mongrelized" Vienna of his youthful frustrations and failures, an attitude he made amply clear in his autobiographical *Mein Kampf*. Indeed, of all Hitler's territorial ambitions, those he harbored toward Austria were the most personal, an expression of his perverted nostalgia.[27]

Yet, at the same time, those ambitions could not ignore Austria's strategic location in the heart of Central Europe, directly adjacent to successor-state Czechoslovakia and with its German-inhabited Sudetenland. In the summer of 1933, after his recent accession to the German chancellorship, Hitler accordingly took his first step toward *Anschluss*—the territorial ingestion of his remnant Austrian neighbor. It was to strangle the little nation's economy. His opening moves in that direction were to levy a prohibitive 1,000-mark visa tax on German tourists who normally spent their vacations in Austria, and to impose equally punitive trade quotas on Austrian imports. Thus far, however, Hitler disdained to exploit Austria's homegrown Nazi Party for his own

---

26 Fürst von Ernst Rüdiger Starhemberg, *Die Reden des Vizekanzlers* (Vienna: Oesterreichischer Bundespressedienst, 1935), 37.
27 Konrad Heiden, *Hitler: A Biography* (New York: Knopf, 1936), 14–16, 22–24.

purposes. His lack of initial interest was understandable. During the 1920s, under the chairmanship of a rabble-rousing Viennese lawyer, Walter Riehl, the Austrian Nazis remained a negligible force in their little nation's politics. Even as late as 1930, under the somewhat more dynamic leadership of Alfred Frauenfeld, a former Vienna stone mason and intermittent stage actor, the party comprised not more than 15,000 members. Most of these were minor civil servants, policemen, and occasional army recruits who had gravitated to Nazism essentially to seek wider economic opportunity for themselves in joinder to Germany.[28]

In 1932, however, the Austrian Nazi Party registered unanticipated signs of life in the little nation's parliamentary elections. As the only faction that had not been part of a national coalition, it could escape blame for the Depression. In that year, Austria's Nazis actually had garnered some 75,000 new votes— 17 per cent of the ballots—enough to return 33 seats among the 165 members of parliament (although essentially at the expense of the German People's and Heimatbloc parties). Taken by surprise at this unexpected electoral upsurge, Hitler then began to discern potential advantage in encouraging Austria's Nazis to destabilize Dollfuss's government.[29] Belatedly, too, he recognized that the party's members could profit by their very anonymity. If some Austrian Nazis simultaneously joined Dollfuss's new Fatherland Front, they were careful to disguise their ongoing Nazi sympathies. Later, when Dollfuss outlawed their party (p. 203), a substantial number of these Hitler loyalists went underground in an effort to protect their employment in Austria's civil service and police.[30]

Still others among Austria's Nazis emigrated directly to Germany to regroup and reorganize with German funding. The chief operative in this migration was Theo Habicht, a former German citizen and minor Wiesbaden alderman whom Hitler had sent to Austria as early as July 1931 with a mandate to serve as Nazi "Inspector-General for Austria." Short, plump, and thickly bespectacled, Habicht proved to be a whirlwind of unscrupulous energy. Even his deportation by the Dollfuss government in late 1932 did not significantly limit his activities. Transferring his headquarters to Lechfeld, Bavaria, he set about organizing other émigré Austrian Nazis as an "Austrian Legion," in effect, as an integral component of Germany's own Nazi Party. Well equipped with training facilities and weaponry, Habicht's uniformed quasi-militia soon

---

28  F. L. Carsten, *Fascist Movements in Austria* (London: Sage Publications, 1977), 199.
29  Carsten, *Fascist Movements*, 79.
30  Carsten, *Fascist Movements*, 133–37.

grew to a strength of some 15,000 members, almost as many as the party's numbers in Austria proper.[31]

Indeed, by mid-1933, Habicht began selectively infiltrating his "legionnaires" back across the Bavarian border to their original homeland. Once in Austria, these transplants embarked on a reenergized campaign of antigovernment and antisemitic smoke bombings in such provincial, middle-sized Austrian cities as Salzburg, Linz, and Klagenfurt—and, intermittently, even in "Red" Vienna (p. 190). For the first time, too, on Austrian soil, they wore swastika-adorned uniforms and engaged in raucous public demonstrations. Habicht's initial purpose in orchestrating this offensive apparently was to force Dollfuss into an early reelection campaign. Far from succeeding, however, the tactic provoked the chancellor into arresting over a thousand Nazi sympathizers and dismissing 387 suspect civil servants and 81 small-town mayors.[32] Then, on June 17, 1933, Dollfuss banned the Austrian Nazi Party outright, half a year even before taking similar action against the Social Democrats (p. 198).

But if the Austrian chancellor speculated that his campaign against the Social Democrats might fend off Hitler and earn some breathing room for his own fascist—Christian Social—regime, he was swiftly disabused. To his confidants, Hitler repeatedly boasted that he would make "short shrift of Dollfuss."[33] The *Völkischer Beobachter*, Nazism's party journal, left no doubt that Berlin would "fight the Dollfuss government tooth and nail so that a new Austria may arise after the Dollfuss system has met its deserved downfall."[34] It was apparent by then that the chancellor could not satisfy Hitler simply by emulating his policies but only by maneuvering his little republic "home to the Reich."[35] Nevertheless, until the autumn of 1933, Dollfuss persisted in sending out feelers to Hitler, requesting a personal meeting, even suggesting that he, Dollfuss, might appoint two Nazis to his own cabinet. His overtures were contemptuously ignored.

On one occasion, however, in October 1933, Hitler intimated through private emissaries that his counterdemand was for Dollfuss to restore legal status to the Austrian Nazi Party, to reserve for the party not two but fully half the seats in the Austrian cabinet, and to appoint Theo Habicht, commander of the émigré "Austrian Legion," as Austrian vice-chancellor "with enlarged

---

31  Jürgen Gehl, *Austria, Germany, and the Anschluss, 1931–1938* (London: Oxford University Press, 1963), 54–56.
32  Gordon Brook-Shepherd, *Dollfuss* (Westport, CT: Greenwood Press, 1978), 195.
33  Hermann Rauschning, *Gespräche mit Hitler* (Vienna: Europaverlag, 1973), 84.
34  Quoted in Large, *Between Two Fires*, 94.
35  Jens Petersen, *Hitler-Mussolini: Die Enstehung der Achse Berlin-Rom, 1933–1936* (Tübingen: Niemeger, 1973), 521.

responsibilities."[36] Although Dollfuss categorically rejected these macabre proposals, he agreed two months later to receive Habicht for exploratory talks on other, less intractable, political issues.[37] But within days of the agreement, a new series of Nazi bombings were launched in Austria, and these continued into January 1934. In reaction, on January 7, 1934, when Habicht's courier airplane from Munich was only 20 minutes from beginning its descent to Vienna's airport, Dollfuss canceled the latter's scheduled visit, and the pilot had to turn back. Enraged by the Austrian chancellor's "insolence," Hitler then lost no further time in ordering Habicht to enlarge the Nazi terror campaign.[38]

Habicht accordingly unleashed his "legionnaires," whether Austrian nationals or transplants smuggled over the Bavarian border, on a climactic onslaught. From mid-May until early July 1934, their rampage surpassed its predecessors both in scope and intensity. Hardly a day passed in these months without a dynamite attack against Austrian electricity grids and water installations, against railways, telephone networks, and government buildings. The assault struck province by province, from Salzburg to Lower Austria, from Styria to South Tyrol.[39] In response, on July 11, with unequivocal assurances of Mussolini's support (p. 199), Dollfuss reconstituted his cabinet on an emergency basis, assumed personal direction of the nation's federal police and army, and ensured that the Heimwehr paramilitaries remained under the control of Ernst von Starhemberg, his trusted lieutenant and newly appointed vice-chancellor. Anyone suspected of Nazi affiliations was subject to arrest and internment.[40] Altogether, in these mid-summer weeks, Austria resembled less a functioning state than a besieged fortress.

## "COORDINATION" OR COUP D'ÉTAT?

But if it was clear by then that Hitler would not be deterred from his subversion of Austrian independence, it was less obvious that he personally organized the plot to overthrow the Dollfuss government.[41] In future years, some historians were persuaded that the concept of a putsch originated with

---

36  Martin Kitchen, *The Coming of Austrian Fascism* (London: Croom Helm, 1980), 149.
37  Heinz Höhne, *Die Zeit der Illusionen: Hitler und die Anfänge des Dritten Reiches, 1933–1936* (Düsseldorf: ECON Verlag, 1991), 223–24.
38  Gerhard L. Weinberg, *Hitler's Foreign Policy: The Road to World War II, 1933–1939* (New York: Enigma Books, 2005), 103–16.
39  Höhne, *Die Zeit der Illusionen,* 289.
40  Félix Kreisler, *Von der Revolution zur Annexion* (Vienna: Europa Verlag, 1970), 210.
41  Weinberg, *Hitler's Foreign Policy,* 103.

Austrian Nazis themselves, reacting in frustration to Berlin's seeming preference for *Gleichschaltung*—a gradual "coordination" of Austrian policies and public institutions with Germany's.[42] If that was the case, it seemed extraordinary that Dollfuss had not managed to identify the most important of these local subversives (with the exception of Habicht, whose headquarters, in any case, were not in Austria).

It developed only later that the arch conspirator was Dr. Anton Rintelen, a native Austrian and, indeed, the person Hitler himself lately had designated as Austria's future chancellor. A middle-aged, heavyset man, whose pince-nez and daintily trimmed moustache gave him the appearance of a larger-scale Heinrich Himmler, Rintelen earlier had served as the governor of Styria, then briefly as minister of education in the first Dollfuss cabinet, and subsequently as rector of the University of Graz. In 1934, he was appointed Austria's minister to Italy. On July 23 of that year, however, Rintelen had returned to Vienna, where he had been instructed to report to the chancellor on "developments" in the Italian government. But Rintelen had not yet reported to Dollfuss—nor did he intend to do so.

A year earlier, suspecting Rintelen of pro-Nazi sympathies, Dollfuss had dismissed him from his assignments within Austria itself, including the governorship of Styria and his seat in the government cabinet, and had "exiled" him to his current diplomatic post in Italy. Now, however, on July 23, once back in Vienna, Rintelen checked into a suite in the Hotel Imperial, on the capital's Ringstrasse. It was there, within the ensuing 48 hours, that he anticipated the overthrow of Dollfuss's government at the hands of others of his secret conspirators, to be followed by his, Rintelen's, ensuing appointment as Austria's chancellor. Among his key liaisons in the conspiracy was a prominent Viennese lawyer, Baron Otto Gustav von Wächter. The 33-year-old son of a former Austrian defense minister, Wächter, a closet Nazi, in recent months had functioned in Vienna as "field commander" of Theo Habicht's Austrian Legion. In that capacity, he had visited Rintelen in June 1934, at the Austrian embassy in Rome, for a well-camouflaged series of meetings. Their mutual purpose was to arrange the final details of a putsch.

In fact, the conspiracy by then had meandered along for almost a year, and its designated operatives still consisted mainly of Austrian Nazis, particularly those whom Dollfuss had driven underground in June 1933, banning their party and expelling their—identified—members from Austrian military service (p. 203). For the time being, most of these Hitler admirers had remained in

---

42 Pauley, *Hitler and the Forgotten Nazis*, 103–16.

Austria, unlike their compatriots who had resumed their activities in Bavaria as members of Habicht's "Austrian Legion."[43] But in late 1933, still at Hitler's orders, the network of Austria's own clandestine Nazis had been mobilized for the first time into a special "shock" unit, "SS Standarte 89," under the command of "SS Sturmbannführer" Fridolin Glass, a much-decorated Austrian war veteran. From then on, it was specifically Glass's camarilla of Austrian plotters that was responsible for an escalating campaign of domestic mayhem. Their prime objective this time was unequivocal. It was the usurpation of the Austrian government itself.[44]

On June 25, 1934, Glass shared in a strategy conference with a group of fellow conspirators. The meeting took place in Zurich. Other participants included Habicht, who had arrived in Switzerland from Bavaria; Rudolf Weydenhammer, Habicht's civilian chief of staff in Bavaria; and Wächter, Habicht's Austrian "field commander." Yet it was Fridolin Glass, ostensibly lowest in rank of the conspiratorial quartet, who took the initiative in outlining his preferred scenario for the imminent putsch. Its objective, he explained, was for "his" SS Standarte 89 to capture Austria's President Miklas and Chancellor Dollfuss in one fell swoop, together with the entire Austrian cabinet, thereby creating a near-total vacuum of public authority. In the process, units of Glass's Standarte 89 simultaneously would take over the Austrian state radio transmitter and the Vienna telephone headquarters. Glass's strategy anticipated, too, that Austrian regular army units would provide active assistance on the instructions of the secret Nazis in their ranks. It was henceforth on these multiple assumptions that the plotters approved the scenario and sent Glass back to Vienna to prepare its details. The entire meeting did not exceed two hours.

Another prominent member of the conspiracy who would have been present at the Zurich conference was Rintelen, the shadow chancellor-in-waiting. But it was deemed expedient for him to remain at his diplomatic post in Rome until the last moment. Nevertheless, he had been kept well informed of the plot's development, both by Weydenhammer and Wächter. Indeed, during the first half of 1934, Wächter had accompanied Weydenhammer on most of the latter's clandestine visits to Rintelen in Italy up to the moment of Rintelen's final secret departure for Vienna on July 23. In their conversations, citing the imminent Dollfuss-Mussolini joint family "vacation" at Riccione (p. 182), it was Rintelen himself who maintained the pressure for the operation to be carried out before the end of July. These repeated exhortations, coming from

---

43 Dieter Ross, *Hitler und Dollfuss: Die deutsche Österreich-Politik, 1933–1934* (Hamburg: Leibniz-Verlag, 1966), 235.
44 Höhne, *Die Zeit der Illusionen*, 224.

the most prestigious figure in the conspiracy, were weighty enough. But so were those of an Austrian army officer, Lieutenant Colonel Adolph Sinzinger, a closet Nazi who commanded Vienna's Second Garrison army headquarters (p. 208). It was the combination of Rintelen's impatience and Sinzinger's treachery that apparently persuaded Habicht and Weydenhammer to strike at the Dollfuss government sooner rather than later.

On July 16, the plotters' last joint meeting took place, this time in Habicht's Munich apartment. Again, Glass dominated the conference, supplying the final details for the putsch.[45] The impending action was code-named "*Operation Sommerfest*" ["Operation Summer Festival"], and its timetable was set for the afternoon of July 24, when the Austrian cabinet was scheduled to meet in its final session before the ministers dispersed for the summer holiday and before Dollfuss himself left to join Mussolini in Italy. Upon this understanding, Wächter, Glass, and their fellow conspirators returned to Vienna. Weydenhammer followed a week later to await Rintelen's secret arrival in the capital on July 23.

In Germany, until the last moment, *Operation Sommerfest* remained strictly a Nazi Party conspiracy. At no time was the Reichswehr leadership involved or informed. Neither was the senior staff of Germany's foreign ministry, whose members continued to advocate *Gleichschaltung*, the peaceful "coordination" of Austria's public institutions by Nazi propaganda and economic pressure. It was assumed that any other, direct action might provoke the retaliation of the Versailles Powers. Indeed, only ten days before the scheduled putsch, Germany's minister to Austria, Dr. Kurt Rieth, was shocked upon hearing ambiguous rumors of a planned uprising. He telegraphed an alarmed inquiry to Berlin. Yet even Rieth was without proper instructions on a putsch or its uncertain fate until the very end, and he scampered around on the fatal day (in the words of a British journalist in Vienna) "like a startled and not very intelligent rabbit."[46]

## "*OPERATION SOMMERFEST*"

In the early evening of July 23, Weydenhammer—Habicht's deputy in Bavaria—arrived in Vienna from Munich. Under a British passport that identified him as "Trevor Williams," a businessman, he visited Rintelen at the

---

45 Andrew Whiteside, "Austria," in *The European Right: A Historical Profile*, ed. Hans Rogger and Eugen Weber (Berkeley, CA: University of California Press, 1966), 308 *ff*.

46 Gordon Brook-Shepherd, *Prelude to Infamy: The Story of Chancellor Dollfuss of Austria* (New York: I. Obolensky, 1961).

latter's suite in the Hotel Imperial. The meeting was brief. Weydenhammer reassured the "chancellor-in-waiting" that the putsch schedule was holding firm. It was to be launched the next day, between 1:00 and 2:00 p.m., when the officers and men of the "SS Standarte 89" would assemble at a gymnasium attached to the garrison headquarters of the Austrian Second Brigade, the unit commanded by Lieutenant Colonel Sinzinger. Once gaining entrance, either by guile or intimidation, and equipping themselves with Austrian army rifles and ammunition, the Standarte contingent would be transported to the chancellory in a fleet of commercial trucks to be supplied by a "Herr Löhner," an Austrian businessman.

A problem developed. The plotters had assumed that they would take into custody not only Chancellor Dollfuss but also President Wilhelm Miklas. The plan was upset, however, when Miklas left Vienna two days earlier for his traditional Carinthian holiday retreat in Velden. Nevertheless, Wächter had taken steps to resolve even this unexpected difficulty. At dinner on the evening of July 23, he revealed to Weydenhammer and the other conspirators that, on his own, he had just dispatched a small task force to Velden with the assignment of "interning" President Miklas the following afternoon, simultaneously with the assault on the chancellory in Vienna. With this assurance, the plotters finished their meal. Later that night, Weydenhammer visited Rintelen's hotel a second time for a lengthier conversation, this one relating to the political reconstruction of the Austrian cabinet after the putsch. It was not until 4:00 a.m. of July 24 that Weydenhammer returned to his own room at the Hotel Cobenzl.

He was up again four hours later, placing calls to the conspirators to reconfirm all details. Yet it was in the same mid-morning that Weydenhammer received an unsettling piece of news. Evidently seeking to clear his desk of other government business, Dollfuss had decided to postpone the date of the cabinet meeting by another 24 hours, to July 25. Immediately, Weydenhammer launched into a frantic series of telephone calls to reschedule the putsch. His exertions were at least partly successful. By the time he met later that morning with Wächter and Glass, every detail of the operation had been recalibrated for the next day. But again, during the morning of July 25, still another last-minute alteration took place. Dollfuss's belated cabinet meeting did indeed begin at 11:00 a.m. The session had only completed its first hour, however, when Major Emil Fey, in his role as Heimwehr "chief of security" for Vienna, approached the chancellor and whispered in his ear. Dollfuss listened intently for a few moments and then addressed the other cabinet members. "I've been given an alert to a possible security threat," he said. "It's not confirmed, but we had better give Fey some time to take precautions. I propose that all of you wait at the ministry of defense until we resume our discussions at four p.m."[47]

The "alert" and subsequent interruption could be traced back to Police Commissioner Johann Dobler and his urgent conversation that very morning with secret Heimwehr official Karl Mahrer at the Café Weghuber (p. 183). By telephone, Mahrer had persuaded three of his Heimwehr colleagues to rush over to the coffee house to interrogate Dobler personally. Upon arrival, the men listened incredulously as Dobler repeated the developing plot to them. Still unsure of its veracity, the senior Heimwehr officer telephoned his superior, Major Karl Wrabel, aide-de-camp to Major Fey, and related Dobler's warning. Wrabel, in turn, telephoned Fey, who himself had just returned to the chancellory for the rescheduled cabinet meeting. Fey also was dubious about the plot, yet he regarded it as his duty to alert Dollfuss. This he did. Upon being informed, the chancellor was equally skeptical, but his decision to interrupt the cabinet session and to have his ministers remain in attendance at the nearby ministry of defense probably saved their lives.

It was Dollfuss alone who disdained to leave the chancellory office. He could not be faulted for his skepticism. Since the days of Metternich, Austria had been a nation of informers and pseudo-informers, and "treason" was their subject of choice. The issue formed the theme of dramas by Franz Grillparzer, Austria's most renowned nineteenth-century playwright; and, among later authors, treason and betrayal similarly were recurrent plots. Stefan Zweig wrote an absorbing biography of Joseph Fouché, Napoleon's minister of police and double agent. Franz Werfel crafted three dramas in which treason played an important role, as did Arthur Schnitzler. The prewar treason of Colonel Alfred Redl, the Habsburg chief of military counterintelligence, although of limited value to Austria's enemies, was a public sensation and scandal. Well inured to this public fascination with conspiracy, the Austrian police after the war tended to greet every report of treason with suspicion. Accordingly, when Major Fey assigned some two dozen additional Heimwehr paramilitaries to the chancellory building, he did not bother to request police reinforcements.

Two hours earlier, at 10:30 a.m. on that same July 25, the 150 members of "SS Standarte 89" crowded into their eight disguised "army" trucks and converged from all over Vienna toward their designated assembly point. This was the equipment depot of the Second Brigade's headquarters garrison. Entering the building, and ignoring its two confused guards, the Nazi paramilitaries headed directly to the supply shelves on the depot's lower

---

[47] Gerhard Jagschitz, *Der Putsch der Nationalsozialisten 1934 in Österreich* (Graz: Verlag Styria, 1976), 106.

level. There, exchanging their civilian clothes for official army uniforms, they strapped rifles on their shoulders, climbed again into their fleet of trucks (several with the name of their business owner, Markus Löhner, painted clearly on the vehicles' side panels), and sped off directly toward the chancellory.

Except for the former royal palaces, the chancellory was Vienna's most impressive public edifice. Sprawling over a full city block, the Ballhausplatz, it had been constructed in 1719 as the dominant icon of the Habsburg government. In 1814–15, it had been the site of the Congress of Vienna, and, in later decades, it housed both the chancellory and foreign ministry. Altogether, the building resonated with tradition. Dollfuss's spacious office was luxuriously furnished with eighteenth-century furniture, artifacts, and paintings. The adjoining "Hall of Mirrors," equally sumptuous, was used for cabinet meetings. In the same building, ascending from the courtyard staircase to the first floor, were the "state" rooms, including the (largely ceremonial) office of the federal president. A multitude of landings, passages, and small offices accommodated the rest of the chancellory's extensive staff.

Toward this phantasmagoria on the Ballhausplatz the procession of eight trucks, bearing their cargo of uniformed and armed "soldiers," continued without interference or even challenge directly into the chancellory courtyard (among the passengers was Johann Dobler, who had just betrayed the entire enterprise at the Café Weghuber). The operation was based on the Nazis' private information that the ceremonial changing of the chancellory guard always took place between 12:50 and 1:00 p.m. It was in this "dead" time zone that the "army reinforcements" disembarked from their trucks and disarmed the building's eight bewildered police guards. Hence, by 12:55 p.m. of July 25, the seat of the Austrian government was in the control of 154 Nazi putschists.

During these same minutes, however, Ignaz Karwinsky, security director of the chancellor's suite of offices, hearing the rumble of truck engines and glancing out of his office window, immediately suspected that the "soldiers" were fraudulent. Turning to Dollfuss, he implored the chancellor to follow him to the third floor, where a remote hallway cloakroom could be used as a hiding place. Yet before Dollfuss could react, his personal attendant, Eduard Hedvicek, suddenly pulled the chancellor by the arm, urging him instead to come with him. They could escape the building altogether, Hedvicek explained, through a side exit at the opposite end of the main floor. Dollfuss complied. But to both men's consternation, they found the exit door locked. Hedvicek then frantically began rummaging in his pocket for a spare key. His search took too long.[48]

---

48 Gottfried Karl Kindermann, *Hitler's Defeat in Austria, 1933–34* (London: C. Hurst, 1988), 103.

A RETURN VISIT FROM AUSTRIA'S TATTERDEMALION SON

## A PLOT BUNGLED

As the troops of SS Standarte 89 careened into the chancellory courtyard, another small group of 15 Austrian Nazis, armed but wearing civilian attire and evidently detached from the chancellory operation, pushed its way into the state radio's central transmitting station on the Johannesgasse. Once inside, the intruders disconnected the building's telephone switchboard and at gunpoint forced the newscaster to broadcast an announcement: "Chancellor Dollfuss has resigned. Doctor Anton Rintelen has taken charge of the new government." The "news flash" was the signal awaited by every clandestine Nazi officer in Austria.[49] Within the hour, in all the nation's federated provinces except those of Lower Austria, Voralberg, and Vienna itself, bands of uniformed Nazis began to parade, unfurling swastika-emblazoned flags on town halls and other public buildings. Initially, local police hesitated to interfere.

Yet, at the same time, Austria's cabinet ministers, who had left the chancellory to re-congregate a mile away in the massive neo-baroque defense ministry, began to consult with their home offices by telephone, querying their staffs on Rintelen's alleged "accession" to power. No one could verify the radio announcement. Certainly, there had been no word from President Miklas. Unknown to the plotters, Miklas and his wife had left their Carinthian vacation retreat at Velden two days earlier to visit relatives in Klagenfurt. When informed of the Nazi radio broadcast, the outraged president immediately ordered the provincial police to seek and intercept any putschists who may have been en route to Velden. Within 90 minutes, the search and interception bore fruit. The two automobiles bearing the Nazi "emissaries" were discovered parked in the woods near the president's assumed chalet at Velden. Their six occupants were arrested on the spot.

Almost at the same time, from the local Klagenfurt radio station President Miklas broadcast a statement, with orders for it to be retransmitted to the ministers in Vienna and to the nation's press. As head of state, he declared solemnly and forcefully, he would not recognize a single decision on behalf of any government official presently in "rebel" captivity or accept any "rebel" political conditions. In the absence of any information on the fate of Chancellor Dollfuss, Miklas continued, he, the president, was appointing Minister of Education Kurt von Schuschnigg as "provisional" chancellor and directing Schuschnigg to ensure the release of any captive ministers, if necessary by force.

---

49 Kindermann, *Hitler's Defeat*, 104.

For all its unyielding obduracy, however, Miklas's order was unable to save the Nazis' most important captive. A few moments before 1:00 p.m. of July 25, as Dollfuss and his bodyguard encountered the mysteriously locked "escape" door in the corner office of the chancellory's main floor, a contingent of uniformed Nazis broke into the room. They were led by a discharged former army sergeant, Oskar Planetta. Pistol in hand, Planetta approached the chancellor and proceeded to shoot him twice at point-blank range. Dollfuss crumpled to the floor, feebly calling for help. An autopsy determined later that he had been shot in the neck and armpit, and the bullet entering his neck had severed his spine. Another Nazi intruder, Corporal Viktor Stiastny, kneeling for a moment beside the bleeding chancellor, unbuttoned Dollfuss's jacket, calmly took out its wallet and relieved it of its cash. Interrogated after the event, the rebels insisted that they had not been authorized to fire on Dollfuss. But subsequent evidence indicated the contrary. Berlin had given orders for the chancellor to be "put out of the way for good."

Meanwhile, Sergeant Planetta and his men left Dollfuss where he lay to search for other government ministers. The only one they found was Major Fey, whom they immediately took captive. During the ensuing 40 minutes, Dollfuss remained on the floor, semiconscious, as groups of putschists intermittently entered and left the room. One of these, Major Hudl, sat at a desk, smoking. When two captured chancellory guards were brought into the room and caught sight of the prostrate Dollfuss, they asked for a physician to be summoned. Hudl refused, although he allowed the guards to carry the chancellor to the office sofa. Dollfuss then revived briefly. "How are my ministers?" he whispered. The guards reassured him of their safety; but the putschists berated their wounded captive, accusing him of persecuting Austria's Nazis. Dollfuss could only murmur: "I have always wanted peace."[50] Then he asked for a priest. The request was denied. Dollfuss lingered for two hours more. His last words were "Ask Mussolini to look after my wife and children." At about 3:30 p.m. he breathed his last.

The attack on the chancellory and the murder of Dollfuss had been the putschists' first success. The second was their broadcast message announcing the "resignation" of Dollfuss and the appointment of Rintelen as his successor. This was also their final success. After the broadcast, Wächter and Weydenhammer had ensconced themselves at the Hotel Imperial, where they intended to guide Rintelen, the "chancellor-elect," in his first executive measures. But it soon became evident that something was amiss. No delegation

---

50  Walter P. Maas, *Assassination in Vienna* (New York: Scribner, 1972), 91–92.

ENGELBERT DOLLFUSS (AT FRONT, LEFT), AT A HEIMWEHR RALLY IN INNSBRUCK TWO WEEKS BEFORE HIS ASSASSINATION IN 1934

came to escort Rintelen to the chancellory. In Vienna, the anticipated pro-Nazi street parades did not materialize.[51]

The answer to the mystery was the last-minute gathering of the other cabinet members in the heavily fortified defense ministry and the urgent mandate they had just received from President Miklas to bring the situation "under control." In fact, their task was comparatively uncomplicated. It developed that the morning interview between Police Commissioner Dobler and senior Heimwehr officials at the Café Weghuber, together with the ensuing interruption of the cabinet meeting, had allowed Major Fey to alert the Heimwehr senior command to the impending danger. At Fey's instructions, some 2,000 Heimwehrer, as well as police and army units, had been held in reserve. It was this combined force that subsequently converged on the chancellory—although 40 minutes after the putschists had gained entrance. At the orders of "Provisional Chancellor" Schuschnigg, the assembled units refrained from rushing the building for fear of jeopardizing the safety of any captives or the life of Dollfuss (whose fate was unknown to them). But they proceeded forthwith to block all chancellory exits.

---

51  Ross, *Hitler und Dollfuss*, 236–43.

From his temporary office in the defense ministry, Schuschnigg then entered into communication with the blockaded rebels. The arrangements were awkward. Schuschnigg's liaison was Vienna's commissioner of police, whose aide had commandeered the telephone of a tobacco kiosk across the street from the chancellery. For the putschists, the intermediary was Major Fey. Appearing on the chancellery balcony with a pistol trained on his back, the Heimwehr minister was forced to announce that Dollfuss (whose mortal wounding he could not disclose) had authorized Rintelen, the "chancellor-designate," to mediate in the dispute and that, until Rintelen's arrival, no aggressive action should be taken. But Rintelen did not arrive, either then or later. It was not until after 5:00 p.m. that the insurgents learned of President Miklas's decisive action in appointing Schuschnigg provisional chancellor. From that point on, Fey was able to persuade his captors that the putsch was doomed. The latter then began to bargain for safe conduct. Schuschnigg's response, at 5:30 p.m., was an ultimatum to surrender within 15 minutes or face the storming of the building. Even then, the confrontation was not resolved. The Nazi plotters continued their bargaining efforts, and Schuschnigg refrained from making good his threat.

Finally, at 8:00 p.m., the main central doors of the chancellery opened and the 154 rebels, encouraged by Schuschnigg's "forbearance," streamed out of the building and to anticipated safety. They did not make it through the courtyard. Exiting with them, Fey confirmed the news of Dollfuss's murder, and Schuschnigg ordered the immediate arrest of the putschists. Although itching to kill their captives on the spot, the Heimwehrer followed orders, bundling them into vans and carrying them off to imprisonment at the police barracks on the Marokkanergasse. Although most of these Nazi "foot soldiers" were later released, the identified plot leaders, including Planetta and ten other members of his "execution squad," were summarily tried, sentenced, and hanged.[52] Wächter and Weydenhammer were seized as they prepared to leave Rintelen's suite at the Hotel Imperial. For the next few days, the two men sought to negotiate with the Heimwehr, to exchange information for their lives. But Prince Starhemberg, the Heimwehr's supreme commander, who had just flown back from his Italian vacation after being notified of the events in Vienna, rejected a deal. Possibly through bribery, however, Wächter and Weydenhammer later "escaped" from jail the day before their scheduled trial and succeeded in making their way across the Czech border.

---

52  Petersen, *Hitler-Mussolini*, 360–66.

Rintelen, the "chancellor-in-waiting," was taken into police custody the same evening of July 25, where he was promptly escorted from his hotel to jail. Yet, en route, he managed to shoot himself with a small pistol that he had concealed in his pocket (although he was careful to wound himself only superficially). Found in Rintelen's pocket, too, was a dramatic farewell note to his family, proclaiming that his name had been "misused." Three weeks later, in mid-August, he was put on trial for treason. The proceedings lasted only a day and half before the court found Rintelen guilty and sentenced him to 25 years imprisonment. He served his time until the German occupation of Austria four years later. On March 12, 1938, Hitler personally ordered his release.[53]

It was more than ironic that Johann Dobler, the district police commissioner who had sought frantically to betray the plot, was captured with the rest of the "Standarte 89" prisoners. Perhaps his change of mind would have gotten him off lightly; but, on July 29, overwhelmed with guilt and fear, he suddenly broke away from his guards while being led upstairs to the central police headquarters' interrogation room and flung himself from a fourth-storey window to his death.

## THE AFTERMATH OF *SOMMERFEST*

The immediate threat of a Nazi putsch did not end in the late afternoon of July 25, 1934. From then until July 30, its aftershocks continued to fuel Nazi violence in the provinces, especially in Carinthia, Styria, and Upper Austria. The combined efforts of the Heimwehr, the police, and the federal army were required to suppress the uprising. On the government side, there were over 100 deaths and 500 wounded; on the Nazi side, approximately 140 deaths and 600 wounded. In all, 13 rebels eventually were executed and over 4,000 suspects were imprisoned without trial,[54] although another 4,000 Austrian Nazis managed to flee to Yugoslavia and several hundred others to Bavaria—despite Hitler's orders against providing them refuge (p. 217). On July 30, the late Dollfuss was given a state funeral. Not less than a million people filed by his bier, including many veteran Social Democrats.

It was Kurt von Schuschnigg, however, who emerged as the hero of the hour. Thirty-seven years old, the son of an imperial military officer, he had been born and reared in the army garrison town of Riva on Lake Garda, near

---

53 Friedrich Funder, *Als Österreich den Sturm bestand* (Vienna: Herold, 1957), 214.
54 Jagschitz, 221 *ff*.

the Italian border, and educated in a Jesuit school. Like Dollfuss, he had served on the Italian front during the war, and, following his demobilization, he too studied law. Upon earning his degree at the University of Innsbruck, Schuschnigg practiced in the same community before going into politics. Subsequently, as a Christian Social, he was elected in 1927 to the upper house of parliament, where he swiftly acquired a reputation for personal rectitude. Dollfuss, upon becoming chancellor in 1932, appointed Schuschnigg minister of justice and, the following year, awarded him the additional portfolio of education. Two years later, in July 1934, Schuschnigg's unflinching role in crushing the putsch effort earned him further respect, both in Austria and elsewhere in Europe. A correspondent in Vienna for the London *Times* described him later as "austere, diligent, sober . . . infused by an almost religious faith in his mission of statesmanship."[55] He would also turn out to be as committed in his ideological fascism as his predecessor (p. 196).

In the summer of 1934, however, it was not only the courage and patriotism of Schuschnigg and President Miklas that prolonged Austria's independence. The diplomatic stance of the German and Italian leadership played an even more critical role. In the case of Germany, that role was ambiguous. Whatever executive advantage Hitler gained by his liquidation of Ernst Röhm and the SA only a month before Dollfuss's murder, he sensed that he was not yet in a position to risk a blatant invasion of his little German-speaking neighbor. The Reichswehr high command had been propitiated, to be sure, and its personal loyalty to Hitler fortified; but the Reichswehr's manpower thus far had not been significantly enlarged, nor had Nazi *Weltpolitik* been tested. Indeed, it was the Führer's reluctance to launch a frontal, military invasion of Austria that persuaded him instead to acquiesce in the sub rosa tactic of a "spontaneous" putsch; and now even that exercise in political duplicity had gone wrong.

Hitler's subsequent objective reduced itself to damage control. In the late afternoon of July 25, his foreign minister, Konstantin von Neurath, received a telephone call from Kurt Rieth, the German minister in Vienna. Rieth related the news of the putsch and of its—as yet—uncertain fate. A few minutes later, after discussing the report with Hitler, Neurath telephoned Rieth to transmit the Führer's orders. These were to avoid conveying even the slightest intimation of German government involvement. Indeed, that evening, Hitler himself still kept to his plans of attending a Bayreuth performance of Wagner's *Rheingold*. Yet he was hardly seated in the opera house when an aide whispered the news that the putsch had failed and that all the conspirators had

---

55  C. Earl Edmondson, *The Heimwehr and Austrian Politics, 1918–1936* (Athens, GA: University of Georgia Press, 1978), 244.

been arrested. Still in whispers, Hitler issued orders for Neurath to prohibit Rieth from any contact with the Austrian "rebels" and to ensure that none of the latter was given refuge in Germany.

Within the hour, Neurath dutifully issued an official statement denouncing the putschists and other Austrian Nazis, and emphasizing that, if any of them as much as attempted to set foot on German soil, they would be arrested.

The next morning, again at the foreign minister's suggestion, President Hindenburg telegraphed Austrian President Miklas, expressing his personal condolences at the death of Dollfuss and pledging "eternal friendship" between their two countries. Later that same day, Neurath telephoned Rieth in Vienna, instructing him to wind up his affairs as minister and return to Germany at once. He was being replaced by Germany's former chancellor, Franz von Papen. Presumably only a suave and experienced eminence such as Papen, performing the role of Catholic emissary to a Catholic nation, could function as a "peacemaker" between the two governments.[56]

It developed only later that Hitler himself, after leaving the opera performance the previous night for his Beyreuth hotel suite, and after a lengthy telephone discussion with Neurath, had personally telephoned Papen. Citing the danger of "another Sarajevo," the Führer importuned the former vice-chancellor to accept the appointment. Papen had reluctantly acquiesced, but only on condition that Habicht be dismissed from his command of the "Austrian Legion" and that no further "adventures" be attempted. Hitler agreed on the spot. The following week he went further, ordering the dissolution of the Austrian Nazi Party's émigré bureau in Munich.

In Vienna, however, outraged at Hitler's clumsy gangsterism, President Miklas and Provisional Chancellor Schuschnigg reacted only grudgingly to the Führer's belated gestures. Indeed, Papen, who arrived in Vienna the evening of July 26, was obliged to visit the Ballhausplatz each day, vainly cooling his heels in the presidential waiting room until August 7, when President Miklas finally and formally received him and stonily accepted his credentials as Germany's minister.[57]

## AN "INTERESTED PARTY" TO THE SOUTH

It was not only Hitler's setback in Vienna that allowed Austria four more years of precarious independence (nor even, in 1938, Schuschnigg's "forbearing" gesture of appointing to his cabinet two pro-Nazi Austrians from

---

56 Franz von Papen, *Der Wahrheit eine Gasse* (Munich: P. List, 1952), 339.
57 Kindermann, *Hitler's Defeat*, 113–15.

the "National Opposition" coalition). The reaction of Benito Mussolini had much to do with Hitler's cautionary retreat. In his first 18 months as Germany's chancellor, Hitler was intent upon maintaining a respectful, even deferential, relationship with Europe's senior Fascist dictator. The practical foundations of the two men's relationship had been laid by Hermann Göring. After Hitler's abortive Munich putsch effort in 1923, Göring, fleeing abroad, had spent a year of his four-year exile in Italy. There he made friends in Italian air force circles. Upon returning to Germany in 1927, he acted as Hitler's unofficial intermediary both with the Vatican and with the Mussolini government.

In the 1920s and early 1930s, Hitler himself had been an ardent admirer of Mussolini. Indeed, in some ways, he modeled his own later regime on the Duce's in Italy, even down to the Roman salute. When he became chancellor in 1933, there was evidence that he and Göring wished Mussolini to approve the list of the new Nazi-Nationalist cabinet. Mussolini's unofficial emissary in Berlin, Giuseppe Renzetti, functioned at first as a kind of lord protector of the Reich; and, for the ensuing three-and-a-half years, Mussolini arguably was the most powerful man in Western Europe. But although the two dictators shared a common ambition for a revision of the Paris peace treaties, other territorial issues lingered between them.

The most serious of these related to Austria. One stumbling block was assumed to be the South Tyrol, the Austrian province that the Western Allies had promised the Italians in the 1915 Treaty of London (p. 37). During the Habsburg era, this region, with its picturesque Alpine countryside and prosperous agricultural population, had encompassed two distinct sectors. The largest and southernmost, directly adjacent to the Italian border and known in Italy as the "Trentino," included at least 400,000 Italian speakers whose discriminatory treatment at the hands of the Habsburg authorities had remained a legitimate source of grievance to the Italian government. In 1919, by terms of the Treaty of Saint-Germain, the sector was transferred to Italy.

Further to the northwest, however, in the same Austrian province of South Tyrol, the Italians similarly claimed the "Alto Adige," a segment that encompassed only 22,000 ethnic Italians among a great majority—some 230,000—of German speakers. This territory also had been promised to Italy in the 1915 Treaty of London. Hence, in 1919, disregarding the last of Woodrow Wilson's original "Fourteen Points," with its promise of national self-determination, and over the anguished protests of Alto Adige's German-speaking majority, the Allied statesmen at Paris transferred to Italy the full composite of South Tyrol, the Trentino and Alto Adige alike, thus bringing Italy's northern boundaries up to the Brenner Pass, the gateway to "integral" Austria. By this award, the

Allies' senior statesmen—Clemenceau, Lloyd George, and Wilson—doubtless imagined that they were placating the Italians, after denying them their even more extravagant territorial demands in the Adriatic littoral (p. 37). But the wound to South Tyrol's German speakers did not heal easily. In the late 1920s, a closing stanza of a regional folk song was eloquent:

> Erhebt nun Eure Hände
> Zum Schwüre hoch und hehr,
> Wir führen es zu Ende
> Bis auf den Bergen wieder
> Der Freiheit Sonne glüht
> Und wir Tiroler wieder
> Im freien deutschen Süd!

> Now lift your hands to heaven
> And take the oath
> That you will never rest
> Until upon the mountains
> Once more the sun of freedom glows,
> And we are again Tyroleans
> In the free German south![58]

Until the rise of Mussolini, Italy's postwar governments adopted a forbearing policy to the inhabitants of Alto Adige, tolerating German-language schools and cultural events and the use of German as a second language in the postal system and in other government offices. After 1924, however, once the embarrassment of the Matteotti murder had been "resolved" (pp. 59–62), the Duce launched a program of forceful *"Italianità"* in the whole of composite South Tyrol, and his government's earlier dispensations were systematically revoked. German-Tyrolean nationalist activities or publications were harshly suppressed, even coupled with isolated murders or with the "disappearance" of pro-Austrian activists. In fact, no permanent solution on the Tyrolean question was ever reached between postwar Italy and postwar Austria.[59]

In his militant pan-Germanism, Adolf Hitler was assumed to be unlikely to forgo the issue. By the early and middle 1930s, however, determined both to absorb remnant Austria and to retain Mussolini's friendship, Hitler kept

---

58 Hans Fingeller, *The Case of German South Tyrol Against Italy* (London: Allen & Unwin, 1927), 96.
59 Dennison I. Rusinow, *Italy's Austrian Heritage, 1919–1946* (Oxford: Clarendon Press, 1969), 163 ff.

clear of the South Tyrol controversy. In April 1934, he went so far as to inform a gathering of his government's foreign ministry personnel that he was prepared to divide Europe with Mussolini at the Brenner Pass, the "frontier indicated by geography," and that a few "unredeemed" German-speakers south of that boundary could be ignored. Hitler also reminded his listeners that, years earlier, in his *Mein Kampf*, he had written that any "diversion" of German diplomacy to the Tyrolean issue should be regarded as a "Jewish-Legitimist conspiracy" aimed at the obstruction of German-Italian rapprochement. Indeed, during his courtship of Mussolini, the Führer intimated that recovery of Alsace-Lorraine from France was a more immediate German priority.[60]

But if Hitler was prepared to consign the issue of South Tyrol to the back burner, this was not the approach he adopted to Austria itself, either in the pages of *Mein Kampf* or in his later career as German chancellor. In his *Weltpolitik*, no European country was a more predestined "racial" candidate than Austria for incorporation in his envisioned Greater Reich. Indeed, the Führer's coveted alliance with Mussolini was based ultimately on the anticipated expulsion of Italian influence from Austria (although Italy, in turn, would be generously compensated in the Mediterranean area). But to Hitler's chagrin, it was a formula that the Duce was not buying.

Mussolini had always taken an active interest in Danubian Europe. Intent on protecting the region's "integrity," he dubbed it "our European hinterland.... Without it, we shall be forced to play the insignificant role of a peninsula on the edge of Europe."[61] In the late 1920s and early 1930s, it was to protect that "hinterland" that he purposefully increased his nation's trade relations with Austria.[62] On November 7, 1933, in an interview with the editor of *Petit Parisien*, the Duce boasted: "If the *Anschluss* [between Germany and Austria], which [would be] ... as dangerous to Italy as to France, has not yet been accomplished, it is to a great extent because ... the Germans know that I have sent more troops to the [Austrian] frontier and that, if they enter Austria, I will intervene by force of arms."[63]

Thus, as the Nazi terror campaign within Austria gained momentum, Mussolini reacted in perturbation and ultimately in outrage. In scope and sheer mayhem, the onslaught threatened to surpass the brutalities that his own *Fascisti* had perpetrated in Italy. Earlier, he had been adamant in

---

60  Elizabeth Wiskemann, *The Rome-Berlin Axis* (London: Collins, 1966), 23–24.
61  Wiskemann, *The Rome-Berlin Axis*, 31.
62  Weinberg, *Hitler's Foreign Policy*, 64–68.
63  Wiskemann, *The Rome-Berlin Axis*, 63.

encouraging Dollfuss to deal harshly with Austria's Social Democrats, and, in pursuit of that approach, he had ensured an ample flow of Italian weapons to the Heimwehr. But after the Austrian "civil war" of February 1934, Mussolini similarly had lent his undisguised support to Dollfuss's campaign against Austria's homegrown Nazis. Hitler was not pleased by the Duce's reaction. Indeed, in June of that year, the two dictators finally agreed that the rising tensions between their two governments warranted no less than a summit conference.

On June 14, Hitler as the "junior" dictator made the rail trip to Italy. The meeting took place at Venice's Alberoni golf club, amidst much ceremony and fanfare. The ensuing conversations between the two leaders started politely enough, with Mussolini's courtesy to his guest only faintly tinctured with condescension.[64] But as the talks approached issues of substance, the Duce felt obliged to issue thinly veiled warnings about Germany's efforts to subvert the Dollfuss government. Hitler riposted that Austria in any case could not realize its true destiny as long as it was infested with Jews and other "mongrel" types. Mussolini reacted coldly to the observation and suggested that the Italian people did not admire the Nazis' racial theories and were particularly distressed by reports of the mistreatment of Germany's Catholic institutions.[65] Although Hitler denied the allegation, Mussolini went on to criticize episodes of Nazi "hooliganism" against Austrian citizens. Again, Hitler protested that the episodes were spontaneous and in no sense instigated by the German government.

Later in the discussions, however, Mussolini apparently conceded that he saw no problem with the inclusion of a few Austrian Nazis in Dollfuss's government.[66] The Venice conference then ended on June 15 with a joint communiqué. "Herr Hitler agrees that the independence of Austria is not in question," it stated, "and that the governments of Germany and Italy should collaborate for a speedy return to normal political conditions in Austria." No mention was made of replacing Dollfuss as chancellor.[67] But at the end of June, upon receiving word of the Röhm purge in Germany, Mussolini also made no secret of his revulsion. "[Hitler] is a cruel and ferocious character,"

---

64  Petersen, *Hitler-Mussolini*, 344 ff.
65  Ivone Kirkpatrick, *Mussolini: Study of a Demagogue* (London: Odhams Books, 1964); Wiskemann, *The Rome-Berlin Axis*, 36.
66  Alfred Rosenberg, *Das politische Tagebuch Alfred Rosenbergs aus den Jahren 1934/35 und 1939/40: Nach der photographischen Wiedergabe der Handschrift aus den Nürnberger Akten* (Göttingen: Musterschmidt-Verlag, 1956), 28.
67  Gehl, *Austria, Germany, and the Anschluss*, chapter 5; Weinberg, *Hitler's Foreign Policy*, 113–14.

he observed to his sister Edvige, "and recalls such legendary characters of the past [as] Attila. The men he killed had been his closest collaborators, [the ones] who [had] raised him to power."[68]

It was only six weeks later that the Austrian Nazis launched their putsch attempt against the Dollfuss government. Shortly after 1:00 p.m. on July 25, Mussolini was preparing to leave his office for the two-hour train journey to Riccione, where he intended to rejoin his family and await Dollfuss's arrival. Suddenly, he was called back to the telephone. Fulvio Suvich, undersecretary of state for foreign affairs, was on the line to inform him of the events taking place in Vienna. By later accounts, Mussolini went pale and then launched into an unrestrained diatribe against Hitler as "a hoodlum," "a depraved sexual maniac." Within the hour, still receiving reports of the apparently indeterminate outcome of the putsch, Mussolini sent for his military chief of staff, General Rodolfo Graziani, to learn which army reserves were available for manning the Brenner Pass. Later that afternoon, Graziani was able to report that two army corps and two squadrons of fighter airplanes could be mobilized at the Brenner within 24 hours. Mussolini immediately gave the order for their activation. "Graziani," he added. "Don't bother to keep the mobilization secret."[69]

That same night, as Hitler attended the performance in Bayreuth's opera house, he was alerted to these Italian military deployments. He remained seated until the opera ended. Afterwards, however, at his suite in the Hotel Royale, when he telephoned Papen and implored him to travel to Vienna immediately, he emphasized the importance of patching up matters not only with the successor Austrian government but with Mussolini.[70] In turn, the Duce, en route to Riccione to offer his personal protection to Dollfuss's widow, Alwine, and her two young children, doubtless was weighing his own course of diplomatic and military action. In ensuing days, he reconfirmed his commitment to Austria's independence, and the Italian press was allowed to condemn the attempted putsch. Pinning responsibility on Berlin, *Il Popolo d'Italia* characterized the Germans as the progeny of "illiterate barbarians" at a time when Rome could boast of "Caesar, Virgil and Augustus."[71]

Six days later, during a long conversation in Ostia with Ernst von Starhemberg, the Heimwehr commander whom he had summoned for an emergency visit, Mussolini launched into a further tirade against Hitler.

---

68  Edvige Mancini Mussolini, *Mio fratello Benito* (Florence: La Fenice, 1957), 147.
69  Wiskemann, *The Rome-Berlin Axis*, 40; C.A. Macartney and Alan W. Palmer, *Independent Eastern Europe: A History* (London: Macmillan, 1966), 326.
70  Kirkpatrick, *Mussolini*, 297.
71  Macartney and Palmer, *Independent Easter Europe*, 326; Kindermann, *Hitler's Defeat*, 100.

Characterizing the Führer as a "horrible sexual degenerate and a dangerous fool [whose] Nazi Party [consisted] of murderers and pederasts," the Duce added a barbed reference to French and British diplomatic inaction: "Others must at least demonstrate *some* interest in Austria and the Danubian Basin."[72] He had not ascended the heights of his country's government, he warned, and transformed his nation into a senior player on the European scene only to be ignored, let alone outflanked, by a political "arriviste," a "depraved sexual maniac" in Berlin. For the immediate future, Mussolini continued, his foreign policy would concentrate on the repair of the ignominy inflicted on his nation's dignity (as well as, presumably, on his own). But afterward, he assured Starhemberg, he would reserve his "freedom of action" in Europe. Less than half a year was to pass before the Duce would keep his promise.

---

72 Starhemberg, *Die Reden des Vizekanzlers*, 26.

CHAPTER SEVEN

# All Roads Lead to Rome

*"Failing in my assignment, I shall accept
death as my penalty. Amen."*

## A SOUTH SLAVIC BIRTH TRAUMA

Among postwar Europe's constellation of "successor states," the newly sovereign or enlarged nations that had been carved out of the moribund empires of the prewar period, it was the South Slav "Kingdom of the Serbs, Croats, and Slovenes" that soon was revealed as the most precarious. None of its fellow beneficiaries, neither Czechoslovakia, Poland, nor Rumania, encompassed a more complex or contentious amalgam of peoples: six, at least, with an equivalent scattering of regional subcultures.

The Serbs remained the largest component among them. In medieval times, their national home actually was known by its self-proclaimed title: "Serbian Empire." During the fourteenth century, however, the Turks, pouring out of Central Asia to overrun the Balkans, laid waste to these imperial pretensions. During the ensuing 500 years, the Serbs lay prostrate under their invader's heel.

It was only in the late eighteenth and early nineteenth centuries, with the subsequent enervation of the Turks' ruling Ottoman dynasty, that the Serbs began to stir again. Indeed, their successive uprisings in 1804 and 1815 led to a gradual resurrection of their autonomy until, by mid-century, they had achieved a de facto independence. Finally, in 1878, at the initiative of tsarist Russia, whose armies recently had defeated the Turks, an international meeting of the Great Powers (the "Congress of Berlin") restored the Serbs to full and formal sovereignty.

Yet it is of note that sovereignty was not a benediction that the congress extended to the Slovenes, the Croats, the Macedonians, the Bosnians, the Herzegovinians, or (with the single exception of tiny Montenegro) to others of the South Slav peoples. Rather, during the seventeenth and eighteenth centuries, although most of these diverse Balkan nationalities also had been wrested from Turkish rule, the feat had been accomplished less by their own or even by the Russian armies than by the armed forces of the Habsburg Empire, which subsequently consigned them to Austro-Hungarian imperial rule. Diverse they remained. In contrast to the Eastern Orthodox Serbs and the Muslim Bosnians and Herzegovinians, the Slovenes and Croats were predominantly Roman Catholic, and they gradually had come to share many of the cultural and social values of their Austrian and Hungarian overlords.

Even in their heterogeneity and parochialism, however, the South Slavic peoples managed intermittently to transcend their remaining political and cultural divisions. By the late nineteenth century, a sizeable minority of Serbian and Croatian secondary-school graduates had become intrigued by the idea of "South Slav" unity. In the mid-nineteenth century, Ilija Garašanin, a charismatic Serbian prime minister, warned his fellow citizens that their country, still undersized when measured by the vast demographic resources of the Ottoman and Habsburg empires, could achieve its full political and economic potential only in political alliance with their South Slav neighbors. In the second half of the century, a Croatian bishop, Juraj Strossmayer, similarly propagated the idea of a confederative South Slav nation.

Although, initially, these speculations achieved only limited popular resonance, a sequence of events in the early twentieth century ignited a broader-based pan-Slav nationalism. In 1908, the Habsburg government repudiated a commitment that it had issued 30 years earlier, at the Congress of Berlin. This was a promise to exempt from Great-Power rule the tiny and recently liberated twin Muslim principalities of Bosnia and Herzegovina, thereby preserving the Russian-Austrian balance of power in Eastern Europe. In 1908, however, the Austrians peremptorily annexed Bosnia-Herzegovina.[1] Although the Serbian and Russian governments launched vigorous protests, these initially were unavailing. Serbia's population numbered barely 4 million, and Russia, traditionally Serbia's patron and protector, was still licking its wounds after its recent defeat in the Russo-Japanese War. More critically yet, Berlin "reminded" the tsarist government of Germany's treaty partnership with the Dual Monarchy. The Russians backed down.

Even as late as 1912 and 1913, when the Serbs on their own managed to achieve a few localized military victories and modest territorial gains against the Turks and Bulgarians, these did not suffice to win over their fellow South Slavs to acceptance of Serbian leadership of a future "Yugoslav"—South Slav—confederation. Neither did the assassination, in the Bosnian capital of Sarajevo, of Habsburg Archduke Franz Ferdinand on June 28, 1914, at the hands of a Serbian nationalist society. Rather, the Serbs' eventual claim to Yugoslav leadership lay in their record of self-sacrifice during the ensuing World War. They bore the brunt of Austrian retaliation for the Sarajevo assassination with a tenacity and stoicism exceeded by no other wartime nation. Indeed, it was not until October 1915 that the Habsburg army, against ferocious Serbian resistance, managed to conquer Belgrade, the Serbian capital, which lay just across the Danube from integral Austria. From then on, however, the Serbs endured the full horror of Austrian occupation. Thousands of their citizens were rounded up and consigned to forced-labor camps, many of them eventually to die of their privation.

By then, too, the little nation's army, together with its ailing, half-paralyzed king, Petar I, and other members of the Serbian government, as well as tens of thousands of civilians, had embarked on a historic exodus through neighboring Montenegro, Albania, and Macedonia. Under the military leadership of Serbia's Prince Regent Aleksandar, who functioned as his father's surrogate, the trek was carried out over snow-clad mountains and through vertiginous defiles, in extremes of cold and heat, of illness and starvation, all in an effort to reach the Macedonian coast and rescue by units of the British and French navies. Of the soldiers and civilians who participated in the epic three-month journey, enduring a nightmare of typhus, dysentery, and mountain frost, at least 70,000—men, women, children—expired in the ordeal. In December 1915, when the survivors finally straggled into the Macedonian port of Salonika, they had been reduced to living skeletons. More than half

---

1 Branimir Anzulovic, *Heavenly Serbia: From Myth to Genocide* (New York: New York University Press, 1999), 30.

of them had to be carried off by Allied naval vessels for convalescence in the military hospitals of Corfu and Corsica.

Even afterward, Serbian soldiers hardly had been nursed back to health when they were returned to battle action in the final Allied offensive on the Balkan front in 1918. By the time the Habsburg government sued for peace, the war had cost Serbia an estimated 1.25 million dead—almost one-quarter of its population, and close to two-thirds of its male population between the ages of 15 and 55.[2] In perspective, the odyssey of the Serbs' courage and sacrifice rivaled any comparable saga in history and was immortalized ever after in their people's folklore.

## THE SOUTH SLAV MODEL IN DIPLOMATIC REALITY

In the autumn of 1916, after the remnants of the Serbian army had left Corfu and Corsica and as other Serbian civilians and soldiers were still undergoing wartime trauma, their veteran prime minister, Nikola Pašić, remained behind in the Aegean island of Corfu to plot the future of his country.[3] A deceptively avuncular figure, with his lengthy white beard and gentle, solicitous manner, Pašić, in fact, was committed to a maximalist vision of a united South Slavic state functioning in essence as a "Greater Serbia." By his formulation, Serbia would amalgamate under its restored central government the former independent kingdom of Montenegro, as well as the former Habsburg provinces of Croatia, Slovenia, Bosnia-Herzegovina, and Temesvar—and perhaps even Greek and Bulgarian Macedonia. It was a grandiose notion. Indeed, it was also one that immediately encountered strenuous opposition.

As early as November 1914, two Dalmatian Croats, Franjo Supilo and Ante Trumbić, both perennial members of the prewar Habsburg imperial parliament, began organizing their own rival South Slav committee. Formally convened in April 1915 under the aegis of 11 Croatian, 4 Slovenian, and even 2 Serbian émigré dissenters, the group had chosen London as its venue, and its mission at first was to represent essentially the Habsburg Empire's Roman Catholic South Slavs, those who had never been citizens of the Serbian kingdom and who were acutely uninterested

---

2 Tim Judah, *The Serbs: History, Myth and the Destruction of Yugoslavia*, 2nd ed. (New Haven, CT: Yale University Press, 2000), chapters 1–2, *passim*; see also Andrej Mitrović, *Serbia's Great War, 1914–1918* (West Lafayette, IN: Purdue University Press, 2007), especially vii.

3 Alex N. Dragnich, *Serbia, Nikola Pašić, and Yugoslavia* (New Brunswick, NJ: Rutgers University Press, 1974), chapters 1–2 *ff*.

in exchanging Austro-Hungarian domination for Serbia's "half-civilized," Eastern Orthodox variety.[4]

Yet, as the months passed, neither London's Yugoslav Committee nor the Serbian government in exile was enamored of other, even less palatable alternatives. The Croats and Slovenes were aware that France and Britain, if victorious in the Great War, would feel obliged to honor the earlier promises embodied in their own—1915—Treaty of London, that is, of territorially rewarding the Italians at the expense of the Habsburg Empire's South Slavic peoples, and particularly at the expense of the Slovenes and Croats who populated the Adriatic Sea's Dalmatian littoral (see below). In March 1917, too, South Slav nationalist ambitions were further imperiled by the Russian Revolution, a political bombshell that appeared likely to remove Serbia's most loyal Great-Power champion from the war.[5] Accordingly, during the ensuing June and July, again on the island of Corfu, Serbian Prime Minister Pašić hosted a series of meetings. In addition to his fellow Serbs, this time the participants included the Croatian representatives, Supilo and Trumbić, together with other original members of the 1915 Yugoslav Committee.

By July 20, 1917, these rival South Slav delegations finally hammered out a diplomatic compromise, to be known ever after as the "Corfu Declaration." Acknowledging that Serbs, Croats, and Slovenes were of the same blood and language, and (presumably) shared the same aspirations for functional cooperation, the document proclaimed that their respective populations would constitute a future state to be known as the "Kingdom of the Serbs, Croats, and Slovenes" and to be governed by a constitutional monarchy under the Serbs' current Karageorgević dynasty (p. 232). Indeed, during the ensuing months, self-appointed assemblies were convened in others of the Habsburg South Slav provinces, including Temesvar, Vojvodina, and Bosnia-Herzegovina, as well as the formerly independent kingdom of Montenegro. In these conclaves, the delegates similarly voted their endorsement of the Corfu Declaration. Finally, on October 29, 1918, as the Habsburg Empire underwent its climactic dissolution, a "National Council of Serbs, Croats, and Slovenes," meeting in Zagreb, Croatia, proclaimed the "formal" independence of their conglomerate nation.[6]

---

4 Ivo J. Lederer, *Yugoslavia at the Paris Peace Conference: A Study in Frontiermaking* (New Haven, CT: Yale University Press, 1963), 11; Ivo Banac, *The National Question in Yugoslavia: Origins, History, Politics* (Ithaca, NY: Cornell University Press, 1984), 90.

5 Lederer, *Yugoslavia*, 6–7.

6 Sabrina P. Ramet, *The Three Yugoslavias: State-Building and Legitimation, 1918–2005* (Bloomington, IN: Indiana University Press, 2006), 42–44.

Still to be resolved, however, was lingering Allied ambivalence to this proposed South Slav confederation. Initially, France alone was its enthusiastic supporter. A French commander, General Louis Franchet d'Esperey, had led the successful Allied military campaign in the Balkans and had ensured that the Serbian army played a preeminent role in that effort. Presumably, the Serbs would remain France's grateful protégés, and not least in blocking Italian efforts to gain more than a modest foothold in the Adriatic entryway to France's Mediterranean empire. On the other hand, Britain's Prime Minister David Lloyd George, cautioned by his "Balkan" adviser, the Cambridge historian R.W. Seton-Watson, remained skeptical in his appraisal of future South Slav unity—whatever its political configuration.[7]

Yet, in the end, it was Woodrow Wilson who exerted the decisive influence in resolving the Allies' divided and equivocal Balkan diplomacy. In February 1919, less than a month after the opening of the Paris Peace Conference, and after conferring at length with Serbia's Prime Minister Pašić, the American president decided to accept the credentials of the new "Kingdom of the Serbs, Croats, and Slovenes."[8]

## AN ITALIAN "DISTRACTION"

As he reached his decision, Wilson was motivated not only by his widely proclaimed ideal of national "self-determination" nor even by the charm and eloquence of old Nikola Pašić (who lost no opportunity to regale Wilson with accounts of Serbian wartime sacrifices). In common with the French, the American president also was influenced by his indignation at Italian post-armistice aggressiveness in the Adriatic Basin.[9] He had not been a signatory of the secret Treaty of London (p. 37), after all, and hence did not regard the United States as bound by the document's generous concession to the Italians of "Venezia Giulia" (the ancient imperial Roman enclave encircling both sides of the upper Adriatic).

Eventually, Wilson's adamant stance on self-determination was accepted by his fellow Allied statesmen. Although Italy would be allowed to retain the South Tyrol, and even Trieste in the upper Adriatic, its Dalmatian littoral aspirations were dramatically foreshortened. At that point Italy's Prime

---

7 John R. Lampe, *Yugoslavia as History: Twice There Was a Country*, 2nd ed. (Cambridge: Cambridge University Press, 2000), 106.
8 Lederer, *Yugoslavia*, 134.
9 Victor S. Mamatey, *The United States and East Central Europe, 1914–1918: A Study in Wilsonian Diplomacy and Propaganda* (Princeton, NY: Princeton University Press, 1957), 181–83, 185–87.

Minister Vittorio Orlando left the Paris Peace Conference in a high dudgeon. It was not until November 1919 that Orlando's successor in office, Francesco Nitti, traveled to the Parisian suburb of Saint-Germain, where he resignedly signed a treaty that relinquished the most far-reaching of Italy's "Venezia Giulia" claims, including the Dalmatian littoral's port city of Fiume, with its substantial Italian population (p. 37).[10]

Even with these compromises, however, the issue of the Dalmatian littoral was not to be that easily resolved. A month before the signing of the Treaty of Saint-Germain, one of Italy's most colorful eccentrics, Gabriele D'Annunzio, a 57-year-old poet-playwright, gigolo, and flamboyant patriot, had taken it upon himself to lead a miscellany of some 2,000 discharged Italian war veterans into Fiume. There, he pronounced the establishment of the "State of Carnaro" over the city's ethnically mixed populations. Declaring it "a searchlight radiant in the midst of an ocean of abjection," D'Annunzio proceeded to issue a "Charter" for Fiume and declare himself the state's self-appointed Italian "magister."[11] But, as he set about issuing bombastic proclamations from his office in Fiume's city hall, his "administration" shortly became dysfunctional, unable even to feed its own population, and reduced to foraging in neighboring cities for food and fuel.[12]

Eventually, in December 1919, exasperated at the poet-patriot's antics and the obloquy these were evoking against Italy at large, Prime Minister Nitti authorized the Italian navy to tighten its blockade of the city, and, in that same month, an Italian naval gunboat lobbed several shells in the vicinity of Fiume's harbor. Hereupon, waiving his oath to fight to the death, and hurriedly emerging with his latest mistress from their tryst in the basement of Fiume's city hall, D'Annunzio sought and obtained a guarantee of safe conduct. As he departed for his home in Venice, however, he loosed a defiant peroration. "We are proud to have given our blood," he declaimed to the handful of journalists still willing to listen to him, "to have shown our devotion to a people [the Italians] of such pure and elevated character.... Only my courage is left

---

10 Mamatey, *The United States*, 201–2.
11 Quoted in Lucy Hughes-Hallett, *Gabriele D'Annunzio: Poet, Seducer, and Preacher of War* (New York: Random House, 2013), 478–79.
12 For D'Annunzio's Fiume adventure, see Rusinow, *Italy's Austrian*, 98–99; Lucy Hughes-Hallet, *Gabriele D'Annunzio: Poet, Seducer and Preacher of War* (New York: Knopf, 2013), 425–26; Enrico Caviglia, *Il Conflitto di Fiume* (Milan: Garzanti, 1948), 74; Michael Arthur Ledeen, *The First Duce: D'Annunzio at Fiume* (Baltimore, MD: Johns Hopkins University Press, 1977), 102–3; Pietro Badoglio, *Rivelazioni su Fiume* (Rome: D. de Luigi, 1948), 107–21 ff.

me."[13] In ensuing years, although the recipient of deference and handsome pecuniary rewards from Italy's successor Mussolini government, D'Annunzio would play no further role in his country's public affairs.

Even in the aftermath of D'Annunzio's flight, however, the ultimate disposition of Fiume remained an embarrassing distraction for the Italian government, which by then faced increasingly critical issues of domestic unemployment (p. 38). But, in June 1920, for the fourth time in 22 years, the veteran Giovanni Giolitti returned to the Italian prime ministry. The wily old politician and his equally experienced foreign minister, Carlo Sforza, set about negotiating their own settlement with the fledgling South Slav government. The discussions took place in the northern Italian resort town of Rapallo, and were consummated in a bilateral treaty. By the document's terms, it was agreed that, officially, Fiume would not be a part of Italy. Instead, it would function as an independent city-state, although one of "Italian character"; while Fiume's most populous suburb, the predominantly Slav-inhabited community of Sušak, would be incorporated into the economy (although not formally into the government) of the new South Slav nation. As compensation, Italy was assigned the neighboring Adriatic port of Zara.

Nevertheless, it remained to be seen whether future Italian governments would accept the Rapallo document's provisions, or the Treaty of Saint-Germain altogether, as a sufficient concession to the Dalmatian littoral's Italian irredenta—or indeed to the national pride of the Italian people at large.

## A PARAGON OF DYSFUNCTIONALISM

Meanwhile, as the South Slav nation in its clamorous diversity entered the privileged circle of newly independent states, its initial, surviving, population of approximately 12 million remained a mirror image of the Balkans at large. In 1920, the three peoples that gave their new state its initial name, "the Kingdom of the Serbs, Croats, and Slovenes," comprised approximately 4.3 million Serbs, 2.9 million Croats, and slightly over 1 million Slovenes. The remaining 4.4 million (some 29 per cent of the population) embraced a heterogeneity of Albanians, Montenegrins, Bosnians, Macedonians, Hungarians, Turks, Romanians, Italians, and Roma ("gypsies").

At the outset of South Slav independence, the task of establishing a viable nation among this mélange of peoples and cultures was infinitely exacerbated

---

13 Anthony R. E. Rhodes, *D'Annunzio, the Poet as Superman* (New York: McDowell, Obolensky, 1960), 261–62.

not only by mutual suspicion but by economic ruination. The armies of the Central Powers had left Serbia and Montenegro a wasteland. The civilian shortages of food and housing were existential. Indeed, anticipating the "NEP" peasants of Bolshevik Russia (p. 115), the South Slavs in their deprivation often refused to send their produce or livestock to urban markets. When the central government in Belgrade imposed taxes on Croatian farmers and sought to register their draft animals, the Croats burned all records of their holdings. Meanwhile, rebel bands, including many deserters from South Slav military units, roamed the countryside, pillaging homes, farms, and warehouses, and vandalizing public utilities.

It was in the midst of this postwar chaos that the task of devising a functional government for the new state's conglomeration of traditions, religions, cultures, dialects, legal systems, and currencies proved desperately challenging.[14] For one thing, the "Kingdom of Serbs, Croats, and Slovenes" had left unresolved the fate of other annexed South Slav constituencies—in Bosnia-Herzegovina, Kosovo, Montenegro, Temesvar, Istria, and Dalmatia. For another, the 1917 Corfu Declaration had established a provisional South Slav authority essentially to cope with the diplomatic challenges of the future Paris Peace Conference, and only afterward to organize a constitutional convention that would establish the nation's governing institutions. Finally, during the interim before the state's first political election of November 28, 1920, Crown Prince Aleksandar, as the South Slavs' provisional dynast, still found himself accepted by an uncertain and shifting plurality even within his assortment of putative subjects.

In his early years, Aleksandar Karageorgević had been known as a modest youth who "knew his place." In 1909, as he reached his 21st birthday, his "place" remained only second in line for the Serbian throne, behind his older brother, George, who was already married and had produced an heir. But, in that same year, Prince George beat a servant to death for alleged incompetence, and an outraged Council of State promptly declared him ineligible to succeed his father, Petar I. In George's stead, Prince Aleksandar was then declared the royal heir presumptive. Five years later, in 1914, and two months before the Austrian invasion of Serbia, the elderly Petar suffered a crippling stroke. Afterward, in the summer of 1914, with the ensuing outbreak of the European war and the initial Serbian military setback at the hands of the Habsburg army, it was left to Aleksandar—now appointed Serbia's "Prince Regent"—to lead the Serbian army on its epic trek across the Albanian mountains and to naval rescue at the ports of Macedonia. Subsequently, in July 1917, with the ongoing

---

14 Alex N. Dragnich, *Serbs and Croats: The Struggle in Yugoslavia* (New York: Harcourt Brace Jovanovich Publishers, 1992), 18–19.

incapacitation of King Petar, it was Aleksandar's task to support Nikola Pašić and other members of Serbia's provisional government in winning recognition for the South Slavs' incipient multinational kingdom and in formulating the Corfu Declaration, with its proposed "Kingdom of the Serbs, Croats, and Slovenes." In the immediate postwar, too, it was Aleksandar who continued working with Pašić to delineate the confederative nation's prospective boundaries and, in 1919, to orchestrate the election of a constitutional convention. It was only upon the death of King Petar in August 1921 that the prince regent's dynastic leadership was officially confirmed and that, at the age of 33, he assumed the throne as Aleksandar I of Yugoslavia.

By then, however, the young monarch had more than paid his dues as reigning sovereign. Indeed, he had fortified his popular reputation in that same year of 1921 by marrying Princess Maria of Romania, a lineal descendant both of Russia's Tsar Alexander II and Britain's Queen Victoria. Subsequently, Maria gave her husband three sons and was worshiped by her subjects, even by the Croats and Slovenes; and Aleksandar, a vigorous, broad-shouldered man, who cultivated a bristling moustache under his generous hawk nose, was determined not to forfeit the ample affection he and his family had achieved among their core Serbian constituency. He shunned the role of autocrat. As a young man, he had learned humility both in peace, as a young "court intern" in the service of Russia's Tsar Nicholas II, and then in war, as Prince Regent of the incipient South Slav kingdom behind his ailing father. He remembered its lessons well, even insisting for many years on wearing his old army uniforms, with their darned handkerchiefs.

It was in this stance of modest stewardship, too, that Aleksandar ensured that the November 1920 constitutional elections were free, secret, and direct. But he also ensured that the elections were based on the proportionate model adopted by most of continental Europe, rather than the constituency—majority-based—model prevailing in the Anglo-Saxon world. For the South Slavs, the choice turned out to be a particularly awkward fit. The constitutional convention's 419 elected delegates may well have reflected the demography of the new South Slav state, but they also reflected its endemic factiousness. The Serbian parties managed to win a plurality and to elect the veteran Nikola Pašić as the kingdom's first prime minister; but the Croats, essentially united in their own Republican Peasant Party, achieved a compact (if distant-second) minority of 56 deputies; and the rest of the South Slav nationalities trailed too far back to engineer a workable coalition either with the Croats, Slovenes or any other of the state's minority delegates.[15]

---

15 William Bartlett, *Croatia: Between Europe and the Balkans* (London: Routledge, 2003), 15.

The Corfu Declaration notwithstanding, it soon became evident that the electoral process created as many problems for the new kingdom as it solved. The Serbs represented a homogeneous people that had been independent for decades. They had made no secret of their intention to "amalgamate" the government apparatus and the military command into the preexisting Serbian administration, and to impose a school curriculum that gave priority to Serbia's history and Eastern Orthodox religious culture.[16] But the Croatian Republican Peasant Party, under the leadership of Stjepan Radić, saw no further need to cooperate with Serbia's politicians, much less to acknowledge the legitimacy of a Serbian-dominated state. Hence, in the national parliament, Radić and his followers managed tenaciously and consistently to disrupt the assembly's sessions and to sabotage the application of its intermittent legislation within Croatia itself.

Radić's was a peasant's stubbornness. Born in a Croatian village, Trebarjevo Desno, he was the ninth of his family's eleven children. Entirely self-educated, a rebel from his early teens, he subsequently was in and out of prison for his shrill denunciations of Austro-Hungarian rule. After 1917, he proved a comparably reluctant supporter of the Corfu Declaration. Indeed, his suspicion of the Karageorgević dynasty became an issue almost before Allied recognition of South Slav independence in the summer of 1919.[17] It was then that King Aleksandar sentenced Radić and the latter's closest political allies to a year's imprisonment for their "disruptive" insistence on a fully autonomous Croatian state. Although the king released the prisoners several months later, hoping that they had learned to cooperate, the gesture was futile. In December 1920, when most assembled delegates approved the new constitution and transformed themselves into the kingdom's first elected parliament, Radić and his party's delegates declined to take their parliamentary seats and rejected all Serbian appeals to accept the legitimacy of a centrally governed state. Back to prison the Croatian deputies then went, in a stagy and well-publicized display of political martyrdom.[18]

Was their obstructionism entirely perverse? Despite its considerable legislative flaws, the South Slav state's newly adopted constitution appeared to be less than autocratic, at least by the standards of Eastern Europe. Under

---

16 Charles Jelavich, "Education, Textbooks and South Slavic Nationalism in the Interwar Era," in *Allgemeinbildung als Modernisierungsfaktor*, ed. Norbert Walter and Holm Sundhaussen (Berlin: Harrassowitz in Kommission, 1994), 127–42, see 134.

17 Marcus Tanner, *Croatia: A Nation Forged in War* (New Haven, CT: Yale University Press, 1997), 115–16.

18 Dragnich, *Serbia, Nikola Pašić*, 18–19, 46–90.

its provisions, each citizen, of whatever background, was equal before the law. So were its religio-cultural traditions, for juridical acknowledgment was extended to the country's separate dialects, alphabets, and communal institutions. But even under these guarantees, the political lockstep between Serbs and Croats did not ease. Prime Minister Pašić was unrelenting in his insistence upon a Serbian-dominated civilian and military administration; and Stjepan Radić (in or out of prison) maintained his intractable opposition to the faintest hint of Serbian centralism and ensured that his followers strictly embraced his credo of "full and unqualified" Croatian autonomy.

In the second parliamentary election of March 1923, the Croatians won a slightly more impressive minority of 70 seats. But again, at Radić's orders, its delegates, lacking a Serbian acknowledgment of full Croatian political autonomy, refused to claim their seats or even to exit their prison cells. The theatrics continued in subsequent elections. Eventually, by 1925, the South Slav kingdom had undergone a turnover of not less than five cabinets (four headed by Nikola Pašić), and seemed terminally afflicted by political tribalism. It was then, in the wake of the 1925 election and alarmed by the clash of ideological agenda that was poisoning almost every echelon of the nation's public life, that King Aleksandar issued an ultimatum.

This time, however, the ultimatum was directed at his own supporters: Prime Minister Pašić, "one of the craftiest and most tenacious of statesmen,"[19] and Pašić's Serbian constituents. For the sake of national "harmony," the king insisted, they would have to swallow a power-sharing agreement with the Croats and other non-Serbs, and distribute a greater number of ministries among them. The ultimatum was accepted. Yet, all but predictably, it exerted little substantive effect. Pašić ensured that the cabinet's key portfolios remained in the hands of his fellow Serbs. In April 1926, equally predictably, Radić and his Croatian followers withdrew from the coalition cabinet and the government fell once again. But, in that year too, Pašić died at the age of 82; and over the ensuing months, as a gesture less of goodwill than of desperation, King Aleksandar decided to ignore the Serbs' majority status. Instead, he offered the prime ministry to Stjepan Radić himself, and this time, for once, a royal inducement appeared successful. Radić "provisionally" accepted the offer. Was an era of political stability dawning at last for the fractious South Slav peoples?

Hardly likely. Ignoring their leader's pleas, Radić's Croatian colleagues refused to serve in a cabinet dominated by a Serbian majority, and by 1927

---

19  Dragnich, *Serbs and Croats*, 32–33.

tension between the two communities' delegations regained its former virulence. Indeed, Radić himself, back in opposition if not in prison, resumed his former role as naysayer and led the catcalls and invective in parliament, vilifying its Serbian members as "thieves," "bandits," "outlaws," "murderers."[20] Finally, on June 14, 1928, internecine bitterness crested when a Serbian delegate drew his pistol in parliament and shot four Croatian deputies. Radić was among them. Three of the victims, including Radić's nephew, died almost instantly. Radić himself lingered a few months before succumbing to his wounds. By then, too, the South Slav kingdom appeared on the threshold of disintegration, and with it the audacious successor-state experiment that had represented arguably the most impressive diplomatic achievement of the Paris Peace Conference.

### RULE BY ROYAL DECREE

During the next months, with the continuing lockstep of intercommunal accusations and imprecations, functional legislation in the South Slav parliament ground to a halt. Eventually, on January 6, 1929, after urgent consultations with legal experts, King Aleksandar suspended parliament altogether and assumed personal rule over his nation. Once the king acted, moreover, he acted decisively, not only suspending parliament but abolishing the constitution, the kingdom's political parties, and authorizing police action against "divisive" organizations, chiefly those based predominantly on nationality or religion. In the process, the king's most decisive innovation was to eliminate the fledgling state's 33 provinces and substitute for them 9 regional units that deliberately cut across ethnic and religious divisions, including those of his native Serbia. By this measure, Aleksandar manifestly sought to prove that he was not a Serbian chauvinist, that he was determined to foster a new political template for his country. Indeed, he went so far as to replace the state's title—the "Kingdom of the Serbs, Croats, and Slovenes"—and to announce that henceforth the realm would be known as the "Kingdom of Yugoslavia."

But in his effort to dispense with the South Slav nation's initial neo-federalism, did Aleksandar become a monarcho-fascist?[21] His decree abolishing the constitution apparently gave all his subsequent edicts the force of absolutism. In the process, too, the king did not hesitate to muzzle the nation's press, or to

---

20 Tanner, *Croatia*, 122–23.
21 Lampe, *Yugoslavia as History*, 127, 132.

apply an iron fist to his political enemies. Although these latter included first and foremost spokesmen for Croatian autonomy, whose parties and political activities he banned altogether, Yugoslavia's other ethnic blocs, including Slovenes, Dalmatians, Montenegrins, Bosnians, Herzegovinians, and Macedonians—whether Roman Catholics, Eastern Orthodox, Muslims, or Jews—also were subjected to political harassment and new constraints on their educational and communal institutions.

It was not long, too, before the king's political police were allowed widening discretion to intimidate his critics. One particularly notorious incident claimed the life of Milan Šufflay, a respected professor of history at the University of Zagreb and an outspoken Croatian nationalist. On several occasions in the latter 1920s, the government had imprisoned Šufflay for reputed political incitement. At first, the confinements were short; but no sooner was the professor released than he embarked again on fiery press criticism of the royal dictatorship. At last, on February 19, 1931, members of the king's intelligence service waylaid Šufflay outside his home and clubbed him to death. The episode aroused outrage both in Yugoslavia and abroad. Albert Einstein and Heinrich Mann were among the international figures whose protests appeared in leading European and American newspapers.

It was of note, however, that most of Yugoslavia's private citizens seemed to accept the royal dictatorship with less protest than did their politicians and intellectuals, let alone their clamorous émigré communities abroad. Even non-Serbs appeared at first to prefer Aleksandar's efficient and comparatively graft-free administration. It did not escape them that, for all his repressive measures, the king had authorized a number of enlightened innovations, among them a significant increase of openings for women in government and a progressive tax schedule. Moreover, an effective program of land reform, initiated in the mid-1920s, was dramatically enlarged after 1928 and applied equitably to all sectors of the population.[22]

Yet, as elsewhere in Europe, it was the advent of the Great Depression that overshadowed both the monarch's transgressions and accomplishments.[23] Earlier, during the mid- and late-1920s, as the hybrid kingdom inched its way upward from its wartime ruination, its economic balance sheet had appeared on the road to recovery. But in 1931 the failure of Austria's Creditanstalt banking network (p. 191) produced a ripple effect throughout the former Habsburg

---

22 Jozo Tomasevich, *Peasants, Politics, and Economic Change in Yugoslavia* (Stanford, CA: Stanford University Press, 1955), 353–82.

23 John R. Lampe and Marvin R. Jackson, *Balkan Economic History, 1550–1950: From Imperial Borderlands to Developing Nations* (Bloomington, IN: Indiana University Press, 1982), 158–73.

Empire. The Balkans were not spared. Croatian and Slovenian banks, holding the majority of Yugoslavia's deposits, were among the nation's principal casualties. They failed, one by one. As economic tariffs and import quotas multiplied throughout Central and Eastern Europe, Yugoslav farmers lost their markets and land; shopkeepers, workmen, and civil servants lost their employment.

Eventually, it was the combination of political deadlock and economic crisis that threatened the nation's royal dictatorship—and the survivability of the Yugoslav experiment altogether. In 1931, seeking to defuse mounting public unrest, the king decided to reissue the constitution and cancel the ban on parliament.[24] But his other political initiatives were grudging. The secret ballot was not reinstated. A revised electoral law, palpably inspired by Mussolini's "Enabling Act" of 1923 (p. 49), decreed that a party winning a plurality of votes in a national election would subsequently be awarded two-thirds of the seats in the Chamber of Deputies; and the king himself would appoint half the members in Yugoslavia's—largely consultative—parliamentary upper house.

Indeed, by the early 1930s the nation's political life had been atomized. The newly named Croatian Peasant Party had grown both in numbers and intransigence, and its current leader, Vladko Maček (the political successor to the murdered Radić), functioned in effect as his province's uncrowned king.[25] In Slovenia the People's Party, under the chairmanship of Anton Korošec, a Catholic priest and undisguised enemy of the king, attracted the majority of his region's voters. So, too, in Bosnia-Herzegovina, did the Yugoslav Muslim Organization, under the direction of Mehmet Spaho. Whatever their professed acceptance of the Yugoslav state, these regional parties remained obdurate, indeed, all but lockstepped, in their political and cultural parochialism.

## A FRAGILITY OF ALLIANCES

Even as he confronted these partisan animosities and economic frustrations, Aleksandar was not lacking in foreign enemies who were prepared to exploit his nation's endemic factionalism. Among them, the Hungarians ranked as perhaps the most unregenerate. Both before and after the establishment of the Habsburg Dual Monarchy in 1867, almost a million of Serbia's citizens, in common with a majority of Croats and Slovenes, had lived under Hungarian rule and oppression.

---

24  Lampe, *Yugoslavia as History*, 169.
25  Vladko Maček, *In the Struggle for Freedom* (University Park, PA: Pennsylvania State University Press, 1957), 161–63.

## NEW NATIONS OF RECONSTRUCTED CENTRAL EUROPE

Hence, at the Paris Peace Conference, the Allied statesmen dealt almost as punitively with Hungary as with Austria. The resultant Treaty of Trianon amputated no less than three-fifths of the Magyar nation's territory, specifically those regions that had encompassed dense enclaves of South Slavs. In their bitterness, postwar Hungarian nationalists made no secret of their intention to reclaim this "abducted" terrain, whether through diplomacy or subversion.

Other liberated successor states shared Serbian concern at the revanchism of the former Central Powers. Their governments included the Bohemian-Moravian politicians who dominated public policy in Czechoslovakia (a republic encompassing its own substantial minority of resentful Germans and Slovaks), and the Polish nationalists who exercised sovereignty over recently annexed enclaves of Germans, Ukrainians, and Jews, and who feared the recrudescence of the former German and Russian empires.[26] Apparently,

---

26  H. James Burgwyn, *Italian Foreign Policy in the Interwar Period, 1918–1940* (Westport, CT: Praeger, 1997), 39–40.

the successor governments' first and logical response to these revanchist and irredentist dangers was to make common cause with each other. This they did. Indeed, their principal accords comprised no fewer than four treaties, negotiated seriatim between 1920 and 1933.

The first of the documents, signed in August 1920, represented the initiative of Czechoslovakia's Foreign Minister Edvard Beneš and took the form of a mutual defense treaty with the South Slavs, a document palpably directed against both Austria and Hungary. By itself, however, the Czechoslovak convention on joint defense did not appear to foreclose Habsburg dreams of returning to power or of retrieving important segments of the monarchy's defunct realm. Indeed, in late March 1921, the former Habsburg Emperor Karl made the first of two brief ceremonial visits to Budapest. Each was a barely disguised attempt to mobilize Hungarian nostalgia for his dynasty. But the tactic proved counterproductive. Reacting to Karl's visit, the South Slav and Czechoslovak governments promptly extended their bilateral treaty to include Romania, another territorial beneficiary of the Paris Peace Conference. Subsequently, in August 1922, ten months after the ex-emperor's second Hungarian visit, the South Slav and Czechoslovak governments transformed their military partnership into a general political agreement, pledging themselves to make "common cause" in international affairs. Finally, in February 1923, the foreign ministers of Czechoslovakia, Yugoslavia, and Romania entered into a "Little Entente," signing a pact both of diplomatic and military cooperation.[27]

Even with these initiatives, however, the "Little Entente" could not have sustained its diplomatic and military credibility without the encouragement and patronage of the Allied Great Powers. The most important of these was France, which had given priority after the Paris Peace Conference to "supplementary" defense treaties against a potentially resurgent Germany. Hence, in the first of these documents, signed in September 1922, the French entered into a ten-year military compact with Poland, whose government and people lived in chronic fear both of German and Russian territorial revanchism. France's next diplomatic foray eastward was toward Czechoslovakia. Again, both nations were sentient to the perils of territorial revanchism: from Germany, in the case of France, and from both Germany and Hungary, in the case of Czechoslovakia. In 1924, under the terms of the Franco-Czechoslovak treaty, the signatories pledged themselves to block a restoration of the Habsburgs in Austria and to stand firm against the even more fearful threat of German armed intervention on behalf of Czechoslovakia's ethnically German Sudetenland citizens.

---

27   Magda Ádám, *The Little Entente and Europe, 1920–1929* (Budapest: Akadémiai Kiadó, 1993), 90–109, 204–17.

But in contrast to the other of the "Little Entente" signatories, it was the government of the South Slavs that found it substantially more complicated to negotiate an alliance with France. This government, after all, was in search of a mutual-defense commitment not only against revanchist Hungary but against acquisitive Italy, which, for its part, continued to nurture ambitions of an Adriatic empire at Yugoslavia's expense (pp. 229–31). The French, on the other hand, were intent on keeping Mussolini's support as a feature of their putative *cordon sanitaire* against a resurgent Germany. Thus, in November 1927, after repeated overtures from Belgrade, the best the French foreign ministry could offer King Aleksandar was a treaty "of amity and understanding" (albeit with a provision to sell weaponry to the Yugoslav army).[28] The king and his advisers had to accept this bland document, understanding well that in no sense did it approach France's military commitments to the Poles, to the Czechs, or even to the notoriously opportunistic Romanians.

## A BELATED GREAT-POWER PATRONAGE

In 1933–34, however, with the rise and consolidation of Nazi rule in Germany, the French government almost overnight found itself obliged to give renewed and urgent attention to an enhanced relationship with the "Little Entente," and this time including Yugoslavia. France's Foreign Minister Louis Barthou was the statesman who made it his diplomatic priority to energize his nation's "eastern policy." A seasoned veteran of French politics, Barthou, at the age of 72 had been involved in France's public affairs for over 40 years: as lawyer, journalist, parliamentary deputy, and cabinet minister. It was a formidable career for a man of distinctly provincial and petit-bourgeois origins.

Barthou had been reared in a Pyrenean village, Oloron-Sainte-Marie, to undereducated parents who operated a neighborhood hardware store. As a precocious student in secondary school, however, he was accepted on scholarship to the law faculty at the University of Bordeaux. Graduated at the top of his class, Barthou subsequently attended the University of Paris to earn a doctoral degree in jurisprudence, again with distinction. During his equally successful law practice, first in his native Pyrenean region and later in Paris, he was drawn increasingly to politics. Years earlier, in 1889, with the encouragement of Raymond Poincaré, his former Sorbonne classmate and subsequently a prominent spokesman for the Democratic Republican Alliance,

---

28 Piotr S. Wandycz, *The Twilight of French Eastern Alliances, 1926–1936* (Princeton, NJ: Princeton University Press, 1988), 104.

Barthou, at the age of 27, stood for the Chamber of Deputies as a member of Poincaré's political bloc. He won his seat by a narrow plurality.

Only five foot six, and less than a charismatic orator, Barthou made up in tactical resourcefulness and sheer intellectual tenacity for his less than impressive persona. Over the turn of the century, as a survivor of the Third Republic's rotating governments, he managed to hold on to his parliamentary seat, to win appointment to several minor cabinet posts, even to serve a brief stint as vice-premier. Eventually, in the spring of 1913, Barthou reached the summit of his prewar political career when his faithful patron and friend, Poincaré (by then president of the Republic), called on him to form a government. It was during his single ensuing year as premier that Barthou accepted the daunting task of negotiating the passage of a bill to fund an extended, three-year term of military conscription. The political battle was tumultuous, carried out against relentless Socialist opposition. Even in victory, Barthou was left exhausted and barely able to hold his government together. Nevertheless, when the World War began, the new conscription law manifestly saved Paris, for it provided the razor-thin edge of manpower that held the line in the First Battle of the Marne.

In his private life, too, Barthou revealed himself as no less than a polymath, managing over the years to churn out a series of erudite essays on Mirabeau, Danton, Lamartine, Baudelaire, and Wagner, as well as incisive and frequently provocative articles on the nation's political culture (indeed, one of his "political" essays aroused the ire of Jean Jaurès, chairman of the French Socialist Party, resulting in a duel in which both men formulaically discharged their pistols in the air). In 1895, Barthou married the only daughter of a wealthy Jewish business family and subsequently enjoyed a self-indulgent life style, replete with trips to the Far East and South America, the purchase of a chalet in Switzerland, and the means to invest heavily in French automotive, aeronautical, and railway technology. Newspaper society columns were full of "little Barthou's" accomplishments: as an homme de lettres, as an athlete who exercised rigorously, as an amateur pilot, as an explorer of mountains and jungles, as a munificent philanthropist, and not least as a devoted husband and father. It was as a parent, too, that he evoked universal compassion in December 1914 when his only son was killed in action on the Western Front.

In 1916–17, serving as chairman of the Chamber's foreign-affairs committee, the wiry little politician-litterateur became known for his advocacy of bitter, relentless, and uncompromising war against the Germans. The very thought of negotiating peace with the enemy, even after France's military reverses and the stalemate of 1917, was anathema to him. "We must level [Germany]," he insisted, "reduce her to impotence and hate her still.... Hate the Germans with all the intensity ensured by our claims against them."[29] Barthou maintained his unforgiving stance well into the postwar, warning that the Versailles Treaty had been poisoned at the well and denouncing Prime Minister Clemenceau for having allowed himself to be "outmaneuvered" by the other Allied leaders (pp. 263–69).

Accordingly, in the political campaign of 1921, assuming office again as defense minister in Aristide Briand's government, Barthou made it his priority to block all German attempts to evade their reparations obligations. Two years later, upon just such a German reparations default, Barthou vigorously supported Poincaré (by then functioning as prime minister) in the dispatch of a combined French-Belgian occupation force to the Ruhr Valley in the effort to reclaim the region's coal and steel for shipment directly to France. In this instance, however, the strategy was counterproductive. German resistance, both active and passive, soon proved to be an economic calamity for Germany and France alike. In the end, Barthou was left with no alternative but to join Poincaré in resigning his ministry.[30]

Nevertheless, from 1929 on, as private citizen, lawyer, editor, and essayist, Barthou maintained his traditional role as nationalist Cassandra; and, with the subsequent rise of Nazism in Germany, he evoked less public skepticism. In February 1934, when Gaston Doumergue, an experienced political deal maker (p. 279), crafted a centrist "Government of National Unity," Barthou was awarded the coveted portfolio of foreign minister. Even in that pivotal role, however, his freedom of maneuver was constrained against Nazi Germany's militant revisionism. For all his previous insistence on German disarmament, Barthou sensed that, without British support, the time evidently was past when France could enforce its demands unilaterally.

It was Alexis Léger, veteran secretary-general of France's foreign ministry, who proposed an alternate strategy. The approach that was needed, he suggested to Barthou, was a fortified *regional* security pact for Eastern Europe, a kind of "eastern Locarno"—adverting to the 1925 treaty in which France, Britain, Italy, and Belgium had secured Weimar Germany's acceptance of a demilitarized Rhineland. In Léger's view, a diplomacy that similarly guaranteed the frontiers of Eastern Europe's successor states against Adolf Hitler's militant *Weltpolitik* might induce even the Soviet Union to join a comparable pact. Barthou reacted to the proposal enthusiastically. Indeed, he lost no time

---

29 Robert J. Young, *Power and Pleasure: Louis Barthou and the Third French Republic* (Montreal: McGill-Queen's Press, 1991), 138.

30 Jacques Bariéty, *Les relations franco-allemandes après la Première-Guerre mondiale: 10 novembre 1918–10 janvier 1925* (Paris: Editions Pedone, 1977), 265.

in putting it into action. In April 1934, he embarked on a series of "good-will" visits to Poland, Czechoslovakia, and Yugoslavia.

Although the foreign minister's journeys were downplayed as essentially ceremonial in nature, they produced agreements of diplomatic substance. In Warsaw, his first stop, Barthou's renewed assurance of France's ongoing friendship induced a skeptical President Józef Pilsudski (who recently had felt it circumspect to sign a preemptive treaty of friendship with Nazi Germany) to acknowledge that his government should also give serious thought to a "safety net" of diplomatic and military ties with France. Barthou's ensuing visit to Prague was more successful yet. He and Czechoslovakia's President Edvard Beneš were personal friends, dating from the latter's wartime refuge in Paris. Inasmuch as there was nothing on the diplomatic horizon in 1934 to cloud Franco-Czech relations, Barthou easily secured Beneš's agreement to refortify the current Franco-Czech defense pact. Moreover, he also persuaded the Czech president to join him in exploring an improvement of Czech ties with the—otherwise reactionary—government of Poland, to reaffirm the Franco-Czech commitment to an independent Austria, and to help protect the Balkans against Hungarian revanchism. Once these understandings were reached, Barthou continued on to Belgrade.

## A CONSPIRACY OF HATREDS

For the government of Yugoslavia, too, a prospective relationship with France was impelled by the animus of its enemies. In some respects, however, the most implacable of these continued to be internal. The Croats' disdain for their Serbian cousins remained barely veiled. The Roman Catholic Croats and Slovenes, they were convinced, with their historically Western associations, represented the economic and cultural elite of their jerry-built kingdom. Indeed, in the postwar as in the prewar, Croatia and Slovenia remained the commercial heartland of the South Slav world. Their exports accounted for nearly half of Yugoslavia's still fragile revenues and provided the endowment for a majority of the country's universities. With these "credentials," Slovenes and Croats of all backgrounds continued to nurture their sectarian resentment of Serbian political dominance.

It was also from the tension of Yugoslavia's intercommunal relations, in 1929, soon after the establishment of King Aleksandar's dictatorship, that one Ante Pavelić, a 40-year-old Croatian lawyer, embarked on a round of visits to his compatriots both in their provincial communities and in surrounding lands. Not for Pavelić the comparatively peaceful (if stubborn) Croatian Peasant Party of the late Stjepan Radić. He was intent, rather, on establishing an *Ustaša* (insurgent) movement—a "Croatian Revolutionary Organization." From his earliest school years, Pavelić had been marinated in his people's anti-Serb embitterment. Before the war, as a law student at the University of Zagreb, he had joined the implacably anti-Serb "Frankist" Party, a faction that had been organized in 1902 by a Croatian-Jewish journalist, Josip Frank, and dedicated uncompromisingly to Croatian self-government.

In the postwar, spared the defunct Habsburg connection, Pavelić maintained the late Frank's legacy and mission both as a practicing attorney in Zagreb and as a deputy in the Croatian Diet. As a lawyer, he defended Croatian, Slovenian, and Macedonian separatists pro bono against Serbian charges of treason. As a politician, he operated in tandem with Frank's son-in-law, Eugen ("Slavko") Kvaternik, to establish a network of ultranationalist Croatian student societies, those that subsequently functioned as the ideological nucleus of the Ustaša.[31] Between 1929 and 1931—again jointly with Kvaternik—Pavelić succeeded in forming Ustašist cells both throughout Croatian Dalmatia and among Croats living in Slovenia and Macedonia, and later in Hungary, Bulgaria, and Italy (pp. 250, 259).

Yet, even as the Ustaša's acknowledged *poglavnik* (leader), Pavelić hardly fitted the description of a terrorist, or even of a man of action. Elegant and fastidious, with a placid and courteous demeanor, he often was described by other South Slavs as "resembling no more than a bourgeois fop."[32] It was only among his fellow Croats that Pavelić never troubled to disguise his revolutionary incendiarism or his unappeasable hatred of King Aleksandar. In the summer of 1932, one of his Ustaša periodicals, *Grič*, published a doggerel that openly acknowledged the movement's determination to do away with the king:

Oh, Croatia, mother dear,
You suffer and you live in fear.
Hey, you Serbs, we'll make you pay.
Time will show what comes your way.
"Beloved" Aleksandar King,
In mourning do the Croats sing:
"Aleksandar, just you wait.
Time for you to meet your fate."[33]

---

[31] Ramet, *The Three Yugoslavias*, 82–84.
[32] François Broche, *Assassinat de Alexandre 1er et Louis Barthou, Marseille, le 9 octobre 1934* (Paris: Balland, 1977), 30.
[33] Ramet, *The Three Yugoslavias*, 91–92.

The tradition of conspiracy and assassination manifestly was not foreign to the South Slav world. It had been well inculcated during more than five centuries of Ottoman repression, torture, and murder. Upon regaining their independence in the nineteenth century, the Serbs themselves proved adroit students of these methods even among their own people. Their earliest and most notable victims were members of the Obrenović family, the Serbian reigning dynasty of the mid- and late-nineteenth century. In the eyes of Serbian ultranationalists, these "lackeys" of the neighboring Austrian Empire had betrayed the cause of South Slav independence for the sake of privileged Serbian access to the Habsburg agricultural market.

The "betrayal" subsequently was rectified in June 1903 when partisans of the rival Karageorgević clan invaded the royal palace, seized young King Aleksandar and Queen Draga in the couple's bedroom, methodically dismembered them with sabers, and disposed of their body parts for a dogs' feast in the palace courtyard. Eleven years later to the month, on June 28, 1914, the "Black Hand," a Serbian secret society, made a comparable statement of nationalist commitment by fatally shooting Habsburg Archduke Franz Ferdinand and his wife, the Duchess Sofia, upon the couple's ceremonial visit to Sarajevo, Bosnia. In the 1920s and 1930s, evidently, the Croatian Ustaša was following a venerated South Slav protocol.

## A NEXUS OF COCONSPIRATORS

### *Bulgaria and Hungary*

Although their organization was officially banned in Yugoslavia, Ante Pavelić and his fellow militants succeeded as early as 1927 in establishing Ustaša offices, newspapers, and paramilitary training camps not only in Croatia but in Bulgaria, Hungary, and Italy.[34] Defeated in the late war, Bulgaria had shared in the loss of thousands of square miles of territory to successor state Yugoslavia. On the one hand, its government initially was hesitant to provoke the Allies by meddling in the Yugoslav cauldron. Bulgaria's King Boris III, as a cousin of Yugoslavia's King Aleksandar, personally was not eager to foster national or filial hatreds. Bulgaria's Prime Minister Aleksandŭr Stamboliĭski, a socialist, preferred to ignore territorial issues altogether in favor of concentrating on his leftist domestic agenda.

---

34  Srdja Trifkovic, *Ustaša: Croatian Separatism and European politics, 1929–1945* (London: The Lord Byron Foundation for Balkan Studies, 1998), 42–43.

But despite King Boris's and Stamboliĭski's reservations, some quarter-million ethnic Macedonians, much of whose habitat had been amputated by the Paris Peace Conference, migrated from the enlarged "Kingdom of the Serbs, Croats, and Slovenes" to relocate in the Bulgarian kingdom's remnant Macedonian province. Before long, it was this enclave that began seething with irredentist vengefulness against the neighboring Yugoslav successor state, and specifically against its Serbian king. Many of the Bulgarian migrants were active partisans of the IMRO, the Internal Macedonian Revolutionary Organization, which smuggled weapons and hired out strong-arm enforcers for its ideological comrades in the Croatian Ustaša (although the IMRO's ranks included not a few hardened criminals who plied guns and explosives throughout the Balkans at large).[35]

In these same postwar years, the Ustaša also operated nine paramilitary camps in Hungary, two of these in the town of Janka Puszta, adjacent to Yugoslavia's Slovenian border. A majority of the trainees were émigré Croatian lumpenproletariat who had enlisted mainly for the promise of room and board. But whatever their original impulsion, they learned shortly to adapt to the Ustašist agenda. That agenda was based undisguisedly on the fascist model, replete with a *poglavnik* (Ante Pavelić) and a "blood oath" committing the trainees to follow Pavelić's orders unquestioningly for the hallowed goal of wresting Croatia from the detested King Aleksandar.

## The Italian Connection

By 1930, as an integral feature of his resurgent imperialism, Benito Mussolini was among those who eventually turned their attention again to the Adriatic. For the Duce, as for most of postwar Italy's rightist politicians, the most urgent territorial objective was the projection of Italy's frontiers to "Venezia Giulia"—the "Julian March's" ancient Roman imperial borders, encompassing not only the Paris Peace Conference award of Trieste and the Trentino but the enticing if yet unclaimed extension of the Dalmatian littoral. He had long shared the nationalist mantra that an aggressive Adriatic venture, if successful, would provide Italy with a protected entryway both into the Mediterranean Sea and the Balkan Peninsula. Indeed, in that ambition, as early as 1919, three years even before seizing political power in his own country, Mussolini had given praise and verbal support to Gabriele D'Annunzio's

---

35 Richard J. Crampton, *A Short History of Modern Bulgaria* (Cambridge: Cambridge University Press, 1987), 102–11.

rogue government in the Dalmatian coastal port of Fiume (pp. 230–231). Following his 1922 march on Rome and the subsequent establishment of his dictatorship, it was assumed that the Duce would evince a comparable muscularity in foreign affairs.

He did, but only on one occasion. In 1923, Greek bandits attacked and murdered several members of a commission that had been appointed by the League of Nations to craft an official Greco-Albanian border. One of the victims was an Italian army officer. In retaliation, Mussolini authorized Italy's navy to launch a brief naval bombardment of the Greek island of Corfu. But the incident was settled quickly when the Greek government agreed to pay restitution to the family of the slain Italian and to the government of Italy. Preoccupied afterward with his political and economic agenda, Mussolini for the while evinced an unexpected forbearance is his international dealings.[36] Perhaps, foreign observers speculated, he would be content from then on to play the role of "good European." [37]

During most of the 1920s, the Duce did indeed give priority to his domestic program. Even in these early years, however, he made it known that he would not allow his country to be limited indefinitely to the peninsular constraints of a second-rate power. Indeed, he emphasized the point as early as 1927 in the "Treaty of Tirana," by formalizing Italy's creeping protectorate over Albania, and later by extensive (if clandestine) arms shipments to the Hungarian army, which he regarded as a potential ally in a future campaign of territorial revisionism.[38] If the Croats and Slovenes were comparably exploitable as proxies of Italian expansion into "Venezia Giulia," Mussolini would not hesitate in using them.

Accordingly, in 1930, when King Aleksandar's "consultative council" imposed an in-absentia death sentence on Ante Pavelić, Mussolini's government was the first to grant the *poglavnik* asylum. The following year, in the northern Italian towns of Brescia and Borgotaro, district police were ordered to cooperate with Pavelić's effort to establish two Ustaša training camps. In Rome, his lieutenants were given access to a rent-free suite of offices as headquarters for their "government in exile."[39] Subsequently, Pavelić's followers in Croatia also began receiving clandestine Italian police transfers of weapons,

---

36   James Barros, *The Corfu Incident of 1923: Mussolini and the League of Nations* (Princeton, NJ: Princeton University Press, 1965), *passim*.
37   Alan Cassels, *Mussolini's Early Diplomacy* (Princeton, NJ: Princeton University Press, 1970), 139–40.
38   Burgwyn, *Italian Foreign Policy*, 39–40.
39   Esmonde M. Robertson, *Mussolini as Empire-Builder: Europe and Africa, 1932–36* (London: Macmillan, 1977), 24.

food, and equipment, and sub-rosa subsidies that, by 1931, reached 100,000 lire a month.[40] In the autumn of 1932, comparably financed and armed, several hundred of Pavelić's men even ventured to cross from the Italian border town of Zara (p. 231) into Yugoslav sovereign territory, where they fecklessly proclaimed a "Croatian Republic" before being scattered by the Yugoslav army.[41]

King Aleksandar by no means underestimated the threat implicit in these Ustašist adventures, particularly the raids that were Italian based and subsidized. But neither could he discount Italy's economic importance to his own country. By 1929, the Italian market absorbed by far the largest quantity— between 25 and 28 per cent—of Yugoslavia's exports.[42] Consequently, as late as the winter of 1933–34, in the depths of the Great Depression, the king continued to exert every effort to protect his fragile relationship with Mussolini. He supported Italy's "special status" in Albania, even secretly offered the Italian government docking facilities at Kotor, the famed Herzegovinian deep-water naval base on Yugoslavia's Adriatic coast.

Nevertheless, regarding these overtures simply as evidence of Aleksandar's weakness, Mussolini remained unresponsive. In May 1934, he disdained to receive Yugoslavia's foreign minister, Bogoljub Jevtić, who had traveled to Rome with his king's offer of pragmatic cooperation. By then, in fact, the enmity between Mussolini and Aleksandar had become personal, with the Duce losing no opportunity of exposing the Yugoslav monarch to ridicule. In June, the Italian newspaper *San Marco* published a detailed historical essay on the South Slavs' catastrophic fourteenth-century defeat at the hands of the Turks at Kosovo. Reacting to the insult, Aleksandar ordered the Belgrade newspaper *Vreme* to print his own personally dictated account of Italy's World War I debacle at Caporetto, with its portrayal of the Italian army as a demoralized mob.[43]

It was in the wake of the *Vreme* article, in the summer of 1934, when the Italian ambassador delivered his government's official protest to the Yugoslav foreign ministry, that Louis Barthou volunteered to mediate between the Yugoslav and Italian governments. In tendering his good offices, the French foreign minister discerned the possibility of achieving a coup for his nation's diplomacy. Mussolini, after all, was known to be increasingly apprehensive

---

40  Trifkovic, *Ustaša*, 46–47.
41  Robertson, *Mussolini as Empire-Builder*, 25.
42  Robertson, *Mussolini as Empire-Builder*, 25.
43  Alan Roberts, *The Turning Point: The Assassination of Louis Barthou and King Alexander I of Yugoslavia* (New York: St. Martin's Press, 1970), 86.

of Hitler's pressure on Austria. In September 1934, in the aftermath of the Dollfuss assassination, the Italian government had joined France and Britain in a communiqué that publicly reconfirmed their joint démarche of the previous February, with its commitment to Austrian independence.[44] Manifestly, it was not Austria alone that the Duce had in mind as he repeated this pledge. He was also sending a message to Hitler. Even as it was not Austria alone that Barthou had in mind by endorsing the tripartite warning; holding out his hand to Austria, he was also renewing France's offer of friendship to Mussolini.[45]

## THE PLOT

In early September 1934, in the Hungarian border town of Nagykanizsa, in an apartment rented by a certain "Emil Horvath," nine Croatian visitors engaged in a lottery. "Horvath's" actual name was Gustav Perčec, and he was a senior Ustašist official, as were his visitors, most of whom had come to Nagykanizsa from Janka Puszta, the Ustaša's principal training camp in Hungary. Three of the men—Zvonimir Pospišil, Mijo Kralj, and Ivan Rajić—now picked the lottery's "winning" black cubes. With his congratulations, Perčec announced that the trio was "chosen" to help liberate Croatia. Immediately, the three responded to Perčec's benediction by repeating the Ustašist oath: "Failing in my assignment, I shall accept death as my penalty, so help me God, Amen."[46] The "assignment" was not specified; but everyone in the room knew that it was nothing less than the assassination of Yugoslavia's King Aleksandar.

The plot was given renewed urgency as a consequence of French Foreign Minister Barthou's recent visit to Belgrade and Barthou's offer to serve as the Yugoslav king's liaison to Mussolini. Aleksandar had accepted the proposal gratefully.[47] However belated, it brought with it the hint of the Duce's cautious interest in a relationship with the "Little Entente," a hint communicated discreetly to Barthou by Pompeo Aloisi, chief of the "Yugoslav Bureau" of the Italian foreign ministry. Indeed, preparing for his spring 1934 tour of Eastern Europe's successor states, Barthou had taken pains in advance to alert King Aleksandar to the multiple advantages of French diplomatic and military patronage, and Aleksandar had taken the foreign minister at his word.

---

44  Wandycz, *The Twilight of French*, 104.
45  Alfred D. Low, *The Anschluss Movement, 1918–1919, and the Paris Peace Conference* (Philadelphia, PA: American Philosophical Society, 1974), 165.
46  Trifkovic, *Ustaša*, 46.
47  Pompeo Aloisi, *Journal, 25 juillet 1932–14 juin 1936* (Paris: Librairie Plon, 1957), 122–25.

Thus, in May 1934, when Barthou arrived in Yugoslavia as the last stop in his East European itinerary, he was given a lavish reception the moment his train crossed the Danube into Yugoslav territory. Serbian cavalrymen raced their horses along the river bank and fired their rifles in the air. Pausing at villages en route, Barthou was greeted by folk dancers performing in native costumes. At Belgrade, King Aleksandar personally welcomed his distinguished guest at the railroad station. The next day, introduced to the Yugoslav parliament, Barthou received a thunderous standing ovation. All the Chamber's delegates, Serbs and non-Serbs, were aware that French soldiers had played a crucial role in liberating the South Slavs from Habsburg rule. When the visiting foreign minister reassured them that France would always be at their side, they believed him. At the evening's banquet in his honor, when Barthou extended King Aleksandar an official invitation to pay a return visit to France, the monarch immediately accepted.

By then, Ante Pavelić and his Ustaša cohorts recognized that they had little time to lose in doing away with the king. If Barthou actually succeeded in brokering an Italian-Yugoslav accord, Croatian hopes for independence might be postponed indefinitely. Yet, by the same token, if an assassination effort were launched, it had to be foolproof. Six months earlier, in December 1933, Pavelić had recruited three Ustašists to murder Aleksandar during the monarch's annual ceremonial visit to the Croatian capital of Zagreb. The attempt failed. As Aleksandar and his entourage were escorted through the city's Jelačića Square, the designated assassins unaccountably froze. The king continued unharmed, and the putative killers were identified and captured. Their fate was gruesome.

This time Pavelić would leave nothing to chance. In addition to the three Nagykanizsa lottery winners, he had ordered eight other recruits to be selected from Ustaša camps in northern Italy. These were chosen by his personal bodyguard, a hulking Macedonian, Vlado Cernozemski, better known as "Vlada" or "Vlada the Chauffeur." Coarse-featured, with glittering brown eyes and a thin slit of a mouth in a Tatar-like face, the brutish Vlada was illiterate and spoke only a barely comprehensible amalgam of Bulgarian and Serbo-Croatian. But Vlada was a crack sharpshooter, an expert bomb maker, and as fearless as he was fanatically loyal to Pavelić. In mid-September of 1934, when the entire assassination team was assembled in its Italian camp outside Brescia, it was Vlada who put its members through their final training exercises.

The assassination strategy was planned elsewhere. This became clearer in late September of 1934 when the three lottery winners—Pospišil, Kralj, and Rajić—were dispatched to Budapest. There they were furnished with railroad tickets to Switzerland, together with a generous supply of Swiss and Italian currency, and counterfeit Hungarian passports. Their instructions were to travel to Zurich on the night of September 27. Upon arrival, they were to wait patiently at the city's railroad station for the appearance of their contact, a personal emissary of the *poglavnik*. All these instructions were meticulously followed. Moreover, upon reaching Zurich, the three prospective assassins were relieved to learn the identity of their contact. He turned out to be Slavko Kvaternik, Ante Pavelić's deputy in chief.

Most recently, Kvaternik had served as the Ustašist "ambassador" in Berlin, where he had been befriended by Gestapo Chief Heinrich Himmler and other senior Nazis. He had returned to Italy only days before to undertake his new assassination assignment. At Kvaternik's side now at the Zurich railroad station was Vlado Cernozemski ("Vlada the Chauffeur"). In the station coffee shop, Kvarternik then showed Pospišil, Kralj, and Rajić a handwritten note. "Execute without discussion whatever orders you will receive from the *Bear*," it stated. The "*Bear*" was Kvaternik's alias. The "signature" on the note was simply "The *Poglavnik*"—Ante Pavelić.

Duly purchasing rail tickets for the lottery winners, Kvarternik and Vlada then joined the other three conspirators on the next train from Zurich to Lausanne. En route, Kvarternik supplied his companions with a new set of counterfeit—Czech—passports. Upon arrival in Lausanne, posing as Czech "businessmen," the conspirators proceeded to register and rest in the city's Hôtel des Palmiers. On the following morning, October 3, the five separated, embarking for France on different trains. Arriving in Paris late that afternoon, they registered at separate hotels. The precautions were not superfluous. The French border police were known to be mounting a special lookout for Croatian visitors. Moreover, only the week before, for similar purposes of deception, the Ustašists had been preceded to the French capital by a man who went by the name of "Petar." "Petar" was accompanied on the Rome-Paris express train by a striking blonde woman, "Maria." In her suitcase, under her packed clothing, "Maria" had stored five grenades, five pistols, and ten boxes of cartridges. These too would be distributed to the Ustašist group— but only in the last hours before the murder attempt.

Days earlier, the French press had published the schedule of King Aleksandar's impending visit. On the afternoon of October 9, the announcement stated, the Yugoslav naval cruiser *Dubrovnik* would bring the monarch and his retinue to Marseille. The visitors would be welcomed at the harbor by Foreign Minister Barthou; by General Alphonse Georges, France's military chief of staff; and by the Yugoslav ambassador to France and other Yugoslav embassy officials. The royal party then would be driven in a procession of limousines for overnight hotel rest in Marseille; and the next morning, October 10, the entire entourage would proceed onward by special train to Paris. On the same evening, France's President Albert Lebrun would host a banquet for the king in the historic palace of Versailles. The ensuing morning and afternoon of October 11 would be devoted to a series of discussions between the Yugoslav visitors and French Prime Minister Gaston Doumergue, Barthou, and other senior foreign ministry officials. Afterward, the king would travel on to Lausanne for a last few days of vacation before returning home.

With this information, the Ustašist assassination team had prepared several alternate scenarios. The first projected the "elimination" of Aleksandar, either upon his arrival at Marseille harbor or at his designated Marseille hotel. If this attempt failed, the king would be waylaid en route to Paris or in Paris itself. Other options envisaged the assassination taking place at the Palace of Versailles, or, as a last effort, at the train station in Lausanne, Aleksandar's final destination before his scheduled return to Yugoslavia. In each of these sites, "Vlada the Chauffeur" would assign two or more of the eight recruits he had selected at the Italian Ustaša camps. Yet the venues of first choice were always Marseille or Versailles-Paris.

On October 6, Pospišil and Rajić, two of the three lottery winners, arrived in Versailles, mingling among the usual crowd of tourists but taking special note of potential ambush positions. That same day Kvaternik (the "bear") and Kralj (the third of the "lottery" winners) joined Vlada in boarding the Paris-Marseille Express. In late afternoon, they detrained in nearby Aix-en-Provence. That night, at their local hotel, they were joined by two strangers whose true identity was known only to Kvaternik and Vlada. These were "Petar" and his blonde consort "Maria," who had arrived by separate train. Upon introducing them, Kvarternik informed Kralj and Vlada that "Petar is our leader, the man we all have to obey."

On October 7, "Petar" and Kralj were driven in Vlada's rented automobile to Marseille. They surveyed the harbor, studied a map of the city, and compared it to newspaper descriptions of King Aleksandar's prospective itinerary. That same evening, as French police began a methodical inspection of Marseille's hotel registries for clues to suspicious guests, the conspirators returned to Aix-en-Provence. There, "Petar" and "Maria" distributed their weaponry and ammunition and then left, never to be seen again by the prospective assassins—with the exception of Vlada, who discovered only afterward that "Petar" was Ante Pavelić, the *poglavnik* himself. "Maria" was his mistress.

That same night of October 7, Kvarternik gave final instructions to his two remaining companions, Vlada and Kralj. He had directed Rajić and Pospišil, he explained, to remain in Fontainebleau, outside Paris, where they would wait "in reserve" if the assassination effort failed in Marseille. But Vlada and Kralj would function as the initial Marseille assassination team. On the afternoon of October 9, they would travel by bus from Aix-en-Provence to Marseille. In Marseille, they would take up their positions on the steps of the city's Palais de la Bourse, flanking the route of Aleksandar's scheduled arrival procession. It was from this vantage point at the municipal stock exchange that Kralj would hurl one of his two grenades into the crowd at the same moment that Vlada began shooting at the king. In the anticipated panic, both men would have the best chance of making their escape.

## DEATH IN THE AFTERNOON

On the morning of October 9, his task in France completed, Kvaternik entrained for Lausanne, where he intended to review the preparations of his reserve team. At 1:00 p.m. of the next day, Vlada and Kralj traveled by bus from Aix-en-Provence to Marseille. Two and half hours later, the Yugoslav destroyer *Dubrovnik* hove into view of the harbor. Within minutes, the ship anchored, still at sea, allowing King Aleksandar and his retinue to descend into an awaiting French naval vedette.

Flying the French and Yugoslav flags, the smaller vessel then maneuvered its way into a "VIP" inlet, the Quai des Belges. Overhead, a squadron of French naval seaplanes passed in formation. In the distance, artillery boomed in salute.

Awaiting the royal company on the dock were Barthou and General Alphonse Georges, together with the mayor of Marseille and other French government and local officials. As the king, dressed in admiral's uniform, led his party down the carpeted gang plank, a squad of French marines stood at attention. Adjoining them, in civilian clothes, an assemblage of some 20 bemedaled French veterans of the wartime Macedonian campaign also stood at attention. The royal entourage and attending French dignitaries shook hands. A young girl stepped forward to present Queen Maria with a bouquet of flowers, and a military band then played the national anthems of both countries. In the distance, behind a substantial police cordon, a large crowd cheered.[48]

Six chauffeured limousines had been placed at the disposal of the royal visitors. The first three were Citroën landaus, fitted with partially retracted leather roofs. Entering the lead vehicle, the king and Barthou were seated

---

48 For the events of October 9, 1935, see Broche, *Assassinat de Alexandre 1er*; Alan Roberts, *The Turning Point, passim*; and Alain Decaux, *Les Assassins* (Paris: Perrin, 1986), *passim*.

KING ALEKSANDAR I (LEFT) WITH FRENCH FOREIGN MINISTER LOUIS BARTHOU

side by side, with General Georges occupying the seat facing them. Yugoslav Foreign Minister Bogoljub Jevtić and the mayor of Marseille took their places in the second limousine, and Queen Maria and her personal retinue occupied the third. Subordinate officials followed in the last three automobiles. As the caravan started out,[49] it was preceded by mounted cavalrymen of France's elite Garde Mobile, wearing their ceremonial plumed helmets and gleaming breastplates. Moving at a leisurely pace, in full view of thousands of applauding bystanders, the procession approached the Bourse. But there, unaccountably, it slowed down, then stopped.

General Georges turned his head to see what had happened to the mounted honor guard. Many of these horsemen appeared to be galloping in the opposite direction of the motorcade. The police, assigned to keep the crowds at bay, seemed confused, facing the street rather than the throngs of spectators. Yet, before the general could appraise the evident confusion, a large man, clad in a brown suit, lurched out of the crowd on the Bourse steps and made

---

49 Roberts, *The Turning Point*, 131.

directly for King Aleksandar's limousine. It was Vlada. Colonel Piollet, one of the few mounted escorts who had held his position, shouted in warning as Vlada clambered onto the running board of the automobile. Yet, even at that moment, assuming that the intruder was simply an over-enthusiastic journalist, Colonel Piollet made no effort to unsheathe his saber.

The limousine's chauffeur was the first to react. Hearing a gunshot and an ensuing gasp from the back seat, he leaned over to open the passenger door in an effort to push Vlada off the running board. Clinging to the retracted limousine roof, however, the burly Macedonian, a large automatic pistol in his right hand, succeeded in firing point-blank at the chauffeur's neck. At the same time, Barthou attempted to fling himself over the king before Vlada could fire again. The effort was useless. Four more bullets struck Aleksandar, three in his torso, one in his jaw. General Georges meanwhile pushed the automobile door open and leaped into the street. He was instantly cut down by Vlada's ensuing two shots. A gendarme then rushed from the sidewalk and grappled with Vlada, at the same time firing his own pistol. His bullet went astray, however, striking Barthou in the arm. Vlada, with his immense strength, then hurled the gendarme aside and resumed his fusillade against the king.

Hearing the succession of pistol shots, the onlookers' cheers turned to shouts and screams.[50] Conceivably, it was their reaction, more than the shots themselves, that impelled Colonel Piollet at last to draw his saber and flail away at Vlada's head and neck, before the burly Macedonian loosened his grip on the limousine. By then, a second gendarme had arrived, firing at Vlada repeatedly before the latter fell to the street. The crowd subsequently burst through the police cordon to beat and kick Vlada' prone body (although, incredibly, he clung to life for another three hours). At the same time, Mio Kralj, Vlada's partner, although under orders to throw a grenade into the midst of the spectators on the Bourse's steps, remained petrified as the havoc continued Finally, in the turmoil of the assassination, he bestirred himself, but only to slip out of the panic-stricken crowd.

Extricating themselves from the second limousine, meanwhile, Yugoslavia's Foreign Minister Jevtić and General Dimitrievic, the nation's military chief of staff, raced to the king's side. They saw instantly that they were too late. After helping the stricken Barthou out of the car, they temporarily laid the king's body across the back seats. Aleksandar's unseeing eyes remained open, but only the seeing eye of a motion-picture camera took in the scene.

---

50  Decaux, *Les Assassins*, 120–22.

It was history's first assassination to be captured on motion picture film. Meanwhile, a gendarme had replaced the chauffeur at the limousine's steering wheel, and Aleksandar was sped off to police headquarters, where his body was removed and carried inside. An urgent call went out then for the police surgeon. But when the doctor arrived, nothing remained for him but to sign the king's death certificate, as well as the chauffeur's. General Georges was more fortunate. Rushed to a hospital and then into emergency surgery, he hovered between life or death for the next six weeks, but eventually recovered.

Louis Barthou shared the fate of King Aleksandar. He had not been a target. The wound he suffered in his arm was later attributed to the stray police bullet. Following the assault on the king, however, and helped out of the limousine, the bleeding and confused French foreign minister bent down for several crucial minutes in an unsuccessful effort to retrieve his glasses. During the ensuing chaos, he was somehow overlooked. By the time he stood up, King Aleksandar and General Georges, as well as their chauffeur, had been sped off for medical attention. Incredibly, Barthou was left alone, with no alternative but to seek a taxi on his own. Some 20 minutes went by before he found one, which then took him through crowded streets to the nearest hospital, the Saint-Charles.

The sequence of later events in the hospital has never been verified. There were reports that Barthou had been left on a gurney to await a blood transfusion, or at least a tourniquet, before a surgeon finally arrived. Yet by then the damage was done. The stray police bullet had severed the humeral artery in his arm, and the loss of blood proved fatal. In late afternoon, the foreign minister was wheeled into the operating room, semiconscious, mumbling a question about his missing glasses. He expired on the operating table.[51]

## A BALKAN AFTERMATH

When informed of the multiple assassinations, French President Albert Lebrun and Minister of the Interior Albert Sarraut rushed immediately by special train to Marseille, where the king's body had been delivered to a temporary resting place, the lobby of city hall. There, Lebrun delivered a moving eulogy, and then returned to Paris. Sarraut remained behind to investigate the circumstances of the multiple killings. It had taken several hours, meanwhile, before news of the event could be verified and telegraphed officially

---

51  Broche, *Assassinat de Alexandre 1er*, 78–102.

from the French foreign ministry to Belgrade. When the telegram arrived, Yugoslav Prime Minister Nikola Uzunović at first refused to believe it. But Prince Paul, the king's cousin, accepted the news immediately. He was also aware that Aleksandar's last will and testament stipulated that he, Paul, was to serve as Yugoslavia's regent until the king's oldest son, Petar, 11 years old, came of age. The boy was then in London, enrolled in an elite private school. He was summoned home directly; and within days, all government officials in Yugoslavia took the oath of allegiance to him as King Petar II.

The speed of the dynastic transition was influenced at least in part by fear of an outbreak of Serbian reprisals against the Croats, and by the specter of a full-blown civil war. Yet, almost miraculously, the fear was unrealized. The assassin, Vlada, was a Bulgarian, not a Croat; and, in Croatia itself, the population appeared as stunned and alarmed as the Serbs. Indeed, three days after the murders, when Aleksandar's body was returned to Yugoslavia, its flag-draped coffin first lay in state in Zagreb, beneath the rotunda of Croatia's provincial diet. Whether out of curiosity or respect, an estimated 200,000 Croats filed by while the Yugoslav flag flew at half mast over Croatia's other public buildings. When the casket was escorted to Belgrade for the national funeral in the Memorial Church of Saint George, Prime Minister Nikola Uzunović had a fiery Slovenian nationalist prelate, Monsignor Anton Korošec, released from prison to attend the ceremonies. "We ought to work and live for Yugoslavia now," Korošec was quoted later. "Everything else is forgotten."[52] In December, the government also released from house arrest Vladko Maček, the veteran Croatian deputy to the slain Stjepan Radić. Maček similarly appealed for unity.

In France, meanwhile, Louis Barthou's body remained on public view at the Marseille prefecture, while cabinet colleagues in Paris made preparations for his state funeral. On October 11, Vice-Premier Pierre Herriot supervised the transfer of the coffin to a special train, which took the slain foreign minister back to Paris. A ceremonial procession led by Prime Minister Gaston Doumergue then accompanied the body to the Quai d'Orsay, where it lay in the foreign ministry's Salon de l'Horloge, surrounded by an honor guard. On October 13, the day of the funeral, all shops in Paris closed. Flags on public buildings flew at half mast. Republican Guards led the solemn procession from the Quai d'Orsay to the Hôtel des Invalides, where the prime minister himself gave the funeral oration.

The obsequies transcended the respectful platitudes traditionally rendered a veteran public servant, even one fallen in the active service of his

---

52  Lampe, *Yugoslavia as History*, 176.

country. Frenchmen of all backgrounds, of the Right and Left, responded with rare emotion to the tributes rendered Barthou's career of service and sacrifice. The foreign minister had been a statesman in the mold of a Thiers or a Clemenceau. In the originality and audacity of his diplomacy, Barthou saw beyond the more commonplace alliances of traditional wartime partners. He pursued his own nation's security interests, to be sure. That was his mandate and function. Yet, in the performance of his responsibilities, the foreign minister evinced a rare glint of imagination, even of idealism, in linking his nation's future alliances not only with the heavyweight imperial governments of the prewar but with the aspiring new successor states that formerly had been consigned to Europe's back door. In espousing their cause as France's own, he was making a gesture that, ultimately, would become the recognized hallmark of a "new" European diplomacy.

For the present, however, amid all the ceremonial and commiseration, was justice present? In the chaos of the assassinations, Mio Kralj, Vlada's companion, managed to elude detection. Later, he made his way from the Bourse to Marseille's central bus terminal and from there to Aix-en-Provence. In his rush to check out of his hotel, forgetting his instructions to discard any remaining weapons in a nearby river, Kralj stuffed his grenades, pistols, and ammunition under the mattress. Then he embarked by train for Paris. At the same time, when news of the assassination was confirmed, the other lottery winners, Pospišil and Rajić, who had prepared to ambush King Aleksandar at Versailles if the initial assault failed, departed Paris by separate trains. But two days later, all three Ustašists were arrested at the Swiss border. France's Sûreté had belatedly identified them from the counterfeit Czech passport numbers in their hotel registrations, as well as from the weapons in Kralj's hotel bedroom. Only the master plotters, Ante Pavelić and his deputy, Kvaternik, had succeeded in making their escape—initially, before the assassinations, from France to Switzerland, and afterward, following the killings, from Switzerland to Italy. In Italy, Mussolini himself issued orders for the two men to be hidden in an island off the Ligurian coast.

Who and what were behind the assassinations? Was it Hungary? Evidently the Yugoslav government thought so. Within the week, the interior minister ordered the eviction from his country of thousands of—completely innocent—ethnic Hungarians.[53] Was the guilty party also Italy? Certain that it was, the Yugoslav ambassador to the League of Nations was preparing formally to accuse the Italian government. Before the accusation could

---

53 Hugh Seton-Watson, *Eastern Europe between the Wars, 1918–1941* (Hamden, CT: Archon Books, 1962), 344.

be delivered to the League Council, however, Pierre Laval, whom France's Prime Minister Gaston Doumergue had appointed as Barthou's successor at the foreign ministry, entrained for Geneva. As Laval had insisted to the cabinet before his hurried departure, whatever the formidable evidence of Italian support for the Ustaša, a Yugoslav accusation before the League would jeopardize the late Barthou's master strategy, and Laval's own. That strategy was at any cost to fortify the "Little Entente" of successor states against both Nazi Germany and Fascist Hungary. The effort would be endangered, Laval argued, if Mussolini were put on the defensive. The Duce might even be provoked into joining a common front with Hitler.[54]

At first, Laval's attempt to forestall diplomatic indictment seemed unavailing. Ten days after the successive funerals, Yugoslav Foreign Minister Bogoljub Jevtić instructed his ambassador at Geneva to request the League to determine whether the "terrorist organizations" were given encouragement and help by "certain governments" (although Jevtić did not openly mention Italy or Hungary). In the last week of November 1934, the League Council duly assembled in special session; and, on December 7, its members appointed a committee to debate the Yugoslav request. By then, however, Laval's preemptive strategy had begun to achieve results. His warning to the Belgrade government of a possible interruption of essential French subventions and armaments was discreet, but eminently decipherable. Nor was the foreign minister alone in seeking to fend off the indictment. Anthony Eden, then Britain's "Minister for League of Nations Affairs," similarly preferred to keep the Mussolini government within the Allied orbit. He supported Laval's diplomacy.

By January 1935, the outline of a compromise was becoming visible. Yugoslav Foreign Minister Jevtić would refrain from pressing his demand for a League condemnation of Italy. Instead, he would accept Laval's offer to focus League attention on the role of Hungary in supporting Ustašist activities. But even in this diversionary tactic, Laval offered the Yugoslavs less than half a loaf. He preferred also to walk softly with the Hungarians. For several weeks, Tibor von Eckhardt, Hungary's representative at the League Council, persisted in denying his government's collusion with the Ustaša. Eventually, in February 1935, much to the chagrin of the Yugoslav government, Laval and Eckhardt agreed on a proposal for Hungary's League delegation simply to accept censure for "border laxity" in failing to block occasional Ustašist forays into Yugoslavia. The League Council then accepted this limp formulation.

---

54   Trifkovic, *Ustaša*, 46–47.

As for Italy, its role in the assassination was not so much as mentioned in Geneva. Henceforth, Mussolini could afford to mute his recriminations against the Yugoslav leadership, even to close the Ustaša camps on Italian soil.[55] He had levered France into his circle of allies, after all, and, in the process, he had conveyed a message to the "depraved sexual maniac" in Berlin. However belatedly, the road toward Italy's imperial future appeared now to be opening: in Yugoslavian Dalmatia, in Ethiopia, perhaps in the Middle East.

Years before, as a young editor, Mussolini had confided to his admirer, Leda Rafanelli:

> I desire to be somebody, do you understand me? . . . I want to rise to the top. . . . The background in which I was raised enslaved me. . . . I must rise, I must make a leap forward, to the top.[56]

By the winter of 1934–35, shrewdly exploiting the effort of the Versailles Powers to defend their new cordon sanitaire of successor states, and Hitler's preference to avoid a rupture with Italy, Mussolini apparently had taken a giant step toward fulfilling his youthful dream. Among the continent's rival sets of adversaries, he had seized the moment to emerge as the most courted government leader in Europe.

---

55  Trifkovic, *Ustaša*, 54–55.
56  Leda Rafanelli, op. cite., 67–69.

CHAPTER EIGHT

# Gallic *Fraternité* under the Third Republic

*"To Die for Danzig? To Die for the Jews?"*

### THE PRICE OF VICTORY

Riding the Paris Metro as late as 1950, passengers could still view the captions stenciled over the choicest seats, those facing or adjoining the carriage doors. "Réservés pour les mutilés de la guerre," they proclaimed. Faded and barely legible, the reminders shared the antiquity of the Metro trains themselves. They alluded not to the recent war of 1939–45 but to the "Great War," the immemorial war, of 1914–18.

For decades even after World War II, the battlefield hemorrhage of its predecessor remained an open lesion in French public consciousness. One in five men alive in 1914 had been mobilized in France's armed services. During the 51 months between August 1914 and November 1918, 1.35 million Frenchmen out of a prewar population of 36 million had perished in combat. Half of the 6.4 million troops who evaded death had sustained wounds, many of them permanently crippling. During the conflict there had been 1.4 million more civilian deaths than births in a nation whose falling prewar birthrate already had been a source of anxiety.[1] By November 1918, three-quarters of a million war orphans had become wards of the state, which paid for their nurture until they reached the age of 18; and, by 1931, a sapping 13.5 per cent of the government's budget also was being disbursed in remittances for widows and orphans.[2]

There were other consequences of the Great War. Although the northeastern territory that had been occupied by the Reichswehr comprised a small part of geographical France, it accounted for 80 per cent of the nation's iron ore and 70 per cent of its coal. The Germans had virtually denuded these resources, even as they had systematically expropriated the region's granaries and livestock for shipment home. Occupying 4,143 French municipalities, the Reichswehr had completely demolished 1,039 of them and damaged some 1,200 others. Eastern France's rail transportation system was also left in chaos.

Hence, in the first years after the war, it was inevitable that the French government and people should have remained obsessed with issues of national security. Twice in a lifetime, in 1870 and 1914, there had been German invasions, with their attendant costs in military bloodshed and economic devastation. By 1918, no one needed a reminder that Germany possessed resources greater than those of France. The Reich itself had escaped invasion, even in defeat. Its own industrial plant was intact. Despite the territorial amputations of the Versailles Treaty, Germany's population of 53 million in the postwar remained 40 per cent larger than France's.

Georges Clemenceau was the voice and conscience of these anxieties. His memory was long. He had lived through the Franco-Prussian War of 1870–71 and had seen the Germans invade his country and occupy Paris. He had been the only parliamentary deputy then who had refused to ratify Prussia's dictated Treaty of Frankfurt. In 1908–9, as a Radical Socialist and ardent disciple of Léon Gambetta ("father" of the Third French Republic), Clemenceau himself had served a brief term as prime minister. Although subsequently consigned to the opposition, he was called back to the premiership in November 1917, at the age of 76.

It was the darkest period of World War I. The Central Powers were on the threshold of victory, and France's Chamber of Deputies was convulsed in

---

1 Antoine Prost, *Histoire générale de l'enseignement et de l'éducation*, vol. 4, *L'école et la famille dans une société en mutation, 1930–1980* (Paris: Éditions de la Nouvelle Librairie de France, 1981), 28.
2 Georges Wormser, *Georges Mandel, l'homme politique* (Paris: Plon, 1967), 17.

turmoil and rage at the ineptitude of the predecessor Viviani and Painlevé cabinets. Accordingly, as he took over the reins of power again, Clemenceau, whom journalists now dubbed the "Old Tiger," almost immediately became a hero to civilians and soldiers alike. His ferocious patriotism and restless energy often led him down into the trenches, where he circulated among the ranks to cheer them on with his racy, biting humor. Doggedly persevering through the climactic German offensive in 1918, Clemenceau stripped other military fronts for the reinforcements that won the Second Battle of the Marne, and then gambled on a massive Allied counterattack that finally compelled Berlin to sue for an armistice. At that triumphant moment, the French people regaled Clemenceau as their national savior.

## THE "TIGER'S CUB"

The year before, as he replaced the floundering Paul Painlevé in the premiership, Clemenceau had appointed the 32-year-old Georges Mandel as his *chef de cabinet*. The office functioned in effect as the general secretaryship of the French wartime government, and, as Clemenceau knew from past experience, his young appointee would exercise his manifold responsibilities with punctiliousness, imagination—and ruthlessness.

Mandel was the son of a middle-class Jewish clothing merchant. His grandfather, Adolphe Rothschild, born in Sulzbach, Bavaria in 1814, moved to Paris 20 years later. His father, Edmond Rothschild, born in Paris in 1843, married Hermine Mandel, a native Parisian. The couple in turn produced three sons. Louis, born in 1884, was the eldest. In 1902, Louis Rothschild became "Georges Mandel." There was no mystery to the transformation. By then, even at the age of 18, Louis Rothschild had begun to write articles for the left-wing journal, *Le Siècle*, and later for the nation's leading anticlerical daily, *L'Aurore*. Although the Dreyfus Affair had wound down by then, its accusations and counteraccusations against the "Rothschild conspiracy" had not entirely disappeared. In reaction, upon entering the realm of public readership, the precocious teenager decided to adopt his mother's maiden name, Mandel, and simultaneously to change his first name from Louis to "Georges" to avoid confusion with his maternal uncle, Louis Mandel.

Sensitivity to antisemitism was an understandable reaction. Yet Mandel's quest for public acceptance approached the threshold of pathology. Refusing to admit that his grandfather had been an immigrant, he took pains to emphasize that his mother was born in Alsace, encompassing the oldest and most acculturated Jewish community in France. During his 1919 campaign for election to the Chamber of Deputies (p. 270), he would invent a grandfather who had fought in the Revolution of 1830. Once, too, he asserted that 30 members of his family had been killed on the battlefields defending France and (equally mendaciously) that two of his brothers had fallen in the World War. Even as a neophyte journalist, short of stature and frail of physique, Mandel adopted the self-conscious demeanor of an aristocrat, dressing entirely in black, carrying a heavy briefcase, and using his parental subsidies to rent a fashionable apartment and hire a personal secretary.[3]

Beneath Mandel's factitious autobiography, however, and his poseur's façade, there lurked a first-rate political mind and an even more aggressive political careerism. His choice of the newspaper *L'Aurore* as his forum was characteristic. It was the political organ of the Radical Socialist Party and hence of Clemenceau, the party's chairman. Indeed, Mandel's intermittent articles, infused with the older man's burning anticlericalism and fiery nationalism, consciously parroted Clemenceau's latest speeches, whether delivered in or out of government. The sycophancy first paid off in 1906, when Clemenceau accepted the portfolio of minister of the interior in the cabinet of Ferdinand Sarrien and appointed Mandel, then 22, as one of his several assistants in the ministry's secretariat.

The young man immediately established himself as an overachiever, making it his business to study the workings of both his and other ministries. In the process, he exhibited a prodigious, near-encyclopedic memory for political details. Two years later, when Clemenceau stepped from his ministerial billet to assume his first premiership, he arranged for Mandel to be appointed deputy to Albert Sarraut, then chef de cabinet (and later premier). In 1909, following the defeat of Clemenceau's initial government, Mandel remained the great man's protégé, this time as political editor of the *Journal de Var*, the Radical Socialists' "house" organ.[4] Indeed, within three years, Clemenceau transferred full responsibility of the journal to Mandel and consulted him daily on issues of party importance. The relationship between the two was cemented in November 1917, when Clemenceau regained the prime ministry and unhesitatingly appointed Mandel as his own chef de cabinet.

By then, the older man's faith in Mandel had become unshakable. As he explained to Raymond Poincaré, France's president, "Mandel will arrange everything. He is amazing. With that Jewish nose of his, he can smell out the weaknesses of [others].... He's really a walking encyclopedia. One could not

---

3 Francisque Varenne, *Mon patron, Georges Mandel* (Paris: Éditions Défense de la France, 1948), 36–39.

4 Varenne, *Mon patron*, 42–44.

ask for a better collaborator."[5] As testimony of that faith, Clemenceau gave Mandel virtually free rein in structuring the new government. The young executive assistant promptly set about the task with a political canniness that belied his age. His methods were not always refined. In one instance, Mandel offered the undersecretariat of the interior to Pierre Laval, a fast-rising Socialist deputy in the Chamber and the lawyer for the Confédération Générale du Travail, but only on condition that Laval monitor his fellow Socialists and harass those ministers who displeased the premier.[6] If journalists or editors proved intransigent and bribes did not succeed in influencing their views, Mandel was not averse to using threats, including prosecution for "illegal traffic in newsprint," or the cancellation of military draft deferments.[7]

Not surprisingly, it was in the process of asserting his role as the "vice-dictator of France" that Mandel struck his critics as "bilious, suspicious, peremptory, vindictive." Their snide allusions to his ancestry ranged from "un Machievelle israélite" to "son Majesté, Jéroboam II."[8] Even Clemenceau, bemusedly noting and approving Mandel's ruthlessness, at times characterized the young man as "un asiatique."[9] Altogether, for the French population, the spectacle of a Jew exercising this omniscience on behalf even of a respected prime minister was unprecedented, and more than a little unsettling.

## AN ILLUSORY *BELLE ÉPOQUE*

Following the liquidation of the Dreyfus Affair in 1898–99, the Third French Republic seemingly had broadened its anchorage in secular egalitarianism. Although bigotry and xenophobia had not entirely vanished even during the nation's celebrated "belle époque," between 1899 and 1914, the forces of royalist and clerical reaction appeared to have atrophied as a credible political force. Nevertheless, the lingering resentments were hardly trivial. Édouard Drumont, the journalist who had sparked the initial anti-Dreyfusard campaign, might have lapsed into a politically crippled figure long before his death in 1917, but there were others who swiftly picked up the torch of reactionary

---

5   John M. Sherwood, *Georges Mandel and the Third Republic* (Stanford, CA: Stanford University Press, 1970), 21.

6   Wormser, *Georges Mandel*, 63–65.

7   Georges Wormser, *La République de Clemenceau* (Paris: Presses universitaires de France, 1961), 364–65.

8   Marcel Berger and Paul Allard, *Les secrets de la censure pendant la guerre* (Paris: Éditions des portiques, 1932), 276.

9   Wormser, *Georges Mandel*, 30.

chauvinism. One of these, Maurice Barrès, coining the phrase *"nationalisme intégral"* as early as the 1898 political campaign, invested patriotism with a new and mystical resonance, emphasizing the "spiritual" character of French blood and soil. A decade later, a group of self-styled "philosophical traditionalists," led by Maurice Pujo and Henri Vaugeois, organized a "Comité d'Action Française," ostensibly dedicated to a reestablishment of the "old Gallic certitudes."

It was Charles Maurras, however, joining the committee a year later, who swiftly became its leader and driving force. Born in a small Mediterranean fishing village in 1868, the son of a provincial tax assessor, the young Maurras had anticipated a career as a naval officer. But upon being rejected for reasons of partial deafness, he departed for Paris, where his parents registered him in a Catholic lycée. It was Maurras's first exposure to an authentically cosmopolitan city. The extensive presence in the capital of North Africans, Middle Easterners, Eastern Europeans, Jews, and other "non-Gallic" types quite shocked him. Nine years later, as a 26-year-old fledgling literary critic for the right-wing newspaper *La Cocarde*, Maurras gave a name to these elements. For him, they were *"métèques,"* perennial aliens, a term he borrowed from the ancient Athenians and which later he enlarged to include Protestants and Freemasons.

In 1908, retrieving the mantle of the discredited Drumont, Maurras and his colleagues of the Action Française, among them the renowned nationalist historian Jacques de Bainville and the literary critic Léon Daudet, set about honing their political strategy for the resuscitation of a monarchical France, a nation that would be purged equally of its *"métèques"* and its political leftists. The program frankly envisaged the use of force. "The crowd," Maurras insisted, "always follows."[10] To mobilize the "crowd," he set about transforming the original Comité d'Action Française into a *ligue*, an ideological consociation. Maurras was not physically impressive. A short, bespectacled man, he compensated for his appearance and semi-deafness with a klaxon-like voice. Yet this former café intellectual revealed himself to be a dynamic and imaginative political operator. Under his guidance, branches of the Action Française were swiftly organized among a wide diffusion of anti-Dreyfusard and nativist elements.

At the same time, the movement established its own newspaper, also titled *L'Action Française*. Henceforth, with Maurras setting editorial policy,

---

10 Edward R. Tenenbaum, *Action Française: Die-Hard Reactionaries in Twentieth-Century France* (New York: Wiley, 1962), 75.

it was Léon Daudet, his managing editor, who guided the paper to financial solvency. Like his father, Alphonse, Daudet was neither a first-class novelist nor a first-class polemicist. But he demonstrated an infallible instinct for public relations and for revenue-generating. Some of his funds came from his own and his wife's family estate; but more were raised from other wealthy contributors and advertisers. Before long, from the densely packed, garishly headlined pages of *L'Action Française* a torrent of xenophobic abuse gained momentum. Its theme was established in the paper's first editorial: "The *métèques* are our foreign guests," Maurras proclaimed, "domiciled or recently naturalized. . . . [T]hey are foreigners, aliens, with an alien disdain for our national traditions or ideals."[11]

Soon, too, in the years immediately before World War I, exploiting the putative threat of alienism rather than the more traditional bête noire of republican parliamentarism, the party drew widening support from military, aristocratic, and petit-bourgeois circles. Its youth organization, a collection of toughs dubbed "Camelots du Roi" (literally, "the king's street vendors"), disseminated antisemitic wall placards, hooted performances by Jewish musicians and artists, heckled Henri Bernstein's plays at the Comédie Française, and organized "*métèque*"-baiting parades on Joan of Arc Day. In this fashion, acting out the gospel of "integral nationalism" not less frontally than Édouard Drumont had managed in his diatribes against Dreyfus, the Action Française emerged by 1914 as the vanguard of a chauvinist revival. Although the outbreak of war inevitably focused all varieties of nationalism on the German enemy, the post-armistice era would reopen the floodgates of a more indiscriminate xenophobia.[12]

## THE SEARCH FOR SECURITY

At the Paris Peace Conference of 1919, if Prime Minister Clemenceau was implacable in his demand for iron-clad territorial and military guarantees, he was animated by more than a quest for vengeance. As he periodically reminded the other two leading Allied statesmen, David Lloyd George and Woodrow Wilson, he knew the Germans too well to discount the possibility of their military resurgence. Yet, while the premier's erstwhile political supporters shared his misgivings, they also judged his tenacious diplomatic struggle as less than successful. Forced to the wall by his British and American colleagues, the "Old Tiger" made several fateful concessions that his critics

---

11  Charles Maurras, *La démocratie religieuse* (Paris: Nouvelle librairie nationale, 1921), 90.
12  Eugene Weber, *The Hollow Years: France in the 1930s* (New York: Norton, 1994), 26–28.

would not forgive. Rather than digging in his heels for an outright annexation of the German Rhineland, Clemenceau settled for "demilitarization" of this strategic frontier zone. Again, at the insistence of Lloyd George and Wilson, he relinquished his original demand for a small German conscript militia and accepted instead an army of "volunteers," which before long would serve as camouflage for a veteran and experienced military nucleus. Conversely, the prime minister's insistence on substantial German reparations payments evoked Lloyd George's public warning of a "Carthaginian Peace" and soon became the object of inter-Allied recriminations.

In the immediate postwar, Clemenceau had been affectionately dubbed "*Père la Victoire* [Father Victory]." Subsequently, as public disillusionment with the Versailles Treaty mounted, the premier became "*Perdre la Victoire* [Lost Victory]." In the January 1920 parliamentary election, his "Union Sacrée" dissolved in the Chamber of Deputies, to be replaced by the "Bloc National," a centrist combination of Republicans and Radical Socialists that settled on Alexandre Millerand as its choice for prime minister. Millerand, however, proved even less successful than Clemenceau in ensuring German compliance with the peace treaty. The reparations provision was its first casualty. The ink on the document was scarcely dry before the German government began protesting the difficulty of meeting its payment schedules. The problem was genuine, given the precariousness of the Weimar Republic's economy. Yet the protest also evinced the German cabinet's shrewd insight into the widening rift in the Allied camp. The British persisted in their warnings against the dangers of a "Carthaginian Peace" and shortly made clear that their previous guarantees of support to France were all but void. The Americans, whose Senate declined altogether to ratify the Versailles Treaty, were obsessed less with German reparations to France than with France's repayment of its war debt to the United States.

Eventually, in January 1923, the German government defaulted on its scheduled reparations installment of coal and steel. Hereupon France's Bloc National government, by now under the premiership of its former wartime president, Raymond Poincaré, lost no time in dispatching two brigades of Algerian troops into the Ruhr Valley, the German industrial heartland. Yet as these imperial contingents set about loading the required supplies for direct shipment to France, the Germans in turn resorted to passive resistance, declining to operate the Ruhr's mines and factories. The French counterreaction was to import additional replacement workers from Belgium. The impasse continued for almost two years. It was in this period that Germany, its economy all but paralyzed, experienced the most catastrophic inflation in modern European history (p. 142).

Yet, at the same time, France's population underwent a parallel economic trauma. The cost of the Ruhr occupation, and its eventual failure to make good the nation's staggering war debt to its own citizens, dramatically eroded the value of France's currency. Before the occupation, the franc had been worth 20 cents to the American dollar. During the Ruhr occupation, the franc plummeted steadily until it struck bottom at 2 cents to the dollar, a loss of 90 per cent of its prewar value. By 1926 the Poincaré government managed finally to stabilize the franc—but at the equivalent of 3.9 cents! In fewer than three years, the nation's petite bourgeoisie had suffered a crippling erosion of their accumulated savings, and thereby of their social status. As in Germany, it was the bitterness of this widening déclassé sector that would fuel the rancor of political extremism.

## THE "TIGER'S CUB" AS SACRIFICIAL LAMB

An augury of the transformation could be discerned as early as the winter of 1919–20, still during Clemenceau's premiership. By then, Georges Mandel as the "Old Tiger's" protégé had established so formidable an administrative record that he decided to test the political waters on his own. In November 1919 he succeeded in winning a parliamentary seat on a hybrid party list of centrist Republicans and rightist Catholics. By this achievement, Mandel was positioned to manage Clemenceau's parliamentary majority from within the Chamber of Deputies, a leverage that had been denied him as a civil servant. Yet the setbacks and disappointments of the Paris Peace Conference could not be overcome. Even Mandel's awesome managerial talents failed to hold Clemenceau's followers in line, and it was in the same month that the prime minister was obliged to relinquish office.

Neither was Mandel able to engineer so much as a consolation prize for his esteemed mentor. That prize was the French presidency. Although the office was essentially ceremonial, Clemenceau's opponent, Paul Deschanel, did not limit his warnings to the dangers of prolonged "Clemencist" rule (pp. 263–66). "If Clemenceau is elected," he predicted direly, "a Mandelian regime will be installed in the Elysée Palace [and] Mandel will become the master of France."[13] The public knew exactly what Deschanel meant, and the exhortation, with its antisemitic undertones, was not lost on Mandel's colleagues in the Chamber, who voted Clemenceau down. Afterwards, with the "Old Tiger" in permanent retirement, Mandel was on his own and politically friendless.

---

13  Marcel Berger and Paul Allard, *Les dessous du traité de Versailles* (Paris: Éditions des Portiques, 1933), 21.

The coalition that had brought him to office declined to offer him a cabinet portfolio, and in the election of 1924 he also lost his parliamentary seat.

It was ironic, even in these early postwar years, when the French economy was wallowing in duress after the Ruhr invasion and the nation's far-rightists were pouncing on "*métèques*" as their scapegoats, that the French government managed to keep the nation's doors open to immigration. Indeed, between 1919 and 1929, it permitted an influx of nearly 3 million foreigners, most of these from Eastern and Southern Europe and the Near East and proportionately the largest postwar immigration wave to be accepted by any single Western nation, including the United States. But the apparent disjunction between economic vulnerability and open immigration was not the result of accident, and surely not of compassion. It traced back, rather, to France's sapping battlefield losses and to the nation's urgent military and economic need for demographic revival. By 1936 (well after free immigration had been terminated), not less than 11 per cent of France's work force was composed of foreigners. These included, besides transplants from French North Africa, fully 720,000 Italians, 245,000 Spaniards, 195,000 Belgians, and 435,000 East Europeans, most of the latter from Poland, Ukraine, and Romania.[14]

Among the influx of Easterners, 185,000 were Jews. Indeed, by 1930, East European Jewish immigrants comprised 60 per cent of the 310,000 Jews in France. A majority of the newcomers tended to gravitate to Paris's lower-middle-class Marais quarter, where they comprised a distinctly insular quasi-ghetto element.[15] For the rightist ligues, in turn, the immigrants presented a choice new target. Maurice Barrès warned that "Russia is disappearing [under the Bolshevik regime] because it is infested with Jews. Rumania is disappearing for the same reasons. . . . [T]he Jews are the masters in the United States and in England."[16] In his unappeasable hatred of Germany, Charles Maurras managed ingeniously to conflate Germany, Jews, and bolshevism as the source of a common peril. Thus, after 1918, he stigmatized Germany as the center of world revolution, the "stem and root" of Russian bolshevism, inasmuch as German Jews were "the masters in Moscow."[17] The editor's warnings were echoed by the *Documentation Catholique* and

---

14 Henri Dubief, *Le déclin de la Troisième République, 1929–1938* (Paris: Éditions du Seuil, 1976), 122.
15 Dubief, *Le déclin de la Troisième*, 26–28.
16 Léon Poliakov, *The History of Anti-Semitism* (New York: Vanguard Press, 1977–1985), 4: 276.
17 Ernst Nolte, *The Three Faces of Fascism: Action Française, Italian fascism, National Socialism* (New York: Holt, Rinehart and Winston, 1965), 124; cf. for a view of ligues as anti-German: René Rémond, *La Droite en France de la Première Restauration à la Ve République*, 2nd ed. (Paris: Aubier, Éditions Montaigne, 1982).

*Revue Internationale des Sociétés Secrétes*. Both journals denounced Jews as fomenters of atheistic bolshevism worldwide, as a "gigantic boa whose constricting coils are tied around an agonizing world, squeezing it, crushing it."[18] Even "respectable" conservatives in the Chamber of Deputies shared in the denunciation, attacking the "cosmopolitan madmen and traitors" who had seized power in Russia.

In May 1920, a series of work stoppages in Paris escalated into a riot. Three workers were killed and over 100 police and gardes républicaines were injured. Although no specifically Jewish involvement was discernable, the violence triggered an explosion of press attacks against "Jewish radicalism." In clerical and other rightist circles, warnings were circulated that defined "Bolshevik terrorism" as the instrument of "Jewish associations" in France itself. For Charles Maurras and Léon Daudet, the political climate by then seemed ideal for intensifying their campaign equally against the older target of a "Judeo-German financial syndicate" and the current putative menace of a "Judeo-Bolshevik" conspiracy. The Consistoire Israélite, French Jewry's representative communal agency, reported in July 1920 that antisemitism in senior military circles was approaching the intensity of the Dreyfus Affair.[19]

## AN INCIPIENCE OF FASCISM

Eventually, in the mid- and late-1920s, the upsurge of postwar xenophobia appeared to be receding. A tentative diplomatic relaxation with Germany was ushered in with the signing of the Locarno treaties in 1925 (p. 346), even as a rescheduling of German reparations payments under the American-sponsored "Dawes Plan" allowed for gradual economic relief in France and Germany alike. Both nations experienced a certain modest social stabilization (pp. 155–56). Yet, in France no less than in Germany, the aura of revived egalitarianism proved deceptive.

One of the war's lingering consequences was the dysfunctionalism it had aggravated in the nation's political structure. With its awkward system of proportional representation and its multitude of splinter parties, government in France seemed all but tailor-made for political bedlam. Between 1876, when a constitutional assembly established France's Third Republic by the margin of a single vote, and 1920, there had been 59 governments. From 1920 until 1939, there would be another 41. Political instability in turn

---

18  Poliakov, *The History of Anti-Semitism*, 4: 263.
19  Poliakov, *The History of Anti-Semitism*, 4: 265–66.

exacerbated France's deeper social lesions. These were substantial. Beyond their Catholic-traditionalist personal values, the politicians of the nation's Right spoke for private property, for the preservation of a notoriously inequitable tax structure, and for vigilance against a possible "bolshevization" of France's laboring classes.

Sharing in their rightist concerns was the nation's largest swing party, the Radical Socialists. The title was a misnomer. With Clemenceau, the "Radicals" had emerged out of the furor of the Dreyfus Affair as champions essentially of secular republicanism. Otherwise, based on peasant proprietors and small businessmen, the party adopted a cautiously moderate approach to political and economic issues. It offered no vision of fiscal reform, no support for an income tax or for any effective political barrier to elitist vested interests. Altogether, following Clemenceau's resignation as premier in 1920, and throughout most of the ensuing decade, it was the right-wing Bloc National that essentially dominated French politics. A united Socialist Party in these years might still have made its impact on public policy. During the war, however, the Socialists, in common with other parties, had joined in the government of the "Union Sacrée"; and afterward, fragmented even among themselves, they vowed never again to participate in a "bourgeois" cabinet. As a result, throughout most of the 1920s, under center-rightist coalitions, parliament evinced no interest in enacting meaningful reforms in the nation's tax structure or in its industrial working conditions.

The Great Depression reached France late in 1931. Within the year, as factories, offices, and shops closed in cities and towns, some 3 million French citizens clogged municipal unemployment offices and food relief lines. Following a national election in June 1932, a certain rickety, arm's-length parliamentary cooperation was achieved between Radicals and Socialists; but the alignment lasted barely six months and accomplished nothing, except to frighten the political Right. From 1933 onward, moreover, fearful that even the centrist Radicals might open the floodgates of leftist extremism, France's traditionally conservative parties began to exhibit a growing susceptibility to fascist ideology.

As elsewhere in Europe, the putative enemies targeted by the far-rightists were not merely the Socialists and Communists, but Jews, Freemasons, even Protestants and other alleged "non-Gallic" elements that offended the population's religious identity and cultural sensibilities. Predictably, Charles Maurras remained primus inter pares among these prophets of reaction. Exploiting the frustrations of the Depression, he and his closest Action Française colleagues, Léon Daudet and Jacques de Bainville, worked overtime in alerting public gatherings to the danger of a Bolshevik, "non-Gallic" France. The ligue's newspaper, also the *Action Française*, with its densely upholstered coverage of political and cultural affairs, continued to lay its principal editorial emphasis upon discipline, hierarchy, and authoritarianism.

Moreover, it was also in the same early and mid-1930s that the "integral nationalism" of the Action Française was taken up by a wider agglomeration of fascist or crypto-fascist ligues.[20] With most of them sharing Maurras's impatience with "effete" parliamentarism, they evinced an instinctive preference for a strong leader of the Mussolini genre, and a growing fascination with violence. Among these groups were such Italian-style *squadristi* as Marcel Bucard's "Françisme" and Antoine Rédier's "Ligue des Patriotes."

An even more serious competitor for ultrarightist loyalties was the "Jeunesses Patriotes." Its founder, Pierre Taittinger, had entered the war as a sergeant and emerged as a twice-wounded, much-decorated captain. With these credentials, Taittinger was elected to the Chamber of Deputies in 1919 as a member of the rightist "Bloc National"; subsequently gaining reelection throughout the 1920s and early 1930s. During these same years, Taittinger used his wife's ample inheritance to pyramid his business fortune into some 20 commercial enterprises, including the champagne company that still bears his name. An ardent admirer of Mussolini, Taittinger in 1924 funded and organized the "Jeunesses Patriotes."[21] Conducting mass marches and demonstrations in full military panoply, with uniforms and torchlights, Taittinger's putative *squadristi* initiated brawls with communists and socialists alike, attacking trade union offices, breaking up workers' strikes.[22] At its peak in 1934, the Jeunesses Patriotes' membership had grown to approximately a quarter-million.[23]

Yet Taittinger's Jeunesses Patriotes and even Maurras's Action Française were eclipsed in sheer critical mass by the "Croix de Feu." Launched in 1927 as a veterans' association, this nominally apolitical confederation achieved major visibility only in 1931 when its command was taken over by Lieutenant Colonel François de La Rocque. A renowned war hero who had served in Marshal Foch's staff on the Western Front, La Rocque in 1920 had been attached to the French military commission that "advised" Poland in its defense of Warsaw against the advancing Red Army. That early confrontation

---

20  Philippe Machever, *Ligues et fascismes en France, 1919–1939* (Paris: Presses universitaires de France, 1974), 7.
21  Jean Philippet, *Les Jeunesses patriotes et Pierre Taittinger, 1924–1940* (Paris: Institut d'etudes politiques, 1967), 47–49.
22  Rémond, *La Droite*, 278–79.
23  Carmen Callil, *Bad Faith: A Forgotten History of Family, Fatherland and Vichy France* (New York: Knopf, 2006), 101–2.

with the Communists was a defining moment for the colonel. Although he had been a law-abiding man in his earlier years, adopting no tendentious political doctrine and refraining then and even subsequently from espousing racism, he soon grasped the presumed urgency of "national vigilance" against "subversive"—that is, leftist—influences.

Henceforth, from the late 1920s on, the Croix de Feu's members, uniformed and highly disciplined under the colonel's leadership, began engaging in massive torchlight parades and pageants. Eventually their ranks also were opened to nonveterans. Some of these belonged to rightist youth organizations, others were simply lumpenproletariat. All, however, were committed to La Rocque's stance of "national vigilance." "If necessary," the colonel promised, "we shall descend into the street . . . to help the army and the police establish order by any means."[24] If the threat was ominous, so was the ligue's sheer emergent bulk. By 1934, with a membership estimated at 400,000, and enjoying the tacit approbation of numerous senior army officers, the Croix de Feu had become the largest and most prestigious of all France's paramilitary organizations.[25]

## THE "EVENTS" OF FEBRUARY 1934

The moment for these rightist ensembles to flex their muscles came in the winter of 1933–34. Mired in the Depression, the citizens of France witnessed nothing but ineptitude in the government's reaction to the economic crisis. Since the 1932 elections, Radicals and Socialists had enjoyed a comfortable majority in the Chamber of Deputies. Yet they had failed to agree on an economic agenda. The Radicals preferred a cautious deflationary approach. The Socialists advocated "reflation" and public spending. Each faction blocked the other's program (p. 273). The results were five governments in 1932–33 alone, and public outrage approaching the threshold of explosion. The spark was provided on Christmas Eve of 1933. It was then that a certain Gustave Tissier, who managed the municipally licensed pawnshop of Bayonne, a middle-sized Atlantic port city, paid a visit to the sub-prefect of his département. He had come to acknowledge an act of malfeasance. Two years earlier, Tissier confessed, he and a group of business partners had sold 200 million francs' worth of the pawnshop's two-year credit bonds. The sale was not insured by

---

24 Jean Plumyène and Raymond LaSierra, *Les Fascismes français, 1923–1963* (Paris: Éditions du Seuil, 1963), 31–32.
25 Robert J. Soucy, *French Fascism: The Second Wave, 1933–1939* (New Haven, CT: Yale University Press, 1995), 114.

collateral. It was assumed that there would be time to cover repayment by milking "other resources." But now the two years had expired, and there were no "other resources." Losing his nerve, Tissier felt obliged to come clean. But as his crestfallen admission emerged, it became apparent that he was merely a small cog in a far larger operation. Its arch-manipulator was Alexandre Stavisky.

Thirty-eight years old, a dapper bon vivant, "Sasha" Stavisky posed as a master of high finance. Sporting a chauffeured limousine and displaying a taste for the company of the rich and famous, he became a familiar presence in trendy watering places from Cannes to Deauville. To the police and judiciary, however, Stavisky was nothing more than "a gentleman among gangsters, and a gangster among gentlemen." Born in Kiev, he had been brought to France as a small boy with his Jewish immigrant parents. His father, a dentist, soon developed a practice comfortable enough to provide his son with quality schooling. But if young Stavisky acquired a certain cultural varnish in his expensive private lycée, he also fell in with a group of sybaritic classmates. Sharing their taste for fast living, he dropped out of school to go into business as a precocious "theatrical entrepreneur." The enterprise served as a front for prostitutes and loan sharks.

In the late 1920s and early 1930s, Stavisky also began accumulating a substantial police record for questionable stock dealings. His modus operandi was brazen. By offering munificent salaries, he lured unsuspecting parliamentary deputies and even several cabinet ministers onto the boards of his "investment companies." One of his first ventures was the municipal pawnshop of Orléans. Purchasing a significant bloc of stock in this semipublic corporation, Stavisky then floated additional shares at vastly inflated prices. When funds had to be repaid, he was already well launched on other flotations for other municipal ventures, using new funds to redeem older issues. For a while, the elaborate subterfuge worked smoothly.

"Le beau Sasha's" crowning achievement, however, was the Bayonne affair. Gaining control of the city's pawnshop soon after it was established, he and his associates set about their customary practice of recruiting a collection of well-paid municipal officials and several parliamentary deputies to serve as board members. Under their cover, Stavisky was able to sell bonds carrying a face value of 200 million francs. During the early winter of 1933, however, the cover blew open when he failed to produce the funds needed to guarantee a maturing issue. It was then that the pawnshop manager lost his nerve and made his Christmas Eve visit to the departmental sub-prefect.

At that point, the Sûreté Générale was alerted and immediately circulated a warrant for Stavisky's arrest. At first, no clues were located. But soon it was discovered that, a few days earlier, on December 23, sensing that his operation was about to be exposed, Stavisky had obtained a new passport at the local police prefecture under the name—actually his bodyguard's—of "Miemancrenko." Further investigation revealed that "Miemancrenko's" passport had been stamped at the Swiss frontier, then restamped when its holder returned to French territory. This was the clue that ultimately brought French police to Chamonix, a border village in the French Alps. At Chamonix, on January 9, 1934, Stavisky was traced to a local villa. The police knocked at its door. At that moment, inside, Stavisky fired a bullet into his brain. Subsequently, a police search recovered only 33,000 francs in his premises, and it was assumed that the rest of his absconded funds had been deposited in a Swiss bank account. Stavisky also left a suicide note for his son, begging forgiveness. This, at least, was the official police version.

But few people in France believed a word of the official version.[26] It was the consensus of political leaders of all parties, and of most of the press, that the police had murdered Stavisky to block exposure of his many connections with public figures. Predictably, the *Action Française* began milking the scandal for all it was worth. Did not the "Affaire Stavisky," the newspaper editorialized, expose the bottomless corruption of parliament and of its so-called respectable politicians? Was this not evidence that Stavisky (to whose Jewish antecedents the paper devoted a full issue) and his avaricious cronies held France's politicians "in thrall"? Soon the *Action Française* had even juicer grist for its mill. Beyond parliament, important government officials evidently had been corrupted by Stavisky's operations.

The revelation became public when an assistant state prosecutor was rushed to the hospital after taking poison and when a deputy minister of agriculture fatally cut his throat in Fontainebleau Forest. If doubt remained of Stavisky's link with senior public officials, it was dissipated altogether by the fate of Judge Albert Prince, former director of the finance department of the nation's public prosecutor's office and the man officially responsible for fraud investigations. On February 21, 1934, Prince's mangled body was found on a railroad track near the town of Dijon. It was subsequently revealed that he had attempted to shield the public prosecutor, Georges Pressard, against charges of delinquency of duty, and Pressard happened to be the brother-in-law of Camille Chautemps, who was none other than the prime minister of France's current Radical Socialist government.

---

26  Paul Lorenz, *Les trois vies de Stavisky* (Paris: Presses de la Cité, 1974), 9.

Shaken by the revelations and accusations, Chautemps promptly authorized a full inquiry, to be conducted by Inspector Marcel Guillaume, a respected senior police official. Guillaume's investigation unearthed much evidence of incompetence and negligence among high government officials, but nothing to impugn Pressard, or the late, unfortunate Prince, or least of all Prime Minister Chautemps. The premier then declared the case closed. Yet by then the political Right had smelled blood. As early as January 9, 1934, even before corpses began to be discovered, the *Action Française* headlined its editorial "Down with the Thieves," and urged "the people of Paris to assemble in large numbers before the Chamber of Deputies . . . to clamor for honesty and justice."[27]

Demonstrations outside the Palais Bourbon, home of the parliament, actually had been mounting for at least a week before the *Action Française*'s call to action, and these were not limited to followers of Maurras and his associates. All the rightist paramilitary ligues now sensed that the moment was ripe for a decisive blow against the Chautemps government, and thereby against the shaky makeshift partnership between Radicals and Socialists. On January 13, 1934, the *Action Française* issued a second editorial appeal for mass demonstrations. This one produced larger crowds and growing violence. So did a third summons of January 22. The protests mounted steadily. Beleaguered on the Right, and given only tepid support by the Socialists, Prime Minister Chautemps was forced to the wall. He submitted his government's resignation on January 28. For the first time in the history of the Third Republic, a parliamentary majority government had capitulated to a mob. Even then, however, the appetites of the rightist organizations had only been whetted. Their demonstrations picked up momentum, day after day.

Meanwhile, the president of the Republic, Albert Lebrun, sought out an acceptable compromise figure among the Radical-Socialist majority as a replacement for Chautemps. His choice fell on Édouard Daladier. Daladier was a decorated war veteran and practicing Catholic, and it was assumed that these credentials might spare him the obloquy of the rightist ligues. But they did not. On February 5, Maurras and other ligue spokesmen exhorted their followers to demonstrate "in force" before the Palais Bourbon the next evening, February 6, when Daladier was scheduled to submit his proposed cabinet to the Chamber of Deputies. But as the paramilitaries mobilized, they achieved little coordination. With the exception of the Action Française, most of the other rightist organizations—Jeunesses Patriotes, Solidarité Française,

---

27 Alexandre Werth, *The Twilight of France, 1933–1940*, trans D.W. Brogan (New York: H. Fertig, 1942), 90.

Ligue des Patriotes, Croix de Feu—seemed uninterested at first in establishing a hard-core dictatorship. Rather, they were intent simply on rioting, on intimidating, on ensuring a more reactionary parliamentary configuration, and with it a more authoritarian government.[28]

But if few of the rioters were agreed on the feasibility of overthrowing the Republic, their climactic "demonstration" of February 6 unquestionably threatened the Chamber of Deputies. On that afternoon, an estimated 10,000 partisans and hangers-on converged at the Place de la Concorde, near the bridges that would carry them across the Seine to the Left Bank and the Palais Bourbon. Bitter clashes with the police and with the Garde Républicaine continued throughout the evening. Finally, about 11:30 p.m., heavy police reinforcements began to push the crowds back, and the worst of the threat to the Chamber of Deputies seemed to ease. By then, however, 14 rioters had been killed and 236 seriously injured. Property damage was estimated at 10 million francs.[29]

Even as the aftershocks of violence continued throughout the late afternoon of February 6, Daladier, the premier-designate, eventually won a slim parliamentary majority in the Chamber of Deputies, this time with the help of the Socialists. But he would derive little comfort from his "victory." The next morning, Marshal Louis Lyautey, one of the nation's most renowned military figures and a far-rightist, warned President Lebrun that if Daladier did not resign, he, Lyautey, would order the Jeunesses Patriotes to march on parliament. Other rumors were circulating of a plan to establish a rogue "provisional" government at city hall. Appalled at the prospect of civil war, Daladier then unexpectedly tendered his resignation. For the second time in ten days, a duly elected government had fallen victim to right-wing intimidation.

At this point, President Albert Lebrun cast about for a prime minister to organize a caretaker "government of national union." He found his man in the elderly Gaston Doumergue, a leader of the Radicals "conservative" wing. For the while, the ligues seemed willing to bide their time, and all the more as Doumergue's cabinet included a selection of veteran conservatives. These included André Tardieu in the omnibus role of "minister of state." Another, rather more militant rightist, Marshal Henri-Philippe Pétain, "the hero of Verdun," was appointed minister of war, and still another admired right-winger, Louis Barthou (pp. 242–43), became foreign minister. Within a few weeks, however, deserted by his Radical-Socialist political base, Doumergue was left with no alternative but to submit his own resignation. In turn, an even

---

28  Werth, *The Twilight of France*, 150–51.
29  Soucy, *French Fascism*, 32.

more unregenerately conservative government was patched together under Pierre Flandin, a veteran political hack. But in June of 1935, Flandin himself would be succeeded as premier by Fernand Bouisson, who lasted only a few days in the position, and then by Pierre Laval; and Laval, in January 1936, was impelled to resign in favor of the equally rightist cabinet of Albert Sarraut.

It was in this fashion, during the nation's ongoing political gyrations and escalating violence, that the forces of militant reaction, with their vanguard camarilla of fascist and crypto-fascist ligues, succeeded in entrenching themselves in the nation's political landscape. Less than 35 years after the denouement of the Dreyfus Affair, the Third Republic now once again found itself in existential danger.

## THE RISE OF LÉON BLUM

A year and a half earlier, on the evening of February 6, 1934, as both ultrarightists and Communists howled down Édouard Daladier in the Chamber of Deputies, the premier-designate found his only source of support among the Socialists. This was an irony. Daladier, a veteran Radical and Léon Blum, the Socialist Party chairman, had long been political rivals. Nevertheless, it was "Blum alone," Daladier later acknowledged, "who advised me to remain in office and fight back."[30] Indeed, Blum himself implacably remained at his seat in the Chamber when the angry mob threatened to invade the Palais Bourbon, and possibly lynch him and other Socialist deputies. In his defiance, he soon emerged as France's man of the hour.

Born in 1872, Blum was one of five sons of an Alsatian Jewish family that had settled in Paris in the mid-nineteenth century. Their father, Auguste Blum, opened a silk-ribbon factory. The enterprise flourished. After the father's death in 1921, "Blum Frères" was managed by three of Léon Blum's brothers, until the Depression of the 1930s and a change in women's fashions ended the firm's profitability. Léon Blum himself, however, shared neither in the business's success nor its failure. His interests were elsewhere. At lycée, and subsequently as a law student at the University of Paris, his private passion remained literature. Attending literary salons, he cultivated the acquaintance of André Gide, Paul Valéry, Marcel Proust, and other renowned authors, and, during these student years, he managed to contribute his own essays to a series of literary magazines.

Even upon receiving his law degree in 1894, obdurate in his eclecticism, Blum chose to forgo a routine business practice in favor of public service.

---

30  Daladier's testimony is available in *Événements* 1 (1947), see especially pages 12–13.

He became an *auditeur*—a citizens' representative—at the Conseil d'État, France's chancery court, dealing with issues of equity appeal against the government. Here he proved a skilled and conscientious advocate on behalf of the nation's private petitioners. At the same time, however, Blum did not forgo his intellectual and social interests. It was the era of the Dreyfus Affair, and those interests turned inevitably to political issues. They also turned to socialism, for it was in 1898 that Blum came to know Jean Jaurès, the dynamic parliamentary leader of France's Socialist Party. Thirteen years younger than Jaurès, Blum almost immediately became the great man's devoted protégé. Indeed, in 1904, he gave up his government responsibilities altogether to accept the editorship of *L'Humanité*, French socialism's party newspaper.

It was of note that, in his editorial capacity, Blum shared Jaurès's abhorrence of the very notion of class revolution. Both men were political revisionists, wedded to the goal of social justice achieved through peaceful, democratic change. The two diverged only on issues of military preparedness. For Jaurès, socialism was pacifism, and there was no room for compromise on this principle. Indeed, his adamance ultimately cost him his life. On July 31, 1914, as war clouds gathered, Jaurès was accosted and fatally shot by a demented ultrapatriot. Blum, on the other hand, was prepared to join his party's revisionists in supporting the national cause against Germany. When three Socialists—Jules Guèsde, Albert Thomas, and Marcel Sembat—agreed to become ministers in René Viviani's government of "Union Sacrée," Blum himself accepted appointment as Sembat's *chef d'office* in the ministry of public works. The experience was an enriching one. By the time he left the government, in March 1917, upon Sembat's own departure, Blum had acquired a penetrating insight into the operation of the public bureaucracy.

In that same year, however, Russia's Bolshevik Revolution opened a fault line in France's Socialist Party. A majority of the party was prepared to move decisively leftward; and, two years later, in March 1919, when the Soviets resuscitated the "Comintern" as their party's international network (p. 120), France's working classes already had veered markedly to the camp of radicalism. The full extent of their ideological transformation became evident in the winter of 1919-20, when the Socialists held their national congress in Tours. As chairman of the party (a role he all but inherited upon the death of Jaurès), Blum issued an impassioned appeal to the assembled delegates not to accept the "false god" of a Bolshevik-style dictatorship.[31] Yet his cri de coeur proved unavailing. A telegram had arrived from Grigori Zinoviev, chairman of the Comintern, insisting that all "dissenters" be expelled from the party.

---

31  Sachar, *Dreamland*, 302.

Accordingly, after the ensuing purge of "right-wingers," Blum among them, the remaining left-wing majority became the French Communist Party.

Blum, in turn, immediately set about reconstructing the remnants of the original, mainstream, Socialist Party. Here it was that the former dandy, the "effete" litterateur, revealed unanticipated political skills as he worked tirelessly to rebuild the party's prewar cadres. In the process, as a member (since 1919) of the Chamber of Deputies, he also augmented his personal reputation for intellectual integrity. Blum was less than a charismatic figure, with his drooping moustache, trademark pince-nez, and frail voice; yet his speeches in the Chamber were models of Cartesian logic and stylistic polish. Deputies of all political factions gave them heed. Throughout the 1920s, too, as Russia's Communist regime proved fully as brutal as he had warned, and as bread-and-butter issues took precedence in France's trade-union confederation, Blum was able decisively to reconstruct his party. Indeed, by 1932, the Socialists had regained their pre-Tours strength. As party chairman, Blum accomplished the feat by refusing to accept a marriage of convenience with the petit-bourgeois Radicals, or with any other party—of the Right or the Left—that would not accept a Socialist initiative in formulating the National Assembly's legislative agenda.

Afterward, however, with the Stavisky affair and the "events" of February 6, 1934, everything changed. It was in the tumultuous eight hours of that day, as Daladier frantically scrambled to patch together a new government, that Blum promised the support of his own Socialist Party for a coalition cabinet. But the offer came too late. Daladier's nerve was gone. The new government, when it finally took shape several days later under the recycled leadership of the 71-year-old Gaston Doumergue, was predominantly of the middle class and the political Right. Blum, dismayed at this new configuration, decided then and there on a bold step. It was to guide the Socialists to a new and totally unanticipated partnership.

On February 12, he appeared with Maurice Thorez, chairman of France's Communist Party, in a joint "antifascist" rally of Socialist- and Communist-oriented labor unions. The rally was the first public intimation that an unprecedented political phenomenon, a coalition of Socialists and Communists, was in the making.

## THE RISE OF THE POPULAR FRONT

The partnership was to be led by an even unlikelier one. Léon Blum's image as an "effete" intellectual was the least of his political vulnerabilities. In the postwar years, as the full impact of reawakened xenophobia focused on "*métèques,*" he became the Right's most obvious target. Indeed, even earlier, before embarking on his political career, Blum had been no stranger to obloquy. In 1907, his provocative little volume, *On Marriage* [*Du Mariage*], evoked howls of outrage for its attack on the double standard of premarital sex. Unrequited anti-Dreyfusards promptly denounced the book as "Jewish pornography," as a "Jewish-Masonic and secularist" plot "to dishonor all the women of France." "Civilized" conservatives also resented Blum's presumptuousness in tampering with "Gallic values."[32] After dining with Blum in 1914, André Gide recorded in his diaries that "the virtues of the Jewish race are not French virtues. . . . [Jews] speak with greater ease than we because they have fewer scruples."[33] Even a fellow Socialist, Hubert Bourgin, described Blum in less than flattering terms: "He was there, nervous, feverish. . . . His eyes shone with a prodigious gleam . . . his moustache revealed a sensual mouth which seemed to be savoring the taste of a voluptuous prey."[34]

But these reservations were the merest prelude to the avalanche of denunciations that would greet Blum in the postwar. In December 1920, Léon Daudet warned his readers in *L'Action Française* that "a simian little *youtre* ['yid'] like Blum is utterly indifferent and even hostile to French interests."[35] During Blum's early parliamentary years, he underwent continual ad-hominem taunting when he arose to address the Chamber. "There's room only for Frenchmen here," heckled a royalist deputy, Eugène Magné, in 1923. Léon Daudet trumped Magné by shouting "To Jerusalem!" Another rightist, historian and journalist Pierre Gaxotte, denounced Blum as a "Palestinian mare" and suggested that he and other Jews be sent to an internment camp in Madagascar.[36] Lamenting Blum's success in rebuilding the Socialist Party, Charles Maurras in his exasperation would write of him in 1928: "There is a man who should be shot, but in the back."[37] A January 1935 issue of *La Solidarité Française,* journal of the Jeunesses Patriotes, carried a full-page photograph of Blum, overlaid with the caption: "Public Enemy Number One."[38]

Nevertheless, during the course of the year, and notwithstanding ligue and other rightist denunciations, the prospects for a leftist partnership gained

---

32   Jean Lacouture, *Léon Blum* (New York: Holmes & Meier, 1982), 84.
33   André Gide, *Journals, 1889–1949,* trans. and ed. Justin O'Brien (London: Penguin, 1967), 195.
34   Hubert Bourgin, *De Jaurès à Léon Blum: l'École normale et la politique* (Paris: A. Fayard, 1938), 508–9.
35   Sachar, *Dreamland,* 305.
36   André Blumel, *Léon Blum: juif et sioniste* (Paris: Éditions de la Terre retrouvée, 1951), 7.
37   Lacouture, *Léon Blum,* 181.
38   Colton, *Léon Blum,* 116.

momentum. Until then, Maurice Thorez, the Communist Party chairman, had been uninterested in defending a "bourgeois republic." In the summer of 1934, however, the Soviet leaders in Moscow, alarmed at the prospect of France succumbing to fascism and cognizant that Hitler by then was well entrenched in Germany, visibly shifted their position. They dropped objections to an alliance of their French protégés with others of France's antifascist elements—even with the hated Socialists. For their part, Blum and his party colleagues then warily consented to enter into interparty discussions.

Eventually, by the spring of 1935, agreement was reached on a modus operandi for the scheduled parliamentary elections of April 1936. Barring the unlikely event that one of the parties would win an instant majority, those candidates of either faction—Socialist or Communist—who scored highest in the first round of voting would be given joint support in the second and presumably decisive round. Indeed, the Socialists and Communists were not alone in signing onto the pact. Early in 1935, fearful lest his own party be marginalized by the Left's new political configuration, Édouard Daladier of the Radical Socialists also persuaded his colleagues to enter the alignment, which subsequently would be termed the "Popular Front." Upon signing on to that compromise, the leadership of the three parties then embarked on the task of engineering a cautiously progressive, Social Democratic–oriented platform (pp. 286–87).

Campaigning began in late autumn of 1935. Initially, the Popular Front was less than effective in transcending its intramural suspicions. Cooperation between its member parties was intermittent and unenthusiastic. By contrast, the rightist factions, amply funded, conducted a vigorous public-relations offensive, systematically invoking the threat of "bolshevism." In the effort, they directed their vitriol specifically against Blum. Even by ligue standards, their assault was unprecedented. On the one hand, antisemitism even during the 1930s was less central an issue in French public life than during the fin-de-siècle Dreyfus Affair. In the years of that earlier trauma, it would have been unimaginable for a Jew to seek the premiership. But the lesson learned during the Dreyfus years, that antisemitism could serve as the cutting edge of an assault on political democracy itself, was put to more systematic use in the France of the late 1920s and 1930s. It was supremely the bitterness of the Depression, and subsequently the fear of provoking a new war with Germany, that fused racism with political and paramilitary neo-fascism.

Indeed, on February 13, 1936, the emergent parliamentary campaign spilled over into naked violence. Blum was being driven home from his office. En route, his chauffeured automobile was halted on the Boulevard Saint-Germain by a huge funeral procession. It turned out that the deceased was none other than Jacques de Bainville, the venerated royalist historian and polemicist of the Action Française. Uniformed lines of Camelots du Roi (p. 268) had formed a guard of honor. Suddenly, members of the crowd recognized Blum. Howling with rage, they converged on his automobile, smashing its windows. Blum was dragged out and savagely beaten, then left on the street, bleeding and unconscious. Eventually, several bystanders intervened to call the police, who rushed Blum to a hospital. In the operating room, a partially severed artery in his neck was repaired. He survived, although he was obliged to convalesce throughout the remaining spring election contest.[39] Ironically, the episode evoked widespread public sympathy for Blum. Three days afterward, half a million marchers participated in a mass protest rally. For a rare moment, like Alfred Dreyfus at the end of the nineteenth century, Blum emerged as a symbol of the Republic itself.

Indeed, France's ensuing national elections, taking place in two rounds of April 26 and May 6, 1936, produced a solid triumph for the Popular Front. As the single largest party in the Chamber, the Socialists at long last would exercise decisive leadership; and Léon Blum, at the age of 64, would become the first authentically Socialist prime minister in French history. His election manifestly represented an even more stunning innovation. None of the ultrarightists had allowed the electorate to overlook Blum's Jewish identity. In the last weeks of the campaign, illustrations in their journals depicted Blum in various guises: as a degenerate, with his drooping moustache and effete oratorical posture; as a sinister androgyne, flaunting painted fingernails; as a jackal, spittle dripping from his fangs.

Neither could Blum's subsequent electoral triumph ensure him the minimal respect traditionally accorded the office of prime minister. On June 7, 1936, the day he submitted the prospective list of his cabinet ministers to the Chamber of Deputies, Xavier Vallat, a one-legged war veteran and stalwart of the Far Right, solemnly addressed Blum. "Your advent, M. le Président du Conseil," he intoned, "is without question a historic occasion. For the first time this ancient Gallo-Roman land is to be ruled by an Israelite. . . . To govern this peasant nation of France, it would be better to have someone whose origins, however modest, lie deep in our soil, rather than a subtle Talmudist. . . . although, contrary to the hopes of 'M. Jéroboam Rothschild,' at least he will be not called Georges Mandel."[40] The Chamber then erupted in a bedlam of taunts and counter-taunts. That same day, Charles Maurras in

---

39 Philippe Bourdrel, *Histoire des juifs de France* (Paris: A. Michel, 1974), 33.
40 Sherwood, *Georges Mandel*, 184; Tony Judt, *The Burden of Responsibility: Blum, Camus, Aron, and the French Twentieth Century* (Chicago: University of Chicago Press, 2007), 76.

the *Action Française* had characterized Blum's inauguration as the "the *youtre's* revenge." Predicting that Blum's colleagues would function as a "cabinet of the Talmud" and consist of "thieves, traitors, and prostitutes," Maurras then proceeded in the 50-line article to describe the new prime minister variously as a "sadist," a "pederast," and a "polymorph."[41]

Although assuming leadership of a nation terrified by economic depression and roiling in strikes and public protests, Blum was not intimidated. Fully recovered from his neck wound, enjoying a solid electoral mandate, and brimming with confidence, he defiantly informed the Chamber that he was prepared and eager to lead France to economic recovery and social justice.

## THE LIFE AND DEATH OF THE POPULAR FRONT

At first, the new prime minister made good on his commitment. The agenda he submitted to parliament in May 1936 included a 40-hour work week; paid vacations; reform of the tax system in favor of the working classes; national unemployment insurance; a far-reaching public-works program; enlargement of free, compulsory schooling; and "emancipation" of the Bank of France from the grip of some 200 powerful families. In launching this ambitious social agenda, moreover, Blum acknowledged that he was inspired by the American New Deal; and like Franklin Roosevelt's celebrated "one hundred days," Blum's "new social charter" won massive parliamentary approval in record time, in this case within 60 days.

But France's ideological and political opposition was not intimidated. The Chamber of Commerce declared war on the 40-hour work week. So did most of the—traditionally ultraconservative—professional associations, notably the legal and medical societies. The army command, following the lead of the revered (if retired) marshals, Henri-Philippe Pétain and Louis Lyautey, publicly opposed the government's commitment to the League of Nations and international disarmament. As for the church hierarchs, their reaction to the Socialist and Communist alliance was one of undisguised alarm. In October 1935, the nation's five cardinals issued a joint warning against the "closed fist" (the Communist salute) among the new government's political supporters.

It was foreign policy, however, arguably more even than domestic tensions, that offered the Popular Front its most critical challenge. In July 1936, a

---

41 Eugene Weber, *Action Francaise: Royalism and Reaction in Twentieth Century France* (Stanford: CA: Stanford University Press, 1962), 374–75.

right-wing military junta in Spain launched an uprising against that nation's left-leaning republican government. In France, Blum had been in office less than a month, but he and Spain's Prime Minister José Giral were old comrades within the Socialist International, and Giral now was appealing to Blum for the immediate delivery of airplanes, artillery, and other military equipment. Blum did not hesitate. Indeed, he prepared to requisition the needed armaments directly from France's own military stocks. But the decision was taken in the midst of a major realignment of political viewpoints on foreign affairs. Until late 1934, France's right wing consistently had preached the need for vigilance against a German military revival. It was the left wing that placed its faith in a more general, universal disarmament, and reliance essentially on the League of Nations.

But in 1935, each side of the French ideological spectrum had begun to modify its position. The Right, endlessly on guard against progressive social legislation, adopted an increasingly companionable attitude to fascism. By contrast, socialism in France gradually was shifting away from doctrinaire pacifism and evincing a heightened suspicion of the dangers posed by Hitler and Mussolini. The emerging Spanish Civil War was a litmus test. In the summer of 1936, when word leaked of Blum's intentions to re-arm Spain's republican Loyalists, protests began flooding in from Rome, Berlin, and even from London, where Stanley Baldwin's Conservative government was in office. Of still greater danger to the Blum government was the political reaction in France itself. The Far Right now began to invoke a phrase heard only intermittently before the Spanish Civil War: "Better Hitler than Blum."[42] The centrist Radicals threatened to pull out of the Popular Front cabinet.[43] With profound reluctance, then, Blum was obliged to retract his offer of aid to his old friend Giral. In turn, immediately and unanimously, France's Communist deputies withdrew their parliamentary support from Blum.

By late autumn of 1936, the prime minister's domestic program also had been placed at risk. Since the promising legislation of the previous June–July, not a single important new economic reform had been adopted. In ensuing months, as industrial productivity continued its downward spiral under the burden of the government's diverse social initiatives, the flight of capital from France increased, and early in 1937 Blum was obliged to decree a "hiatus" in public spending. Then, on March 16, a sudden crisis erupted in the Paris industrial

---

42 Nathaniel Greene, *Crisis and Decline: The French Socialist Party in the Popular Front Era* (Ithaca, NY: Cornell University Press, 1969), 80.

43 Bourdrel, *Histoire des juifs*, 111.

suburb of Clichy. During a meeting at a local theater, the rightist Parti Social Français, the political incarnation of the former Croix de Feu (p. 274) clashed with a counterdemonstration of trade unionists. In the mêlée, police fired on the workers, killing or wounding some 200 of them. Alerted to the violence while attending an opera performance, Blum himself, in white tie and tails, rushed off to Clichy. Upon his limousine's arrival at the scene of the violence, the premier and his party were met by the jeers of thousands of workers and their families. The leftist press next day execrated Blum as "the assassin of Clichy."

With its political coalition all but fractured, the Popular Front entered a long death agony. Industrial strikes multiplied. On June 16, 1937, almost drained of gold reserves, the Blum government in its desperation asked parliament for "emergency powers" to ban free trading in gold. The Senate forthwith rejected the appeal. It was then, on June 21, that the despondent premier saw no alternative but to submit his resignation. He asked only that his fellow Socialists continue to participate in the ensuing government, this one under the Radical leadership of Camille Chautemps. Blum declared his willingness to serve as Chautemps' vice-premier in a cabinet he still gallantly titled a "Popular Front."

But, during its ensuing 13 months in office, the Chautemps cabinet all but reversed Blum's former legislative agenda, raising taxes and retrenching on important public-works projects. Subsequently, in January 1938, with the Communists disdaining to reenter a restructured Popular Front government, Prime Minister Chautemps also was obliged to tender his resignation. Once more, Blum was called upon to form a coalition. Yet his subsequent effort to pick and choose among a spectrum of parties failed, and, in January 1938, Chautemps was recalled to organize a makeshift government, this time without Blum or any other Socialist. His cabinet was comprised exclusively of centrist Radicals.

The political crisis engendered a final postscript. In March 1938, Chautemps revealed his diplomatic pusillanimity during Nazi Germany's unopposed annexation of Austria (p. 394). For a second time, his government collapsed; and once again Blum was recalled to office. But after three weeks of political jockeying, his effort to patch together a cabinet failed. In April, the apparently indestructible Édouard Daladier, whose last attempt to form a government had been torpedoed by the Stavisky crisis four years earlier, accepted a mandate to form a government dominated by Radicals, buttressed this time with a scattering of far-rightists.

Barely a month passed, too, before Daladier set about burying the remaining accomplishments of Blum's Popular Front experiment. Dismantling the

40-hour work week, his Center-Right coalition similarly eviscerated Blum's remaining public-works programs. Under the rubric of "military emergency," the cabinet proceeded to crush a series of workers' protest strikes in the nation's mines and railroads. Daladier's management of foreign affairs proved no less calamitous. In September 1938 and March 1939, he collaborated meekly in British Prime Minister Neville Chamberlain's two-stage sacrifice of Czechoslovakia to Nazi Germany.

Unrecognized at the time, Daladier's foreign and domestic policies were closely linked. International crises gave him the pretext both for reversing social reforms and restricting civil liberties. In September 1939, exploiting public outrage at the Nazi-Soviet Non-Aggression Pact (p. 322), which had been signed only the month before, Daladier closed down the nation's Communist press and later outlawed the Communist Party altogether— even ordering the imprisonment of 44 Communist parliamentary deputies. As the prime minister saw it, a harsh stance toward the political Left would help placate Hitler and Mussolini. Indeed, shrewdly cultivating that illusion, Germany's ministry of "public enlightenment" proceeded to buy up a collection of small-circulation French newspapers and news agencies and ensured that they subsequently parroted Berlin's assurances of goodwill toward France. As early as 1935, too, the Nazis had founded and funded a Comité France-Allemagne under the chairmanship of Count Fernand de Brinon, a closet fascist (p. 371). Predictably, the committee made imaginative use of native pacifism, anticommunism and antisemitism. In the effort, it enjoyed the active and enthusiastic support of France's rightist ligues.

The hostility of these crypto-fascist alliances was all but foreordained by one of the former Popular Front government's initial decrees, dating back to June 1936. Although the Sarraut government earlier had dissolved the Action Française after the latter's February 13 physical assault on Blum (pp. 284–85), other reactionary ligues had remained intact. Consequently, Blum's initial Popular Front government, in one of its first legislative acts upon entering office, banned these cabals outright. Yet, even then, the Far Right was not about to go gently into political oblivion. Upon being terminated as a ligue, the Croix de Feu immediately and ingeniously reconstituted itself as a political party, the Parti Social Français (PSF). Its leader, Colonel François de La Rocque, anticipated that the subterfuge eventually would allow his followers to emerge as a "respectable" alternative to the parliamentary system. Possibly he was right. By 1938, in its disciplined muscularity and its avoidance of any overt embrace of antisemitism, the PSF was estimated to have increased its membership to 600,000.[44] Its rolls included 3,000 mayors, some 1,000 municipal councilmen, and a dozen parliamentary deputies.

Meanwhile, barely trailing the—transformed—Croix de Feu in decibel power and public visibility, if not in numbers, was the Parti Populaire Français (PPF). A late bloomer, the PPF was organized as a party ab initio in 1936. Its founder, Jacques Doriot, had begun his career as a Communist. In 1934, however, undergoing a crise de conscience, he decided that France's true salvation was to be found in the authoritarian models of Mussolini and Hitler. To that end, Doriot established the PPF for those who shared his preference for "decisive action," and by 1938 his party had attracted some 170,000 members. Possibly the most ominous of these newly camouflaged ligues, however, was the smallest, with a membership rarely exceeding 30,000. This was the Comité Secret d'Action Révolutionnaire, informally to be known as "*La Cagoule* [The Cowl]." Established as early as 1935, the Cagoulards typically came from the existing aggregation of rightist ligues (although most of them were former Camelots du Roi, the lazzarone associated with Maurras's Action Française). Fascist by temperament, these street brawlers chafed at their leader's apparent hesitation in escalating verbal incitement to full-fledged revolutionary violence. The Cagoule was their alternative.

It was the brainchild of Eugène Deloncle, a 46-year-old marine engineer who, in turn, received generous financial subventions from Eugène Schueller, the owner of France's cosmetics giant, L'Oréal. A graduate of the elite École Polytechnique, Deloncle had played a leading role in designing France's greatest ocean liner, the *Normandie*. From 1935 on, however, he diverted his formidable organizational and technological skills to the formation of a secret "army," which he divided into military units, ranging from squads to brigades. Under his direction, the Cagoulards set about fabricating workshops for the assembly of weapons parts smuggled in from police and army contacts—even from Fascist Italy. In 1936, they managed the formidable exploit of sabotaging a shipment of French military airplanes bound for the republican forces in Spain.[45] That same year, Cagoule explosives were detonated in the Paris offices of the Socialist Party and in the headquarters of the Confédération Générale du Travail.

Thus far, however, and notwithstanding the extensive damage the attacks managed to inflict, the Cagoule had caused no fatalities. This was about to change.

---

44  Soucy, op. cit., pp. 116–17.
45  Bourdrel, *Histoire des juifs*, 138.

## THE BROTHERS

In 1937 the Cagoule proved its rightist bona fides with a sensational act of brutality, a gesture of "reciprocity" carried out on behalf of the "OVRA," the secret service of Italy's Fascist Party. Among Italy's diminishing minority of anti-Fascists were two noted young historian-journalists, the brothers Carlo and Nello Rosselli. Descendants of one of Italy's oldest and most respected Jewish families, the Rossellis as late as 1926 persevered openly as stalwarts of the socialists and liberals who set about publishing an anti-Fascist periodical, "*Non Mollare!* [Don't Give In!]." In the furor precipitated by the Matteotti murder in 1924 (pp. 57–60), Mussolini found it circumspect at first to tolerate the little group's heresies. In 1926, however, his patience worn thin by Carlo Rosselli's outspoken ideological socialism, the Duce struck back. At his orders, Rosselli and several of the latter's colleagues were arrested, tried, and sentenced to a five-year internment on the prison island of Lipari.

Nello Rosselli, Carlo's younger brother, was allowed to remain in Florence, with the proviso that he limit himself to "nonpolitical" research in his field of Renaissance studies. But, two years later, refusing to abide by the constraint, Nello and a group of ideological comrades journeyed to French Tunisia. Purchasing a motor launch from a ship chandler in Bizerte, they subsequently embarked from Tunisia to Lipari. Incredibly, almost under the noses of the island's lackadaisical prison guards, the little band of socialist buccaneers rescued Carlo Rosselli and several of his fellow internees. With its newly freed passengers, the vessel then returned to Tunisia, and, from there, the brothers and their comrades were transported by steamer to France and to a hero's welcome from their fellow Italian expatriates. Indeed, during the ensuing years, the Rosselli group remained the core of France's vibrant community of Italian anti-fascist refugees. By then predominantly democratic socialists, they dubbed their movement "Giustizia e Libertà," after the title of the book Carlo Rosselli secretly had managed to write during his Lipari internment.

In 1936, when the Spanish Civil War began, Carlo Rosselli characteristically was among the first of these transplants to offer his services to Spain's republican cause. As the leader of several hundred fellow expatriate volunteers, he took an active role in organizing the "Garibaldi Battalion," later to be incorporated into the Loyalists' famed "International Brigade." It was the Garibaldi Battalion that played a leading role in the successful republican defense of Guadalajara, in early 1937. Yet Rosselli himself was not present at this precocious (and evanescent) victory. Suffering from acute phlebitis, he had resigned his command in December 1936 and returned to

CARLO AND NELLO ROSSELLI, 1934

Paris, from there to embark on a series of anti-fascist broadcasts to Italy. In ensuing months, the shortwave transmissions became a serious provocation to the Mussolini regime. Although Rosselli's writings often were intercepted by Italian postal authorities, it proved difficult to jam his broadcasts. More decisive action evidently was necessary. Foreign Minister Galeazzo Ciano allowed the OVRA to take that action. Contacts were promptly made in France with the Cagoule.

Early in June 1937, Rosselli drove from Paris to Bagnoles de l'Orne, a spa in Normandy renowned for the therapeutic effect of its mud baths. He anticipated that these would relieve his phlebitis. At Bagnoles, he was joined by his brother Nello. It was on the morning of June 9, 1937, while taking a morning drive through the nearby Couterne forest, that the Rossellis were forced to a stop. An apparently disabled automobile blocked their way. As they parked to offer help, a band of Cagoulard cutthroats that had been lying in wait suddenly fell upon the brothers, stabbing them repeatedly. The assailants then dragged their victims a short distance, left them in the underbrush, and sped off. Two days later, a group of picnickers stumbled across the Rosselli brothers' bodies.

In France, news of the homicide stunned the brothers' admirers and followers. An estimated 25,000 mourners, Italian and French alike, attended their funeral services in Paris. Afterward, the cortege made its way to the Père Lachaise cemetery, accompanied by violinists performing strains from Beethoven's Seventh Symphony. Weeks later, a monument was erected there. Its inscription read

Carlo and Nello Rosselli
Murdered Together
9 June 1937
Expect Together
That the Sacrifice of Their Youth
Will Hasten

The Victory of Their Ideals
Justice and Liberty[46]

At the last moment, the stonecutter had eliminated the phrase "In Italy" and left an ellipsis in its place. The order had come from Prime Minister Daladier, who feared offending Mussolini. But no one was deceived. In the words of the historian Gaetano Salvemini, "All roads lead to Rome."[47] By then, in the 1930s, the ancient maxim already had been invoked in other countries (p. 224).

In June–July of 1937, under public pressure, the French ministry of justice was obliged to open an inquiry into the double murder. The role of the Cagoule was shortly uncovered. More than 100 of its members then were detained, although not more than five were put on trial. Two confessed. According to their testimony, the assassinations had been carried out in

---

46  Stanislao Pugliese, *Carlo Rosselli: Socialist Heretic and Anti-Fascist Exile*, trans. (Cambridge, MA: Harvard University Press, 1999), 220.
47  Gaetano Salvemini, *Carlo e Nello Rosselli*, 2nd ed. (Paris: Ed. di "Giustizia e libertà," 1948), 258–59.

payment for the clandestine delivery to the Cagoule of 700 Italian carbines. Indeed, the murder vehicle actually was Eugène Deloncle's personal automobile. One of the defendants, Fernand Jakubiez, insisted on relating the gruesome details of the crime, describing the repeated knifings and the unexpected time and energy required to confirm that the Rosselli brothers finally had expired.

For reasons of "contradictory evidence," however, no charges were brought against Deloncle himself. Of the three Cagoulards who were given the death penalty, these were the three who conveniently had disappeared after the murders. Five other members of the conspiracy team were tried and convicted in court, where they were given varying sentences of imprisonment. But, three years later, in June 1940, after France's surrender to Nazi Germany and the ensuing establishment of the collaborationist Vichy regime (pp. 335–37), France's "Head of State," Marshal Henri-Philippe Pétain, ordered the prisoners released.[48]

## "TO DIE FOR THE JEWS?"

Although the Cagoule in its political configuration was dissolved and forced into hiding after the Rosselli murders, other proto-fascist ligues continued to regroup either as political parties or under such façades as the "Association Marius Plateau," the "Institut d'Action Français," or the "Institut Royale." Whatever their rightist agenda, or the army and police contacts that provided them with their information and weaponry, the threat presented by these cabals was less military or even political than psychological. In their incendiary anticommunism, antiparliamentarism and antisemitism, they fanned the internecine hatreds that enfeebled France's diplomatic and military resolve in a period of growing European crisis.

The nation's economic doldrums alone would have compounded the vulnerability of the Jews as the favorite target of the Cagoule and other ligues. In the Depression-ridden 1930s, as some 55,000 new Jewish refugees poured into France from the growing Nazi empire, they were singled out as competitors in the labor market and as a threat to Gallic culture. Most recently, too, the suspicion grew that the Jews, immigrants and established residents alike, were eager to embroil the nation in complications with Germany. The public's mood in the 1930s still favored peace at almost any price.[49] Even

---

48  Stanislao Pugliese, *Carlo Rosselli*, 222.
49  Charles A. Micaud, *The French Right and Nazi Germany, 1933–1939* (New York: Octagon Books, 1964), 209.

right-wing veterans' organizations and other former ligues convinced themselves that Hitler, as an ex-soldier, was uninterested in another war. Indeed, following the Munich conference of September 1938 and its surrender to Germany of Czechoslovakia's Sudetenland, such French public reactionaries as Maurras, Doriot, and La Rocque issued testimonials in praise of the Daladier government for "keeping the peace." Subsequently, on May 4, 1939, as Nazi pressure grew upon Poland to return the Baltic port-city of Danzig to Germany, Marcel Déat, a former Socialist Party member turned right-wing activist, emblazoned a "query" across the front page of his party newspaper, *L'Oeuvre*: "To Die for Danzig?" The notion plainly was unthinkable.

Even less imaginable was the prospect of "dying for the Jews." Throughout 1938 and 1939, other ultrarightist publications—*L'Action Française, Candide, Gringoire, Je Suis Partout*—insisted that the Jews alone were fomenting the series of war crises. In his editorial "Attention les Juifs!" Charles Maurras spoke for the Far Right in warning the Jews that they would pay dearly for their "warmongering" effort to "deliver the world to bolshevism."[50] In the spring of 1939, during the last months before the outbreak of World War II, a confidential and entirely apolitical police report on subversive pro-Nazi activity in France provided 66 pages of data on "specialized" hate organizations whose one and exclusive motif was antisemitism. Citing the names, addresses, and biographies of their leaders, the report left no doubt that each of them was intimately enmeshed with Nazi Germany, and often accepted German guidance and money.[51]

Five months earlier, in September 1938, confronting both the Sudeten crisis and the upsurge of native xenophobia, the Daladier government instructed the police to impose even tighter surveillance on foreigners. The order did not refer to Nazi subversives but to the swelling tide of refugees from Germany. Henceforth, prefects of frontier *départements* were authorized to "relocate" these aliens at their own discretion. Aware, however, that refugees could not simply be repatriated to Nazi-controlled territory, the government offered a palliative. The newcomers would be relocated "temporarily" from France's larger cities to remote provincial towns where they could be more carefully monitored. Under this constraint, from late 1938 on, refugees found themselves in limbo between deportation or quasi-internment.

---

50 Sachar, *Dreamland*, 318.
51 Paul J. Kingston, *Anti-Semitism in France during the 1930s: Organisations, Personalities, and Propaganda* (Hull, UK: University of Hull Press, 1983), 7–64.

Finally, in November 1938, the Daladier government followed its initial directive with another. It stipulated that French nationality might be withdrawn even from those foreign-born individuals who years and decades earlier had been officially naturalized, should they now be judged "unworthy of the title of French citizen." Jews and other refugees from Nazism were not specifically mentioned in the directive. By then, there was no need.

CHAPTER NINE

# The Hunt for Leon Trotsky

*"No man, no problem."*

## A PERIPATETIC EUROPEAN REFUGE

In February 1929 Leon Trotsky, Natalia Sedova, and their 22-year-old son "Liova" arrived in Istanbul. After several weeks of subsisting on the hospitality of the Soviet consul, who gave over a wing of the consulate building for their living quarters, the family, at its own request, was transported to a modest villa on one of the suburban Prinkipo Islands. Remaining there under discreet police protection, the Trotskys continued to be treated deferentially by Soviet and Turkish authorities alike. The consulate provided them with an initial subvention of 5,000 dollars for resettlement expenses, and the money was augmented by foreign newspapers that were willing to pay well for articles by the "cofounder of the Soviet Union". With these resources, from 1929 on, Trotsky also defrayed the living costs of three secretaries to whom he dictated his memoirs and his innumerable newspaper and journal articles and who also helped him complete his extensive book-publishing commitments.[1] Among these commitments was a weighty two-volume autobiography, *My Life*, released both in Germany and the United States in 1930, and an even more formidable three-volume *History of the Russian Revolution*, appearing in Great Britain between 1932–33.[2]

Yet, in his privacy no less than his demeanor, Trotsky was cautious about jeopardizing his friends and allies in Russia or elsewhere in Europe.[3] No word on Soviet mismanagement or cruelty escaped from his lips or writing.[4] It was hardly a secret that Stalin was appealing to foreign socialists and even "idealistic" communists to wage war against "reactionaries" and "backsliders."[5] Indeed, Stalin was not alone in appealing to the loyalty of Soviet citizens. Even his critics were aware that Leftist factionalism had played a critical role in the Nazi rise to power.[6] It was an argument that exerted some influence among Soviet anti-Stalinists, many of whom for the time being were constrained even from public criticism. Trotsky, perhaps, initially counted himself as among them.

But despite the tolerable conditions of his personal exile, the early 1930s were also the years of Trotsky's mounting family tragedies. He received word that Zina Volkova, his surviving daughter by his former wife, Alexandra Sokolovskaya, recently had been taken ill. Suffering from an undiagnosed neurological malady, Zina was obliged to give over her children, as well as those of her late sister, Nina, to the care of her aging mother. There was no one else, for Man Nevelson, Nina's husband, had been arrested earlier and dispatched to a Siberian work camp; and Zina's own husband, Platon Volkov, under party suspicion, also would fall victim shortly to Stalin's purges (pp. 300, 329).

Early in 1931, however, at the intercession of French Communist leaders, Zina was allowed to leave the Soviet Union to join her parents in Turkey and

---

1 Jean Van Heijenoort, *With Trotsky in Exile: From Prinkipo to Coyoacán* (Cambridge, MA: Harvard University Press, 1978), passim.
2 George Breitman and Sarah Lovell, eds., "Introduction," in *The Writings of Leon Trotsky*, by Leon Trotsky, vol. 1 (New York: Pathfinder Press, 1975).
3 Robert Conquest, *The Great Terror: A Reassessment* (New York: Oxford University Press, 1990), 413; Bertram David Wolfe, *Three Who Made a Revolution: A Biographical History* (Harmondsworth: Penguin Books, 1966), 520.
4 Adam B. Ulam, *The Bolsheviks: The Intellectual and Political History of the Triumph of Communism in Russia* (New York: Macmillan, 1965), 139–42.
5 Isaac Deutscher, *The Prophet Outcast: Trotsky, 1929–1940* (London: Oxford University Press, 1963), 139–42.
6 Edward H. Carr, *Twilight of the Comintern, 1930–1935* (New York: Pantheon Books, 1982), 343, 346; Albert Glotzer, *Trotsky: Memoir and Critique* (Buffalo, NY: Prometheus Books, 1989), 60–67.

to bring with her the younger of her two children, a five-year-old boy, "Seva" (Vsevolod). The joy of the family reunion was sweet. Yet it was also short-lived. In autumn of the same year, Zina's neurological illness deteriorated so alarmingly that Trotsky was obliged to arrange treatment for her at a Berlin clinic. At his direction, her half-brother Liova later joined her in Berlin. Although Trotsky also had arranged for his son to monitor German political activities, even to edit a German-language edition of his defiant little *Bulletin of the Opposition*, Liova understood that his principal responsibility was to assure Zina's safety.

Yet, despite the best efforts of the Berlin clinic, Zina's condition worsened. After six weeks of futile treatment, including experimental electric shock therapy, her doctors suggested that she be reunited with her son. Liova then dutifully returned to Turkey to pick up Seva and bring him to Berlin. But the reunion failed to alleviate Zina's illness. Eventually, speculating that she might benefit from more extensive contact with her family, her physicians proposed releasing her from the clinic altogether. In early January 1933, however, before the doctors' recommendation could be tested, Liova sorrowfully telegraphed his parents that Zina had just taken her own life. She had inhaled gas in her Berlin rented room. Upon receiving the news, the grief-stricken Trotsky acquiesced in his son's decision to remain in Europe with Zina's child.[7] It was not certain that the Turkish government would continue to provide sanctuary for the family. There was no one else to share responsibility for the boy. Trotsky and Natalia's younger son, Sergei, had remained behind in the Soviet Union. Unwilling to jeopardize his budding career as a physicist, he had severed all ties with his parents.

Yet, by then, even in Turkey, the family's direst forebodings were beginning to be confirmed. As Stalin intensified the campaign against his political opposition, he revoked Trotsky's Soviet citizenship and that of all family members who had gone into exile with him.[8] As stateless persons, they instantly became vulnerable to Turkish expulsion, and perhaps even to extradition back to the Soviet Union. It soon became a matter of urgency, possibly of life or death, for them to obtain asylum elsewhere.

In July 1933, after protracted negotiations on Trotsky's behalf by Socialist Party members in France, the incumbent Daladier government consented to provide that asylum. Within the month, replicating the circumstances of the family's original departure from Odessa to Istanbul, Turkish

---

7 Deutscher, *The Prophet Outcast*, 180.
8 Victor Serge, *Mémoires d'un Révolutionnaire, 1901–1941* (Paris: Éditions du Seuil, 1951), 257.

detectives escorted the couple onto an awaiting freighter, and remained on watch until the ship embarked. Subsequently, upon their arrival in Marseille, the Trotskys were sped away in an unmarked police van. Their destination this time was a villa in Grenoble. Again, Trotsky was under government orders to adopt a low profile, to refrain from sending articles to French journals or even from visiting Paris.[9] Only his son, Liova, by then working in Paris as a stringer for several leftist journals, was permitted intermittently to visit his parents, bringing little Seva with him (p. 308).

But despite all precautions, the Trotskys' arrival in Grenoble soon became known. Newspaper reporters immediately converged on his villa, seeking to report the family's every visible move. More welcome to Trotsky were respectful visits by British Labourite MPs, by Social Democratic parliamentarians from Belgium and the Netherlands, and by refugee German Communists. Yet, at all times, he scrupulously observed the terms of his asylum, refraining from newspaper interviews or visits to Paris, confining his writings to private diary reflections on contemporary political and cultural events in the Soviet Union and Western Europe (which included his pungent characterization of Léon Blum as a "rightist Social Democrat," capable only of "parlor trivialities").[10]

It was on December 1, 1934, however, that the Kirov assassination took place in Leningrad, followed by its attribution to "Trotskyites," "Zinovievites," and "closest Fascists" and its attendant wave of imprisonments, Siberian deportations, and executions.[11] Studying these developments, Trotsky anticipated the impact they would have on his remaining family in the Soviet Union. He was not wrong. Early in 1935, his sons-in-law, Platon Volkov and Man Nevelson, both serving penal sentences in the "Gulag Archipelago," had their sentences extended for an additional ten years. Alexandra Sokolovskaya, Trotsky's former wife, in her late sixties and prostrated by grief after the death of both her daughters, was expelled from Leningrad to a remote settlement in Omsk province. Her grandchildren, formerly in her care, had to be taken in by her aged and equally impoverished sister.

By then, too, the French government was unwilling any longer to risk a Soviet-instigated vendetta on its soil. Altogether, it was not an opportune moment for a diplomatic contretemps with the Russians. In May 1935, Pierre Laval, who the previous year had been appointed his country's foreign

---

9 Serge, *Mémoires*, 182–83.
10 Leon Trotsky, *Trotsky's Diary in Exile, 1935* (New York: Atheneum, 1963), 4.
11 See Stalin's closed letter to the party, January 1935, in *Reabilitatsiia: Politicheskie protsessy 30–50-kh godov* (Moscow: Politzdat, 1991), 191–95.

minister, had gone to Moscow to negotiate a Franco-Soviet treaty to protect Eastern European's successor states against a resurgent Germany. This time, Stalin had proved receptive, both to the treaty and to a "Popular Front" alliance of the Communist and Socialist parties in France (pp. 286–89). But the concession unquestionably would come with a price. Monitoring these developments, Trotsky anticipated the likelihood of his own imminent expulsion. "The Sûreté [French Intelligence] is obviously showing off its knowledge of the circumstances of my life," he wrote morosely in his diary on May 15.[12]

In search of an alternate European sanctuary, he began exploring a potential opportunity in Norway. A recent parliamentary election had brought that country's Labor Party to office. Vigorous in their ideological socialism, the Norwegian Laborites in the early postwar had voted to join the Comintern; and, although later withdrawing that affiliation, they continued to maintain equable relations with the "idealistic," Trotskyite wing of their nation's minuscule Communist Party.[13] Consequently, in May 1935, at Trotsky's request, his European admirers interceded with the Norwegian government; and, the following month, the cabinet agreed to provide Trotsky and Natalia with refugee visas.

As in France, the agreement was rigorously conditional. The Trotskys' residence could not be closer than 40 miles from Oslo, the capital; and when the couple subsequently disembarked at the port of Bergen on June 18, 1935, the awaiting foreign ministry officials tactfully reminded them to abstain from political activity of any kind. Even under these constraints, however, the sanctuary appeared less grudging than its predecessor in France. Konrad Knudsen, a member of the Norwegian parliament and editor of Labor's party newspaper, invited the Trotskys to share his country home in the hamlet of Vexhall, and the offer was accepted. In Vexhall, too, Labor politicians and journalists, as well as occasional Socialist Party notables from other countries, paid the refugee couple respectful visits.

Yet Trotsky soon drew the wrong conclusions from Norwegian hospitality. Despite periodic government reminders, he refused to be deterred from political writings. Indeed, he completed his newest manuscript, *The Revolution Betrayed*, in Konrad Knudsen's country home. Sent to a Paris publisher in 1936, the manuscript was no secret to Stalin. Indeed, extracts were published in the *Bulletin of the Opposition* and parts were sent to Stalin long before the book's May 1937 publication date. It outlined a strategy for overthrowing Russia's Stalinist regime, thereby enabling communism to embark on an alternate, less

---

12  Trotsky, *Trotsky's Diary*, 117.
13  Heijenoort, *With Trotsky in Exile*, 77–78.

radical course. More explicitly than ever before, the volume also called for the establishment of a "Fourth International," with its leadership not to be confined to the Soviet Union. The challenge to Stalin could scarcely have been more frontal. As Trotsky's hosts had feared, the Kremlin was swift to react.

In June 1936, Norwegian Foreign Minister Halvdan Koht was "invited" to visit Moscow. Upon arrival, he was alerted to Soviet concern that, in extending sanctuary to Trotsky, Norway's government was harboring an anti-Soviet "agent provocateur." With the wave of Stalinist purge trials against "Trotskyites" and "Zinovievites" already spilling over into the realm of Soviet foreign policy (pp. 140–41),[14] Koht was sobered by the veiled warning. Indeed, two months later, Soviet Ambassador Pavel Yakubovich underscored his government's suspicions in a note delivered to the Norwegian foreign ministry. This one demanded that Trotsky be expelled for using Norway as "the base for his conspiracy ... [against the Soviet Union]."[15] As an opening shot, the Soviets threatened to cease their importation of Baltic fish, a staple of Norway's foreign trade. It was at this point that the Norwegian cabinet dispatched Minister of Justice Trygve Lie to intervene personally with Trotsky.

The two men had a long acquaintance, dating back to Lie's first visit to Moscow in 1921. An enthusiastic Socialist and internationalist, Lie in the 1920s was among the small group of his party colleagues who had briefly joined the Comintern. Now, 15 years later, he welcomed the opportunity to visit again with Trotsky. Their discussions at Vexhall were friendly. Yet neither man gave ground. Lie insisted that Trotsky abstain from open criticism of the Soviet government. Trotsky riposted that he would denounce Stalin's regime by any and every means. A week later Lie visited Trotsky again. With both men holding firm in their positions, the conversation this time became strained, and eventually was broken off. Finally, in November, the ministry of justice informed Trotsky that it would "cooperate" in seeking alternate sanctuary for him and his family.

Although it was evident by then that no European state would accept them, the Norwegians had sounded out another prospective haven. This was Mexico, which nurtured its own vigorous revolutionary tradition. Lázaro Cárdenas, the nation's far-leftist president, recently had signed a decree parceling out substantial numbers of confiscated latifundias to Mexico's impoverished peasants. Currently, he was embarked on an equally radical agenda to nationalize American and British oil installations. Hence, when the president's close friend, Diego Rivera, a renowned muralist and lifelong

---

14   Vladimir Petrov, *Empire of Fear* (London: Andre Deutsch, 1956), 220.
15   Quoted in Deutscher, *The Prophet Outcast*, 274.

Communist, interceded to endorse the Norwegian government's request, Cárdenas acquiesced. Apprized of this development, Trotsky in turn insisted that Trygve Lie at least guarantee "secure" transportation arrangements for him and his wife. Lie willingly complied. Indeed, on December 18, he informed the Trotskys that the Norwegian government itself had secretly chartered an oil tanker for the couple's transatlantic voyage. The ship would be leaving within 24 hours.

The following afternoon, Trotsky and Natalia were sped off to Oslo in a police van. Once at the city's harbor, under cover of darkness, they were conducted on board the awaiting vessel. The tanker embarked before dawn. The Trotskys were its only passengers, except for a Norwegian police escort. During the ensuing journey, they were treated as "internees," with their cabin put under 24-hour guard and their meals served in a screened corner of the crew's dining room. The precautions were not unwarranted. By the mid-1930s perhaps as many as 15,000 Soviet intelligence agents were working abroad, many of them under orders to hunt down Trotskyite oppositionists. Nevertheless, on January 9, 1937, after a 20-day voyage, the tanker managed to dock without incident at the drab little Mexican oil port of Tampico.

## THE FATE OF "COUNTERREVOLUTIONARIES"

During the two preceding years, much was happening in Trotsky's Soviet homeland. In February 1935, a special commission had been appointed under the co-chairmanship of Karl Radek and Nicholai Bukharin (the latter evidently back in Stalin's good graces) to draft a new constitution, with provisions for decentralizing and ostensibly liberalizing the Soviet state. When the document was made public, in June 1936, Bukharin proclaimed it a model for all nations, for it contained its own "bill of rights," guaranteeing freedom of speech, assembly, and press, as well as freedom from arbitrary arrest. One of the constitution's purposes apparently was to cosmeticize the participation of Communist parties in the Popular Front governments of France and Spain. But soon it became obvious that the document also was intended to occlude a more sinister initiative.[16]

As early as the autumn of 1935, Stalin evidently was contemplating an extensive purge both of suspect "Old Bolsheviks" and of a wider reservoir of potential domestic rivals.[17] Indeed, for the impending onslaught, he had at his

---

16  Stephen F. Cohen, *Bukharin and the Bolshevik Revolution: A Political Biography, 1888–1938* (New York: Vintage Books, 1975), 356–57.

17  Boris I. Nicolaevsky, *Power and the Soviet Elite* (New York: Praeger, 1965), 224.

disposal all the necessary tools. In the wake of the Kirov assassination in 1934, his "December Law" (p. 137) had laid the basis for a penal code that stipulated an extensive variety of crimes, including participation in "counterrevolutionary" organizations and in the dissemination of "counterrevolutionary" propaganda. In addition to armed revolt, terrorism, espionage, and sabotage, the document listed "verbal incitement" as a category that also could be identified as "counterrevolutionary." With these definitions and classifications in hand, Stalin accordingly made ready to launch a second, post-Kirov wave of purgation.[18]

The offensive began in January 1936 in the town of Gorki, when the NKVD—the agency in charge of internal affairs and law enforcement—announced the arrest of a former police informer, Valentin Olberg, a Baltic German who had taken refuge lately in Soviet Russia. Under the promise of immunity, Olberg now was induced to "confess" his membership in an alleged "Trotskyite ring" that ostensibly had laid plans to assassinate the Soviet Union's senior political leadership, including Stalin himself.[19] On March 31, actively monitoring the details of the pretrial interrogations, Stalin personally reviewed the cases of the 82 alleged "plotters" with NKVD Commissar Genrikh Yagoda and Prosecutor General Andrei Vyshinski. Only a minority of the accused had been partisans of Trotsky. Most were mid-level bureaucrats who had not troubled to align themselves with Stalin in the early years after Lenin's death, and whom Stalin now simply wanted out of the way. Accordingly, the defendants were spared open trial and given perfunctory, although harsh prison sentences.

But also included among the remaining 16 defendants were 5 regional party chairmen, as well as the former Politburo eminences Grigori Zinoviev and Lev Kamenev. Although the latter two already had been transported to the Gulag, apparently Stalin had never ceased to regard them as potential threats, even in their Arctic exile. In February 1936, he issued orders for their return to Moscow to await retrial. Subsequently, during the spring of 1936, and under Stalin's personal monitoring, Prosecutor General Vyshinski subjected Zinoviev, Kamenev, and the other 14 prisoners to relentless interrogation.[20] Most of them adamantly defended themselves against the charges of antiparty treason or of plotting the late Kirov's murder

---

18  F. Beck and W. Godin, *Russian Purge and the Extraction of Confession* (New York: Viking Press, 1951), 47; Bertram D. Wolfe, *Khrushchev and Stalin's Ghost* (New York: Frederick A. Praeger, 1957), 90.
19  Aliksandr Orlov, *The Secret History of Stalin's Crimes* (London: Jarrolds, 1954), 61–62.
20  Orlov, *The Secret History*, 96; Simon Sebag Montefiore, *Stalin: The Court of the Red Tsar* (New York: Knopf, 2004), 185.

(pp. 135–37), let alone the assassination of Stalin. Some went on hunger strikes. On July 3, however, in a bizarre confrontation, the 16 were granted an audience with Stalin. Brought from their cells to the dictator's Kremlin office, they were given his "personal" assurance, "in the name of the Politburo," that neither they nor their families would face execution if they agreed to plead guilty in open court.[21] The promise was apparently unrefuseable. Indeed, the government in short order was able to notify its party branches that all "spies, provocateurs, White Guards, kulaks, Trotskyites and Zinovievites" had surrendered, and their trials, together with those of a collection of former regional party chairmen, would begin on August 19 in the supreme court's military collegium.[22]

The courtroom itself was a relatively small chamber, accommodating fewer than 200 persons. No relatives of the accused were admitted. Neither were defense attorneys. Although the chief judge, Vassili Ulrikh, was a uniformed NKVD colonel with much experience in political cases, the "star" of the trial remained Prosecutor General Vyshinski. A relentless bulldog, Vyshinski proceeded to charge the defendants with acting as "the direct organizers of the assassination of Comrade S.M. Kirov" and also of plotting to murder other Soviet party leaders, including—here Vyshinski's voice dropped to an appalled whisper—no less than "Comrade Joseph Stalin."[23] In response, as if on cue, all 16 defendants admitted to each and every accusation. Kamenev actually elaborated on his "monstrous crime," emphasizing his alleged connections with Trotsky and even with Trotsky's younger son, Sergei. Zinoviev, in turn, meekly admitted that his "defective bolshevism became transformed into anti-bolshevism and, through Trotsky, arrived at fascism."[24] As the trial continued, the prisoners vied with each other in acknowledging both their own guilt and the guilt of their fellow defendants—even going so far as to cite "evidence" of their murder plots (many of which foreign press observers later described as logistically impossible).[25]

Although Stalin himself had returned to his summer vacation dacha at Sochi after the first week of proceedings, he received daily transcripts of the trial. Vyshinski's notations were ravenous and sycophantic. Invariably, they ended with the initialed recommendation "VMN"—death by shooting. By

---

21 Robert Conquest, *Stalin and the Kirov Murder* (Oxford: Oxford University Press, 1989), 87.
22 Montefiore, *Stalin: The Court of the Red Tsar*, 187.
23 Roy Aleksandrovich Medvedev, *Let History Judge: The Origins and Consequences of Stalinism* (New York: Knopf, 1976), 169.
24 Quoted in Conquest, *The Great Terror: A Reassessment*, 103–4.
25 Orlov, *The Secret History*, 165–67.

August, too, the Soviet press had been competing with the prosecution in its frenzied denunciation of the prisoners. Workers in the Kiev Red Flag Factory and Stalingrad's Dzerzhinski tractor plant, in Kazak kolkhozes and Leningrad trade unions, similarly demanded the death penalty. The trials of the 16 accused finally ended on August 23, 1936. The judges then retired for consultation. Twenty-four hours later, they returned to the courtroom with their verdicts. All 16 of the "senior" defendants were pronounced guilty, all were sentenced to death, and the following morning, on August 25, all were shot. Stalin's earlier promise to them had been given its characteristically eccentric interpretation.

It had been a promise, moreover, not only to spare the prisoners' lives but to refrain from exacting retaliation against their families. Yet, by then, the fate of the slain convicts' relatives was equally predictable. Ursula Olberg, the German-born wife of the original informer, Valentin Olberg, was dispatched to an undisclosed labor camp. In September 1940, 13 months after signature of the Molotov-Ribbentrop Pact, she was sent back to Germany and handed over to the Gestapo, never to be heard from again. Also disappearing and presumably executed were the son of Grigorii Evdokimov and the wives of Ivan Bakayev and Yefim Dreitzer. As for the doomed Kamenev, his wife had been arrested in March 1934 and sentenced to Arctic exile. Upon being brought back to Moscow and retried in January 1938, she was returned to the Gulag, where she was shot in the autumn of 1941. The Kamenevs' elder son was arrested in August 1936, sentenced to prison in May 1937, and shot in 1939. Zinoviev's sister, a physician, was sent to the notorious Vorkuta labor camp and shot there at an undisclosed date. Three of Zinoviev's brothers and three of his sisters were dispatched to labor camps, together with two nephews, a niece, a brother-in-law, and a cousin. They were never heard from again. Zinoviev's younger son, for whom the father had made a special appeal directly to Stalin, was arrested and shot in 1937.

A week after the liquidation of Zinoviev, Kamenev, and their fellow "senior" defendants, Stalin ordered NKVD Commissar Yagoda to select and arrange the execution of 5,000 of the "oppositionists" already serving time in penal camps.[26] The order was carried out during the winter of 1936–37. In early summer 1937, a further mass execution was ordered at Vorkuta and at other camps in the Gulag. From then until the end of 1938, prisoners were

---

26 Montefiore, *Stalin: The Court of the Red Tsar*, 190; Robert Conquest, *Great Terror: Stalin's Purge of the Thirties* (New York: Collier Books, 1973), 98.

shot once or twice a week in groups of 40 or 45. Of their surviving families, only children under 12 were spared.[27]

## TROTSKY IN MEXICO

At noon of January 9, 1937, as the Norwegian tanker bearing the Trotskys approached the Mexican port of Tampico, a small naval vessel approached, with passengers including a Mexican general and a half-dozen other government officials. Boarding the tanker, the visitors brought with them the cordial personal greetings of President Cárdenas, and assurance that the presidential train was en route to carry the Trotskys directly to Mexico City. On the pier of Tampico, calling out greetings, were a dozen veteran Trotskyites, most of them American. On hand, too, was Frida Kahlo, Diego Rivera's wife and an accomplished artist in her own right. She personally accompanied the refugee family as it was waved through customs.

At 11:00 that night, the president's armored train, guarded by two carriages of soldiers, arrived to pick up the little group and its entourage of welcoming officials. It was mid-morning of the next day before the party arrived at the capital's suburban rail depot of Coyoacán. There, Diego Rivera himself stood beaming on the platform. Embracing Trotsky, the famed muralist insisted on putting his Coyoacán summer villa, the famous "Blue House," at the couple's personal disposal, and the Trotskys gratefully accepted. The comfortable, flower-encircled dwelling would be their home for the ensuing year and a half.

Yet the villa was not altogether a tranquil sanctuary. Within days of settling in Coyoacán, Trotsky became the object of threats from Stalinists both in the Soviet Union and Mexico. President Cárdenas soon was obliged to assign a permanent police guard outside the Blue House. Trotsky himself made it clear at the outset that he did not intend to play the role of passive scapegoat, nor did his partisans elsewhere, for whom he remained the venerated symbol of Communist idealism. Indeed, only two weeks after his arrival in Mexico, as the second wave of Stalin's purge trials began in the Soviet Union (pp. 304–05), additional pro-Trotsky committees were organized throughout the world, including the United States. One American committee, consisting of a half-dozen left-leaning intellectuals and labor leaders, was led by the famed Columbia University philosopher Professor John Dewey. In April 1937, it

---

27 Orlov, *The Secret History*, 179; Deutscher, *Prophet Outcast*, 416–18; see also Timothy Snyder, *Bloodlands: Europe between Hitler and Stalin* (New York: Basic Books, 2010), 84–85, and Timothy Snyder, "Hitler vs. Stalin: Who Killed More?" *New York Review of Books*, March 10, 2011.

was this committee that undertook extensive investigations of the Stalinist charges, and then traveled en bloc to Mexico to conduct 12 days of detailed interviews with Trotsky in the Coyoacán Blue House itself. Their report, rushed to book publication in December 1937 and fully "exonerating" Trotsky, was given wide press coverage.[28]

But whatever Trotsky's gratification at these supportive gestures, it was overshadowed by a further sequence of bitter family losses. In the spring of 1937, the mounting Stalinist terror claimed the life of Trotsky and Natalia's younger son, the 30-year-old Sergei Sedov. A promising physicist and adjunct member of the Soviet Academy of Sciences, Sergei had assiduously shunned personal contact with his exiled father and even had adopted his mother's surname. Nevertheless, he was arrested in early May on charges of attempting a "mass poisoning" of factory workers, ostensibly at his father's orders.[29] Upon learning of this development, and consumed with alarm for their estranged "Seryozha," Natalia Sedova dispatched repeated letters to Stalin's son, Yakov, a former schoolmate of Sergei's, begging the latter's intercession with his father. Her appeals went unanswered. Two years later, it was belatedly discovered that Sergei had been sent to the Gulag, where he was consigned to the grim Vorkuta camp, there to be secretly executed, either in late 1937 or early 1938.[30]

For the Trotskys, the fate of their older son, Liova, was even more devastating. With the five-year-old Seva still in his care, Liova had remained in Paris as a freelance columnist for a pair of left-wing newspapers (p. 300). There, his major energies were devoted to his father's cause. In late 1936, together with his companion, Jeanne Molinier, he published an extensive indictment of the Soviet purge trials.[31] If Liova by then had premonitions of his vulnerability to Stalinist assassins, his concern evidently was shared by French police detectives. They trailed him discreetly, on the lookout for ambushes. Once, in the autumn of 1937, investigating the murder of Ignace Reiss, a former NKVD agent who subsequently had converted to Trotskyism, the detectives warned Liova that his own life was in equally imminent danger and suggested that he leave France altogether. Liova rejected the suggestion.

---

28 Bertrand M. Patenaude, *Trotsky: Downfall of a Revolutionary* (New York: HarperCollins, 2009), 38–56; Heijenoort, *With Trotsky in Exile*, 108–10; John Dewey, *Report of the Commission of Inquiry into the Charges Made Against Leon Trotsky in the Moscow Trials* (New York: Monad Press, 1937), *passim*.
29 Trotsky, *Trotsky's Diary*, 63.
30 Trotsky, *Trotsky's Diary*, 130–31.
31 Lev Sedov, *Livre rouge sur le procès de Moscou* (Paris: Éditions populaires, 1936), *passim*.

By then he had found a seemingly loyal and dependable alter ego. This was Mark Zborowski, a Soviet émigré and former university sociologist. Describing himself as a penniless fugitive from Stalin's terror campaign, Zborowski had ingratiated himself with Jeanne Molinier, who in 1936 recommended him to Liova as an assistant. A small man, described as possessing a "sullen, frowning face" and a somewhat "colorless manner," Zborowski over the next year and a half amply fulfilled Jeanne Molinier's recommendation.[32] He made himself indispensable to Liova as a researcher. Yet he made himself even more useful to the NKVD. Since 1933, Zborowski had operated in France as a Stalinist "mole," and had figured as a secret informer in several earlier NKVD ambushes.[33]

In February 1938, the overworked Liova experienced a painful gastrointestinal attack. Zborowski immediately entreated him to book himself into a small private clinic in the Paris suburb of Auteil. It was staffed by Russian émigré doctors, Zborowski explained, all of them trustworthy refugees from the Stalinist regime. Liova accepted the advice. That same afternoon he registered at the clinic under the name of "Martin." Upon examination, he was diagnosed as suffering from acute appendicitis and underwent immediate surgery. The operation apparently succeeded. Indeed, over the next few days, Liova appeared to be on the way to a normal recovery, and the private nurse Zborowski had ordered for him was removed. Then, suddenly and unaccountably, he took a violent turn for the worse. Despite repeated blood transfusions, he died on the morning of February 16, at the age of 32.[34]

Upon receiving the news in Mexico, the horrified Trotsky immediately launched a secret investigation of the "indispensable" Zborowski. He entrusted the matter to Rudolf Klement, a former aide and subsequent participant in Trotsky's Fourth International (p. 302). Yet, before Klement managed to complete his inquiries in Paris, a NKVD agent, Ale Taubman, lured him to a Left Bank apartment. There, with the help of two other Soviet enforcers, Taubman strangled Klement, and subsequently dumped his body in the Seine. When Klement's headless corpse washed ashore in the ensuing August, it was identified by friends from a scar on one hand. Although Zborowski personally had not committed the murder, he seemed to have played the key role as "finger man."

---

32 Patenaude, *Trotsky: Downfall*, 112; Elizabeth K. Poretsky, *Our Own People* (Ann Arbor, MI: University of Michigan Press, 1970), 239.
33 Patenaude, *Trotsky: Downfall*, 139–46.
34 Isaac Don Levine, *The Mind of an Assassin* (New York: Farrar, Straus, and Cudahy, 1959), 399–40.

It was not until two decades later, in 1958, after moving to the United States and securing a teaching position at Columbia University as a "social anthropologist," that Zborowski was exposed and convicted by a federal court. Ironically, the charge against him was not of complicity in Liova Sedov's murder but of perjury in disguising his Communist connections during his earlier American immigration hearings. Eventually, four years after his appeal and retrial, Zborowski was sentenced to a modest five- to seven-year prison term, but was paroled after serving fewer than three years.[35]

In February 1938, meanwhile, when the news first arrived of Liova's death, Trotsky had kept his emotions as private as his suspicions. He and Natalia had closed themselves in their bedroom for three days, all but paralyzed with grief. As he later wrote a friend, "Liova was part of us, our younger part. . . . With our son's death, everything that still remained young in us has also died."[36]

## AN APOTHEOSIS OF PURGATION

In the Soviet Union, the trials of the mid-1930s, with their systematic convictions, imprisonments, and liquidations of putative "Trotskyites," continued through 1936 and beyond. On January 10, 1937, still another group of defendants was arraigned on vague charges of "treason" and brought to trial in the NKVD's military collegium. In contrast to the prominent defendants of the previous August, however, the 17 latest accused had never been serious rivals to Stalin. They were second-level bureaucrats who evidently had been tainted by their routine office contacts with the earlier "Zinovievite-Trotskyite Conspiracy" of 1934. Nonetheless, Stalin wanted a clean sweep of them. On January 30, 1937, the hapless prisoners were routinely and swiftly convicted. Thirteen of them were condemned to death and summarily shot. The remaining four were sentenced to varying terms of imprisonment—although eventually, between 1939 and 1941, they too were executed.

The earlier August 1936 mass trial of "Trotskyites" had evoked a credulous response from the Soviet public. But this latest judicial travesty in January 1937 evoked tremolos of doubt—and then of widespread fear. Who would be next? The answer was not long in coming. In late February and early March of the same year, during a series of meetings of the Communist Central Committee, Stalin's closest henchmen began leveling charges against the surviving "rightists" of the Old Bolshevik era, and specifically against its senior figures, Nicholai Bukharin, Alexei Rykov, and Nicholai Krestinsky. Together

---

35 Conquest, *The Great Terror: A Reassessment*, 415.
36 Deutscher, *Prophet Outcast*, 401.

with the accusation of "conspiracy" to murder Stalin, the charge this time was "implication" in a plot to return capitalism to the Soviet Union through "Fascist interventionism." Included among the 17 "conspirators" (a number reduced from the original 21) was Genrikh Yagoda, the former NKVD commissar. Evidently, Stalin wished to dispose of him for being privy to the rigged scenario of the Kirov assassination.

During ensuing months, the alleged conspirators were deprived of their posts, then imprisoned and subjected to the usual—and by then perfected—regimen of intimidation. At last, on March 2, 1938, the hapless defendants were brought to formal trial. Although the proceedings were held in the supreme court, these too were conducted under NKVD auspices, with the sinister Andrei Vyshinski once again orchestrating the prosecution of "this foul-smelling heap of human garbage . . . these hired murderers, saboteurs, and wreckers in the service of fascism."[37] Here, for the first time, several press correspondents and foreign diplomats were admitted as spectators. It was apparent that Vyshinski anticipated the identical self-abasing "confessions" elicited by the previous trials. For the most part, he got them, together with incriminating mutual charges among the defendants themselves. The trial ended on March 12. After one day of deliberation, the judges pronounced death sentences on Bukharin, Rykov, and the other defendants. All 17 were immediately shot.

Neither were their families spared. Bukharin's widow, Anna, was arrested soon afterward, to spend six months in a Moscow cell, and 18 ensuing years at hard labor in the Gulag. His crippled former wife, Nadia, had written Stalin several times to plead Bukharin's innocence. Shortly after Bukharin's execution, Nadia too was arrested. In March 1940, after languishing in prison for three years and being deprived of her medications, she was shot. Her brothers, brothers-in-law, and other relatives also were arrested, to be executed, left to die in prison, or to disappear in the Gulag. By then, Stalin had managed to eliminate virtually all of Lenin's original senior staff dating from the days of the November Revolution, eradicating in the process any further possibility of a Trotskyite "shadow" government.[38]

## OVERTURE TO A STRATEGIC REVOLUTION

While the spring 1938 trial was the more far reaching in its chain reaction of arrests, imprisonments, and executions, it was preceded by an unexpected and even more traumatic Stalinist witch hunt. In its origins, however, this

---

37  Cohen, *Bukharin*, 370–71, 374.
38  Glotzer, *Trotsky: Memoir*, 236.

purge was motivated less by political than by military considerations. It was on May 11, 1937 that Marshal Mikhail Tukhachevsky, who doubled as chief of staff of the Red Army and Soviet deputy commissar of defense, was relieved of his offices and demoted to army commander for the Volga District. Two weeks later he was arrested and remanded for court martial. At the same time, six other respected military commanders—Generals Iona Yakir, Yan Gamarnik, Alexei Volovich, Dmitri Schmidt, Mikhail Medvedev, and Boris Feldman—also were arrested and imprisoned. The charges against them were "espionage on behalf of Nazi Germany."[39]

For the Soviet public, news of these arrests evoked acute astonishment and horror. Mikhail Tukhachevsky was renowned as the finest brain in the Red Army. The son of a minor aristocrat, he had served gallantly in an elite guards regiment during the World War. When captured by the Germans in 1915, he had attempted five escapes before he was transferred to the high-security fortress of Ingolstadt (where his fellow prisoners included a young French captain, Charles de Gaulle). Eventually, in 1917, Tukhachevsky was returned to Russia in a POW exchange. After the November Revolution, he joined the Bolshevik cause, volunteering his services to the emerging Red Army. In 1920, appraising this 27-year-old officer's leadership qualities, Trotsky gave him command of the army corps that subsequently counterattacked a Polish offensive and surged to the gates of Warsaw before being repulsed only at the last moment by the intervention of the French army (p. 274). Eight years later, Tukhachevsky was promoted to chief of Soviet strategic planning and afterward, in 1935, at the age of 42, to the rank of army senior marshal and vice-commissar of defense.

By then, the precocious commander also had dedicated himself to a fundamental reorganization and modernization of the Soviet armed services, with emphasis on an expanded armored corps and air force. A professional to the core, Tukhachevsky did not suffer fools lightly. In the process of reconfiguring Soviet defense forces, apparently he aroused the ire of veteran partisan commanders of Russia's civil war, among them such old Bolshevik war horses as Kliment Voroshilov and Semyon Budyenny, cronies whom even Stalin trusted and over the years similarly had anointed as marshals.[40] But without compelling reasons of his own, Stalin possibly would not have given heed to allegations of disloyalty against Tukhachevsky, whom he recently had promoted even in the midst of the country's "civilian" purge trials. Foremost

---

39  Orlando Figes, *Revolutionary Russia, 1891–1991: A History* (New York: Henry Holt and Company, 2014), 195.

40  Montefiore, *Stalin: The Court of the Red Tsar*, 221–22.

among Stalin's motives, apparently, was concern that his army command might obstruct an eventual rapprochement with Hitler's emerging Reich.[41]

Relations between the German and Soviet military leadership predated even the postwar diplomatic Treaty of Rapallo (p. 100). As early as the winter of 1921, the governments of these former wartime enemies had permitted their senior army officers to enter exploratory discussions on military cooperation. The Soviet command urgently needed modern armaments factories and updated military academies. The Germans, restricted by the Versailles Treaty from maintaining more than a de facto militia, coveted the flat steppes of Russia for secret and expanded military maneuvers and new weapons-testing. It was to meet these diverse requirements that an arrangement was negotiated as early as April 1922 and maintained in secrecy until September 1933, fully nine months after Hitler had come to power in Germany. As Tukhachevsky himself admitted that year, "[T]he Reichswehr has been the teacher of the Red Army, and [its contributions] will never be forgotten."[42] Although military cooperation eventually languished with the consolidation of the Nazi regime, the two nations still carried on an extensive trade as late as 1935, and Stalin was hesitant to relinquish those ties.

But the Soviet dictator was even more hesitant to risk a new military confrontation with Germany. His nation had not yet recovered from the effects of World War I, from the ensuing civil war, and from the starvation of the early and mid-1920s; and it had not so much as begun to recover from the more recent trauma of rural collectivization and urban industrialization. Thus, while sentient to the Nazi leadership's enmity to bolshevism and contempt for the Slavic race, Stalin preferred to buy time with Hitler and the emerging German Wehrmacht. The alternative notion, of making common military cause with the principal Western democracies, whose postwar leadership had disdained meaningful contacts with Moscow—indeed, who had sought to strangle the Communist experiment at birth—was beneath the Soviet leader's consideration. As early as December 1936, an NKVD agent in Paris confided to his colleague, Walter Krivitsky, that "[w]e have set our course toward an understanding with Hitler. It will only be a matter of [time]. . . . There's nothing for us in this rotting corpse of France."[43]

---

41 David Clay Large, *Between Two Fires: Europe's Path in the 1930s* (New York: Norton, 1990), 297–98; Hans von Herwarth, *Zwischen Hitler und Stalin: Erlebte Zeitgeschichte, 1931–1945* (Frankfurt am Main: Ullstein, 1985), 59.

42 Walter Laqueur, *Russia and Germany: A Century of Conflict* (New Brunswick, NJ: Transaction Publishers, 1990), 143.

43 W. G. Krivitzsky, *I was Stalin's Agent* (London: Hamish Hamilton, 1940), 31.

Unlike Stalin and his political advisors, however, the USSR's senior generals had dismissed the likelihood of peaceful coexistence with Nazi Germany. Mikhail Tukhachevsky was preeminent among these skeptics. Despite his German contacts and his past willingness to exploit German military expertise, the marshal took with increasing seriousness the racism of the Nazi government and its denigration of the Slavic peoples as "Mongol *Untermenschen.*" By 1935, he did not bother to disguise his preference for a strengthened relationship with the Western democracies. Stalin, on the other hand, was not pleased with the shift of the high command's strategic assessment. It threatened his evolving strategy of buying time with Hitler, possibly by a joint partition of Poland, or by the reclamation of Russia's former Baltic provinces.

Even into the mid-1930s, however, without unassailable evidence of disloyalty, Stalin perhaps would have been reluctant to move against his senior commanders. But that "evidence" suddenly was presented by Germany itself. In late 1936, Walther Schellenberg, chairman of the Sicherheitsdienst, the Nazi office of party security, formulated a plan for the transfer of "disinformation" to Moscow.[44] It was based on an alleged revelation of Tukhachevsky's "secret collusion" with the German military leadership in a plot to assassinate Stalin. If the "plot" could be leaked to the Soviet dictator, conceivably it could doom Tukhachevsky and others of the Soviet armed forces' senior leadership. Schellenberg discussed the idea with Heinrich Himmler, the commander of the Schutzstaffel (SS), the office of state security, who in turn brought it to Hitler. The Führer gave it his personal approval.

Subsequently, in March 1937, Reinhard Heydrich, Himmler's deputy, ordered the preparation of a spurious "dossier." The dossier contained copies of an apparent exchange of correspondence between Tukhachevsky and members of the Wehrmacht high command, outlining a plot against Stalin. In actuality, there was no plot. A German master engraver had been engaged to transpose Tukhachevsky's signature from an earlier document of 1926 relating to German-Soviet military cooperation. The engraver had also copied the signatures (artfully "lifted" from local bank checks) of alleged lower-level Reichswehr military conspirators. Eventually, in May 1937, the bogus documents were "leaked" to the Soviet Union through known German Communist agents. Days later, they were in Stalin's hands. Seemingly authentic, they offered the evidence he needed to target the Soviet high command for "cleansing." As in his civilian purges and in his depiction of "conspiring" former politicians,

---

44 Walter Schellenberg, *Labyrinth* (New York: Harper & Brothers, 1956), 25–28; Montefiore, *Stalin: The Court of the Red Tsar,* 224–25.

he would link the "conspiracy" of Soviet military leaders with the ideological "conspiracy" of Trotskyism.

On June 2, 1937, Tukhachevsky and eight senior military commanders were arrested by detachments of NKVD police and nine days later were placed on trial in a special military tribunal before Chief Judge Vassili Ulrikh. This time Ulrikh's fellow judges were the old Stalin cronies, Marshals Semyon Budyenny and Kliment Voroshilov. Their respective cross-examinations of Tukhachevsky and his colleagues were unrelenting. Yet it was Prosecutor-General Vyshinski who determined the trial's agenda and ensured that Trotsky remained its principal defendant in absentia. Indeed, from the trial's beginning to its end, Vyshinski lost no opportunity, however incongruous, to cite Trotsky's alleged "secret agreements" with Hitler—even with Japan's Emperor Hirohito!—in the effort to "do away" with Stalin; to "dismember" the Soviet Union; to "sabotage" the nation's coal mines, factories, and railways; and to perpetrate "mass poisonings" of Soviet workers.

The trial of the nine principal military defendants was completed in a single day. At 11:35 p.m. on that same June 11, all were pronounced guilty and sentenced to death. Minutes later, on being telephoned, Stalin instantly confirmed the sentences. The executions were carried out early the following morning, in the presence of Chief Judge Ulrikh and Nikolai Yezhov (the latter serving as Genrikh Yagoda's recent successor as NKVD commissar). Unable to restrain his curiosity, Stalin telephoned Yezhov that same day. "What were Tukhachevsky's last words?" he asked. "The snake said he was dedicated to the Motherland and Comrade Stalin," was Yezhov's reply.[45]

In June 1937, following the trial and execution of Tukhachevsky and his colleagues, the net closed on scores of other senior officers, including 3 marshals, 21 corps commanders, 37 division commanders, 20 younger generals from the Moscow Central Military Kommandatura, and the entire teaching faculty of the Frunze Military Academy. In the navy, of nine fleet admirals and admirals first class, only one survived the purge. The victims included Admiral Vladimir Orlov, the naval chief of staff. The provinces witnessed a comparable chain reaction of trials and executions. In the Kiev military district alone, more than 700 younger officers were secretly arrested, tried, and shot. By late 1938, when the wave of executions finally abated, some 40,000 military, naval, and air force officers, many of them heroes of the Russian Revolution, had been shot or had "disappeared" in their Siberian exile. Whether or not Stalin

---

45 Montefiore, *Stalin: The Court of the Red Tsar*, 224–25.

had destroyed a potential or (more likely) an imagined threat to his political authority, in the process he had also inflicted almost irreparable damage on the Soviet state's defensive capacity.[46]

## AN INTERIM POSTMORTEM

As for those millions of civilians whose lives in the 1930s were not deliberately taken, the circumstances of their imprisonment or Siberian exile were little short of homicidal. Most were herded into the network of labor camps stretching across the Soviet Union's eastern reaches, from the Urals to the frozen wastes of the Arctic. There, they were put to work on such basic infrastructure projects as dredging the White Sea and Moscow-Volga canals, double-tracking the Trans-Siberian Railway, gold mining in the Kolyma waste fields, logging, constructing factories, or other tasks that the central economic planners deemed essential to fulfill the requirements of the nation's current Five-Year Plan. In any one year through the 1930s, as many 1.5 million prisoners served their varying sentences in the Siberian wasteland—and cumulatively, by the end of 1938, as many as 8 million.[47]

Robert Conquest, a prolific author on the Stalinist terror, has calculated that, from the mid-thirties to late 1941—whether directly or indirectly at Stalin's orders, whether in prisons or in the Gulag—some 13 million Soviet citizens perished of execution, malnutrition, exposure, or exhaustion.[48] Later calculations by Timothy Snyder, another respected authority on the Soviet purges, have reduced the estimate to between 6 and 7 million.[49] But even if the "Great Terror" had continued at the lower of the two rates, it was uncertain that any semblance of organized life could have endured in the Soviet Union in the decade before World War II. The question still resonates: in countenancing this trauma, why did Stalin find it necessary to include among the imprisonments and executions tens of thousands of teachers, physicians, engineers, and the most senior or promising of the nation's military officers, all of whose efforts were critical for the growth and security of the state? What was his purpose in destroying the victims' extended families, and

---

46 Seweryn Bialer, ed., *Stalin and His Generals* (New York: Pegasus, 1969), 59.
47 Conquest, *The Great Terror: A Reassessment*, 485–86.
48 Robert Conquest, *Inside Stalin's Secret Police: NKVD Politics, 1936–1939* (London: Macmillan, 1985), 30.
49 Robert Conquest, *The Great Terror: Stalin's Purge of the Thirties* (London: Macmillan, 1973), 30. For an alternate appraisal, compare Snyder, *Bloodlands*, 81–84.

thereby the very moral underpinnings of the Soviet nation? Even if a wife of a condemned suspect was not herself arrested, she and her children usually lost their employment, their pensions, their lodgings, their local residency permits, and were obliged ultimately to sell their most basic possessions and subsist on the charity of relatives.[50]

Many historians of this period have suggested that Stalin was the victim of a paranoia that approached the threshold of madness. It is at least agreed that he operated in the devious and cunning tradition of his native Caucasus. The perverse logic of his crimes apparently was to sweep away the possibility not only of any alternate government but of all centers of independent thought and action within the party and government, thereby leaving the entire nation reliant on his leadership.[51] If that indeed was Stalin's objective, his campaign to extirpate the threat of a rival, "shadow" Communist leadership manifestly was not to be confined to the frontiers of the Soviet Union alone.

## THE SPANISH CONNECTION

Despite his recent family losses, Leon Trotsky in the summer of 1938 stubbornly persisted in his efforts to establish just such a shadow leadership. With the aid of a devoted European protégé, Alfred Rosmer, who had befriended him in his years of European exile before World War I, preparations were made for the founding congress of a rival "Fourth International" (the "Third International" having largely disintegrated with the imprisonment and subsequent execution of Zinoviev, its former leader). Although Trotsky himself, as presumptive leader of the anticipated body, could not risk leaving his Mexican refuge, he appointed Rosmer as his spokesman. The "congress" accordingly was convened at Rosmer's village home, outside Paris, on September 3, 1938.

It was a modest, even rather pitiable, gathering of a mere 21 delegates, veteran Communist Party members all, who claimed to represent the Trotskyite organizations of 11 countries. The meeting lasted a single day. Electing Trotsky as chairman of the "Fourth International," it confirmed the program he himself had sent from Mexico, with its harsh condemnation of Stalin's terror machine and its appeal for all gradations of socialism to unite

---

50  Evgeniia Ginzburg, *Journey into the Whirlwind* (New York: Harcourt, Brace & World, 1967), 137, 185.
51  Beck and Godin, *Russian Purge*, 248–58.

against the common menace of fascism and Nazism. The impact of the feeble affair was nil. By then, virtually all oppositionist cells in the Soviet Union had been eradicated and the Communist Party altogether had been destroyed in Germany, Austria, Italy, and Spain, as it had been earlier in the East European proto-fascist successor states of Poland, Romania, and Hungary.

In Mexico, too, Trotsky was becoming less comfortable even with some of his most intimate friends and collaborators. Diego Rivera surely had been the most loyal of these. But when the famed muralist lately had accused Mexico's President Cárdenas—the man who generously had given refuge to Trotsky—of being a "traitor to socialism" for decrying Stalin's reign of terror, Trotsky reacted in shock and consternation.[52] Indeed, he decided shortly afterward to remove his family from Rivera's villa. The decision to seek another residence was not easily made, for it entailed serious financial commitments. In the process of moving, Trotsky was compelled to purchase and furnish another villa, this one several blocks away from the "Blue House," on Coyoacán's Avenida Viena.

In October 1939, moreover, fearing Stalin's retaliation for hosting the "Fourth International," Alfred and Marguerite Rosmer arrived in Mexico from France. Trotsky instantly provided the couple with a modest stipend from his own resources and then lodged them with Natalia and himself in his new villa. Burdensome as the financial disbursements and physical congestion were, in this case, they were tempered with a "prize" the Rosmers had brought with them. It was the late Zina's son, Seva, now almost 11 years old, whom Liova Trotsky had reared until his own death two and a half years before. The Rosmers had obtained a French court order consigning Seva to their interim guardianship, pending the boy's return to family members. His safe arrival with the Rosmers over the wartime Atlantic now became the consolation of Trotsky's life.

Indeed, the need to ensure his grandson's ongoing safety, more than Natalia's or his own, impelled Trotsky to launch into the fortification of his new home. The villa's basic structure already was sound. Its walls were thick. It stood in its own plot, well separated from the street and neighboring villas. Yet, as rumors of impending Stalinist conspiracies circulated, Trotsky had a watchtower erected by the entrance gate and iron bars and electric alarms installed on all doors. By mid-January of 1940, at heavy personal expense, his renovations were completed. The Cárdenas government supplemented these by assigning 24-hour police patrols to the house and the adjoining

---

52  Heijenoort, *With Trotsky*, 110–11.

street. Inside the courtyard, a contingent of "handymen"—actually several American Trotskyite volunteers—functioned as private guards.[53] If the Trotskys or the Rosmers wished to visit Mexico City or other nearby communities, they traveled in great secrecy by automobile, accompanied by several of these plainclothesmen.

The precautions were more timely than the Trotskys could have anticipated. Three months before, in late October of 1939, a delegation of eight Spanish Communists had set out from Barcelona for Mexico on the passenger ship *Manuel Arnuz*. Among their members was a handsome, 44-year-old woman, Eustaquia Caridad Mercader del Rio Ocuvite Hernández. Although "Caridad" was born in Cuba, her affluent Spanish-born parents had sent her as a girl to private Jesuit schools in Paris and Barcelona, before themselves later resettling in Barcelona. It was there, at the age of 18, that Caridad was married off to Pau Mercader Marina, a young man from a respected local family. She bore him five children. Rather than settling into the life of a homemaker, however, the spirited young society matron eventually rebelled against her pedestrian husband and his fashionable milieu. By the late 1920s, she had been attracted to radical political causes.

Barcelona's surrounding province of Catalonia abounded in them, from regional nationalism (against Spanish sovereignty) to anarcho-syndicalism (against wealthy property owners). It was in this ideological hothouse, no less than in the strife of an increasingly contentious marriage, that Ramón Mercader, Caridad's second child, was reared. In 1932, a year after the revolution that overthrew the Spanish monarchy, Ramón, age 18, was conscripted into the Spanish republican army, where he eventually achieved the rank of lieutenant. By then, separatist mini-revolutions were erupting both in Catalonia and in the Basque province of Asturias. Ramón himself participated in the bloody (although abortive) Catalonian revolt. Simultaneously, under Caridad's influence, he became an outspoken Communist, and in June 1935 he was arrested for his radical activities and sentenced to four months in prison.[54]

Fortunately for the young Mercader and other imprisoned leftist extremists, a "Frente Popular" coalition shortly afterward assumed government office in Madrid and amnestied them. But the interlude of political liberalism was brief. In July 1936, a fascist uprising was launched against the republican government. When Spain's beleaguered Prime Minister José Giral (p. 287) called for volunteers to form a defense force, Caridad and her son were

---

53 Glotzer, *Trotsky: Memoir*, 244.
54 "Secrets of an Assassin: Brilliant Probe Bares the Identity, Twisted Mind of Trotsky's Killer," *Life*, 28 September 1959, 104–110, 112–122, see especially page 109.

among the first to enlist. Although Caridad was preoccupied essentially with winning recruits for the republican cause, it was Ramón Mercader's effectiveness as a political officer in his loyalist regiment, as well as his courage and resourcefulness in battle, that attracted the attention of experienced Soviet "observers."

One of those "observers" was Leonid (Nahum) Eitingon, a veteran of the Bolshevik Revolution and Red Army and subsequently a valued specialist in political assassinations on the Kremlin's behalf. In the early 1930s, the stocky, bearded Eitingon had been functioning as deputy director of Soviet intelligence operations in France. In late 1936, after the outbreak of the Spanish Civil War, he was reassigned to assume the same role in Madrid as deputy to the legendary Soviet intelligence chief, Aleksandr Orlov. Two years into his mission, Eitingon was reassigned yet again, this time to organize an elite team of Spanish Communists for a special "liaison" mission. The order had come straight from Moscow, from the NKVD commissar Nikolai Yezhov, and actually had little to do with events in Spain.[55] Rather, Eitingon's mandate henceforth was to organize an assassination "mission" to Mexico. Its intended victim was Trotsky.

For ideological as well as linguistic reasons, the selection of Spanish-speaking Communists for the "mission" was logical. Eitingon's ensuing choice of the designated assassin, Ramón Mercader, Caridad's iron-nerved son, was inspired.[56] In March 1938, Eitingon first dispatched the 24-year-old Mercader to Moscow for three months of NKVD special training. In the Kremlin itself, with the help of Russian translators, the young man was put to work studying the voluminous files assembled on Trotsky and, specifically, the circumstances of Trotsky's Mexican exile, his physical surroundings, his friends, associates, and guards. Afterward, Mercader's destination was Paris, where a "mark," an unsuspecting dupe, had been selected for him.[57]

The "mark" was an American woman, the Brooklyn-born Sylvia Ageloff, who had been recommended to Eitingon by Dr. Gregory Rabinowitz, a part-time New York University lecturer in Slavic Studies—and a secret NKVD agent.[58] Sylvia had been a student of Rabinowitz's and an unabashed

---

55 Petrov, *Empire of Fear*, 222.
56 Pavel Sudoplatov and Anatolii Sudoplatov, *Special Tasks: The Memoirs of an Unwanted Witness, a Soviet Spymaster* (New York: Little, Brown and Company, 1994), 239.
57 See "Secrets of an Assassin," *Life*, 28 September 1959, for details of the plan.
58 United States Congress, House Committee on Un-American Activities, *American Aspects of the Assassination of Leon Trotsky: Hearings* (Washington, DC: U.S. Government Printing Office, 1951), viii–ix.

Trotskyite, as was her older sister, Ruth Ageloff, who, for several months in 1937, had worked as Trotsky's volunteer secretary in Mexico. Upon earning her undergraduate degree at New York University and subsequently a master's degree at Columbia, Sylvia had obtained her current position as a clinical psychologist for the New York Board of Education. Twenty-seven years old, angular, and quite plain, she had been diligently saving her overtime payments for a long-anticipated "romantic" vacation in France with her best friend, Ruby Weil Lewis.

Ruby Lewis was a committed Stalinist. Sensing an opportunity to use the bland Sylvia for her political agenda, Ruby first conferred with Rabinowitz, who in turn wrote Eitingon in care of the latter's office in Moscow. As Ruby had hoped, Eitingon at once grasped the opportunity to use Sylvia as an unwitting collaborator in the secret "Trotsky operation." To that end, through Rabinowitz, Eitingon transmitted funds to Ruby to allow her to "share"—in effect, to underwrite—Sylvia's travel expenses. In late October 1938, shortly after the two women arrived in Paris, Ruby introduced Sylvia to another visiting American, Louis Budenz, editor of the United States' miniscule Communist newspaper. It was Budenz, in turn, who introduced Sylvia to Alfred and Marguerite Rosmer,[59] the hosts of Trotsky's incipient Fourth International "congress" (p. 302). Budenz also introduced Sylvia to "Jacques Mornard." A tall, handsome, multilingual young man, characterized by Budenz as the son of a respected Belgian diplomatic family, "Mornard" described himself as a sports journalist for a Belgian newspaper. Unknown to the Rosmers, however, or even to Budenz, "Mornard" was Ramón Mercader.

Following the scenario devised earlier with Eitingon, Mercader promptly set about wining and dining Sylvia in Paris. In the process, he displayed no apparent interest in communism or in politics of any sort, only in his journalistic activities—and in her. Besotted, Sylvia in short order became Mercader's lover. When the time came for her to return to New York with Ruby Lewis, Mercader prevailed upon her to remain behind. He explained that he had made arrangements with the management of the "Argus Publishing Company" to purchase, at a handsome fee, any articles Sylvia would write for them on "educational psychology." Sylvia agreed on the spot, not even questioning Mercader's reluctance to bring her into personal contact with the "Argus" editorial staff or, later, to show her the printed versions of her articles. She received her payments, too, exclusively through Mercader, who periodically returned to "Belgium" or traveled elsewhere in Europe, ostensibly for his journalistic assignments.[60]

---

59  Louis F. Budenz, *This Is My Story* (New York: McGraw-Hill Book Company, 1947), 239.
60  Albert Goldman, *The Assassination of Leon Trotsky* (New York: Pioneer Publisher, 1940), 14.

Months later, however, in February 1939, Mercader informed Sylvia that his newspaper lately had appointed him its American "sports correspondent," and thus it would be more logical for her to return to New York, where he would join her "shortly." As always, she complied, eventually securing a new position at the New York Home Relief Bureau. But in ensuing months, Mercader delayed his arrival. His letters to Sylvia alluded vaguely to "administrative" matters that prevented their early reunion. In fact, the "administrative" matters were the final preparations for the assassination of Trotsky. The orders had come directly from Stalin. In March 1939, the Soviet dictator had confided to his NKVD commissar Lavrenti Beria (by then Nikolai Yezhov's successor) that "Trotsky should be eliminated within the year."[61]

Time was indeed becoming a crucial factor. Five and a half months later, on August 23, 1939, responding to increasingly urgent initiatives from the German foreign ministry, the Soviet government would sign a "Non-Aggression Treaty" with the Nazi Reich. The document's inducements for a mutual territorial partition of Poland and the Baltic republics were barely veiled. As Stalin contemplated formulation of the treaty, it was of some urgency for him to arrange the "disposal" of Trotsky before the "Fourth International" could organize a campaign to exploit the pact's shocking cynicism.

## MISSION TO MEXICO

Early in September 1939, a week after Europe was plunged into war, Mercader belatedly turned up at Sylvia Ageloff's New York apartment. He explained that he had only just managed to depart before the French army could draft him as a French "permanent resident." Indeed, to evade arrest, he had been obliged to travel on a false Canadian passport under the name "Frank Jacson." The original passport holder was an actual person, Tony Babich, a Canadian who had been killed fighting in the Spanish republican army. The Soviet NKVD later had collected these passports and altered their identities for its own purposes—although, in this instance, the NKVD had misspelled the passport's fake signature, "Frank Jackson," as "Frank Jacson." Hence, as "Mr. and Mrs. Jacson," Mercader and the unsuspecting Sylvia proceeded forthwith to resume their "married life."

Barely five weeks went by, however, before Mercader informed Sylvia that he had been offered still another assignment, this one in Mexico City, where he would lead a "raw-materials purchasing commission" on behalf of France and Britain. Although he needed to leave without delay, he promised that

---

61 Montefiore, *Stalin: The Court of the Red Tsar*, 295.

he would send for her "shortly." Again, she did not cavil. It was accordingly in mid-October, after providing Sylvia with an ample supply of cash for her daily expenses, that Mercader departed for Mexico. Once arrived, posing as "Frank Jacson," a wealthy Canadian mining engineer, he rented a comfortable apartment, purchased a Buick sedan, and in ensuing weeks passed himself off at Mexico City's fashionable cocktail parlors as a devoted supporter of the Allied cause. Secretly, however, he entered into intensive discussions with Leonid Eitingon and with his own mother, the iron-willed Caridad. They had arrived in November on the *Manuel Arnuz* as participants in the Mexican "mission."

In January 1940, Mercader notified Sylvia that the moment was opportune for her to join him. Overjoyed, she required less than four days to book an airplane reservation and embark for Mexico City, where she and Mercader resumed their "married" life. In January, too, at Mercader's initiative, Sylvia agreed to contact their mutual acquaintances Albert and Marguerite Rosmer, who were known to be ensconced as guests in the Trotsky villa. Indeed, for Sylvia, it was the recent arrival of the Rosmers, her earliest friends in Paris, that possibly was consolation for the absence of her own Brooklyn family. In telephoning the couple, however, she felt obliged to explain to them her "husband's" draft-dodging rationale for his new alias as "Frank Jacson." The Rosmers accepted the explanation and agreed with alacrity to a reunion.

Two days later, upon arrival at the Trotsky villa, Sylvia secured admittance after only a perfunctory interrogation by the guards (one of whom remembered Ruth, her older sister). Mercader discreetly remained outside the courtyard gate. But afterward, the two couples dined together at a neighboring restaurant. From then on, too, the Rosmers gratefully accepted their young friends' invitations to accompany them on excursions to places of interest. Mercader also volunteered to deliver the medications Alfred Rosmer periodically ordered from a local Coyoacán pharmacy. Soon the guards at the Trotsky compound routinely admitted Mercader into the courtyard. On one occasion, Natalia Sedova invited him into the house itself to meet her husband and share their breakfast coffee.

Meanwhile, in its admiration for Stalin and the Soviet Union, and at the Kremlin's instigation, Mexico's Communist press had been engaging in a furor of anti-Trotsky propaganda, calling for the expulsion of the "notorious counterrevolutionary." In the annual May Day parade of 1940, 20,000 marchers flaunted anti-Trotsky placards demanding that the government "throw out the sinister and dangerous traitor."[62] Evidently, it was this

---

62 Levine, *The Mind of an Assassin*, 81.

climactic pro-Stalinist shift of the Mexican Left that convinced Eitingon and the NKVD assassination team to forgo their original, cautious plan of infiltrating Ramón Mercader into the Trotsky entourage. They would strike for the jugular immediately.

On the night of May 23–24, 1940, an eminent Mexican muralist, José Siqueiros, a veteran Communist who had gained fame as "General Carlos," a republican brigade commander in the recent Spanish Civil War, toured Coyoacán in his chauffeured limousine. Both he and the passenger seated beside him were outfitted in counterfeit Mexican police uniforms, as was the 16-man detachment Siqueiros now commanded. Most of its members were veterans of his civil war brigade. But while Siqueiros gave them their orders, it was his fellow passenger, "Felipe," who had planned and now supervised the operation. "Felipe" was Leonid Eitingon.

At 11:10 p.m., as both men watched from their automobile, their "police" contingent made for the courtyard of the Trotsky villa. Intimidated by their uniforms and badges, a guard opened the gate—and was promptly knocked unconscious. The full complement of attackers then swarmed inside the courtyard and disarmed the compound's remaining guards. Shooting open the locks on the main entrance door, they made immediately for two of the villa's bedrooms. Again, they fired their weapons through locked doors, although refraining from entering the bedrooms themselves in suspicion that these had been booby-trapped for the night.[63] Then they withdrew. Miraculously, the Trotskys had survived the fusillade by burrowing under their mattress. Seva, Trotsky's grandson, who awoke screaming in his modest bedroom-playroom, was barely grazed by a bullet that penetrated his sofa bed.[64] As for the Rosmers' bedroom, it was not touched. The attackers had verified in advance that the couple was visiting friends (and within the week the panicked Rosmers departed by coastal steamer from Veracruz to Miami).[65]

Altogether, the scope and brutality of the assault on the aging Trotskys and a young grandson had been a public-relations disaster for the Kremlin. Beyond Mexico itself, expressions of outrage poured in from European and American sympathizers. The protests often were accompanied by cash contributions, and these in turn enabled the family to engage an American engineer to transform the Coyoacán villa into a virtual fortress, encircling it with barbed wire and two new guard towers and reinforcing it with bomb-proof walls and

---

63  Levine, *The Mind of an Assassin*, 86–87.
64  Leon Trotsky, *Stalin's Gangsters* (London: New Park Publications, 1977), 77–78.
65  Leandro A. Sánchez Salazar, *Murder in Mexico: The Assassination of Leon Trotsky* (London: Secker & Warburg, 1950), 18–25.

floors.⁶⁶ Ironically, it was Trotsky himself who viewed these alterations with ambivalence. As the former battle-hardened commissar of the Red Army, he was hardly a shrinking violet. Although concerned for the safety of his wife and grandchild, he himself refused to wear a bulletproof vest, noting disdainfully that "a single agent of the NKVD who could pass himself off as my friend could murder me."⁶⁷

## A CONSPIRACY CONSUMMATED

Trotsky's evaluation by then had been re-embraced by the Kremlin. Lavrenti Beria, latest in the sequence of NKVD commissars, agreed that too many participants had been involved in the attack. At Beria's orders, the assassination plot would revert to its original strategy of infiltration, and the killer, after all, would be a single person, Ramón Mercader. When Eitingon shared this revived scenario with Caridad, she too accepted it stoically. Through Eitingon, however, she demanded—and received—the Kremlin's assurance that her son would be provided with maximum opportunity for escape after completing his mission. Eitingon and Mercader then worked closely on the details of the plot. In Moscow, earlier, their NKVD overseers had reminded them that Trotsky had been reared in the early Leninist technique of attracting disciples mainly by intellectual persuasion. Hence, they encouraged Mercader now to adopt the stance of a confused but potential Trotskyite disciple. Trotsky presumably would rise to the bait.

He did. As the hoax was recalibrated during the summer of 1940, Mercader visited the Trotskys five more times, four of them with Sylvia but once alone. On each occasion, he feigned a gradual conversion to Trotsky's politics. Finally, in mid-August of 1940, when Mercader requested Trotsky to peruse the draft of an article he had written on "Communist theory," the latter readily agreed. When Mercader delivered the draft two days later, Trotsky suggested that he return at the end of the week, when they would discuss its contents.

The murder scenario itself, "Operation Duck," had been hatched in Moscow by Lavrenti Beria and approved personally by Stalin.⁶⁸ It was modeled on the recent assassination in Australia of a Soviet intelligence defector. The killer had used a steel bar to administer a single, surgical blow to the head of his

---

66 Patenaude, *Trotsky: Downfall*, 264–65.
67 Victor Serge and Natalia Sedova Trotsky, *Vie et Mort de Léon Trotsky* (Paris: Amiot Dumont, 1951), 36.
68 Patenaude, *Trotsky: Downfall*, 271; Levine, *The Mind of an Assassin*, 111.

victim. Once the plan had been related to Eitingon and then to Mercader, both men accepted it on the spot. They too assumed that a single blow with a steel bar would kill Trotsky instantly and silently, without giving him time to press the alarm button on his wall. Mercader would then leave Trotsky's office, leisurely stroll out of the house and enter his automobile to make his carefully prearranged escape. His initial destination would be a suburban air strip, where a private airplane and its pilot would be waiting. A false United States passport already had been prepared for him by the Communist apparat in the Mexican government. It was anticipated that, within hours, Mercader would be in a different country with yet a new name and nationality. No provision had been made for Sylvia.

On the late afternoon of August 20, Mercader drove off for his scheduled appointment with Trotsky. Although the sun was shining, he wore a raincoat. One of its pockets contained a *piolet*, a mountain-climber's ax. With its heavy wooden stock cut down for easy concealment and its seven-inch steel claw tempered to the sharpness of an ice pick, it was a formidable weapon. Mercader also carried a letter in his jacket, in the event he was captured, purporting to explain the motive for his impending deed. In this "confession," he claimed to be a disillusioned follower of Trotsky, who allegedly had solicited him to travel to the Soviet Union and arrange to assassinate Stalin. "For me," Mercader wrote, "this . . . was the last straw." The letter concluded with the assertion that "Sylvia Ageloff"—Mercader wrote her true name—had known nothing of his actual identity or purpose and that no guilt should be imputed to her.

Arriving at the Trotsky compound, Mercader entered the courtyard, where the guards casually waved him into the house. In the hall, Trotsky greeted him personally and ushered him into the study. It was then, as Trotsky opened his desk drawer to retrieve his visitor's draft article, that Mercader removed the *piolet* from his raincoat and brought it down full force onto Trotsky's head. But instead of slumping soundlessly to the floor, the aged but still wiry veteran of tsarist prisons, Siberian work gangs, and civil war gave a hoarse shout and threw himself at Mercader. In the house and adjoining guard tower, the shout was heard, together with the sounds of struggle. Natalia Sedova was the first to rush into the office, where she witnessed her husband staggering, blood streaming down his face. Behind her, an accompanying guard proceeded to flail at Mercader's head with the butt of his pistol, until the young Spaniard collapsed.

Within minutes of the attack, two ambulances and a police escort arrived to rush Trotsky, Natalia, and the unconscious Mercader to the "Green Cross" hospital, one of Mexico City's best equipped. X-rays there revealed that the elderly victim would need an immediate craniotomy, and neurosurgeons were promptly summoned to trepan his skull. But the ensuing surgery was

LEON TROTSKY DYING IN HOSPITAL AFTER THE ATTACK BY RAMÓN MERCADER, AUGUST 20, 1940

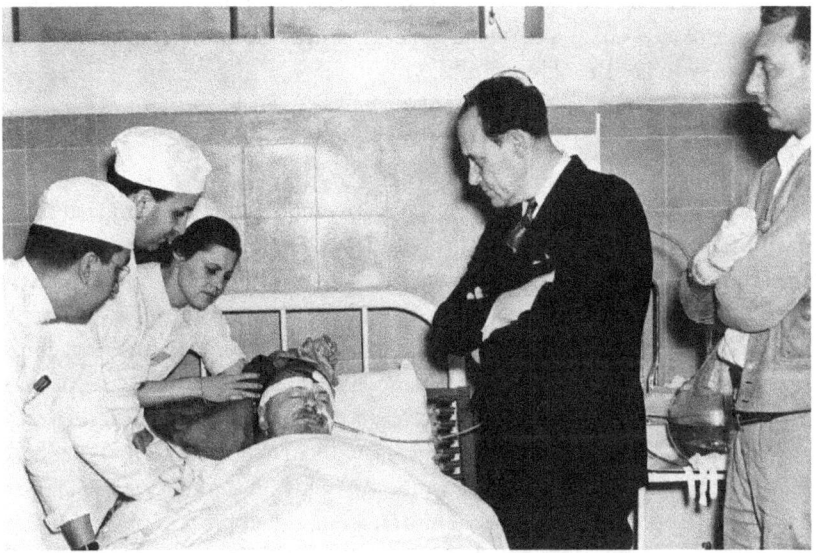

unsuccessful. Although Trotsky clung to life for another 26 hours, with Natalia uninterruptedly at his bedside in the emergency room, he expired in the late afternoon of August 21.

At 7:45 of the previous evening, Sylvia Ageloff received an urgent telephone call from one of Trotsky's guards, alerting her that a police car was en route to pick her up. She was given no further information until she was driven to the nearby station house. There, relating to her the events of the last few hours, the police booked her as an "accomplice." At that moment, Sylvia's world disintegrated. Hysterical, in and out of fainting spells, she was driven under guard to the hospital where Trotsky lay dying and, ironically, where the badly mauled Mercader was confined under police watch in a nearby recovery ward. Sylvia remained in the hospital for another two days of continual interrogation, until the police finally were convinced of her innocence.

Preparing to depart, however, she suddenly encountered Mercader as he was being wheeled from the recovery ward to a private room. Flinging herself at him, clawing his face before she was restrained, she screamed at the man she had known only as Jacques Mornard: "Scoundrel! Murderer!"—then to the police: "He is a Stalinist agent! He used me! Kill him! Kill him!"[69] Nine

---

69 Levine, *The Mind of an Assassin*, 129–30.

days later, still under police protection and intermittent sedation, Sylvia was driven to the border railroad depot of Brownsville, Texas, where she was escorted onto a train bound for Chicago, with an ensuing connection to New York. A broken woman, she traveled silently and alone on the two-and-a-half-day journey to her Brooklyn family.

## A POLITICAL POSTMORTEM

On August 26, when Mercader himself recovered enough to be moved from the hospital, he was transferred to Mexico City's highest-security prison. Subsequently, an interrogating magistrate required him to undergo extensive psychological examination. The process continued for no fewer than six months. During that time, Mercader said nothing of his sponsors or accomplices, or even of his true identity. Inasmuch as capital punishment in Mexico had long since been eliminated, a panel of judges sentenced Mercader to a 20-year term of imprisonment for murder, with an extra year for "false entry" into the country. But although he would serve his full sentence, the Stalinist *apparat* in the government assured him treatment of unprecedented leniency, including a spacious private cell, with its own bookshelf, radio, and record player, and meals prepared for him by nearby restaurants.

His mother was also the recipient of special consideration. On August 20, 1940, the afternoon of her son's attack on Trotsky, Caridad Mercader and Leonid Eitingon had been stationed down the street in different automobiles. It was then that the sirens of approaching ambulances and police cars alerted them that the murder scenario evidently had gone awry. They lost no time in racing off. With the help of the Communist network, both were smuggled out of the country by separate routes, Caridad by automobile to neighboring Guatemala, Eitingon by Soviet freighter directly from an Acapulco loading inlet to international waters and eventually to the Soviet Union.[70]

In late September, Caridad herself reached Moscow. Upon being driven to the Kremlin, she received a heroine's welcome. Lavrenti Beria personally escorted her to Stalin's office. Kissing Caridad's hand, the Soviet dictator then awarded her the Order of Lenin for her part in liquidating a dangerous enemy of the people. He followed the award with another for her son, "Hero of the Soviet Union," entrusting the medallion to Caridad's safekeeping until Mercader's release and promising that everything would be done to rescue him as soon as the circumstances of the war permitted (France recently had

---

70 Levine, *The Mind of an Assassin*, 131.

fallen to the Germans, and the Battle of Britain was raging). In the meanwhile, Caridad was given a private apartment and a pension, allowing her to live in Moscow in relative comfort.

It was not until 23 years later that she and her son were reunited. The meeting took place in June 1963, a year and a half after Mercader's release from prison. The site was Havana, the city of Caridad's birth and now of her son's newest home. Cuba's President Fidel Castro had welcomed him there and provided him with "honorary citizenship" and an apartment. An account of the family reunion is lacking, except that it was brief. Shortly afterward, Caridad relocated to Paris, where she lived with her daughter and the latter's family in their working-class apartment. Until her death seven years later, she neither saw nor mentioned her son again. Mercader himself died in 1978 and was cremated under his adopted name of "Ramón Ivanovich López." In 1990, the jar bearing his ashes was taken from its Havana locker, flown to Moscow, and interred in the city's Kuntsevo Cemetery, the resting place of Soviet heroes.[71]

In the non-Communist world, Leon Trotsky was consigned to the mists of history within months of his assassination. But neither before nor after the events of August 1940 was his extended family permitted the safety of anonymity. It is recalled that, of Trotsky's daughters by Alexandra Sokolovskaya, the elder, Zina, had committed suicide (p. 299). Zina's husband, Platon Volkov, who had been exiled to the Gulag, later was shot, as was Man Nevelson, the husband of Trotsky's younger daughter, Nina, who herself had succumbed to tuberculosis in 1928. In 1935, Sergei Sedov, Trotsky's younger son by Natalia Sedova, was arrested and sent to the notorious Vortuga work camp in the Arctic Circle, where he either died or was executed, probably in 1937. It was the Trotskys' older son, Liova, who perished mysteriously a year later outside Paris in an émigré Russian clinic.

The scythe of Stalin's relentlessness continued to swing widely. Trotsky's parents, David and Anna Bronshtein, had produced six children. Two of them had died in infancy; but three of the four survivors—Alexander, Elizaveta, and Olga—together with their spouses and offspring, also became Stalin's victims. Alexander was arrested in 1937 and shot in 1938. Trotsky's sister, Olga, who had been married briefly to the doomed Lev Kamenev, was arrested in 1935 and shot in 1941. Trotsky's younger sister Elizaveta died,

---

71 Slava Katamidze, *Loyal Comrades, Ruthless Killers: The Secret Services of the USSR, 1917–1991* (Miami, FL: Lewis International, 2003), 85.

apparently of natural causes; but her son, Lev, was exiled to Kazakhstan and died there in 1960.

The Stalinist purge continued into the second and third generations of Trotsky's family. Trotsky's grandson (also Lev) and his granddaughter Volina (the children of his younger daughter, Nina) simply disappeared after their mother's death, and their fate remains unknown. Another granddaughter, Alexandra (from his older daughter, Zina), was arrested in 1939 and exiled to Kazakhstan, where she died in mysterious circumstances at an unknown date. Trotsky's nephew, Boris, older son of his brother, Alexander, was shot in 1937. Alexander's younger son (again, Lev), died ten years later, after an extended term of Siberian imprisonment. Alexander's oldest daughter, Matilda, died in the Potlura concentration camp in 1952. His middle daughter, Evgenia, was exiled to Kazakhstan in 1946, where her fate remains unknown. His third and youngest daughter, Anna, similarly was arrested in 1946 and never heard from again. Alexander's grandson, Valeri, was arrested in 1948 and sentenced to exile in the Arctic labor camp of Kolyma, where he expired four years later.[72]

Only Trotsky's second wife, Natalia Sedova; his grandson Seva (the child of Zina); and his great-granddaughter Nora Volkova (the daughter of Zina's surviving child) managed to live out their lives in peaceful exile. Natalia eventually moved from Trotsky's Coyoacán villa to Paris in 1960, and died there two years later. Seva, the grandson, together with his subsequent wife and children, continued to reside in the same villa until his death in 1990.[73] In 1968, Nora Volkova emigrated from the Soviet Union to the United States, where she achieved a distinguished career as program director for neurology at the National Institutes of Health in Bethesda, Maryland.

Otherwise, in the elimination of individuals whom he regarded as active or potential threats to his authority, Stalin was fond of repeating the brusque aphorism, "no man, no problem," that he had adopted in Russia's civil war, when as commissar of supply in Ukraine he had ordered the mass execution of captured White soldiers. In the case of Leon Trotsky, the Soviet dictator's formula likely could have been extended: "No man, no woman, no children, no descendants or kin of any generation or degree—then, and *only* then, no problem."

---

72 Valery Bronstein, "Stalin and Trotsky's Relatives in Russia," in *A Trotsky Reappraisal*, ed. Terry Brotherstone and Paul Dukes (Edinburgh: Edinburgh University Press, 1992), 8–15; Montefiore, *Stalin: The Court of the Red Tsar*, 132–33.

73 Patenaude, *Trotsky: Downfall*, 295.

CHAPTER TEN

# Gallic *Fraternité* under Vichy's Armistice

*"I had been Georges Mandel's friend for thirty years....*
*His death was a great shock to me."*

## THE "TIGER'S CUB" DEFANGED

In the parliamentary elections of 1924, Georges Mandel lost his seat in the Chamber of Deputies. Temporarily exiling himself from Paris, he purchased a small newspaper in his Gironde constituency and devoted himself to editorializing, mainly on issues of foreign policy. But his hiatus from politics was brief. In 1928, standing again for the Gironde, Mandel succeeded in reclaiming his seat in the Chamber. He would never again relinquish it in peacetime. For all his characteristic hauteur and spleen, and his personal vulnerability as a Jew, his fellow deputies gave him their full attention whenever he took the floor, and specifically when he addressed them on matters of diplomacy and military security.[1]

---

1 Francisque Varenne, *Mon patron, Georges Mandel* (Paris: Editions Défense de la France, 1948), 140.

In 1934, the center-rightist Doumergue government was impressed enough by Mandel's *gravitas* to offer him his first cabinet portfolio, as minister of posts. He accepted this minor assignment as a necessary step toward the resuscitation of his former wartime eminence. Two years later, however, during the short-lived Sarraut premiership, Mandel's cabinet responsibilities were enlarged, allowing him to serve in the dual capacity of minister of posts and high commissioner of Alsace-Lorraine. Eventually, in 1938, for reasons of political "balance," Prime Minister Édouard Daladier awarded Mandel the colonial ministry in a reincarnated "Popular Front" government. The portfolio still was not quite in the front ranks. Nevertheless, Mandel was vigorous in his efforts to improve military intelligence in the empire and to recruit half a million additional native troops for the imperial army.[2]

By the spring and summer of 1938, too, as hostilities with Nazi Germany threatened to erupt over the Sudetenland, Mandel's admirers, aware of his indispensable wartime role under Clemenceau, regarded his cabinet presence as proof of governmental fortitude. Yet if they judged Mandel rightly, they judged the prime minister wrongly. Mandel was among the small minority of cabinet members who implored Daladier to stand firm against Hitler. Daladier chose instead to stand with Britain's Prime Minister Neville Chamberlain in surrendering the Sudetenland to the German Reich. It was only when news of the Hitler-Stalin Non-Aggression Pact reached Paris on August 23, 1939, and the entire nation sensed that war with Nazi Germany was imminent, that Daladier procrastinated no longer in ordering a general mobilization. But even when the German army invaded Poland on September 1, the prime minister waited a crucial 60 hours before acknowledging, along with Britain, that "a state of war exists." More ambivalently yet, once the German Wehrmacht overran Poland in a devastating, two-week "*Blitzkrieg*," the Allied armies responded with a timorous "*Sitzkrieg*" on the Western Front, a defense-oriented war of fixed positions and desultory, intermittent shelling.

Again it was Mandel, together with two of his cabinet colleagues, Paul Reynaud of the Democratic Alliance and Auguste Champetier de Ribes of the Christian Democrats, who implored Daladier and his military commanders to take the strategic initiative in the West before the Reich could absorb its territorial gains in Poland. "If we do not mount a full-scale offensive against the Germans while they are occupied in Poland," they warned, "we may never

---

2 Georges Catroux, *Deux actes du drame indochinois: Hanoï, juin 1940, Dien Bien Phu, mars–mai 1954* (Paris: Pion, 1959),146–48; Fred Kupferman, *Laval, 1883–1945* (Paris, Balland, 1987), 205.

again have such a chance."³ But once more Daladier's response was ambivalent. In March 1940, he proposed withdrawing troops from the Western Front altogether and dispatching them northward to assist beleaguered Finland, which was engaged in its "winter war" against the Soviet Union's invading armies. Although advocates of a Finnish rescue mission were not lacking, Daladier's trial balloon this time was too grotesque even for the most credulous of the Chamber's deputies. A majority of them voted their lack of confidence in him and, on March 20, replaced him with Paul Reynaud.

The new prime minister, a veteran and implacable foe of Nazism, swiftly and decisively patched together a coalition government of Socialists, Radical Socialists, and two smaller center-rightist parties. After installing his new cabinet, Reynaud flew to London where he signed an agreement with Neville Chamberlain pledging their governments to wage a war of active partnership, and, under no circumstances to conclude a separate peace with Germany. Both prime ministers also agreed to impose an immediate naval blockade of Norwegian waters, with the aim of precluding German access to vital supplies of Norwegian iron ore. On April 9, however, within ten days of the incipient naval blockade, the Allied operation was preempted by the Nazi Wehrmacht's land invasion of Norway and the capture of the iron mines themselves. The ruthless German masterstroke against a neutral country was almost instantly followed by a larger and even more decisive offensive, one that had been in preparation for at least five months. It encompassed the invasion of the Dutch Netherlands, Belgium, and, ultimately, of France itself.

Until the German spring offensive of 1940, the French army was reputed to be the finest in the world. In fact, the reputation was undeserved. Obsessed with memories of the human sacrifices of the previous war, the French military commander, General Maurice Gamelin, and most of his senior staff were committed to a strategy of defense and fixed lines of combat, with dependence specifically on the reticulation of underground fortresses that comprised the "Maginot Line." By contrast, the Wehrmacht's strategists had embraced the doctrine of rapid armored movement. They had detected a potentially exploitable invasion route. This was the hilly, wooded terrain of the Ardennes Forest, a sector that the French military leadership had dismissed as impassable for a modern army and that they had not bothered to fortify. The German strategy was vindicated. In early May, in a swift and

---

3 John M. Sherwood, *Georges Mandel and the Third Republic* (Stanford, CA: Stanford University Press, 1970), 225.

pulverizing blitzkrieg into the Belgian Netherlands, the Nazi Wehrmacht then imaginatively and preemptively maneuvered its main force of tanks through the undefended Ardennes. The flank assault took the French high command by almost total surprise. Fanning out behind the Maginot Line, the Wehrmacht's armored columns proceeded to create havoc in the Allied rear. By the third week in May, there appeared little to stop them as they drove southwestward toward Paris.

## THE WAGES OF DEFEAT

On May 28, 1940, still unshaken in his determination to blunt the onrushing German offensive, Prime Minister Reynaud restructured his cabinet. Taking over the defense ministry himself, he awarded Mandel the latter's first major portfolio, the ministry of the interior. It was the closest approximation of the role Mandel had played 23 years before, when he had served as Clemenceau's chef de cabinet. In his element now, Mandel did not hesitate to arrest former ligue crypto-fascists, closing their newspapers and offices with the same remorselessness that he had displayed in 1917–18. In turn, responding to his decisiveness of purpose, many even of his former political enemies now closed ranks behind him.

Elsewhere in Reynaud's cabinet configuration, however, the prime minister committed a fatal miscalculation, one that soon vitiated his strenuous political and inter-Allied diplomacy. Just a few days earlier, intending to stiffen the nation's morale, he announced that he was appointing as his deputy prime minister Marshal Henri-Philippe Pétain, the renowned World War I "hero of Verdun." Simultaneously, he replaced General Maurice Gamelin as military chief of staff with General Maxime Weygand, who, as commander of French occupation forces in the Levant, had broken a 1925 Syrian guerrilla insurrection. In 1940, Pétain was 84. Weygand was 73. Their appointments and hesitant "containment strategy" exerted no inhibiting effect whatever on the Nazi juggernaut. Rather, German armored columns by then were converging on Paris, and Albert Lebrun, president of the Republic, was speculating openly about the prospect of a separate peace with Germany. In an emergency meeting of the reformulated cabinet, Pétain and Weygand were the first to translate the president's "speculation" into unambiguous defeatism. On May 28, Pétain sent Reynaud a private note, questioning the wisdom of the prime minister's commitment to fight on at the side of Britain. It was a reservation that the old marshal shared the same afternoon in a private meeting with General Edward Spears, Britain's military liaison to the French government. Indeed, in early June, General Weygand ordered a general withdrawal of French detachments along the Channel to protect Paris, but the new "Weygand Line" began to come apart despite stiff French resistance. Then, on June 10, Italy's Mussolini government, sensing the opportunity of territorial spoils, declared war on France, and Reynaud promptly ordered his own senior government officials to begin decamping from Paris to Bordeaux. During the transfer, the panicked cabinet ministers urgently debated the question of an armistice; and, by the time they regrouped in Bordeaux on June 13, Marshal Pétain had won a majority of them over to his position: that only a termination of hostilities could salvage the French nation and avoid civil disorder. Even at that late date, however, and notwithstanding Pétain's defeatism, Reynaud pleaded with his colleagues to heed the offer of Winston Churchill, who on May 7 had succeeded Neville Chamberlain as British prime minister. It was to accept a functional "act of union" that would share imperial resources between France and England in a fight to the death against Hitler. Yet, with the exception of the cabinet's three die-hards—Mandel, Champetier de Ribes, and Reynaud himself—the ministers shot the proposal down sine die.

On June 16, moreover, Pétain dramatically announced his "resignation" as vice-premier. The move was transparently designed to force Reynaud's hand, and it succeeded. With his political leverage gone, the premier submitted his own resignation within hours and disconsolately advised President Lebrun to offer the prime ministry to Pétain himself. When Lebrun complied, Pétain unhesitatingly accepted. The next day, even before taking office, the "hero of Verdun" requested the intercession of the Spanish embassy in seeking armistice terms from Germany. Berlin's answer came two days later. Its conditions were rigorous but appeared initially to be less than draconian. Both governments agreed that the details would shortly be clarified between military delegations of the two countries.

The meeting took place on June 22 at the town of Rethondes, in the Compiègne forest. Hitler had chosen the site personally. Twenty-two years before, on November 11, 1918 (p. 77), in the same Compiègne forest, sitting in his private rail carriage, Marshal Ferdinand Foch had dictated armistice terms to the German high command. Now, at Hitler's orders, German engineers trundled the same rail carriage from its nearby museum pavilion for use in the current meeting. After dancing his famously photographed victory jig, the Führer then sat in on the conference briefly to savor the Reich's moment of vengeance before exiting the carriage, leaving his officers and their Italian counterparts to dictate terms to the French military delegation.

The terms were harsher than they had originally appeared. Alsace-Lorraine would revert to Germany. The Pas-de-Calais area on the English Channel also

## OCCUPIED AND VICHY FRANCE

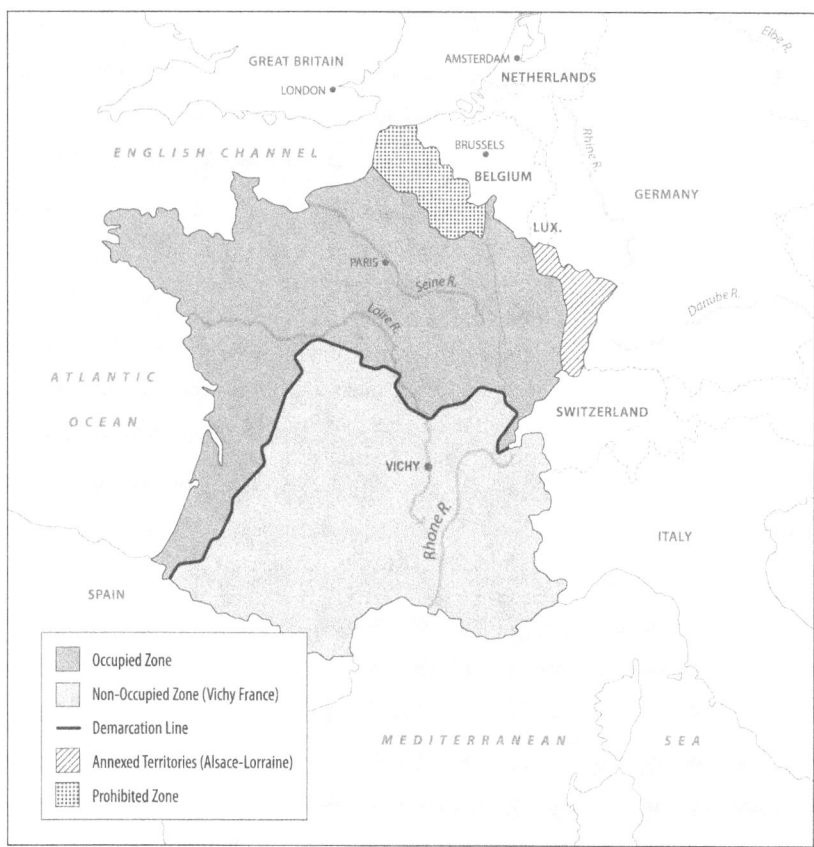

would be ceded to German occupation. Otherwise, "integral" France would be divided into a northern "occupied zone," encompassing some three-fifths of the country, including Paris and most of the Atlantic coast, as well as virtually all of the nation's richer, industrialized sectors. The "unoccupied zone," in turn, would comprise the remaining two-fifths of France, essentially the southeastern part of the country, and manifestly would serve Hitler as a guarantee of French ongoing passivity both in the remainder of geographical France and in the French overseas empire. In theory, the laws promulgated by the French government in the unoccupied zone would apply to the whole of territorial and imperial France. In practice, however, German military headquarters in the occupied zone would carve out increasingly larger areas of their "administrative authority."

That authority was geographical, to include strategic sectors reserved exclusively for German military rule, and economic, to administer the collection from the French population of a huge "reparations" debt (estimated initially at 400 million francs a day), as well as an additional sum—as yet unspecified—to cover the expense of provisioning the German occupying forces. The government of the unoccupied zone would be allowed a token army of 100,000 men (by no coincidence, the limit allowed Germany under the 1919 Treaty of Versailles). The fate of almost 1.3 million French prisoners of war, however, would be left to "future negotiations" (similarly unspecified) on a permanent Franco-German peace treaty; in fact, the Germans left the fate of both the prisoners and peace negotiations undefined to guarantee French quietude both in the unoccupied zone and in the empire. Meanwhile, if there were redeeming features in the otherwise inflexible armistice terms, one was that Hitler's ally, Mussolini, was comparatively modest in Italy's claims. These were limited to an Italian presence in a 50-mile-wide armistice zone, essentially in the French Riviera. The other redeeming feature was the latitude reserved for the France's empire and navy.

## IMPERIAL FRANCE AND THE ORDEAL OF GEORGES MANDEL

Even before the French military delegation set out for Rethondes, on the morning of June 22, Marshal Pétain instructed General Charles Huntziger, the delegation's chairman, immediately to break off negotiations with the Germans if the latter should demand control either of the empire or the navy. But in fact the German delegation had no intention of issuing these demands. Hitler and his advisors were well aware that the Reich possessed neither the sea power to gain access to France's overseas possessions nor the civilian or military personnel to govern terrain of such magnitude and diversity. Neither could Germany effectively lay claim to the French navy, most of which was kenneled in French North African ports. It was more practicable to let these ships remain under the "sovereignty" of France's unoccupied zone. Pétain presumably would not take the risk of turning them over to Britain's Royal Navy, if only for fear of German retaliation against metropolitan France.

Yet, even before Pétain ascended to the premiership and almost to the eve of the Rethondes armistice, some members of the French parliament had indeed contemplated evacuating the nation's remaining army divisions to North Africa and carrying on the war from there, in tandem with the British. This had been Winston Churchill's urgent plea to Reynaud, and subsequently to Pétain. Reynaud needed no persuasion to accept. Neither did some three dozen members of the French parliament. But their reaction was not that of the despondent parliamentary majority, and surely not of Pétain, who rejected the proposal out of hand. Three days before taking over the premiership, the marshal had warned the nation that a cabinet-in-exile might lose all control of metropolitan France, and most of the deputies had agreed.

Provisionally, however, the cabinet decided on June 17 to authorize President Lebrun's "visitation" to Morocco, together with senior members of parliament and the civil service, as a symbol of France's ongoing imperial rule. At first, Pétain accepted the decision; but, two days later, he had second thoughts, and unilaterally ordered the police to block the departure of all but a selective minority—29 members—of the prospective delegation. Except for Lebrun, the latter included men known to be active or potential "militants." It was evident that Pétain wanted them out of the country before the onset of armistice talks with the Germans.

One of these parliamentarians was Georges Mandel. After the original German breakthrough at the Ardennes, Mandel proved more obdurate even than Reynaud in pressing for continuation of the war, if necessary from North Africa. Indeed, on June 14, at an emergency cabinet meeting at Bordeaux, it was Mandel alone who opposed the very notion of an armistice. Two days later, when Reynaud—still prime minister—received a final, emergency telephone call from Churchill in London, restating the latter's offer of political union between France and Britain, the proposal was again brought before the French cabinet. This time, the ministers disdained even to table the offer. Their reaction brought Mandel to his feet. "There are present," he stated acidly, "two sorts of men: the brave and the cowardly."[4] He demanded then that each minister stand up and be counted: for or against the armistice. But his proposal met with jeers, catcalls, even epithets. It was thus at 10:00 p.m. of the same evening that the despairing Reynaud submitted his resignation, and almost immediately afterward that President Lebrun offered the premiership to Pétain himself.

Moreover, upon replacing Reynaud, Pétain made it his first order of business to remove Mandel from the cabinet and to have the latter's makeshift office surrounded by police. The next morning, June 17, Pétain went further, ordering Mandel's arrest, ostensibly for preparing a "coup d'état." Only the shocked intercession of President Lebrun persuaded the marshal to countermand his order. Ironically, just the day before, Britain's military liaison officer, General Edward Spears, was preparing to fly back from Bordeaux to England,

---

4 Mandel's speech is available in *L'Illustration*, nos. 5117–5129, 656.

and he begged Mandel to accompany him. Mandel declined in words that Spears would never forget: "General, I am grateful for your concern," he answered. "You fear for me because I am a Jew. Well, it is just because I am a Jew that I will not go with you tomorrow. It would be interpreted as an act of cowardice, as if I were running away."[5]

If Mandel was prepared to "escape," it was not to England but to French Morocco, together with the small minority of parliamentary deputies and government officials who evidently shared his resolution to continue the war from the empire. Thus, he joined the other 28 passengers in boarding the packet boat *Massilia* at the harbor of Port Vendres. The ship weighed anchor on June 21. It was only when the little group was well out to sea that its members discovered that Pétain and his remaining cabinet had made the irretrievable decision to seek an armistice. Yet, even then, the *Massilia* passengers had confidence that General Charles Noguès, the resident general of French Morocco and a much-decorated World War I veteran, would support their efforts to continue military resistance. But, arriving in Casablanca three days later, they learned to their dismay that Pétain had cabled Noguès to abide by the Rethondes armistice, and the resident general had obeyed.

At Pétain's orders, too, Noguès dispatched a police contingent to "escort" Mandel from the *Massilia* to the nearby Moroccan resort town of Ifranc, where he was placed under house arrest. The other passengers were shielded from the knowledge that Pétain, regarding Mandel as the principal threat to his defeatist cabinet, was stripping him of his parliamentary immunity. Indeed, as part of its subterfuge, the government at first kept the other passengers on ship, under the pretext that the newly appointed German armistice commission had forbidden the *Massilia* to return. But, on July 8, Pétain cabled Noguès "to begin judicial proceedings against 'X' [Mandel] at the Permanent Court at Casablanca [on charges of treason]. As soon as the session of Parliament [in France] is closed, the case can be changed into one naming Mandel expressly."[6] Three days later, on July 11, with Mandel in internment and the brief, intervening session of parliament over (p. 338), Pétain ordered that the other *Massilia* passengers be returned to France, where they could be more closely watched. Only Mandel would stay behind.

In the second week of July, Mandel's overseas trial began in the military court of Meknès. But to the government's consternation, the assigned prosecutor, Colonel Henri Loireau, soon discerned no credible evidence of treason

---

5 Benjamin F. Martin, *France in 1938* (Baton Rouge, Louisiana State University Press, 2006), 221.
6 Sherwood, *Georges Mandel*, 264.

or of any other crime against the defendant. Loireau then petitioned Noguès for Mandel's release. Instead, summarily rejecting the petition, the resident general ordered Mandel to be kept under house arrest pending "further investigations." The trial then was resumed on July 26. Once more, Mandel was charged with plotting against the security of France. This time, too, the Pétain government began organizing a widespread press campaign against him, denouncing him as an "arch-deserter." But again Colonel Loireau interrupted the court proceedings. A latter-day Georges Picquart (the intelligence officer who had famously championed Dreyfus's innocence in fin-de-siècle France), Loireau insisted that, in good conscience, he could not continue the prosecution. Moreover, on September 7, in a breathtaking act of defiance, he cabled Pétain that he was officially dismissing all charges against the defendant.

Before Mandel could be set free, however, or Loireau brought to heel, the Pétain government dispatched a special police contingent to Morocco by airplane. Mandel was immediately rearrested, carried off to the Casablanca airport, and flown back to metropolitan France. On September 10, he was transported under guard to Bourasel, a small town in the province of Clermont-Ferrand in unoccupied France, where he was placed in "administrative internment" in the Château de Chazeron. Together with seven other senior government figures, he would await trial in the nearby town of Riom on charges of engaging in a "plot against France."

## THE MARSHAL AND "REBORN" FRANCE

Whatever Henri-Philippe Pétain's temperament or political ideology, during his long life he could not have been accused of personal careerism. Although he had served as war minister in the Doumergue government after the Stavisky riots of February 1934 (pp. 277–78), he would not allow his name to be submitted for the presidential elections of the 1930s. In March 1939, for reasons of simple patriotic duty, he had accepted appointment as France's ambassador to Spain, where he was considered likely to improve his country's relations with the Franco government. In May 1940, patriotism was similarly his impulsion in accepting Reynaud's invitation to serve as vice-premier and, subsequently, in accepting the premiership itself. Indeed, Pétain was far from oblivious to the aura his reputation as the "hero of Verdun" projected among an entire generation of Frenchmen. On June 17, as he entered office and announced over the radio that he was bestowing upon his country "the gift of my person," his listeners experienced a profound sense of reassurance. To them, the marshal was a revered father figure, the quintessence of all France's martial and civic virtues.

There is little evidence that the 84-year-old Pétain was senile. It is incontestable, however, that he was an arch-reactionary. His political philosophy reflected that of Barrès and Bainville (pp. 267, 285), although he himself had only cursory acquaintance with the inner politics of the Action Française. During the 1930s, the Stavisky affair had increased Pétain's distaste for the fractious parliamentarianism of republican government. By the time World War II began, he had begun to advocate a merger of the powers of the prime minister and the president. Yet, even then, Pétain's "integral" and decidedly Catholic view of the state reduced itself essentially to his favored aphorism, soon to be the triptych of his regime: "travail, famille, patrie." In the summer of 1940, the people of France, without necessarily understanding the full implications of Pétain's homely maxim, trusted him more than any other of the nation's public figures, and continued to do so almost unquestioningly during the first two years of his governance.

Consequently, Pétain faced little organized opposition as he set about forming a cabinet. With few exceptions, his choices were archetypes of the Right, although, initially, two of his most trusted and influential counselors did not hold senior portfolios. These were Raphaël Alibert, a former professor of constitutional law, a royalist, and a secret member of the Cagoule (p. 290), whom Pétain appointed minister of justice, and Dr. Bernard Ménétral, Pétain's personal physician, who functioned in effect as the marshal's private secretary, although soon he was given the ceremonial rank of deputy minister of state. As confirmed a reactionary as Alibert, Ménétral was invested with the power to screen all the marshal's visitors. Even Pierre Laval, as "minister of state"—in effect, deputy prime minister—deferred at first to these éminences grises.

It was only when his cabinet was in place and when the armistice negotiations at Rethondes were completed that Pétain's government moved on from its temporary venue in Bordeaux to the resort town of Vichy, in the département of Auvergne. Renowned for its natural springs, its gracious parks and buildings, its gambling casinos, its modern telephone system, and its numerous hotels (including the Park Hotel, which Pétain chose as the headquarters of his executive offices), Vichy was a natural and comfortable choice as administrative center of the new unoccupied zone. It could have functioned as the site for a permanent French parliament, as well; but on July 10, pressed by Alibert and Laval, Pétain hesitated no longer in revealing the kind of government he envisaged for "reborn France." As more than 600 deputies and senators descended on Vichy and took their seats in the town's Grand Casino, Pierre Laval, on Pétain's behalf, delivered the address that would establish the raison d'être of unoccupied France.

Citing the disastrous "shortsightedness" of the republican government in declaring war and the "treachery" of France's British ally, the minister of state warmed to the government's central theme. This was the innate fragility and corruptibility of parliamentary democracy and the urgent need for its replacement. In the name of the government, Laval then proposed that the assembled dignitaries surrender their legislative powers to Marshal Pétain. The latter henceforth would bear the title "Head of State." At a later date, Laval suggested, the nation's deputies and senators would be called back into session to vote a new constitution; but for the present, he asked them to approve the fundamentals of a "reborn" France. This they did, by a vote of 569 to 80 (and 17 abstentions).[7] In fact, the "new constitution" was never promulgated, and parliament never reconvened. Government, in effect, was directed afterward by a "National Council," its members appointed by the marshal. All appointees were obliged to take their oath of allegiance to Pétain as "Head of State." Thus perished France's Third Republic.

In historical perspective, the vote for the reconfigured new government was less an endorsement of ideological fascism than a gesture of pragmatic support for Pétain's effort to seek a bearable accommodation with Germany. Indeed, the resolution might not have passed at all, except for a tragic event that took place just the week before. Britain's Prime Minister Winston Churchill, intent on blocking the Pétain government from wilting under Hitler's pressure and dispatching the French fleet for "internment" to German-designated ports, had resolved on a drastic measure. Its full implications became clear at 6:00 a.m. on July 3. It was then that a British naval task force, dispatched from Gibraltar two days earlier, steamed out of the morning mist to within firing range of the Algerian port of Mers-el-Kebir, the largest naval base in the French Empire. There, the British commander, Vice Admiral Sir James Somerville, signaled an ultimatum to his French counterpart: British marines were to be allowed on board the base's capital ships to deactivate the latter's firing mechanisms. Afterward, the vessels would be escorted to the French West Indies, to remain there under British naval supervision for the ensuing course of the war.

Alerted by cable to the ultimatum, Pétain and his ministers rejected it out of hand. When the rejection was transmitted to Mers-el-Kebir and then to Somerville, the consequences were grim. The British flotilla proceeded to launch an avalanche of shells and torpedoes against the main battleships and cruisers of the French navy, sinking most of them and inflicting a loss of

---

7 James Shields, *The Extreme Right in France: From Pétain to Le Pen* (New York: Routledge, 2007), 17.

approximately 1,300 French personnel. In his subsequent address to parliament, Laval's enraged response to the tragedy was to declare that "France has never had, and never will have, a more treacherous enemy than Great Britain."[8] The assembled legislators greeted his remarks with tumultuous applause.

Indeed, by mid-summer of 1940, the reaction of the nation at large had shifted in its appraisal both of France's past alliances and its future priorities. The "Cult of the Marshal" was increasingly and extensively embraced, and Pétain's agenda for a "National Revolution" was accepted by large elements of the population, in the occupied and unoccupied zones alike. That agenda was devoted essentially to a restoration of the "Gallic certitudes"—Catholic, pietistic, agrarian—of royalist France. Traditional Catholic education now became mandatory. Labor unions were banned. Persons suspected of Freemasonry or even of vaguely leftist political allegiances were removed from government employment, from the school system, or from any other public position. The "National Revolution," in sum, repudiated all the "moral delinquencies" of modern French history, those that ostensibly had led to the recent military catastrophe. It should have come as no surprise that Charles Maurras hailed the program as a "divine surprise" or that the papal nuncio described it as the "Pétain miracle" (choosing to overlook the marshal's marriage to a divorced woman). Above all, it was the French people in their millions who evidently supported Pétain in his self-proclaimed role as leader of the nation's "moral recovery."

## A "POWER BEHIND THE THRONE"

By contrast, a "national revolution" or any other variety of "moral recovery" almost certainly was not the guiding motif of Pierre Laval. From the beginning to the end of his Vichy career, the minister of state/vice-premier was obsessed with a single goal. It was to develop a functional strategy for sparing France the worst ravages of German occupation. In the effort, Laval brought with him a lifetime of experience as political and diplomatic negotiator. Although only 57 years old in the summer of 1940, he had been a prime minister twice, a foreign minister three times, and the holder of four other cabinet portfolios, as well as—intermittently—a seat in the Chamber or Senate for 22 years. In private life, he had developed one of the most successful law practices in the nation; and, whether in or out of parliament, his reputation as a political deal maker was legendary.

---

8 Henri Michel, *Vichy: Année 40* (Paris, Robert Laffont, 1966), 226.

Laval's beginnings were modest. Born in the village of Châteldon, in the Auvergne region of central France, he was the son of a butcher who doubled as an innkeeper. His mother possibly was of North African extraction. Dark of skin and heavy-lidded, she transmitted her features to her children. Although Laval worked with his father after school, he studied hard and achieved a creditable record at lycée and, subsequently, at the University of Lyon's faculty of law. In 1909, he passed the national bar examination. By then, he had a married a woman of upper-middle-class background, to whom he remained faithful for the rest of his life. Laval also had joined the Socialist Party, and, as a matter of principle, he opened his first office in a working-class district of Paris. There, notwithstanding his slovenly, tobacco-stained appearance, the young lawyer quickly built a solid practice among trade-union clients.

In 1914, at the age of 30, Laval was himself elected to the Chamber of Deputies from the département of the Seine. A few months later, as a committed pacifist, he refused to vote for mobilization when the World War broke out, and in 1917 he joined the international group of socialist pacifists that traveled to Stockholm to vote in favor of a peace resolution. Indeed, by then, Laval's horror of the ongoing battlefield carnage transcended his socialist principles. His brother-in-law had been killed in action, together with eight members of his extended family. It was French security afterward that remained his guiding obsession. Thus, at the postwar French Socialist Party (SFIO) Congress at Tours in 1920, when a majority of the delegates voted to join the Soviet-dominated Third International and create the French Communist Party (PCF), Laval resigned his membership.

Subsequently, as he drifted to the political center and his law practice and personal business investments began to flourish, Laval's clients and admirers elected him mayor of Aubervilliers, a town that would remain his political base for the rest of his career. Under French law, these "extracurricular" local responsibilities did not preclude membership in the Chamber of Deputies, or even in the national cabinet. Hence, in 1925, Laval became minister of public works in the center-leftist Painlevé government. Later the same year, he was appointed undersecretary of state in the government of the renowned internationalist, Aristide Briand, the architect of the 1925 Locarno treaties (p. 243) and a statesman whose adroitness Laval much admired. The respect was mutual, for Laval himself had fashioned the treaties' language. Indeed, even as Briand delighted in the title of "poet of peace," he generously identified his undersecretary as the "engineer of peace." Afterward, Laval won equivalent praise as a master craftsmen of domestic legislation. In 1930, as minister of labor in the government of the avowedly right-wing André Tardieu, he brilliantly guided the premier's social-insurance program through both houses of parliament.

With these multiple achievements, Laval emerged almost inevitably, after the fall of the Tardieu cabinet in December 1930, as the center-rightists' compromise choice for the prime ministry. Assuming office in January 1931 (after the short-lived Théodore Steeg cabinet), he held the premiership for the ensuing 13 months, by then something of a record on the nation's fractious political scene. Ironically, it was an issue of foreign policy—Laval's favored métier—that unseated his government. He had exerted much energy in attempting to preempt German rearmament by proposing a general European disarmament treaty. In effect, the initiative was Laval's signature project in international relations. But, in January 1932, at a League of Nations–sponsored disarmament conference in Geneva, the Germans rejected his plan, and the Chamber then denied him a vote of confidence. Soon afterward, Laval returned to private life—and to private compensation. For the next two years, devoting himself to his business career, he succeeded in accumulating valuable properties in real estate (including a luxurious home for his family in his native village of Châteldon), as well as two newspapers and a radio station. Indeed, by 1934, in the depths of the Depression, Laval had emerged as one of France's most successful entrepreneurs.

It was the sequence of "events" in February 1934—the Stavisky affair, the ensuing mass riots, and the fall of the Chautemps government (pp. 277–78)—that brought Laval back to the cabinet. Characteristically, it was he who masterminded Gaston Doumergue's "national coalition." Yet he returned to the center of France's political scene as foreign minister only after the assassination of Foreign Minister Louis Barthou, in October 1934 (pp. 270–71). By then, Hitler had come to power in Germany, and Prime Minister Doumergue and the Chamber of Deputies understood well that a man of Laval's negotiating skills was needed in a more sustained effort to block German militarism and expansionism. In that effort, Laval fully matched the late Barthou in his preoccupation with containment diplomacy. Unlike Barthou, however, who had laid emphasis on strengthened relations with the "Little Entente" of successor states, Laval concentrated upon striking a deal with Italy and Britain. To that end, in December 1934, exploiting Mussolini's alarmed reaction to Hitler's recent putsch attempt against Austria (pp. 221–30), Laval negotiated a secret understanding with the Duce. Under its terms, France would send troops to support Italy if Hitler renewed his aggression against Austria, and Mussolini would provide air support to France if Germany attempted to reoccupy the Rhineland.

In March 1935, when Hitler, in flagrant defiance of the Versailles Treaty, announced the reintroduction of military conscription in Germany, Laval reacted with determination and imagination. Within the month, he succeeded in negotiating the "Stresa Front" both with Italy and Britain, an agreement for the three governments to "consult with each other" if Germany violated the earlier, 1925, Treaty of Locarno (in which the signatories had pledged mutual nonaggression). Indeed, the "Stresa Front" may have represented postwar European diplomacy at its most vigorous and decisive. So, too, did Laval's visit to Geneva later that same April, where he elicited the League Council's unanimous condemnation of Germany for its violation of its treaty obligations. And so, not least of all, did his ensuing trip to Moscow in early May 1935, where he persuaded the Soviet government to join France in a tripartite agreement with Czechoslovakia to "consult" together in the event of German aggression in Eastern Europe. It was accordingly in tribute to Laval's impressive statecraft that the National Assembly invited him to return to the prime ministry in June 1935.

It was a rather briefer premiership than his first, however. In October 1935, Mussolini launched his long-threatened invasion of Ethiopia. The Duce's palpable aberration from the spirit of the "Stresa Front" was an acute embarrassment to Laval, as it was to Britain's Foreign Secretary Samuel Hoare. Nevertheless, unwilling to give up on the Italian connection, Laval and Hoare hastened to confer in Paris in December and to devise a "compromise" offer to Mussolini that would acknowledge Italy's de facto hegemony over the largest part of Ethiopia. The tentative deal leaked. In an uproar over a proposal that, in effect, rewarded Italy's act of naked aggression, Britain's House of Commons forced Hoare's resignation. In France's Chamber of Deputies, Laval's own resignation followed in January 1936. Although retaining his parliamentary seat, the ex-premier afterward returned to his private business affairs, noting bitterly to his colleagues: "This Chamber vomited me up. The next time France is confronted by a similar crisis, I'm going to vomit it up."[9]

Even out of the cabinet, however, Laval did not remain silent on issues of foreign policy. In September 1938, when Britain's Prime Minister Chamberlain and France's Prime Minister Daladier betrayed Czechoslovakian security at Munich, wilting before Nazi Germany's annexation of the Sudetenland, Laval was scalding in his denunciation of the two Allied statesmen. The consequence he foresaw came to pass only too quickly. In March 1939, Hitler

---

9 Paul Baudouin, *Neuf moir au government: avril–décembre, 1940* Paris: Éditions de La Table Ronde, 1948), 219.

annexed the remaining Bohemian heartland of Czechoslovakia. As Laval warned Foreign Minister Georges Bonnet, the abandonment of the Czechs, with their impressive mountain fortifications and well-equipped army, made the defense of neighboring Poland a military impossibility; and France should at all costs refrain from entering a war against Germany in a "hopeless" endeavor. Four years later, in November 1943, he would remind a group of French mayors: "I did not want war.... A nation must fight only when it is attacked. In 1939 we were not attacked.... It was untenable to fight for the Polish Corridor or Danzig."[10]

If the war that Laval had desperately feared became a reality in September 1939, so too did the military defeat that he similarly had predicted. In late May of 1940, when the Battle of France approached its climax, Laval raced by automobile from his family retreat at Châteldon for Bordeaux. Over his wife's objections, he was intent on reentering the government, unseating Prime Minister Reynaud in favor of Marshal Pétain, and then taking its administration in hand and speedily terminating the war. By the time Laval arrived in Bordeaux on June 14, however, he learned that Reynaud was contemplating a transfer of government to French North Africa and continuing the war from overseas. It was not to be, of course (p. 334). The cabinet rejected the notion, and it was two days later that Reynaud himself resigned in favor of Pétain. The marshal forthwith submitted his list of potential ministers to President Lebrun. Laval was on the list, tentatively penciled in as minister of justice. In fact, this was not the portfolio that Laval, as a two-time former prime minister, had in mind. He declined the offer, waiting for Pétain to reconsider. His wait was not long.

On June 20, while the terms of a proposed armistice were being discussed, Reynaud, out of power but still a member of the French cabinet, once again raised the proposal of transferring the government to North Africa. At that moment Laval burst into the room with his entourage of supporters and launched an impassioned denunciation of a "government in exile," let alone a continuation of the war.[11] The nation's priority, he insisted, was to win an "honorable" peace and then to work for a tolerable "coexistence" with Germany. Pétain and most of the equally dispirited cabinet members did not have to be convinced. Two days later, when the ministers received and accepted to Hitler's Rethondes armistice terms, Pétain asked Laval to

---

10 Pierre Laval, "Discours du 9 novembre 1943 aux maires du Cantal à Vichy," in *Les discourse de Pierre Laval, 1942–1944* (Paris: Fondation José et René Chambrun, 1999), 124–27.

11 Jacques Benoist-Méchin, *À l'épreuve du temps: Souvenirs*, vol. 2, *1940–1947* (Paris: Julliard, 1989), 428.

assume the portfolio of minister of state, a title that shortly would be changed to vice-premier and combined with that of foreign minister. This time, Laval accepted.

Two weeks later, once the government transferred itself to Vichy, Laval completed the speech that he would present to parliament on July 10. Although delivered in the marshal's name, the address in effect was Laval's personal blueprint for abolishing France's democratic constitution and establishing in its stead a kind of latter-day version of the French Revolutionary Directorate. Nothing less, Laval emphasized, would keep the nation alive under the Nazi heel. To his critics, he noted that "[w]e are paying today for the fetish that chained us to democracy . . . while around us, and leaving us behind, Europe was forging a new world inspired by new principles."[12] It was a declaration that eventually would come back to haunt Laval and seal his fate.

## IN QUEST OF FRANCO-GERMAN "PARTNERSHIP"

In common with Pétain and others of the marshal's advisers, Laval assumed that the Vichy administration was essentially a staging post in the government's way back to a redeemed if somewhat attenuated France, with Paris again as its capital.[13] Thus, in his diplomacy, the vice-premier devoted his principal efforts to a relaxation of the occupation, to the release of French prisoners of war, and, most important, to the formulation of a peace treaty that would relieve France of the incubus of prolonged German interference in the nation's internal affairs. To achieve these multiple objectives, however, Laval first had to identify his likeliest German interlocutor. He soon found his man in Otto Abetz, the personal representative in Paris of German Foreign Minister Joachim von Ribbentrop.

Only 37 years old, Abetz was already an experienced French hand. A gymnasium art teacher in his native Karlsruhe, near Mannheim, and a profound admirer of French culture, the young francophile in the late 1920s and early 1930s had enthusiastically arranged meetings between French and German youth organizations. It was at one of these that he met and married a French girl. In 1934, Ribbentrop appointed Abetz director of the French section of the foreign ministry's research and information bureau. Six years later, in June 1940, the foreign minister sent Abetz back to Paris, first as his

---

12   Geoffrey Warner, *Pierre Laval and the Eclipse of France* (London: Eyre & Spottiswoode, 1968), 206–9.
13   For general introduction to Vichy period, see Robert O. Paxton, *Vichy France: Old Guard and New Order, 1940–1944* (New York: Knopf, 1972).

"personal representative" but shortly afterward as ambassador to unoccupied France. Keeping offices both in Paris and Vichy, Abetz in fact bore wide responsibility for dealing with all political questions in both occupied and unoccupied France.

Laval found Abetz congenial, and the younger man in turn was impressed by Laval, who struck him as a "canny Auvergnoit" and a "true French patriot."[14] After several appeals to Berlin, Abetz won permission for Laval to travel across the sealed frontier to Paris. Over the ensuing weeks, as Abetz wined and dined Laval, the two men developed a productive working relationship. It was in early August 1940, in an extended conversation, that Laval put his cards on the table. He proposed that Germany countenance a generous final settlement with France on the basis of shared interests, including the defeat of Britain (which was taken for granted by then). A peace of reconciliation, Laval emphasized, would usher in a new age of Franco-German cooperation.[15] But the peace could not offend French pride, he emphasized, and first and foremost Germany would have to find a way of relaxing its choking grip on occupied France. Abetz listened sympathetically. Although he was not in a position to make any promises, he succeeded in arranging a meeting between Laval and Hitler.

With Abetz serving as intermediary and translator, the meeting took place on October 22, in Hitler's private train, at Montoire-sur-Loire, in the heart of occupied France and conveniently on Hitler's route to Hendaye, the site of his scheduled appointment the next day with the Spanish dictator, Francisco Franco. The Führer was correct but unforthcoming with Laval.[16] It was not yet the time to consider Vichy's request for a definitive peace treaty, he emphasized, unless the Vichy government shared in Germany's ongoing war with Britain. Although Hitler did not insist that France engage actively in the hostilities, he expected its leadership to provide "full cooperation" with the German occupation administration in all civilian affairs. Laval, not venturing any objections, simply listened to Hitler's terms and accepted them in principle. Two days later, on October 24, en route back from his conference with Franco, Hitler also received Pétain at Montoire. This meeting, too, was mutually respectful; but the Führer again made clear that only if France mobilized at Germany's side would the burden of surrender and recompense be shifted

---

14 Otto Friedrich Abetz, *Das offene Problem: Ein Rückblick auf zwei Jahrzehnte deutscher Frankreichpolitik* (Cologne: Greven, 1951), 146.
15 Hubert Cole, *Laval: A Biography* (New York: Putnam, 1963), 99–100; see also Marc Olivier Baruch, *Servir l'État français: L'Administration en France de 1940 à 1944* (Paris: Fayard, 1997), 177.
16 H. R. Kedward, *Occupied France: Collaboration and Resistance, 1940–1944* (Oxford: Blackwell, 1985), 32.

from "defeated France" to "defeated Britain." Neither Laval nor Pétain seemed to grasp that Hitler had no intention of easing his demands, or of signing a peace treaty with the Vichy government.

It was in the aftermath of the Montoire discussions that Pétain had issues of his own to resolve with Laval. The two men ostensibly functioned as alter egos. Laval raised no objections to Pétain's "national revolution," and Pétain did not intervene in Laval's "pragmatic" negotiations with Abetz in Paris. The tensions that developed between them were less of policy than of authority. From the beginning of Laval's incumbency, Pétain's other confidants—Alibert, Ménétral, and Admiral François Darlan, commander of the French navy—distrusted Laval, especially after July 1940, when he had been given seniority over them as minister of state and (shortly afterward) as vice-premier and foreign minister. Laval, in turn, disdained their jealousy. "They know what I'm likely to extract from the Germans," he confided to his staff. "If necessary, I'll pound on the table and [my critics] will all rush off like rabbits into burrows. I'll save my country in spite of them."[17] Nevertheless, in the weeks after the Montoire interviews with Hitler, Laval's vigorous pursuit of his own "pragmatic" diplomacy became increasingly offensive to Pétain, the more so as it was conducted without deferential reference to him.

For the marshal, the climactic provocation occurred in mid-November, 1940, after Ribbentrop vetoed Laval's request to Abetz that the French government be allowed to move from Vichy back to Paris. On his own, then, Pétain "informed" the Germans that he, as "Head of the French State," would forthwith be moving his government to Versailles, just outside Paris. Learning of this feckless ultimatum, an embarrassed Laval suggested to Abetz that Pétain probably would be satisfied with a single, "symbolic" visit to the historic royal palace at Versailles. But the veto of his public announcement left Pétain humiliated and infuriated. On December 13, 1940, he called a surprise meeting of his cabinet. Before the full plenum of 32 ministers, he announced that he was "accepting" Laval's "resignation," and then followed his bombshell by ordering Laval confined to house arrest.[18] Upon being apprized of this development, Abetz rushed to Vichy to browbeat Pétain, warning that "the Führer considers the conduct of the French government [to be] a personal offense."[19] Pétain agreed then to release Laval. Yet he was adamant in vetoing

---

17 Yves Frédéric Jaffré, *Les derniers propos de Pierre Laval, recueillis par son avocat* (Paris: A. Bonne, 1953), 160.
18 Warner, *Pierre Laval*, 255–56.
19 Paul Baudouin, *Neuf mois au gouvernement, avril–décembre, 1940* (Paris: Éditions de la Table ronde, 1948), 242–45 *ff.*

Laval's return to government. Getting nowhere, Abetz then invited Laval and his family to accompany him back to Paris, where they could live under his protection in private life. Instead, the Lavals chose to return to their family estate at Châteldon.

Pétain, in turn, after acceding to the brief transitional premiership of Pierre-Étienne Flandin, decided on February 9, 1941 on a permanent replacement for Laval. This was the 59-year-old Admiral François Darlan, commander of the French navy. Although Darlan came from an old republican family and actually owed his naval command to Léon Blum's Popular Front government, he personally shared Pétain's contempt for republican democracy. Since the previous July, when a British task force sank the pride of France's battle fleet at Mers-el-Kebir, Darlan's raging anglophobia had surpassed even the marshal's. Now, inheriting Laval's cluster of ministries, he professed himself seized by a "Grand Design." Ostensibly, it was Laval's, that is, to provide France with a collaborative role within Hitler's new "continental system," thereby safeguarding the French Empire and navy from "British clutches" and providing a "bulwark against bolshevism." Yet Darlan was not simply a collaborator, or even an undisguised fascist who himself had gone through the ranks of the Action Française and the Croix de Feu. He was also a vulgar careerist, who loved and lived for titles, honors, decorations, and personal luxuries. It was probably this careerism that animated his uxorious deference to Pétain and acceptance of the old marshal's compliance with German dictates under the façade of French "rebirth."

But if Darlan's objectives may not have differed substantially from Laval's, at least Laval had bargained relentlessly in his negotiations for German concessions: on the treatment of French POWs, French workers, French Jews. Even out of office, with Abetz's secret approval, Laval continued to write Hitler, seeking a forthcoming policy to France.[20] In contrast, Darlan found himself conceding more and more, until he approached the threshold of wartime partnership with Germany. In May 1941, when Hitler needed Vichy bases in Syria to support an anti-British revolt in Iraq, he got them. Instead of concessions, however, the Führer presented Darlan with new demands, including access to the Tunisian port of Bizerte as a supply route for General Rommel's Afrika Korps and the construction of a German submarine base at Dakar. Again, Darlan was forthcoming—and received nothing in return.[21] As

---

20 Kupferman, *Laval, 1883–1945*, 286.
21 Jean-Baptiste Duroselle, *Politique étrangère de la France*, vol. 2 *L'abîme: 1939–1944* (Paris: Imprimerie nationale, 1986), 281–301.

Abetz informed the crestfallen admiral, it was only after total German victory in Europe that more "distant matters" could be discussed.

Indeed, the most galling aspects of the occupation remained unchanged, and more frequently were aggravated. These included a steady increase of reparations imposed on the Vichy government, soaring from 400 million francs a day in June 1940 to almost 500 million francs a day by the opening of 1942.[22] It was under Darlan's aegis, too, that the most sinister aspects of Vichy collaboration were either introduced or intensified. These included recruitment of French civilians for labor in Germany, the formation of a "Légion des Volontaires Français" to fight at the side of the Wehrmacht on the Russian front, as well a wholesale expulsion of French and refugee Jews into the Vichy zone—and then elsewhere (pp. 362–63).[23]

In February 1942, recognizing the extent of Darlan's failure to protect the nation's residual privileges, Pétain resignedly called Laval back from Châteldon and reinstated him, even augmenting his title to "Prime Minister and Head of Government" (although keeping Darlan on as minister of defense). By then, however, the momentum of German-French "collaboration" seemed all but irreversible.[24]

## THE RETURN OF GEORGES MANDEL

Back in September 10, 1940, upon being transported under guard from Morocco to France, Georges Mandel was consigned to "internment," first in the Château de Chazaron and later in a small private hotel in the town of Riom. In Riom, Mandel awaited trial before France's supreme court, which similarly had been transplanted from the occupied to the Vichy zone. With him waited seven other public figures, including the former prime ministers Blum, Daladier, and Reynaud. Under guidelines laid down by Pétain himself, the initial charges against these men were their failure adequately to prepare France for war and their subsequent "unconstitutional manipulation" of France into the conflict. If proven, the accusation carried a sentence of life imprisonment.

In ensuing weeks, before the Riom judges, all the prisoners vigorously defended their records. In Blum's case, it was a defense of the entirety of the

---

22  Ian Ousby, *Occupation: The Ordeal of France, 1940–1944* (New York: Cooper Square Press, 2000), 66.
23  Eberhard Jäckel, *Frankreich in Hitlers Europa* (Stuttgart: Deutsche Verlags-Anstalt, 1966), 13–24; see also, Paxton, *Vichy France: Old Guard, passim*.
24  Jacques Benoist-Méchin, *A l'épreuve du temps: Souvenirs II: 1940–1947* (Paris: Julliard, 1989), 51–63.

1936–37 Popular Front government. Steadfastly and defiantly, in day after day of personal testimony, the 70-year-old former premier retraced the history of his administration. He denounced his accusers for acquiring their "information" from the paramilitary ligues and other right-wing groups. "*These* are the men who should be in your dock," he protested. "*These* are the ones who are responsible for this misery, this suffering."[25] Blum's fellow internees matched him in the vigor of their defense. The proceedings consumed 24 public sessions over nearly 5 months, and the prisoners' bravura performance ultimately became a public-relations embarrassment for the Vichy government. In mid-April 1941, under pressure from Otto Abetz, Pétain suspended the court hearings "pending future judicial action"—although Blum and the five other defendants were kept under indefinite internment.

Two of the latter, moreover, were not spared active and extended prosecution. These were Paul Reynaud and Georges Mandel, the stalwarts who had insisted upon continuing the war, even from the overseas empire. Among the charges they faced was "conspiracy with a foreign power" (Britain) to prolong the war. It took less than a week for the Riom judges to dismiss the accusation. But in December 1941, the Vichy government rather desperately enlarged the supreme court's jurisdiction to include cases of "ministers, former ministers . . . accused of embezzlement, corruption, or misuse of funds . . . by speculating on the value of the national currency or by misappropriating funds with which they were entrusted."[26] Although the clumsy maneuver evoked the scorn even of several pro-Vichy journalists, it succeeded in its transparent purpose of keeping the government's case on the docket.[27]

It also sufficed to fuel a firestorm of "cathartic" native racism. Thus, Xavier Vallat, director of Vichy's newly established "Commission for Jewish Affairs" (p. 373), wrote German officials that he considered Mandel "to be one of the most despicable specimens of the Jewish race."[28] Columnists in the fascist journal *Je Suis Partout*, among them Robert Brasillach, the "poet of integral nationalism," vied with each other in demanding that Mandel be hanged.[29] Several of Mandel's old political enemies echoed the demand, vilifying him in the press and conjoining him with Léon Blum, Pierre Mendès-France, and other Jewish political liberals. Jean-Louis Tixier-Vignancour,

---

25  Léon Blum, *L'histoire jugera* (Paris: Éditions Diderot, 1945), 265.
26  Sherwood, *Georges Mandel*, 269.
27  Paul Soupiron, *Bazaine contre Gambetta, ou le procès de Riom* (Lyons: Lugdunum, 1944), 41.
28  John M. Sherwood, *Georges Mandel and the Third Republic*, 271.
29  Michael Marrus and Robert O. Paxton, *Vichy France and the Jews* (New York: Basic Books, 1981), 20.

director of (unoccupied) France's national radio system, embellished on the hate campaign, asserting that "I want to see a Jew hanged from every branch in the park." Jacques Doriot, cofounder (with Marcel Déat) of the xenophobic Parti Populaire Français and later of the Légion des Volontaires Français, a French military brigade attached to the Wehrmacht, demanded that "the Jews Mandel and Blum simply be put against a wall and shot."[30] Even Philippe Henriot, Mandel's former parliamentary colleague from the Gironde and, in 1940, Vichy's director of propaganda, demanded that Pétain "free us from the Jews."[31]

Meanwhile, Germany's offices and institutions in occupied France were not about to be overshadowed by their Vichy counterparts. They had their own scores to settle with the most prominent and vulnerable of Germany's enemies. As Abetz explained to Reynaud's lawyer in January 1941, "We are not really interested in the Riom trial, but we *are* interested in the men who were responsible for the war . . . Reynaud and Mandel."[32] He could have added "*especially* Mandel," whom the Germans remembered well in his World War I incarnation as "the Tiger's Cub." Consequently, from the first days of the Wehrmacht's entrance into Paris in June 1940, Gestapo agents began ransacking Mandel's vacant office and apartment, seeking evidence that would link him with the United States government or with international Jewish organizations. In ensuing months, Abetz and others of Ribbentrop's emissaries pressed the Vichy government to find a way to "eliminate" Mandel.

During his foreshortened tenure as Vichy's head of government, Admiral Darlan had seemed prepared to comply. But on August 8, 1941 Pétain intervened, explaining that, much as he himself desired to see Mandel and Reynaud punished, he could hardly single them out without punishing the others still under indictment at Riom. Eventually, however, in late October of 1941, Pétain would change his tune. Under intense German pressure, the marshal in his "personal" capacity as head of state decided that he was empowered after all to prolong Reynaud's and Mandel's indictment. "[R]ecent investigations," he declared, had uncovered "grounds for new charges" against the two men, "the gravity of which might be sufficient to condemn [them] to perpetual imprisonment and even, perhaps, to death." The "grounds" were never revealed.[33]

On November 14, 1941, after 14 months of confinement, Mandel, Reynaud, and the other internees were transferred from Riom to the Fort

---

30  Sherwood, *Georges Mandel*, 272.
31  Marrus and Paxton, *Vichy France and the Jews*, 339.
32  Otto Friedrich Abetz, *D'une prison* (Paris: Amiot-Dumont, 1949), 197–98.
33  Paul Reynaud, *Au cœur de la mêlée, 1930–1945* (Paris: Flammarion, 1951), 90–99.

du Portalet in the Pyrenees, a more primitive facility than their original quarters in the Château de Chazaron. Mandel was kept in isolation from the others, even from Blum. Again, the move evoked protests, this time from the former president of the French Senate, Jules Jeanneney, and from Michel Clemenceau, son of the World War I premier.[34] Although these intercessions did not spare Mandel his unique status as a candidate for "elimination," he was at least allowed visits from his mistress, Mme. Béatrice Bretty, and their 12-year-old daughter. The latter had rented quarters in a nearby village and were permitted to join Mandel in the private meals they brought with them. Otherwise, security at the fortress was elaborate, replete with searchlights and barbed wire.

After Pierre Laval returned to Vichy in April 1942, this time as prime minister *and* head of government, Mandel's intermediaries, including Jeanneney and Michel Clemenceau, found a more understanding response. While never close, Laval had maintained correct relations with Mandel during their years in the French parliament. He reacted with interest now when his visitors suggested that Mandel be "allowed" to escape. But after giving the proposal further consideration, he regretfully and courteously demurred. As he explained, Mandel was less a political prisoner of the French government than a hostage of the German government. Abetz had made clear that Germany's occupation authorities would probably retaliate against him, Laval, and perhaps against the marshal himself, if Mandel should "mysteriously" evade the Fort du Portalet's formidable penal arrangements. The "internment," if not the trial, would have to continue.[35]

## THE FASCIZATION OF FRANCE

### *The Occupation*

After returning to office, Laval had given his major attention to foreign affairs, his first preference. Yet here too, as in his consideration of the Mandel case, his room for maneuver had been curtailed. Previously, France's navy and overseas empire had been his most valuable assets when dealing with Berlin. By spring of 1942, however, these assets were rapidly diminishing. After the armed intervention of British and Free French units the previous summer, the formerly Vichy-ruled territories of Syria, Lebanon, and French

---

34 Herbert R. Lottman, *Pétain: Hero or Traitor?* (New York: W. Morrow, 1985), 250.
35 Lottman, *Pétain*, 281–82.

Equatorial Africa had come under the control of General Charles de Gaulle's Committee of National Liberation.

Moreover, on the night of November 7–8, 1942, the Americans launched their own long-planned "Operation Torch," an amphibious invasion of French North Africa that engaged fully 650 ships and 100,000 troops.[36] Although President Franklin Roosevelt had dispatched a preemptive message to Vichy, assuring his "old friend, Marshal Pétain" that the operation was simply a precautionary measure to anticipate further German military action, Pétain reacted in scalded outrage. At first he ordered France's colonial forces to mount a vigorous resistance. But the next day Laval persuaded the marshal to withdraw his order (although for several days, French colonial troops in Algeria managed to sustain a spirited, if erratic, defense). Hitler, it turned out, had just interposed his own demand: that the Vichy government immediately declare war on the United States and Britain and turn over the full complement of its North African bases to Germany. Neither French leader was willing to go that far. Pétain accepted Laval's suggestion simply to announce that Vichy was breaking off diplomatic relations with Washington. In response, on November 11, the infuriated Führer ordered German military forces to cross the demarcation line from occupied to unoccupied France. And once more, as in the case of the American invasion, Pétain's first impetuous reaction was to order his modest Vichy constabulary to resist. But two hours later, again at Laval's intercession, the marshal canceled the futile gesture.

As late as November 1942, Vichy still had controlled most of France's North African empire, its principal bargaining chip in dealing with Germany. But, within weeks, Algeria and Morocco, the largest part of that extensive terrain, would be relinquished in favor of the Allies; and Tunisia would fall to American and British occupation the following spring.[37] The Vichy government would have to accept the inevitable in its future dealings with the German Reich, including the presence of the Wehrmacht in France's previously unoccupied zone. Even then, Laval speculated, perhaps not all was lost. Hitler still had not denounced the Rethondes armistice or the concept of "unoccupied France." Indeed, the original demarcation line between the country's two segments would remain nominally in place for two additional years, and with it the putative authority of the Vichy government over

---

36 William L. Langer, *Our Vichy Gamble* (New York: Knopf, 1947), 386–98; Arthur L. Funck, *The Politics of Torch: The Allied Landings and the Algier Putsch, 1942* (Lawrence, KS: University Press of Kansas, 1974), 236–48.

37 Rick Atkinson, *An Army at Dawn: The War in North Africa, 1942–1943* (New York: Henry Holt & Co., 2002), 150–58, 257.

occupied and unoccupied France alike. But, plainly, with Germany's military and administrative apparatus now ensconced in the totality of geographical France, that "authority" was reduced to a sham—and with it the residual negotiating room of Pierre Laval.

Nowhere was this atrophy of diplomatic leverage more evident than in the transformations of Vichy's domestic political agenda. Well before Hitler's retaliatory incursion into southwestern France—indeed, as far back as June 1940, in the immediate aftermath of the Rethondes armistice—the new Pétain government had set about establishing an increasingly fascisized state. The suspension of parliamentary government was only one of its features. Before long, alleged "Communist" and "Masonic-Jewish" conspiracies were being singled out for identification and repression. By early 1941, the prefectures of southern France were inundated with lists of potential "leftist subversives." Anonymous denunciations were encouraged, private telephones were tapped, newspapers and journals were censored.

## Deracinating the Jews

Perhaps the surest weathervane of France's transformed political climate was the fate of the nation's Jewish minority. In the early twentieth century, before and after World War I, that climate was influenced by France's decades-long obsession with the "purity" of Gallic culture (pp. 281, 287). During the 1920s and 1930s, however, a more sinister consideration obtruded. Even moderate politicians began to suspect Jews as alien radicals or as competitors in the nation's employment market or, increasingly, as obstructionists to peace with Germany (pp. 353–54).

Approximately 340,000 Jews lived in France by the outbreak of World War II (p. 271). Some 50,000–55,000 of them were newly arrived refugees from the Nazi Reich. The rest, French citizens, were divided roughly between veteran, acculturated Jews and more recent, essentially post–World War I, immigrants from Eastern Europe and French North Africa (p. 285). Once the Rethondes armistice was signed in June 1940, veteran and foreign-born Jews alike immediately began fleeing southward to the Vichy zone until, by the end of the year, an estimated 195,000 of them, refugees and veterans alike, had taken up residence there. For the time being, the German occupation authorities in northeastern France, short of manpower and focusing their major energies on the continuing war against Britain, preferred to leave to Vichy the expense and time of dealing with civilian matters, including the fast-accumulating Jewish presence. At the initiative of the German *Judenreferat* (Jewish Desk) in Paris, Jews who remained in the occupied zone were ordered to register with their sub-prefectures and to carry stamped Jewish identity papers; and they were denied ownership of vehicles and admittance to public schools or public parks. Nevertheless, in the first months after the armistice, the German administration placed its greatest emphasis upon "encouraging" Jews to flee southward to the Vichy zone—a strategy that the Pétain government protested with increasing vehemence.

Even without direct German prompting, however, an indigenous French antisemitism was at work in unoccupied France, a homegrown program that rivaled and occasionally surpassed the anti-Jewish measures that Abetz and his colleagues were developing in the north (p. 375). In this fashion, the Vichy government intended not only to solve the "Jewish Question" but to reassert its administrative authority over the whole of metropolitan France and the overseas empire. Indeed, between October 1940 and December 1941, the Pétain regime published no less than 109 anti-Jewish laws and decrees. French judges accepted these measures unanimously and routinely sent on to the Gestapo in Paris copies of all verdicts and sentences, anticipating that these would be applied to the whole of mainland France.

The list of decrees was based essentially on the Vichy government's October 3, 1940 "Statut des Juifs," which laid down a racist definition of Jews, and was applied with a growing series of enactments that established a new branch of French law, a "Jewish civil status." It was this specialized "status" that drastically reduced or eliminated the Jews' individual freedoms, including their access to government employment and selected private vocations, as well as to bank accounts, business property, or various categories of personal dwellings. A Vichy edict of October 7, 1940, swept away the "Crémieux Decree" of 1870, a law that had granted French citizenship to the substantial community of Jews in Algeria. Cancellation of the decree was followed by a drastic attenuation in the legal status of foreign-born Jews living in France itself. Even if their naturalization dated back as far as 1927, Jewish immigrant families were summarily reclassified now as "stateless." In short order, the fate of these "stateless" persons was to become grim, and prefigured the darkest chapter of the Vichy period altogether. By early 1941, among the scores of thousands of Jews who had fled from occupied France to take up hurried residence in the Vichy zone, 13,000 newly decreed "stateless" individuals—men, women, and children alike—were packed into 52 Vichy internment camps under penal conditions, 3,000 of them ultimately to die of their mistreatment.[38]

---

38  Warner, *Pierre Laval*, 305.

Pétain himself had no role in framing his government's racial program. He was reputed even to have interceded on behalf of several highly decorated Jewish military veterans who were known to him. Neither did the old marshal ever mention Jews in his public speeches. Yet his years in the army and his temperamental affinity for the rightist ligues had nourished his tolerance for racist legislation. The essence of his crime was inaction, his unwillingness to cancel a single one of Vichy's antisemitic measures.[39] As for Pierre Laval, his peacetime career had generated no discernable record of overt antisemitism. In 1940, coping with major foreign-policy and imperial issues during his initial, foreshortened term as Pétain's deputy, he played no substantive role in Vichy's first racial laws. Like Pétain, he left the field to zealots, and especially to Raphaël Alibert, a rightist ligue veteran whose ministry of justice first drafted the October 3 Statut des Juifs.[40]

It was only on March 29, 1941, under Darlan's vice-premiership, that the Vichy government established its first "Commissariat Générale aux Questions Juives," a commission for Jewish affairs with offices both in Vichy and in Paris. Its first director was Xavier Vallat, a right-wing deputy in the parliament of the 1930s (p. 299). His version of militant Catholicism, absorbed in his rural childhood in Provence, had been shaped by the rabidly antisemitic Catholic journal *Le Pèlerin*. As a committed xenophobe, Vallat subsequently became an ardent protégé of Charles Maurras. Yet, as a French patriot, a decorated veteran who had lost a leg and an eye in World War I, Vallat was determined to eliminate Jews from the nation's economy and body politic in a French, not a German, way. On the one hand, he set about widening the list of occupations from which Jews were to be excluded. By July 1941, his registry completed and with teams of gendarmes available as enforcers, Vallat launched into an intensified economic purge, requisitioning Jewish property, "aryanizing" Jewish businesses, and evicting Jews from their offices and increasingly from their homes.[41] Although this vocational "cleansing" applied both to occupied and unoccupied France, principal attention was given to the Vichy zone, the "haven" to which some three-fifths of French Jewry had fled by then (p. 372).[42]

---

39  *HaAretz*, December 4, 2010.
40  Warner, *Pierre Laval*, 16–20.
41  Warner, *Pierre Laval*, 80–112; Henry Rousso, "L'aryanisation économique: Vichy, l'occupant et la spoliation des Juifs," *Yod, revue d'études hébraïques, modernes et contemporaines* 15–16 (1982): 51–60, see page 53.
42  Marrus and Paxton, *Vichy France and the Jews*, 123–28; In the same text, for information on increasing movement by July 1941 to the occupied zone, see 133 *ff*.

Thus far, however, the commission for Jewish affairs had not condoned physical brutality or imprisonment. It was accordingly the suspicion of SS Captain Theodor Dannecker, chief of the *Judenreferat* in occupied France, that Vallat was still too "Catholic," too "soft," in dealing with the Jews. As late as December 1941, the combined Jewish presence in occupied and unoccupied France had not been significantly diminished. To repair this lacuna, Dannecker set about undermining Vallat's position in the Vichy government. His campaign was soon lent decisive momentum by events taking place elsewhere in Europe. On January 20, 1942, at Grossen Wannsee, a lakeside retreat outside Berlin, Reinhard Heydrich, chief of the Reich Main Security Office charged with Germany's internal security, addressed a gathering of senior SS officials. With the Reich currently at war with the Soviet Union, Heydrich explained, and with the British navy forestalling a mass emigration of Jews overseas, an alternative "final solution" to the Jewish Question had to be found. Heydrich's meaning did not have to be deciphered. It was mass emigration by land—and to the Nazi concentration camps of Eastern Europe.

In May 1942, moreover, under Abetz's virtual ultimatum, Pétain and Darlan dismissed Vallat and replaced him with a commissioner general even more congenial to German purposes. This was Louis Darquier, the son of an eminently respectable family from the Gascon region of south-central France. His father and older brother were medical doctors. Another brother was a physicist. Only Louis Darquier had developed into a black sheep. Not bothering to complete his secondary education, he became a gambler, an idler who never managed to hold steady employment. Although earning a creditable World War I military record as a sub-lieutenant, he continued in the postwar to sponge off his family. Married to an equally disoriented and habitually drunken Australian woman, with whom he lived in an assortment of threadbare hotels, Darquier sported a monocle, gave himself a fake aristocratic suffix, "de Pellepoix," manufactured an equally fake employment record as a "successful businessman," and then morphed into an hysterical antisemite and an obsequious acolyte of his idol, Charles Maurras. Through Maurras, in turn, during the late 1930s, Darquier was put in touch with other leading members of the nation's fascist ligues; and, in 1940, after the surrender of France, Maurras brought Darquier into the social circle of several Vichy cabinet members. It was due to these connections in May 1942, at the age of 44, that Darquier was installed in Vichy as Vallat's successor at the Commissariat Générale aux Questions Juives, and allowed to operate as Germany's dutiful functionary in the execution of the "Final Solution."[43]

---

43 Carmen Callil, *Bad Faith: A Forgotten History of Family, Fatherland and Vichy France* (New York: Knopf, 2006), 254.

## The "Final Solution"

A month before Darquier's appointment, Pétain had made the decision to replace Darlan as vice-premier, keeping him on nominally as defense minister and military commander in French North Africa. Laval then was invited back to serve in the newly augmented executive role of head of government. With Pétain left to tinker with his mythos of a "national revolution," the Nazis had in Laval a man whom they believed evoked more credibility among the French people. Time now was critical. In May 1942, Reinhard Heydrich, the RHSA chief, accompanied by his deputy Adolf Eichmann, paid a visit to Paris to acquaint Abetz and Dannecker with their new "Jewish" assignments. As Heydrich explained, it was previously the Führer's intention that the Jews of France, whether "native" or "refugee," be dumped from occupied France into the Vichy zone. But even this measure was viewed as provisional. Hitler's eventual master plan had envisaged a sweeping transplantation of French Jewry, indeed, European Jewry at large, for "internment" in the French island of Madagascar in the Indian Ocean.

In recent months, however, Eichmann continued, reprising his earlier explanation at Grossen Wannsee, the Wehrmacht's massive invasion of the Soviet Union, coupled with the intimidating presence of Britain's Royal Navy in the Indian Ocean, had mandated a fundamental revision, a "Final Solution" of the Jewish Question. Henceforth, European Jewry would have to be dispatched by land to alternate "relocation centers." The application of Eichmann's directives in France required that refugee Jews should systematically be "deported back" to the occupied zone, where they could be re-transported "to the east."[44] As at Grossen Wannsee, the euphemism did not have to be interpreted. Formerly, in 1941 and early 1942, even under the aegis of Darlan and Vallat, some 2,500 Jews of foreign origin had been deported from occupied France to Drancy, a rail depot outside Paris that originally had been used for cattle shipments. From Drancy, the prisoners were loaded into boxcars and dispatched to Poland—and to the Nazis' principal liquidation center of Auschwitz. Now, under the mandate of the "Final Solution," these Drancy deportations were to be vastly enlarged to include Jewish internees both in the Vichy zone and in occupied France. To that end, the distinction between "foreign" and "veteran" Jews should now be eliminated.

In the summer of 1942, however, the challenge of enlarged Jewish deportations was presenting complications to the Vichy government. For an

---

44 Hans-Jürgen Döscher, *Das Auswärtige Amt im Dritten Reich: Diplomatie im Schatten der "Endlösung"* (Berlin: Siedler, 1987), 215–20.

undertaking of this scope, the active cooperation of France's national police was required. Under terms of the Rethondes armistice, the national police, in occupied and unoccupied France alike, remained under the authority of the Vichy government. Would Vichy order this force to cooperate in the massive roundup and deportation of Jews? On June 11, 1942, the Germans tested the waters by demanding that Vichy authorize the expulsion of no fewer than 100,000 Jews, foreign and veteran alike, and from both zones. For his part, Darquier was only too eager to cooperate. Presumably, the reinstatement of Laval as prime minister would ensure that cooperation.

It did not. Laval required only two days to formulate his answer. Without consulting Darquier, for whom he felt only contempt, he presented Abetz and the SS officials in Paris with his counter-formula.[45] Vichy would deliver from its unoccupied zone a maximum of 10,000 foreign Jews, but with the proviso that native French Jews still living in the occupied zone would be deported only if the total of foreign Jews fell short of German quotas. In this way, the prime minister hoped to protect both French Jewish nationals and Vichy's autonomy. To all Germany protests, Laval remained firm. Indeed, in the Vichy zone, the initial police roundup produced barely half the promised 10,000 foreign Jews. The rest would have to be sought in occupied France.

On July 16, therefore, and in apparent defiance of Laval's orders, "special" police units conducted a lightning raid in the Paris region, collecting from prepared lists some 13,000 Jews, foreign and native alike, and depositing them under guard in an open sports arena, the Vélodrome d'Hiver. There, the prisoners—men, women, and children—remained for three days, under a blazing sun and with only the food and water they had brought with them, until enough rail cars could be assembled at Drancy to convey them to their final destination of Auschwitz. But upon learning of this horror and at the intercession of American consular and Quaker volunteer groups in Vichy, Laval issued impassioned protests to the German administration. Jews could not be handed over "as in a supermarket," he protested, "as many as you want for the same price."[46] The qualification, "for the same price," offered the key to Laval's frantic bargaining. He was intent at the least on exchanging immigrant Jews for native French Jews.

For the Germans, however, the formula was unacceptable. On August 15, 1942, SS Commandant Geissler, the Gestapo representative at Vichy, telephoned Colonel Knochen, the SS commandant in Paris, to complain that

---

45  Paxton, *Vichy France*, 184.
46  Paxton, *Vichy France*, 184–85.

"Laval refuses . . . to put the French police . . . at our disposal."⁴⁷ A month later, Geissler further protested to Knochen that Laval "often receives calls from Jews or persons who intervene on their behalf. Certain members of his entourage are friends of the Jews. One must distrust him altogether, for he will refuse to support our anti-Jewish action even though many segments of the French population regard it sympathetically." The postwar testimony of Jean Chaigneau, prefect of the Alpes-Maritimes, was typical of scores of depositions still extant at the Hoover Institution in Palo Alto, California: "With regard to the measures taken against the Jews and Freemasons," it stated, "we always found [Laval] at our side . . . protecting [us] in the actions we took to ensure that these new measures should be as ineffective as possible."⁴⁸ In conversations with Pinkney Tuck, the American chargé d'affaires in Vichy, Laval suggested "that the United States send ships to Marseille to save as many foreign Jewish children as possible."⁴⁹

On December 10, 1942, however, a month after the Wehrmacht poured across the demarcation line in the wake of Allied North African landings, Hitler himself ordered the indiscriminate arrest and deportation of all Jews, whether immigrant or native, in the unoccupied and occupied zones alike. And still Laval continued to bargain.⁵⁰ On one occasion, in August 1943, confronted on this issue by Knochen and other members of Germany's Jewish *Referat*, Laval exploded: "I will not serve [Germany] as *rabbateur* and beat the woods for hunted [Jewish] game."⁵¹ But neither, as head of government, would he divert his attention or energies on behalf of foreign Jews, to whom he felt no obligation. In any case, by then a majority of the captives tended to be foreign Jews, whose paper trail of naturalization applications, available in government offices, exposed them to deportation. In the summer of 1942, when representatives of the Quaker mission in France sought to intercede on behalf of naturalized or refugee Jews, even Laval brushed their protests aside, remarking that "these foreign Jews have always been a problem in Paris and the [Vichy] government [is] content that [the Germans at least give] France an opportunity to get rid of them."⁵² Indeed, during the entire course of the "Final Solution," not 1 of the 85 convoys of Jewish deportees from Drancy was derailed by French railroad personnel or otherwise impeded,

---

47  Jacques Baraduc, *Les Archives secrètes du Reich* (Paris: L'Élan, 1949), 192.
48  René de Chambrun, *Pierre Laval: Patriot or Traitor?* (New York: Scribner, 1984), 83.
49  Chambrun, *Pierre Laval*, 84.
50  Warner, *Pierre Laval*, 299–301.
51  Marrus and Paxton, *Vichy France and the Jews*, 344.
52  Warner, *Pierre Laval*, 374–77.

even in the twilight period of German occupation.⁵³ Altogether, after the Wehrmacht's occupation of the Vichy zone, an estimated 74,000 French Jews were deported to the Polish morgue. Another 16,000 to 18,000 died as a result of detention-camp brutality or spot executions. At first estimate, the proportion of Jewish victims seemingly was less draconian than elsewhere in Western Europe.⁵⁴ Although Hitler, by the end of the war, had wiped out perhaps 80 per cent of the Jews in other countries under German occupation, in France 80 per cent of the prewar French population, even 40 per cent of the foreign Jewish population, remained alive. In Western Europe only Danish and Italian Jewry exceeded this survival rate.⁵⁵

But there was another facet to the equation. It was also in Western Europe that the French government's record was by all odds the most unsavory. As President Jacques Chirac sadly acknowledged a half-century later, in July 1995, the collaborative role of much of Vichy's political leadership and bureaucracy, as well as of others of France's homegrown racist vigilantes (p. 354), was a painfully authenticated fact of modern history.⁵⁶

## THE RELÈVE

In the late spring of 1941, evaluating the implications of a prolonged war against Britain, Otto Abetz and his colleagues in Paris imposed schedules of increased food deliveries from occupied France to Germany. Although the unoccupied zone as yet was unaffected by the schedules, the Vichy government also contributed from its own limited resources in the effort at least to sustain its moral authority among its compatriots in the north. More ominously yet, as Polish and Ukrainian slave laborers were being worked literally to death in German armaments factories, the Nazi government turned to Western Europe for alternate supplies of foreign workers. Responsibility for coordinating that "recruitment" was delegated to Fritz Sauckel, a veteran Nazi bureaucrat and most recently the gauleiter of Thuringia. On May 15, 1941, Sauckel visited Paris as "Deputy Plenipotentiary for Labor Deployment" with an order for Abetz to convey to Laval.

---

53 Marrus and Paxton, *Vichy France and the Jews*, 344; see also "SNCF, French Railroad, Apologizes for Holocaust Role Before Florida Bid," *The Huffington Post*, November 14, 2010, http://www.huffing tonpost.com/2010/11/14/sncf-railroad-holocaust-apology-_n_783417.html.
54 Cole, *Laval: A Biography*, 211.
55 Marrus and Paxton, *Vichy France and the Jews*, 344.
56 Howard M. Sachar, *Israel and Europe: An Appraisal in History* (New York: Knopf, 1999), 350.

The order presented Laval with a harsh choice: either increase the supply of "voluntary" French laborers for the Reich or accept the conscription of "involuntary" workers. Characteristically, Laval temporized by presenting a counterproposition. If Germany left in place its post-armistice offer of decent wages and working conditions for French volunteers, Laval would do everything possible to encourage his countrymen to accept. Reluctantly and provisionally, Sauckel agreed. But the tentative agreement survived barely two months. The number of French volunteers leveled off at approximately 110,000. Sauckel had anticipated three times that many.[57]

Moreover, fewer than five weeks after Sauckel's initial visit, Hitler launched his armies on their invasion of the Soviet Union. Germany's need for foreign labor soon doubled and tripled. During the ensuing year, Sauckel, who in March 1942 was promoted to chief plenipotentiary with responsibility for the Europe-wide deployment of foreign laborers, intensified his pressure on Vichy to provide thousands of additional French workers. Accordingly, in September, Laval resorted to another tactic of desperation. It was a proposal for a *relève*—an "exchange."[58] In "exchange" for every three French industrial workers who volunteered to accept employment in Germany, three French POWs who came from agricultural backgrounds would be released from their German captivity to work on farms in France. Upon consideration, the German negotiators accepted the formula. But within a matter of weeks, the relève proved to be inadequate. The number of French volunteers remained static and intermittently even declined. The number of French POWs who were sent home also remained static. No fewer than 1 million remained in their German imprisonment.

Eventually, at the end of 1942, the putative "exchange" was abandoned, and Sauckel set about enforcing his original demand for outright conscription. During the first six months of 1943, with most of Vichy France under German military occupation, and with the cooperation of the French police, some 390,000 French industrial workers were drafted for labor in German factories. By year's end, the figure had climbed to 694,000, and France by then had become Germany's single largest source of foreign skilled labor and was second only to Poland as Germany's largest source of foreign labor altogether. Even with the increase, however, Laval succeeded in mitigating the relève's most serious hardships. Although French workers in German factories were consigned to barracks under armed guard, they were paid and allowed to remit

---

57 Warner, *Pierre Laval*, 299–301.
58 Warner, *Pierre Laval*, 307–10.

their salaries to their families. With few exceptions, they were not reduced to the abject slavery and starvation of Polish and other Slavic factory workers. During the winter of 1942–43, moreover, Laval managed to convince Albert Speer, Hitler's armaments chief, that the additional thousands of Frenchmen already producing military supplies for Germany in French factories should be exempted from the relève. But these concessions made little psychological impression on the French people. Rather, they counted the relève as the single most detestable feature of the German occupation.

## The Milice Française

In ways large and small, the fabric of the nation's life continued its deterioration under the German heel, and most dramatically after November 1942 and the Wehrmacht's occupation of the Vichy zone. A condition of the original Rethondes armistice was the payment by the Pétain government of "reparations," a cost originally set at the equivalent of 400 million francs a day. By the onset of 1943, however, due to inflation and continued German manipulation of the exchange rate, the actual cost had risen to 500 million francs and to 590 million by June 1944. At the same time, enforced shipments of agricultural goods to Germany left food and other basic necessities increasingly scarce, even on France's active black market. Meanwhile, police roundups of Jews and suspected *résistants* were exacerbated by the appearance of a chilling innovation. This was a homegrown militia.

In the early summer of 1943, an unexpected slowdown had occurred in the number of Jewish deportees. By then the SS had arrested most of the foreign Jews. Impatient to get the "Auschwitz Express" rolling again, the Nazis subsequently demanded that Vichy "denaturalize" all Jews of foreign origin, including those who had acquired French citizenship before January 1927. Once again, Laval strenuously protested. The law would overtax the capacity of the Commissariat of Jewish Affairs, he argued. It might also create problems with the Italians, who wanted no part of Hitler's "Final Solution." Laval then came up with an alternate proposal. In place of the "denaturalization" feature, he persuaded the Germans to let him deal with these "internal" matters through Vichy's own special Milice Française. This was a militia whose establishment Laval himself had countenanced in June as an offshoot of the Service de L'Ordre Légionnaire (SOL), the paramilitary wing of the former prewar Légion Française des Combattants.

The milice functioned under the command of Joseph Darnand. A World War I veteran, Darnand had since acquired an unsavory fascist record, passing successively through the ranks of Maurras's Action Française, Jacques

Doriot's Parti Populaire Français, and even the murderous Cagoule. Although Laval abhorred Darnand's politics, he recognized that the easiest means of combating the Résistance, and thus of defanging German retaliation, was to detach the SOL from the Légion to form its own paramilitary force. Darnand accepted the proposal. With the assurance of French police support, the milice then succeeded in recruiting some 30,000 young toughs, who zealously set to work hunting down Jews, Communists, and members of the Résistance. While not execrated in the same degree as the relève, the depredations of the milice's cutthroats, their pitiless hounding, abductions, collaborative deportations, torture, and spot executions of thousands of innocent Frenchmen was the least defensible measure of Laval's wartime *Realpolitik*.[59]

It was also his last. When the Allies launched their invasion of France on June 6, 1944, Laval was on the radio to broadcast his government's refusal to declare war on Germany. "France is not in the war," he declared to his nation, in warning them against joining the Résistance. "You must refuse to aggravate a foreign war with the horrors of civil war. . . . Think of France and of her alone."[60] In July, as the Allied offensive gained momentum, the Vichy regime heeded the German "request" to transfer itself to Paris, where it was still allowed to maintain its façade as the government of France. But, in mid-August, with the "transfer" of the skeletal Pétain-Laval administration from France to Germany only a week before the entrance into Paris of Allied troops, the four-year façade collapsed altogether.

## THE RETURN OF GEORGES MANDEL

Two and a half years earlier, if Georges Mandel ever had envisioned Vichy's help in an arranged "escape" from his internment at the Fort de Portalet, the hope vanished after the Allied landings in North Africa in November 1942. The event was not kept secret from the fort's prisoners. Mandel immediately sent word to Béatrice Bretty, his mistress, to have his friends in Paris telegraph a personal message from him to Pétain.

> M. le Maréchal [he wrote]: I wish to remind you [that] . . . for the last twenty-nine months, without even [the court in Riom] having heard my defense . . . you have kept me imprisoned in defiance of all law. Leaving me in Portalet when all

---

59 Warner, *Pierre Laval*, 387–88.
60 Cole, *Laval: A Biography*, 253–54.

of France is going to be occupied is equivalent to turning me over to the enemy. I wish to warn [you] of this so that it will be clearly established before the court of history that you are personally responsible for this crime.[61]

There was no reply.

As Mandel predicted, the German army occupied the Vichy zone three days later, on November 11. Four days after that, a German SS contingent, led by Colonel Knochen, arrived at the Fort du Portalet with orders to transfer Mandel and Reynaud back to Paris. At first, the prison commandant, a Major Vidala, denied the Germans access to the two men until instructions arrived from Vichy. During the respite, friends of Mandel and Reynaud interceded with Laval, entreating him to prevent the Germans from carrying out their abduction. "So long as I am in power," Laval reassured them, "the prisoners will not be handed over to the Germans."[62] But Laval's promise notwithstanding, Colonel Knochen assumed charge of the prisoners on November 20. Apparently, Major Vidala had received orders directly from Pétain's office to resist only "passively." The next day, Laval himself traveled from Vichy to Paris to register his protest. It was equally unavailing.

Until April 1943, the fate of Reynaud and Mandel remained unknown. It developed only later that they had been transported from Portalet directly to Berlin, and from there to the neighboring Oranienburg prison camp. Confined in separate cells, Mandel and Reynaud were kept in total isolation. But in April 1943, their circumstances unaccountably improved. In that month the Germans transferred the other political prisoners—including Blum, Daladier, and General Gamelin—to the same prison, and treated them correctly. Mandel and Reynaud shared in this improvement, and Mandel was allowed again to correspond with Béatrice Bretty and their daughter. In July, however, Reynaud, Daladier, and Gamelin were transported to a camp in Austria. As Jews, Blum and Mandel were separated from the others. Blum was shipped to Buchenwald in Germany, and Mandel followed several weeks afterward.

Even in Buchenwald, however, the conditions of the two men did not deteriorate significantly. They were interned in a small, makeshift cottage several hundred yards apart from Buchenwald's notorious concentration camp; they were given separate bedrooms and shared a kitchen and radio. Blum, a widower like Mandel, was given permission to marry, and his new

---

61 Louis Noguères, *Le veritable procès du Maréchal Pétain* (Paris: A. Fayard, 1955), 2: 342–43.
62 Noguères, *Le veritable procès*, 2: 347–51.

wife, Jeanne Reichenbach (née Levylier) was allowed to live with him. The camp commandants provided the Blums and Mandel with books and writing materials. The reprieve from the aridity of prison cells continued for almost 14 months. Blum later recalled of Mandel:

> Nothing has changed in his face, in his behavior, in his attitude, or in his dress. He even continued to wear those high stiff collars . . . [which Mme. Blum ironed] and his gloves whenever he went for a walk on the little enclave between the barred walls of the prison. . . . Toward the officers of the camp he was even more imperious than he used to be with his staff at his ministry. In everything . . . he maintained a disdainful, even contemptuous dignity, which in those circumstances and at that time was actually a form of heroism.[63]

But, on May 30, 1944, Hitler himself decreed that, in reprisal for any assassinations of German personnel or French collaborationist officials, Blum, Reynaud, and Mandel would be turned over to the Vichy government to be shot. The threat registered, and a Gaullist military court in Algiers commuted the death sentence it had earlier pronounced on Admiral Louis Derrien, the collaborationist former commander of the Bizerte naval base. Reynaud, Blum and Mandel also were reprieved. On June 13, the Algiers court pronounced a second death sentence, this time against Colonel Magnien, leader of the equally collaborationist "Phalange Africaine." Two days later, Otto Abetz alerted Laval that the three French prisoners were to be shot. This time Laval himself protested to the Algiers authorities, who again postponed the execution.

For Mandel, however, time had run out. On the night of June 27–28, the Résistance assassinated Philippe Henriot, the former Vichy minister of propaganda. Within hours, Mandel received orders from the Buchenwald commander to pack for his return to France. In the morning, he calmly breakfasted as usual with the Blums. Blum recalled: "[Mandel] had not the slightest illusion about the fate that awaited him. . . . [Y]et there was not the slightest change in the gesture of his hands, in his demeanor, in his articulation or in the intonation of his voice. We never saw him more calm, more poised, more lucid."[64]

On June 29, Mandel was flown to Rheims in a German courier airplane and taken from there by automobile to Paris, where he was kept for three

---

63  Léon Blum, "Georges Mandel: Anniversaire 1848," Archives Nationales 544AP/79, Dossier 2: Imprimés 1946–1967, 8.
64  Sherwood, *Georges Mandel*, 288.

GEORGES MANDEL SPEAKING AT AN INAUGURATION CEREMONY, NOVEMBER 16, 1938

days in an SS cell. Colonel Knochen, the SS commander in Paris, then arranged for Mandel to be transferred to the authority of the dreaded milice. Subsequently, on July 6, Max Knipping, chief of milice operations in the Vichy zone, arrived in Paris to supervise Mandel's transfer to the capital's formidable La Santé prison. Within hours, the transfer was carried out. The next afternoon, Knipping arrived at La Santé accompanied by three carloads of miliciens. Mandel was escorted out of his cell, placed in the lead automobile, and informed that he would be driven to Vichy "for trial." The convoy set out on the Fontainebleau Road.

After some 45 minutes, in the midst of the forest, the automobiles stopped. All the passengers were ordered out. At that point, one of the miliciens approached Mandel and fired a pistol into the latter's chest. Another man emptied his pistol into Mandel's prostrate body, while others sprayed the first automobile with bullets, apparently as "evidence" that the miliciens had been attacked by Résistance partisans. Then the remaining two automobiles returned to Paris, where an ambulance carried Mandel's body to the municipal morgue in Versailles. The assassins evidently hoped that it would not be identified and simply be buried in an unmarked grave. But an attending doctor recognized the corpse and notified Joseph Besselère, the lawyer who had been Mandel's personal assistant for 15 years. It was Besselère who arranged a private burial in a local cemetery.

On July 8, Laval learned of Mandel's death from Fernand de Brinon, Vichy's "ambassador" to the German administration in occupied France. Horrified, the prime minister summoned Joseph Darnand, the milice commander, and accused him of complicity in the murder.[65] Darnand professed innocence. Laval was not having it. Telephoning his "friend," Otto Abetz, he bitterly protested the behavior of the German government in consigning a statesman like Mandel to the tender mercies of a "Gestapo."[66] Everyone who saw Laval that day agreed that he was furious at the murder.[67] On July 12, he ordered the ministry of justice to begin investigations of the case and to arrest those responsible, "even if the guilty ones are members of the government."[68] By August 17, however, the day Laval himself was deported to Germany with other Vichy officials (p. 381), the investigation still had not been completed. In July 1945, at his own trial in liberated France, Laval would remind the court of his 30-year political association with Mandel. "His death was a great shock to me," he insisted, "all the more tragic because for a time I thought I had saved his life." The statement was accurate. The minutes of the secret Vichy cabinet meeting of July 23, 1944, corroborated Laval's horror and outrage.[69]

### THE RETURN OF THE MARSHAL

For all Laval's premonitions and warnings, the Allied invasion of France in June 1944 did not degenerate into a civil war. Vichy officials generally cooperated in the transfer of power to the Free French military units who participated in the Allied campaign. If the Libération produced spontaneous acts of vengeance against Vichyites, these were not of engorged proportions, especially when contrasted with the purges that wracked liberated Belgium, Holland, and Denmark—and least of all when contrasted with the Vichy regime's own purge of republican officials in the aftermath of the 1940 Rethondes armistice. Vichy's apologists later compared the early post-Libération to a Robespierran "Reign of Terror," producing as many as 100,000 victims. The figure was

---

65 Pierre Laval, *The Unpublished Diary of Pierre Laval*, ed. Malcolm Muggeridge (London: Falcon Press, 1948), 117–19.
66 Fernand de Brinon, *Mémoires* (Paris: L.L.C., 1949), 233.
67 Varenne, *Mon patron*, 213–14.
68 Pierre Taittinger, . . . *et Paris ne fut pas détruit* (Paris: L'Élan, 1948), 287.
69 Laval, *The Unpublished Diary*, 118; Brinon, *Mémoires*, 233.

exaggerated. Although some 125,000 Frenchmen were "detained" in these months, fewer than 10,000 of them were slain and most of those killed were the random prey of vigilantes.[70]

Yet the post-Libération judicial process lurched into operation with frustrating slowness. A backlog of fully 311,000 cases of treason or collaboration had to be processed and assigned to postwar France's understaffed hierarchy of courts, and this number did not include other thousands of trials consigned to professional organizations that were authorized to set up their own investigative committees. Nevertheless, some 171,000 cases eventually were processed and judged, and, in three-quarters of these, sentences were pronounced. Of the latter, 6,763 were death sentences—3,910 issued in absentia and 767 actually carried out. Life sentences were meted out to 2,777 defendants, and shorter prison terms to 34,116 others.[71] Very few identified collaborators escaped punishment altogether.

Among these few, however, was the sadistic Louis Darquier, who as Vallat's successor in the Commissariat for Jewish Affairs was the arch-administrator of Jewish deportations to Auschwitz. While Vallat himself was seized, tried, and sentenced to a ten-year imprisonment, Darquier escaped even that fate. As the Allied armies liberated France, he was smuggled into Spain. Together with several hundred miliciens and other French war criminals, he was allowed to live there under an assumed name to the end of his days. He died in bed in 1980.[72]

France's High Court of Justice was the tribunal that exercised jurisdiction over Vichy's most senior officials. Its cases were heard before 3 judges and 24 jurors. Among the defendants, 18 received death sentences. Ten of the sentences (including Darquier's) were pronounced in absentia. Of the eight death sentences pronounced in the presence of the accused, only three were carried out. Two of these were Joseph Darnand, commander of the milice, and Fernand de Brinon, Vichy's "ambassador" to occupied France.

One of those whose trial was most eagerly awaited was Henri-Philippe Pétain. Within two weeks of the Allied invasion of France, on June 6, 1944, detachments of German soldiers began transporting the old marshal around the country from one "safe" house to another. On September 8, he was

---

70 Alain Brossat, *Les Tondues: Un carnaval moche* (Paris: Levallois–Perret, 1992), 247–56; see also Julian Jackson, *France: The Dark Years, 1940–1944* (London: Oxford University Press, 2001), 577; John F. Sweets, *Choices in Vichy France* (New York: Oxford University Press, 1986), 233–38.
71 Jackson, *France*, 77; see also Herbert Lottman, *The Purge* (New York: Morrow, 1986), *passim*.
72 Louis Noguères, *La Dernière Étape: Sigmaringen* (Paris: A. Fayard, 1956), 19.

carried off to Germany and lodged in the venerable Hohenzollern castle of Sigmaringen. Thereafter, Pétain refused to participate in the charade of a "government in exile" and, in effect, ceased to head the Vichy government. In ensuing weeks he was moved again, to Schloss Zeil north of Wangen. Finally, on April 22, 1945, the marshal's guards escorted him across the German border to Switzerland. There, two days later, Pétain demanded that the Swiss government have him repatriated to France, and his demand was granted with alacrity.[73] Charles de Gaulle, by then serving as prime minister of his nation's provisional government, actually had hoped that Pétain could be tried quickly in absentia, to avoid stirring up old loyalties and emotions. But the "hero of Verdun" was determined to render his account to the French people, and on April 26 he set foot again on his native soil, where he was formally received by General Pierre Koenig, De Gaulle's senior combat general. Standing stiffly at attention, Koenig refused to salute or shake the hand of his old commander. The marshal was driven to Paris and sent directly to his "suite" of prison cells.

Pétain's trial began on July 23, 1945 and continued for three weeks. He was allowed to read a prepared statement. It continued for five hours and in essence made the case that the armistice of 1940 actually had contributed to the Allies' eventual victory in Europe by delaying German occupation of North Africa and that the Vichy government had acted as a shield to "protect" the French people. The statement then ended with Pétain's post-factum refusal to accept the court's jurisdiction. He would participate no further in its proceedings, he declared. In ensuing days, the marshal adhered to this position, maintaining his silence, occasionally falling asleep in the courtroom.[74] The prosecution, in turn, began its case by asserting that Pétain's assumption of power in June 1940 was the climax of his long-standing plot to bring down the Third French Republic. The argument was less telling with the jurors, however, than the evident obsequiousness of the marshal's collaboration with the Nazis, the abominations of the relève, the milice, and the deportations of innocent civilians that were committed under the imprimatur of Pétain's Vichy regime. During the course of the trial, many of the leading figures of the prewar Republic appeared as prosecution witnesses to give damning testimony. These included Reynaud, Daladier, Blum, and Lebrun.

---

73  Noguères, *La Dernière Étape*, 20–22.
74  *Le procès du Maréchal Pétain* (Paris: Imprimerie des journaux officiels, 1945); Lottman, *The Purge*, 368.

After deliberating for seven hours during the night of August 14–15, the jury delivered a unanimous guilty verdict and recommended that the marshal receive the death sentence—although suggesting that Pétain's advanced age could be taken into account. The panel of judges accepted both the verdict and its accompanying suggestion. So did De Gaulle, who promptly announced his commutation of Pétain's sentence to life imprisonment. Subsequently, the "hero of Verdun" was transported to the prison citadel of Yeu, an island off the coast of Brittany. He remained there for six years, matching the exile of his more illustrious predecessor in Saint Helena, until he expired on July 23, 1951, at the age of 95.

## THE RETURN OF PIERRE LAVAL

Pétain's defense had not been helped by the unexpected appearance in court on August 3, 1945 of none other than Pierre Laval as a witness for the prosecution.[75] Haggard and emaciated, Laval had aged dramatically, but his mental facilities still were intact. Indeed, for over three hours, with precision and eloquence, he made the case that all of his own collaborative actions as Vichy's prime minister and head of government—the relève of almost 700,000 French workers, the deportations of tens of thousands of Jews, even his declared support for Germany's invasion of the Soviet Union—were made either at the initiative or with the approval of Pétain, as head of state. Whatever the prosecution's intention, the role Laval was playing in court was transparently a rehearsal for his own impending trial, and the reaction of jury members and spectators alike was one of shouts, catcalls, and expletives. The political cartoon appearing on the front page of *Paris-Soir* the evening of August 3 depicted judges, jury, and journalists holding their noses as Laval entered the courtroom.

Laval's delivery into the hands of his vindictive countrymen had taken rather longer than Pétain's. On June 9, 1944, three days after the Allied landings, German Foreign Minister Ribbentrop notified Abetz that the French government would have to be transferred immediately to Belfort, in the east of France. Laval and his wife consequently were left no choice but to depart Vichy in a German convoy. Arriving in Belfort on August 18, the couple was joined three days later by the marshal and his entourage. In early September, Pétain, Laval, and their former Vichy colleagues were transferred yet again, to Sigmaringen Castle (p. 387). In December, when Laval refused to cooperate

---

75  Jules Roy, *The Trial of Marshal Pétain* (New York: Harper & Row, 1967), 127.

in the formation of a French government in exile, he and his wife were carried off still a third time, to a modest nearby farmhouse (Pétain had made the same decision but had been treated more circumspectly). Yet, by April 1945, the American Third Army was approaching the area, and the French exiles were left to seek their own escape. Laval found his through the cooperation of Spanish Foreign Minister José Félix de Lequerica. On May 2, the Lavals were flown in a Luftwaffe transport aircraft to Barcelona. On their arrival, they were greeted at the airport by the city's civil governor, who promptly had them carried off to their own apartment in the city's Monjuïc district, where they were officially "interned."

The De Gaulle government subsequently left no stone unturned in seeking Laval's extradition as a traitor. Laval insisted that he was a political refugee. Foreign Minister Lequerica agreed, and he persuaded Francisco Franco, Spain's caudillo, that Laval at least could be used as a bargaining card, perhaps in a "trade" for Juan Negrín, a former leader of the Spanish Republic who was currently a refugee in France. Lequerica then announced that extradition was impossible inasmuch as diplomatic relations had not yet been reestablished between the two countries. The deadlock continued into mid-summer. But in July Laval's position began to deteriorate. The Franco government was exposed to the full force of Allied diplomatic and economic pressure and, in the end, decided that Laval's presence was not worth the effort. On July 31, the Lavals were flown from Barcelona to Horsching, Austria, in the American zone of occupation. From Horsching they were driven under escort to the French occupation zone near Innsbrück and then flown again to Paris the next day.[76] In Paris, Laval was formally arrested and escorted through back streets to the capital's Fresnes prison. His wife occupied a cell in another section of the prison but was released the next month.

Pétain's trial was then in session, and it was barely 36 hours after arriving in France that Laval was called upon to testify as a prosecution witness—and make the case that all his own actions had been approved by the marshal. The response his testimony received (p. 374) was the merest prelude to the reception he would get at his own trial. First, however, he would have to undergo the obligatory *interrogatoire*, the pretrial hearing. This began on September 23. Even earlier, on August 21, Laval's two senior defense lawyers, Albert Naud and Jacques Baraduc, had been assured that the *interrogatoire* would be a long affair, lasting into November. But

---

76 Noguères, *La Dernière Étape*, 9–12.

only five sessions took place before the defense was informed that the hearing was over and the actual trial would begin almost immediately, on October 4.[77] The government had required that all court proceedings be completed before campaigning began for parliamentary elections, which were scheduled for October 21. At this point, in protest against the successive departures from judicial protocol, Laval's lawyers decided to recuse themselves from the defense, and they recommended that Laval follow their example.[78]

Instead, Laval sought to act as his own lawyer.[79] But, after a day and a half, encountering a fusillade of insults from the jury members (which the three-judge panel did nothing to suppress), he too decided to remain seated and mute.[80] By then, the courtroom had fallen into an uproar so ungovernable that even Léon Blum termed the trial "a scandal and a mistake," and Minister of Justice Pierre-Henri Teitgen felt obliged to rebuke the judges.[81] To no avail. On October 9, the jurors unanimously issued a guilty verdict on all counts of treason and national betrayal, and the judges the same afternoon pronounced the sentence: "[According] to Articles 87 and 75 of the penal code," its president intoned, "the court sentences the defendant to death, declares him convicted of national unworthiness and, as a result, [also] sentences him to national degradation and the confiscation of all his property." The execution was set for October 15.[82]

On October 10, Laval was transferred to the prison's "condemnation" bloc. In the ensuing days, his lawyers, Naud and Baraduc, launched into a frantic attempt to win support for a new trial.[83] In their effort, they sought the intercession of such luminaries as Léon Blum, François Mauriac, and British Ambassador Alfred Duff Cooper (vainly, except in the case of Blum). On October 12, the lawyers were received by Charles de Gaulle. As the general sat smoking, Naud and Baraduc drew his attention to the scandalous improprieties of the judicial proceedings and observed meaningfully that the "execution" of a former prime minister after such a mockery of a trial would set a precedent that could be used against future heads of government. They did not embellish on the hint. When

---

77 Jacques Baraduc, *Tout ce qu'on vous a caché: Les archives secrètes du Reich* (Paris: Editions de l'Élan, 1949), 31.
78 Albert Naud, *Pourquoi je n'ai pas défendu Pierre Laval* (Paris: A. Fayard, 1948), 242.
79 Henry Rousso, *Vichy, l'événement, la mémoire, l'histoire* (Paris: Gallimard, 2001), 489–552.
80 Warner, *Pierre Laval*, 411–12.
81 *Le procès Laval: Compte rendu sténographique* (Paris: A Michel, 1946), 248–66.
82 *Le procès Laval*, 262.
83 Naud, *Pourquoi je n'ai pas défendu*, 155–87.

the lawyers finished, De Gaulle stood up, shook their hands, and assured them that he would consult immediately with Minister of Justice Teitgen. This he did. The minister's answer came the next day. It declared that the "regrettable" events of the trial had been provoked by Laval himself and that the verdict and sentence were just and should be allowed to stand.[84]

During his two remaining days, Laval, who was not allowed visits from his wife and daughter, worked on his lengthy reply to the prosecution's charges. The effort apparently was intended for history. Naud and Baraduc recalled that, as late as October 14, the day before Laval's scheduled execution, he had appeared at peace with himself. He expressed his gratitude to them and assured them of his readiness to die: "I await and accept death with serenity."[85] At 8:00 a.m. the following day, three government limousines arrived at the Palais de Justice to pick up Naud and Baraduc. Joined by the attorney general and other members of the prosecution team, the group was driven to Fresnes prison. A phalanx of guards then escorted the visitors to Laval's cell. The prisoner was waiting. Dressed in civilian clothes, he nodded his greeting but remained seated on his bed.

Suddenly, Laval pulled the bed sheet up to his face and swallowed the contents (later determined to be cyanide) of a small vial that he had hidden in his mattress. Moments afterward, he began to convulse. Prison doctors were hurriedly summoned and began injecting Laval with antidotes. As he continued to writhe from side to side, a rubber stomach pump was thrust down his throat. During the next 2 hours, he would undergo 17 such purges before his pulse began to quicken. By 11:00 a.m., the doctors confirmed that Laval was "saved." At this point, Naud whispered to him, "Monsieur Laval, I implore you, try to breathe, try to stand. France is watching." Laval nodded feebly. Shortly before noon, with his lawyers' help, Laval staggered toward the awaiting prison van. Although tormented by an agonizing thirst, he was unable to keep down any of the water offered him. From the windows of his cell block, other inmates could be heard to cheer, although it was not certain that it was Laval they were cheering or his imminent death. The van carried the prisoner and his escort to a stockade abutting the far side of the building's main wall. Here Laval was manacled to a stake bearing the scars of innumerable bullets. At the sergeant major's offer of a blindfold, he shook his head. Moments later, as the firing squad took up its position, Laval managed to croak out the formulaic "Vive la France!" The execution was then carried out,

---

84 Warner, *Pierre Laval*, 415.
85 René de Chambrun, *Pierre Laval devant l'histoire* (Paris: Editions France-Empire, 1983), 244.

followed by the sergeant major's prescribed coup de grâce to Laval's head. Two minutes later, at 12:23 p.m., the prison warden dialed an open line to De Gaulle's office to report the death of a man who had been a four-time prime minister and a three-time foreign minister of France. Fourteen years later, describing the episode in his published memoirs, De Gaulle allowed himself the terse observation: "He died bravely."[86]

---

86  Charles De Gaulle, *War Memoirs*, 3 vols. (New York: Simon & Schuster, 1950–1959), 3: 251.

CHAPTER ELEVEN

# The Humanist of Yesterday

*"I, all too impatient, take my leave in advance."*

## THE PRECOCITY OF AFFLUENCE

On August 7, 1936, Stefan Zweig, a renowned 54-year-old Austrian belletrist, literary critic, and biographer, embarked from Southampton, England on the Royal Mail liner *Alcantara*. His destination was Rio de Janeiro. The Brazilian government had invited him there to deliver a series of lectures on contemporary European literature. Afterward, he would continue on to the international PEN conference in Buenos Aires, Argentina. The prospect of a two-week ocean voyage was a congenial one for Zweig. It would give him time to put Europe's escalating political dangers behind him, even as the sea air and his spacious cabin facilities would allow him ample comfort for writing. Most important, upon arrival he could savor a long-awaited opportunity to explore the physical and cultural terrain of a new continent.

Zweig's expectations were not disappointed. From the moment the *Alcantara* docked at the harbor of Rio, he was deluged with hospitality and honors. A representative of the Brazilian foreign ministry boarded the ship to tender him official welcome. Upon disembarking, Zweig was driven to his guest quarters, a luxurious flower-bedecked apartment facing Rio's celebrated Copacabana esplanade. A limousine and chauffeur were put at his disposal. During the course of his 12-day Brazilian visit, Zweig was mobbed by journalists as he made the rounds of scheduled appointments. His hosts included Brazil's President Getúlio Vargas as well as the nation's ministers of education and foreign affairs. His speeches and seminars (in German, French, and English) at the University of Rio de Janeiro were given prominent coverage in the Brazilian press. His keynote address, "The State of Contemporary European Literature," was attended by an overflow audience at Brazil's Academy of Arts and Letters.

Zweig's sojourn was interspersed by private guided tours: to São Paolo, where the local university awarded him an honorary degree; to neighboring Brazilian islands; to Petrópolis, the exotic "jewel" of Brazil's cities. By the time he boarded an Argentinian coastal steamer for his three-day visit to Buenos Aires, he had been overwhelmed (if exhausted) by the warmth and effulgence of his Brazilian reception. "It's fantastic," Zweig wrote in one of his letters home, "to think of the experiences I've had these last twelve days in this indescribably beautiful country where I should like to live for years."[1] Yet he did not regard his welcome as more than his due. In the 1930s, with his books published in over 40 languages, Stefan Zweig had become the single most widely read contemporary author in the world (p. 400). A fluent and eloquent polymath, he was also an internationally esteemed lecturer on modern Europe's cultural achievements.

Vienna, the city of Zweig's birth, shared luster with Paris as the fount of that effervescence. Before 1914, the Austrian capital had attracted ambitious and creative talents both from the wide-flung Habsburg Empire and from other, neighboring lands. Zweig's maternal grandfather, Josef Brettauer, was one of those overachievers. Originally a German citizen, Brettauer subsequently had transferred his banking and underwriting enterprises to Vienna, where he purchased a handsome mansion on the Schottenring and later provided an ample dowry for his daughter, Ida, on her marriage to Moritz Zweig. Moritz, on his own, already had become a precociously successful

---

1 Stefan Zweig and Friderike Maria Burger Winternitz Zweig, *Stefan and Friderike Zweig: Their Correspondence, 1912–1942*, ed. and trans. Henry G. Alsberg (New York: Hastings House, 1954), 180.

textile manufacturer in Prague before transplanting his business to Vienna. Both he and Ida were well educated, conversed easily in French and English, loved classical music, and were familiar with serious works of contemporary literature. Their spacious apartment on Vienna's Rathausstrasse mirrored the family's quiet elegance.

Born in 1881, Stefan Zweig was Moritz's and Ida's second son, and he fully shared in his parents' refinement. With his older brother, he received private instruction in French, English, and piano. By the time he entered gymnasium, he and his classmates, most of them products of comparably affluent families, were eager to participate in Vienna's effulgence of cultural resources. The libraries were their hunting ground and the coffee houses the forums in which they discussed and dissected the latest works by fashionably "important" writers.[2] Altogether, Jewish families of Zweig's social status tended to labor overtime as Europe's most ardent intellectual patrons, clients, and "practitioners."

Certain it was that Vienna never had a more committed litterateur than Stefan Zweig himself. In 1895, at the age of 14, he achieved publication of his first critiques in *Die Gesellschaft*, the empire's preeminent German-language journal of literary "moderns," as well as in Maximilian Harden's avant-garde *Die Zukunft*. While still in gymnasium, the young prodigy's essays appeared in an even wider assortment of journals and newspapers. Later, at the University of Vienna, where he "read" philosophy and literature, Zweig managed simultaneously to produce a veritable cascade of these feuilletons and, in 1901, to achieve publication of his first book of verse, *Silver Strings* [*Silberne Saiten*]. That same year, Theodor Herzl, literary editor of the prestigious *Neue Freie Presse*, published one of Zweig's poems on the literary section's front page. Thrilled at the honor, Zweig's father readily agreed that his son should "broaden" himself by spending his ensuing academic semester at the University of Berlin. The experience stood Zweig in good stead, principally by launching him on a future of correspondence, travel, and friendships with literary eminences both in Germany and elsewhere in Europe.

In 1904, upon earning his doctorate with his dissertation on Hippolyte Taine, a nineteenth-century critic and literary historian, Zweig set himself up in a comfortable Viennese apartment and embarked on a full-time literary career: writing the foreword to an album of paintings by Ephraim Lilien; translating into German the verses of the hitherto underappreciated Belgian poet, Émile Verhaeren; publishing his own first collection of short stories, *The Loves of Erika Ewald* [*Die Liebe der Erika Ewald*]; and conducting research for

---

2 Donald A. Prater, *European of Yesterday: A Biography of Stefan Zweig* (Oxford: Clarendon Press, 1972), 9.

his well-regarded biographical essays on Honoré de Balzac and Victor Hugo. It was also in the final years in this antebellum false dawn that Zweig's own blank-verse drama *Tersites* was produced in four German theaters. By 1914, in his 33 year, Zweig was firmly established as the youngest member in the "*Jung-Wien*" constellation of Vienna's most esteemed literary talents.

## HUMANITY OVER NATIONHOOD

In July–August 1914, notwithstanding his respect for the colleagues and cultures of other lands, Zweig initially found himself swept up in Europe's wartime passions.[3] Writing to his long-time Berlin publisher, Anton Kippenberg (himself currently serving in the German army), he acknowledged that

> [my great ambition] . . . is to be an officer . . . over with you . . . in France, the France that one must chastise because one loves her. It is strange to think that against no one would I have had more nationalist resentment than those who have stood highest in my esteem, for it was [France's] presumptuousness that was the beginning of all misfortunes. . . . I have no hatred for Russia, for she, like Germany, is fighting for an enlarged nationhood; but France fights for her image, her frivolity, and England for her money bags. . . .[4]

At Zweig's initial medical examination, the army pronounced him unfit for military service, evidently due to the lingering effect of rib surgery two years before. Through connections, however, he managed to wangle assignment to Vienna's War Archives Office (essentially a government propaganda agency) and was permitted to wear an army uniform.

But it was in the army, too, that Zweig's more characteristic humanism soon resurfaced. In April 1915, his office dispatched him to Galicia, an economically underdeveloped Habsburg province that the Austrians lately had recaptured from the Russians. Zweig's mission was to gather evidence there of the hardships unleashed by tsarist "barbarism." He found instead that the carnage suffered by Galicia's Polish-speaking civilians had been inflicted by both armies, Austrian and Russian. From then on, Zweig's dispatches reflected an increasingly indiscriminate horror and condemnation of war. When his dispatches were blue-penciled by his superiors, he translated several of them into French and arranged for friends in Switzerland to have them circulated in France.

---

3  Stefan Zweig, *The World of Yesterday: An Autobiography* (London: Cassell, 1943), 205–6.
4  Zweig, *The World of Yesterday*, 72.

It was also in the autumn and winter of 1915–16 that Zweig devoted his free hours to a drama that would express his growing revulsion for chauvinism and militarism. Titling the work, *Jeremiah* [*Jeremias*], he projected the ancient Hebrew prophet as the voice of revulsion and castigation for those rabid for bloodshed and vengeance. The play's nine scenes were crafted in pseudo-biblical style, with a chorus of "The People" howling for war—and then, belatedly, after defeat, clamoring for peace. "Ye all wanted war, all, all!" Jeremiah scornfully flings their entreaties back at them. "Your hearts are fickle and ye sway in the wind like reeds. The very ones who now shout for peace, I have heard howling for war. . . . Woe unto ye, O people! Ye speak with two voices, and sway before every breeze. Ye have fornicated with war. Ye have played with the sword, and shall now taste its edge!"[5]

Production of *Jeremiah* hardly was to be expected in wartime Austria; but Vienna's Burgtheater, as well as several German theaters, promised to stage the play immediately at the end of hostilities. Indeed, Zweig did not have to await peace for *Jeremiah* to find a German-speaking audience. Late in 1917, Zurich's Stadttheater agreed to produce the drama; and the Austrian government, whether out of forbearance or indifference, granted Zweig travel permission to Switzerland for consultation in the last phase of production, which was scheduled for February 1918. Presumably the drama was "general" enough in its pacifism not to be ascribed to any one government. Indeed, it was well received later even among many discriminating Austrians of high station, who resented being tethered to Prussian militarism. Despite the play's turgid, pseudo-apocalyptic format, ensuing productions of *Jeremiah* in the theaters of postwar Europe virtually canonized Zweig as a prophet of international brotherhood.

## THE FRUITS OF DOMESTICITY

The war's end also gave Zweig leeway to settle long-neglected family issues. A decade earlier, in 1908, a striking young woman had caught his attention at a concert. This was Friderike Burger Maria von Winternitz. The daughter of a Jewish father, Ephraim Burger, she had been raised as a Catholic and only recently had been married to Felix von Winternitz, a minor civil servant 14 years her senior. The couple in short order produced a daughter, and Friderike would give birth to another daughter ten months later. Even in these first years, however, the Winternitzes began to experience marital pressures.

---

5  Stefan Zweig, *Jeremiah: A Drama in Nine Scenes* (New York: Viking Press, 1939).

Friderike was increasingly alarmed at her husband's indiscipline in financial matters. To help cope with the family's mounting debts, she began giving private lessons in history and literature. In the process, reviving a youthful talent, she succeeded also in placing her own short stories and literary critiques in several Austrian and German newspapers.

It was at the concert in 1908 that Friderike reciprocated Zweig's attention. Besides his distinguished appearance and manifest refinement of demeanor, his growing reputation intrigued her. Taking pains afterward to read through his diverse oeuvres, she found herself altogether captivated. Five more years would pass before she would venture an admiring letter to him. From then on, however, the two began corresponding and then meeting privately. As their letters and trysts increased in frequency and fervor, Friderike made no effort to conceal these contacts from her husband.[6] Winternitz shrugged them off. Eventually, in the autumn of 1913, Zweig encouraged her to seek "annulment" of her marriage (divorce being impossible in Catholic Austria). Again, Winternitz registered no objection.

Even a legally sanctioned annulment, however, would have left Friderike in precarious financial straits. With custody of two little girls and lacking an independent income, she faced an uncertain economic future. This was not a problem for for Zweig. He insisted on assuming financial responsibility for her daughters. Zweig's parents accepted Friderike and her children equally warmly. During the war, the two couples' apartments were close by, and Zweig, Friderike, and her children dined frequently at his parents' home. In December 1919, too, the new postwar Austrian Republic, its government coalition dominated by Social Democrats, finally legalized divorce. To both families' relief, Zweig and Friderike were married the following month in a civil ceremony. It was time to reap the fruits of peace and "normalcy."

## THE SEIGNEUR OF CAPUCHIN HILL

The circumstances of early postwar Austria manifestly were anything but normal. Stripped of its former empire, the tiny remnant nation had to wrestle with a near-prostrate economy and a politically fragile government that teetered at the edge of revolution (pp. 182–236). Inevitably, Austria's turmoil extended to cultural life. In Zweig's recollection, the younger postwar generation, "[revolting] against the mayhem caused by their 'elders' and 'leaders,'... [also] rebelled against every [artistic and aesthetic] tradition... against every

---

6  Stefan Zweig and Friderike Zweig, *Stefan*, 45–46.

legitimate [form of expression] for the mere pleasure of revolting, even against the order of nature, against the eternal polarity of the sexes." Zweig found this revolution, whether in art, music, or literature, deeply offensive. "There remained [no alternative]," he wrote later, "but to withdraw into my work, quietly, and in retirement.... [f]or I declined any ape-like conformism."[7]

Zweig's "withdrawal" was both intellectual and geographic. In 1918, en route home from Switzerland, he and Friderike had taken a brief detour to vacation in Salzburg. Even in the postwar, Salzburg had remained a provincial Austrian town, offering essentially peace, quiet, and attractive scenery. At the "dying edge" of the Alpine chain, it also provided convenient—peacetime— access to Munich, Zurich, and Venice. During their initial Salzburg visit, too, the family happened across an empty wooden schloss rumored to have been used by a Capuchin archbishop as a private hunting lodge. Leaking and unheated, the ramshackle structure was uninhabitable. With its nine rooms, however, and its relative isolation on "Capuchin Hill," it offered Zweig the potential advantages of amplitude and privacy. On the spot, he decided to purchase it. A year and a half were required for the dwelling to be renovated; but in April 1919, Zweig, Friderike, and her two daughters left Vienna to take up permanent residence in their Alpine aerie.

The move served Zweig's purposes ideally. Favored by tranquil surroundings and under his disciplined writing schedule, his output was hardly less than phenomenal, particularly in his increasingly favored métier of the novella. It was also uncompromising in his choice of technique and subject. However much the older tenets of thematic romanticism and stylistic craftsmanship were under assault in the postwar era, they survived and flourished in Zweig's fiction. In such novellas as *Amok* and *Clerambault* and in short stories as diverse as "Leporella," "Mendel the Bookseller [Buchmendel]," "The Heart's Impatience [Ungeduld des Herzens]," "Fear [Angst]," "A Confusion of Feelings [Verwirrung der Gefühle]," and scores of others that eventually were included in the collected volumes of his work, Zweig's mastery of the sheer narrative art of storytelling was enhanced by an undercurrent of *Weltschmerz*, a sensitivity to the plight of victims of injustice and helplessness.[8] Even literary critics acknowledged that they were moved by the deaths of Zweig's conflicted dramatis personae. Altogether, in the compulsion of its narrative and the acuity of its human insights, Zweig's fiction was unsurpassed in sheer

---

7 Zweig, *The World of Yesterday*, 299.
8 Ann Clark Fehn and Ulrike S. Rettig, "Narrative Technique and Psychological Analysis in Two Novellas by Stefan Zweig," in *The World of Yesterday's Humanist Today*, ed. Marion Sonnenfeld (Albany, NY: SUNY Press, 1983), 168–76.

audience appeal and in its adaptability, both to foreign translation and even to stage and screen production.⁹

Increasingly, too, throughout the 1920s and 1930s, Zweig devoted his literary energies to the production of an extensive series of popular historical biographies, many of them to be assembled later under the title *Great Moments of Mankind* [*Sternstunden der Menschheit*]. His favored technique was to group in a single volume three figures of similar epochs and literary or political interests and attempt to find among them a common "spiritual" denominator. Thus, in 1922, Zweig's first collection in this genre, *Three Masters* [*Drei Meister*], took the form of comparative biographical studies of Balzac, Dickens, and Dostoyevsky. The second volume, published in 1925, bore the intriguing title, *Struggle with the Demons* [*Der Kampf mit dem Dämon*] and devoted its analysis to the figures of Hölderlin, Kleist, and Nietzsche, all of whom eventually had succumbed to mental illness and suicide. In 1929, the last in the trilogy, *Three Writers: Their Lives* [*Drei Dichter ihres Lebens*], explored the memoirs of Casanova, Stendhal, and Tolstoy for clues to their lives and writings.

In ensuing years, others of Zweig's biographies focused on personalities as diverse as Mary Stuart, Marie Antoinette, Joseph Fouché (Napoleon's sinister police minister), and the explorers Ferdinand Magellan, Christopher Columbus and Amerigo Vespucci. Perhaps more even than his fiction and dramaturgy, these lucid and popular biographical histories established Zweig's international reputation. Their astonishing "marketability" was revealed in 1930 by a League of Nations cultural committee, which confirmed that Zweig by then was the single most translated author in the world.¹⁰ In November 1931, on his 50th birthday, his publisher Insel-Verlag printed an international bibliography of "Zweigiana." It included publications in almost every language of Europe, the Americas, and Asia, as well as in various exotic Pacific and Caribbean dialects. Over the years, selections of his works became required reading in the curricula of national and provincial school systems.

Although most of Zweig's biographical studies did not survive the research standards of later scholarship, their popularity demonstrated the author's shrewd awareness of a growing segment of upper-middle-class readers—in

---

9   Mimi Grossberg, "Zweig in Film," in *The World of Yesterday's Humanist Today*, ed. Marion Sonnenfeld (Albany, NY: SUNY Press, 1983), 314–19; see also Leon Botstein, "Introduction," in *Jewish Legends*, by Stefan Zweig, trans. Eden and Cedar Paul (New York: M. Wiener, 1987), i–iv.

10  Zweig, *The World of Yesterday*, 321.

business, government, the professions—and enabled him to act in his self-described role as "a broker between the world of journalism and politicians and that of the intellectuals; as a spokesman to a wider audience for the concerns of writers and thinkers."[11] If less than modest, Zweig's sentience to the potential amplitude of his readership was not cynical. He was convinced that *Bildung* (education) was the indispensable key to social and political progress. For him, "the world of readers, writers, artists, and scientists comprised an ideal commonwealth within a corrupt world."[12] By no coincidence, too, the illusion of charter membership in an "international commonwealth of the spirit" was the defining characteristic of many Jews of Zweig's generation, who sought to transcend bigotry and cultural parochialism by embracing international humanism.[13]

## THE "PROPHET" OF HUMANISM

In his dedication to that vision, and with his enlarged Salzburg residence accommodating a vast private library and a treasure trove in collected mementos of Mozart, Beethoven, Blake, Claudel, Rolland, and other magisters of European culture, Zweig presided like a philosopher-king over an endless stream of bien-pensant houseguests from other countries. Lists of his visitors read like entries from a cultural "Who's Who": among them, Béla Bartók, Maurice Ravel, Bruno Walter, Jakob Wassermann, Moritz Brandes, Arthur Schnitzler, H.G. Wells, Paul Valéry, as well as Zweig's cherished "soul mate," Romain Rolland (pp. 402). Zweig, in turn, enthusiastically reciprocated the pilgrimages of these kindred spirits. Although longer journeys were not convenient in the first postwar years, Italy and France lay near. After 1924, when the European economic crisis eased, trips to Germany also resumed a semblance of normalcy. Passports and visa restrictions were relaxing, currency fluctuations were subsiding.

In his autobiography, Zweig made much of his resistance to public honors or to public gatherings in neighboring lands. "Anonymity in every aspect of life is a necessity to me," he insisted.[14] Yet the facts belied him. Although his keenest personal indulgence lay in visits to friends, he rarely turned down the scores of well-paying lecture invitations that came his way or the

---

11  Botstein, "Introduction," xi.
12  Wilma Iggers, "*The World of Yesterday* in the View of an Intellectual Historian," in *The World of Yesterday's Humanist Today*, ed. Marion Sonnenfeld (Albany, NY: SUNY Press, 1983), 10–19.
13  Botstein, "Introduction," xii–xiv.
14  Zweig, *The World of Yesterday*, 324, 326–27.

opportunity to address his fellow authors of the PEN society. "I spoke in French in the Palais des Arts at Brussels," he acknowledged years later, not without pride, "in Italian at Florence in the historic Sala dei Duecenti where once Michelangelo and Leonardo had sat, and in English in America on a lecture tour from the Atlantic to the Pacific" (pp. 409).[15] In 1928, for the Soviet government's commemoration of the centenary of Tolstoy's birth, Zweig accepted an invitation to visit Moscow, where his personal host was Maxim Gorky, who himself had written the introduction to the ten-volume Russian translation of Zweig's works. In letters home to Friderike, Zweig rapturously described his impressions of these foreign visits, the beauties of Paris and the German North Sea coast, the warmth and friendship of the Russian people, the competition between his hosts and foreign booksellers to wine and dine him.[16]

Yet Zweig's travels were not mere exercises in self-indulgence, or even in honoraria acquisition. In whichever country he lectured, he rarely lost an opportunity to emphasize the uniqueness of the European heritage, the ineradicable tradition of *humanus* that obliged former enemies to reconcile. Neither was it mere chance that bound Zweig and Romain Rolland in lifelong intellectual and personal devotion. The two writers had met in Paris shortly before the outbreak of war and in short order became mutual admirers. Rolland had foreseen the impending catastrophe (as Zweig had not) and described its emergent pathology in the last of the ten volumes of *Jean-Christophe*, his epic *bildungsroman*. With the onset of hostilities, Rolland in his outspoken pacifism then fled to Switzerland to escape the wrath of his fellow citizens. In empathy and admiration, perhaps even in guilt for his early martial ardor, Zweig made a point of sustaining his respectful, almost adoring correspondence with his revered friend.[17]

After the war, too, he continued to characterize Rolland as the embodiment of a desperately needed internationalism. Hence, in 1921, he delivered himself of a hagiography of his soul mate and, in 1926, of an equally reverential tribute in the Festschrift compendium that he himself had organized.[18] "I had already known [Rolland] earlier," Zweig confessed in its introduction.

---

15 Zweig, *The World of Yesterday*, 326–27.
16 Stefan Zweig and Friderike Zweig, *Stefan*, 122–24, 167.
17 Helene Kastinger Riley, "The Quest for Reason: Stefan Zweig's and Romain Rolland's Struggle for Pan-European Unity," *The World of Yesterday's Humanist Today*, ed. Marion Sonnenfeld (Albany, NY: SUNY Press, 1983), 20–31, see page 21.
18 Stefan Zweig, *Romain Rolland: Der Mann und das Werk* (Frankfurt am Main: Rütten & Loening, 1921).

"I had loved him earlier. . . . [B]ut the breadth and incomparable greatness of his cultural presence I experienced only in my darkest, unforgettable, and terrible days in the abyss of war."[19]

It was a presence that remained vibrant during Zweig's ensuing postwar lecture tours throughout Europe and the Western Hemisphere. By his own acknowledgment, it was principally under Rolland's inspiration that he, Zweig, a younger man but (unlike Rolland) a virtuoso linguist, rapidly emerged as the senior voice of humanist internationalism.[20] More than any of his fellow authors, he mastered the art of addressing his rapt audiences of intellectuals manqués in their own languages and in response to their own cultural aspirations.

In Zweig's travels and lectures, however, it was notable that he consciously avoided taking a stand on tendentious political issues. Thus, after corresponding in the early 1920s with Count Richard Coudenhove-Kalergi, a Czech-born political theorist whose concept of "Pan-Europa" had elicited his interest, Zweig eventually rejected the role of international organizations, even the League of Nations, as essentially "mechanistic." He preferred more culture-driven models. In his lecture at the University of Florence in 1932, he managed to finesse his way around Mussolini's press censorship by equating the ideal of humanistic fellowship with the Duce's conceit of "Roman" unity and "Catholic" internationalism. In 1934, as Hitler increased his pressure for an *Anschluss* with Austria, Zweig invoked the same model by refusing all appeals to declare his unequivocal support of Austrian independence. During that same year, without embarrassment, he even struck up a correspondence with Karl Haushofer, a noted German professor of geopolitics and an equally prominent apologist for Nazi expansionism.

In this "apolitical" pose, Zweig differed profoundly from Romain Rolland, who did not hesitate to espouse political causes, whether Mahatma Gandhi's campaign of nonviolence in India or (far more naively) the "progressive socialism" of Soviet Russia. Well into the 1930s, in his reverence for the "authentic" internationalism of culture, Zweig refused to follow Rolland's path, or any sectarian political creed. There were possibly several explanations of this reluctance to step down from his ivory tower. Zweig was an undisguised elitist. Unlike the majority of Austria's Jews, who had moved recently from poverty-stricken Galicia and Bukovina to Vienna's Leopoldstadt ghetto, he had been born to economic security and effortless attunement to

---

19  Stefan Zweig, ed. *Liber Amicorum Romain Rolland* (Zurich: Rotapfel-Verlan, 1926), 387.
20  Riley, "The Quest for Reason," 25–31.

a world of culture and refinement. He could not visualize himself as engaging in the rough and cynical interplay of practical politics. As late as August 1934, in a letter to a former secretary, he confessed, "I tie myself to no party or group.... [E]verything I do, I try to do *quietly*.... There is nothing of the so-called heroic in me. I was born a conciliator, and must act according to my nature."[21]

Even in his self-defined intellectual asceticism, however, Zweig was less than candid. As one of his most discerning biographers has suggested,

> Zweig's sense of himself as an aristocrat of the mind ... was yet another form of transmuting his identity as a Jew into a less vulnerable form.... [I]n the race-based national politics of the age, refuge as a [member of] an apparently spiritual aristocracy ... [was] a serious option for an elite of Jews. For Zweig, his success and fame among the gentile reading audiences could [presumably] secure his place.[22]

But eventually he had to abandon this illusion. Despite his initial distaste for the pungent ethnicity of Vienna's East European Jewish immigrants, he came to accept that Central European antisemitism made little distinction between *Kaiserjuden* and *Ostjuden*. Although he himself took no part in Jewish communal life, he had never repudiated his Jewish identification. The opposite was the case. In addition to Zweig's wartime *Jeremiah*, several of his stories and novellas—"Buchmendel [Mendel the Bookseller]," "Der begrabene Leuchter [The Buried Candelabrum]", and his *Jewish Legends* collection [*Jüdische Legenden*]—dealt respectfully with biblical themes. In a newspaper interview in 1931, he acknowledged "another influence in my life that made me a Jew in heart and soul, as well as through birth.... [This was] Theodor Herzl [the founder of modern political Zionism]. He showed me the greatness of our race. From that friendship really stems my immense interest in Jewish matters."[23] Eleven years later, Zweig returned to the touchstone of that interest even more forthrightly (p. 398) in his autobiographical *The World of Yesterday* [*Die Welt von Gestern*].

---

21 Leon Botstein, "Stefan Zweig and the Illusion of the Jewish European," in *The World of Yesterday's Humanist Today*, ed. Marion Sonnenfeld (Albany, NY: SUNY Press, 1983), 82–110, see pages 90–93, 100.
22 Botstein, "Stefan Zweig and the Illusion," 103; see also Ken Frieden, "The Displacement of Jewish Identity in Stefan Zweig's 'Buchmendel,'" *Symposium: A Quarterly Journal in Modern Literatures* [Special Issue on Judaic Literature: Identity, Displacement, and Destruction] 52, no. 4 (1999): 232–39.
23 Prater, *European of Yesterday*, 217.

## THE HUMANIST OF YESTERDAY

### A PROPHET OF WANDERINGS

Until 1933, Zweig had ventured no public comment on Hitler's rise to power in Germany. By the spring of that year, however, the political lesions of his native Austria were widened by the growth of Nazism on both sides of the Austro-German frontier. Zweig experienced their consequences personally. On May 10, 1933, during the infamous Nazi book-burning ceremonies in Berlin, Nuremburg, and several other German cities, his own publications were among the first to be thrown on the pyres. His most recent German publishing house, Insel-Verlag (itself extensively Jewish in staff), was forced to terminate relations with him. Earlier, in October of 1931, Zweig had accepted a commission from Richard Strauss to produce a libretto for the renowned composer's new comic opera, *The Discreet Wife* [*Die schweigsame Frau*]. The two men worked together on the project intermittently for 30 months, both in Zweig's Salzburg aerie and in Strauss's villa in Garmisch, Bavaria. But when the opera opened in Dresden in September 1934, after Strauss courageously had resisted all official warnings to disavow Zweig's collaboration, the Nazi regime banned further performances and divested Strauss of his honorific role as president of Germany's Reichsmusikkammer.

From his retreat in Salzburg, meanwhile, Zweig enjoyed a clear view of the Bavarian Alps. During the mid-1930s, Hitler's vacation lodge of Berchtesgaden was under construction only 28 miles from the Austro-German frontier. By then, it required no stretch of Zweig's imagination to anticipate Nazism's lurking dangers to Austria, and especially to its vibrant Jewish minority. Although he himself remained characteristically taciturn on all political matters, his non-Jewish acquaintances began avoiding him in the street or else suggesting that their meetings take place in private. Others advised him to leave Salzburg altogether.

Until February 1934, Zweig had resisted the very notion of uprooting himself from his mountain retreat. But early that month he traveled to Vienna to visit his widowed mother and his publisher. It was the period of the Heimwehr-Schutzbund "civil war" (pp. 190–92). Although Zweig himself witnessed nothing of the conflict, he encountered a shocking surprise when he returned to Salzburg. That same week, a trio of policemen came to his door with orders to search for hidden Schutzbund weapons. Upon being admitted and after casually exploring the house and finding nothing of interest, they left with equally perfunctory apologies. For Zweig, the episode was decisive. He would not remain, either in Salzburg or elsewhere in Austria. His home, his books, his priceless mementos—all would be abandoned. As he wrote Rolland, "Let them [the Austrian government] take the lot, I don't care. On the contrary, I shall be freer when all this no longer weighs on my shoulders."[24]

Leaving Friderike with the thankless task of closing up the lodge, Zweig relocated in London. By then, he had made several visits to the British Museum for material on his impending biography of Mary Stuart. In the process, he had found that he was comfortable among the British, whose language he spoke quite fluently and whose cool reserve and civilized manners were a welcome contrast to the turmoil and overheated passions of Central Europe. Subsequently, in the spring of 1934, he decided to rent an apartment on Portland Place. Even before his decision to leave Austria permanently, Zweig had written his friend and fellow author Joseph Roth, "I offer up a prayer of thanks every morning that I am free [to get on with my work] in England."[25]

The move was not without its costs, however. It brought to a head Zweig's increasingly problematic relationship with Friderike. Before and after their marriage, he had made little effort to engage her as a partner in his public activities. With a few exceptions, such as their wartime journey to Switzerland to oversee the production of *Jeremias* and their occasional visit to postwar Germany, he did not invite her to accompany him on his lecture or research trips. His frequent letters home invariably were fulsome and enthusiastic, overflowing with detailed accounts of his meetings with foreign colleagues and dignitaries, the banquets tendered in his honor, the ovations that greeted his lectures, the sumptuousness of his hotel accommodations, the beauties of Paris, Brussels, Florence, and Milan. Like any husband, he anticipated that Friderike would share in the gratifications and rewards of his prestige. She did, but only vicariously. Her most tangible compensations were the soirées she cohosted for Zweig's glittering array of Salzburg house guests. Even then, her daughters were confined to their own quarters when the family was entertaining or when Zweig was writing in his memento-laden office suite.

By the autumn of 1934, although Friderike dutifully closed up the Salzburg home, shipping many of the family belongings to London and packing her children off to school in Switzerland, she had made the decision to reside mainly in her small Vienna apartment. Zweig did not demur. As in the past, he provided for her every material need and for those of her daughters. Before returning to Vienna, Friderike in turn interviewed potential secretaries for her husband. The person they eventually chose was Charlotte ("Lotte") Altmann. A tall, pale 26-year-old, the granddaughter of a rabbi whose

---

24  Stefan Zweig, *Briefe*, 4 vols. (Frankfurt am Main: S. Fischer, 1995–2005), 4: 426.
25  Prater, *European of Yesterday*, 218–19.

son had married a gentile, she had emigrated to England from Frankfurt with her brother two years before, and their widowed mother had joined them shortly afterward. Serious and earnest, if somewhat timorous, the young woman was as adept in English as in German. She soon proved herself indispensable to Zweig as secretary and research assistant.

Within a few months, too, awestruck at the opportunity of working for a world-renowned author, Lotte Altmann would become Zweig's most devoted "admirer." In December 1934, as he put the finishing touches on his Mary Stuart biography, he reserved a hotel suite in Nice for a working vacation. On this occasion, he invited Friderike to join him, and she agreed. Lotte also accompanied Zweig, ostensibly in her role as secretary. She was lodged in the same hotel, in a separate room on the same floor, and shared in the Zweigs' entourage as the latter mingled with other vacationing luminaries. One afternoon, however, Friderike, returning from the hotel veranda to their suite for a change of clothing, discovered Zweig and Lotte "compromised" together. No scene ensued, but under Friderike's ultimatum the mortified Zweig immediately banished Lotte to a neighboring hotel and promised his wife to terminate the latter's employment. The promise was not kept. Although Friderike did not raise the issue again, neither did she and Zweig resume their lives together.

In ensuing years, Friderike in Vienna and Zweig in London managed to sustain their mutual regard and friendship. Periodically, she visited her husband, even located a larger and more comfortable London apartment for him. Back in Austria, she exerted every effort to sell their Salzburg home and finally succeeded in 1937 (although for much less than its true value). Zweig, in turn, had made arrangements for a major part of his ample royalties to be paid directly to Friderike. From time to time, he suggested that they go on vacations together, but the gesture came too late and she refused. Both of them knew that their marriage had ended. In 1936, on one of Friderike's trips to England, Zweig did not trouble to deny that he and Lotte were living together; and, when his wife raised the issue of legal separation, he did not object. There were no recriminations. Rather, at Zweig's request, Friderike still attended to his publishing and business affairs. But when he entreated her to relocate to the safety of Switzerland, assuring her that he would cover all her expenses, she declined. Her daughters were back in Vienna, making their own careers there, and she would not leave them.

## AUSTRIAN INTERREGNUM

Events in Europe ultimately determined the family's course of action. Hitler's earlier putsch attempt in Austria had been a humiliating setback for the Nazi führer. In its aftermath, Austria's president, Wilhelm Miklas, appointed Kurt von Schuschnigg, whom he first had designated as "provisional" chancellor (p. 211), to replace the murdered Dollfuss. Settling into office, the 36-year-old Schuschnigg swiftly made plain that the rule of law, if not of democracy, would prevail in his little country. In that stance, he appeared to have won the support of the nation's "respectable" middle-class and rural populations. Yet no one appreciated more than Schuschnigg that Austria's survival ultimately depended on the protection of Fascist Italy. Hence, assiduously cultivating Mussolini's goodwill, he emulated the late Dollfuss in preserving the Italian "corporative" model for his government.

Within less than two years, however, Schuschnigg's tightwire gamble on the Duce proved ineffective. By 1936, isolated diplomatically by France and Britain after his military invasion of Ethiopia, Mussolini began contemplating a foreign-policy realignment with Nazi Germany. Alarmed in turn at this erosion of Italian support, the Austrian chancellor was left with no alternative but to visit Berlin and negotiate an "understanding" of his own with Hitler. On July 11, 1936, under the provisions of their agreement, the Führer promised to respect Austrian sovereignty. Schuschnigg, for his part, consented to appoint Austrian Nazis to several key positions in the cabinet. It was a fatal bargain. From then on, a German Sword of Damocles hovered over the little Austrian Republic.

The sword dropped in the winter of 1938. On February 12 of that year, Schuschnigg was summoned to Hitler's Berchtesgaden retreat, where he was ordered forthwith to link Austria's economic and foreign policies to those of Germany—in effect, to give over his government to the rule of its Nazi cabinet members. At first, under Hitler's browbeating, Schuschnigg saw no alternative to capitulation. Upon returning to Vienna, however, he apparently regained some of the iron resolve that had seen Austria through the putsch crisis four years earlier. On March 9, he announced that he was scheduling a national plebiscite to determine if his fellow Austrians actually wished an *Anschluss*, a governmental amalgamation with Germany. It was the chancellor's instinct that his Catholic nation still would prefer to maintain its independence and that the German government accordingly would be stripped of any diplomatic pretext for Austrian subservience to the Nazi Reich. But Schuschnigg did not yet know his Hitler. Two days later, on March 11, the enraged Führer sent detachments of his army into Austria to effect a "voluntary union" of the two countries. No resistance was offered, either by the Versailles Powers, by Mussolini, or least of all by the Austrian people. Indeed, Hitler's subsequent triumphal entry into Vienna was greeted by hundreds of thousands of cheering Austrians, each striving to outdo the others in a counterfeit display of rapture at their instant citizenship in the Nazi Reich.[26]

As this sequence of events took place, Friderike and her daughters were vacationing in France. Before they could return, their apartment in Vienna was confiscated, together with the cartons of Zweig's manuscripts and memorabilia that Friderike had retrieved from Salzburg. Mercifully, the family's absence at least spared it from physical abuse. Zweig's widowed mother still resided in Vienna, but (equally mercifully) she expired of natural causes the following month. In December 1938, Friderike and Zweig officially and amicably secured a Swiss divorce. Afterward, Friderike settled with her daughters, temporarily in Switzerland, then in France, and, eventually, with Zweig's contacts and financial support, in the United States (p. 411). The two continued to write each other frequently and cordially. Perhaps it was no coincidence, however, after the bittersweet episode of their final separation, that Zweig embarked on his compelling novella *Ungeduld des Herzens* (most frequently translated as *Beware of Pity*), with its tragic denouement of emotional indifference supplanted by compassion.

The *Anschluss*, meanwhile, had left him stateless, residing in England as a "temporary visitor." The loss of his much beloved Austrian homeland was wrenching enough. But his distress was exacerbated in September 1938 by an even more spectacular and shocking Nazi victory. This was Hitler's success in blackmailing the governments of France and Britain to accede in the cession of Czechoslovakia's Sudetenland to Nazi Germany. Characteristically, Zweig refrained from public comment. His rationale never varied. Open denunciation of political behavior, he insisted, would only exacerbate the plight of Europe's victims. Yet, privately, his dispensations to these victims were unstinting. His London apartment functioned as a virtual welfare office where he supplied guarantees and financial subventions for the refugees' entry permits and initial subsistence. The experience was exhausting and dispiriting.

Above all, it was expensive. In his rescue effort, Zweig soon felt obliged to commit himself to an enlarged lecture schedule. An American booking agency had guaranteed him a cumulative honorarium of 15,000 dollars for a series of 25 lectures in the United States and Canada. Book signings in each city would supplement that total. Sailing to New York, Zweig then proceeded to soldier through the full complement of North American cities, coast to

---

26  Zweig, *The World of Yesterday*, 405 ff.

coast, south to north. In March of 1939, he returned to England with substantially augmented funds to distribute. That same month, however, Hitler dispatched his army for a bloodless occupation of Bohemia and Moravia—of "integral" Czechoslovakia. The threat of another European war crisis loomed even larger. So, in July, Zweig moved with Lotte to the English provincial town of Bath. By his own account, he anticipated peace and quiet there to work on his biography of Balzac and (not less important) to be spared from involvement in a public campaign of anti-Nazism.

Two months later, however, in September 1939, the Nazi Wehrmacht launched its invasion of Poland, triggering a second European war. Under British law, Zweig and Lotte became instant "enemy aliens." Fortunately, Zweig's contacts in the Foreign Office sped the process of his naturalization as a British citizen. Less than a week after acquiring these credentials, he married Lotte in a private ceremony before a justice of the peace, thereby allowing her to share his new legal status. But in July 1940, following the surrender of France and with the Battle of Britain gaining momentum, Zweig apparently experienced a nervous collapse and sought a retreat from England altogether. He accepted another lecture tour in the United States. Once his decision became known, however, many of his former European admirers and friends severely criticized him for opportunism, even cowardice. Whether as a result of this obloquy or in anticipation of further recourse to the American lecture market, Zweig resolved never to return to England.

Arriving with Lotte in New York in late September, he set forth on his earlier regimen of a city-by-city tour. Less than two months into his American itinerary, however, exhausted and disconsolate, he suddenly canceled his remaining engagements. Instead, he booked a room in a New Haven hotel for several weeks, availing himself of the research facilities of the Yale University Library and simultaneously regaining his physical strength. It was also during this New Haven interlude, in the autumn of 1940, that Zweig made preparations for a second voyage to Brazil. Ostensibly, his purpose was to expand into book form his earlier essay "Short Journey to Brazil [Kleine Reise nach Brasilien]," published after his original 1936 visit. Yet he did not attempt to disguise the growing temptation this vast and exotic nation exerted on him for a more extended stay. For its part, the Brazilian government willingly facilitated Zweig's trip, and, in late October 1940, he and Lotte sailed for Rio de Janeiro.

Upon arrival, the couple spent two months revisiting the principal cities of Zweig's earlier journey, but this time adding a lengthy tour of the mysterious Amazon region. Before returning to the United States in January 1941, Zweig was able to complete the final draft of his enlarged manuscript *Brasilien: ein Land* and arrange for its translation and publication in New York later that year as *Brazil: Land of the Future*. Intended as a love letter to the country that he now anticipated as his own future, the book actually was flawed in its indiscriminate praise for Brazil's ethnic pluralism and in its failure to acknowledge either the nation's extremes of wealth and poverty or its restiveness under the heavy-handed presidency of Getúlio Vargas. In Brazil itself, critics would give the work mixed reviews. The ambivalent response left Zweig undeterred. He had decided on his future home.

In New York, he first accepted the British Broadcasting Corporation's request to deliver (in English and German) several messages of hope to the British people and to the Europeans who had fallen under the Nazi heel. Zweig recorded the messages in New York, and the BBC subsequently transmitted the recordings from London. It was also during this New York interregnum that he and Lotte met with Friderike, who had braved the wartime Atlantic crossing with her daughters for an introductory visit to American relatives. The reunion was entirely cordial and ended with promises of further meetings. Indeed, during the ensuing fortnight, the promises were kept. But, in September 1941, on his last day in the United States before his impending third trip to Brazil, Zweig murmured cryptically to Friderike: "Do you realize that we shall probably never meet again?"[27]

## THE WORLD OF YESTERDAY

In mid-October, after their vessel docked in Rio de Janeiro, Zweig and Lotte spent the ensuing two weeks in a transit hotel near the harbor. This time their applications for an extended stay met with an unanticipated bureaucratic delay. Brazil's immigration authorities were struggling with a tidal wave of European refugees. Even for the renowned Zweig and his wife, the best arrangements that could be negotiated were for six-month visas, and even these subject to the lengthy ordeal of periodic renewal. Once the initial formalities were completed, however, the Zweigs lost no time in making for the neighboring mountain community of Petrópolis.

A kind of Brazilian equivalent of Austria's summer retreat of Bad Ischl, Petrópolis had enchanted Zweig on his previous two visits, and this time he and Lotte arranged in advance for friends to lease a "suitable" villa for them.

---

27 Friderike Maria Burger Winternitz Zweig, *Stefan Zweig: Wie ich ihm erlebte* (Stockholm: Neuer Verlan, 1947), 256.

Although photographs of its premises did not arrive before the Zweigs left New York, upon arrival at Petrópolis, they found that the villa fulfilled their every hope. Spacious, with ample library and office facilities, it also possessed an attractive garden, redolent with exotic tropical fruits and flowers. Most of the nearby neighbors were cultured and multilingual. Among them were Gabriela Mistral, a renowned Chilean poet (and future Nobel Prize laureate), with whom the Zweigs spent many congenial evenings in mutual visits. Other neighbors included Ernst and Erna Feder, a cultivated German-Jewish couple who became the Zweigs' closest friends.

With his daily regimen devoted to literary projects, Zweig also took time over the months to correspond faithfully and extensively with Friderike. Their letters dealt with family matters, news (mostly bleak) of their mutual refugee friends, accounts of visits and recommended books, or simply exchanges of congratulations upon each other's birthdays and his warm regards to her children and hers to Lotte. Invariably, she signed her letters "Always your Fritzi," and he, "In love and friendship." But despite the comparative ease of life in Petrópolis, Zweig's sense of isolation increased day by day (as he wrote Friderike), together with his sense of hopelessness in using the German language to write into "empty space."

It soon became clear that Zweig was afflicted by an inconsolable nostalgia for a world gone by, the prewar world of 1914, the unrecoverable "World of Yesterday," whose *Stimmung* he was nevertheless intent on recapturing from his newest home in the "Land of the Future." He did not reprise that older world uncritically. In Zweig's handwritten pages, little nostalgia was evinced for the way Central Europe had educated its young people, hypocritically repressing their sexuality, their furtive instinct for political extremism, and others of their churning emotions.[28] Although not minimizing the heroic efforts of friends such as Romain Rolland and Émile Verhaeren to rescue the community of letters from its surrounding political and emotional prejudices, he acknowledged that their warnings had gone largely unheeded.

Yet, as the draft of his memoirs took shape, Zweig himself palpably distorted others of the Old World's latent realities. His beloved Vienna, for him the epicenter of European enlightenment, was not the fin-de-siècle Vienna later resurrected by more objective post–World War II historians, who analyzed the many ways that Zweig's idealized universe of cultural humanism

---

28 George Iggers, "Some Introductory Observations on Stefan Zweig's *World of Yesterday*,) in *The World of Yesterday's Humanist Today*, ed. Marion Sonnenfeld (Albany, NY: SUNY Press, 1983), 1–9, see pages 3, 7.

actually had lapsed into a state of deep crisis well before 1914.[29] For all his intellectual acumen, Zweig in his reconstruction evinced little sense of the powerful currents of nihilism that had been gestating beneath the European surface, including the Nietzschean fascination with death. Even the writers he knew and still revered—Romain Rolland, Henri Barbusse, Georges Duhamel, Maxim Gorky, George Bernard Shaw—were essentially the "Europeans of Yesterday," the relics of a bygone era. Perhaps most surprising, in light of his characteristic *Judenschmerz* (the emotional pain of identifying with his fellow Jews), Zweig failed to analyze the underlying malevolence of European antisemitism, a racism that actually had burgeoned up as early as the 1880s and 1890s, not only in the Habsburg and Hohenzollern empires but even in republican France. Altogether, in his obsession with reconstructing the luminous "certitudes" of pre-1914 Europe, Zweig had remained largely oblivious to the abnormality of its political climate. For him, Hitler seemed to have come out of nowhere.[30]

Zweig's *The World of Yesterday* [*Die Welt von Gestern*], begun in New York and finished in his Petrópolis villa in January 1942, was neatly typed by Lotte and mailed back to New York. It was published early in 1943, in Stockholm in its original German and in New York the same year in English. Afterward, Zweig returned to his prospective biography of Michel de Montaigne, the renowned sixteenth-century courtier-essayist. But his energy for writing appeared to slacken. In advance of his 60th birthday, in November 1941, he had declined all proposals of Festschriften. His thoughts were elsewhere, and apparently they were mordant. Did his vanished world of yesterday, the loss of his European *Heimat*, the seemingly implacable tide of the Nazi Reich's military triumphs prefigure a climactic demise of his revered European civilization? *The World of Yesterday*'s epigraph conveys that impression: "Choose and speak for me, ye memories, and at least give some reflection of my life before it sinks into the dark."[31]

Or did the clue to Zweig's deepening melancholy lie elsewhere? Friends later confirmed that, even as a university student, he had exhibited a curious fascination with suicide. In his early poetry, such as "Life Song [Lebenslied]," written when he was 19, there appear prefigurations of a death wish: "Only by death that binds every wound is my soul's prayerful plea fulfilled."[32]

---

29  Carl E. Schorske, *Fin-de-Siècle Vienna: Politics and Culture* (New York: Knopf, 1980), chapter 1.
30  Schorske, *Fin-de-Siècle Vienna*, 161 ff.
31  Zweig, *The World of Yesterday*, ix.
32  Rosi Cohen, "Emigration: A Contributing Factor to Stefan Zweig's Suicide," in *The World of Yesterday's Humanist Today*, ed. Marion Sonnenfeld (Albany, NY: SUNY Press, 1983), 254–61, see page 257.

Indeed, very few of his fictional characters survive death or attempted death, particularly in his tales and novellas of unrequited love—"The Governess [Die Gouvernante]," "Letter from an Unknown Woman [Brief einer Unbekannter]," "Leporella," and "Beware of Pity [Ungeduld des Herzens]." In all of these, the heroine ends her life by suicide. In other stories, "Amok" and "Moonbeam Alley [Die Mondscheingasse]," the protagonists' motives are even more complex, usually involving altruistic concerns; although, in "Twenty-Four Hours in a Woman's Life [Vierundzwanzig Stunden aus dem Leben einer Frau]," it is a hopelessly addicted young gambler who shoots himself.[33]

Years later, preoccupied with the mounting suicides of friends and colleagues, Zweig displayed a morbid curiosity for details of the poisons they used. In 1940, meeting in New York with a fellow refugee, the writer Carl Zuckmayer, he confided that he himself did not expect to linger on beyond 1941, when he would be in his 60th year. Characterizing his imminent birthday as "the ominous, somber day," he murmured, "Sixty, I think that's enough."[34] If Zweig postponed his decision by a few months, it was almost certainly to complete his autobiography. But, in the summer of 1941, in his last meeting with Friderike before his third and final departure for Brazil, when he confessed that they should probably never meet again, she must have recalled that, in his periods of depression, Zweig had suggested that she join him in death.

## "ALL TOO IMPATIENT"

It was during the winter of 1941–42, in his Petrópolis haven, that Zweig's interludes of creativity alternated with increasingly frequent bouts of despair. Lotte and his friends sought to reassure him that his writings had lost none of their vigor, that his current draft essay on Montaigne was among his best work. In February 1942, he reluctantly agreed to accompany Lotte and the Feders to Rio's annual carnival. But on the 15th of that month, news of yet another Axis triumph—Japan's capture of Singapore, Britain's heavily fortified Pacific naval bastion—left Zweig in a state of deep depression. Four days later, he returned to Rio to deposit a copy of his last will and testament at the office of his lawyer, João Melamud. Later it was revealed that the document confirmed Zweig's imminent suicide and his desire to be buried in a simple

---

33 Rosi Cohen, "Emigration," 257.
34 Cohen, "Emigration," 257.

STEFAN AND LOTTE ZWEIG, SHOWN IN THEIR HOME AFTER THEIR DEATHS ON FEBRUARY 22, 1942

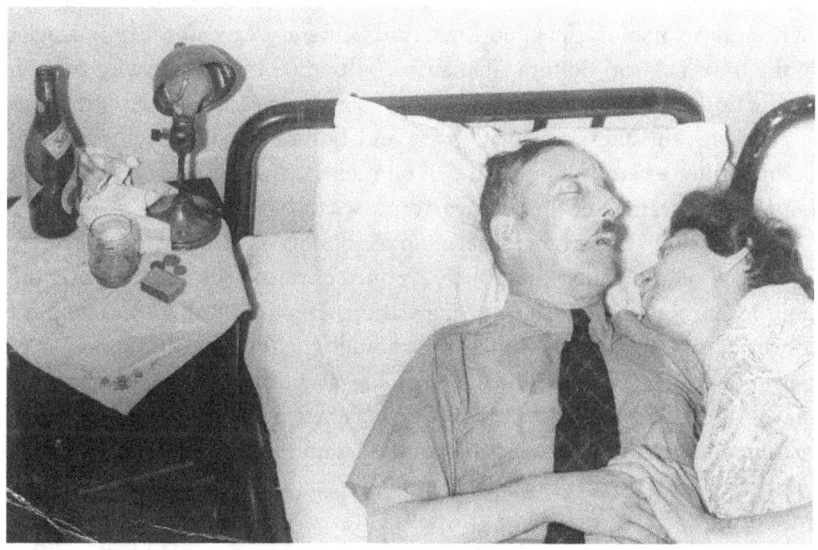

grave in Petrópolis. On February 20, back in his villa, he dispatched a letter to Romain Rolland, acknowledging his emotional desolation and expressing gratitude for their many years of friendship.

Had Lotte agreed by then to accompany her husband in his last act? The evidence is not clear. On the morning of Saturday, February 21, she went shopping as usual and purchased her usual variety of groceries. Zweig spent the time arranging or discarding his papers. Later, neighbors recalled smoke arising from a small bonfire in the Zweigs' back garden. That same evening, Lotte invited the Feders to stop by for dessert and drinks. The couple noted then that Zweig appeared reserved and depressed. When they left, Zweig returned to his office to complete his farewell letters. The most heartfelt of them was to Friderike. Confessing his terminal despair, he wrote, "Dearest Fritzi, I send you these lines in my last hours, you who cannot possibly imagine how relieved I feel since I have taken the decision. Please give my love to your children.... Love and friendship, and be of good cheer, knowing me to be at peace. Always, your Stefan."[35]

---

35  Stefan Zweig and Friderike Zweig, *Stefan*, 344; Prater, *European of Yesterday*, 338.

The servants were not present on Sunday, February 22, and there was no witness to the final events of that day. It is known, however, that Zweig put his bank accounts in order, wrote out a few last modest bequests, and consigned all his manuscripts and drafts to his literary executor, Abrão Kogan of the Brazilian firm Editora Guanabara. Subsequently, upon leaving written instructions for his own burial, he penned a more intimate death note. It was evidently in the afternoon that Zweig and Lotte each drank full bottles of the barbiturate veronal and lay down on their beds, he in full dress, she in a kimono, and waited for the massive overdoses to take effect.

The servants discovered the couple's bodies the following morning, February 23, and called the police. Upon recovering the suicide note, the police summoned the Feders for translation. Apparently, there was no need for an autopsy. The police then summoned Claudio de Souza, mayor of Petrópolis, who functioned as Zweig's liaison with President Vargas. The mayor immediately placed a call to Vargas's office, relaying his somber information and asking for instructions on the couple's interment. Less than an hour later, the president's secretary called back, confirming that the burial would indeed take place in Petrópolis. Moreover, despite Zweig's wishes for a private ceremony, full state honors were to be accorded him and his wife—an unprecedented departure in Brazil, which reserved state funerals for national luminaries.

The president's staff also assumed that the burial, scheduled for February 24, would take place in the town's largest Christian cemetery. But as soon as Rio Jewry's senior rabbi Heinrich Lämmle got wind of the decision, he and others of Brazil's Jewish leadership sped to Petrópolis to insist that Zweig and Lotte (who actually had been reared as a Catholic) be interred in the town's tiny Jewish cemetery. After a spirited argument with Claudio de Souza, the mayor eventually acquiesced. At the funeral the next day, both Rabbi Lämmle and a cantor presided. Among the eminences in attendance was President Vargas himself. Several of Brazil's most prestigious literary figures delivered memorial addresses. Afterward, the Zweigs' joint grave was designated by an unadorned black marble stone, which eventually bore the couple's names and dates, in Portuguese and Hebrew.

During the extended funeral cortege from the mortuary to the cemetery, shopkeepers in Petrópolis had shuttered their doors in tribute. A bas-relief of Zweig subsequently was commissioned and even now looks over a square in Bahía. A Stefan Zweig B'nai B'rith lodge also still functions in Penha, in Brazil's southern province of Santa Catarina. For many years into the postwar, a Stefan Zweig literary society held scheduled meetings in Vienna, and much later a tablet was attached to the house of Zweig's birth. The path ascending to Zweig's former Salzburg retreat continues to bear his name, as do obscure streets both in Vienna and Rio de Janeiro.

Yet, for decades afterwards, the mystery of the double suicide persisted. Zweig's note, consisting of hardly more than a paragraph, was written in the first person. In it, he thanked the government and people of Brazil for their hospitality, for the welcome given him and his work. He expressed the past satisfactions of his career but alluded to his despair at the world crumbling about him, and his determination to have done with life. Yet it remains of interest that the farewell he bade was only to *his* friends and *his* life. Lotte did not so much as exist in the document.

Was Lotte's death, then, a voluntary suicide? Her glass on their night table was as empty as Zweig's. Her bed sheets displayed no evidence of struggle. No bruises or other contusions were found on her body, which lay in her husband's arms. Timorous, obedient, even worshipful of Zweig in their foreshortened seven years together, Charlotte Altmann Zweig manifestly was not the unsuspecting victim of a homicide. But neither, in her husband's surrender to the romanticized memory of a vanished world, did the "quintessential humanist" trouble to spare Lotte her fate as his sacrificial collaborator.

> *So halte ich es für besser, rechtzeitig und in aufrechter Haltung ein Leben abzuschliessen, dem geistige Arbeit immer die lauterste Freude und persönlich Freiheit das höchste Gut dieser Erde gewesen. Ich grüsse alle meine Freunde! Mögen sie die Morgenröte noch sehen nach der langen Nacht! Ich, allzu Ungeduldiger, gehe ihnen voraus.*[36]

Hence, I consider it far better in a timely and proper manner to end a life that has been continually dedicated to the incomparable joy of intellectual endeavor, and that has regarded personal freedom as the highest goal on this earth. I send affectionate greetings to all my friends! May they yet be privileged to see the dawn after the long night. I, all too impatient, take my leave in advance.

---

[36] Prater, *European of Yesterday*, 358.

# BIBLIOGRAPHY

Note: Some items are listed, as appropriate, in more than one chapter.

## CHAPTER ONE: SOCIAL DEMOCRACY'S WHITE TERROR

Angress, Warner T. *Stillborn Revolution: The Communist Bid for Power in Germany, 1921–1923.* Princeton, NJ: Princeton University Press, 1963.

Basso, Lelio. *Rosa Luxemburg: A Reappraisal.* New York: Praeger, 1975.

Bayer, Hans. *Von der Novemberrevolution zur Räterepublik in München.* Berlin: Rütten & Loening, 1957.

Berghahn, Klaus L., ed. *The German–Jewish Dialogue Reconsidered: A Symposium in Honor of George L. Mosse.* New York: Peter Lang, 1996.

Berghahn, Volker K. *Der Stahlhelm: Bund der Frontsoldaten 1918–1935.* Düsseldorf: Drosto, 1966.

Bornstein, Joseph. *The Politics of Murder.* New York: Sloane, 1951.

Carr, Edward H. *German-Soviet Relations between the Two World Wars, 1919–1939.* Baltimore, MD: Johns Hopkins Press, 1951.

Carr, Edward H., ed. *Studies in Revolution.* London: Macmillan, 1950.

Coper, Rudolf. *Failure of a Revolution: Germany in 1918–1919.* Cambridge: Cambridge University Press, 1955.

Dunayevskaya, Raya. *Rosa Luxemburg, Women's Liberation, and Marx's Philosophy of History.* Urbana, IL: University of Illinois Press, 1991.

Eisner, Kurt. *Gesammelte Schriften*, 2 vols. Berlin: P. Cassirer, 1919.

Ettinger, Elzbieta. *Rosa Luxemburg: A Life.* Boston: Beacon Press, 1986.

Fishman, Sterling. "The Assassination of Kurt Eisner." In *The German–Jewish Dialogue Reconsidered: A Symposium in Honor of George L. Mosse*, edited by Klaus L. Berghahn, 141–54. New York: Peter Lang, 1996.

Flechtheim, Ossip K. *Die KPD in die Weimarer Republik.* Offenbach: Bollwerk-Verlag K. Drott, 1948.

Florence, Ronald. *Marx's Daughters: Eleanor Marx, Rosa Luxemburg, Angelica Balabanoff.* New York: Dial Press, 1975.

Friedrich, Otto. *Before the Deluge: A Portrait of Berlin in the 1920's*. New York: Harper & Row, 1972.

Frölich, Paul. *Rosa Luxemburg: Gedanke und Tat*. Frankfurt: Europäische Vergasanstalt, 1967.

Frölich, Paul. *Rosa Luxemburg: Her Life and Work*. London: Victor Gollancz, 1940.

Gordon, Harold J. *The Reichswehr and the German Republic, 1919–1926*. Princeton, NJ: Princeton University Press, 1956.

Grossman, Kurt R. "Deutsche Juden auf der Linken." In *Gegenwart im Rückblick*, edited by Herbert Arthur Strauss and Kurt R. Grossmann, 86–105. Heidelberg: L. Stiehm, 1970.

Gumbel, E.J. *Vier Jahre politischer Mord*. Berlin: Verlag der Neuen Gesellschaft, 1922.

Hitler, Adolf. *Mein Kampf*. Boston: Houghton Mifflin Company, 1943.

Hochdorf, Max. *Rosa Luxemburg: Das Leben einer Revolutionärin*. Berlin: Verlag der Neuen Gesellschaft, 1930.

Howard, Dick, ed. *Selected Political Writings of Rosa Luxemburg*. New York: Monthly Review Press, 1971.

Knütter, Hans. *Die Juden un die deutsche Linke in der Weimarer Republik 1918–1933*. Düsseldorf: Droste, 1971.

Kolb, Eberhard. *Die Arbeiterräte in der deutschen Innenpolitik, 1918–1919*. Düsseldorf: Droste, 1962.

Large, David C. *The Politics of Law and Order: A History of the Bavarian Einwohnerwehr, 1918–1921*. Philadelphia, PA: American Philosophical Society, 1980.

Levi, Paul. *Unser Weg: Wider den Putschismus*, 2nd ed. Berlin: Vereinigung Internationaler Verlags-Anstalten, 1922.

Leviné-Meyer, Rosa. *Aus der Münchener Rätezeit*. Berlin: Vereinigung Internationaler Verlags-Anstalten, 1925.

Lowenthal, Richard. "The Bolshevization of the Spartacus League." In *International Communism*, edited by David Footman, 23–71. Carbondale, IL: Southern Illinois University Press, 1960.

Luhrssen, David. *Hammer of the Gods: The Thule Society and the Birth of Nazism*. Washington, DC: Potomac Books, 2012.

Luxemburg, Rosa. *Briefe an Karl and Luise Kautsky*. Berlin: E. Laub, 1923.

Luxemburg, Rosa. *Comrade and Lover: Rosa Luxemburg's Letters to Leo Jogiches*. Edited by Elizbieta Ettinger. Cambridge, MA: MIT Press, 1979.

Luxemburg, Rosa. *Die industrielle Entwicklung Polens*. Leipzig: Duncker & Humblot, 1898.

Luxemburg, Rosa. *Der Krise der Sozialdemokratie: Juniusbroschüre*. Berlin: Rote Fahne, 1919.

Luxemburg, Rosa. *Die russische Revolution, eine kritische Würdigung*. Berlin: Verlag Gesellschaft und Erziehung, 1922.

Luxemburg, Rosa. *The Letters of Rosa Luxemburg*. Edited by Stephen E. Bronner. Boulder, CO: Westview Press, 1978.

Luxemburg, Rosa. *The Russian Revolution and Leninism or Marxism?* Edited by Bertram D. Wolfe. Ann Arbor, MI: University of Michigan Press, 1961.

Mattes, Wilhelm. *Die bayerischen Bauernräte: Eine soziologische und historische Untersuchung über bäuerliche Politik.* Stuttgart: Cotta, 1921.

McMeekin, Sean. *July 1914: Countdown to War.* New York: Basic Books, 2013.

Mitchell, Allan. *Revolution in Bavaria, 1918–1919: The Eisner Regime and the Soviet Republic.* Princeton, NJ: Princeton University Press, 1965.

Nettl, J.P. *Rosa Luxemburg.* 2 vols. London: Oxford University Press, 1966.

Noske, Gustav. *Von Kiel bis Kap: Zur Geschichte der deutschen.* Berlin: Verlag für Politik und Wirtschaft, 1920.

Oelssner, Fred. *Rosa Luxemburg: Eine kritische biographische Skizze.* Berlin: Dietz, 1951.

Roland Holst-Van der Schalk, Henriette. *Rosa Luxemburg: Ihr Leben und Wirken.* Zürich: Jean Christophe-Verlag, 1937.

Rosenberg, Arthur. *Die Enstehung und Geschichte der Weimarer Republik.* Frankfurt am Main: Europäische Verlagsanstal, 1955.

Sachar, Howard M. *Dreamland: Europeans and Jews in the Aftermath of the Great War.* New York: Alfred A. Knopf, 2002.

Schade, Franz. *Kurt Eisner und die bayerische Sozialdemokratie.* Hanover: Verlag fur Literatur und Zeitgeschehen, 1961.

Scheidemann, Philipp. *Memoiren eines Sozialdemokraten.* 2 vols. Dresden: Reissner, 1928.

Schorske, Carl. E. *German Social Democracy, 1905–1917: The Development of the Great Schism.* Cambridge, MA: Harvard University Press, 1955.

Schwend, Karl. *Bayern zwischen Monarchie und Diktatur: Beiträge zur bayerischen Frage in der Zeit von 1918 bis 1933.* Munich: R. Pflaum, 1954.

"Rosa Luxemburg Mystery: DNA of Great-Niece May Help Identify Headless Corpse." *Der Spiegel,* July 21, 2009, http://www.spiegel.de/international/germany/rosa-luxemburg-mystery-dna-of-great-niece-may-help-identify-headless-corpse-a-637385.html.

Stampfer, Friedrich. *Erfahrungen und Erkenntnisse: Aufzeichnungen aus meinem Leben.* Cologne: Verlag für Politik und Wirtschaft, 1957.

Teller, Judd. *Scapegoat of Revolution.* New York: Scribner, 1954.

Toller, Ernst. *I Was a German: The Autobiography of a Revolutionary.* New York: Morrow, 1934.

Waite, Robert G.L. *Vanguard of Nazism: The Free Corps Movement in Postwar Germany, 1918–1923.* Cambridge, MA: Harvard University Press, 1952.

Waldman, Eric. *The Spartacist Uprising of 1919 and the Crisis of the German Socialist movement: A Study of the Relation of Political Theory and Party Practice.* Milwaukee: Marquette University Press, 1958.

Watt, Richard M. *The Kings Depart: The German Revolution and the Treaty of Versailles, 1918–19.* Harmondsworth: Penguin, 1969.

Wheeler-Bennett, J.W. *Wooden Titan: Hindenburg in Twenty Years of German History, 1914–1934.* New York: W. Morrow & Co., 1936.

Wistrich, Robert S. *Socialism and the Jews: The Dilemmas of Assimilation in Germany and Austria-Hungary.* Rutherford, NJ: Fairleigh Dickinson University Press, 1981.

Zimmermann, Werner G. *Bayern und das, Reich 1918–1933.* Munich: R. Pflaum, 1953.

# BIBLIOGRAPHY

## CHAPTER TWO: THE DEATH OF GIACOMO MATTEOTTI

Anderson, Robin. *Between Two Wars: The Story of Pope Pius XI*. Chicago: Franciscan Herald Press, 1977.

Balabanoff, Angelica. *Il traditore*. Rome: G. Popolizio, 1942.

Balbo, Italo. *Diario 1922*. Milan: Mondadori, 1932.

Battistrada, Lucio. *Il delitto Matteotti*. Bologna: Cappelli, 1973.

Ben-Ghiat, Ruth. *Fascist Modernities: Italy, 1922–1945*. Berkeley, CA: University of California Press, 2001.

Binchy, Daniel A. *Church and State in Fascist Italy*. London: Oxford University Press, 1941.

Bosworth, R.J.B. *The Italian Dictatorship: Problems and Perspectives in the Interpretation of Mussolini and Fascism*. London: Arnold, 1998.

Bosworth, R.J.B. *Mussolini: A Biography*. New York: Oxford University Press, 2002.

Bosworth, R.J.B. *Mussolini's Italy: Life under the Dictatorship, 1915–1945*. New York: Penguin Books, 2006.

Burgwyn, H. James. *The Legend of the Mutilated Victory: Italy, the Great War, and the Paris Peace Conference, 1915–1919*. Westport, CT: Greenwood Press, 1993.

Cardoza, Anthony L. *Benito Mussolini: The First Fascist*. New York: Pearson Longman, 2006.

Casanova, Antonio. *Matteotti, una vita per il socialismo*. Milan: Bompiani, 1974.

Colarizi, Simona. *Dopoguerra e fascismo a Puglia, 1919–1926*. Bari: Laterza, 1971.

De Begnac, Ivon. *Palazzo Venezia: Storia di un Regime*. Rome: La Rocca, 1950.

Delzell, Charles F. *Mussolini's Enemies: The Italian Anti-Fascist Resistance*. Princeton, NJ: Princeton University Press, 1961.

Dresler, Adolf. *Mussolini als Journalist*. Berlin: De Gruyter, 1938.

Dumini, Amerigo. *Diciassette colpi*. Milan: Cammeo, 1951.

Dunnage, Jonathan. *Twentieth-century Italy: A Social History*. London: Longman, 2002.

Fermi, Laura. *Mussolini*. Chicago: University of Chicago Press, 1961.

Grandi, Dino. *Origini e la missione del fascismo*. Bologna: L. Cappelli, 1922.

Gregor, A. James. *Mussolini's Intellectuals: Fascist Social and Political Thought*. Princeton, NJ: Princeton University Press, 2005.

Gregor, A. James. *Young Mussolini and the Intellectual Origins of Fascism*. Berkeley, CA: University of California Press, 1979.

Hughes-Hallett, Lucy. *Gabriele d'Annunzio: Poet, Seducer, and Preacher of War*. New York: Alfred A. Knopf, 2013.

Kent, Peter C. *The Pope and the Duce: The International Impact of the Lateran Agreements*. New York: St. Martin's Press, 1981.

Kertzer, David I. *The Pope and Mussolini: The Secret History of Pius XI and the Rise of Fascism in Europe*. New York: Random House, 2014.

Kirkpatrick, Ivone. *Mussolini: Study of a Demagogue*. London: Odhams Books, 1964.

# BIBLIOGRAPHY

Lussu, Emilio. *Enter Mussolini: Observations and Adventures of an Anti-Fascist.* London: Methuen, 1936.

Lyttle, Richard B. *Il Duce: The Rise and Fall of Benito Mussolini.* New York: Atheneum, 1987.

MacGregor-Hastie, Roy. *The Day of the Lion: The Life and Death of Fascist Italy, 1922–1945.* New York: Coward-McCann, 1963.

Mack Smith, Denis. *Mussolini.* New York: Knopf, 1982.

Megaro, Gaudens. *Mussolini in the Making.* Boston: Houghton Mifflin, 1938.

Mussolini, Benito. *My Autobiography.* New York: C. Scribner's Sons, 1928.

Mussolini, Benito. *The Political and Social Doctrine of Fascism.* London: Hogarth Press, 1933.

Pernot, Maurice. *L'expérience italienne.* Paris: B. Grasset, 1924.

Pini, Georgio, and Duilio Susmel. *Mussolini l'uomo e l'opera.* 2 vols. Florence: La Fenice, 1953–1955.

Pugliesi, Stanislao G. *Fascism, Anti-Fascism, and the Resistance in Italy: 1919 to the Present.* Lanham, MD: Rowman & Littlefield Publishers, 2004.

Rafanelli, Leda. *Una donna e Mussolini.* Milan: Rizzoli, 1946.

Rhodes, Anthony. *The Vatican in the Age of the Dictators, 1922–1945.* New York: Holt, Rinehart and Winston, 1973.

Rocca, Massimo. *Come il fascismo divenne una dittatura, storia interna del fascismo dal 1914 al 1925: Seguita da La fine e il socialismo di Mussolini.* Milan: Edizioni Librarie Italiane, 1952.

Rossi, A. [Angelo Tasca]. *The Rise of Italian Fascism, 1918–1922.* London: Methuen, 1938.

Rossi, Cesare. *Il delitto Matteotti nei Procedimenti Giudiziari e nelle Polemiche Giornalistische.* Milan: Ceschina, 1965.

Rossi, Cesare. *Mussolini com'era.* Rome: Ruffolo, 1947.

Rossi, Romualdo. *Mussolini nudo alla meta.* Rome: Edizioni de La Rinascita d'Italia, 1944.

Rusinow, Dennison. *Italy's Austrian Heritage, 1919–1946.* London: Oxford University Press, 1969.

Salandra, Antonio. *Il Diario.* Milan: Pan, 1969.

Salvemini, Gaetano. *The Fascist Dictatorship in Italy.* New York: H. Fertig, 1967.

Salvemini, Gaetano. *Mussolini diplomatico: 1922–1932.* Bari: Laterza, 1952.

Sarfatti, Margherita. *Dux.* Milan: Mondadori, 1926.

Schiavi, Alessandro. *La Vita e l'opera di Giacomo Matteotti.* Rome: Opere Nuove, 1957.

Seton-Watson, Christopher. *Italy from Liberalism to Fascism, 1870–1925.* London: Methuen, 1967.

Silverman, Dan P. *Reconstructing Europe after the Great War.* Cambridge, MA: Harvard University Press, 1982.

Silvestri, Carlo. *Matteotti, Mussolini, e il dramma italiano.* Rome: Ruffolo, 1947.

Wiskemann, Elizabeth. *The Rome-Berlin Axis: A Study of the Relations between Hitler and Mussolini.* London: Collins, 1966.

BIBLIOGRAPHY

## CHAPTER THREE: A POSTHUMOUS IMPERIAL VENGEANCE

Albrecht, Philipp, ed. *Die Ursachen des deutschen Zusammenbruches im Jahre 1918*. 9 vols. Berlin: Deutsches Verlagsgesellschaft für Politik und Geschichte, 1925.

Anderle, Alfred. *Rapallo und die friedliche Koexistenz*. Berlin: Akademie-Verlag, 1963.

Bane, S.L., and R.H. Lutz, eds. *The Blockade of Germany after the Armistice: Selected Documents of the Supreme Economic Council, Superior Blockade Council, American Relief Administration, and Other Wartime Organizations*. Stanford, CA: Stanford University Press, 1942.

Berglar, Peter. *Walther Rathenau: Seine Zeit, sein Werk, seine Personlichkeit*. Bremen: Schunemann Universitatsverlag, 1970.

Blücher, Wipert von. *Deutschland's Weg nach Rapallo: Erinnerungen eines Mannes aus dem zweiten Gliede*. Wiesbaden: Limes Verlag, 1951.

Böttcher, Helmuth M. *Walther Rathenau: Persönlichkeit und Werk* . Bonn: Athenäum-Verlag, 1958.

Brandenburg, Erich. *Deutschlands Kriegsziele*. Leipzig: Quelle & Meyer, 1917.

Brecht, Arnold. "Walther Rathenau and the German People." *The Journal of Politics* 10, no. 1 (February 1948): 20–48.

D'Abernon, Edgar V. *Versailles to Rapallo: The Diary of an Ambassador, 1920–1922*. New York: Doubleday, 1929.

Dampierre, Robert de. "Dix années de politique français à Rome." *Revue des Deux Mondes* 21 (1953): 14–38.

Dorpalen, Andreas. *Hindenburg and the Weimar Republic*. Princeton, NJ: Princeton University Press, 1964.

Epstein, Klaus. *The Genesis of German Conservatism*. Princeton, NJ: Princeton University Press, 1966.

Epstein, Klaus. *Matthias Erzberger and the Dilemma of German Democracy*. Princeton, NJ: Princeton University Press. 1959.

Eschenburg, Theodor. *Mattias Erzberger: Der grosse Mann des Parlamentarismus und der Finanzreform*. Munich: R. Piper, 1973.

Eynern, Maximilian von. *Walther Rathenau in Brief und Bild*. Frankfurt am Main, 1967.

Federn-Kohlhaas, Etta. *Walther Rathenau: Sein Leben und Wirken*. Dresden: C. Reissner, 1927.

Felix, David. *Walther Rathenau and the Weimar Republic: The Politics of Reparations*. Baltimore, MD: Johns Hopkins Press, 1971.

Fischer, Rudolf. *Karl Helfferich*. Berlin: Verlag, 1932.

Friedrich, Otto. *Before the Deluge: A Portrait of Berlin in the 1920's*. New York: Harper & Row, 1972.

Gall, Lothar. *Walther Rathenau: Porträt einer Epoche*. Munich: C.H. Beck, 2009.

Gordon, Harold J. *The Reichswehr and the German Republic, 1919–1926*. Princeton, NJ: Princeton University Press, 1956.

Grady, Tim. *The German-Jewish Soldiers of the First World War in History and in Memory*. Liverpool, UK: Liverpool University Press, 2011.

Gugelmeier, Erwin. *Der schwarze Jahr, 1917–1918: Erlebes aus dem letzten Kriegsjahr.* Freiburg: J. Bielefelds Verlag, 1926.

Hard, William. *Raymond Robins' Own Story.* New York: Harper & Brothers, 1920.

Hausmann, Conrad. *Schlaglichter: Reichstagsbriefe und Aufzeichnungen.* Frankfurt: Frankfurter Societätadruckerei, 1924.

Holborn, Hajo. "Diplomats and Diplomacy in the Early Weimar Republic." In *The Diplomats 1919–1939*, edited by Gordon Craig and Felix Gilbert, 123–71. Princeton, NJ: Princeton University Press, 1953.

Joll, James. "Walther Rathenau: Prophet without a Cause." In *Intellectuals in Politics: Three Biographical Essays*, edited by James Joll, 59–129. London: Weidenfeld and Nicolson, 1960.

Karlweiss, Marta. *Jakob Wassermann.* Amsterdam: Querido Verlag, 1935.

Kennan, George F. *Soviet-American Relations, 1917–1920.* Princeton, NJ: Princeton University Press, 1956.

Kessler, Harry. *In the Twenties: The Diaries of Harry Kessler.* Translated by Charles Kessler. London: Weidenfeld and Nicolson, 1971.

Kessler, Harry. *Walther Rathenau: His Life and Work.* Translated by W.D. Robson-Scott and Lawrence Hyde. New York: Harcourt, Brace and Co., 1944.

Kollman, Eric C. "Walther Rathenau and German Foreign Policy: Thoughts and Actions." *Journal of Modern History* 24, no. 2 (July 1929): 127–142.

Krausnick, Michail, and Günter Randecker. *Mord Erzberger!* Norderstedt: Books on Demand, 2005.

Löffler, Hans F. *Walther Rathenau: Ein Europäer im Kaiserreich.* Berlin: Verlag A. Spitz, 1997.

Lotz, Walter. *Die deutsche Staatsfinanzwirtschaft im Kriege.* Stuttgart: Dt. Verl.-Anst., 1927.

Luckau, Alma. *The German Delegation at the Paris Peace Conference.* New York: Columbia University Press, 1941.

Ludendorff, Erich. *The General Staff and its Problems*, 2 vols. London: Hutchinson, 1920.

Ludendorff, Erich. *My War Memories: 1914–1918*, 2 vols. London: Hutchinson, 1919.

Macmillan, Margaret O. *Paris 1919: Six Months that Changed the World.* New York: Random House, 2001.

McMeekin, Sean. *July 1914: Countdown to War.* New York: Basic Books, 2013.

Mosse, Werner E., and Arnold Paucker, eds. *Deutsches Judentum in Krieg und Revolution, 1916–1923.* Tübingen: J.C.B. Mohr, 1971.

Niewyk, Donald L. "The Economic and Cultural Role of the Jews in the Weimar Republic." *Leo Baeck Institute Yearbook* 16, no. 1 (1971): 163–173

Orth, Wilhelm. *Walther Rathenau und der Geist von Rapallo.* Berlin: Buchverlag der Morgen, 1962.

Palmer, Cristophe, and Thomas Schnabel. *Matthias Erzberger, 1875–1921: Patriot und Visionär.* Stuttgart: Hohenheim, 2007.

Pulzer, Peter. *Jews and the German State: The Political History of a Minority, 1848–1933.* Detroit: Wayne State University Press, 2003.

Pulzer, Peter. *The Rise of Political Anti-Semitism in Germany and Austria*. New York: Wiley, 1964.

Rathenau, Walther. *Schriften und Reden*. Edited by Hans Richter. Frankfurt am Main: S. Fischer, 1964.

Rathenau, Walther. *Tagebuch, 1907–1922*. Edited by Hartmut Pogge von Strandmann. Düsseldorf: Droste Verlag, 1967.

Reichsverband Jüdischer Frontsoldaten. *Die jüdischer Gefallenen des deutschen Heeres, der deutschen Marine und der deutschen Schutztruppen, 1914–1918: Ein Gedenkbuch*. Berlin: Reichsband Jüdischer Frontsoldaten, 1932.

Riedler, A. *Emil Rathenau und das Werden der Grosswirtschaft*. Berlin: Verlag von Julius Springer, 1916. http://dx.doi.org/10.1007/978-3-642-94487-1.

Rosenbaum, Eduard. "Reflections on Walther Rathenau." *Leo Baeck Institute Yearbook* 4, no. 1 (1959): 260–270.

Rosenberg, A.J. *Der deutsche Krieg und der Katholizismus*. Berlin: Germania, Aktien-Gesellachaft für Verlag und Druckerei, 1915.

Sabrow, Martin. *Der Rathenaumord*. Munich: R. Oldenbourg, 1994.

Sachar, Howard M. *Dreamland: Europeans and Jews in the Aftermath of the Great War*. New York: Alfred A. Knopf, 2002.

Scheidemann, Philipp. *Memoiren eines Sozialdemokraten*, 2 vols. Dresden: C. Rerissner, 1928.

Schulin, Ernst. *Walther Rathenau: Repräsentat, Kritiker, und Opfer seiner Zeit*. Göttingen: Musterschmidt, 1979.

Stern, Fritz. *Einstein's German World*. Princeton, NJ: Princeton University Press, 1999.

Steuer, Wilfried. *Matthias Erzberger (1875–1921): Staatsmann und Demokrat*. Biberach: Biberacher Verlagsdruckerei, 1986.

Volkmann, Erich O., Albrecht Philipp, and Walther Schücking, eds., *Die Annexionfragen des Weltkrieges: Gutachten*, 2 vols. Berlin: Deutsches Verlagsgesellschaft für Politik und Geschichte, 1926–1931.

Volkov, Shulamit. *Walther Rathenau: Weimar's Fallen Statesman*. New Haven, CT: Yale University Press, 2012.

Watt, Richard M. *The Kings Depart: The Tragedy of Germany—Versailles and the German Revolution*. New York: Simon and Schuster, 1968.

Wheeler-Bennett, J.W. *The Forgotten Peace: Brest-Litovsk, March 1918*. New York: W. Morrow, 1939.

Wheeler-Bennett, J.W. *Wooden Titan: Hindenburg in Twenty Years of German History, 1914–1934*. New York: W. Morrow, 1936.

Winz, Alfons. *Erzberger zu den neuen Problemen der Gegenwart*. Singen: Singener Zeitung, 1921.

Wirth, Josef. *Reden währen der Kanzlerschaft*. Berlin: Germania, 1925.

Zechlin, Egmont. *Die deutsche Politik und die Juden im Ersten Weltkrieg*. Göttingen: Vandenhoeck & Ruprecht, 1969.

Zinnecke, Fritz. *Erzberger gegen Helfferich*. Berlin: Berliner Kommissionsbuchhandlung, 1920.

# BIBLIOGRAPHY

## CHAPTER FOUR: WHO KILLED SERGEI KIROV?

Abramovich, Raphael R. *The Soviet Revolution*. London: George Allen & Unwin, 1962.

Andrew, Christopher, and Oleg Gordievsky. *KGB: The Inside Story of Foreign Operations from Lenin to Gorbachev*. New York: Harper Collins, 1990.

Applebaum, Anne. *GULAG: A History of the Soviet Concentration Camps*. London: Doubleday, 2003.

Bauer, Raymond A., and Edward Wasiolek. *Nine Soviet Portraits*. Westport, CT: Greenwood Press, 1979.

Beck, F., and W. Godin. *Russian Purge and the Extraction of Confession*. London: Hurst & Blackett, 1951.

Carr, Edward H. *The Bolshevik Revolution*. Harmondsworth: Penguin, 1966.

Ciliga, Ante. *The Russian Enigma*. London: Routledge, 1940.

Cohen, Stephen F. *Bukharin and the Bolshevik Revolution: A Political Biography, 1888–1938*. New York: Knopf, 1973.

Conquest, Robert. *The Great Terror: A Reassessment*. New York: Oxford University Press, 1990.

Conquest, Robert. *The Harvest of Sorrow: Soviet Collectivization and the Terror-Famine*. London: Oxford University Press, 1986.

Conquest, Robert. *Stalin and the Kirov Murder*. Oxford: Oxford University Press, 1989.

Deutscher, Isaac. *The Prophet Armed: Trotsky, 1871–1921*. London: Oxford University Press, 1954.

Deutscher, Isaac. *The Prophet Unarmed: Trotsky, 1921–1929*. London: Oxford University Press, 1959.

Deutscher, Isaac. *Stalin: A Political Biography*. New York: Oxford University Press, 1967.

Fainsod, Merle. *How Russia is Ruled*. 2nd ed. Cambridge, MA: Harvard University Press, 1963.

Figes, Orlando. *A People's Tragedy: A History of the Russian Revolution*. New York: Viking, 1997.

Fitzpatrick, Sheila, Alexander Rabinowitch, and Richard Stites. *Russia in the Era of NEP: Explorations in Soviet Society and Culture*. Bloomington, IN: Indiana University Press, 1991.

Getty, J. Arch. *The Origins of the Great Purges: The Soviet Communist Party Reconsidered, 1933–1938*. Cambridge: Cambridge University Press, 1985. http://dx.doi.org/10.1017/CBO9780511572616.

Glotzer, Albert. *Trotsky: Memoir and Critique*. Buffalo, NY: Prometheus Books, 1989.

Grin'ko, V.A. *The Bolshevik Party's Struggle against Trotskyism*. Moscow: Progress Publishers, 1969.

Hard, William. *Raymond Robins' Own Story*. New York: Harper & Brothers, 1920.

Kirilina, Alla A. *L'assassinat de Kirov: Destin d'un Stalinien, 1888–1934*. Paris: Éditions du Seuil, 1995.

Knight, Amy. *Who Killed Kirov?: The Kremlin's Greatest Mystery*. New York: Hill and Wang, 1999.

Krivitzky, Walter G. *I Was Stalin's Agent*. London: H. Hamilton, 1940.

Lenoe, Matthew E. *The Kirov Affair and Soviet History*. 2nd ed. New Haven, CT: Yale University Press, 2010.

Lincoln, W. Bruce. *Passage through Armageddon: The Russians in War and Revolution, 1914–1918*. New York: Simon and Schuster, 1986.

MacKenzie, David, and Michael W. Curran. *A History of the Soviet Union*. 3rd ed. Chicago: Dorsey Press, 1987.

Mahoney, H.T. *The Saga of Leon Trotsky*. San Francisco: Austin & Winfield, 1998.

Medvedev, Roy. *Let History Judge: The Origins and Consequences of Stalinism*. London: Spokesman Books, 1976.

Medvedev, Roy. *On Stalin and Stalinism*. London: Oxford University Press, 1979.

Medvedev, Zhores, and Roy Medvedev. *The Unknown Stalin: His Life, Death, and Legacy*. Woodstock, NY: Overlook Press, 2003.

Molyneux, John. *Leon Trotsky's Theory of Revolution*. New York: St. Martin's Press, 1981.

Montefiore, Simon S. *Stalin: The Court of the Red Tsar*. New York: Knopf, 2004.

Montefiore, Simon S. *Young Stalin*. New York: Alfred A. Knopf, 2007.

Naumov, Oleg V. *The Road to Terror: Stalin and the Self-Destruction of the Bolsheviks, 1932–1938*. New Haven, CT: Yale University Press, 1999.

Nicolaevsky, Boris I., *Power and the Soviet Elite: "The Letter of an Old Bolshevik" and Other Essays*. Edited by Janet D. Zagoria. New York: Praeger, 1965.

Orlov, Aleksandr. *The Secret History of Stalin's Crimes*. New York: Random House, 1953.

Patenaude, Bertrand M. *Trotsky: Downfall of a Revolutionary*. New York: Harper, 2010.

Payne, Robert. *The Life and Death of Trotsky*. New York: McGraw-Hill, 1977.

Phillips, Stephen. *Lenin and the Russian Revolution*. Oxford: Heinemann, 2000.

Rabinowitch, Alexander. *The Bolsheviks Come to Power: The Revolution of 1917 in Petrograd*. Chicago: Haymarket Books, 2004.

Rabinowitch, Alexander. *Prelude to Revolution: The Petrograd Bolsheviks and the July 1917 Uprising*. Bloomington, IN: Indiana University Press, 1968.

Rabinowitch, Alexander, and Janet Rabinowitch, eds. *Revolution and Politics in Russia: Essays in Memory of B. I. Nicolaevsky*. Bloomington, IN: Indiana University Press, 1972.

Riasanovsky, Nicholas V. *A History of Russia*. 6th ed. New York: Oxford University Press, 1963.

Reswick, William. *I Dreamt Revolution: A Memoir of the Right Wing Bolsheviks*. Chicago: Henry Regnery, 1952.

Sachar, Howard M. *A History of the Jews in the Modern World*. New York: Knopf, 2005.

Schapiro, Leonard. *The Communist Party of the Soviet Union*. New York: Random House, 1959.

Segal, Ronald. *Leon Trotsky: A Biography*. New York: Pantheon Books, 1979.

Serge, Victor. *Memoires d'un Révolutionnaire, 1901–1941*. Paris: Éditions du Seuil, 1951.

Serge, Victor, and Natalia Sedova Trotsky. *The Life and Death of Leon Trotsky*. New York: Basic Books, 1975.

BIBLIOGRAPHY

Sinclair, Louis. *Trotsky: A Bibliography*. Aldershot, UK: Scolar Press, 1989.

Slusser, Robert M. *Stalin in October: The Man Who Missed the Revolution*. Baltimore, MD: Johns Hopkins University Press, 1987.

Snyder, Timothy. *Bloodlands: Europe between Hitler and Stalin*. New York: Basic Books, 2010.

Souvarine, Boris. *Stalin: A Critical Survey of Bolshevism*. London: Secker and Warburg, 1964.

Thatcher, Ian D. *Leon Trotsky and World War I: August 1914–February 1917*. Basingstoke, UK: Palgrave Macmillan, 2000. http://dx.doi.org/10.1057/9781403913968.

Ticktin, Hillel, and Michael Cox. *The Ideas of Leon Trotsky*. London: Porcupine Press, 1995.

Trotsky, Leon. *1905*. New York: Random House, 1971.

Trotsky, Leon. *My Life*. New York: Grosset & Dunlap, 1960.

Trotsky, Leon. *Stalin: An Appraisal of the Man and His Influence*. Translated by Charles Malamuth. New York: Harper & Bros., 1941.

Tucker, Robert C. *Stalin as Revolutionary, 1879–1929: A Study in History and Personality*. New York: W. W. Norton, 1973.

Tucker, Robert C. *Stalin in Power: The Revolution from Above, 1928–1941*. New York: W.W. Norton, 1990.

Tucker, Robert C., and Stephen F. Cohen, eds. *The Great Purge Trial*. New York: Grosset & Dunlap, 1965.

Ulam, Adam. *The Kirov Affair*. San Diego: Harcourt Brace Jovanovich, 1988.

Ulam, Adam. *Stalin: The Man and His Era*. New York: Viking, 1973.

Volkogonov, Dmitriĭ. *Trotsky: The Eternal Revolutionary*. Translated by Harold Shukman. New York: Free Press, 1996.

Wheeler-Bennett, J.W. *The Forgotten Peace: Brest-Litovsk, March 1918*. New York: W. Morrow, 1939.

Wistrich, Robert. *Trotsky: Fate of a Revolutionary*. New York: Stein and Day, 1979.

CHAPTER FIVE: "RICHARD III" IN GERMANY

Bennecke, Heinrich. *Die Reichswehr und der "Röhm-Putsch"*. Vienna: Günter Olzog, 1964.

Bennecke, Heinrich. *Hitler und die SA*. Munich: Günter Olzog, 1962.

Bessel, Richard. *Political Violence and the Rise of Nazism: The Storm Troopers in Eastern Germany, 1924–1934*. New Haven, CT: Yale University Press, 1984.

Conway, John S. *The Nazi Persecution of the Churches, 1933–45*. London: Weidenfeld & Nicolson, 1968.

Deuerlein, Ernst. *Der Hitler-Putsch*. Stuttgart: Deutsche Verlags-Anstalt, 1962.

Domarus, Max. *Der Reichstag und die Macht*. Warburg: Selbstverlag, 1968.

Dorpalen, Andreas. *Hindenburg and the Weimar Republic*. Princeton, NJ: Princeton University Press, 1964.

Fest, Joachim C. *Hitler*. Vol. 1. New York: Harcourt Brace Jovanovich, 1974.

Frank, Hans. *Im Angesicht des Galgens: Deutung Hitlers und seiner Zeit auf Grund eigener Erlebnisse und Erkenntnisse*. 2nd ed. Neuhaus: Eigenverlag Brigitte Frank, 1955.

Franz-Willig, Georg. "Munich: Birthplace and Center of the National Socialist German Workers' Party." *Journal of Modern History* 29, no. 4 (December 1957): 319–334.

Franz-Willig, Georg. *Putsch und Verbotszeit der Hitlerbewegung, November 1923–Februar 1925*. Oldendorf: K.W. Schütz, 1977.

Gallo, Max. *The Night of the Long Knives*. New York: Harper & Row, 1972.

Goebbels, Joseph. *Das Tagebuch von Joseph Goebbels, 1925/26*. Schriftenreihe der Vierteljahrshefte für Zeitgeschichte No. 1. Edited by Helmut Heiber. Stuttgart: Deutsche Verlags-Anstalt, 1960.

Gordon, Harold J. *Hitler and the Beer Hall Putsch*. Princeton, NJ: Princeton University Press, 1972.

Gordon, Harold J. *The Reichswehr and the German Republic, 1919–1926*. Princeton, NJ: Princeton University Press, 1956.

Görlitz, Walter. *History of the German General Staff, 1657–1945*. Translated and edited by Brian Battershaw. London: Hollis & Carter, 1953.

Gritschneider, Otto. *Der Führer hat sie zum Tode verurteilt. . . . Hitlers "Röhm-Putsch": Morde vor Gericht*. Munich: C. H. Beck, 1993.

Hallgarten, George W.F. *Hitler, Reichswehr, und Industrie*. Frankfurt am Main: Europäische Verlagsanstalt, 1955.

Hanfstängl, Ernst. *15 Jahr mit Hitler: Zwischen Weissem und Braunem Haus*. Munich: Zürich Piper, 1980.

Heyen, Franz Josef. *Nationalsozialismus im Altag*. Boppard: Boldt, 1967.

Hitler, Adolf. *Mein Kampf*. Boston: Houghton Mifflin, 1943.

Hitler, Adolf. *The Speeches of Adolf Hitler*. Vol. 1, *April 1922–August 1939*. Edited by Norman Hepburn Baynes. New York: Oxford University Press, 1942.

Höhne, Heinz. *Mordsache Röhm*. Hamburg: Rowohlt, 1982.

Hossbach, Friedrich. *Zwischen Wehrmacht und Hitler, 1934–1938*. Göttingen: Vandenhoeck & Ruprecht, 1965.

Kershaw, Ian. *Hitler*. 2 vols. New York: W. W. Norton, 1999–2001.

Kissenkötter, Udo. *Gregor Strasser und die NSDAP*. Stuttgart: Deutsche Verlags-Anstalt, 1978. http://dx.doi.org/10.1524/9783486703436.

Kühnl, Reinhard. *Die nationalsozialische Linke, 1925–1930*. Meisenheim: A. Hain, 1966.

Landauer, Carl. 1923. "The Bavarian Problem in the Weimar Republic, 1918–1923: Part I." *Journal of Modern History* 16, no. 2 (1944): 93–115.

Large, David C. *Between Two Fires: Europe's Path in the 1930s*. New York: W. W. Norton, 1990.

Larson, Erik. *In the Garden of Beasts*. New York: Crown, 2011.

Lohse, Hinrich. "Der Fall Strasser." Typescript MS in the possession of the Forschungsstelle für die Geschichte des Nationalsozialismus in Hamburg, n.d.

Longerich, Peter. *Die braunen Bataillone: Geschichte der SA*. Munich: Beck, 1989.

Machtan, Lothar. *The Hidden Hitler*. New York: Basic Books, 2001.

Mommsen, Hans. "The Reichstag Fire and Its Political Consequences." In *Republic to Reich: The Making of the Nazi Revolution*, edited by Hajo Holburn, 351–413. New York: Pantheon Books, 1972.

Mosse, Werner E. *The German–Jewish Economic Elite, 1820–1935*. Oxford: Clarendon Press, 1989.

Müller, Klaus. *Das Heer und Hitler*. Stuttgart: Deutsche Verlags-Anstalt, 1969. http://dx.doi.org/10.1524/9783486595581.

Orlow, Dietrich. *History of the Nazi Party, 1919–1933*. Pittsburgh: University of Pittsburgh Press, 1969.

Papen, Franz von. *Der Wahrheit eine Gasse*. Munich: Paul List, 1952.

Pulzer, Peter. *The Rise of Political Anti-Semitism in Germany and Austria*. New York: Wiley, 1964.

Rauschning, Hermann. *The Voice of Destruction*. New York: G.B. Putnam, 1940.

Reck-Malleczewen, Friedrich. *Diary of a Man in Despair*. New York: Macmillan, 1970.

Rhodes, Anthony. *The Vatican in the Age of Dictatorship, 1922–1945*. London: Hodder and Stoughton, 1973.

Röhm, Ernst. *Die Geschichte eines Hochverräters*. Munich: F. Eher Nachf, 1934.

Rosinski, Herbert. *The German Army*. Washington, DC: The Infantry Journal, 1944.

Sauer, Wolfgang. "Die Mobilmachung der Gewalt." In *Die nationalsozialistische Machtergreifung: Studien zur Errichtung des totalitären Herrschaftssystems in Deutschland 1933/34*. 2nd ed. Edited by Karl Dietrich Bracher, Wolfgang Sauer, and Gerhard Schultz, 685–966. Cologne: Westdeutscher Verlag, 1962.

Schleunes, Karl A. *The Twisted Road to Auschwitz: Nazi Policy Toward German Jews*. Urbana, IL: University of Illinois Press, 1970.

Scholder, Klaus. *Die Kirchen und das Dritte Reich*. Frankfurt am Main: Propyläen, 1977.

Shirer, William L. *Rise and Fall of the Third Reich*. New York: Simon and Schuster, 1960.

Stachura, Peter D. *Gregor Strasser and the Rise of Nazism*. London: Allen & Unwin, 1983.

Strasser, Otto. *Hitler und Ich*. Konstanz: J. Asmus, 1948.

Turner, Henry A. *German Big Business and the Rise of Hitler*. New York: Oxford University Press, 1985.

Tyrell, Albrecht. *Führer befiehl ... Selbstzeugnisse aus der "Kampfzeit" der NSDAP*. Düsseldorf: Droste, 1969.

Tyrell, Albrecht. *Von "Trommeler" zum "Führer."* Munich: W. Fink, 1975.

Wheeler-Bennett, J.W. *The Nemesis of Power: The German Army in Politics, 1918–1945*. New York: St. Martin's Press, 1953.

Wheeler-Bennett, J.W. *Wooden Titan: Hindenburg in Twenty Years of German History, 1914–1934*. New York: W. Morrow, 1936.

BIBLIOGRAPHY

## CHAPTER SIX: A RETURN VISIT FROM AUSTRIA'S TATTERDEMALION SON

Andics, Hellmut. *Der ewige Jude: Ursachen und Geschichte des Antisemitismus.* Vienna: Molden, 1968.

Andics, Hellmut. *Der Staat den keiner wollte: Österreich 1918-1938.* Vienna: Herder, 1962.

Ardelt, Rudolf G. *Zwischen Demokratie und Faschismus: Das deutschnationales Gedankengut in Österreich, 1919-1930.* Vienna: Geyer, 1972.

Bärnthaler, Irmgard. *Die Vaterländische Front: Geschichte und Organisation.* Vienna: Europa Verlag, 1971.

Beller, Steven. *Vienna and the Jews, 1867-1938: A Cultural History.* Cambridge: Cambridge University Press, 1989.

Benedikt, Heinrich, ed. *Geschichte der Republik Österreich.* Vienna: Verlag für Geschichte und Politik, 1954.

Binder, Dieter Anton. *Dollfuss und Hitler: Über die Aussenpolitik des autoritären Ständestaates in den Jahren 1933/34.* Graz: Verlag für die Technische Universität Graz, 1979.

Bischoff, Günter, Anton Pelinka, and Alexander Lassner, eds. *The Dollfuss/Schuschnigg Era in Austria: A Reassessment.* London: Transaction Publishers, 2003.

Braunthal, Julius. *The Tragedy of Austria.* London: V. Gollancz, 1948.

Brook-Shepherd, Gordon. *Dollfuss.* Westport, CT: Greenwood Press, 1978.

Brook-Shepherd, Gordon. *Prelude to Infamy: The Story of Chancellor Dollfuss of Austria.* New York: I. Obolensky, 1961.

Bukey, Evan Burr. *Hitler's Austria: Popular Sentiment in the Nazi Era, 1938-1945.* Chapel Hill, NC: University of North Carolina Press, 2000.

Busshoff, Heinrich. *Das Dollfuss-Regime in Österreich.* Berlin: Duncker & Humbolt, 1968.

Buttinger, Joseph. *In the Twilight of Socialism: A History of the Revolutionary Socialists of Austria.* New York: F. A. Praeger, 1953.

Carsten, F.L. *Fascist Movements in Austria: From Schönerer to Hitler.* London: Sage Publications, 1977.

Carsten, F.L. *Revolution in Central Europe, 1918-1919.* Berkeley, CA: University of California Press, 1972.

Cassels, Alan. *Mussolini's Early Diplomacy.* Princeton, NJ: Princeton University Press, 1970.

Corvaja, Santi, *Hitler and Mussolini: The Secret Meetings.* New York: Enigma Books, 2001.

Deakin, Frederick. *The Brutal Friendship: Mussolini, Hitler, and the Fall of Italian Fascism.* New York: Harper & Row, 1962.

Edmondson, C. Earl. *The Heimwehr and Austrian Politics, 1918-1936.* Athens, GA: University of Georgia Press, 1978.

Eichstadt, Ulrich. *Von Dollfuss zu Hitler: Geschichte des Anschlusses Österreichs, 1933-1938.* Wiesbaden: F. Steiner, 1955.

Fingeller, Hans. *The Case of German South Tyrol Against Italy.* London: Allen & Unwin, 1927.

Fingeller, Hans. *Die Wahrheit über Südtirol nach Verbürgtem Tatsachenstoff.* Munich: Huber, 1926.

# BIBLIOGRAPHY

Fodor, Marcel William. *Plot and Counterplot in Central Europe: Conditions South of Hitler*. Boston: Houghton Mifflin, 1937.

Funder, Friedrich. *Als Österreich den Sturm bestand*. Vienna: Herold, 1957.

Gehl, Jürgen. *Austria, Germany, and the Anschluss, 1931–1938*. London: Oxford University Press, 1963.

Glaser, Ernst. *Im Umfeld des Austromarxismus: Ein Beitrag zur Geistesgeschichte des österreichischen Sozialismus*. Vienna. Europaverlag, 1981.

Goldhammner, Leopold. *Die Juden Wiens: Eine statistiche Studie*. Vienna: R. Löwit Verlag, 1927.

Grandi, Dino. *La politica estera dell'Italia dal 1929 al 1932*. Rome: Bonacci, 1985.

Gulick, Charles A. *Austria from Habsburg to Hitler*, 2 vols. Berkeley, CA: University of California Press, 1948.

Hanfstängl, Ernst. *15 Jahr mit Hitler: Zwischen Weissem und Braunem Haus*. Munich: Zürich Piper, 1980.

Heer, Friedrich. *Der Kampf um die österreichische Identität*. Vienna: Böhlau, 1981.

Heiden, Konrad. *Hitler: A Biography*. New York: Knopf, 1936.

Höhne, Heinz. *Die Zeit der Illusionen: Hitler und die Anfänge des Dritten Reiches, 1933–1936*. Düsseldorf: ECON Verlag, 1991.

Jagschitz, Gerhard. *Der Putsch der Nationalsozialisten 1934 in Österreich*. Graz: Verlag Styria, 1976.

Kendrick, Clyde K. "Austria under the Chancellorship of Engelbert Dollfuss, 1932–1934." PhD dissertation, Georgetown University, Washington DC, 1958.

Kerekes, Lajos. *Abanddämmerung einer Demokratie: Mussolini, Gömbös, und die Heimwehr*. Vienna: Europa Verlag, 1966.

Kindermann, Gottfried K. *Hitler's Defeat in Austria, 1933–34*. London: C. Hurst, 1988.

Kirk, Tim. *Nazism and the Working Class in Austria: Industrial Unrest and Political Dissent in the "National Community"*. Cambridge: Cambridge University Press, 1996. http://dx.doi.org/10.1017/CBO9780511599576.

Kirkpatrick, Ivone. *Mussolini: Study of a Demagogue*. London: Odhams Books, 1964.

Kitchen, Martin. *The Coming of Austrian Fascism*. London: Croom Helm, 1980.

Kreisler, Félix. *Von der Revolution zur Annexion*. Vienna: Europa Verlag, 1970.

Lamb, Richard. *Mussolini as Diplomat*. New York: Fromm International, 1999.

Leichter, Otto. *Otto Bauer: Tragödie oder Triumph*. Vienna: Europa Verlag, 1970.

Litschel, Rudolf W. *1934–Das Jahr der Irrungen*. Linz: Oberösterreichischer Landesverl, 1974.

Low, Alfred D. *The Anschluss Movement, 1918–1919, and the Paris Peace Conference*. Philadelphia, PA: American Philosophical Society, 1974.

Maas, Walter P. *Assassination in Vienna*. New York: Scribner, 1972.

Macartney, C.A., and Alan W. Palmer. *Independent Eastern Europe: A History*. London: Macmillan, 1966.

Macmillan, Margaret O. *Paris 1919: Six Months that Changed the World*. New York: Random House, 2001.

Miller, James W. *Engelbert Dollfuss als Agrarfachmann*. Vienna: Böhlau, 1989.

Mitrany, David. *The Effect of the War on Southeastern Europe*. New Haven, CT: Yale University Press, 1936.

Musman, Richard. *Hitler and Mussolini*. London: Chatto & Windus, 1968.

Michaelis, Meir. *Mussolini and the Jews: German-Italian Relations and the Jewish Question in Italy, 1922–1945*. Oxford: Clarendon Press, 1978.

Mussolini, Mancini Edvige. *Mio fratello Benito*. Florence: La Fenice, 1957.

Oxaal, Ivar, Michael Pollak, and Gerhard Botz, eds. *Jews, Antisemitism, and Culture in Vienna*. London: Routledge & Kegan Paul, 1987.

Papen, Franz von. *Der Wahrheit eine Gasse*. Munich: Paul List, 1952.

Pasvolsky, Leo. *Economic Nationalism of the Danubian States*. New York: Macmillan, 1928.

Pauley, Bruce F. *Hitler and the Forgotten Nazis: A History of Austrian National Socialism*: Chapel Hill, NC: University of North Carolina Press, 1981.

Petersen, Jens. *Hitler-Mussolini: Die Enstehung der Achse Berlin-Rom, 1933–1936*. Tübingen: Niemeger, 1973.

Rauschning, Hermann. *Gespräche mit Hitler*. Vienna: Europaverlag, 1973.

Rosenberg, Alfred. *Das politische Tagebuch Alfred Rosenbergs aus den Jahren 1934/35 und 1939/40: Nach der photographischen Wiedergabe der Handschrift aus den Nürnberger Akten*. Göttingen: Musterschmidt-Verlag, 1956.

Ross, Dieter. *Hitler und Dollfuss: Die deutsche Österreich-Politik, 1933–1934*. Hamburg: Leibniz-Verlag, 1966.

Rintelen, Anton. *Erinnerungen an Österreichs Weg*. Munich: F. Bruckmann, 1941.

Rusinow, Dennison I. *Italy's Austrian Heritage, 1919–1946*. Oxford: Clarendon Press, 1969.

Sachar, Howard M. *Dreamland: Europeans and Jews in the Aftermath of the Great War*. New York: Alfred A. Knopf, 2002.

Schausberger, Norbert. *Der Griff nach Österreich: Der "Anschluss"*. Vienna: Jugend und Volk, 1978.

Schuschnigg, Kurt von. *Austrian Requiem*. Translated by Franz von Hildebrand. New York: G.P. Putnam's Sons, 1946.

Schuschnigg, Kurt von. *Im Kampf gegen Hitler: Die Überwindung der Anschlussidee*. Vienna: Molden, 1969.

Stadler, Karl R. *The Birth of the Austrian Republic, 1918–1921*. Leiden: A. W. Sijthoff, 1966.

Starhemberg, Ernst Rüdiger, Fürst von. *Between Hitler and Mussolini: Memoirs of Ernst Rüdiger Prince Starhemberg*. New York: Harper, 1942.

Suval, Stanley. *The "Anschluss" Question in the Weimar Era: A Study of Nationalism in Germany and Austria, 1918–1932*. Baltimore, MD: Johns Hopkins University Press, 1974.

Sweet, Paul R. "Democracy and Counterrevolution in Austria." *Journal of Modern History* 22 (1950): 52–58

BIBLIOGRAPHY

Villari, Luigi. *Italian Foreign Policy under Mussolini*. New York: Devin-Adair, 1956.

Von Klemperer, Klemens. *Ignaz Seipel: Christian Statesman in a Time of Crisis*. Princeton, NJ: Princeton University Press, 1972.

Weinberg, Gerhard L. *Hitler's Foreign Policy: The Road to World War II, 1933–1939*. New York: Enigma Books, 2005.

Whiteside, Andrew G. "Austria." In *The European Right: A Historical Profile*, edited by Hans Rogger and Eugen Weber, 308–363. Berkeley, CA: University of California Press, 1966.

Wiskemann, Elizabeth. *The Rome-Berlin Axis: A Study of the Relations between Hitler and Mussolini*. London: Collins, 1966.

## CHAPTER SEVEN: ALL ROADS LEAD TO ROME

Ádám, Magda. *The Little Entente and Europe, 1920–1929*. Budapest: Akadémiai Kiadó, 1993.

Albrecht-Carrié, René. *Italy at the Paris Peace Conference*. Hamden: CTL Archon Books, 1966.

Aloisi, Pompeo. *Journal: 25 juillet 1932–14 juin 1936*. Paris: Librairie Plon, 1957.

Anzulovic, Branimir. *Heavenly Serbia: From Myth to Genocide*. New York: New York University Press, 1999.

Badoglio, Pietro. *Rivelazioni su Fiume*. Rome: D. de Luigi, 1948.

Banac, Ivo. *The National Question in Yugoslavia: Origins, History, Politics*. Ithaca, NY: Cornell University Press, 1984.

Bariéty, Jacques. *Les Relations franco-allemandes après la Première-Guerre mondiale: 10 novembre 1918–10 janvier 1925*. Paris: Éditions Pedone, 1975.

Barros, James. *The Corfu Incident of 1923: Mussolini and the League of Nations*. Princeton, NJ: Princeton University Press, 1965.

Bartlett, William. *Croatia: Between Europe and the Balkans*. London: Routledge, 2003.

Benedetti, Giulio. *La pace di Fiume dalla conferenza di Parigi al trattato di Roma: I documenti delle trattative diplomatiche e della lotta di Fiume, l'organizzazione tecnica, industriale, marittima, economica della citta e del porto, il testo integrale del trattato di Roma*. Bologna: N. Zanichelli, 1924.

Bonodeo, Alfredo. *D'Annunzio and the Great War*. Madison, NJ: Fairleigh Dickinson University Press, 1995.

Bonsal, Stephen. *Suitors and Supplicants: The Little Nations at Versailles*. New York: Prentice-Hall, 1946.

Broche, François. *Assassinat de Alexandre 1er et Louis Barthou*. Paris: Balland, 1977.

Burgwyn, H. James. *Italian Foreign Policy in the Interwar Period, 1918–1940*. Westport, CT: Praeger, 1997.

Burgwyn, H. James. *The Legend of the Mutilated Victory: Italy, the Great War, and the Paris Peace Conference, 1915–1919*. Westport, CT: Greenwood Press, 1993.

Cassels, Alan. *Mussolini's Early Diplomacy*. Princeton, NJ: Princeton University Press, 1970.

Clark, Christopher M. *The Sleepwalkers: How Europe Went to War in 1914*. New York: Harper, 2013.

Clissold, Stephen. "The Marseille Murders, 1934." *History Today* 29 (October 1979): 631–638.

Cohen, Lenard J. *Broken Bonds: The Disintegration of Yugoslavia.* Boulder, CO: Westview Press, 1993.

Colombani, Roger, and Jean-René Laplayne. *La Mort d'un roi: La Vérité sur l'assassinat d'Alexandre de Yougoslavie.* Paris: A. Michel, 1971.

Crampton, Richard J. *A Short History of Modern Bulgaria.* Cambridge: Cambridge University Press, 1987.

Curtis, Glenn E., ed. *Yugoslavia: A Country Study.* Washington, DC: Federal Research Division, Library of Congress, 1993.

Deakin, Frederick. *The Brutal Friendship: Mussolini, Hitler, and the Fall of Italian Fascism.* New York: Harper & Row, 1962.

Decaux, Alain. *Les Assassins.* Paris: Perrin, 1986.

Denitch, Bogdan Denis. *Ethnic Nationalism: The Tragic Death of Yugoslavia.* Minneapolis, MN: University of Minnesota Press, 1996.

Dragnich, Alex N. *The First Yugoslavia.* Stanford, CA: Hoover Institution Press, 1983.

Dragnich, Alex N. *Serbs and Croats: The Struggle in Yugoslavia.* New York: Harcourt Brace Jovanovich Publishers, 1992.

Dragnich, Alex N. *Serbia, Nikola Pašić, and Yugoslavia.* New Brunswick, NJ: Rutgers University Press, 1974.

Duroselle, Jean-Baptiste. *Le conflit de Trieste, 1943–1954.* Brussels: Éditions de L'Institut de Sociologie de L'Université Libre de Bruxelles, 1966.

Hoptner, Jacob B. *Yugoslavia in Crisis, 1934–1941.* New York: Columbia University Press, 1962.

Hughes, H. Stuart. "The Early Diplomacy of Italian Fascism, 1922–1932." In *The Diplomats, 1919–1939,* edited by Gordon Alexander Craig and Felix Gilbert, vol. 1, 213–17. Princeton, NJ: Princeton University Press, 1953.

Hughes-Hallett, Lucy. *Gabriele D'Annunzio: Poet, Seducer and Preacher of War.* New York: Knopf, 2013.

Jelavich, Charles. "Education, Textbooks, and South Slav Nationalism in the Interwar Era." In Allgemeinbildung als Modernisierungsfaktor, edited by Norbert Walter and Holm Sundhaussen, 127–142. Berlin: Harrassowitz in Kommission, 1994.

Jones, John Rison. "The Foreign Policy of Louis Barthou, 1933–1934." PhD dissertation, University of North Carolina at Chapel Hill, 1958.

Judah, Tim. *The Serbs: History, Myth and the Destruction of Yugoslavia.* 2nd ed. New Haven, CT: Yale University Press, 2000.

Kaplan, Robert D. *Balkan Ghosts: A Journey Through History.* New York: St. Martin's Press, 1996.

Kelly, Cecile. "The Foreign Policy of Louis Barthou." PhD dissertation, Georgetown University, Washington, DC, 1959.

Lamb, Richard. *Mussolini as Diplomat.* New York: Fromm International, 1999.

Lampe, John R. *Yugoslavia as History: Twice There Was a Country.* 2nd ed. Cambridge: Cambridge University Press, 2000.

Lampe, John R., and Marvin R. Jackson. *Balkan Economic History, 1550–1950*. Bloomington, IN: Indiana University Press, 1982.

Ledeen, Michael A. *The First Duce: D'Annunzio at Fiume*. Baltimore, MD: Johns Hopkins University Press, 1977.

Lederer, Ivo J. *Yugoslavia at the Paris Peace Conference: A Study in Frontiermaking*. New Haven, CT: Yale University Press, 1963.

Ljubisic, Davorka. *Politics of Sorrow: The Disintegration of Yugoslavia*. Montréal: Black Rose Books, 2004.

Maček, Vlado. *In the Struggle for Freedom*. Translated by Elizabeth and Stjepan Gazi. University Park, PA: Pennsylvania State University Press, 1957.

Mamatey, Victor S. *The United States and East Central Europe, 1914–1918: A Study in Wilsonian Diplomacy and Propaganda*. Princeton, NJ: Princeton University Press, 1957.

McDonald, Gordon, ed. *Area Handbook for Yugoslavia*. Washington DC: U.S. Government Printing Office, 1973.

Mittleman, Earl N. *The Nationality Problem in Yugoslavia: A Survey of Developments, 1921–1953*. PhD dissertation, New York University. UMI No. 22,962. Ann Arbor, MI: University Microfilms, 1975.

Mojzes, Paul. *Yugoslavian Inferno: Ethnoreligious Warfare in the Balkans*. New York: Continuum, 1994.

Moodie, A.E. *The Italo-Yugoslav Boundary: A Study in Political Geography*. London: G. Philip & Son, 1945.

Noël, Léon. *Les illusions de Stresa: L'Italie abandonée à Hitler*. Paris: France-Empire, 1975.

Papy, Michel, ed. *Barthou: Un homme, une époque: Actes du colloque de Pau, 9 et 10 novembre 1984*. Paris: Pau, 1987.

Ramet, Sabrina P. *The Three Yugoslavias: State-Building and Legislation, 1918–2005*. Bloomington, IN: Indiana University Press, 2006.

Rhodes, Anthony Richard Ewart. *D'Annunzio: The Poet as Superman*. New York: McDowell, Obolensky, 1960.

Roberts, Alan. *The Turning Point: The Assassination of Louis Barthou and King Alexander I of Yugoslavia*. New York: St. Martin's Press, 1970.

Robertson, Esmonde M. *Mussolini as Empire-Builder: Europe and Africa, 1932–36*. London: Macmillan, 1977.

Rusinow, Dennison I. *Italy's Austrian Heritage, 1919–1946*. Oxford: Clarendon Press, 1993.

Sadkovich, James J. *Italian Support for Croatian Separatism, 1927–1937*. New York: Garland, 1987.

Salvemini, Gaetano. *Mussolini diplomatico*. Translated by Antonino Castellett. Bari: Laterza, 1952.

Seton-Watson, Christopher. "The Anglo-Italian Gentleman's Agreement in French Diplomacy and its Aftermath." In *The Fascist Challenge and the Policy of Appeasement*, edited by Wolfgang J. Mommsen and Lothar Kettenacker, 267–82. London: Allen & Unwin, 1988.

Seton-Watson, Hugh. *Eastern Europe between the Wars, 1918–1941*. 3rd ed. Hamden, CT: Archon Books, 1962.

Stavrianos, L.S. *Balkan Federation: A History of the Movement toward Balkan Unity in Modern Times*. Hamden, CT: Archon Books, 1964.

Stavrianos, L.S. *The Balkans since 1453*. New York: Holt, Rinehart and Winston, 1963.

Tanner, Marcus. *Croatia: A Nation Forged in War*. New Haven, CT: Yale University Press, 1997.

Tomasevich, Jozo. *Peasants, Politics, and Economic Change in Yugoslavia*. Stanford, CA: Stanford University Press, 1955.

Toscano, Mario. *The Origins of the Pact of Steel*. Baltimore, MD: Johns Hopkins Press, 1967.

Trifkovic, Srdja. *Ustaša: Croatian Separatism and European Politics, 1929–1945*. London: S.C. Aiken, 1998.

Vucinich, Wayne S., ed. *Contemporary Yugoslavia*. Berkeley, CA: University of California Press, 1969.

Wachtel, Andrew. *Making a Nation, Breaking a Nation: Literature and Cultural Politics in Yugoslavia*. Stanford, CA: Stanford University Press, 1998.

Wandycz, Piotr S. *The Twilight of French Eastern Alliances, 1926–1936*. Princeton, NJ: Princeton University Press, 1988.

West, Rebecca. *Black Lamb and Grey Falcon: A Journey through Yugoslavia*. New York: Viking Press, 1943.

Wiskemann, Elizabeth. *The Rome-Berlin Axis: A Study of the Relations between Hitler and Mussolini*. London: Collins, 1966.

Woodhouse, John Robert. *Gabriele D'Annunzio: Defiant Archangel*. New York: Oxford University Press, 1998.

Young, Robert J. *In Command of France: French Foreign Policy and Military Planning, 1934–1940*. Cambridge, MA: Harvard University Press, 1978.

Young, Robert J. *Power and Pleasure: Louis Barthou and the Third French Republic*. Montreal: McGill-Queen's University Press, 1991.

CHAPTER EIGHT: GALLIC *FRATERNITÉ* UNDER THE THIRD REPUBLIC

Allen, Luther A. "The French Left and Soviet Russia: Origins of the Popular Front." *World Affairs Quarterly* 30 (July 1959): 91–121.

Anderson, Malcolm. *Conservative Politics in France*. London: Allen & Unwin, 1974.

Audry, Colette. *Léon Blum, ou la Politique du Juste*. Paris: R. Julliard, 1955.

Baudouin, Paul. *Neuf mois au government: avril–décembre, 1940*. Paris: Éditions de La Table Ronde, 1948.

Berger, Marcel, and Paul Allard. *Les secrets de la censure pendant la guerre*. Paris: Éditions des Portiques, 1932.

Bernard, Philippe. *Le Fin d'un monde, 1914–1928*. Paris: Éditions du Seuil, 1975.

Bloch, Marc. *Strange Defeat*. Oxford: Oxford University Press, 1949.

Blumel, André. *Léon Blum: juif et sioniste*. Paris: Éditions de la Terre retrouvée, 1981.

Bourdrel, Philippe. *La Cagoule*. Paris: Éditions J'ai lu, 1973.

## BIBLIOGRAPHY

Bourdrel, Philippe. *Histoire des juifs de France.* Paris: A. Michel, 1974.

Bourgin, Hubert. *De Jaurès à Léon Blum: l'École normale et la politicque.* Paris: A. Fayard, 1938.

Caron, Vicki. *Uneasy Asylum: France and the Jewish Refugee Crisis, 1933–1942.* Stanford, CA: Stanford University Press, 1999.

Colton, Joel. *Léon Blum: Humanist in Politics.* New York: Knopf, 1966.

Dubief, Henri. *Le déclin de la Troisième République, 1929–1938.* Paris: Éditions du Seuil, 1976.

Duroselle, Jean Baptiste. *La décadence, 1932–1939.* Paris: Imprimerie Nationale, 1979.

Fysh, Peter, and Jim Wolfreys. *The Politics of Racism in France.* New York: St Martin's Press, 1998. http://dx.doi.org/10.1057/9780230373273.

Greene, Nathaniel. *Crisis and Decline: The French Socialist Party in the Popular Front Era.* Ithaca, NY: Cornell University Press, 1969.

Guérin, Daniel. *Front Populaire, révolution manquée.* Paris: F. Maspero, 1970.

Hughes, H. Stuart. *The Obstructed Path: French Social Thought in the Years of Desperation, 1930–1960.* New York: Harper & Row, 1968.

Jackson, Julian. *France: The Dark Years, 1940–1944.* Oxford: Oxford University Press, 2001.

Kedward, H. Rod. *France and the French: A Modern History.* Woodstock, NY: Overlook Press, 2006.

Kingston, Paul J. *Anti-Semitism in France during the 1930s: Organisations, Personalities, and Propaganda.* Hull, UK: University of Hull Press, 1983.

Lacouture, Jean. *Léon Blum.* New York: Holmes & Meier, 1982.

Larkin, Maurice. *France since the Popular Front: Government and People, 1936–1986.* New York: Clarendon Press, 1997.

Lorenz, Paul. *Les trois vies de Stavisky.* Paris: Presses de la Cité, 1974.

Lottman, Herbert R. *The Left Bank: Writers, Artists, and Politics from the Popular Front to the Cold War.* Boston: Houghton Mifflin, 1982.

Machever, Philippe. *Ligues et fascismes en France, 1918–1939.* Paris: Institut d'etudes politiques, 1974.

Macmillan, Margaret O. *Paris 1919: Six Months that Changed the World.* New York: Random House, 2001.

Maurras, Charles. *La démocratie religieuse.* Paris: Nouvelle librairie nationale, 1921.

Micaud, Charles A. *The French Right and Nazi Germany, 1933–1939.* New York: Octagon Books, 1964.

Namier, L.B. *Diplomatic Prelude, 1938–30.* London: Macmillan, 1948.

Namier, L.B. *Europe in Decay: A Study in Disintegration, 1936–1940.* London: Macmillan, 1950.

Noiriel, Gérard. *Les origines républicaines de Vichy.* Paris: Hachette Littératures, 1999.

Nolte, Ernst. *The Three Faces of Fascism: Action Française, Italian fascism, National Socialism.* New York: Holt, Rinehart and Winston, 1965.

Paxton, Robert O. *The Anatomy of Fascism.* New York: Vintage Books, 2005.

Pertinax (Géraud, André). *The Gravediggers of France*. Garden City, NY: Doubleday, Doran & Co., 1944.

Philippet, Jean. *Les Jeunesses patriotes et Pierre Taittinger, 1924–1940*. Paris: Institut d'etudes politiques, 1967.

Plumyène, Jean, and Raymond LaSierra. *Les Fascismes français, 1923–1963*. Paris: Éditions du Seuil, 1963.

Poliakov, Léon. *The History of Anti-Semitism*, 4 vols. New York: Vanguard Press, 1977.

Prost, Antoine. *Histoire générale de l'enseignement et de l'éducation*, vol. 4, *L'école et la famille dans une société en mutation, 1930–1980*. Paris: Éditions de la Nouvelle Librairie de France, 1981.

Pugliese, Stanislao G. *Carlo Rosselli: Socialist Heretic and Anti-Fascist Exile*. Cambridge, MA: Harvard University Press, 1999.

Pugliese, Stanislao G. "Death in Exile: The Assassination of Carlo Rosselli." *Journal of Contemporary History*. 32, no. 3 (1997): 305–319.

Rémond, René. *La Droite en France de la Première Restauration à la Ve République*. 2nd ed. Paris: Aubier, Éditions Montaigne, 1982.

Sachar, Howard M. *Dreamland: Europeans and Jews in the Aftermath of the Great War*. New York: Alfred A. Knopf, 2002.

Salvemini, Gaetano. *Carlo et Nello Rosselli*. 2nd ed. Paris: Ed. di "Giustizia e libertà", 1948.

Sarkozy, Nicolas. *Georges Mandel: Le moine de la politique*. Paris: B. Grasset, 1994.

Sherwood, John M. *Georges Mandel and the Third Republic*. Stanford, CA: Stanford University Press, 1970.

Shirer, William L. *The Collapse of the Third Republic*. New York: Simon and Schuster, 1969.

Sorlin, Pierre. *"La Croix" et les juifs*. Paris: B. Grasset, 1967.

Soucy, Robert J. *French Fascism: The Second Wave, 1933–1939*. New Haven, CT: Yale University Press, 1995.

Sternhell, Zeev. *La droite révolutionnaire: Les origines françaises du fascisme, 1885–1914*. Paris: Éditions du Seuil, 1978.

Talmon, Jacob L. *The Origins of Totalitarian Democracy*. London: Secker & Warburg, 1955.

Tenenbaum, Edward R. *The Action Française: Die-Hard Reactionaries in Twentieth-Century France*. New York: Wiley, 1962.

Varenne, Francisque. *Mon patron, Georges Mandel*. Paris: Éditions Défense de la France, 1948.

Weber, Eugene. *Action Française: Royalism and Reaction in Twentieth Century France*. Palo Alto, CA: Stanford University Press, 1962.

Weber, Eugene. *The Hollow Years: France in the 1930s*. New York: W. W. Norton, 1994.

Werth, Alexandre. *The Twilight of France, 1933–1940*. Translated by D.W. Brogan New York: H. Fertig, 1942.

Wormser, Georges. *Georges Mandel, l'homme politique*. Paris: Plon, 1967.

Wormser, Georges. *La république de Clemenceau*. Paris: Presses universitaires de France, 1961.

BIBLIOGRAPHY

CHAPTER NINE: THE HUNT FOR LEON TROTSKY

Abramovitch, Raphael R. *The Soviet Revolution, 1917–1939*. London: Allen & Unwin, 1962.

Alexander, Robert J. *Trotskyism in Latin America*. Stanford, CA: Hoover Institution Press, 1973.

Applebaum, Anne. *GULAG: A History of the Soviet Concentration Camps*. London: Doubleday, 2003.

Beck, F., and W. Godin. *Russian Purge and the Extraction of Confession*. New York: Viking Press, 1951.

Bialer, Seweryn, ed. *Stalin and His Generals*. New York: Pegasus, 1969.

Breitman, George, and Sarah Lovell, eds. *The Writings of Leon Trotsky*, 12 vols. New York: Pathfinder Press, 1971–1978.

Bronstein, Valery. "Stalin and Trotsky's Relatives in Russia." In *A Trotsky Reappraisal*, edited by Terry Brotherstone and Paul Dukes, 8–15. Edinburgh: Edinburgh University Press, 1992.

Budenz, Louis F. *This Is My Story*. New York: McGraw-Hill, 1947.

Callelo, Osvaldo. *Trotsky y la revolución en America Latina*. Buenos Aires: Ediciones de la Izquierda Nacional, 2002.

Carr, Edward H. *The Twilight of the Comintern, 1930–1935*. New York: Pantheon Books, 1982.

Ciliga, Ante. *The Russian Enigma*. London: Routledge, 1940.

Cohen, Stephen F. *Bukharin and the Bolshevik Revolution: A Political Biography, 1888–1938*. New York: Knopf, 1973.

Conquest, Robert. *The Great Terror: A Reassessment*. New York: Oxford University Press, 1990.

Conquest, Robert. *The Great Terror: Stalin's Purge of the Thirties*. New York: Collier Books, 1973.

Conquest, Robert. *The Harvest of Sorrow: Soviet Collectivization and the Terror-Famine*. London: Oxford University Press, 1986.

Conquest, Robert. *Inside Stalin's Secret Police: NKVD Politics, 1936–1939*. London: Macmillan, 1985.

Conquest, Robert. *Stalin: Breaker of Nations*. New York: Viking, 1991.

Conquest, Robert. *Stalin and the Kirov Murder*. Oxford: Oxford University Press, 1989.

Cookridge, E.H. *The Soviet Spy Net*. London: F. Muller, 1954.

Deriabin, Peter, and Frank Gibney. *The Secret World*. New York: Doubleday, 1959.

Deutscher, Isaac. *The Prophet Outcast: Trotsky, 1929–1940*. London: Oxford University Press, 1963.

Deutscher, Isaac. *Stalin: A Political Biography*. New York: Oxford University Press, 1967.

Dewey, John, ed. *The Case of Leon Trotsky: Report of Hearings on the Charges Made against Him in the Moscow Trials*. New York: Merit Publishers, 1968.

Dewey, John. *Report of the Commission of Inquiry into the Charges Made against Leon Trotsky in the Moscow Trials*. New York: Monad Press, 1937.

BIBLIOGRAPHY

Doerries, Reinhard R. *Hitler's Intelligence Chief Walter Schellenberg*. New York: Enigma Books, 2009.

Dyadkin, Iosif G. *Unnatural Deaths in the USSR 1929–1954*. New Brunswick, NJ: Transaction Books, 1983.

Erickson, John. *The Soviet High Command: A Military-Political History, 1918–1941*. London: Macmillan, 1962.

Fainsod, Merle. *How Russia Is Ruled*. 2nd ed. Cambridge, MA: Harvard University Press, 1963.

Figes, Orlando. *Revolutionary Russia, 1891–1991: A History*. New York: Henry Holt and Company, 2014.

Fischer, George. *Soviet Opposition to Stalin: A Case Study in World War II*. Cambridge, MA: Harvard University Press, 1952. http://dx.doi.org/10.4159/harvard.9780674333987.

Getty, J. Arch. *The Origins of the Great Purges: The Soviet Communist Party Reconsidered, 1933–1938*. Cambridge: Cambridge University Press, 1985. http://dx.doi.org/10.1017/CBO9780511572616.

Ginzburg, Evgeniia. *Journey into the Whirlwind*. New York: Harcourt, Brace & World, 1967.

Glotzer, Albert. *Trotsky: Memoir and Critique*. Buffalo, NY: Prometheus Books, 1989.

Goldman, Albert. *The Assassination of Leon Trotsky*. New York: Pioneer Publisher, 1940.

Hansen, Joseph, ed. *Trotsky: The Man and His Work*. New York: Merit Publishers, 1969.

Katamidze, Slava. *Loyal Comrades, Ruthless Killers: The Secret Services of the USSR, 1917–1991*. Miami, FL: Lewis International, 2003.

Knight, Amy. *Who Killed Kirov?: The Kremlin's Greatest Mystery*. New York: Hill and Wang, 1999.

Krivitzky, Walter G. *I Was Stalin's Agent*. London: H. Hamilton, 1940.

Laqueur, Walter. *Russia and Germany: A Century of Conflict*. New Brunswick, NJ: Transaction Publishers, 1990.

Large, David C. *Between Two Fires: Europe's Path in the 1930s*. New York: W.W. Norton, 1990.

Levine, Isaac Don. *The Mind of an Assassin*. New York: Farrar, Straus, and Cudahy, 1959.

Medvedev, Roy. *Let History Judge: The Origins and Consequences of Stalinism*. New York: Knopf, 1976.

Montefiore, Simon Sebag. *Stalin: The Court of the Red Tsar*. New York: Knopf, 2004.

Morros, Boris. *My Ten Years as a Counterspy*. New York: Viking Press, 1959.

Mosley, Nicholas. *The Assassination of Trotsky*. London: Joseph, 1972.

Nicolaevsky, Boris I. "The Kirov Assassination." *New Leader*, August 23, 1941, 1–6.

Nicolaevsky, Boris I. *Power and the Soviet Elite*. New York: Praeger, 1965.

Orlov, Aliksandr. *The Secret History of Stalin's Crimes*. London: Jarrolds, 1954.

Patenaude, Bertrand M. *Trotsky: Downfall of a Revolutionary*. New York: HarperCollins, 2009.

Poretsky, Elizabeth K. *Our Own People*. Ann Arbor, MI: University of Michigan Press, 1970.

Petrov, Vladimir. *Empire of Fear*. London: Andre Deutsch, 1956.

*Reabilitatsiia: Politicheskie protsessy 30–50-kh godov*. Moscow: Politzdat, 1991.

Roberts, Geoffrey. *The Unholy Alliance: Stalin's Pact with Hitler*. London: I.B. Tauris, 1989.

Sachar, Howard M. *A History of the Jews in the Modern World*. New York: Knopf, 2005.

Salazar, A. Sánchez. *Murder in Mexico: The Assassination of Leon Trotsky*. London: Secker & Warburg, 1950.

Schellenburg, Walter. *The Schellenburg Memoirs*. London: A. Deutsch, 1956.

Sedov, Leon. *Livre Rouge sur le procès de Moscou*. Paris: Éditions populaires, 1936.

Serge, Victor, and Natalia Ivanovna Sedova Trotsky. *Vie et Mort de Léon Trotsky*. Paris: Amiot-Dumont, 1951.

Slezkine, Yuri. *The Jewish Century*. Princeton, NJ: Princeton University Press, 2004.

Snyder, Timothy. *Bloodlands: Europe between Hitler and Stalin*. New York: Basic Books, 2010.

Sudoplatov, Pavel, and Anatoliĭ Pavlovich Sudoplatov. *Special Tasks: The Memoirs of an Unwanted Witness, a Soviet Spymaster*. New York: Little, Brown and Company, 1994.

Thurston, Robert W. *Life and Terror in Stalin's Russia 1934–1941*. New Haven, CT: Yale University Press, 1996.

Trotsky, Leon. *Les Crimes de Staline*. Paris: Bernard Grasset, 1937.

Trotsky, Leon. *Stalin's Gangsters*. London: New Park Publications, 1977.

Trotsky, Leon. *Trotsky's Diary in Exile, 1935*. New York: Atheneum, 1963.

Tucker, Robert C. *Stalin in Power: The Revolution from Above, 1928–1941*. New York: W.W. Norton, 1990.

Tucker, Robert C., and Stephen F. Cohen, eds. *The Great Purge Trial*. New York: Grosset & Dunlap, 1965.

Ulam, Adam. *Stalin: The Man and His Era*. New York: Viking, 1973.

United States Congress. House Committee on Un-American Activities. *American Aspects of the Assassination of Leon Trotsky: Hearings*. Washington, DC: U.S. Government Printing Office, 1951.

Van Heijenoort, Jean. *With Trotsky in Exile: From Prinkipo to Coyoacán*. Cambridge, MA: Harvard University Press, 1976.

Von Herwarth, Hans. *Zwichen Hitler und Stalin*. Frankfurt am Main: Ullstein, 1985.

Weissberg, Alexander. *The Accused*. New York: Simon and Schuster, 1951.

## CHAPTER TEN: GALLIC *FRATERNITÉ* UNDER VICHY'S ARMISTICE

Abetz, Otto Friedrich. *Das Öffene Problem: Ein Rückblick auf zwei Jahrzehnet deutscher Frankreichpolitik*. Cologne: Greven, 1951.

Abetz, Otto Friedrich, *D'une prison*. Paris: Amiot-Dumont, 1949.

Adler, Jacques. *The Jews of Paris and the Final Solution*. Oxford: Oxford University Press, 1987.

Algazy, Joseph. *La Tentation néo-fasciste en France de 1944 à 1965*. Paris: Fayard, 1984.

Aron, Robert. *Histoire de Vichy, 1940–1944*. Paris: Fayard, 1955.

Atkin, Nicholas. *Pétain*. London: Longman, 1998.

Atkinson, Rick. *An Army at Dawn: The War in North Africa, 1942–1943*. New York: Henry Holt and Company, 2002.

Baraduc, Jacques. *Tout ce qu'on vous a caché: Les archives secretes du Reich*. Paris: Editions de l'Élan, 1949.

Baruch, Maurice Olivier. *Servir l'état français: L'administration en France de 1940 à 1944*. Paris: Fayard, 1997.

Baudouin, Paul. *Neuf mois au government: avril–décembre, 1940*. Paris: Éditions de La Table Ronde, 1948.

Beevor, Antony, and Artemis Cooper. *Paris After the Liberation: 1944–1949*. New York: Doubleday, 1994.

Benoist-Méchin, Jacques. *À l'épreuve du temps: Souvenirs II: 1940–1947*. Paris: Julliard, 1989.

Benoist-Méchin, Jacques. *Sixty Days that Shook the West: The Fall of France, 1960*. Edited by Cyril Falls. London: Cape, 1963.

Bleustein-Blanchet, Marcel. *Sur mon antenne*. Paris: M. Dodeman, 1947.

Blum, Léon. *L'histoire jugera*. Paris: Éditions Diderot, 1945.

Brinon, Fernand de. *Mémoires*. Paris: L.L.C., 1949.

Brody, J. Kenneth. *The Trial of Pierre Laval: Defining Treason, Collaboration, and Patriotism in World War II France*. New Brunswick, NJ: Transaction Publishers, 2010.

Brossat, Alain. *Les Tondues: Un carnaval moche*. Paris: Levalois–Perret, 1992.

Bùhrer, Jules (General X). *Aux heures tragiques de l'Empire, 1938–1941*. Paris: Office Colonial d'Édition, 1954.

Burrin, Philippe. *La France à l'heure allemande, 1940–1944*. Paris: Éditions du Seuil, 1995.

Callil, Carmen. *Bad Faith: A Forgotten History of Family, Fatherland and Vichy France*. New York: Knopf, 2006.

Catroux, Georges. *Deux acts du drame indochinois: Hanoï, juin 1940, Dien Bien Phu, mars–mai 1954*. Paris: Pion, 1959.

Chambrun, René de. *Pierre Laval: Patriot or Traitor?* New York: Scribner, 1984.

Chambrun, René de. *Pierre Laval devant l'histoire*. Paris: Éditions France-Empire, 1983.

Cliadakis, Harry. "Neutrality and War in Italian Policy, 1939–1940." *Journal of Contemporary History* 9, no. 3 (July 1974): 171–190.

Cointet, Jean-Paul. *La Légion Française des Combattants: La Tentation du Fascisme, 1940–1944*. Paris: A. Michel, 1995.

Cointet, Michèle. *L'Église sous Vichy, 1940–1945: La Repentance en Question*. Paris: Perrin, 1998.

Cole, Hubert. *Laval: A Biography*. New York: Putnam, 1963.

Curtis, Michael. *Verdict on Vichy: Power and Prejudice in the Vichy France Regime*. New York: Arcade Publishers, 2002.

# BIBLIOGRAPHY

De Gaulle, Charles. *War Memoirs*. 3 vols. New York: Simon & Schuster, 1950–1959.

Delperrié de Bayac, Jacques. *Histoire de la Milice, 1918–1945*. Paris: Fayard, 1994.

Döscher, Hans-Jürgen. *Das Auswärtige Amt im Dritten Reich: Diplomatie im Schatten der "Endlösung."* Berlin: Siedler, 1987.

Duroselle, Jean-Baptiste. *Politique étrangère de la France, 1939–1945*, vol. 2, *L'abîme: 1939–1944*. Paris: Imprimerie nationale, 1986.

Evrard, Jacques. *La Déportation des travailleurs français dans de IIIième Reich*. Paris: Fayard, 1972.

Ferro, Marc. *Pétain*. Paris: Fayard, 1987.

France. High Court of Justice. *Le procès du Maréchal Pétain*. Paris: Imprimerie des journaux officiels, 1945.

France. Ministry of Foreign Affairs. *Procès Laval: Compte rendu sténographique*. Paris: A. Michel, 1946.

Funck, Arthur L. *The Politics of Torch: The Allied Landings and the Algier Putsch, 1942*. Lawrence, KS: University Press of Kansas, 1974.

Gildea, Robert. *Marianne in Chains: In Search of the German Occupation, 1940–1945*. London: Pan Books, 2002.

Herbert, Ulrich. *Hitler's Foreign Workers: Enforced Foreign Labor in Germany under the Third Reich*. Cambridge: Cambridge University Press, 1997.

Hirschfeld, Gerhard, and Patrick Marsh. *Collaboration in France: Politics and Culture During the Naze Occupation, 1940–1944*. New York: Berg, 1989.

Jackson, Julian. *France: The Dark Years, 1940–1944*. London: Oxford University Press, 2001.

Jaffré, Yves. *Les derniers propos de Pierre Laval, recueillis par son avocat*. Paris: A. Bonne, 1953.

Jennings, Eric Thomas. *Vichy in the Tropics: Pétain's National Revolution in Madagascar, Guadeloupe, and Indochina, 1940–1944*. Stanford, CA: Stanford University Press, 2001.

Kedward, H.R. Occupied France: Collaboration and Resistance, 1940–1944. Oxford: Blackwell, 1985.

Kedward, H.R. *Resistance in Vichy France: A Study of Ideas and Motivation in the Southern Zone, 1940–1944*. Oxford: Oxford University Press, 1978.

Kedward, H.R., and N. Wood, eds. *The Liberation of France: Image and Event*. Oxford: Berg Publishers, 1995.

Kupferman, Fred. *Laval, 1883–1945*. Paris: Balland, 1987.

Langer, William L. *Our Vichy Gamble*. New York: Knopf, 1947.

Laqueur, Walter. *The Terrible Secret: Suppression of the Truth about Hitler's "Final Solution."* London: Weidenfeld and Nicolson, 1980.

Laval, Pierre. *The Diary of Pierre Laval*. Edited by Josée Laval. New York: C. Scribner's, 1948.

Laval, Pierre. *Les discourse de Pierre Laval, 1942–1944*. Paris: Fondation José et René Chambrun, 1999.

Laval, Pierre. *The Unpublished Diary of Pierre Laval*. Edited by Malcolm Muggeridge. London: Falcon Press, 1948.

## BIBLIOGRAPHY

Lloyd, Christopher. *Collaboration and Treason in Occupied France: Representing Treason and Sacrifice*. New York: Palgrave Macmillan, 2003. http://dx.doi.org/10.1057/9780230503922.

Lottman, Herbert R. *Pétain: Hero or Traitor?* New York: W. Morrow, 1985.

Marrus, Michael, and Robert O. Paxton. *Vichy France and the Jews*. New York: Basic Books, 1981.

Martin, Benjamin F. *France in 1938*. Baton Rouge: Louisiana State University Press, 2006.

Melton, George E. *Darlan: Admiral and Statesman of France, 1881–1942*. London: Praeger, 1998.

Michel, Henri. *Vichy: Année 40*. Paris: Robert Laffont, 1966.

Naud, Albert. *Pourquoi je n'ai pas défendu Pierre Laval*. Paris: Fayard, 1948.

Noguères, Louis. *Le véritable procès de Maréchal Pétain*. Paris: Fayard, 1955.

Novick, Peter. *The Resistance versus Vichy: The Purge of Collaborators in Liberated France*. New York: Columbia University Press, 1968.

Ousby, Ian. *Occupation: The Ordeal of France, 1940–1944*. New York: Cooper Square Press, 2000.

Paxton, Robert O. *The Anatomy of Fascism*. New York: Knopf, 2004.

Paxton, Robert O. *Vichy France: Old Guard and New Order, 1940–1944*. New York: Knopf, 1972.

Pétain, Henri-Philippe. *Verdun*. New York: Dial Press, 1930.

Reynaud, Paul. *Au coeur de la mêlée, 1930–1945*. Paris: Flammarion, 1951.

Rigoulet, Pierre. *Les Enfants de l'épuration*. Paris: Plon, 1993.

Rouquet, François. *L'Épuration dans l'administration française: Agents de l'État et collaboration ordinaire*. Paris: CNRS Éditions, 1993.

Rousso, Henry. "L'aryanisation économique: Vichy, l'occupant et la spoliation des Juifs." *Yod, revue d'études hébraïques, modernes et contemporaines* 15–16 (1982): 51–60.

Rousso, Henry. *Pétain et la fin de la collaboration: Sigmaringen, 1944–1945*. Brussels: Editions Complexe, 1984.

Rousso, Henry. *Vichy, l'événement, la mémoire, l'histoire*. Paris: Gallimard, 2001.

Roy, Jules. *The Trial of Marshal Pétain*. New York: Harper & Row, 1967.

Sachar, Howard M. *Dreamland: Europeans and Jews in the Aftermath of the Great War*. New York: Alfred A. Knopf, 2002.

Servent, Philippe. *Le mythe Pétain: Verdun, ou, les tranchées de la mémoire*. Paris: Payot, 1992.

Sherwood, John M. *Georges Mandel and the Third Republic*. Stanford, CA: Stanford University Press, 1970.

Shields, James. *The Extreme Right in France: From Pétain to Le Pen*. New York: Routledge, 2007.

Soupiron, Paul. *Bazaine contre Gambetta, ou le procès de Riom*. Lyon: Lugdunum, 1944.

Spears, Edward. *Assignment to Catastrophe*, 2 vols. London: Heinemann, 1954–1955.

Sweets, John F. *Choices in Vichy France: The French Under Nazi Occupation*. New York: Oxford University Press, 1986.

Varenne, Francisque. *Mon patron, Georges Mandel*. Paris: Éditions Défense de la France, 1948.

Warner, Geoffrey. *Pierre Laval and the Eclipse of France*. London: Eyre & Spottiswoode, 1968.

Wieviorka, Olivier. *Une certaine idée de la résistance: Défense de la France, 1940–1949*. Paris: Éditions du Seuil, 1995.

Williams, Charles. *Pétain: How the Hero of France became a Convicted Traitor and Changed the Course of History*. New York: Palgrave Macmillan, 2005.

Wormser, Georges. *Georges Mandel, l'homme politique*. Paris: Plon, 1967.

Zay, Jean. *Carnets sécrets de Jean Zay (de Munich à la guerre)*. Paris: Éditions de France, 1942.

## CHAPTER ELEVEN: THE HUMANIST OF YESTERDAY

Allday, Elizabeth. *Stefan Zweig: A Critical Biography*. Chicago: J.P. O'Hara, 1972.

Alsberg, Henry G., ed. *Stefan and Friderike Zweig: Their Correspondence, 1912–1942*. New York: Hastings House, 1954.

Arens, Hanns. *Der grosse Europaër Stefan Zweig*. Munich: Kindler, 1958.

Gehl, Jürgen. *Austria, Germany, and the Anschluss, 1931–1938*. London: Oxford University Press, 1963.

Matuschek, Oliver. *Three Lives: A Biography of Stefan Zweig*. London: Pushkin, 2012.

Nedeljković, Dragoljub Dragan. *Romain Rolland et Stefan Zweig*. Paris: Klincksieck, 1970.

Prater, Donald A. *European of Yesterday: A Biography of Stefan Zweig*. Oxford: Clarendon Press, 1972.

Schorske, Carl E. *Fin-de-Siècle Vienna: Politics and Culture*. New York: Knopf, 1980.

Sonnenfeld, Marion, ed. *The World of Yesterday's Humanist Today*. Albany, NY: SUNY Press, 1983.

Stern, Léopold. *La Mort de Stefan Zweig*. Rio de Janeiro: Ed. Civilizaçao Brasileira, 1942.

Strauss, Richard. *A Confidential Matter: The Letters of Richard Strauss and Stefan Zweig, 1931–1935*. Berkeley, CA: University of California Press, 1977.

Zohn, Harry. *Wiener Juden in der deutschen Literatur: Essays*. Tel-Aviv: Edition Olamenu, 1964.

Zweig, Friderike Maria Burger Winternitz. *Stefan Zweig: Wie ich ihn erlebte*. Stockholm: Neuer Varlan, 1947.

## STEFAN ZWEIG: SELECTED NON-FICTION

Zweig, Stefan. *Adepts in Self-Portraiture: Casanova, Stendhal, Tolstoy*. New York: Viking Press, 1928.

Zweig, Stefan. *Amok, a Story*. New York: Viking Press, 1931.

Zweig, Stefan. *Brazil: Land of the Future*. New York: Viking Press, 1941.

Zweig, Stefan. *Briefe* [Letters]. 4 vols. Frankfurt am Main: S. Fischer, 1995–2005.

Zweig, Stefan. *Briefe an Freunde*. Frankfurt am Main: S. Fischer, 1978.

Zweig, Stefan. *Jewish Legends*. New York: M. Wiener, 1987.

Zweig, Stefan. *Liber Amicorum Romain Rolland*. Zurich: Rotapfel-Verlag, 1926.

Zweig, Stefan. *Romain Rolland: The Man and His Work*. London: Allen & Unwin, 1921.

Zweig, Stefan. *Sternstuden der Menschheit: Zwölf historische Miniaturen*. Frankfurt am Main: Fischer Taschenbuch Verlag, 1978.

Zweig, Stefan. *The World of Yesterday: An Autobiography*. London: Cassell, 1943.

Zweig, Stefan. *Zeit und Welt: Gessamelte Aufsätze und Vorträge, 1904–1940*. Berlin: Bermann-Fischer, 1946.

# INDEX

Note: Page numbers in italics indicate maps.

Abetz, Otto
   anti-Jewish measures in France and, 358, 360, 361, 362
   background, 348–49
   against Georges Mandel, 354, 355
   as Nazi liaison, 349, 350–51, 352, 364, 369
   Pierre Laval and, 349, 371
   reparations from France and, 364
   Vichy trials of former French leaders and, 353, 354, 369
*Action Française* (newspaper), 267–68, 274, 277, 278, 283, 295
Action Française (organization), 267–68, 273–74, 278, 285, 289
Adler, Viktor, 187
AEG (Allgemeine Elektrizitäts Gesellschaft), 94–95
Ageloff, Ruth, 321
Ageloff, Sylvia, 320–23, 325, 326, 327–28
Ahlwardt, Hermann, 89–90, 143
Albania, 248, 249
Aleksandar I (Serbian king), 246
Aleksandar I (Yugoslav king)
   1920 elections and, 233
   acceptance of Louis Barthou's help, 250
   assassination of, 254–57
   dictatorship of, 236–37, 238
   enthronement, 233
   exodus during WWI, 226, 232
   foreign enemies of, 238
   marriage to Maria of Romania, 233
   Mussolini and, 249
   plot to kill, 250–54
   political ultimatum issued by, 235
   as regent, 232–33
   Stjepan Radić and, 234
   visit to France, 251, 252–53
   *See also* Kingdom of the Serbs, Croats, and Slovenes; Yugoslavia
Alekseev, M.V., 113
Alexander II (Russian tsar), 2
Alexandra (Russian tsaritsa), 107
Algeria, 356
Alibert, Raphaël, 341, 350, 359
Alldeutscher Verband, 93
Allgemeine Elektrizitäts Gesellschaft (AEG), 94–95
Alliluyeva, Nadezhda, 132
Aloisi, Pompeo, 250
Alsace, 264
Alsace-Lorraine, 76, 78, 81, 220, 335
Altmann, Charlotte (Lotte), 392–93, 396, 397–98, 399, 401, 403
"Alto Adige," 218, 219
Amendola, Giovanni, 59–60, 61
Anatolian Railway Company, 85

*Anschluss*, 186, 200–1, 220, 389, 394
antisemitism
    Boycott Day, 165
    in Christian Social Party (Austria), 188–89
    in France, 271–72, 284, 295–96
    against Georges Mandel, 353–54
    in Germany, 89–91, 92–94, 97–99, 165
    of Hitler, 144–45, 148, 164
    *Judenzählung* (census), 93–94
    against Léon Blum, 283, 285–86, 354
    Scheunenviertel district attacked, 98–99
    Stefan Zweig's failure to recognize, 399
    in Vichy government, 358–59
    in Vienna, 189
    *See also* Jews
Aosta, Duke of, 32, 60
Arco auf Valley, Anton von, 25–26
Armenia, 81
Arnhold, Eduard, 92
Aryan racism, 98, 143
Association Marius Plateau, 294
Auer, Erhard, 23, 26
August Wilhelm (German crown prince), 161
Austria
    1932 elections, 202
    annexed by Germany, 288, 394–95
    *Anschluss*, 186, 200–201, 220, 389, 394
    attack on Schutzbund and Social Democrats, 197–99
    Bosnia-Herzegovina annexed by, 225–26
    concordat with Vatican, 193
    Dollfuss government, 191, 192–93, 194, 199
    Enabling Law, 193–94
    fascistization of, 193–94, 197–99
    in Great Depression, 191, 192–93
    Hitler and, 394
    independence affirmed, 250
    Mussolini and, 183, 194–97, 200, 394
    new constitution by Dollfuss, 199
    Operation Sommerfest, 184, 205–17, 222
    paramilitary groups in, 189–90
    at Paris Peace Conference, 185–86, 218–19
    post–WWI, 184–86, 384
    Rome Protocols, 200
    Seipel government, 187–88, 189, 190, 195
    South Tyrol, 36–37, 77, 186, 218–20
    Streeruwitz government, 190, 195
    transition to republic, 186–87
    treason viewed in, 209
    Treaty of Saint-Germain, 185–86, 190
    *See also* Christian Social Party (Austria); Dollfuss, Engelbert; Habsburg Empire; Nazi Party (Austria); Social Democratic Party (Austria)
Austrian Legion, 202–4, 206, 217. *See also* Nazi Party (Austria)
*Avanti* (newspaper), 40–41, 42, 44
Aventinians, 59–60, 61
Axelrod, Tovia, 27
Azerbaijan, 81

Babich, Tony, 322
Bainville, Jacques de, 267, 273, 285
Bakayev, Ivan, 306
Balabanoff, Angelica, 39, 40, 42
Balbo, Italo, 31, 45
Baldwin, Stanley, 287
Ballin, Albert, 90, 92
Baraduc, Jacques, 375–76, 377
Barbusse, Henri, 399
Barrès, Maurice, 267, 271
Bartels, Adolf, 92–93
Barthou, Louis
    Aleksandar I's visit to France and, 251, 252–53, 254–55
    background, 241–42
    death of, 256–57
    in Doumergue's government, 279
    Eastern Europe diplomacy by, 241, 243–44, 345

INDEX

funeral for, 258
against Germany, 242–43
offer to mediate between Italy and
    Yugoslavia, 249–50
tributes for, 259
in Yugoslavia, 251
Bartók, Béla, 387
Bauer, Gustav, 83
Bauer, Max, 93
Bauer, Otto, 187, 191, 199
Bavaria
    acceptance of German sovereignty, 26
    Eisner government, 22–23
    extremist groups in, 146–47
    Hoffmann government, 26–27, 28
    independence of, 22–23, 25, 26
    Landtag elections, 25
    monarchy, 20, 22
    "pure" soviet government, 27–28
    revolution in during WWI, 11
    socialist governments in, 20–21
    Soviet Republic of, 27
Bavarian Red Army, 28
Bebel, August, 4, 6, 91
Belarus, 81
Belgium, 76, 333, 371
Beneš, Edvard, 240, 244
Beria, Lavrenti, 322, 325, 328
Bernstein, Eduard, 5–6, 7
Bernstorff, Johann von, 80, 83
Besselère, Joseph, 371
Bethmann-Hollweg, Theobold von,
    70, 85, 91
Bianchi, Michele, 31
Bismarck, Otto von, 35
Black Hand, 246
Blackshirts, 31–32, 45, 46, 50, 61. See
    also Fascist Party (Italy)
Bloc National (France), 269, 273
Blomberg, Werner von, 167, 169, 170,
    172, 173, 181
Blum, Auguste, 280
Blum, Léon
    antisemitism against, 283, 284,
        285–86

background, 280–81
Daladier's government and, 280, 282
on Georges Mandel, 369
Giacomo Matteotti's murder and, 58
imprisonment by Germans, 368–69
Leon Trotsky on, 300
physical attack of, 284–85
on Pierre Laval's trial, 376
in Popular Front, 284
as prime minister, 285, 286–88
Socialist partnership with
    Communists, 282
Socialist Party (France) and, 281–82
Spanish Civil War and, 287
testimony at Pétain's trial, 373
trial of by Vichy government,
    352–53
Bohusz, Maria, 2
Bolsheviks
    vs. Mensheviks, 110
    revolution by, 9, 107–8, 112, 281
    Rosa Luxemburg on, 9, 14–15
    supplanted by Stalin, 141
    See also Social Democratic Party
        (Russia)
Bonnet, Georges, 347
Bonomi, Ivanoe, 46
Borgotaro, 248
Boris III (Bulgarian king), 246–47
Borisov, Mikhail, 137, 138
Bosnia-Herzegovina, 225–26, 227, 228,
    232, 238
Bosnians, 225, 231, 237
Bouisson, Fernand, 280
Bourgin, Hubert, 283
Boycott Day, 165
Brandes, Moritz, 387
Brandler, Heinrich, 30
Brasillach, Robert, 353
Brauchitsch, Walther von, 169
Brazil, 379–80, 397
Brescia, 248
Brettauer, Ida, 380–81
Brettauer, Josef, 380
Bretty, Béatrice, 355, 367

# INDEX

Briand, Aristide, 243, 344
Brinon, Fernand de, 289, 371, 372
Britain. *See* Great Britain
Brockdorff-Rantzau, Ulrich von, 80, 81, 83
Bronshtein, David and Anna, 108, 329
Brownshirts. *See* Sturm Abteilung (SA)
Bucard, Marcel, 274
Budenz, Louis, 321
Budyenny, Semyon, 311, 315
Bukharin, Nicholai, 120, 121, 122, 130, 310–11
   new 1935 constitution and, 303
Bulgaria, 246–47
*Bulletin of the Opposition* (journal), 299, 301
Bülow, Bernhard von, 96–97
Burger, Ephraim, 383

Café Weghuber, 183, 209
*Cagoule* (Comité Secret d'Action Révolutionnaire), 290–91, 292–94
Camelots du Roi, 268, 285, 290
*Candide* (newspaper), 295
capitalism, 5–6
Cárdenas, Lázaro, 302, 303, 307, 318
Carnaro, State of, 230–31
Castro, Fidel, 329
Catholic Action (Piusverein), 193
Catholic Church, 163, 193. *See also* Vatican
Catholic Youth Organization, 163
Center Party (Germany)
   1920 elections, 30
   1932 election, 158
   Enabling Act and, 162
   in Hitler's cabinet, 158
   Matthias Erzberger in, 86
   monarchist views of, 172
   positions on WWI, 71
   Treaty of Brest-Litovsk and, 72
   Treaty of Versailles and, 83
Cernozemski, Vlado, 251, 252, 253–54, 256, 258

Chaigneau, Jean, 363
Chamberlain, Houston Stewart, 143
Chamberlain, Neville, 289, 332, 333, 335, 346
Champetier de Ribes, Auguste, 332, 335
Chautemps, Camille, 277–78, 288
Cheka, 118, 121, 124. *See also* GPU; NKVD
Chicherin, Georgi, 101
Chirac, Jacques, 364
Christian Social Party (Austria)
   antisemitism of, 188–89
   Dollfuss and, 192, 194
   in government, 187, 191, 194
   Heimwehr as branch of, 190, 194
   Ignaz Seipel in, 187
   influence of on Nazi Party, 145
   Mussolini and, 195
   suspension of, 194
   *See also* Heimwehr
Chudov, Mikhail, 136, 138
Churchill, Winston, 335, 337, 342
Ciano, Galeazzo, 292
civil purgation, 132
Clemenceau, Georges, 219, 243, 263–64, 265–66, 268–69, 270
Clemenceau, Michel, 355
Cohen, Hermann, 92, 93
Comintern (Communist International), 120, 124, 281, 301. *See also* Third International
Comité d'Action Française. *See* Action Française (organization)
Comité France-Allemagne, 289
Comité Secret d'Action Révolutionnaire (*La Cagoule*), 290–91, 292–94
Committee of National Liberation (France), 356
communism. *See* Bolsheviks; Comintern (Communist International); Fourth International; Soviet Union; Third International; *and individual communist parties*

# INDEX

Communist Central Committee (Russia)
  awards for Leon Trotsky, 114
  Lenin's last testament and, 122–23
  post–WWI, 113, 114–15
  purges and, 130–32
  Treaty of Brest-Litovsk and, 74
  Trotsky vs. Stalin and, 121, 124
  See also Communist Party (Russia); Soviet Union
Communist Party (Austria), 318
Communist Party (France), 282, 284, 287, 288, 289, 344
Communist Party (Germany)
  1932 elections, 157–58
  1933 elections, 160
  destruction of, 318
  formation of, 15
  Nazi Party against, 160
  Paul Levi as leader of, 19, 30
  revolution attempted by, 15–16
  second attempted revolution, 17–18
  third attempted revolution, 30
  See also Spartakusbund
Communist Party (Hungary), 318
Communist Party (Italy), 45, 48, 61, 318
Communist Party (Norway), 301
Communist Party (Poland), 318
Communist Party (Romania), 318
Communist Party (Russia)
  naming of, 113
  office of party secretariat, 115, 118
  Stalin and, 121–22, 141
  against Trotsky, 123
  See also Communist Central Committee (Russia); Soviet Union
Communist Party (Spain), 318
Community of German People's Unions, 97–98
Confédération Générale du Travail, 290
Congress of Berlin, 225
Conquest, Robert, 316

Conservative Party (Germany), 70–71, 90
Consistoire Israélite, 272
Constitutional Democratic Party (Kadets; Russia), 107
Cooper, Alfred Duff, 376
Corfu Declaration, 228, 232
corporation laws (Italy, 1926), 64
Cosattini, Giovanni, 52
Coudenhove-Kalergi, Richard, 389
Creditanstalt, 191, 193, 194, 237–38
Croatia, 195, 227, 244, 258. See also Croats; Pavelić, Ante; Radić, Stjepan; Ustaša
Croatian Peasant Party, 238, 244. See also Republican Peasant Party
Croats
  in 1920 elections, 233
  in 1923 elections, 235
  in Habsburg Empire, 225
  post–WWI, 232
  self-perception of, 244
  in South Slav union, 228, 231, 234–36
  South Slav unity and, 225
  See also Croatia
Croce, Benedetto, 58, 59
Croix de Feu, 274–75, 278–79, 288, 289. See also Parti Social Français (France)
Cuba, 329
Czechoslovakia
  annexation of, 289, 295, 332, 346–47, 395, 396
  mutual defense agreements by, 239–40, 244, 346

D'Abernon, Edgar, 102
Daladier, Édouard
  antisemitic directives of, 295–96
  asylum for Leon Trotsky, 299
  closure of Communist Party by, 289
  Czechoslovakia and, 295, 346–47
  imprisoned by Germans, 368
  Léon Blum and, 280
  in Popular Front, 284

as prime minister, 278, 279, 280, 282, 288–89
Rosselli brothers' tombstone and, 293
testimony at Pétain's trial, 373
trial of by Vichy government, 352
WWII and, 332–33
Dalmatia, 200, 232
Dannecker, Theodor, 360, 361
D'Annunzio, Gabriele, 44, 47, 230–31, 247–48
Danzig, 295
Darlan, François, 350, 351–52, 354, 359, 360, 361
Darnand, Joseph, 366–67, 371, 372
Darquier, Louis, 360, 362, 372
Daudet, Alphonse, 268
Daudet, Léon, 267, 268, 272, 273, 283
Dawes Plan, 155–56, 272
De Bono, Emilio, 31, 49, 51, 54, 61
De Capitani d'Arzago, Giuseppe, 48
De Gaulle, Charles
  Mikhail Tukhachevsky and, 312
  Pierre Laval's trial and death, 375, 376–77, 378
  trial of Pétain and, 373, 374
  in WWII, 356
De Stefani, Alberto, 48
De Vecchi, Cesare, 31
Déat, Marcel, 295, 354
December Law, 137, 139, 304
Del' Giudice, Mauro, 56, 62
Deloncle, Eugène, 290, 294
Denikin, Anton, 113
Denmark, 371
*Der Stürmer* (newspaper), 165
Derrien, Louis, 369
Deschanel, Paul, 270
Deutsch, Julius, 197–98, 199
Deutsche Bank, 85
*Deutschland* Pact, 170, 181
Dewey, John, 307
*Die Gesellschaft* (journal), 381
*Die Rote Fahne* (*The Red Flag*), 14, 16
*Die Zukunft* (journal), 381

Diels, Rudolf, 170, 171
Dietrich, Otto, 174
Diez, Karl, 87–88
Disarmament Conference, 166–67
Dobler, Johann, 183–84, 209, 210, 213, 215
*Documentation Catholique* (journal), 271–72
Dollfuss, Engelbert
  Anton Rintelen and, 205
  attack on Social Democrats, 198–99
  Austrian Nazi Party and, 202, 203
  background, 191–92
  concordat with Vatican, 193
  death of, 212
  elected chancellor, 191
  Enabling Law and, 193–94
  fascistization of Austria by, 193–94, 197–99
  funeral for, 215
  Hitler and, 201, 203–4
  League of Nations and, 192–93
  Mussolini and, 182–83, 194–96, 199–200
  new constitution by, 199
  Operation Sommerfest and, 208, 210, 212
Dollfuss, Josefa, 191
Doriot, Jacques, 290, 295, 354
Doumergue, Gaston
  appointment of Georges Mandel, 332
  at Louis Barthou's funeral, 258
  Pierre Laval and, 260, 345
  as prime minister, 243, 279, 282, 345
Draga (Serbian queen), 246
Dreitzer, Yefim, 306
Drexler, Anton, 145, 146, 150, 151
Dreyfus, Alfred, 285
Dreyfus Affair, 264, 266, 284
Drumont, Édouard, 266, 268
Duhamel, Georges, 399
Dühring, Eugen, 98, 143
Dulles, John Foster, 82
Dumini, Amerigo, 53, 54, 56, 60, 63
Dzerzhinski, Feliks, 118, 121

# INDEX

Ebert, Friedrich
  birth of German republic and, 11–12
  as chancellor, 12–13, 16, 29
  Eisner government in Bavaria and, 23
  eulogy for Walther Rathenau, 104
  Treaty of Versailles and, 83
  welcoming troops home, 79
Eckart, Dietrich, 147–48
Eckhardt, Tibor von, 260
Eden, Anthony, 260
Ehrhardt, Hermann, 147
Ehrhardt Brigade, 102
Eichmann, Adolf, 361
Einstein, Albert, 237
Eisner, Kurt, 20, 21–23, 25
Eitingon, Leonid (Nahum), 320, 321, 323, 324, 325, 326, 328
Enabling Act (Germany), 161
Enabling Law (Austria), 193–94
Epp, Franz von, 147
Erzberger, Matthias
  antisemitism of, 89, 93
  armistice implemented by, 79–80
  armistice negotiations led by, 67–68, 69, 76, 78–79
  assassination of, 87–88, 147
  background of, 70
  as finance minister, 84, 86
  Karl Helfferich against, 85–86
  murder attempt against, 86
  public opinion against, 80
  reactions to death of, 88–89
  on reparations, 86–87
  threat against, 83–84
  Treaty of Brest-Litovsk and, 72, 75
  Treaty of Versailles and, 83
  WWI views of, 69–70, 71
Erzberger, Oskar, 68
Estonia, 81
Ethiopia, 346, 394
Evdokimov, Grigorii, 306
*Evolutionary Socialism* (Bernstein), 5

Facta, Luigi, 32, 46, 195
Fasci di Combattimento (Combat Squads), 43–44. *See also* Fascist Party (Italy)
Fascist Grand Council (Italy), 58, 60, 63–64
Fascist Party (Italy)
  in 1919 elections, 44
  in 1921 elections, 45
  1924 elections and, 50
  assassination of Rosselli brothers, 291
  consolidation of power by, 60–61
  "enabling act," 49–50
  formation of, 43–44
  march on Rome, 31–33, 47
  membership, 45, 47
  paramilitary operations by, 45–46
  political coups in northern Italy, 46–47
  *See also* Italy; Matteotti, Giacomo; Mussolini, Benito
*Fascists Exposed* (Matteotti), 52
Fatherland Front, 183, 194, 196, 199, 200, 202. *See also* Heimwehr
Feder, Ernst and Erna, 398, 402
Feder, Gottfried, 145, 146
Federzoni, Luigi, 58
Feldman, Boris, 311
Ferrara, 46
Fey, Emil, 196–97, 198, 208–9, 212, 213, 214
Filippelli, Filippo, 54, 56
Finland, 81, 333
Finzi, Aldo, 56, 57
Fischer, Hermann, 102, 103
Fiume, 230–31, 247–48
Flandin, Pierre-Étienne, 280, 351
Foch, Ferdinand, 10, 69, 78, 335
Fourth International, 317–18, 322
France
  1936 elections, 284–85
  antisemitism in, 271–72, 284, 295–96

belle époque period, 266
Czechoslovakia and, 240, 244, 346
in Great Depression, 273, 275
immigration to, 271
Mussolini and, 241, 345
paramilitary and Far Right groups in, 267–68, 274–75, 278–79, 280, 289–90, 294
at Paris Peace Conference, 268–69
Poland and, 240, 244
political instability in, 272–73, 275, 278–80, 288–89
post–WWI, 263
pro-Nazi activity in, 295
reparations to, 269, 272
Ruhr Valley takeover by, 98, 142, 148, 243, 269–70
Spanish Civil War and, 287
Stavisky affair, 275–78, 282
in Stresa Front, 346
USSR and, 300–301, 346
work stoppages in Paris, 272
in WWI, 262–63, 264
in WWII, 333–34, 335–37
Yugoslavia and, 229, 241
*See also* Barthou, Louis; Blum, Léon; Clemenceau, Georges; Daladier, Édouard; Doumergue, Gaston; Vichy government
Franchet d'Esperey, Louis, 229
Françisme, 274
Franco, Francisco, 375
Frank, Josip, 245
Frank, Ludwig, 91
Frankist Party (Croats), 245
Franz Ferdinand (archduke), 226, 246
Franz Josef (Habsburg emperor), 189
Frauenfeld, Alfred, 202
Freikorps
 attempt on Rosa Luxemburg, 15
 Bavarian branch, 147
 Communist uprisings and, 16, 18, 30
 Spartacists and, 15
 White Terror in Bavaria, 28

Wolfgang Kapp uprising and, 29
French Equatorial Africa, 355–56
Frick, Wilhelm, 154, 159
Fritsch, Theodor, 92, 93
Fritsch, Werner von, 170, 173
Fürstenberg, Carl, 90

Galicia, 382
Gamarnik, Yan, 311
Gambetta, Léon, 263
Gamelin, Maurice, 333, 334, 368
Garašanin, Ilija, 225
Garibaldi Battalion, 291
Gasparri, Pietro, 58
Gaxotte, Pierre, 283
Geissler, Hugo, 362–63
George (Yugoslav prince), 232
Georges, Alphonse, 252, 254, 255, 256, 257
Georgia, 81
German Democratic Party (DDP), 30, 83, 99–100
German Labor Party, 145. *See also* Nazi Party (Germany)
German National Party, 98
German National People's Party (DNVP), 30, 158
German National Socialist Workers' Party (Austria), 201
German People's League for Protection and Defiance, 97–98
German People's Party (Austria), 200, 202
German People's Party (Germany), 30
Germany
 1919 elections, 28
 1920 elections, 30
 1928 elections, 156
 1930 elections, 156
 1932 elections, 156–58
 1933 elections, 160
 1934 plebiscite on Hitler, 181
 annexation of Austria, 288, 394–95
 annexation of Czechoslovakia, 289, 295, 332, 346–47, 395, 396

# INDEX

annexation policy during WWI, 70–71
*Anschluss* and, 200, 201
Ebert government, 11–13, 16, 23, 29–30
Enabling Act (1933), 161
foreign workers in, 364–66
against France's Spanish Civil War aid, 287
at Genoa conference, 100–1
Great Depression and, 156, 164
invasion of Poland, 332
Kaiser Wilhelm II's abdication, 11–12
military conscription in, 346
in occupied France, 354, 356, 368
at Paris Peace Conference, 80–81
post–WWI, 82–83, 84, 142–43, 155–56, 263
purchase of French newspapers, 289
reparations, 76, 81–82, 86, 100, 142, 148, 152, 155–56, 243, 269, 272
Ruhr Valley takeover, 98, 142, 148, 243, 269–70
as socialist heartland, 4
Treaty of Brest-Litovsk, 71–75, 76, 82
Treaty of Bucharest, 82
Treaty of Rapallo, 101
Treaty of Versailles, 36, 81, 83, 86–87, 166, 168, 312
USSR and, 101, 289, 322, 332, 365
Wolfgang Kapp uprising, 29, 146
WWI, protests against, 68–69
in WWI, 7, 10–11, 70–71, 263
WWI armistice, 67–68, 76, 78–80
WWI peace treaty, 29
in WWII, 332–34, 335–37
*See also* Communist Party (Germany); Hitler, Adolf; Nazi Party (Germany); Social Democratic Party (Germany); Weimar Republic
Gestapo, 170, 173, 176, 177

Gide, André, 283
Giolitti, Giovanni, 35, 45, 50, 59, 231
Giral, José, 287, 319
Giustizia e Libertà, 291
Glass, Fridolin, 206, 207, 208
Goebbels, Joseph
  1930 elections, 156
  captured by SA, 167
  coeditor of *Völkischer Beobachter*, 154
  cult of Hitler and, 161
  on Edmund Heines, 174
  Ernst Röhm against, 169
  ideological change of, 154
  Nazi installation ceremony and, 161
  in Night of the Long Knives, 174, 175
  post–beer hall putsch, 152
  Strasser brothers and, 155
Gömbös, Gyula, 200
Göring, Hermann
  1933 elections and, 159–60
  Ernst Röhm and, 169, 177
  in Hitler's cabinet, 159
  Mussolini and, 218
  in Night of the Long Knives, 172, 173, 174, 176–77, 179
  post–beer hall putsch, 152
  on SA, 171
  trip to Vatican, 162
Gorky, Maxim, 388, 399
GPU, 124, 125, 126–27, 131. *See also* Cheka; NKVD
Graziani, Rodolfo, 222
Great Britain
  attack on Mers-el-Kebir naval base, 342–43
  against France's Spanish Civil War aid, 287
  naval blockade of Germany in WWI, 96
  reparations and, 82, 269
  South Slav union and, 228, 229
  in Stresa Front, 346
  Sudetenland and, 332, 346, 395
  support for Austrian independence, 250

WWII and, 332
Great Depression
  in Austria, 191
  in France, 273, 275, 294
  in Germany, 156, 164
  Nazis and, 156
  in Yugoslavia, 237–38, 249
Greece, 248
*Grič* (journal), 245
Grillparzer, Franz, 209
*Gringoire* (newspaper), 295
Gröner, Wilhelm, 11–12
Guèsde, Jules, 281
Guidi, Rachele, 39–40, 65
Guillaume, Marcel, 278
Gumbel, E.J., 99
Günther, Martin, 102
Gutmann, Hugo, 144

Haas, Ludwig, 93
Haase, Hugo, 8, 91, 99
Haber, Fritz, 92
Habicht, Theo, 202–4, 206, 207, 217
Habsburg Empire
  Balkans in, 225
  dismantling of, 184–85, 186, 228
  new nations formed from, 239
  nostalgia for in Austria, 200
  political autonomy given to subject peoples, 34
  in Serbia during WWI, 226
  *See also* Austria; Hungary
Hammerstein, Kurt von, 166
Hanfstängl, Ernst ("Putzi"), 150
Harden, Maximilian, 99, 381
Haushofer, Karl, 389
Hedvicek, Eduard, 210, 212
Heimatbloc, 191, 196, 202
Heimwehr
  against *Anschluss*, 200–1
  as Christian Social Party (Austria) militia, 190, 194
  as Fatherland Front militia, 183
  formation of, 190

Heimatbloc as political wing of, 191, 196
  Nazi uprising and, 215
  Operation Sommerfest and, 213, 214
  against Schutzbund, 197, 198
  weapons from Italy for, 196, 200, 221
Heines, Edmund, 174
Helfferich, Karl, 84–86, 101
Henderson, Arthur, 58
Henriot, Philippe, 354, 369
Herriot, Pierre, 258
Hertling, Georg von, 71
Herzegovinians, 225, 237. *See also* Bosnia-Herzegovina
Herzl, Theodor, 381, 390
Hess, Rudolf, 26, 151–52, 154, 162, 169
Heydrich, Reinhard, 172, 173, 314, 360, 361
Himmler, Heinrich
  Ernst Röhm against, 169
  Eugen Kvaternik and, 252
  at meeting about SA, 170
  at memorial for Walther Rathenau's murderers, 104
  in Night of the Long Knives, 172, 173, 177, 179
  plot against Mikhail Tukhachevsky, 314
  on SA, 171
Hindenburg, Oskar von, 180, 181
Hindenburg, Paul von
  on armistice, 68, 69, 79
  ban on SA, 157
  burning of Reichstag and, 160
  death of, 180
  Ebert government and, 11–12
  on Hitler as chancellor, 158, 159
  illness of, 170, 172
  last will and testament, 180–81
  leadership of, 70
  monarchist views of, 172, 180–81
  at Nazi installation ceremony, 161
  on Night of the Long Knives, 179
  Operation Sommerfest and, 217

INDEX

as president, 156–57, 158
SA conflict and, 169
Treaty of Brest-Litovsk, 73, 74, 75
WWI final offensive and, 10
Hirsch, Julius, 92
Hirschfeld, Oltwig von, 86
Hitler, Adolf
  1930 elections, 156
  1932 political negotiations, 157–59
  1933 elections, 159–60
  1934 plebiscite on, 181
  antisemitism of, 144–45, 148, 165
  Austria and, 201, 203–4, 216–17, 220
  Austrian Nazi Party and, 201–2
  background, 143
  beer hall putsch, 149–51
  on Blum, Reynaud, and Mandel, 369
  burning of Reichstag and, 160
  challenge from Franz von Papen, 172
  as chancellor, 159
  cult of, 161–62
  Enabling Act (1933), 161
  Ernst Röhm and, 168–69, 170–71, 174–75, 177–78
  expansionist plans of, 200, 201
  family relations, 145
  Final Solution and, 363
  Gustav von Kahr and, 147
  Hindenburg's last will and testament and, 181
  industrial support for, 154
  invasion of USSR, 365
  *Mein Kampf*, 144, 145, 151–52, 201, 220
  military conscription and, 346
  Mussolini and, 218, 219–20, 221–22, 222–23
  Nazi Party founding and, 145–46, 148
  Night of the Long Knives, 172–75, 177–78, 179
  Operation Sommerfest and, 204–5, 222

  plot against Mikhail Tukhachevsky, 314
  Reichswehr and, 153, 165–67, 168, 173, 179
  relationship with Geli Raubal, 145
  SA and, 153, 165, 167–70, 170–71
  Strasser brothers and, 154–55
  Vichy government and, 349–50, 356
  "visibility" tactics of, 146
  in WWI, 143–44
  *See also* Nazi Party (Germany)
Hitler Youth (Hitler Jugend), 161–62, 163
Hoare, Samuel, 346
Hobson, John, 5
Hoffmann, Johannes, 26–27, 28
Hoffmann, Max, 71–72, 73
Holland, 333, 371
Horthy, Miklós, 183
Hugenberg, Alfred, 154
humanist internationalism, 387, 389
Hungary
  blamed for Aleksandar I's assassination, 259, 260
  Communist government under Bela Kun, 27
  Italian arms to, 248
  loss of territory after WWI, 185, 239
  Mussolini and, 195, 200
  in Rome Protocols, 200
  rule in Balkans, 238
  *See also* Habsburg Empire
Huntziger, Charles, 337

*Il Mundo* (newspaper), 51, 60
*Il Popolo d'Italia* (newspaper), 42, 43, 52, 66, 222
Imperial Hammer League (Reichshammerbund), 92
imperialism, 5
IMRO (Internal Macedonian Revolutionary Organization), 247
Independent Social Democratic Party (Bavaria), 21, 22, 25, 26–27

# INDEX

Independent Social Democratic Party (Germany), 8, 11, 12–13, 15–16
Insel-Verlag, 391
Institut d'Action Français, 294
Institut Royale, 294
Internal Macedonian Revolutionary Organization (IMRO), 247
International Brigade, 291
international humanism, 387, 389
*Iskra* (newspaper), 110
Istria, 232
Italian Liberal Party (PLI), 35, 36
Italian Popular (Catholic) Party (PPI), 44
Italian Social Democratic Party, 48
Italian Socialist Party (PSI)
    1913 and 1914 gains, 41
    in 1919 elections, 44
    Fascist government and, 48
    Matteotti murder and, 59
    Mussolini and, 39, 40, 42
    role in Italian politics, 35
    schisms within, 44–45
    against WWI, 41
Italy
    1919 elections, 44
    1921 elections, 45
    1924 elections, 50, 52
    Albania and, 248, 249
    Aleksandar I's assassination and, 259–61
    Austria and, 194–97, 200
    Corfu incident, 248
    economic modernization in, 35
    "enabling act," 49–50
    Fascist government, 47–48, 60–61, 63–66
    Final Solution and, 366
    Fiume and, 230–31
    France and, 287, 335, 345
    march on Rome, 31–34
    Matteotti murder fallout, 57–60
    at Paris Peace Conference, 43, 186, 218–19, 229–30
    political coups by Fascists, 46–47
    post–WWI, 37–38, 43
    *Risorgimento*, 34
    South Tyrol, 36–37, 77, 186, 218–20, 229
    in Stresa Front, 346
    territorial aspirations, 36–37, 229–30, 261
    Treaty of Saint-Germain, 186, 218, 230, 231
    Vatican and, 64–65
    voting rights in, 34–35
    WWI and, 35–37, 41–42
    WWII against France, 335, 337
    Yugoslavia and, 231, 249–50
    *See also* Fascist Party (Italy); Mussolini, Benito

Jakubiez, Fernand, 294
Japan, 400
Jaurès, Jean, 242, 281
*Je Suis Partout* (newspaper), 295, 353
Jeanneney, Jules, 355
Jentya, Aleksandra, 2
*Jeremiah* (Zweig), 383
Jeunesses Patriotes, 274, 278–79, 283
Jevtić, Bogoljub, 249, 255, 256, 260
Jews
    in Alsace, 264
    in Bavarian socialism, 25
    East European, 89, 91, 98, 145, 271, 390
    Final Solution, 360, 361–64, 366
    in France, 271–72, 294, 295–96, 357–58, 363–64
    in Germany, 89–90, 92, 98, 163–64
    Nazi Party and, 148
    patriotism of German, 92
    political murders of, 99
    political views of East European, 3, 90
    as Social Democrats, 91
    in Vichy France, 352, 357–64
    in Vienna, 144, 189
    in WWI, 92
    *See also* antisemitism

Joffe, Adolf, 72, 73, 124–25
Jogiches, Leo
   against attempted revolution, 16
   death of, 18, 99
   ideology of, 91
   in Poland's 1905 October uprising, 6
   political activities of, 3, 4, 9
   relationship with Rosa Luxemburg, 3–4, 6–7, 9, 14
   on Rosa Luxemburg's death, 17
   Spartakusbund and, 13, 17
*Journal de Var*, 265
*Judenzählung* (census), 92–93
Jung, Edgar, 172, 177
Junius, 8. *See also* Luxemburg, Rosa

Kadets (Constitutional Democratic Party; Russia), 107
Kahlo, Frida, 307
Kahr, Gustav von, 146, 147, 149–50, 177
Kamenev, Lev
   death of, 306
   defense of Stalin by, 122
   family of purged, 306
   partial pardon of, 133
   party schism and, 121
   in Politburo, 120
   purges of, 124, 132, 140, 141
   Treaty of Brest-Litovsk and, 72
   trial for Sergei Kirov's murder, 304–5
   Trotsky and, 123
Kapp, Wolfgang, 29, 146
Karageorgevič dynasty, 246. *See also* Aleksandar I (Yugoslav king); Petar I (Yugoslav king)
Karl (Habsburg emperor), 184–85, 188, 240
Karl-Marx-Hof, 198
Karwinsky, Ignaz, 210
Kautsky, Karl, 8
Kempka, Erich, 174
Kerensky, Aleksandr, 112
Kern, Erwin, 102, 103
Kessler, Harry, 96, 103
KGB, 141

Khrushchev, Nikita, 134, 139
*Kievskaya Mysl* (newspaper), 111–12
Kingdom of the Serbs, Croats, and Slovenes
   1920 elections, 233
   1923 elections, 235
   election process in, 234
   ethnic composition of, 231
   founding of, 227–28
   France and, 241
   governance assumed by Aleksandar I, 236–37, 238
   international support for, 229, 231
   in Little Entente, 240
   name changed to Yugoslavia, 236
   political challenges in, 232, 234–36
   post–WWI, 232
   precariousness of, 224
   *See also* Aleksandar I (Yugoslav king); Yugoslavia
Kirdorf, Emil, 154
Kirov, Sergei
   assassination of, 135–37
   background, 133
   funeral for, 138–39
   in government, 133–34
   investigation of death, 137–38
   Joseph Stalin and, 134–35
   against political executions, 131
   trials for death of, 139–40, 300–1, 304–5
Klement, Rudolf, 309
Knilling, Eugen von, 149–50
Knipping, Max, 370
Knochen, Helmut, 362–63, 368, 370
Knudsen, Konrad, 301
Koenig, Pierre, 373
Kogan, Abrão, 402
Koht, Halvdan, 302
Kolchak, Alexander, 113
Kornilov, Lavr, 112, 113
Korošec, Anton, 238, 258
Kosovo, 232
Kralj, Mijo, 250, 251–52, 253–54, 256, 259

Krestinsky, Nicholai, 310–11
*Kreuzzeitung* (newspaper), 89
Krivitsky, Walter, 313
Krupp von Bohlen, Alfried, 154
Krupskaya, Nadya, 119, 122–23
Kühlmann, Richard von, 71, 72, 73, 74, 75
*kulaks*, 128–29, 132
Kun, Bela, 27
Kvaternik, Eugen ("Slavko"), 245, 252, 253–54, 259

*La Cocarde* (newspaper), 267
La Rocque, François de, 274–75, 289, 295
*La Solidarité Française* (newspaper), 283
Labor Party (Norway), 301
Labour Party (British), 52
*L'Action Française* (newspaper). *See Action Française* (newspaper)
Lämmle, Heinrich, 402
Landauer, Gustav, 25, 27, 28, 99
Landbund (Austria), 191
Larina, Anna, 311
Lateran "Concordat" and "Treaty," 65
Latvia, 81
*L'Aurore* (newspaper), 265
Laval, Pierre
  Aleksandar I's assassination aftermath and, 260
  antisemitic measures and, 359
  background, 344–45
  Bernard Ménétral and, 341
  deportation to Germany, 371
  Ethiopia and, 346
  execution of, 377–78
  Final Solution and, 362–63, 366
  foreign workers (*relève*) and, 365
  Franco-Soviet treaty and, 300–1
  Georges Mandel and, 266, 355, 368, 369, 371
  German occupation and, 343, 348, 350
  against a government-in-exile, 347
  Hitler and, 349–50
  Mers-el-Kebir naval base attack and, 343
  Milice Française and, 366–67
  Mussolini and, 345
  Otto Abetz and, 348, 349
  post-Vichy, 374–75
  as prime minister, 345, 346
  on Reynaud, Mandel, and Blum's death sentences, 369
  on Reynaud and Mandel's imprisonment, 368
  Stresa Front and, 346
  suicide attempt by, 377
  testimony at Pétain's trial, 374
  trial of, 375–77
  in Vichy government, 347–48, 350–51, 352, 355, 361
  Vichy government formation and, 342, 348
  WWII and, 347, 356, 367
*Le Pelerin* (journal), 359
League of Nations, 166–67, 192–93, 248, 260, 346, 389
League of the Upright, 102
Lebanon, 355–56
Lebrun, Albert
  Aleksandar I's assassination and, 257
  Aleksandar I's visit and, 253
  German WWII invasion and, 334
  political instability under, 278, 279
  testimony at Pétain's trial, 373
  Vichy government and, 335, 338, 347
  visit to Morocco, 338
Léger, Alexis, 243
Légion des Volontaires Français, 352, 354
Légion Française des Combattants, 366
Lenin, Vladimir
  Bolshevik revolution and, 107–8, 112
  death of, 122
  illness, 119, 120
  last will and testament, 119–20, 122–23

Leon Trotsky and, 109–10, 112, 118–19
postwar collectivization and, 114–15
Stalin and, 115, 118, 119–20, 122–23
Treaty of Brest-Litovsk and, 71, 73, 74, 75
views on political organization, 119
in Zurich, 3
Lequerica, José Félix de, 375
Levi, Paul, 14, 19, 30
Levien, Max, 27
Leviné, Eugene, 27
Lewis, Ruby Weil, 321
*L'Humanité* (newspaper), 281
Liberal Party. *See* Italian Liberal Party (PLI)
Lie, Trygve, 302, 303
Liebknecht, Karl
  death of, 16–17
  *Die Rote Fahne (The Red Flag)* and, 14
  imprisonment of, 9
  Rosa Luxemburg and, 4
  Spartakusbund and, 13, 15
  against WWI, 7
Liebknecht, Wilhelm, 6, 21
Ligue des Patriotes, 274, 278–79
Lilien, Ephraim, 381
Lindner, Alois, 26
Lipp, Franz, 27
Lippert, Michael, 178
Lithuania, 81
Little Entente, 240, 241, 250, 260
Lloyd George, David, 82, 100, 219, 229, 268–69
Locarno treaties, 156, 243, 272, 344, 346
*L'Oeuvre* (newspaper), 295
Löhner, Markus, 208, 210
Loireau, Henri, 339–40
Lossow, Otto von, 149, 150
Lübeck, Gustav, 5
Ludendorff, Erich
  armistice supported by, 68
  in beer hall putsch, 149–51
  dismissed from Reichswehr, 76
  leadership of, 70
  Treaty of Brest-Litovsk and, 73, 74, 75
  in Wolfgang Kapp's uprising, 29
  WWI final offensive planned by, 10
Ludwig III (Bavarian king), 22
Lueger, Karl, 145, 189
Lukina, Nadia, 311
Lüttwitz, Walther von, 28
Lutze, Viktor, 171, 173
Luxemburg, Rosa
  attempted revolution supported by, 16
  background of, 2–3
  on Bolsheviks, 9, 14–15
  burial of, 19
  death of, 1, 16–17, 99
  *Die Rote Fahne (The Red Flag)* and, 14, 16
  ideological influence of, 4, 5, 7
  ideology of, 91
  imprisonments, 6, 8, 9–10, 13–14
  as Junius, 8
  marriage to Gustav Lübeck, 5
  misplaced body of, 20
  move to Germany, 4–5
  murder attempts on, 15
  in Poland's 1905 October uprising, 6
  political formation of, 1–2
  relationship with Leo Jogiches, 3–4, 6–7, 9, 14
  release from prison, 13–14
  retrospective assessment of, 19
  against revisionism, 5–6
  socialism of, 3
  Spartakusbund and, 13
  against WWI, 7–8, 9
Lyautey, Louis, 279, 286
Lyushkov, Genrikh, 140

MacDonald, Ramsay, 58
Macedonia, 227
Macedonians, 225, 231, 237, 247
Maček, Vladko, 238, 258

Magné, Eugène, 283
Mahrer, Karl, 183–84, 209
Malacria, Augusto, 54
Maltzan, Ago von, 101
*Man Without Qualities, The* (Musil), 95
Mandel, Georges
    antisemitism against, 270
    arrest and trial in Morocco, 339–40
    arrest by Pétain, 338
    assassination of, 369–71
    background of, 264–65
    in cabinet, 332
    falsified background of, 264–65
    Georges Clemenceau and, 264, 265–66, 270
    hiatus from politics, 331
    interned and trial in France, 352–55, 367–68
    interned by Germans, 368–69
    as minister of interior, 334
    against Nazi aggression, 332, 335, 338
    refusal to escape France, 339
Mandel, Hermine, 264
Mann, Heinrich, 237
Maria of Romania (Yugoslav queen), 233
Marinelli, Giovanni, 53, 54, 56, 62
Marne, First Battle of the, 41, 242
Marne, Second Battle of the, 10, 264
Marr, Wilhelm, 98
Martov, Julius, 3
Matteotti, Giacomo
    career, 51–52
    discovery of body, 60
    against Fascists, 52
    investigation of murder, 54–57
    kidnapping and murder of, 53–54
    plot against, 52–53
    political fallout of murder, 57–60
    trial for murder, 61–63
Matteotti, Velia, 54, 62
Mauriac, François, 376
Maurras, Charles
    Action Française and, 267–68, 273
    antisemitism of, 271, 272, 295
    background of, 267
    on Léon Blum, 283, 285–86
    Louis Darquier and, 360
    propaganda of, 271
    protests organized by, 278
    support for Vichy government, 343
    against war with Germany, 295
Maximilian of Baden (chancellor), 11, 67, 68, 99
Medved, Filip, 138
Medvedev, Mikhail, 311
Mehring, Franz, 13
*Mein Kampf* (Hitler), 144, 145, 151–52, 201, 220
Melamud, João, 400
Mendès-France, Pierre, 353
Ménétral, Bernard, 341, 350
Mensheviks, 110
Mercader, Caridad, 319–20, 323, 325, 328–29
Mercader, Ramón, 319–20, 321–23, 325, 326, 327, 328–29
Mercader Marina, Pau, 319
Mers-el-Kebir naval base, 342–43
Mexico, 302
Michaelis, Georg, 71
Miklas, Wilhelm, 182, 208, 211, 217, 393
Milan, 46
Milice Française, 366–67, 370
Millerand, Alexandre, 269
Mistral, Gabriela, 398
Molinier, Jeanne, 308, 309
Molotov, Vyacheslav, 138
Montenegrins, 231, 237
Montenegro, 225, 227, 228, 232
Morocco, 356
Moscow, 121
Mühsam, Erich, 25, 27, 28, 99
Munch, Edvard, 95
*Münchener Post* (newspaper), 21
Munich conference, 295
Musil, Robert, 95
Mussolini, Benito
    1924 elections, 50

Aleksandar I's assassination and, 259
ambition of, 41, 261
in the army, 39, 42–43
Austria and, 220–21, 394
*Avanti* and, 40–41, 42, 44
childhood of, 38
consolidation of power by, 60–61
Corfu incident, 248
cult of, 66
as dictator, 63–64
Dollfuss and, 183, 194–96, 199–200
"enabling act," 49–50
European tour, 46
Fascist Party and, 43–44, 45
Germany and, 394
health problems, 49
Hitler and, 218, 219–20, 221–23, 249–50
*Il Popolo d'Italia* and, 42, 43
imprisonment, 40
invasion of Ethiopia, 346, 394
Italian Socialist Party and, 39, 40, 42
*italianità* policy, 196–97, 219
in journalism, 39, 40
march on Rome, 31–34, 47
Matteotti murder and, 52, 54–55, 57–59
on Operation Sommerfest, 222
as prime minister, 47–50, 66
relationship with Rachele Guidi, 39–40, 65
Rosselli brothers and, 291
sexual promiscuity of, 49
support for Ante Pavelić and Ustaša, 248–49
in Switzerland, 38–39
territorial expansionist plans, 195, 220, 247–48
Vatican and, 65
in WWI, 42–43
*See also* Fascist Party (Italy)

Naldi, Filippo, 56
Narodnaya Volya (People's Will) party, 3
National Liberal Party (Germany), 71, 91
National Socialism (Nazism), 143. *See also* Nazi Party (Germany)
National Socialist Freedom Party (Germany), 152, 153
National Socialist German Workers' Party, 146, 154. *See also* Nazi Party (Germany)
*nationalisme intégral*, 267
Nationalist Party (Italy), 58
Naud, Albert, 375–76, 377
Naumann, Friedrich, 83–84
Nazi Party (Austria)
in 1932 elections, 202
banned by Dollfuss, 203
formation of, 202
Hitler and, 201–2, 203–4
Operation Sommerfest, 184, 205–17, 222
*See also* Austrian Legion
Nazi Party (Germany)
1928 elections, 156
1930 elections, 156
1932 elections, 156–58
antisemitism of, 148, 164
Anton von Arco auf Valley and, 26
Bamberg conference, 154
beer hall putsch, 149–51
book burnings by, 391
Boycott Day, 165
Catholic Church and, 162–63
Comité France-Allemagne and, 289
Enabling Act (1933), 161
founding of, 145–46, 148
Gustav von Kahr and, 147
ideological basis for, 143, 154
industrial support for, 154
installation ceremony for, 161
membership, 146, 155
memorial for Walther Rathenau's murderers, 104
Night of the Long Knives, 172–79
in northern Germany, 153
one party rule of, 161

Operation Sommerfest and, 207
post-beer hall putsch, 152–53
Treaty of Versailles and, 146, 148
"visibility" tactics of, 146
*Völkischer Beobachter*, 147–48
See also Hitler, Adolf; Sturm Abteilung (SA)
Nazi-Soviet Non-Aggression Pact, 289, 322, 332
Negrín, Juan, 375
Netherlands, 333, 371
*Neue Freie Presse* (newspaper), 381
Neurath, Konstantin von, 165, 216–17
Nevelson, Man, 298, 300, 329
Nevelson, Nina, 126, 329
New Economic Policy (USSR), 115, 121, 123, 127
Nicholas II (tsar), 106–7
Night of the Long Knives, 172–80
Nikolaev, Leonid, 135–37, 138, 139
Nitti, Francesco, 230
NKVD
    Leon Trotsky's assassination and, 320, 322, 324, 325
    Mark Zborowski as mole for, 309
    passports collected and used by, 322
    purges and, 139, 140, 310, 311
    role of, 140, 304
    See also Cheka; GPU
Noguès, Charles, 339, 340
*Non Mollare!* (journal), 291
Norway, 301, 333
Noske, Gustav, 16, 18, 19, 28
*Novy Mir* (newspaper), 111

Oberndorff, Alfred von, 69, 78, 79
Obrenovič dynasty, 246
Olberg, Ursula, 306
Olberg, Valentin, 304
*Oletzkoer Zeitung* (newspaper), 89
Operation Sommerfest, 184, 205–17, 222
Operation Torch, 356
Ordzhonikidze, Grigori, 118
Organization Consul, 102, 147

Orlando, Vittorio, 37, 38, 50, 59, 230
Orlov, Aleksandr, 320
Orlov, Vladimir, 315
Orsenigo, Cesare, 162–63
Ottoman Empire, 225
OVRA, 61, 291, 292

Pabst, Waldemar, 17
Pacelli, Eugenio, 102–3, 162
Painlevé, Paul, 264
Pan-Europa concept, 389
Papen, Franz von
    challenge to Hitler, 172
    as chancellor, 157, 158
    Hindenburg's last will and testament and, 180
    as minister to Austria, 217, 222
    monarchist views of, 172
    in negotiations with Hitler, 158–59
    Night of the Long Knives and, 176–77
    Vatican concordat and, 162, 163
Paris, 272
Paris Metro, 262
Paris Peace Conference
    Austria at, 185–86, 218–19
    France at, 268–69
    Germany at, 80–81
    Habsburg Empire at, 185–86
    Italy at, 43, 186, 218–19, 229–30
    provisions of, 81
    Romania and, 240
    USSR "successor states" and, 113
    See also Treaty of Saint-Germain; Treaty of Trianon; Treaty of Versailles
Parma, 46
Parti Populaire Français (France), 290, 354
Parti Social Français (France), 288–90. See also Croix de Feu
Pašić, Nikola, 227, 228, 229, 233, 235
Paul (Yugoslav regent), 258
Pavelić, Ante
    assassination of Aleksandar I and, 251, 252, 253, 259

background, 244–45
  Mussolini and, 248, 259
  Ustaša and, 245, 246, 247, 248
  Yugoslav death sentence for, 248
People's Party (Germany), 89
People's Party (Slovenia), 238
People's Will (Narodnaya Volya) party, 3
Perčec, Gustav, 250
Perovskaya, Sophia, 1–2
Pétain, Henri-Philippe
  antisemitic measures and, 359
  armistice negotiations with Germany, 334–35, 337, 339, 347
  against Blum government, 286
  career of, 340
  in Doumergue government, 279
  exile and death of, 374
  Georges Mandel and, 367–68
  against a government-in-exile, 338
  Hitler and, 349–50
  Jewish Affairs director and, 360
  on Mandel and Reynaud indictments, 354
  military action in WWII and, 356
  "National Revolution" of, 343
  patriotism of, 340
  Pierre Laval and, 350–51, 352
  political philosophy of, 341
  post-Vichy, 374
  as prime minister, 335, 338, 341, 347
  in Reynaud government, 334
  Roselli brothers' murderers and, 294
  trial of, 373–74
  Vichy government and, 342, 351, 361, 372–73
Petar I (Yugoslav king), 226, 232–33
Petar II (Yugoslav king), 258
Petrograd, 121
Pfeffer von Salomon, Franz, 153, 167, 168
Pilsudski, Józef, 244
Pius XI (pope), 58–59, 65, 162–63, 183, 193
Pius XII (pope). *See* Pacelli, Eugenio

Piusverein (Catholic Action), 193
Planetta, Oskar, 212, 214
Plekhanov, Georgi, 3
Poincaré, Raymond, 241, 242, 243, 269, 270
Poland
  1905 October uprising, 6
  diplomatic agreements signed by, 244
  fear of Central Powers, 239–40
  foreign workers in Germany from, 365
  invasion of, 332
  Rosa Luxemburg on tsarist, 3
  Treaty of Versailles and, 81
Politburo (Russia), 120, 121, 130–32, 134
Popular Front (France), 284, 285, 286, 287, 288, 289
Pospišil, Zvonimir, 250, 251–52, 253–54, 259
*Pravda* (newspaper), 111
Pressard, Georges, 277
Prince, Albert, 277
Progressive People's Party (Germany), 71
Proletariat (Polish workers' party), 2
Pugliese, Umberto, 32
Pujo, Maurice, 267

Rabinowitz, Gregory, 320, 321
Radek, Karl, 303
Räder, Erich, 170
Radić, Stjepan, 234, 235–36
Radical Socialists (France), 265, 269, 273, 284, 287, 333
Rafanelli, Leda, 41, 261
Rajić, Ivan, 250, 251–52, 253–54
Rasputin, Grigori, 107
Rathenau, Emil, 94–95
Rathenau, Walther
  assassination of, 101–3, 147
  in government, 99–100
  industrial career, 94–95
  Jewishness of, 96–97
  Kaiser Wilhelm II and, 90

love for Germany of, 97
mourning for, 103–5
social and intellectual life of, 95–96
trial for murder of, 104
WWI involvement of, 92, 94, 96
Ratti, Achille. *See* Pius XI (pope)
Raubal, Geli, 145
Ravel, Maurice, 387
*Red Flag, The* (*Die Rote Fahne*), 14, 16
Rédier, Antoine, 274
Redl, Alfred, 209
Reich Defense Council, 166
Reichenbach, Jeanne, 368
Reichshammerbund (Imperial Hammer League), 92
Reichstag, burning of, 160
Reichswehr
  against Communist final uprising, 30
  *Deutschland* Pact, 170, 181
  Hitler and, 153, 165–67, 168, 173, 179, 181, 216
  *Judenzählung* (census), 93
  new German republic and, 12
  in northeastern France during WWI, 263
  Soviet armed forces and, 312
  Treaty of Versailles and, 168
  White Terror in Bavaria, 28
  Wolfgang Kapp uprising and, 29
Reiss, Ignace, 308
Renner, Karl, 186, 187
Renzetti, Giuseppe, 218
reparations
  from Austria in WWI, 185
  Dawes Plan and, 155–56, 272
  from Germany in WWI, 76, 81–82, 86, 100, 148, 152, 243, 269
  proposed for Treaty of Brest-Litovsk, 73
  Ruhr occupation for, 98, 243, 269
  from Vichy France in WWII, 337, 352, 366
Republican Peasant Party, 233, 234. *See also* Croatian Peasant Party

Republicans (France), 269
Reventlow, Ernst, 92–93
revisionism, 5–6
*Revolution Betrayed* (Trotsky), 301–2
Revolutionary Workers' Soviet (Bavaria), 26
*Revue Internationale des Sociétes* (journal), 271–72
Reynaud, Paul
  against Germany, 332, 335
  imprisoned by Germans, 368
  as prime minister, 333, 334
  resignation as prime minister, 335, 338, 347
  support for French army-in-exile, 337, 347
  testimony at Pétain's trial, 373
  trial of by Vichy government, 352, 353, 354–55
Ribbentrop, Joachim von, 348, 350, 374
Riehl, Walter, 202
Rieth, Kurt, 207, 216–17
Rintelen, Anton, 205, 206–8, 212–13, 214, 215
*Risorgimento*, 34
Rivera, Diego, 302–3, 307, 318
Robins, Raymond, 74
Röhm, Ernst
  background, 148
  beer hall putsch, 149–51
  death of, 177–78
  Hitler and, 149, 170–71, 174–75, 177–78
  in Night of the Long Knives, 173, 174–75
  plans for "second revolution," 171
  post-beer hall putsch, 152, 153
  on Reichswehr, 171
  Sturm Abteilung and, 147, 153, 168
Rolland, Romain, 387, 388–89, 398, 399, 401
Romagna, 38
Roman Catholic Church. *See* Vatican
Romania, 240
Rome, 31–34, 46–47

Rome Protocols, 200
Roosevelt, Franklin, 356
Rosenburg, Alfred, 26, 152, 154
Rosmer, Alfred, 317, 318, 321, 323
Rosmer, Marguerite, 318, 321, 323
Rosselli, Carlo, 291–93
Rosselli, Nello, 291–93
Rossi, Cesare, 50–51, 52–53, 56, 60, 62, 63
Rothschild, Adolphe, 264
Rothschild, Edmond, 264
Rothschild, Louis, 264. *See also* Mandel, Georges
Ruhr Valley
  French occupation of, 98, 142, 148, 243, 269–70
  government raids on Communists in, 30
  threat of revolution in, 27
Russia (tsarist)
  1905 October Revolution, 110
  Bolshevik revolution, 9, 107–8, 112, 281
  Serbian sovereignty and, 225
  White armies for, 113
  *See also* Soviet Union
Russian Social Democratic Labor Party. *See* Social Democratic Party (Russia)
Rykov, Alexei, 122, 130, 133, 310–11
Ryutin, Martemyan, 130–32, 134
Ryutin platform, 131

SA. *See* Sturm Abteilung
Salandra, Antonio, 32, 33, 36, 37, 50, 59
Salomon, Ernst von, 102, 104
Salvemini, Gaetano, 293
*San Marco* (newspaper), 249
Sarfatti, Cesare, 41
Sarfatti, Margherita, 41, 49
Sarraut, Albert, 257, 265, 280
Sarrien, Ferdinand, 265
Sauckel, Fritz, 364–65
Schacht, Hjalmar, 154
Scheidemann, Philipp, 29, 81, 83

Schellenberg, Walther, 314
Schleicher, Kurt von, 157, 158–59, 171, 176, 179
Schleunes, Karl, 164
Schmidt, Dmitri, 311
Schmitt, Carl, 180
Schmutz, Leopold, 191
Schnitzler, Arthur, 209, 387
Schober, Johann, 188
Schönerer, Georg von, 145
Schueller, Eugène, 290
Schuschnigg, Kurt von, 211, 213–14, 215–16, 217, 393–94
Schutzbund (Protective League), 190, 194, 196, 197–98
Schutzstaffel. *See* SS (Schutzstaffel)
SDKP (Social Democratic Party of the Kingdom of Poland and Lithuania), 3
Sebottendorf, Rudolf von, 26
Sedov, Lev ("Liova")
  in Berlin with Zina, 299
  death of, 308–9, 310, 329
  in exile, 125, 126–27, 297
  nephew raised by, 318
  in Paris as journalist, 300
Sedov, Sergei, 299, 308, 329
Sedova, Natalia
  death of, 330
  death of Leon Trotsky and, 326–27
  exiles of, 111, 124, 125, 126–27, 297, 301, 303
  holiday to Black Sea, 122
  Liova Sedov's death and, 310
  Ramón Mercader and, 323
  relationship with Leon Trotsky, 110
  Sergei Sedov's death and, 308
Seipel, Ignaz, 187–88, 189, 190–91, 195
Seitz, Karl, 198
Sembat, Marcel, 281
Serbia, 226
Serbs
  in 1920 elections, 233
  history of, 224–25
  leadership claims by, 226

in South Slav union, 231, 234
South Slav unity and, 225
in WWI, 226–27
Service de L'Ordre Légionnaire (SOL), 366–67
Seton-Watson, R.W., 229
Sforza, Carlo, 231
Shaw, George Bernard, 399
Simon, Ernst, 93
Singapore, 400
Sinzinger, Adolph, 207
Siqueiros, José, 324
Slovenes, 225, 228, 231, 237, 244
Slovenia, 227, 238, 244
Snyder, Timothy, 316
Social Democratic Party (Austria)
   background of, 187
   banning of, 197–99
   Catholic Church and, 193
   coalition with Christian Social Party, 186–87
   Dollfuss and, 194
   in Great Depression, 191
   Karl-Marx-Hof and, 198
   Schutzbund as armed wing of, 190
Social Democratic Party (Bavaria), 23, 25
Social Democratic Party (Germany)
   1919 election, 28
   1933 elections, 160
   against Communist final uprising, 30
   Ebert government, 11–13, 16, 23, 29–30
   as Europe's largest, 4
   ideological stance of, 7
   Jews in, 91
   loss of government by, 30
   model for Treaty of Brest-Litovsk by, 72
   Nazis against, 160
   post–WWI, 143
   schism in, 8–9
   against Treaty of Versailles, 81
   view of Walther Rathenau, 100
   WWI and, 7, 71

Social Democratic Party (Russia), 107, 110, 111, 116–17. *See also* Bolsheviks
Social Democratic Party of the Kingdom of Poland and Lithuania (SDKP), 3
socialism, 2
Socialist Party. *See* Italian Socialist Party
Socialist Party (Belgium), 52
Socialist Party (France)
   Bolshevik revolution and, 281
   bombing of offices by *Cagoule*, 290
   Daladier government and, 279
   economic agenda of, 275
   Léon Blum and, 282
   Leon Trotsky's asylum and, 299
   Pierre Laval and, 344
   political stance of, 273
   in Popular Front, 284, 285
   in Reynaud government, 333
Sokolnikov, Grigori, 75
Sokolovskaya, Alexandra, 109, 110, 126, 298, 300
SOL (Service de L'Ordre Légionnaire), 366–67
Solidarité Française, 278–79
Somerville, James, 342
Sonnino, Sidney, 36
South Slavs, 225, 227–28, 245. *See also* Croatia; Croats; Kingdom of the Serbs, Croats, and Slovenes; Serbs; Yugoslavia
South Tyrol, 36–37, 77, 186, 218–20, 229
Souza, Claudio de, 402
Soviet of Workers' and Soldiers' Deputies (Russia), 107
Soviet Republic of Bavaria, 27
Soviet Union
   1923 industrial strikes, 121
   1935 constitution, 303
   1936 census, 130
   armed forces, 311, 312–16
   assassination of Leon Trotsky, 320–27

# INDEX

Bolshevik revolution, 9, 107–8, 112, 281
collectivizations, 114–15, 128–29, 132
famines in, 115, 129
five-year plans, 129, 130, 132–33, 316
Nazi-Soviet Non-Aggression Pact, 289, 322, 332
New Economic Policy, 115, 121, 123, 127
at Paris Peace Conference, 113
post–WWI, 113, 114
purges in, 303–7, 310–11, 314–17, 316–17, 329–30
Red Army, 113–14
Stalin's policies, 127–30
Treaty of Brest-Litovsk, 71–75, 108
Treaty of Rapallo, 101
treaty with France, 300–1
tripartite agreement with France and Czechoslovakia, 346
war with Finland, 333
in WWI, 106–7
*See also* Bolsheviks; Communist Central Committee (Russia); Communist Party (Russia); Lenin, Vladimir; Russia (tsarist); Stalin, Joseph; Trotsky, Leon
Spaho, Mehmet, 238
Spain, 319–20, 375
Spanish Civil War, 287, 291, 319
Spartakusbund, 8, 13, 14, 15. *See also* Communist Party (Germany)
Spears, Edward, 334, 338
Speer, Albert, 366
SS (Schutzstaffel), 169, 173, 174, 177, 208
SS Standarte 89, 206, 209–10
Stalin, Joseph
1923 industrial unrest and, 121
1934 relaxation by, 132–33
background, 115–16
Caridad Mercader and, 328
criminal life in Georgia, 116–17
death of wife, Nadezhda Alliluyeva, 132

December Law, 137, 139, 304
Germany rapprochment and, 311–12, 314
Lenin and, 115, 118, 119–20, 122
Lenin's last testament and, 120, 122–23
*vs.* Leon Trotsky, 119–20, 121–22, 123, 124, 125, 127, 299
*vs.* Martemyan Ryutin, 131
in party secretariat, 115, 118
party support for, 120, 121–23, 141
policies of, 127–30
political formation of, 117–18
purges by, 130–32, 139–41, 303–7, 310–11, 314–17, 329–30
Sergei Kirov and, 134–35, 137–39
at Tsaritsyn, 117
views on political organization, 119
Stalingrad, 117
Stamboliĭski, Aleksandŭr, 246
Starhemberg, Ernst von, 196–97, 200–1, 214, 222
State of Carnaro, 230–31
Stavisky, Alexandre, 276–77
Stavisky affair, 282, 341, 345
Steeg, Théodore, 345
Stennes, Walther, 167–68
Stiastny, Viktor, 212
Stöcker, Adolf, 90
Stolypin, Pyotr, 40
storm troopers. *See* Sturm Abteilung (SA)
Strasser, Gregor, 152, 153–55, 171, 175–76
Strasser, Otto, 152, 154–55, 175
Strauss, Richard, 391
Streeruwitz, Ernst von, 190, 195
Streicher, Julius, 152, 165
Stresa Front, 346
Stresemann-Briand nonaggression pact, 156
Strossmayer, Juraj, 225
Stubenrauch, Hans, 102
Sturm Abteilung (SA)
1930 elections and, 156
1933 elections and, 160–61
antisemitic attacks, 164–65

457

ban on, 157
beer hall putsch, 150
conflict with Hitler, 167–70
Ernst Röhm and, 148, 153, 168–69, 171
establishment of, 147, 148
Franz Pfeffer von Salomon as leader, 153, 167, 168
Night of the Long Knives, 172–79
plans for "second revolution," 171, 173
post-beer hall putsch, 152, 153
violence by, 157, 158
Stürmer, Boris, 107
Sudetenland, 201, 240, 295, 332, 346, 395
Šufflay, Milan, 237
Supilo, Franjo, 227, 228
Sušak, 231
Suvich, Fulvio, 196, 222
swastika, 26, 146
Syria, 355–56

Taine, Hippolyte, 381
Taittinger, Pierre, 274
Tardieu, André, 279, 345
Taubman, Ale, 309
Techow, Ernst-Werner, 102, 103, 104
Techow, Gerd, 102
Teitgen, Pierre-Henri, 376, 377
Temesvar, 227, 228, 232
Thierschwald, Otto, 53, 54
Third International, 30, 44, 317, 344. *See also* Comintern (Communist International)
Thomas, Albert, 281
Thorez, Maurice, 282, 284
Thule Society (Thule Gesellschaft), 25–26, 145
Thyssen, Fritz, 154
Tissier, Gustave, 275–76
Tivoli Convention, 90
Tixier-Vignancour, Jean-Louis, 353–54
Toller, Ernst, 27, 28
Tomsky, Mikhail, 130

Toscanini, Arturo, 58
Treaty of Brest-Litovsk, 10, 71–75, 76, 82, 108
Treaty of Bucharest, 82
Treaty of Frankfurt, 263–64
Treaty of Locarno. *See* Locarno treaties
Treaty of London, 37, 42, 43, 195, 218, 228, 229
Treaty of Rapallo, 101, 312
Treaty of Saint-Germain, 77, 185–86, 190, 218, 230, 231
Treaty of Tilsit, 75
Treaty of Tirana, 248
Treaty of Trianon, 185, 186, 239
Treaty of Versailles
    "articles of shame" in, 81–82
    German army and, 166, 168, 313, 346
    German reaction to, 29
    German signing of, 29, 83
    German territorial losses by, 36
    Nazi Party (Germany) and, 146, 148
    reparations in, 142
    *See also* reparations
Treitschke, Heinrich von, 89–90
Trentino, 37, 218, 247
Trepov, Fyodor, 1
Trieste, 229, 247
Triple Alliance, 35, 37
Triple Entente, 37, 42
Trotsky, Leon
    assassination of, 326–27
    background, 108–9
    Bolshevik revolution and, 112
    *Bulletin of the Opposition*, 299, 301
    collectivization and, 114–15
    defense of, 123, 307–8
    exile, internal, 123–26
    exile in France, 299–301
    exile in Istanbul, 126–27, 297–98
    exile in Mexico, 302–3, 307, 318–19
    exile in Norway, 301–3
    exiles, pre-revolution, 109–10, 111–12
    failed assassination attempt on, 324
    family of purged, 329–30

family tragedies, 126, 298–99, 300, 307–10
Fourth International and, 317–18
in government, 118–19
Lenin and, 109–10, 112, 118–19
Lenin's death and, 122
on Léon Blum, 300
literary output, 297–98
Mikhail Tukhachevsky and, 311
opposition to, 120–24
plot to murder, 320–26
Red Army and, 113–14
relationship with Alexandra Sokolovskaya, 109, 110, 126
relationship with Natalia Sedova, 110, 124, 125, 126–27
*The Revolution Betrayed*, 301–2
Sergei Kirov's death and, 140
in Social Democratic circles, 110, 111
vs. Stalin, 119–20, 121–22, 123
Treaty of Brest-Litovsk and, 73–75
views on political organization, 119
Trumbić, Ante, 227, 228
Tsaritsyn, 117
Tsederbaum, Iulii, 3
Tsokos, Michael, 19–20
Tuck, Pinkney, 363
Tukhachevsky, Mikhail, 311, 313, 314, 315
Tunisia, 356
Turati, Filippo, 59
Turks, 224–25, 231

Ukraine, 81, 129
Ulrikh, Vassili, 305, 315
Union of Revolutionary National Socialists (Germany), 155
Union Sacrée (France), 269, 273, 281
United Kingdom. *See* Great Britain
United Socialists (Italy), 51
United States of America, 10, 11, 229, 269, 356. *See also* Wilson, Woodrow
University of Zurich, 2–3
USSR. *See* Soviet Union
Ustaša

assassination of Aleksandar I, 250–57
establishment of, 245, 246
in Hungary, 247, 260
in Italy, 248–49, 261
Uzbekistan, 81
Uzunović, Nikola, 258

Valéry, Paul, 387
Vallat, Xavier, 285, 353, 359, 360, 372
van der Lubbe, Marinus, 160
Vandervelde, Emile, 4
Vargas, Getúlio, 380, 397, 402
Vatican
against Aventinians, 61
concordat with Austria, 193
concordat with Italy, 64–65
Matteotti murder and, 58–59
Nazi Party and, 162–63
Vaugeois, Henri, 267
Venezia Giulia, 229–30, 247, 248
Verhaeren, Émile, 381, 398
Vichy government
end of, 371
fascist policies of, 357
formation of, 342, 348
French assumptions of, 348
Hitler and, 349–50, 349–51
Jews and, 352, 357–64, 366
Mers-el-Kebir naval base attack, 342–43
Milice Française, 366–67, 370
"National Revolution" of, 343
post-liberation judicial processes, 372
purges of, 371–72
reparations imposed on, 352, 364, 366
transfer to Paris, 367
trial of former French leaders by, 352–55
workers to Germany (*relève*) from, 352, 364–66
in WWII, 351–52, 355–57
*See also* Laval, Pierre; Mandel, Georges; Pétain, Henri-Philippe
"Vidoni Palace" agreement, 64
Vienna

## INDEX

Austria and, 186
chancellory, 210
civil violence in, 198
creative talents in, 380
Jews in, 144, 189
Viola, Giuseppe, 54
Vittorio Emanuele II (Italian king), 64
Vittorio Emanuele III (Italian king), 32, 33, 34, 46, 58, 60
Viviani, René, 281
Vlada. *See* Cernozemski, Vlado
Vogel, Kurt, 17
Vojvodina, 228
*Völkischer Beobachter* (newspaper), 147–48, 154, 173
Volkov, Platon, 298, 300, 329
Volkov, Seva, 299, 300, 308, 318, 324, 330
Volkova, Nora, 330
Volkova, Zina, 298–99, 329
Volovich, Alexei, 311
Volpi, Albino, 53, 54
Voroshilov, Kliment, 118, 138, 311, 315
*Vorwärts* (newspaper), 21
*Vreme* (newspaper), 249
Vyshinski, Andrei, 118, 138, 304, 305, 311, 315

Wächter, Otto Gustav von, 205, 206, 207, 208, 212, 214
Walter, Bruno, 387
Warburg, Max, 90
Wassermann, Jakob, 92, 387
Weimar Republic
  beer hall putsch against, 149–51
  constitution, 17, 26, 29
  fiscal deficit of, 83
  founding of, 17, 29
  as "Jew Republic," 97, 98
  political instability of, 30
  Wolfgang Kapp uprising against, 29
  *See also* Germany
Wells, H.G., 387
Werfel, Franz, 209
Weydenhammer, Rudolf, 206, 207–8, 212, 214

Weygand, Maxime, 69, 78, 334–35
*White Book of the Purge, The*, 179
White Terror (Bavaria), 28
Wilhelm II (German kaiser)
  abdication of, 12, 78
  acceptance of democracy by, 11, 68
  on Jews, 90–91
  Maximilian of Baden as chancellor, 11, 68, 76
  Treaty of Brest-Litovsk and, 72, 73, 75
  WWI and, 10–11, 71
Wilson, Woodrow
  conditions of for peace with Germany, 11, 68
  Fourteen Points, 81–82, 218
  on indemnities and reparations, 81–82
  South Tyrol and, 219
  WWI armistice and, 76
  Yugoslavia and, 229
Winternitz, Felix von, 383–84
Winternitz, Friderike Burger Maria von
  Austria annexed and, 395
  marriage to Felix von Winternitz, 383–84
  relationship with Stefan Zweig, 384, 388, 392, 393, 395, 397, 398
  in Salzburg, 385, 392
  Stefan Zweig's depression and, 400
  Stefan Zweig's suicide and, 401
  trip to America, 397
Wirth, Josef, 88, 100, 102–3, 104–5
World War I
  armistice, 10–11, 67–68, 78–80
  France in, 262–63, 264
  Italy and, 35–37, 41–42, 43
  Jews in, 92
  Kurt Eisner on, 21–22
  mutiny in German navy during, 11, 68–69
  new nations formed after, 239
  Russia in, 106–7, 113
  Serbs in, 226–27
  Social Democrat Party (Germany) support for, 7

460

*See also* Paris Peace Conference; reparations; Treaty of Brest-Litovsk; Treaty of Saint-Germain; Treaty of Versailles
World War II, 332–34, 355–56, 365, 400
Wrabel, Karl, 209

Yagoda, Genrikh, 137–38, 304, 306, 311
Yakir, Iona, 311
Yakubovich, Pavel, 302
Yezhov, Nikolai, 137–38, 315, 320, 322
Yudenich, Nikolai, 113
Yugoslav Muslim Organization (Bosnia-Herzegovina), 238
Yugoslavia
    Aleksandar I's assassination and, 258, 259–60
    against Ante Pavelič, 248
    constitution of, 234–35
    Croats and Slovenes against, 244
    governance assumed by Aleksandar I, 236–37, 238
    in Great Depression, 237–38, 249
    Italy and, 249
    name changed to, 236
    *See also* Aleksandar I (Yugoslav king); Kingdom of the Serbs, Croats, and Slovenes

Zara, 231, 249
Zasulich, Vera, 1
Zborowski, Mark, 309–10
Zentrum. *See* Center Party (Germany)
Zetkin, Klara, 13
Zhdanov, Andrei, 138
Zimmerwald Manifesto, 111
Zinoviev, Grigori
    Comintern (Third International) and, 281, 317
    death of, 306
    defense of Stalin by, 122
    family of purged, 306
    partial pardon of, 133
    party schism and, 121
    in Politburo, 120
    purges of, 124, 132, 140
    trial for Sergei Kirov's murder, 304–5
    Trotsky and, 123
Zuckmayer, Carl, 400
Zurich, 2–3, 111
Zweig, Moritz, 380–81
Zweig, Stefan, 96
    booked burned by Nazis, 391
    Brazil, first visit to, 379–80
    Brazil, move to, 397–98
    Brazil, second visit to, 396–97
    childhood, 381
    collaboration with Richard Strauss, 391
    in England, 396
    friends of, 387
    funeral for, 402
    international humanism of, 387, 389
    *Jeremiah*, 383
    Jewishness of, 390
    last will and testament of, 400–1
    lectures given by, 387–88, 395–96
    literary output, 381–82, 385–87, 390, 395, 399
    in London, 392, 395
    messages recorded for BBC, 397
    in New York, 396
    nostalgia for past, 398–99
    political stances avoided by, 389–90, 395
    on post-WWI generation, 384–85
    relationship with Friderike von Winternitz, 384, 388, 392, 393, 395, 397, 398, 400, 401
    relationship with Lotte Altmann, 393, 401–2, 403
    Romain Rolland and, 387, 388–89, 401
    in Salzburg, 385, 391
    self-perception of, 390
    suicide, fascination with, 399–400
    suicide of, 400–2, 403
    in WWI, 382–83